'THESE STRANGE CRIMINALS': AN ANTHOLOGY OF PRISON MEMOIRS BY CONSCIENTIOUS OBJECTORS FROM THE GREAT WAR TO THE COLD WAR

In many modern wars, there have been those who have chosen not to fight. Be it for religious or moral reasons, some men and women have found no justification for breaking their conscientious objection to violence. In many cases, this objection has lead to severe punishment at the hands of their own governments, usually lengthy prison terms. Peter Brock brings the voices of imprisoned conscientious objectors to the fore in *'These Strange Criminals.'*

This important and thought-provoking anthology consists of thirty prison memoirs by conscientious objectors to military service, drawn from the United Kingdom, the United States, Canada, Australia, and New Zealand, and centring on their jail experiences during the First and Second World Wars and the Cold War. Voices from history – like those of Stephen Hobhouse, Dame Kathleen Lonsdale, Ian Hamilton, Alfred Hassler, and Donald Wetzel – come alive, detailing the impact of prison life and offering unique perspectives on wartime government policies of conscription and imprisonment. Sometimes intensely moving, and often inspiring, these memoirs show that in some cases, individual conscientious objectors – many well-educated and politically aware – sought to reform the penal system from within either by publicizing its dysfunction or through further resistance to authority. The collection is an essential contribution to our understanding of criminology and the history of pacifism, and represents a valuable addition to prison literature.

PI [illegible] or emeritus in the Department of History at the University of Toronto.

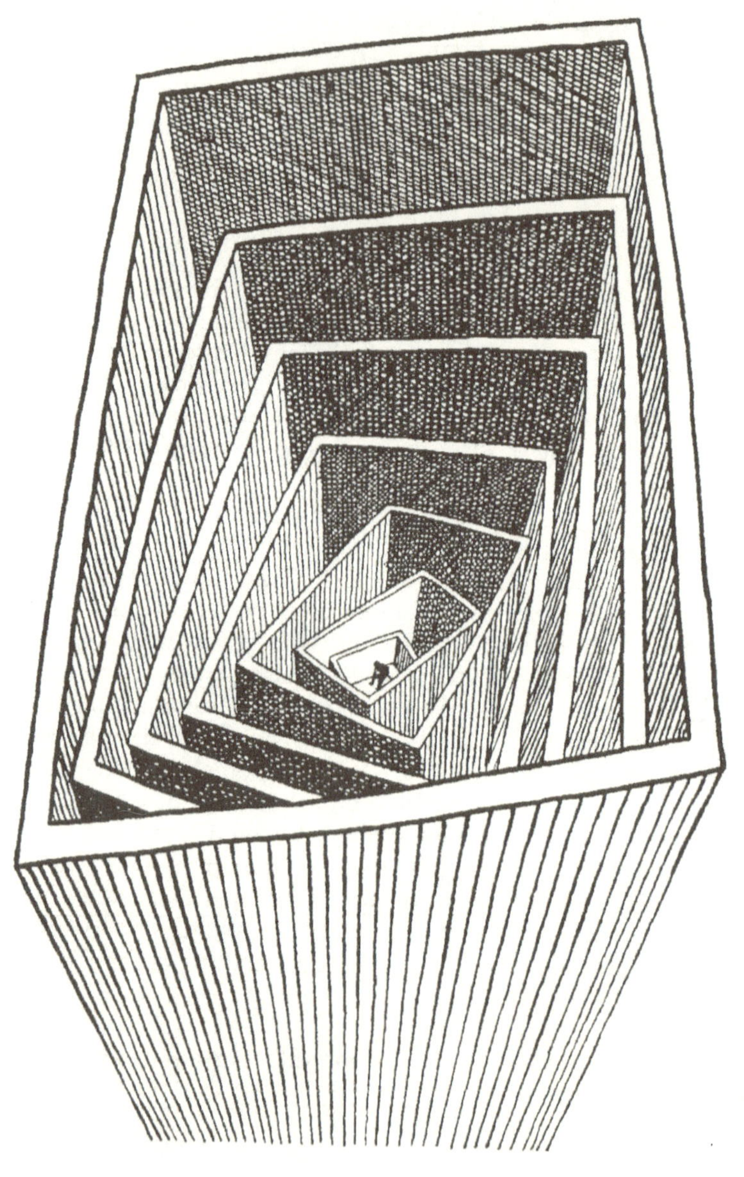

Illustration by Lowell Naeve

'THESE STRANGE CRIMINALS'

An Anthology of Prison Memoirs by Conscientious Objectors from the Great War to the Cold War

Edited by Peter Brock

UNIVERSITY OF TORONTO PRESS
Toronto Buffalo London

Toronto Buffalo London

Reprinted in paperback 2014

ISBN 978-0-8020-8707-2 (cloth)
ISBN 978-0-8020-8661-7 (paper)

Printed on acid-free paper

National Library of Canada Cataloguing in Publication

'These strange criminals' : an anthology of prison memoirs by conscientious objectors from the Great War to the Cold War / edited by Peter Brock.

Includes bibliographical references.
ISBN 978-0-8020-8707-2 (bound)
ISBN 978-0-8020-8661-7 (pbk.)

1. Conscientious objectors – Biography. 2. World War, 1914–1918 – Conscientious objectors. 3. World War, 1939–1945 – Conscientious objectors. 4. World War, 1914–1918 – Prisoners and prisons. 5. World War, 1939–1945 – Prisoners and prisons. 6. World War, 1914–1918 – Personal narratives. 7. World War, 1939–1945 – Personal narratives. I. Brock, Peter, 1920–

UB341.T43 2004 355.2'24'0922 C2003-906492-1

University of Toronto Press acknowledges the financial assistance to its publishing program of the Canada Council for the Arts and the Ontario Arts Council.

University of Toronto Press acknowledges the financial support for its publishing activities of the Government of Canada through the Book Publishing Industry Development Program (BPIDP).

Contents

Part Two: The Good War

Part Three: Cold-War America

Foreword

This anthology presents the accounts of the prison experiences of conscientious objectors (COs) during three eras of armed conflict in the twentieth century. The editor, Peter Brock, tells us that his intent is to contribute to the ethnographic study of the prison and prison(er) culture, and to add the distinctive perspective of this category of prisoners to the literary genre of prison writing. Firmly located within the twentieth-century history of pacifism and antiwar movements, this collection introduces a spirited group of political dissidents, their view of the prison and the societies that created them, and it succeeds brilliantly. The prison emerges from these narratives, its characteristic features highlighted by their numbing repetition, and the spirit and resistance of the authors shines through as testimony to their significance as moral and political commentators of their eras. The historical organization and contextualization of the narratives, and the representative scope of this selection allow Peter Brock to capture the heartbeat of the universal prison experience: the essential loss of freedom and self-determination to the dominating and immutable power of the prison. In recounting their carceral experiences, these writers also succeed in elucidating their age and societies, and the moral philosophies that inform their movements and communities.

The editor's introductions to each historical period, the biographical sketches of the writers, and the footnotes provide the essential context for broadly locating these narratives, and serve to connect them to a multiplicity of academic disciplines and interests. They ground the ideological positions of the writers within their traditions of radical dissent. They also locate the prison, and its changing forms of penal discipline and regime. The editor's decision to provide long narrative pieces contributes significantly to this accomplishment. The broad range of writers selected and their order of presentation combines to produce a flowing and integrated exploration of political dissent and its penal suppression in the twentieth century. The majority of the writers are well educated, articulate, and politically conscious. Their accounts provide critical insights into the operation of the prison. Generally progressive for their era, often their analysis and understanding predates similar discoveries and conclusions in penology. For example, Hobhouse, Lonsdale, Axford, and Hassler present the essentials of the 'proven failure of imprisonment' argument that only becomes established in penology in the 1970s. Indeed, Price provides a distinctly 'penal abolitionist' argument that is consistent with the contemporary analysis of that social movement.

This selection of prison writing also mirrors the range of styles and formats that characterize this genre through the centuries. In memoirs, letters home, political tracts and pamphlets, the reader encounters a plethora of traditional voices. These include the astonishment and horror of the innocent and naive's first encounter with penal justice (Wigham); the moral denunciation of the reformer (Hobhouse); and the 'How to Resist' strategies of the prisoner activist (Miller). While these narratives are generally defiant, the 'bitter humour' of Hamilton epitomizes the defiant contempt of the carnivalesque style of prison writing. These resisters write from the heart and accost the prison, 'the insolence of its sadistic staff' (Hamilton), and the 'endless round of petty routine, overlaying the ever present fear and hostility' (Hassler) that constitute its regimes.

These accounts provide an opportunity to study the ethnography of the prison from a unique set of lenses, that of prisoners of conscience, who successfully overturned the debilitating stigma of criminalization, and were able to resist the consequent transformation of their social identity into that of the socially discredited criminal and convict. Unlike common 'criminals,' they are able to take the moral and intellectual high ground, from which they cast moral condemnation upon their captors and the prison institution. The absence of guilt or remorse is obvious: 'Four years of my life for refusing to kill?' (Osborne), 'I was rather proud of my status' (Brock). Outside community and political support served to further legitimate their stance and strengthen their resolve to resist.

Ioan Davies (1990) in *Writers in Prison* argues that many prisoners of conscience write from the margins of their society and the prison. This is clearly the case for most of these writers, especially those imprisoned in the regime of 'silence and solitude' dominant during the first two world wars. Their marginal position provides the distance and relative detachment desired in the participant observer and ethnographer of the prison. Often their accounts evoke the alienated detachment of

Mersault in Albert Camus's *L'Etranger* or the wonder and incredulity of Kafka's 'A Report to the Academy' and 'In the Penal Colony.' Those incarcerated for long periods (Hamilton) and, to a lesser extent, those imprisoned in the congregate labour and reformative regimes of the United States (Osborne, Miller) are drawn into the centre of prison culture and prisoners' traditional resistance to the domination of the prison. In Hamilton we encounter the perfect synthesis. The radical humanist / political agitator integrated into the collective resistance of the prisoner community for whom 'resistance is the only outlet for independence.' This is another instance in which the selection of writers enriches the text.

These narratives serve to illuminate the prison. There is a consistency in the prisoners' accounts, produced by their encounters with the universals of the prison institution. This consistency attests to the immutable and enduring characteristics of the carceral. The induction into the prison and its routinized humiliations stands out as a defining moment in the experience of incarceration. The loss of autonomy, the mortifying invasion of privacy (strip searches, showers, lavatory), poor diet and lack of medical attention, the cell, and the transformation of social identity into that of convict are thoroughly addressed in these accounts. 'It was just awful. It was degrading to think that your fellow human beings could treat you like that, it's almost too horrible to describe because you can't really believe that conditions could exist like that in 1942' (Wigham, p. 251 below).

The growing sense of lost autonomy that envelops the prisoner, though resisted, permeates these accounts. This experience of the loss of control was heightened during the air raids on Britain during the Second World War. 'And then you'd hear the sirens going, and hear gunfire and bombs dropping, and then this would aggravate the girls; you know there would be terrible tension ... All night you were left hearing and knowing that you're trapped, knowing you can't get out, you can't possibly ... you had no escape' (Wigham, 250–1).

Of particular note are the abusive and harassing 'screws' who feature prominently in the pervasive degradation of the carceral experience. Save for the accounts of a few imprisoned souls resting in the bosom of the Lord, the staff is usually portrayed as 'sullen and officious,' the 'hectoring and sadistic type,' and a major source of the pains of imprisonment. The analysis of the deference and demeanour relationships of 'convict and screw' are insightful, and elucidate the power relations of the total institution in the daily routines of carceral life. For the penologist, the diverse locations and penal eras from which these narratives are drawn provide a clear depiction of the enduring features of penal domination and regime.

While the physical hardships of imprisonment play a part, especially in the accounts of First World War COs, it is the psychological hardship, and the recognition of the debilitating effects of imprisonment upon the mental, spiritual, and social well-being of the prisoner that are most discussed. The constant surveillance of the panoptic gaze, the loss of control and self-determination, the mental debilitation of isolation and solitary confinement all feature prominently in these accounts, as they do in penology and prison ethnography generally. Surviving prison necessitates resistance to its domination, 'so as not to assist in [one's] own imprisonment' (Wetzel). Above all, these are accounts of the resistance of the righteous, whose moral position and political insights, educated and articulate voices, stand in condemnation of the prison and the society that imprisons. This is writing as resistance. These are consciously constructed moral denunciations of the prison as an institution whose intent is to 'break the spirit,' and which succeeds only in creating the delinquent, hardening criminality and ensuring recividism.

Though some of these biographical narratives were written years or decades after the experience of imprisonment, these authors still rankle at the pervasive degradation they endured and their treatment at the hands of staff, which attests to the indelible marks left by the experience. This seems to be the case for editor and contributor Peter Brock, whose own carceral experiences underscore this endeavour, adding a rare and insightful dimension to the organization and selection of the texts.

The multilevel analyses and diverse discourses of this anthology provide a wealth of information, and suggest new research questions for a range of scholarly disciplines and interests. The vitality of this marvellous cast of characters stands out as a testimony to the human spirit. Their moral and political commentary is as pertinent to the present as it was to the past. Indeed, in the current age of mass imprisonment, such moral direction is badly needed. Brock's anthology rescues these voices from the dustbin of history and gives them new life and relevance. This anthology significantly adds to the timeless portrait of the universal prison, and reaffirms the indictment of this institution as 'treason to social justice.'

Robert Gaucher, PhD
Department of Criminology
University of Ottawa
November 2003

Preface

The narratives printed in this anthology represent a sampling from prison memoirs composed by conscientious objectors (COs) from five countries (and a sixth in an appendix). They deal with the two world wars and the Cold War era. There were, of course, COs in other countries during the period covered by this book as well as during other time periods than the ones included here – for instance, the interwar years. I trust, though, that I have presented sufficient materials to be of use to at least two classes of readers.

First come students of penology, to whom the observations of 'these strange criminals' (the phrase is that of Britain's pacifist Bishop E.W. Barnes of Birmingham in 1941) should prove a useful addition to the prison ethnography produced during the same period by 'common criminals.' In fact, I do not think penologists, even the new school of 'convict criminology,' have realized the extent of prison memoir writing by twentieth-century conscientious objectors (indeed by COs since the 1890s). One of the purposes I hope this volume will fulfil is to bring this genre of prison literature to their notice. Second, students of peace history cannot, I believe, fail to find here a new understanding of what it has meant to be a pacifist in wartime – whether the war was a great war, a good war, or a cold war, or the Vietnam War. 'Are they embittered, or have they an inward spiritual peace? Does anger distort their vision ...?' asks Bishop Barnes of these memoirists. The narratives printed here, from the pens of religious objectors as well as from 'non-religious' whose inspiration has been humanist or philosophical or political, will answer the bishop's questions.

Introducing the report he compiled in 1948 on British wartime prisons, Mark Benney, ex–professional burglar turned amateur penologist, wrote that 'if it is agreed that ex-prisoners are not the most trustworthy of witnesses ... conscientious objectors are obviously a class apart from the ordinary run of prison inmates ... No one,' he went on, 'will believe them prone to deliberate misrepresentation or distortion of fact ... On the other hand, the very qualities of conscience which sent them to prison will make them perhaps more rigorous in their judgments and certainly more limited in their experience than is wholly desirable in a prison witness.' Yet every historic witness has his or her shortcomings, which the careful reader should be trained to take into consideration while assessing the value of any memoir.

I have chosen to give fairly extensive extracts from my sources instead of the gobbets and snippets favoured by some anthologists. The latter method may sometimes be appropriate, though I have usually felt rather frustrated by its use. In the present instance I trust readers will find the ample space permitted each author to be rewarding.

The documents printed below, though limited in terms of gender (because among the few women COs – in the eyes of the law – very few have been jailed) and in the time span and area covered, do, I believe, add a new dimension to our perception of the carceral experience over the last century.

The introductions in this book are intended merely as background to the prison narratives that follow. They do not aim at providing a detailed account of pacifism and conscientious objection in the countries and during the periods covered. For this, I would refer readers to the relevant sections of my book, co-authored with Nigel Young, *Pacifism in the Twentieth Century* (Syracuse, NY: Syracuse University Press, 1999). Some readers, of course, may wish to move straight to the narratives themselves, which form the core of the book. Good luck to them! I do indeed think that these texts, together with the notes appended to them, can be read with profit without further introduction. On the other hand, the introductions can assist a reader needing more informational support.

I should note that I have interpreted the term 'memoir' rather more broadly than is perhaps usual, so as to include fragments as well as self-contained units. I have also, in two cases (Lonsdale and Wigham, pp. 232 and 243), extended the definition of conscientious objection *'to military service'* so as to include women objectors in Second World War Britain who were jailed for refusing, respectively, to perform fire-watching duties under compulsion (a libertarian objection) and to obey a direction under wartime industrial conscription. The terms 'jail' and 'prison' have been used interchangeably here. But in the United States jails are city or county institutions, intended primarily for persons with short sentences, whereas those sentenced to more than twelve months, after a brief stay in a jail, are sent to a prison of one type or another, whose inmates are usually known as convicts or felons.

I would like to thank Christine Chattin for producing a neatly typed diskette out of the untidy materials I presented to her. I would also like to thank William Hetherington, Honorary Archivist of the Peace Pledge Union (London), for helping me in my search for documentation, and Malcolm Thomas, Joanna Clark, and Josef Keith, who provided me with the same kind of assistance at the Library of the Religious Society of Friends (London). The staff of the Imperial War Museum (London) Sound Archive were also most helpful during my visits to the museum. At the University of Toronto Press Len Husband, Humanities Editor, and Frances Mundy, Editor, Managing Editorial Department, have been very supportive of my project, while John St James proved an extremely competent copy-editor. My warm thanks go out to the three of them. Lastly – but by no means least – it is a pleasure to express my gratitude to the Interlibrary Loan department of the Robarts Library, University of Toronto, for their assistance to me throughout the years.

Peter Brock
Toronto

Document Credits

I would like to express my gratitude for permission to reprint to the following:

- Cape Catley Ltd, for Archibald Baxter's memoir
- The Bentley Historical Library, University of Michigan (Ann Arbor), for Arthur Dunham's memoir
- Annette Voth and the Mennonite Library and Archives, Bethel College, for Albert Voth's memoir
- Alexander Bryan for his memoir
- Robert Hockley (via his son David Hockley), for his memoir
- The publishers Leo Cooper, for Ernest Spring's memoir
- The Imperial War Museum (London) Sound Archive, for Kathleen Wigham's interview account
- Auckland University Press (my efforts to trace the current copyright holder having been unsuccessful), for Ian Hamilton's memoir
- Al Hassler's widow, Mrs Dorothy Hassler, for his diary extracts
- Lowell Naeve, for his memoir and his two drawings reproduced here
- The Pilgrim Press, for Donald Benedict's memoir
- The Permanent Press, for Donald Wetzel's memoir
- Bradford Lyttle, for his *Guide*
- Gerald R. Gioglio, for Jeffrey Porteous's account
- The Westminster John Knox Press, for J.K. Osborne's diary extracts
- Brassey's Inc., for extracts from the 'Johnson' interview
- David Miller and the Grove Press, for extracts from his 'manual,' co-authored with Howard Levy
- Klartext Verlag (Essen, Germany) for the documentary appendix.

With respect to the Hassler diary, the present handlers of the copyright have requested the insertion of the following statement: From the book *Diary of a Self-Made Convict* by Alfred Hassler. Copyright © 1954

In two instances I have been unable to trace the present owners of copyright. With respect to Phil Hancox's autobiography excerpts (p. 298) the publisher no longer exists and the author has died. The Parker extract (p. 336) was taken from a slim volume printed privately by the author, the late Malcolm Parker. I trust that Max, staunch pacifist that he was, would not have objected to my including extracts from his writings in this anthology. I even hope that he would have been pleased.

If inadvertently I have omitted to obtain permission for a document on which there is still copyright, I hope this will be pardoned me. I don't think either the author or the publisher of any such item will lose from being included in an anthology of this kind.

PART ONE: THE GREAT WAR

In English-speaking countries conscientious objection to military service was not a new phenomenon in 1914. It was associated there, in particular, with three religious sects, the Quakers (known also as the Society of Friends), the Mennonites, and the German Baptist Brethren (known today as the Church of the Brethren). Mennonites and Brethren, who had sought refuge in North America from their original homeland in Central Europe, rarely went to jail on account of their conscientious refusal to bear arms, since they usually succeeded in reaching an acceptable modus vivendi with the state on this issue. Not so the Quakers – either in Great Britain, where the sect had originated in the 1650s, or in the West Indies or in North America, where Quakers were already to be found in comparatively large numbers in the colonial era.

Throughout the seventeenth and eighteenth centuries, on both sides of the Atlantic, the authorities imposed a draft for service in the militia, which mustered regularly and in case of a military emergency. It was, however, always possible to opt out by paying a small fine in lieu of serving. Mennonites and Brethren did not object to paying this, since they regarded it simply as rendering to Caesar his due. But Quakers believed it was wrong to do so and 'disowned' members of their Society who paid a fine: a penalty that, of course, they also imposed on those who actually bore arms (until the practice of disownment lapsed in the course of the nineteenth century). The state, according to the Quakers, had no right to demand money from its citizens because they were acting according to what their consciences told them was right. As a result, Quaker militia-draftees had their goods distrained for their refusal to pay commutation in lieu of bearing arms, or, if they did not possess sufficient property, they were briefly jailed.

The traditional British militia draft eventually faded out in the 1830s. Henceforward military recruitment relied solely on the voluntary system, although in the early years of the twentieth century, especially among Conservatives, voices were heard calling for the imposition of conscript service for the country's youth. Most Liberals and Socialists, by contrast, opposed military conscription as undemocratic and contrary to the English idea of freedom.

In the United States – and in Canada, too – the militia system had become increasingly moribund during the antebellum period. After the outbreak of the Civil War in 1861, military conscription was imposed both in the North and in the Confederate States. All the peace sects encountered difficulties in preserving their pacifist witness intact; in the South they were associated in the minds of the authorities with anti-slavery. Although on both sides of the fighting line some COs suffered imprisonment, peace came in 1865 before there was time for more rigorous conscription laws to come into effect. The United States then returned to the voluntary system until in 1917 conscription was reintroduced.

Meanwhile, throughout the European continent, universal military service became the rule, with a loophole for non-resistant Mennonites who, in Prussia and Russia, could perform respectively non-combatant army and civilian forestry service in lieu of bearing arms.[1] Though during this age of Realpolitik English-speaking countries were fortunately free of the burden of military conscription, compulsory military training for teenagers, the so called 'boy conscription,' was introduced in Australia and New Zealand in 1911 and continued until the outbreak of war. In both countries the small minority of pacifists, including some Quakers, resisted the implementation of the law and were willing to see their sons go to prison rather than train.

Opponents of boy conscription also included a number of socialist antimilitarists. These people were not necessarily absolute pacifists. They certainly condemned international war between capitalist states unreservedly, but most expressed willingness to fight in defence of a post-revolutionary regime and also, when the right moment arrived, to take up arms in order to achieve the new socialist order. Many of the British and American COs jailed in the First World War were drawn from this category of antiwarist: the authorities were often unsympathetic to their claim to CO status – as they were to humanist objectors – since they did not usually base it on any religious motivation.

The outbreak of war in August 1914 had changed the situation radically. In Britain public pressure to introduce military conscription grew, even though some members of the Liberal government still regarded the idea with abhorrence. In July 1915 came national registration of male adults, and in January of the next year the first Military Service Act was passed. It came into force in March. At first only unmarried men between the ages of eighteen and forty-one were affected, but by the beginning of 1918 all able-bodied males between eighteen and fifty-six became liable to conscription.

Provision was made for conscientious objectors; on paper, at any rate, this was remarkably generous. Tribunals could grant COs, including non-religious objectors whom they judged to be sincere, either unconditional exemption or assignment to civilian employment considered 'of national importance' or to non-combatant service in the army.

The flaw lay in the fact that the tribunals, whether local or appeal, which made the decisions were not set up specifically to deal with conscientious objection. Their major concern was in fact to deal with the growing manpower shortage. A military officer sat on every tribunal; his view usually carried most weight in CO as well as in other cases heard. Thus unconditional exemption was granted very rarely, assignment to the army's Non-Combatant Corps, unacceptable to a large number of COs, being the most frequently imposed condition of exemption. Tribunals also tended to disfavour non-religious objectors, even when these men were clearly sincere in their objection to fighting.

Pacifists and antimilitarists soon began to organize to resist conscription and to support war resisters after its introduction. The No-Conscription Fellowship, set up near the end of 1914, became the focal point of resistance. Membership eventually reached almost 10,000, with 6000 members belonging to the socialist Independent Labour Party (ILP) and Quakers forming the next largest component. Many young Quakers adopted the 'absolutist' stand and steadfastly refused to accept anything but unconditional exemption. The Quaker Society of Friends, while it did not officially take a stand on this issue, gave full support to all its members who went to jail as absolutists.[2] Almost all denominations produced at least a few COs. Yet there were scarcely any Catholics and not many Anglican COs. All but a handful of the established church's clergy supported the war. An exception was E.W. Barnes, the future Bishop Barnes, who, as Master of the Temple in London, courageously voiced his pacifism.

Quaker absolutists, and ILP unconditionalists like Clifford Allen or Fenner Brockway, constituted the majority of those COs who went to prison in the First World War. But other COs found themselves in jail, too, if their application had been rejected or their tribunal had given them an unacceptable alternative to combatant service. A few libertarians had refused to apply for exemption at all and thus had not appeared before any tribunal. According to Constance Braithwaite,[3] 'up to the end of July 1919 a total of 5739 objectors were sentenced by court martial.' Arrests had begun as early as March 1916 – either for failing to obey an army call-up notice or for ignoring assignment to civilian alternative service when the assignee was 'deemed' to be a soldier 'in the reserve.'

In that case, writes Braithwaite, 'the usual procedure was for the man to be arrested by the police and ... taken before a magistrate ... formally fined £2 (very often never paid) and handed over to the military escort who took him to the unit to which he had been called up ... On arrival at his unit the objector, if determined to continue his resistance, soon committed some act of technical disobedience, such as refusing to salute or to wear khaki. He was now ... subject to the provisions of army law.' Court martial and imprisonment followed. A few COs were shipped to the battle zone in France and there subjected to various brutalities and even sentenced to death, though this was finally commuted to ten years' penal servitude as the result of protests at home.

Most CO defaulters did not have to face the possibility – probability – of death as this group had done. Still, their fate was still not an easy one. To quote Braithwaite again: 'A sentence of imprisonment did not release from the army: at the end of his sentence an objector was returned to his army unit where, if he again disobeyed orders, he spent a few days in the guardroom and then received a further sentence from a court-martial.' From a total of nearly 6000 jailed objectors, around 850 'were in prison for twenty months or more' and 'some were in prison for nearly three years' as a result of the same kind of cat-and-mouse treatment that had been handed out to suffragettes in the pre-war years. In addition, most COs were sentenced to 'hard labour ... considered by the law to be the most severe form of imprisonment.'

Before long, owing in part to pressure from the COs' friends inside parliament and outside, the British government made certain concessions. In the first place, in July 1916 it set up what became known as the Home Office Scheme, a system of civilian alternative service under semi-penal conditions. Most jailed COs, who were not absolutists, accepted the Scheme and were released from prison. In addition, the conditions of imprisonment for those COs who refused to accept the Scheme were alleviated in a number of ways. Provision, for instance, was made for the release of those in poor health; the preliminary period of solitary confinement of men sentenced to hard labour was shortened; visits were allowed more frequently as well as conversation at exercise periods, although the silence rule remained otherwise in force; and COs exchanged the broad-arrow prison uniform they had worn hitherto along with ordinary criminals for their own clothes.

The Armistice came on 11 November 1918, but COs remained in jail. Release of those who still had time to do took place between April and August 1919.

In New Zealand conscription came into force in June 1916. The small Labour Party, which opposed the war, took a strong anticonscriptionist stand, and several of its leaders were jailed for sedition as a result of carrying on antiwar propaganda. The government provided for conscientious objection, but, in contrast to the mother country, it interpreted this in a very narrow spirit. In fact, it granted exemption only to members of pre-war pacifist sects – and then only with respect to combatant service. As a result, the CO exemption clause of the conscription act in practice applied only to Quakers and Christadelphians, both very small denominations and both conscientiously opposed to serving in the armed forces. Thus, this kind of exemption failed to provide any relief to either Quaker or Christadelphian COs, and they ended up in jail too. Unaffiliated Christian pacifists, like the Baxter brothers for instance, had no option, of course, except prison – or worse – if they chose to remain loyal to their principles.[4]

The United States did not enter the war until 6 April 1917. The Selective Service Act passed by Congress next month exempted from combatant service only COs who belonged to a pacifist sect. All males between the ages of twenty-one and thirty were required to register for service. Registration took place on 5 June. What exactly would be required of COs whom the local boards found to be genuine within the meaning of the act remained unclear. Thus, even on paper American CO legislation proved much less liberal than the corresponding English legislation. Its implementation only added to the confusion; in practice it frequently proved unfair and harsh.[5] Apart from a few non-registrants, almost all COs found themselves in one of the army camps set up throughout the country. This unsatisfactory situation stemmed in large part from the weakness of the American pacifist movement at this time and its almost total lack of representation in Congress. The three peace churches – Quakers, Mennonites, and Brethren – supported their COs but lacked a political ally such as the No-Conscription Fellowship furnished in Britain. True, the American Socialist Party courageously opposed the war, but its leaders, such as Eugene V. Debs, were savagely persecuted by the wartime authorities. And much the same harsh treatment was meted out to the country's conscientious objectors who resisted conscription.[6]

Eventually the president, recognizing the legitimacy of non-religious objections to military service, had designated the Medical, Quartermaster, and Engineering Corps as suitable locations for conscientious objectors. But while over 16,000 of the COs deemed sincere by their local boards had agreed to serve in the army either as combatants or non-combatants, 3500 men remained in camp. During the final months of the war most of these men were furloughed to work on farms or in hospitals, or with the American Friends Service Committee on overseas relief. However, some COs were not offered this alternative or rejected it on principle. Considered 'sullen and defiant,' they were put on trial.[7] Courts martial then sentenced 450 COs to periods of imprisonment of up to twenty-five years; a few were given life or even sentenced to death (though this was never carried out). Among those convicted were members of the peace churches or other Christian denominations as well as socialist, anarchist, and humanist objectors. A CO from one of America's German peace sects, Maurice Hess, expressed the convictions of this group of objectors in the following words: 'I do not think I am seeking martyrdom ... But ... I know the teaching of Christ, our Savior. He taught us to resist not evil [and] to love our enemies ... I pray God for strength to remain faithful.'[8] Typical of the absolutists was the socialist CO Jacob Wortsman, who in 1917 stated to his court martial: 'I cannot accept military service in any capacity or perform work of any sort under compulsion ... I remain firm by my conviction and will suffer any length of incarceration ... in preference to submitting to a violation of my principles.'[9] But others, ready to accept civilian alternative service, did not escape harsh prison terms. In prison COs, along with ordinary criminals, were frequently subjected to various brutalities,[10] not present usually in British jails of that time. At least one CO, 'unable to withstand the isolation and torment of confinement,' committed suicide.[11] In the fearsome Fort Leavenworth detention barracks, COs, led by Evan Thomas, went on strike in November 1918 to protest prison conditions for COs there. After a couple of months success was gained. 'Emboldened by this example, the entire inmate population gained a new respect for the war resisters.'[12] In January 1919 a general strike at Fort Leavenworth, undertaken jointly by COs and other inmates, took place; and again the strikers met with success. Through the COs' influence, no violence had been used by the strikers; the prison administration promised a number of reforms. (Once the COs had been released, however, the authorities reneged on these promises.)

Release for American COs in jail came even more slowly than for their British counterparts. But by the end of November 1920 no more COs remained in prison. Despite the inordinately extended sentences handed out to COs, as to other military offenders, in fact no objector was kept in prison for much longer than three years. Still, more than enough time would, I think, be fair comment here!

We may note that in contrast to English-speaking countries France, though the homeland of modern democracy, made no provision of any kind for conscientious objectors of any sort – until the mid-1960s. Indeed, universal military service had made its first appearance with the French Revolutionary government's *levée en masse* of 1792. In France almost all those who called themselves 'pacifists' supported the idea of national defence if *la patrie* was in danger. The egalitarian democracy that produced this measure did not favour the claims of a dissident antimilitarist minority. The conscript sufferings that French anarchist and anarcho-syndicalist antimilitarists – and a handful of religious pacifists, too – continued to endure over the decades are largely explained by this background.[13]

Notes

1 Prussia (via the new North German Confederation) introduced universal military service in 1867 and the Russian Empire followed in 1874. Other countries on the European continent adopted this system at various dates during the second half of the nineteenth century. Conscientious objectors, other than the Prussian and 'Russian' Mennonites, were usually jailed for shorter or longer terms depending on the laws and practice of the country concerned. COs, of course, were nowhere very numerous, although some were to be found in small numbers in Russia, as well as in Germany, Austria-Hungary, Serbia and Bulgaria, Scandinavia, Switzerland, and the Netherlands. I know of only two European CO prison memoirs composed before 1914. One of them I have co-edited in an English translation, Peter Brock and John L.H. Keep, eds., *Life in a Penal Battalion of the Imperial Russian Army: The Tolstoyan N.T. Iziumchenko's Story* (York, UK: William Sessions Ltd, 2001). The other memoir is also by a Tolstoyan, this time a Slovak medical doctor named Albert Škarvan, who, after induction into the Austro-Hungarian army, refused further service on grounds of conscience. He published his prison memoir in Russian and Slovak versions. For an abridged English version of this work, see Peter Brock, ed., *Life in an Austro-Hungarian Military Prison: The Slovak Tolstoyan Dr. Albert Škarvan's Story* (Syracuse: Syracuse University Press, 2002).

2 For Quaker absolutist COs, see Thomas C. Kennedy, *British Quakerism, 1860–1920: The Transformation of a Religious Community* (Oxford and New York: Oxford University Press, 2001), 1–3, 9, 329–40, 348–56, 366. Chapters 7, and 9–11 are invaluable for the study of Quaker pacifism in the early twentieth century.

3 See Constance Braithwaite, *Conscientious Objection to Various Compul-*

sions under British Law (York, UK: William Sessions Ltd, 1995), 147–56 ('The Fate of the Law-Breakers'). For background, reference may also be made to John Rae, *Conscience and Politics: The British Government and the Conscientious Objector to Military Service, 1916–1919* (London: Oxford University Press, 1970) and David Boulton, *Objection Overruled* (London: MacGibbon and Kee, 1967). Rae is critical of some of the assertions found in the classic treatment by the Quaker John W. Graham, *Conscription and Conscience: A History, 1916–1919* (London: George Allen and Unwin, 1922), whereas Boulton follows Graham's interpretation fairly closely. A new approach to the study of COs and antiwarism in First World War Britain can be found in Cyril Pearce, *Comrades in Conscience: The Story of an English Community's Opposition to the Great War* (London: Francis Boutle, 2001). The community dealt with here is left-wing Huddersfield. Pearce stresses 'the importance of the local experience and ... perspectives anchored firmly outside London' (p. 25) and calls for the revision of previous views on the subject. Another very useful addition to the literature, though also covering a restricted field, is David Rubinstein, *York Friends and the Great War*, Borthwick Paper no. 96 (Borthwick Institute of Historical Research, University of York, 1999), esp. 17–20. 'The Quakers were usually recognized as genuine pacifists ... The tribunals had more difficulty with lesser known sects ... and even more trouble with members of groups (like the Wesleyans ...) who did not go along with ... their church' in support of the war – and especially with non-religious objectors. See A.J. Peacock, *A History of York from 1900 to 1918*, vol. 2: *York in the Great War: 1914 to 1918* (York: The Settlement Trust, 1993), 395, 537.

4 See P.S. O'Connor, 'The Awkward Ones – Dealing with Conscience, 1916–1918,' *New Zealand Journal of History* 8, no. 2 (October 1974), 118–36.

5 David M. Kennedy, *Over Here: The First World War and American Society* (New York and London: Oxford University Press, 1980), 163.

6 See Stephen M. Kohn, *Jailed for Peace: The History of American Draft Law Violators, 1658–1985* (Westport, CT: Greenwood Press, 1986), 25–43. Norman Thomas, *Is Conscience a Crime?* (New York: Vanguard Press, 1927), though outdated, remains unsuperseded. For the later 'Catholic Worker' Ammon Hennacy's account of his incarceration as a CO in Atlanta Prison in 1917–19, see his memoir printed in Staughton Lynd and Alice Lynd, eds., *Nonviolence in America: A Documentary History*, rev. ed. (Maryknoll, NY: Orbis Books, 1995), 104–19; repr. from A. Hennacy, ed., *Two Agitators: Peter Maurin – Ammon Hennacy* (New York: The

Catholic Worker, 1959), 6–19. Hennacy had entered prison an anarchist atheist not a pacifist. In prison, 'locked up ... in solitary,' he read the New Testament for the first time since childhood; the Sermon on the Mount converted him to Christian pacifism. Hennacy became a Catholic in 1952.

7 Kennedy, *Over Here*, 163–5.

8 Ekkehart Krippendorff and Christian Bartolf, eds., *Pazifismus in den USA: Materialien* (Berlin: John F. Kennedy Institut für Nordamerikastudien, Freie Universität Berlin, 1986), vol. 2: 389, 390.

9 Quoted in Kohn, *Jailed for Peace*, 26.

10 Ibid., 29–33 ('Torture and Mistreatment').

11 Ibid., 32. Ernest Gellert, a humanist pacifist, took his life on 8 April 1918.

12 Ibid., 35.

13 See Michel Auvray, *Objecteurs, insoumis, déserteurs: Histoire des Réfractaires en France* (Paris: Editions Stock, 1983), which runs from pre-revolutionary times to the early 1980s. For religious conscientious objection during the interwar years, especially with reference to the Protestant church, read Peter Farrugia, 'The Conviction of Things Not Seen: Christian Pacifism in France, 1919–1945,' 101–16 in Peter Brock and Thomas P. Socknat, eds., *Challenge to Mars: Essays on Pacifism from 1918 to 1945* (Toronto: University of Toronto Press, 1999). The antimilitarist *réfractaire* Louis Lecoin (1888–1971), who devoted almost the whole of his adult life to the struggle for peace, has left an account of his time in prison as a First World War CO. See Louis Lecoin, *De prison en prison* (Antony-Seine, published by the author, 1947), 87–94, 96–105 (also found in another version of his autobiography, self-published in Paris under the title *Le cours d'une vie*, in 1965). Clearly, conditions in the military prisons in which Lecoin was incarcerated outdid in horror those existing in the jails where British and Americans COs were lodged. The United States might have its Alcatraz, but after all Devil's Island was French! Lecoin was finally released from prison a couple of years after the armistice.

Britain

STEPHEN HOBHOUSE

In the First World War, imprisoned COs in British jails had a rough time. Indeed, they were not singled out for especially harsh treatment; towards the end of the war the government even conceded them a few privileges not granted to common criminals. Still, despite some recent reforms, conditions in British jails in that period reflected the severe regimen of the penitentiary system introduced some fifty to a hundred years before.[1] In particular, prisoners regarded the rule of silence, dietary punishment, and the broad-arrow uniform with abhorrence. Jailed COs came to share their feelings as they had come to share their plight. After the war was over, two CO ex-prisoners collaborated to produce a lengthy and extensively researched report that constituted a devastating critique of the whole British prison system. It appeared in 1922 under the title *English Prisons Today*. Its joint authors were the saintly Quaker Stephen Hobhouse and the fiery socialist Fenner Brockway.[2] Their work, which was sponsored by the Prison System Enquiry Committee (not an exclusively pacifist body), initiated a new wave of prison reform, the impact of which is still felt today.

Stephen Hobhouse (1881–1961) was born into a wealthy Liberal patrician family. Brought up as a member of the established Church of England, he was given a sound classical education, first at Eton College and then at the University of Oxford. As the eldest son he was expected to follow in his father's footsteps in politics or one of the liberal professions. Instead, influenced by the prophetic writings of Tolstoy, Stephen, with the support of his wife Rosa, renounced his inheritance and adopted voluntary poverty as his lifestyle; the couple went to live in Hoxton, a slum district in East London. At the same time, they joined the Quaker Society of Friends: a move that strengthened their attachment to pacifism. Husband and wife now became active in Quaker service.

When conscription came in 1916, Hobhouse, along with many other young Quaker activists, took the unconditionalist stand and, as a result, soon found himself in prison.

In his pamphlet *An English Prison from Within*, largely reprinted below,[3] Hobhouse foreshadows the critique that he and Brockway were to present in their famous report.

[My] aim ... is to give the reader a record of the writer's impressions of our prison system, and, in particular, of its moral and mental effect upon convicted prisoners. It is based upon some twelve months' experience of prison life, of which four months were spent in a large London prison, and nearly eight months in a smaller county gaol. My offence happened to be that of 'disobedience' to military orders on the ground of conscientious objection to all war; but I do not wish to lay any stress on the nature of the offence, or on the justice of the two successive sentences imposed, except in so far as these considerations gave us a different outlook from the ordinary 'criminals' occupying the adjoining cells. We objectors to conscription were not conscious of any guilt involved in the act for which we were committed to gaol; on the contrary, we were, more or less powerfully, sustained in our endurance by a faith in the righteousness, and, in many cases, in the supremely Christian character of the cause for which we conceived ourselves to be suffering loss of liberty and a measure of persecution. Rightly or wrongly, this was our conviction, and it reacted, of course, upon our impressions of prison, and differentiated them in some important respects from those of a hardened or a penitent 'offender.' But the main tendencies of the system, its general effects on character and mentality, seemed to me to be sufficiently clear, and to be of a similar nature for all prisoners involved. Almost all conscientious objectors court-martialled have received sentences of 'hard labour' (which may be repeated indefinitely) varying from 112 days to two years; and, until the last week of my imprisonment* we were treated, with a few unimportant exceptions, in the same way as other prisoners undergoing 'hard labour' in the third division. At the end of 1917, a few privileges were accorded to objectors who had been at least twelve months under sentence; of these the only ones of value were the permission to have books sent in from the outside, and the provision daily of two periods of exercise, at which talking in pairs is allowed ...

... The prison system as it exists to-day, with but slight variations, throughout the British Isles ... was inaugurated during the second half

* I was discharged in December 1917, as the result of the Government's undertaking to release men suffering materially in health.

of the eighteenth century in one or two local experiments that came to nothing; it was given a partial trial at the famous Millbank Penitentiary opened in 1816, but was only really developed in the forties of the last century, when the principle of entire separation was adopted by the Government as the result of a Commission of enquiry into the methods of American penitentiaries. During the period 1840–60 some sixty new 'cellular' prisons were built, beginning with the 'model' institution at Pentonville as we have it to-day. Only from 1877, when the Prison Act placed all gaols under the newly-formed board of Prison Commissioners, has the present uniformity of discipline held sway. Before the opening of Millbank, with its 1000, and Pentonville, with its 520 separate cells, indiscriminate herding together of offenders was the general rule. Practically, therefore, the present regime of silence and solitude is less than eighty years old. Have its results in any way justified even this term of existence?

It may be premised that the usual 'hard labour' sentence begins with a month of strict confinement to one's cell (apart from exercise and chapel), accompanied by a fortnight's plank bed and other disabilities. After the first month, good conduct secures one the privilege of 'associated' but silent labour during part of the day.

The characteristics of the system, as impressed upon me by many dreary weeks of experience, seemed to group themselves around three main heads, which I propose to illustrate successively: firstly, discomfort for the body and starvation for the soul; secondly, the attempt to crush out the sense of individuality and the instinct to serve others; and, lastly, entire absence of trust, and government by fear. These characteristics are dominant enough to give the impression that they represent the guiding objects of the system; and they seem to stamp it as essentially deterrent and punitive, without the reformative elements that one would hope to find there.

As might be expected, the most obvious feature of prison is the disappearance of every kind of luxury and comfort, and the restriction of 'supplies' to those required to satisfy the most elementary needs of food, clothing, housing, and cleanliness. To the general principle of this the idealist can take little exception; and, though unpleasant and, in some respects, damaging to health, it need have no terrors to a man who is robust in body and determined in will. But, unfortunately, months of forced abstemiousness seem unable to kill a man's desire for self-indulgence. We found that the solitude and monotony, combined with other circumstances, led us to devour our food with a greed of which we should have been heartily ashamed elsewhere; and a typical inscription on doors or walls was: 'Roll on, another week, and then I'll have a good smoke outside.' The insistence upon the daily cleaning of cell and utensils tends, doubtless, towards good habits; but, to one accustomed to a daily bath, the hurried weekly prison bath, and the wearing of the same underclothing day and night for a fortnight, seemed a mockery reminiscent of 'white-washed sepulchres,' when associated with the requirement of a constant and scrupulous daily polish of the 'tins' which form the cell's chief furniture.

While, however, bodily needs are cared for up to a certain point, social and spiritual needs, so essential for the purposes of reformation, are almost completely neglected. To those of us who were registered as Quakers, our fortnightly half-hour of united worship, and our fortnightly ten minutes with our visiting minister, were brief glimpses of Heaven; and other prisoners who were Catholics or Nonconformists may have had advantages of a similar kind, though far too fragmentary to be of much avail. But the usual prisoner, nominally 'Church of England,' is supposed to subsist entirely, as far as his soul is concerned, on three or four 'chapels' a week, for the most part formal and unspiritual in character, together with occasional visits from the chaplain, who, it is to be feared, usually finds that the professional nature of his appearances erects insurmountable barriers between him and the occupant of the cell. I say this while rendering an admiring tribute to the efforts which I know some chaplains make to touch the souls of their imprisoned flock. But, in the main, the system neutralises their efforts; and, in all probability, few of them understand the psychology of the prisoner's mind.

The result of this neglect of the soul – and I have more to say which will emphasise this – is well described in a letter written from a London prison by a man who is now in the second year of his sentence.

'Men,' he writes, 'are animalised here. The Governor is responsible to the State for keeping the bodies of the men it sends him for the period stated. I have seen the book marked "Body Receipt Book." It took me some time to find a fitting comparison for this well-run machine, clean and regular, but it is that we are treated as bodies without souls. The reforming zeal of John Howard surely did not intend the solitary system to become (I cannot describe it better otherwise) *a human dog-kennel*.'

This treatment of a man as a dog, or, by an equally apt comparison, as a component part of a machine that needs little or no attention beyond watching and oiling at fixed intervals, leads on naturally to my second point. Nearly every feature of prison life seems deliberately arranged to destroy a man's sense of his own personality, his power of choice and initiative, his possessive instincts, his conception of himself as a being designed to love and to serve his fellow-man. His very name is blotted out, and he becomes a number; A.3.21 and D.2.65 were two of my designations. He and his fellows are elaborately counted, whenever moved about from one location to another, in the characteristic machine-like way;– '15 men, correct,' '38 men, correct'; so the warder has to report many times in the day. He is continually, of course, under lock and key, ignored except as an object for spying. When not locked up, he can hardly move a muscle except under orders. There is usually a fixed and unvarying monotony about the daily and weekly round. In default of other interests, one's soul dwells longingly on the few incidents like the weekly bath, the weekly change of socks and towel, the daily dinner and march round the exercise-ring, that break the dulness of life. The scanty contents of one's cell must be arranged, subject to the daily inspection, in exact uniformity with the arrangement of every other cell. This does not, it is true, apply to the evening and night-time; and it is a real satisfaction to be able to choose on which portion of one's cement floor the bed board is to be laid down. There is an almost complete denudation of personal property, and of that sense of self-expression and choice in things which is its chief spiritual value. The only articles that I could call absolutely my own were my spectacles, my wife's letters, four small photographs, and two books – the Weymouth New Testament and Fellowship Hymn-book – which are allowed to Quakers. Otherwise everything is on loan, usually for short periods, until mending or washing is required, or until one is shifted to another, but barely distinguishable cell.*

Still more detrimental than this more than monastic suppression of self is the deliberate removal of all a man's opportunities to serve his fellow, to do him a good turn, to interchange thoughts and greetings with him. On a large printed card, which forms one of the chief features of the cell-landscape, there is written:– 'Rule 1. Prisoners must observe silence. Rule 2. They must not communicate, or attempt to do so, with one another.'[4] Two other keystones of the system, which appear lower down, read to the effect that no prisoner must 'leave his cell or other appointed location without permission'; and that no prisoner may,

* From a hygienic point of view, the promiscuous wearing of different articles of underclothing (often inadequately washed) is a defect that needs attention.

'without express authority, hand to, or receive from, another prisoner any article whatever.' Even apart from the specific mental injuries caused by the enforced silence, it is clear how completely these rules destroy the healthy, normal activities of human intercourse. Designed to prevent collusion and conspiracy among the prisoners, and to make it difficult for them to corrupt one another, they succeed in making courtesy, friendliness, and acts of goodwill either an impossibility or a crime.

One instance, within my own experience, will give an idea of the monstrous folly of such regulations. Since April 1917, the prison rations have been severely curtailed; and there is good evidence to show that many men are suffering seriously from underfeeding. Nearly all of us constantly knew what hunger means; and an extra crust of dry bread would be to most a great prize. A friend of mine was seen by one of the warders handing to another prisoner, who, as he doubtless supposed, needed it more than himself, a piece of bread. He was reported to the Governor for breaking the last rule quoted above. (To do warders justice, I believe most of them would wink at such an offence.) And for this crime my friend had all his 'privileges' suspended; his term of imprisonment was prolonged by a day or two; and he was awarded three days of solitary confinement in his cell on a diet of bread and water, the cell being absolutely stripped of every movable thing except his stool and his bible. The receiver of the bread suffered a similar punishment. What are we to think of a system which treats as crimes, requited by savage penalties, acts that, outside a prison, are among the most lovable and beautiful that human life can show?

It is needless to say that this prohibition of intercourse, this driving of a man back exclusively upon himself, his own defects, his own grievances, his own needs, promotes the habit of selfishnes to a most grievous extent. I found myself that almost the only outlet for the altruistic instincts was praying for others; a fine art in which, it is to be feared, the majority of ordinary prisoners have not been taught any proficiency. And prayer without scope for action is woefully insufficient.

At the same time, the cruel contempt with which one appeared to be treated roused bitter and aggrieved feelings which it needed a great effort to suppress. Apart from actual brutality, harsh words sank in deep. I remember one Sunday so foggy that my small window did not admit enough light for either sewing or reading. As it happened, we had no morning chapel, and there was nothing to do except pace mournfully round one's chilly cell. On remonstrating in the evening with a friendly warder for not having given us some artificial light, he answered smilingly, 'You aren't worth it; it's not a work day.' And this rebuff chanced to come immediately after evening chapel, at which I allowed myself to get hopelessly self-conscious and irritable, because, while I was singing the Te Deum and looking round about me to get a sense of fellowship with the other faces, the warder's harsh voice broke in with 'Number Two Sixty-five, look to your front.' It is a hard struggle for men to keep back bitter thoughts, when almost the only breaks to the deadly monotony are such remarks as these.

There are, it is true, one or two redeeming features, which must be mentioned, so as not to exaggerate this aspect of my subject. Out of every thirty or forty men, one fortunate man, selected as 'cleaner,' has freedom to move about his landing and do small things for the various occupants of the cells, *e.g.* empty their slops and fill their water-tins, and assist the warder in the distribution of rations. There was one such man whom I was tempted to consider something of a materialist. His philosophy of life was 'to be honest with oneself.' But then he told me that by being 'honest with himself' he meant, *e.g.*, not putting aside one of the larger pieces of bread for his own consumption, when handing them out at meal time, although hunger sorely tempted him to do so at the expense of some other prisoner. And there are a few, but very few, other privileged occupations in prison which afford opportunities for active goodwill.

Again, what I have said above as to the absence of the power of choice and the sense of possession must be qualified in two or three ways. First there is a certain amount of choice allowed as regards the library and 'educational' books, which may be changed weekly. Then, some outlet for one's feelings is supplied by the possession of a slate on which inscriptions may be made and erased at one's pleasure (though this is no real substitute for the use of pen or pencil). And – of much greater value – there are the monthly visits from the outside world, and the monthly letters in and out, which are allowed, under restrictions, after the first three months. The brightest ornaments of one's cell are one's little pile of books, the photographs of family and friends, of which four may be sent in, and the letters from home, for which, by a flash of rare illumination, the Prison Commissioners provide a little wooden rack. But these few exceptions do not touch the tendency of the whole system, though they represent small but praiseworthy efforts to redeem it. The vast majority of men work away mechanically at their mat-making or mail-bag sewing, and have no opportunities such as those of the 'cleaner' or library-assistant. And I am afraid that a considerable proportion of ordinary prisoners have not learnt to aspire to any books beyond a sensational novel or magazine, and have no homes capable of acting as sources of inspiration to the monthly letter or visit.

It will be readily inferred from what I have already said that prisons are characterised by an almost complete absence of trust in the honour or obedience of the prisoner; and that the warders and Governor rule not by love but by the fear which punishment and the threat to punish inspire. The regulations that hang on the wall of each cell give a portentous list of some twenty or thirty different forms of activity, for which punishment is prescribed; and the attempt to indulge in any one of these is punishable equally with the activity itself. As we were moved about to and from chapel or workshop or exercise-ring, warders were stationed at different vantage points, with the object of cutting off every effort to communicate with the next man. 'Keep that tongue quiet or you'll soon be having a change of diet,' was a frequent exhortation. Every step and action is watched and spied upon. The gardening gang, for instance, has to move about as if they were roped together. Whenever one man has the smallest job in another part of the garden, *e.g.* emptying out some weeds or fetching some vegetables for replanting, the whole party has to down tools and accompany him; otherwise the warder in charge would be temporarily out of sight or hearing of one portion or other of his gang. The whole effect is ridiculous in the extreme, and not calculated to produce good work.

Compared with this constant and wearing bondage outside one's cell, the stern walls, barred windows, and locked door of that small chamber furnish a certain sense of freedom. But even here there is no true privacy. About once a month there is a surprise search of everything in one's cell and of one's clothing, to detect forbidden articles. One's person is searched too on the return from the laundry or the garden, lest a piece of soap or a raw vegetable should be hidden there – and, in fact, so hungry were we, that I have seen many a root grabbed from the soil surreptitiously, at exercise or while gardening. Every cell door is provided with a glass spy-hole, through which the inmate can be inspected at any hour of the day or night. The warder walks about outside in soft slippers like a cat, and noiselessly slips aside the spy-hole's cover. In this way, even when one's daily task is fully completed, one may be threatened with punishment by a harsh voice for lying down before bedtime or for standing upon one's stool to gaze longingly out of the scanty and heavily-barred window – an action which exposes one to the suspicion of attempting to communicate with the man in one of the adjoining cells.

The want of confidence in the prisoners is accompanied by a corresponding want of confidence in the warders. These officers are also spied upon by the Chief Warder and Governor; and such is the fear of collusion or bribery, that a warder is forbidden to engage in 'familiar' conversation with a prisoner, and is not supposed to say anything to him that does not bear upon his work or the prison rules. This rule is largely disregarded, but, as warders themselves have complained to me, it makes it practically impossible for them to exercise a lasting reformative or uplifting influence on a prisoner. Yet, if any one could help to reform him, it would be, not the Chaplain or Governor, but the warder, who has to supply all his needs, direct his work and control his movements. The harshness and solitude of prison make one peculiarly sensitive to any token of kindness or compassion that breaks through the machine-like routine; and I have often poured blessings inwardly upon a warder for some kindly look or word. I have heard the better warders denounce the present system as 'tyranny' from their point of view also, and express regret, on grounds of humanity, that they ever entered the prison service. Considering the nature of the tasks imposed upon them, it is less surprising that some of them should become harsh task-masters than that others should preserve, in spite of it all, so much of the milk of human kindness. The only criticism one can make of most warders – and that only tentatively – is that they do not relinquish a profession in which daily actions of direct or indirect harshness to their fellow-beings are inseparable from the routine of duty.

I will add one little incident to show that the trouble usually lies much less with the character of the warders than with the system which they have to enforce. At one of the monthly visits allowed after the first three months of a sentence, I was given the exceptional privilege of seeing my wife, with only a long table between us, instead of through the usual double set of bars or wire gauze. One of the strictest warders was 'taking' the interview, and at the end my wife asked to be allowed a parting kiss. The warder bluntly refused, and the interview ended. Whereat I, knowing that other warders (in defiance, of course, of the rules) would have allowed it, forgot my principles and murmured a vicious 'You brute!' beneath my breath.[5] But I had not long been back again in my cell and was trying to change my curse into a blessing, when I heard a key in the lock, and the tyrant of our visit came in, and, in a way that indicated how deeply moved he was, begged me to believe that he felt as unhappy over the incident as we must be feeling, and that there was nothing more hateful than having the duty of 'standing between man and wife.' My faith in humanity was renewed.

Such being the leading characteristics of the system, I will now attempt to illustrate further from my own personal experience what I regard as the most deplorable and immoral of all the rules. This is the attempt to enforce complete silence and separation upon prisoners. In the first place, this regulation, together with the absence of trust that is so conspicuous, brings to bear upon almost every prisoner an overpowering temptation to swerve more and more from the path of truthfulness and openness of conduct, and to fall into varying degrees of dishonesty, deception, and artfulness.

In point of fact hardly any prisoners keep the absolute rule of silence during a single day of their term. Some warders, sensitive to the inhuman nature of the restriction, wink more or less openly at talking between prisoners, at least whenever there is no danger of a sudden invasion from the Chief Warder or Governor; but they do this at considerable risk, for they may be fined, and even discharged, for allowing conversation. On the other hand, it is practically impossible for the strictest and most dutiful warder to detect all breaches of the rule. There are brief occasions on the exercise-ring or elsewhere, when the prisoner is actually too far away from him to be overheard; more often it is due to the simple fact that the warder's eyes cannot be turned in the direction of every prisoner at once. Talking without detection in a special kind of whisper, that will not carry more than a yard or two, becomes a fine art; as does also the swift handing of a note or other harmless article to one's neighbour, while the warder's attention is directed elsewhere. It is easy to imagine to what a pitch of skill the professional thief or burglar develops this artfulness. I used to watch them as we sat together in the workroom, where, at regulated intervals, some thirty of us were sewing our bags in apparent silence.

Under the pressure of the cruel and unnatural restrictions nearly all of us conscientious objectors were also driven to similar forms of underhand communication. From the first, I personally took every opportunity of exchanging cheerful greetings and scraps of news with my companions in misfortune. Apart from the much-needed outlet for self-expression, it seemed a religious duty to pass on words of cheer and interest. At one time a single brief remark could be thrown out, at another a considerable conversation, protracted probably by interruptions, might even be carried on. In this way one's various companions gradually became distinct personalities, and one could love them and pray for them with far more reality. And one's efforts, some successful and some unsuccessful, to communicate with different men added a spice of adventure to the monotony of the day. But gradually, as the months passed by, I felt increasingly the disloyalty to the spirit of absolute Truth entailed by the calculation and concealment without which the prohibited conversation would have been impossible. The sin against Truth was of a very subtle and excusable kind, but it was real; and one slight shade of untruthfulness led on to another of a darker hue. Words thrown out quickly and boldly, when one was momentarily out of range of the warder's eyes and ears, might be blameless enough. But it is different when one habitually turns round to examine that officer's location and attentiveness, before venturing a whispered remark; or when one actually contracts the habit of closely watching his eyes, and regulates one's speech or silence in accordance with their direction at the moment, adopting involuntarily expressions of innocence when those suspicious eyes are turned upon oneself. And even when an unusually friendly warder openly winked at our whispered conversation, *we* were really involved in the deception, which he, by secretly allowing us to break the rules, was practising on the authorities responsible for the discipline.

Some may think it ridiculous to be conscientious about such minute and excusable breaches of the code of truth, but there seems to me no doubt that their cumulative effect was to create an atmosphere of falsehood, suspicion, and dishonesty which affected adversely every one in the prison; and that, to those who had previously acquired no rooted love of truth, prison was a school of artfulness and deceit, as effective as human ingenuity could devise. In any case certain incidents, into which I need not enter here, caused me, when I had spent about eight months in prison, to decide that, cost what it might, I must once and for all break the meshes of calculating concealment in which I, along with the others, was entangled, and must make an open protest to the Governor against the inhuman rule which lay at the root of the whole trouble. The result was that, in order to prevent my carrying out my intention of talking openly to my fellow-prisoners, I was removed to a cell at a distance from the others, had a separate track to myself for the daily exercise, and spent the rest of my time, with the exception of four (or at most five) weekly periods of 'chapel,' in solitary confinement in my cell, where, of course, talking to other men was impossible. On an average nearly twenty-three hours of every twenty-four were spent inside my locked door for about four months preceding my release.

I was now almost completely removed from temptation to untruthfulness, but, on the other hand, I felt the full pressure of the undiluted 'solitary' or 'separate system,' as distinguished from the 'system of silent association' – for so they were called when first introduced. I rejected the very few opportunities that brought me within speaking range of fellow-prisoners, and was entirely dependent for conversation on the warders and the three chaplains, two Church and one 'Quaker.' The occasional visits of the chaplains amounted in the aggregate to fifteen or twenty minutes in the week; and the warders, though, for various purposes, they mechanically unlocked my cell door nine or ten times in the twenty-four hours, were as a rule either unwilling or too busy to listen to one's remarks or to say anything beyond the different formulas of the day, 'All right?' 'Exercise,' 'Empty slops!' 'More bags or thread wanted?' etc.* At first, indeed, I used to treasure up remarks on some rare point of interest, which I might fire off, so to speak, as a means of relief, when the warder next faced me; but the opportunity even for this seldom occurred, and failures so depressed me that, as the weeks passed by and mental stagnation increased, I almost ceased to make the effort to address my keeper. I had a Greek Testament and other good books from the prison library, but my tasks of sewing, cell-cleaning, etc., left me little time to read; and, in any case, the isolation weakened the power of mental attention, so that I seemed to have no capacity for reading beyond about an hour daily.

Thus cut off from new impressions, and having no outlet for the expression of the obvious and the casual, my mind tended to become choked with trivialities and the somewhat sordid details of one's cell life. Besides, I was in a poor state of health, and my ailments were increased by the overpowering temptation to dwell upon them. A foolish rhyme or jingle would form itself in my brain, and go on repeating itself endlessly in the most wearisome fashion. And it may be imagined that there was a weakening of one's power of resistance to more positive temptations of evil, to complaint and bitterness, to ill-will and despair. More, however, than the restless dwelling on trivialities and the battling with temptations I dreaded the occasional appearance

* This is, in actual practice, what the advocates of the regime have called *association with the prison staff*, insisting that it is a *separate*, and not a *solitary* system!

of a spell of dazed vacancy of mind, of indifference to everything; for this seemed to be the prelude to the decay of mind and will, which, as I had been told by a prison chaplain, is a not uncommon result of long imprisonments. And in my case I felt that a complete physical breakdown also could only be avoided by a maintenance of my will-power unbroken; for, in the confinement of my small and often very cold cell, the measure of health that I had was dependent upon a daily regime of physical exercises and other devices undertaken often very much against the grain and with the sacrifice of much of my leisure time.

That no permanent mental damage made its appearance during this last and hardest phase of my imprisonment, I attribute entirely to the spiritual equipment with which I was providentially, thanks to my past life, endowed. My principal means of salvation during this period were these: my faith in a personal God revealed in a human Christ; the practice of prayer, especially prayer for others; the habit of talking aloud to God and to my wife; the sense of the love of friends outside; the sense of the justice and holiness of the cause for which I was suffering; and the sight of the courage of my companions in that cause. I am mentioning these facts, in order to emphasise the point that I had means of resistance to the deadliness of prison conditions, which very few, if any, of the ordinary offenders for whom prisons are intended could be expected to possess. I entered prison with all the advantages of a robust philosophy of life, buoyed up by the belief that I was fighting in a good cause, and without any sense of guilt other than that which is inseparable from the Christian outlook upon the world. Yet, with all these advantages, I seem only to have just managed to preserve my mental balance up to the time of my release. I ask myself how I could possibly have survived, if I had possessed little or no faith in a spiritual world, if I had been the victim of unregulated and violent passions, if I had done things for which my conscience smote me, and over which my solitude forced me to brood unceasingly, if I had felt myself friendless, unloved, and unloving, cast out by the society to whose sins against me I imputed my own misery.

It is not difficult to conceive the tortures of soul, to which the complete isolation of prison must drive an individual to whom this description might apply. And in a greater or less degree it probably applies to a large proportion of the occupants of our prisons. Some men, I suppose, are so hardened that the sensitiveness to mental torture is almost absent. But, if so, prison life does nothing to bring about the revolution which would be their only salvation, and only confirms them in their desperate condition. For other men, where penitence or the capacity for it is present, the possibility of amendment is almost removed. Man is essentially a social being; and to take away altogether the healing power of human intercourse, the opportunities for self-expression, and the possibility of doing a good turn to others, is a crime against nature, a deliberate assault upon the citadel of mental and moral life. The human brain is not proof against more than a very limited amount of mental suffering; and both common sense and the actual results of the discipline indicate that, where prison does not simply confirm a man in his hardened state of vice, it ends by breaking down his mind and will-power, so as at least to render him a useless member of society and, in the worst cases, to drive him to insanity.

To sum up, the wickedness of the regime of enforced silence lies herein: if observed, it inevitably tends to produce mental as well as moral decay; if surreptitiously disregarded, it promotes a special form of demoralisation, an undermining of the standard of truthfulness and sincerity. The present method is a mixture of the two systems which competed with one another for favour in the minds of the 19th-century reformers, viz. the 'solitary' or 'separate system,' and the 'silent associated system.' My own experience of some months of associated labour and opportunities for stealthy intercourse, followed by four months of solitary confinement, enabled me to isolate the effects of each method. In the experience of most prisoners, the two systems, with their characteristic features, are intermingled in varying proportions, but without, I think, much loss of the evil effects of each ...

In the upbuilding of a new world out of the ruins of to-day, which is the hope and desire of every patriot, the reform of our prisons will be not the least important part. If the evidence of some of those, who are passing through prisons now, may serve to establish true principles, by which these institutions may become schools of reformation instead of places of demoralisation and torture, their imprisonment, whatever its other results, will not have been in vain.

Notes

Source: Stephen Hobhouse, *An English Prison from Within* (London: George Allen and Unwin, 1919), 13–34, 36.

1 Philip Priestley, in his anthology of modern prison writings, *Jail Journeys:*

The English Prison Experience since 1918 (London and New York: Routledge, 1989), 2, 3, states that, although 'in 1895 the report of the Departmental Committee on Prisons, the Gladstone Report ... declared a policy in which "deterence *and* reformation" were to be the "primary and concurrent objects," ... so far as the male adult prisoners were concerned, twenty years went by and the conscientious objectors of the First World War arrived in their hundreds at Wormwood Scrubs, Wandsworth, and other prisons up and down the country, to find regimes as harsh and as destructive in their effects on human beings as anything the Gladstone Committee had felt moved to criticise.' My italics.

2 Brockway included a lively account of his incarceration as a First World War CO in the two versions of his autobiography, *Inside the Left: Thirty Years of Platform, Press, Prison and Parliament* (London: New Leader Ltd, 1947), originally published by George Allen and Unwin in 1942, and *Towards Tomorrow* (London: Hart-Davis, MacGibbon, 1977). He spent time in Walton Prison, Liverpool, and the prison at Lincoln as well as three London jails – Pentonville, Wandsworth, and Wormwood Scrubs.

3 For another version of his experiences as a CO, see *The Autobiography of Stephen Hobhouse: Reformer, Pacifist, Christian* (Boston: Beacon Press, 1952), 155–68, 171–5; published in the United Kingdom in 1951 as *Forty Years and an Epilogue* by James Clarke and Co.

4 In his unpublished autobiography ('Escape from Paganism,' Library of the Religious Society of Friends, London, TEMP MSS 4-12, fol. 47), another CO, John H. Brocklesby, records the damage the silence rule did to him as a result of spending around two and a half years in prison. After release, he writes, 'I found myself with a peculiar mental defect which was a direct result of the silent system in prison. In conversation I would suddenly become tongue-tied. I was fully aware of the idea I wished to express but the words to express it would not come ... The prison authorities allowed us to exercise our legs; also our digestive faculties at meal times, [which] were not impaired, rather the contrary. But one's faculty of communicating with one's fellows ... is made to rust away.'

5 In August 1917 Hobhouse's aunt, Kate Courtney, and her husband, the distinguished statesman and publicist, Leonard Lord Courtney of Penwith, both of them convinced pacifists, had visited Hobhouse in Exeter Prison. Kate wrote in a privately published *War Diary*: 'We went into a long bare room with a table on one side of which we sat, while Stephen came and sat on the other, and a good-natured warder sat a little way off ... I don't know if I broke prison rules, but I kissed [Stephen] heartily coming and going. Rosa had warned me not to do so, as she had asked the warder if she might

kiss her husband ... Ask a warder if I might kiss my own nephew, certainly not! So I just put my arms around his neck and gave him a good hug, and the warder like a true gentleman, looked out of the window!' Quoted in Sybil Oldfield, *Women against the Iron Fist: Alternatives to Militarism, 1900–1989* (Oxford: Basil Blackwell, 1989), 39.

E. WILLIAMSON MASON

Soon after the introduction of conscription early in 1916 the author of the following document, a young pacifist socialist, had received the first of three successive court-martial sentences of imprisonment for refusing induction into the army. As an absolutist, Edward Williamson Mason refused on each occasion to accept alternative service of any kind. He served his first sentence of 112 days' hard labour in Durham Prison. In letters to a friend, dated 27 and 28 November 1916 and written soon after his release from prison in the army camp at Catterick, he gives his impressions of life in jail and discusses, too, whether COs should, or should not, accept the Home Office Scheme of alternative service under semi-penal conditions, recently promulgated by the government in an effort to clear the jails of their mounting CO population. Mason writes sensibly, but occasionally his style becomes rather stilted. Then too many clichés give his narrative an artificial flavour. Still, the letters he wrote after his release to a friend describing his prison experiences often have a vividness that conveys what these meant to a sensitive individual.

... So you want to know all about my prison life? ...

Prison either makes or blasts a man. It either makes him self-reliant or else it stuns him into a coma, a mental vacuity which time and habit turn into an inability to do anything except under obedience. Unless one has something self-assertive within one that thwarts the ravages of silence and isolation one will be surely damned. The sepulchral silence or reverberating noises of a prison ward seem to wrap one in an impenetrable cloak that suffocates. The banging of iron doors and gates, the jingling of keys, the heavy, measured tread of the officers as they walk along the galleries, the jangling of food tins, the clanking of the rope mill, all, all, have at first a deadening effect upon the brain. The dull monotony, the weary repetition of commands, the regular meal times, the same rotation of food, and the systematic working of all departments, work their depressing ravages upon prisoner and warder alike. Initiative, self-assertion, individuality, are crimes – nay, almost impossibilities.

Prison discipline enforces habits, rigid habits, of the body; and, in cases of men of ordinary mental powers, of the mind as well. It is this sub-conscious struggle between discipline and mind that embitters the first few months of a first offender's imprisonment. But with those who can live the life of the mind, the mind gradually becomes detached, as it were, from the working of the body. The rigid discipline facilitates this process, the machinery of one's life becomes so stereotyped that any one whose mind is active can ignore it. Slowly but surely one becomes a being of bodily habit and mental endurance and cheer – that is, if one has the necessary mental strength. The prison routine is rarely noticed, except, strangely enough, upon the one day (Sunday) when it is suspended or different from the weekday.

Once the mind is free the prisoner has worked out his salvation, he has little to fear and much to hope. The pleasure of having worn away another day or week without pain or grief adds to his steadily growing stock of fortitude; the satisfaction of finding himself still undismayed, still courageous, although all alone in a cold bare cell, is an emotion which makes him swell with pride and joy. To this type of man imprisonment for a principle is the greatest blessing that can befall him.

But there are other types who unfortunately commence the prison routine struggle with a determination in excess of their powers of resistance. Up to a certain point their endurance awakens admiration, they resist the gnawings and filings of discipline with apparent success. But suddenly, alas, their hard case of courage is penetrated and the soft inside ruthlessly shattered, and they pine away in a silence and despair most pitiful to see.

Others, a splendid, glorious few, of whom I was not, stood firm and defiant come what might. And yet they too suffered. With some their eyes were wild, with others kindly and sympathetic, yet others were furtive and appealing for a word of sympathy and encouragement. But alas, who could give it them? Could their fellow C.O.'s, who were suffering through youthfulness and struggling for themselves? All were mere lads, unaccustomed to spiritual strife or emotional conflict, all called suddenly to face a test which might have shaken the wisdom and experience of a man of fifty.

I hear that some of our cause call traitors those who accepted the Home Office offer of work. We who are now absolutists do not do that, we who have perhaps been fortunate in getting spiritual succour to inspire us. No, those alone who were absolutists from the first have perhaps the questionable right to call the alternativists traitors, but they do not, for they alone know through sympathy and experience what their brethren suffered.

Not one of those who accepted was older than thirty, many, very many, were mere lads of nineteen or so; what can you expect from such immature material? I know you will say the question is not one of age; I submit that has a great deal to do with it. Lads, full of frolic and caprice, intense lovers of sport, conversant, in so far as it is possible to be conversant in clubs and debating societies, with modern social problems, the majority regular attendants at nonconformist chapels, I say they did well, but undoubtedly they might have done better. To make a decision requires mental strength; to carry it out, courage; to persist until the final triumph, the mettle of a martyr. I say they did well, and I only wish they had done as I did in rescinding their decision to accept alternative service. But I at least cannot blame them, I at least should understand and sympathise with them, for I was of them until you showed me the higher way. Knowing what I suffered and knowing that I should have fallen irredeemably without exterior aid, I deprecate the stigmatisation of those who fell as I fell, and had no helping hand to raise them as your hand raised me.

Oh, it was pitiful to see the men who at first refused the Home Office scheme* gradually dwindle in number as, one by one, they slunk down to the Governor and asked him to write to the Home Office rescinding their decision. To see a man one day pacing the exercise yard with resolute step, steady eye, and open mien and bold, gradually, as time wore on, look as though he had been whipped and had his tail between his legs, fearing to look at you in case you penetrated his secret intention of accepting Home Office work, endeavouring to appear so as to avert or allay suspicion; oh, it was pitiful. But the furtive look was in his eyes. That was the sign of spiritual defeat, the curse of the furtive eye. At last he would slink down to the Governor, and if asked by a fellow-

* What is said here is of course only applicable to a certain percentage of those who accepted the Home Office Scheme. Many conscientious objectors are convinced believers in Alternative Service, and were able to accept the scheme without any conscientious scruples.

C.O. why he had been 'cased' (to be 'cased' is to go before the Governor as a case of disobedience or what not) he would bluster, blush, ejaculate something unintelligible and hurry away. Or he would lie a brazen lie, or give some ridiculous excuse of childish explanation; but his furtive eye betrayed him. He was under that human necessity to justify himself to himself, in order that his ego should not be affronted before itself and droop its head before the searing truth that he was not strong enough to stand the test he was undergoing. They were men to be pitied, and I sympathise with them with all my heart, but words of cheer were of no avail; they gave in and went, two by two, to Wakefield[1] or elsewhere. And although we felt a pang of regret at their departure – the fall of a comrade – we were more determined than ever to go on come what might. 'The gentleman C.O.'s,' as we were called, walked the parade-ground with a firmer and a merrier tread than ever. The fall of a comrade is a painful sight, especially when he tries to excuse his failure by brazen subterfuges. One feels humiliated at his degradation and squirms at the sight of his furtive eye ...

Prison trials are mostly spiritual rather than material to a sympathetic nature. But to some the physical discomforts are predominant. How [my friend,] poor Fleckner used to complain of insufficient food, and dozens of others, too, unfortunately! The first words I overheard upon my first visit to Chapel were:

'By gum, when I *do* get out I'll eat and eat.'

Food obsessed the prisoners' minds, and most surely were they punished for their incapacity to rise superior to the obsession. How often did I counsel Fleckner, for his own sake, not to think of nothing else but food, to try to forget it, to tighten up his trouser straps as hungry navvies do. But no, not a snatch of secret conversation but contained some reference to hunger. He certainly punished himself far more than prison need punish any man. The warning of his example, I hope and believe, was not wasted upon me.

I often used to listen during the long hours of the night to the many disturbances which broke the heavy silence. The muffled boots of the warder as he went from cell to cell to peep in to see what the prisoner was doing; the delirious man suffering from hallucinations, shouting in sheer terror and despair through being alone in the dark with the horrors of his mind, screaming out to a warder:

'Oh God, oh God, talk to me. Say anything, only for God's sake talk to me.'

And the warder's response, both kindly and soothing, but expressing inability to do anything for the suppliant. Then the groan of despair from the wretched prisoner as the warder went away and left him in his mental hell.

Imagine the thrill of horror felt by a young conscientious objector who overhears all this as he lies upon his sleepless bed, his heart yearning for those he loves and overwhelmed by the thought that he must be away from home two years in a prison. Imagine further, what horror and anguish he would feel at the sight of a convict suddenly stopping near-by and clutching his (the convict's) face until the blood ran from his cheeks because of his finger nails tearing the flesh, shuddering, sweating, bending over at the knees, gasping out spasmodically exclamations of sheer terror and despair, as the full realisation of the meaning of a two years' sentence flooded his not too powerful mind; and then falling in a heap like a limp rag.

The warders meanwhile look on with indifference, saying to the horror-stricken C.O.:

'Oh, he'll get over that.' ...

How horrible it is to see eyes usually submissive burst out into wild fires of passion, and the prisoner shout out, stamp, rave, and smash something in desperation at the suffocating blanket of discipline, and after the fury has passed relapse into his usual quiet demeanour. The prison system which compels youths or first offenders to witness such sights is an accursed thing, and the responsibility for hardening such men into confirmed criminals rests upon those who defend it. Some of the sights I saw I shall never forget, and had my prison clothes been a criminal's garb and not a suit of honour, I should have left the prison a worse criminal than I entered it.

Prisoners have a mania for doing things that are punishable if discovered, and spend hours scheming to do them by force or cunning. Mostly they are ridiculously trivial, such as having a nail or a piece of glass either in one's cell or upon one's person. It is not that the nail or glass is of any use, but that its possession is forbidden that constitutes the attraction ... The convict who possesses an object forbidden flatters his vanity by the reflection that, despite the cleverness and vigilance of the warders, he must be cleverer than they because he can circumvent them. And in the prison, which otherwise would crush him, he saves his ego from entire defeat by the secret possession of a nail or a pin or a pencil, anything so long as it is forbidden. The mania for doing wrong things simply because they are prohibited and involve punishment if discovered arises from this craving of the convict to delude himself as to his own powers and freedom. 'I am too sharp, too clever for the warders and the Governor,' is a reflection that soothes his incarcerated vanity, and he will cheerfully bear pain and discomfort to maintain this good opinion of himself ...

One thing above all, the criminals are democratic and generous. They will share food with a man under punishment, or even steal some for him; and they will share any forbidden plunder, such as a raw onion or a carrot, although in procuring it they have risked three days' bread and water. I shall never forget having a piece of raw onion given me one morning. I took it from a convict who sidled up to me and whispered:

''Ere's a bit treat for 'e, lad.'

I took the object and thanked him without knowing what it was, grateful not so much for the gift as for the generosity and regard of which it was the sign. I put the onion in my only pocket, which happened to be just above the heart, and consequently only a few inches from the eyes and nose. As my body warmed the onion, its effluvium increased, and my eyes began to water furiously. I dared not offend my generous friend by throwing his gift away, moreover that would have been sacrilege, seeing the spirit in which it was made, and yet I could not eat the wretched thing to save my life. I endured tortures until I could throw away the onion out of sight of the donor, who, by the way, would have been punished with three days' bread and water had his theft been discovered. Was it not noble of him to risk so much for a lad of whom he knew nothing?

Sometimes the prisoners used to fight, and were severely punished by the Governor. The cause of nearly all the fights I witnessed was some joke anent the chastity of the wife of one of the combatants. The prisoners, although generally filthy and obscene in their jokes, would fight furiously at any slighting reference to the honour of their wives. It was rather droll to see a man who had just been wallowing in filth (verbally, *bien entendu*) suddenly become inflamed with passion and rush at another man because the latter made some remark about his wife, mild in comparison with *his* recent obscenities.

Another droll thing was that man and wife were often in prison together – in separate sections of course. When a man was sentenced, his wife would steal something and get arrested in order to be supported by the State whilst also under its charge. Upon release they would have a spell of liberty, love, and housekeeping together so long as the husband could pursue his profession without awakening the vulgar and offensive curiosity of the police, and when he was caught they would arrange to rest and recuperate together in prison again. A merry fellow told me it required the nicest discrimination upon the part of his wife to select an offence calculated to bring about an imprisonment coterminous with his. Truly our prison system is worthy of all admiration!

So far as my experience at Durham goes, it would appear that the same men turn up in prison time after time. Prison is a deterrent in *imagination*, but when one has experienced the reality, one sees that prison terrors are to a certain extent fictitious. Of course prison has its discomforts, even its terrors, but habit deadens them, and one comes to endure them with equanimity. There are many things worse, and it speaks ill for our social system that to some its punishment should be preferable to its protection. To many men in prison, life would offer worse things were they honest, so they can accept with equanimity an existence three parts of which may be spent in prison.

There are some temperaments to which prison is preferable to the Army. There were men at Durham who were there as a deliberately provoked alternative to being soldiers. After all, I suppose that if a man does not care particularly for his country it is small wonder that he goes to prison rather than fight for it ...

At first I felt my loss of liberty most when I attended chapel. I shall never forget the first time. The prisoners enter in single file and take their seats, which are overlooked by warders seated upon raised platforms. There are the usual pulpit and altar at one end of the building. The Governor sat beside the altar in a pew commanding a view of all the prisoners. At the foot of his pew was an organ harmonium, terribly out of tune. Upon the altar were a brass cross and two vases of flowers flanked by two tall anaemic candles, which looked as though they were going over at the knees.

One of our C.O.'s played a march as the men entered and took their seats, and the War notices were given out as soon as he had finished.

Then came the service. Some fine chanting from the prisoners and some hymns, which all sang with desperation, regardless of time ... – just one great overwhelming offensive until the hymn was finished. The sermons, without exception, were insipid and boring; in fact, to listen to them comprised the 'hard labour' of our sentence. Both Chaplain and criminals were hard-hearted, and no one, especially the Chaplain, refrained from displaying boredom at the whole business ...

When the dreadful sermon was at last over, the prisoners revived their drooping spirits by attacking another hymn and carrying it by assault. They let themselves go, and sang with an almost terrific gusto. Piety there was none, only a poor silent prisoner's delight in noise. And yet there is something, an indefinable something, which touches one's heart at the sound of three hundred male voices singing a hymn. I sometimes think they sing so hard because they try to smother the pang that chills and the weary ache of heart engendered by their isolation and desolation.

Although one may sometimes be inspirited by the chanting and singing, in general the services are disheartening and depressing. I am entirely devoid of any religious belief myself, but even I felt they were a sacrilege. If a body of atheists had been compelled by law to attend a Christian service every day, the result could not have been worse. As the warder said to me when I entered Durham, the services are a break in the weary hours; but what an awful break they must be to any one who is really a Christian.

Notes

Source: E. Williamson Mason, *Made Free in Prison* (London: George Allen and Unwin, 1918), 134–43, 145, 146.

1 The location of one of the Home Office Scheme work centres.

HUBERT W. PEET

One of the best descriptions of what it was like to be in a British local prison early in the twentieth century came from the pen of the thirty-year-old Quaker socialist journalist Hubert W. Peet (1886–1951). It originally appeared as a supplement to the April 1917 issue of the paper that Peet coedited, *The Ploughshare: A Quaker Organ of Social Reconstruction.* Active in Quaker work, Peet was then organizing secretary of the radically anticonscriptionist Friends' Service Committee and a leading figure in the Quaker renascence of that period, which had helped to reinvigorate the Society of Friends after a prolonged period of decline. Like many of his colleagues in this movement who were of military age, Peet took an absolutist position, rejecting not only non-combatant service in the army but also alternative civilian work. At his tribunal he had asked for the unconditional exemption for which the Military Service Act had provided. But the tribunal turned down his request and ordered his induction into the forces as a non-combatant soldier.

In his uncompromising stance Peet enjoyed the support not only of his wife but of his Society of Friends as well. After his arrest he did his best, too, to explain his position to his three small children. 'I expect it is difficult for you to understand why I am not at home with you all,' he wrote them. 'I would be if I could, but I am not allowed to. Someday you will understand all about it.'[1]

Court-martialled in November 1916, Peet served his 112 days' hard labour in two London prisons, Wormwood Scrubs and Wandsworth. After the completion of this sentence, he was returned to his regiment at Hounslow, where he spent 'a fortnight's quasi-liberty' in the unit's guardroom. In these comparatively free surroundings, he writes, 'I was conscious of the awful weight of prison life on one's soul and mind. Memory and contrast surged through my brain.' He now recalled 'the loneliness of the cell ... the hurried whispered word in prison ... the nervous tension – tension arising from the habit of listening to every sound re-echoing in the prison galleries and the attempt to visualise what the sounds may signify.' 'There was the relief of realising that no eye of a watchful officer was at the spy-hole in the cell door, transforming the solitary into the most public of lives.'

Yet at the end of that fortnight, on 15 March 1917, Peet was again court-martialled for refusing to obey military orders, receiving a sentence this time of two years' hard labour. The war was nearing its end by the time he was released, and he did not leave a record of his second imprisonment.

The extracts from Peet's pamphlet given below conflate his experiences in the two prisons in which he was incarcerated.

'To prison' and 'to isolate' are practically identical terms. I understood this when on reaching my cell on my first night I found my sole remaining links with ordinary life were my spectacles, every shred of clothing and other possessions having been replaced by prison garb. Then the first rule read, 'Prisoners must preserve silence,' and from the moment of entering till that of leaving the prison, to hold the slightest communication with another prisoner renders one liable to punishment.

A Prison Day

Perhaps the outsider will imagine that temptations to break the rule occur on more occasions than is actually the case. Of this they can judge from a rough time-table of the day's happenings. This is as follows: – 5.30 a.m. – Get up, wash, make bed, put plank bedstead and mattress (the latter is supplied after 14 days) against wall, sweep out cell. 6.00 a.m. – Warder opens door. Put slops out. Ward Officer walks round to note any applications to see the Governor, doctor or chaplain or any small complaints. Door closed while cleaners empty tins, leave clean water, etc., outside. Begin work in cell, for everyone has a canvas task to perform during the day. 7 a.m. – Breakfast served. 8 a.m. – Half an hour's exercise. 12 noon. – Dinner served. 1.30 p.m. – Dinner tins, slops, etc., collected. 4 p.m. – Supper served. 8 p.m. – Lights out. On Wednesday and Saturday morning there is 'Chapel' before exercise. On Sunday, prisoners do not rise till seven, and go to Chapel twice, at 10.30 and 3. Of course, no work is done on this day. During the first month, at all events, the only time one sees another human being is for the few moments when the door is opened for meals, etc., at exercise, and at Chapel.

After this period has elapsed, prisoners are supposed to work in association in the morning and afternoon in canvas, brush or tinsmith's shops, laundry, bakery, etc. In my case, however, owing, I believe, to the congestion in these departments, I worked over ten weeks of my prison life alone in my cell, in practically solitary confinement; the only alleviation being that on three afternoons my cell door was left open and I could see passers-by along the gallery. There were even some cases, however, of men working all the time in their cells. In any case, it will be noted that prisoners are entirely isolated for fourteen hours between supper and 6 a.m. Think what the effect of such life must be on ordinary prisoners who can find no joy in reading after finishing work in the evening, or on the 'juvenile adult,' the poor little boy thieves and *hoc genus omne*[2] in their teens during these empty hours.

Prison Diet

The Food Controller has not yet interfered with the diet. The 'A' menu is practically nothing but bread and porridge. It is served for the first seven days, but during the rest of the time I was on 'B' diet, which is as follows: – Breakfast. – A pint of gruel and 8 oz. of bread. Supper. – The same quantity of bread and a pint of porridge. Dinner. – 6 oz. of bread and nominally 8 oz. of potatoes, but, owing to war shortage, rice or haricots are sometimes substituted for part of the latter. In addition is served on Sunday 4 oz. of cold preserved meat, i.e., a small slice of pressed beef. On Monday, 10 oz. of haricots with 2 oz. of crude fat bacon ('beans in candle grease'). On Tuesday and Friday, 1 pint of soup – usually thick and good, and meat *has* been found in it. On Wednesday and Saturday, 10 oz. of suet pudding made with brown flour – good if received still hot; and on Thursday, 4 oz. of cooked meat without bone, but not without fat or gristle. As a rule the porridge could not be bettered, and the wholemeal bread though [dense] is thoroughly good. One would welcome the opportunity of tasting it with butter. The only condiment is salt, sugar not being tasted in the ordinary way till 'C' diet is reached, after a four months' imprisonment, when cocoa is served. At Wandsworth prison a drink called 'tea' was given to those who did a certain amount of work in excess of the minimum task. It, however, disappeared from my breakfast table after Ash Wednesday, according to rumour, either in consequence of the Chaplain's sermon on fasting in

Lent or as a war economy! Personally, I found I kept in the best health if I ate about two-thirds of my food, but most prisoners, I think, were always ready for a little more had it been obtainable.

Habitat

A prison cell is about 7 feet wide, 11 feet 6 inches long, and 9 feet high. Its furniture consists of stool, table (sometimes fixed by the frosted window through which light is received at night, and sometimes movable), a plank bed, with mattress, two sheets, two blankets, rug and pillow; mug, spoon, tin knife (which bends if used on a crust); slate and slate pencil; and a set of pots, pans and brush. At Wormwood Scrubs the floor is of boards, but in the older prison [i.e., Wandsworth] my cold feet were a perpetual reminder that I was living on tiles. In such a winter as we have been having this fact was perhaps the greatest physical hardship of imprisonment, bearing in mind that often I was only absent from the cell for half-an-hour out of the twenty-four. Those who wish to reproduce the test are advised to try working, sleeping and eating in their scullery.

The clothing consists of grey cloth collarless suit, liberally sprinkled with broad arrows; underclothing – the latter is always clean, but there is only one size for everybody, and a button a garment is liberal fare – stockings and shoes. Usually, little capes are available for extra warmth during exercise in cold weather. All garments are dated, and one day I noted a cape that had been in use for 21 years! I have also seen a man with his trousers turned up at least eight inches to make them fit.

The great luxury of prison life is the weekly bath. The bath-house resembles a loose-box stable with a bath for each man. One can have as much warm water as one wants without the worry of thinking whether the kitchen boiler is empty or not! How chills and colds are avoided is extraordinary, for one comes straight out of a hot bath, for instance, into the snow and east wind without putting on an overcoat; while once, when unfortunate enough to be in the box next the door, I was nearly blown out of the water by the wind that blew in on the advent of new bathers every few minutes.

Oddities of the Exercise Ground

This is a monotonous perambulation in single file round an asphalted circle, vigilant warders keeping their ears open for surreptitious conversation the while. Exercise provides, however, the chance of seeing at least the faces of one's friends, and the solemnity and dullness of the proceedings [were] relieved by many a touch of humour ... A sense of humour evoked by trivial incidents is of inestimable value in prison. It tonics the whole man. It creates to be sure a special temptation – to try to share the zest with one's fellows.

What struck me most forcibly in my earliest experience of prison exercises was that ... [n]ever had I seen such a disreputable-looking company – sallow, red-nosed, scrubby-bearded, and most amazingly garbed, the clothes bursting across the backs of some and hanging loosely around others. Some shuffled along with ill-fitting footwear; some obviously fagged by even this slight physical effort. A few enwrapped and shrouded in ascetic contemplation as if they were old-world mendicant monks walking round and round some monastery garden. If, however, the prison face and mien as noted in the exercise ground seemed to be stamped with some features common to all, in chapel the case was different. Juxtaposition in that more compacted crowd made differences in type more evident. But whether on the exercise ground or in the chapel one could not but be somewhat thankful for the utter absence of mirrors. Happily prisoners cannot 'see oorsels as ithers see us.'

Shaving and haircutting take place occasionally at the hands of a prisoner with a clippers and with an uncertain amount of experience. Up till Christmas men fell out during exercise and were barbered in the open air, even when snow was on the ground. At no time during the first two months did the direct rays of the sun shine on me when in the open air, owing to the earliness of the hour of exercise and the position of the yard.

Chapel and Chaplain

It will seem very curious one day again to attend a religious service at which the congregation is not regimented and watched closely by warders throughout the proceedings. Perhaps the officers are getting used by now to obvious and sometimes, I confess, almost discourteous differences of opinion with the preacher when he states, for instance, as a rebuke to the C.O. portion of his audience, that as a maker of tents Paul was an army contractor who was 'proud to do his bit for his Empire.' ...

Quaker Meetings in Prison

Attendance at the Quaker meetings once a fortnight was a joy, though the presence of the officers with a reminder 'You have come here to a religious meeting, not to enjoy yourselves,' and also the shortness of time available did not assist in the creation of the 'atmosphere.' But to see people one knew and to listen either to their short address or the voice offering of one of the prisoners 'speaking to our condition' made red-letter records in our life.

The Library

... A prison chaplain with the best will in the world cannot avoid being just one of the officials on the staff, each and all of whom form part of the State machinery of punishment. Nevertheless, he may be looked upon as 'Officer of the Humanities,' for he is responsible for the library, the source of what is practically the sole alleviator of prison life – books. On entry one is given a Bible, Prayer Book, and Hymn Book. In the ordinary way these would be supplemented by a curious little manual of devotion entitled 'The Narrow Way,' but at the Scrubs Quakers were mercifully allowed in its place the Fellowship Hymn Book and the Friends' Book of Discipline. The beauty and helpfulness of the latter was a revelation ...

In addition to these books two educational volumes may be allowed during the first month. The difficulty, however, at Wormwood Scrubs was that the presence of the objectors meant demand for books in this category that the library was not used to and could not stand. I personally was particularly lucky in being given Boswell's Johnson on entry, but when I applied to the chaplain for it to be changed all I could get was a school prize volume, 'Brave Deeds by Brave Men,' which I would rather have titled 'Treachery by Traitors.' Other men whispered, however, that all they had, for instance, was a historical reader or a mental arithmetic! Conditions were better at Wandsworth, as the proportion of C.O.'s to ordinary prisoners was far less, and there was some chance of getting eventually books one applied for after making a choice in the catalogue which one is allowed to see.

The range shown in the latter was extensive and peculiar ... During the second month, besides the educational book – if the library has one left – you may have a work of fiction. In the third month and onwards there may be two novels, though on request a volume of poetry or essays may be substituted for one of the latter, while, on the other hand, instead of two books, a bound magazine volume may be had – and is, I believe, the choice. The last allowance may sound quite generous, but it must be remembered that reading at meal times alone would occupy three hours a day, or at least eighteen hours a week, not counting the work-free hours of Sunday ... [and] it must be remembered that reading or meditation is the sole manner of recreation, and one can absorb a great deal. My library list varied considerably in quantity and quality ...

Prison's Worst Torture

It was, however, in connection with my prison reading and the consequent chance of study which the rush of life outside deprives us of that I experienced especially the deprivation of any opportunity of writing, except for ephemeral purposes on the cell slate. There is in prison no method of recording permanently thoughts that occur to one during reading or meditation, or noting for future reference passages that may be found helpful or striking, or of making notes for plans on return to ordinary life. Perhaps such a lack is felt particularly by a journalist, whose memory becomes accustomed to the stimulus of notes, and personally the one single alteration which would go to make gaol life more tolerable than anything else would be the provision of pencil and paper, and the permission to retain the latter on release. So nervous are the prison officers, however, that unauthorised writing shall be indulged in that when a man is writing the three quarter page letter allowed at the end of two months (and thereafter in six weeks and then at monthly intervals) he has to put outside his cell all his books and all the official rules, diet, and 'Prisoners' Aid Society' cards that hang on the walls.

No Self-expression

Yet this is only another aspect of the absence of opportunity for self-expression which weighs so heavily on the prisoner. He has a registered number which is permanent, but is usually referred to by his officer by his cell number. This alters, of course, with any change of location. (At Wormwood Scrubs I was 2176 and occupied Cells B 3/36, B 3/57 and C 4/7; at Wandsworth I was 2031 and lived in Cell 3/33.)

Any trivial incident which [allows self-expression] is most welcome. The visit of the chaplain and the chance of a little talk, the answer to such an inquiry on the part of a warder as 'What was you before you was a soldier?' and the explanation amongst other things that you were not a soldier, or, more exceptionally, the striking suggestion made me by a lively young officer who, bringing me back to my cell after an official visit which had detained me until supper was being served, offered to race me down the path to a certain gate – all such things have an extraordinarily exhilarating effect because of their scarcity.

In a similar manner the C.O. prisoner feels the utter lack of trust imposed in the individual. Prisoners are accompanied everywhere by a warder, and are always under supervision. Surprise searches of cells take place at intervals to detect the presence of contraband of any sort; while the individual is searched. Each time I came in from the laundry while working there I and my fellows had to line up on returning to their hall, hold our handkerchiefs and caps above our heads, while a warder searched one's single pocket in the outside jacket and ran his hands over one's person on the chance of finding – I don't know what, unless we might be tempted to secrete extra clothing or soap about us.

The Cell's Public Privacy: The Peephole

It will be good one day in the future again to live in a room in which there is not a peephole in the door. The prisoner never knows when he is being watched, and however innocent his action it is unpleasant to feel that complete privacy can never be relied on. During the evening officers wear silent felt slippers, and their visits are only known by the slight click of the shield over the hole as he moves it to look through. It was disconcerting, for instance, when engaged one morning in saying my prayers, suddenly to be accused by a voice on the other side of the door of being the author of tapping signals which were going on through the wall somewhere in the neighbourhood, and on my denying the charge, to be told that at any rate you had just been using 'foul langwidge'! A few nights later, the tapping still continuing, and evidently still suspicious of me, the same officer declared I had attempted to deceive him by getting into bed with my trousers on, having heard him about. I was, as a matter of fact, sitting up in bed with my jacket round me finishing a book before lights out, but it was only by getting out of bed I was able to prove that I had taken as many of my clothes off as it is possible to divest oneself of under conditions in which nightwear is not provided!

Our Prussian Penal System

The tone of voice used by some officers has a very depressing effect. Their speech was too often a mere shout, the voice in which one would herd cattle. I have many a time been cheered up for the whole afternoon just by one word from a genial curious officer, who when you told him how many feet of mail bags or dozens of tabs you had made or sewn on, used to say 'Good' in a tone that showed some acknowledgment of your being a human creature. And yet I came to realise that the officers were the victims of the system as much as the prisoners ... [W]ith a few exceptions I found that even with a prison warder the appeal to the best in them evoked the right response ... [On the whole, though, our] civil penal code is, on the other hand, calculated, scientific, soulless cruelty – Prussian in the true meaning of the term.

'No One the Better for Being in Prison'

In the short talks I have been able to get with warders, or before arrest with policemen, I have never discovered one who could admit that any man was ever the better for being in prison. Personally I can imagine nothing more calculated to put a man permanently on the road to ruin. God forbid that I should ever be responsible for sending a man, woman, or child to prison, for any injury to me or mine.

The attempted imposition of silence is unmoral, even if not immoral; the isolation drives the man into himself and tempts him at every turn to fulfil the human instinct of communication with his fellows, a course only possible by the exercise of some petty deceit or the breaking of a rule.

Evil Brooding

The opportunity for brooding over grievances is a corrosive evil. What it must be to the ordinary prisoner – victim of social conditions – I can well imagine from the effect on myself of the mountain of annoyance aroused within me by the molehill incident of delay in getting the promised privilege of a pint of breakfast tea, owing to a temporary error in allocating me the proper marks which entitled me to this addition to the menu.

Punishment

Punishment may take either of several forms. These include the forfeiting of privileges in the way of books, visits, etc., for a period; the performance of the daily task in the cell instead of in association with other prisoners; the loss of remission marks, that is the loss of good behaviour marks by which a prisoner would earn a remission not exceeding one-sixth of his sentence; and the putting of the prisoner on punishment diet. Punishment diet consists of one pound of bread and water per day. This dietary must not be continued for more than three consecutive days. If 'P.D.' is imposed for a longer period 'B' diet must be given during each alternate period of three days.

Ugliness Everywhere

One of my most conscious lacks in prison was the entire outward absence of beauty. All that ministered outwardly to this vital human need was an occasional glimpse of a sunset, the lines, curves, and distant frescoes of the fine Renaissance Chapel at Wormwood Scrubs, and even the warm brown and green of the worsted bedding. A thrill came over me when at exercise – under leaden sky and between lowering walls at Wandsworth – I one day saw flying overhead some seagulls, stragglers from the winter visitors to the Thames a mile or two away. Their graceful form, their easy motion, their association in one's mind with the free and open life of sea and shore, ... were as a refreshing breeze which blew away some of the gaol cobwebs in the mind ...

Prison Life – 'Meals and Mail Bags'

The prison régime provides every temptation to atrophy, and to let oneself vegetate. Several times I felt acutely the danger that my pacifism might merely become passivism, and that if not watchful I might let my life develop into meals and mail bags. It was almost with resentment that any little interference with the mechanical daily régime was received, even when it afforded a chance of such a change as the transference to Wandsworth. Many a time the truly horrible question arose in my mind, 'Is our whole system of civilisation based on prison and a fear of it?' Sometimes I thought with shame that it was; but, No. Bad as our present social order is I do not believe it would be plagued one whit more with crime and criminals were our present penal system abolished to-morrow. The total crime I am certain would not be increased; indeed, I believe it would be definitely diminished, for fear of punishment does little or nothing to deter the hardened criminal, while the stigma of having been to prison (which now almost inevitably turns the weak man who has fallen once into a permanent gaolbird) would be absent. It is pitiful to see the old, bent, grey-haired men who have evidently become habituated to prison as their home, and still more tragic to watch the 'juvenile adults' branded as criminals almost before they have left school, whose defiant eyes contrast strikingly with the dull look of older prisoners.

What a generation of prison reformers we should make – and must make.

Think of what Elizabeth Fry and John Howard effected, and how much greater will be our advantages when we can back our proposals not merely as the result of investigation but of personal experience, back them by the unescapable authentic warrant of those who can say, 'We have been in prison and we *know*.'[3]

The allowing of books, letters, visits, these of course are all steps in the right direction. In the visits, to be sure, one's friends are seen, or not seen, through two thicknesses of wire gauze. It is really an interview in semi-darkness. Four photos are allowed after a month – another right step. Yet another was the practice of the prison chaplain to announce from the front of the altar after service a few items of war news ... [L]et me acknowledge that all these are welcome moves in the right line; it remains to add when that acknowledgment is made that they do but touch the merest surface of the problem.

Wanted – A Prison Newspaper

... The regular provision of a prison journal of some sort, even of one that was heavily censored, would be of the utmost value as a relief to the deadening, debilitating, soul-destroying influence of prison monotony. It would greatly increase the opportunity for some reforming influences being brought to bear upon the prisoners.

No C.O. Privileges Wanted

Any alleviation, however, must apply to the treatment of all prisoners, whether C.O.'s sentenced for refusal to commit what they believe to be a crime, or poor little sneak thieves convicted of some trespass against the community ... We do not invite suffering, but we are only too willing to pay this price rather than that the fundamentals of our stand should be in danger of being obscured.

Notes

Source: Hubert W. Peet, *'112 Days' Hard Labour'*: *Being Some Reflections on the First of My Sentences as a Conscientious Objector* (London: 'The Ploughshare,' 1917), 5–16.

1 Quoted in Felicity Goodall, *A Question of Conscience: Conscientious Objection in the Two World Wars* (Stroud, UK: Sutton Publishing, 1997), 55. Among other sources Goodall quotes from the unpublished prison memoirs of two First World War COs, Harold Blake and Harry Stanton, to which I did not have access.

2 Rough translation: their like ...

3 In the tradition of the great pioneers of the British prison reform movement, Howard and Fry the Quaker, the COs of First World War Britain after the war was over carried the movement one step further.

JOHN HOARE

John Hoare (christened Joseph Edward and known to family and friends as Ted), though some of his ancestors had been Quakers, was brought up in the Church of England. Both his parents were Anglican missionaries, his father becoming Bishop of Victoria, Hong Kong, shortly before his death in 1906. Four years later his widow sent their son to the well-known English 'public' school, Repton, where he came under the moral influence of its dynamic headmaster, William Temple, later Archbishop of York. Early in the war Hoare, still a teenager, had – along with his elder brother – become a pacifist mainly as a result of his own cogitations. But he was already in contact with the newly established Fellowship of Reconciliation when he left school to become a classics student at the University of Oxford in the autumn of 1915.

Next year he was called up for military service; his tribunal assigned him to the army's Non-Combatant Corps. Since this alternative was not acceptable to young Hoare, he was arrested, court-martialled, and sentenced to six months' hard labour. He entered Wormwood Scrubs Prison on 28 September 1916. The document printed below, exactly as it was written by Hoare, was composed for information of his family, who indeed were all most supportive of his stand. Though critical of conditions in the prison the account is by no means entirely negative. In an interview he gave for the Imperial War Museum Archive many years later, Hoare stated that he had 'on the whole ... enjoyed' his sojourn in Wormwood Scrubs. 'I was among other C.O.s for one thing, and I had no conscience at all about what I was in for, and of course things were fairly new. I found that it gave me quite an opportunity of thinking things out and so on.' In fact his stay in prison this time was brief because after only three weeks he left for the Home Office Scheme work centre at Wakefield.

He continued in the Scheme, though increasingly uneasy and with a growing feeling that his place was back in prison. Finally, in May 1918 he left the Princetown work centre, to which he had transferred earlier on from Wakefield. He was soon arrested, once again court-martialled, and sentenced to two years' hard labour, which he served in Wandsworth Prison. 'They sentenced me today,' he wrote in his journal, 'and I am soberly but intensely happy.'

His decision unfortunately caused his mother intense pain, which was compounded by a simultaneous loss of his own religious belief. Until his arrival at the Dartmoor Work Centre he had regarded himself as a loyal Anglican; now he became an atheist, though remaining as convinced a pacifist as before. 'God had ceased to mean anything to me,' he wrote a few years later. 'I often used to muse, as I gazed out through the bars at Wandsworth, on the possibility, nay the probability, of ... loyalty to truth or to love ... finally perishing with all human effort good or bad on a dead world in a universe devoid of any moral purpose whatever. Yet I still knew that I would rather die than surrender.'

In prison again, Hoare from the beginning refused to cooperate with the iniquitous rule of silence, then prevailing as we know in British jails. Other COs joined him in this protest. Refusal to cooperate led to punishment, including bread-and-water and solitary confinement.

After almost a year in Wandsworth Prison, Hoare was at last released in April 1919. His 'spiritual pilgrimage' continued. Though a brilliant scholar first in school and then at university, Hoare decided not to return to Oxford, becoming a social worker instead. Eventually regaining his Christian faith he joined the Society of Friends and engaged in Quaker service for the rest of his active career.[1] John Hoare was a man of exceptional integrity, idealism, and intelligence. What he wrote about prisons and about his own experiences in jail is always worth reading.

I have abridged the document that follows. It was originally a letter Hoare wrote to his family from Wakefield Work Centre on 25/26 October 1916, not long after his release from Wormwood Scrubs Prison. Hoare had spent a brief period in another London prison, Pentonville, before his incarceration at the Scrubs.

I stood on the windswept parade ground at Mill Hill Barracks with (I was told) 'an angelic smile' on my face & heard the Adjutant read out after a long rigmarole, 'We do therefore sentence the accused Private Joseph Edward Hoare to be imprisoned for six months with hard labour.' It was on the seventh day of my sentence that you said Goodbye to me with Serjeant Norton's leave before the great gate of Wormwood Scrubs with the medallion of Elizabeth Fry gazing down at her great-grand-nephew going to prison. The white washed walls of the little cubicles in which we [eight COs] waited for some time & had our tea were covered with the names & messages of C.O.s who had gone before. We could talk to one another as the partitions between did not reach to the roof, & we made good use of our last opportunity. We came across the only criminals with whom we had to do in the prison that first evening ...

All our clothes & goods were taken from us & we arrayed ourselves, not in the drab uniform I wore at Pentonville, but in the black of Court Martial prisoners, with white arrows. We were also given underclothes like a hermit's hair shirt to the skin. I only endured them one day. We were all most ridiculous sights & could do nothing but roar with laughter in spite of the warders' remonstrances. After the Governor had come & we had declared to him our sentence, religion, & money, & had been warned to behave well, the Schoolmaster doled out our books to us. You know that at Pentonville, after I had told him that I was an Oxford undergraduate, he insisted on my reading and writing a sentence to make sure that I was really possessed of those accomplishments. The Scrubs man, an utterly soulless looking man, terrified us more. He asked Holcombe [another CO] abruptly 'Can you do practice?' Now practice is only a dim memory to me: I have not the remotest idea how you set out a practice sum. Holcombe said he used to be able & when pressed further said he could now. (May he be forgiven!) Fortunately no one else was asked that question. There was an amusing sequel to the incident. One day when I came in from exercise I saw my slate on my table with a sum on it. Horror! I thought, here is the Schoolmaster really testing my knowledge! It was only a simple interest sum for three loans for three different periods. I set to work & did it. Later Crawford, our senior officer, a nice old man came in. Had I been able to do that sum? he wanted so much to know what he owed his insurance company and would be so glad if I could tell him what it came to. How I laughed!

It was quite dark when we moved off to B Block. I [should tell] you what a prison looks like in the day: each hall is a long narrow building with stone-paved floor & a vista of iron doors stretching down to the far end, & gallery above gallery, with their iron railings, rising to the lofty roof, a couple of bridges across on each floor & steep & narrow iron staircases leading up to them. That night it was very quiet & gloomy, & looked like a great Cathedral, with a few lights burning here & there at the desks on the ground floor, & warders in felt-soled shoes moving noiselessly about. Up we clattered to our cells & our doors banged behind us. We had mattresses that night: in fact they did not take them away till Saturday, (the night we had the extra hour and changed from Summer time) & then only till the following Thursday by which time we had served a fortnight and were then entitled to them again. For the first hour of the first night I seemed to be all protuding bones: after that I never felt the slightest inconvenience. The cells had wooden floors, a great boon, instead of the stone floors of Pentonville and Wakefield: the furniture was just the same – table and stool, bed-board, water pot, slop pail, basin, brush & dust pan, & a box of cleaning powder, &, most important of all, a plate & pint pot, with knife & spoon. Brush & comb, soap, towel, dish cloth & two sheets were provided: for tooth brushes we had to wait a week as they had to be specially applied for, & the Governor had not had such wholesale demands for them. The slate & pencil came in useful for writing long messages, and it was quite easy to exchange slates with a neighbour in the morning when they were meant to be put outside with applications, if any, to the Governor or Chaplain written on them ...[2]

I learnt more about the regular daily programme than in those hurried few days at Pentonville. I still do not know whether the first bell went at 5:30 or 6: I think at 5:30. After exchanging a rat-tat-tat through the wall to Muirhead [another CO] I washed & put up my bed board with the clothes neatly over the top, all in a dim twilight. At six the door flew open – 'Slops out.' I usually managed to keep my door open some little time [to] get brief conversation with the men who passed up & down with big pails for our dirty water or cans to fill our waterpots. Then when there was no further excuse for dawdling & an officer appeared in sight I slammed the door & set to work on Muller's Swedish exercises & polishing my metal basin & water pot. At about 6:45 there was a rattle at the door & a hand deposited a loaf on the table: a few seconds later the can-bearer appeared, followed by an officer with a ladle. He filled the pint pot I presented on my plate & banged the door almost before I could say 'Thank you.' They were so little used to 'Thank you's' that they were quite disconcerted & at first wondered if we were being insolent. I used to read at meals and spin them out: when it was scrubbing morning, about three times a week, there was no time to waste: otherwise I ate & washed up in a leisurely way, brushed my cell & sat waiting till a little before 8: we repeated the proceeding of first unlocking. A little after 8, the doors were unlocked again & we waited in the doorway for the familiar voice from below 'Lead out C.O.'s.' Then down we clattered & out to the exercise ground.

The paths at the Scrubs were elongated ovals, one inside the other with paths joining them & grass between, instead of the gravel that there was at Pentonville, & quite nice flower beds. Over the wall at the North end we could see the tossing tops of trees that line the edge of the Scrubs. Round & round, sometimes conversing with the man in front in the gaps in between the little platforms on which four officers stood: 164 paces on the outer ring & 120 on the inner, watching the clouds or the tree tops, the sparrows, or the wind in the long grass, or the faces of the eighty other men as they passed up the far side. There was one huge tall fellow with the bottom of his trousers well above his ankle & sleeves to match. In Chapel one day a warder who did not know him called from his perch at the side 'Kneel down there, kneel down, do as I tell you.' The poor man was kneeling down all the time but his legs were so long that it looked as if he were sitting on the bench. Then there was a little dumpy man, rather like an ourang-outang in build, with short curving arms & head buried in his hunched shoulders & a bulging lower jaw with a week's growth of black beard on it. His trousers were turned up to his knees. I always wanted to see him next to the tall man but it never came off. Like several others he was physically incapable of keeping in step & it was maddening to be near him. Exercise lasted an hour and then we went back to our cells & settled down to our work. Dinner came a little after 12, & we were unlocked a little before 2, to put out our pots for water etc. again. At 4:15 supper arrived and the door was shut for the last time. The bell went for us to get ready for bed just before 7 & the lights went out at varying lengths of time after that. So except on Chapel days, we were alone from 9:15 a.m. for the rest of the day except for these brief unlockings. Men without hard labour do not have this solitary confinement but work from 9–12 & 2–4 with others in the sheds, or at odd jobs like cleaning, as I did at Pentonville. Hard labour men also work 'in association' after the first month or else with their cell door open.

The only work I did was sewing tabs onto mail bags: the thread had to be waxed, & the ring sewn onto the top of the tab: then the tabs were sewn on at equal distances over the edge of the mail bags, four tabs to a bag, & about fifty stitches to a tab. It may sound easy but sometimes the needle had to go through nine thicknesses of coarse canvas: I have at times got the point in at the proper place, put the head against the door & my two hands on the other side of the canvas on each side of the place where I wanted the point to come through, & leaned against it with all my weight. Usually however one good push with the thimble did the trick. The thimble had no top, & fitted on between the first & second joints of the first finger. In the first few days the needle's head if it did not slip off the thimble at the top or bottom & bury itself in the knuckle would slip off to the side & rend my second finger or the ball of my thumb. So I improvised other thimbles out of bits of canvas & would have looked soon like a regular old rag bag if I had not acquired more skill in manipulating my tools. Nine bags was the full day's task but we were sometimes given less & yet always marked with full marks. Fifty-six marks a week procured a remission of one-sixth of the sentence (so mine would expire on Feb 20th) & earns the first letter & visit at the end of eight weeks. Marks are of course forfeited for idleness or misconduct. No work is set on Sunday but marks are given on the average of the previous week's work. I usually got done in time for an hour or two reading by my bad electric light before going to bed. The books I had in turn given me were Gibbon's Decline & Fall, Down the Orinoco in a Canoe (a book of amusing travel) & Miss Brandon's 'Thou art the Man.' A library catalogue was available after the first month & choice might be made. I read the second of the three at meals for a day or two: it was very short. Otherwise I confined myself to getting to know my Bible better. If ever you are in prison make a sort of 'Retreat' of it: especially the first month of solitary confinement: it is a priceless opportunity & an experience of a lifetime. In many ways my time in the Scrubs was the happiest of my life.

I found it hard to think consecutively while I worked: I played with pleasant memories, & with imagining the great Might-Have-Beens. I wove dreams around the mysterious sounding fog horns on the river after dark: the whistles & cries of the football games that covered the Scrubs on Saturday afternoons, brought a flood of Repton memories: I held broken conversations with friends. At night I was always nicely tired and slept beautifully. There were usually some excitements to fill in the outline program I have given. On Monday we had clean clothes: on Wednesday after exercise we marched off for a bath: on Saturday & Wednesday we had Chapel before exercise: on Friday we had an afternoon Quaker Meeting. About twice a week in the middle of the morning a heated officer would fling the door open & shout '..Orshun.. Stanmar..' whereupon dropping my work I bounded to the wall & stood against a black paint mark until the Governor passed with a retinue of warders & gave a swift look inside: I discovered later that the warning was a corruption for 'Governor's inspection, stand to the mark.' Also there were odd jobs to be done. One day [four of us] were called out, as being lusty looking fellows to carry four great sacks of dirty clothes to the laundry. They were the heaviest I have ever met. Getting down three flights of steep iron steps with one of them on your neck & shoulders is no joke, especially as the railings at each landing were too high to get them over without giving a great jerk which nearly upset me once. I felt the weight of the bag some[where] down on the back of my head instead of on my shoulders: I don't know how I saved myself. Davies got his sack jammed & the mouth, opening, dropped from his bent head a stream of shirts & socks that solemnly pattered down the stairs in front of him. It looked so utterly ridiculous that we could hardly move for laughter.

The Chapel was a far finer building than that at Pentonville: very light, having an apse with nine large internal Norman arches round & frescoes in the tympanum of each ... Of course we were packed on our benches like sardines & the warders were offensively suspicious, perched on their high stools down the aisles & each side of the low wooden wall of partition down the centre ... [In my cell] I found great consolation in climbing on my stool & looking out through my window. I looked East. Opposite was the grim front of C Block over which the sun rose. The bricks were not at all an unpleasant colour & the tiles of the roof showed great splashes of brightness like a Turkish carpet. To the right, between C Block and the Chapel I could see far away to a great block of buildings on the horizon, two graceful spires & a tall tower, a very restful bit of landscape to the eyes. To the left, being on the top floor, I could see over the wall down to the Scrubs & beyond that to the silent snake-like brown & white electric trains on the embankment & the steam railway with its rushing clouds of white smoke. There was usually a solitary figure or two strolling on the Scrubs, & there were some very fine effects of light & shadow chasing one another over the stretch of close grass. Nearer at hand there was the grass & the flowers waving in the wind in the exercise ground below: a tabby cat with brilliant white legs stalking her dinner on the roof of the colonnade that joined B Block to the bake-house in between & the bake-house to C Block: the pigeons feeding down below & whirring up as a warder passed by, leaving their crumbs to less timid sparrows: or the same birds going to nest at night in the interlacing Norman arches in the roof of the Chapel & fighting one another for possession. My fourteen by seven foot cell seemed very dingy for a time when I descended at night.

At night I clambered up sometimes behind the blanket that curtained the window when the lights were on, & looked at the search lights playing on the clouds, or the flashes of brilliant white light that marked the course of the electric trains, or best of all the stars & the rising moon. But as the blanket completely muffled my head & climbing up to the windows was forbidden, it was a risky pleasure to indulge in when there were stealthy footed warders about.

As C.O.'s we had several little excitements of our own. On the first day the Deputy Governor, a rather nasty little man with a sandy moustache ('He ... tries to assert himself' was [the Quaker prison chaplain] Gillett's verdict) sent for us & asked what prison work we would consent to do, to avoid awkwardness later, & argued with us over why we would not work on War Office or Admiralty contracts. Then after we had been in a fortnight the chief warder came out on the exercise ground & called out about thirty numbers, B4,77 amongst them. We fell out & were presented with papers informing us that the Central Tribunal would attend shortly at the Prison to judge if we had conscientous objections, & telling us that if we convinced them we would be ... placed outside the Army Act. That same afternoon we were marched down & stood in the great courtyard between the main gateway & the visiting magistrates' room (where the Tribunal sat), looking towards the green lawn & gay flower beds that lie in front of the Chapel. The Tribunal were over an hour late. At last a motor drew up outside & hooted, the great iron gates swung slowly in, & in drove – a draper's van. Later somebody nearly pulled the bell down. 'That's them' said one warder. 'Do they always ring like that?' said the second. 'Sure,' said the other. Sure enough in came a nice looking old man with rather a long face & side whiskers (Lord Salisbury, the Chairman, so I was told), a middle aged man with pince-nez & a tail coat, looking very brisk but rather worried, & a third man who made no impression on me at all. One of the two was G.N. Barnes, the Labour M.P. We waited in [an] ante-room in the corner of which there was a door with two large panes in it through which a warder looked into the room, out of earshot but in sight. Through this door I was pushed at last & found myself in a closely railed & wired-in dock. 'You are Joseph Edward Hoare?' said the Chairman. 'Yes' 'Your age?' 'Twenty.' 'You were granted non-combatant exemption by the Oxford Local and Appeal Tribunals?' 'Yes.' 'Did you produce any testimonials?' 'Yes, from Mr. Temple.' 'What, William Temple [the future Anglican Archbishop of Canterbury]?' 'Yes.' 'Thank you, that will do.' Exit, adjudged sincere! Some had slightly longer innings, but not many. The following Monday we were again marched across the Court yard & waited in the colonnade outside the Deputy's office. He came out & read the conditions of the Home Office Scheme to us & we then went in one by one to his office. The one question asked was 'Are you willing to do work of National Importance?' I answered 'Yes.' Then he told me to sign the agreement promising to obey all present & future regulations of the Home Office. I refused & after a slight argument he said 'Well it makes no difference: you will instead of signing a paper beginning "I agree to accept the conditions stated below" receive a paper saying "You are released on the conditions stated below"' ... Then we [COs] returned to our stitching & the silence of our cells.

Many men accepted [the Home Office Scheme] on principle: a few because they were broken men. I have talked to several men of my age & size, that is to say men who are still growing & are neither short nor slight, & they all say that they felt the lack of food considerably. The small men, & the men getting on in years, could not eat all that was given them: I ate it all & found it about right, though I found it increasingly difficult to last through my exercises in the morning which shewed that I was losing strength a bit. The psychological effect of prison varied immensely in different cases. I was not in long enough, lover of solitude as I am, to feel the waves of desolation that some men felt though I experienced it in some degree in my short stay in Pentonville. In the Scrubs I found the sight of so many men in there for conscience sake, & the knowledge of their presence & companionship kept me entirely cheerful, & the kindliness of the warders on our landing contributed to it in no small degree. Also we had a good view from our windows, a priceless treasure. There is a pitiful wistfulness in the eyes of some of the men here who have been four months or more in Durham & Newcastle Prisons, as they describe how they could only see a blank wall & were conscious of glorious days going by & Summer passing into Autumn, bringing nothing but bitterness to them. You know that my ideas on how to meet crime are somewhat unusual, but granted that a prison system must exist there is far too much repression & far too little chance for reformation in prison. I believe that regular work & solitude make a good background for a man's development. But the criminal's mind cannot be expected to dwell on what is beautiful & good without a cue from anybody, & if he does not become a mere jelly fish, solitude will only make him more vicious & bitter. There ought to be more air & sunlight, there ought to be beautiful pictures & colour for him to see. Above all he ought to be able to meet not only with the everlasting nagging officer or the frightfully official chaplains, but with real friends. That would need men willing to give their lives to the work, & men who would have to live down the reputation of being spies: it would also be quite unworkable unless there was real social life: they have regular self-governing communities in Sing-Sing & other American prisons & it is not an impossibility. And supposing the criminal, whose whole mind is far more susceptible to moulding in prison, began really to see it was better & happier to love than hate, some such social life is the only thing to prevent it turning to sourness & hopelessness as all emotional impulses do that have no practical outlet. Prison must make many weak sinners into hardened criminals. Pardon this moralising.

On Wednesday we knew that we were coming out the following day & said a warm & regretful farewell to our friends who thought it right to stay behind. On Thursday morning, three weeks after we came in, we were taken down & given two suits of corduroys etc. & departed a party of seventeen, in two motor brakes to the 1:30 at King's Cross, with untidy great brown paper parcels, leaving some hundreds of friends inside, some still to come before the Tribunal, many who had refused alternative service. We had made a wretched lot of prisoners, we were too cheerful for one thing. Even I, one of the 'gloomy & morose Hoares' was greeted with 'Hello, here's Sunny Jim' when I emerged in prison dress the first evening: at the supreme moment before going in to the Central Tribunal, Muirhead had to caution me 'Now you really must not laugh this time,' & at the end Snowdon said he had never seen me without a smile on my face.[3]

Just one other thing is worth remarking on. I was more than ever impressed with the truth of what Barratt Brown[4] had said in Pentonville, that the warders suffered morally from prison as much as the prisoners. In Chapel it was very noticeable how many of them had not only the keen expression of men who were always on the alert but the arrogant look & loud voice of men who are always bullying & nagging. They have to enforce strict rules & their reputation for smartness & their promotion seem to depend on their proficiency in cowing the men they have to deal with, they hardly have a chance of shewing real kindness. The senior warders were generally less harsh in voice & look: they could afford to be as there were always the junior officers to blame if discipline got slack. It is very striking now at Wakefield[5] to see how hard the warders, who are now in plain clothes & act as instructors &

supervisors, find it to get out of their old habits. They answer questions as if they considered it an impudence in us to speak to them: they shout out orders as if we were dogs, & push men out of the way & then suddenly realise the position, when we go quietly on as before, – and stop abruptly. The warders' life is very bad for them, especially as it is the more uneducated soldiers & therefore those who are more likely to be spoilt by their unlimited opportunities of tyrannising, who are put on prison work.

Notes

Source: Richard J. Hoare, ed., *John Hoare: A Pacifist's Progress – Papers from the First World War* (York, UK: Sessions Book Trust, 1998), 13, 82–94, 167, 209, 210.

1 For John and his wife Margaret's wartime work for the Quakers' 'peace service training centre' in Devonshire, see Stanley Smith, *Spiceland: Quaker Training Centre, 1940–1946* (York, UK: William Sessions Ltd, 1990), passim.

2 The Quaker absolutist Wilfrid E. Littleboy described as follows his first impressions of the Scrubs, where one evening early in January 1917 he began a sentence of '112 days' hard labour': 'Inside Wormwood Scrubs Prison you leave your own possessions and array yourself in prison garb ... the fit both of suit and shoes being approximate. Then you are marched to one of the four great halls. The jangling of keys echoes in the evening silence, though around you are perhaps 300 prisoners, each in his own cell, of which there are four tiers opening out from the main hall. Up an iron staircase, along a gallery a door is opened and clangs to behind you. And that's that! ... Bars on the high window; the locked door; a light over which one had no control; the shuffle of felt slippers outside; the faint click of the spy-hole ... In prison it is assumed that you will know without being told what is expected of you: observation will get you some way, but at first you feel lost. It is best to feel amused when shouted at like a naughty little schoolboy.' 'The way to get through prison,' he adds, 'with the least strain was to let oneself be carried along by the routine – obeying the rules, not under any sense of obligation, but just sufficiently to avoid trouble to one-self or to an officer in charge. Then one could live one's own mental life ...' From Littleboy, '1914–1918: "I Remember ..." VIII. – With the C.O.s in Prison,' *The Friend* 92, no. 38 (21 Sept. 1934), 859, 860. Littleboy, a chartered accountant, became Clerk of the Quaker London Yearly Meeting during the Second World War.

3 On Hoare's arrival at Wormwood Scrubs the Quaker chaplain there had told his sister 'that he looked very well and so bright and cheerful.'

4 Alfred Barratt Brown was a Quaker absolutist CO. After the war he became principal of Ruskin College, a centre at the University of Oxford for extramural students mainly of working-class origin.

5 I.e., Wakefield Work Centre, to which Hoare had transferred after accepting alternative service under the Home Office Scheme.

GEORGE EWAN

George Alfred Ewan (1877–1949) wrote the account of his experiences as an absolutist CO in the First World War, extracts from which I print below, for his family and not for publication. The memoir was composed in 1942 – in the midst of a second global conflict. The description of his sojourn in Wormwood Scrubs and Portsmouth prisons possesses a serenity that other CO prison memoirs sometimes lack. This seems to reflect Ewan's happy disposition and his deep religious faith. He was a member of Stirchley Friends Meeting in Birmingham for over forty years. After his death his meeting described him as 'a man of transparent sincerity of purpose ... always ready with help for those in trouble and with encouragement for those who were seeking the right.'

At the time of his call-up in mid-1917 he was aged forty, already a mature individual therefore in contrast to many other COs (like the twenty-year-old John Hoare, a fellow sojourner in the Scrubs), who had been conscripted while still in their late teens or early twenties. It is interesting to compare their responses to what was essentially the same experience.

His daughter Margaret Keeble wrote of Ewan: '[When arrested] he was employed by the Ten Acres and Stirchley Co-operative Society. He could have been exempted for his essential work but refused this because his junior would then have been conscripted and would have gone to fight.' He was arrested on 4 June 1917 and held in the army guardroom in Warwick for about three weeks before being court-martialled.

The Court [Martial] was assembled, and I was presented before them to answer my charge in refusing to obey an order to put on military clothing. I think I pleaded guilty to the charge, but submitted that I did so with the utmost respect to those with whom I had to contend. The

Adjutant read my statement, and read it with much feeling, and the whole court was to me like a Friends' service. I felt the prayers of those who were not there and God's presence and was filled with a quiet calm.

I have stated a doubt of my pleading, but think I am right in what I have quoted. I believe they interpreted my statement as 'Not Guilty' to get a clear and definite trial. My statement and the statements of witnesses were read and they were interviewed and their statements confirmed. 'Did I wish to be questioned, to question these witnesses?' 'With goodwill to these men I would say I have no questions to ask.' I was proved guilty and sentence would be confirmed later. This, I think, was Thursday.

'Read Out' on Parade Ground

On the day I heard my sentence read, which I think was a Monday, I was taken on the parade ground. There on the square in front of the soldiers on parade, with their officers standing in front of them, it was an uncanny feeling to feel all eyes on me whilst the adjutant read my charge and the confirmation of the Court decision of a sentence of 112 days hard labour.

I was then taken back to the guard room. In my Fellowship Hymn Book I pushed a photo of my wife and fellow teachers of the primary class of our Sunday school. This was to accompany me to Wormwood Scrubs ...

In the morning an escort was to take me to Wormwood Scrubs, and hand my body to the authorities. So it was goodbye to many solid friends I had made with men of all shades of thought and I feel good feeling for the associates of officers and men alike. I do hope my witness at Warwick was one which witnessed for Christ whose law is love and not force. I left Warwick feeling I left behind friends who, not agreeing, respected my God.

To the 'Scrubs'

The walk to the station was refreshing. My wife and children had been to see me, the military police had been kind, I had enjoyed visitors and the Quaker chaplain, and was leaving many friends behind. Now on my way to prison. Other ways I could have found, but I felt a wonder at the calm thought 'I am on my way to prison.'

We boarded the train, and sped on our way. The escort was correct and kind in bearing, and I entered into friendly talk with him. He shared with me food my wife had brought me on the bus taking us on the last stages of the brief liberty. He, at my request, shared some of my food with a passenger who was aboard.

We passed two girls who gave us a look that showed their disgust at our destination. Wormwood Scrubs reached, one felt a happy feeling to see in stone above the Great Gate the figures of Elizabeth Fry and John Howard, who worked for prison reform. Would God use our lives in this effort too?

Imprisoned in the 'Scrubs'

The gate opened and we entered, waited fifteen minutes in a waiting room, documents changed hands and my body was handed over to prison authorities. My escort wished me goodbye.

I was then taken and locked up in a cell awaiting further results. Dinner was brought us, corned beef and bread. All the newcomers were assembled and then called to a room one by one. An officer invited us to empty our pockets, and he entered into a large day-book the contents. Our outer clothes were taken off, and two prisoners ... took them. We were then in our shirts and invited to stand behind a clothes horse with clean sheets around it. Then I faced another officer who said 'Before you take off your shirt let me see the colour of your eyes.' He described them 'brown.' 'Now you have nothing to fear here if you do as you are told.' He really was being friendly. 'Take off your shirt then take a sheet and go into the bathroom.' This was very refreshing after three weeks sleeping in our clothing. Prison clothes awaited us. All the prisoners in reception were CO's and got in a word of cheer when they could. Whilst in the bath they sized you up and put out clothing accordingly. The bathrooms have a small door open at the bottom about two feet and about three feet high, so that the officer has oversight of the prisoners at any time he wishes.

The bath over, we assembled on forms to confirm our sentences by the governor, who reads them out, and gives us advice that the half loaf of bread given us with our pint of cocoa is for supper and breakfast. Then we are sent to the doctor. We are instructed that when we enter the doctor's presence we take our shirt off, let down our trousers, turn our backs on him, then face him and reclothe ourselves. This was the 'medical inspection,' and confirms the hard labour duties. Then we are marched to the inner prison, doors open and clang, and we are locked in. It is night. We are in a great hall, four stories high. I was in B ward. It was whitewashed and each cell lighted up. It looked strange, looking up I saw wire netting across the middle of each storey. What a good fowl run!

At a desk the warder in charge told us to sign our names, which was a notification to our nearest relative that we were safely in Wormwood Scrubs, with a notification that if of good behaviour we will be able to write in fifty-six days. The warder then took me to my cell. 'Get your bed down and get to bed right away, be as quiet as you can.' The door clangs to and we are in prison.

Prison Routine

Morning 5.30 bell rings very violently for about five minutes. We get up, the lights are lit, and at six o'clock the doors are opened about three at a time. We empty our slops and get fresh water. Doors closed at 7 a.m. Great commotion in the halls. The shuffling of feet running backwards, a prisoner, who is a cleaner, holding a five-gallon can of porridge. A warder opening the door and measuring out 1 pt. each. With 3 oz. of bread this is our first meal. After partaking the sumptious feast the cell has to be cleaned up, swept and the tin knife, spoon, dust shovel, lid of chamber, all to be placed on the floor (to be inspected by the governor, who visits every landing in the hall about 10 a.m.) – the chamber to be placed on its side.

The doors are unlocked at 8 a.m., and we all turn out into the exercise yard – a large ring and a smaller one, with four platforms. At one portion the lavatories in charge of an officer. The walk commences of 40 minutes each way, to the voice usually saying 'left, left, left right left (C2/24 keep step – or get back – or stop talking).' Anyone wishing to leave the ring lifts up hand and the officer gives consent if you catch his eye, or next time round. Another officer may be in charge of hair cutting and clipping our beards. (Now in 1942 prisoners shave.)

When time is up, those who go out to work – to book binding shop, part-worn store or other shop, are collected together and marched off to their work. The cleaners and men on first stage, 28 days confined to cell sewing, are taken back to the hall.

Noon dinner men leave shops and march to the halls; there they take their handkerchief out of pocket and hold hands over heads. Their officer then runs his hands over each body to see that he has not taken anything from the workshop, then dismisses them and all walk to their respective cells, a warder being on each landing, which in a big establishment are usually four.

Dinner one pint stew, 4 oz. potatoes 3 oz. bread, varied by 2 kippers and corned beef, Sunday suet pudding in stew, Wednesdays bacon and beans, or minus bacon for Jews, extra beans for bacon. Work in cells after dinner twice a week, either breakfast or dinner time the cleaner puts a bucket of water and cloth in your cell for you to wash and scrub floor, bedboard and table and stool during that time in question.

In the cells we are supposed to work after meals at sewing mailbags or work of that description, beside the work in the workshops. 1.30. I think the warder re-appears, cleaner collects dinner tins and takes them to the kitchen. We empty slops and get fresh water if required, then re-assemble – all who return to workshops until 4 p.m., when the same search took place (usually a matter of form), and we re-enter our cells for supper, 3 oz. bread ° oz. margarine 1 pt. cocoa and then work in cells. A quick worker could get a bit of reading in from 7 to 8 when lights were put out and bed.

Chapel and Chaplains

Every Wednesday morning those who put in their desire to worship with the C. of E. went to the chapel for ° hour divine service and war news after breakfast or after the 40 minutes in the exercise yard, and Sunday morning 10 to 11.30 and afternoon 2 to 3.30. The chaplain or one of his assistants took charge of the service. On raised seats scattered all over the chapel the warders would sit and their watchful eyes would be over the chapel. What I liked to think was that we all could worship God. At Wormwood Scrubs I did not assemble with the worshipers[1] because of the chaplain's conversation with me, I will relate what transpired. All prisoners are taken at the commencement of their sentence before the spiritual adviser of the prison, 'The Chaplain.' I had put in for the C of E service, together with my claim as a Quaker to have a Quaker chaplain and to attend their service. On confronting the C. of E. chaplain, he said 'I see you want to attend C. of E. service.' 'Yes, I would like to worship God with you.' 'You will have to listen to the war news,' was the retort. 'Oh, I beg your pardon, I would like to worship God with you, may I withdraw?' 'Yes, we have enough of your sort here.' 'Thank you,' and my interview with this spiritual adviser was over ...

First Prison Work

On commencing a sentence a prisoner was in the first stage (different now I believe) and spent the first twenty-eight days in the cell, except for exercise. He works at sewing. He is allowed a Bible, hymn book and prayer book, and an educational book. After twenty-eight days he can have a fiction book or another book. I personally enjoyed the quiet, and found spiritual help in it. The first blow was the fifty-six days which my wife and I must undergo before we could pledge to each other our proud faith in the other's trust in God, and we felt a nearness of God's love bridging the gulf.

Eight mailbags a day was expected to be sewn. On my first day the taskmaster found me in my cell. I should have been in the exercise yard, and for some unexplained circumstance I was in my cell ... The taskmaster took me to the warder in charge of the Halls, who was astounded to see me and sent me out, calling to the warder in charge of the exercise 'Another for you.' He said 'Where have you come from? Get in there.' I started my first walk round and round. All these men were CO's.

Men under sixty, for the first fourteen days, sleep on their base board, no mattress, two sheets, a pillow, two blankets in summer and a quilt. I was in five cells in four days. In some way or other I always had my mattress in Wormwood Scrubs.

After twenty-eight days we are given a stripe to put on our sleeves, and we go to the chief warder, who finds us work in some shop. I was asked if I was willing to make 'ship fenders.' I said 'No.' 'Why?' I said I did not want to do work of a character which would cause a man to have to go into military service through my doing work which might be his. 'You can't shoot ship fenders. Do you know what they are?' 'Yes!' 'Oh well, you will have to work there, ship fenders have been made from time immemorial.' But I found he gave me very nice work in the partworn stores, and taking in the washing and putting up the clean clothing, boots, clothing, cell utensils. For nearly two months I worked there.

The Clothing Store

A group of men [were] brought in overnight. The warder and his cleaner bring in the clothes of these men, together with the handcuffs if [they are] brought in from another prison. Those prison clothes are washed and sent back to that prison.

A warder brings in so many boots for repair, and requires the same number back in exchange, similarly other wearing apparel. For my own landing my warder brought in boots and I gave him in return some old boots. He looked at them. He could not say much, but said 'You are a rum one.' So I saw humour. He prided himself on his men looking as smart as any. I would oblige him and after that I gave him, for every pair he brought in, a brand new pair. Before my sentence was over there was many a new shoe on that landing! Neither spoke to the other about the matter.

'Have these men been searched?' 'Yes sir.' We had not! On one occasion a warder who had taken us, it was summer time, July, the warder had been gardening and was tired. At 6.30 he had fallen asleep in the store with five prisoners in his charge. I heard the chief warder approaching the store, and dropped a chamber lid, and as the chief came in I was regretting my clumsiness to the warder, who was now awake. 'Your men all correct?' 'Yes sir.' The incident was closed.

I used to lift the flap of the counter for the governor every morning. My warder asked me to do so, and usually thanked me for it. He brought in an inspector one morning. I, as usual, held the flap up with one hand in the air, the other at my side so as not to appear at attention. Staring at me with wonderment he said, standing right underneath the flap, which was heavy, 'Put your hand down!' I looked and half smiled. He, getting very red in the face, 'Do you hear, put your hand down!' I looked at the governor and my warder and fellow prisoners, half smiling, and he got furious. After a time the governor said quietly 'I think you will see if you look he is doing you a service.' The silly little puppy said 'Oh yes, a good work, a good work' and left the department, much to the amusement of the rest of us. My warder said 'It would have served him right if you had carried out his request' ...

I remember the warder in the partworn department at Wormwood Scrubs wanting to go to the lavatory, and he had to take six of us with him and leave us outside the lavatory under the eye of another officer in the wash house. Another time we were collecting some goods for various places of the prison, and nature's call to our warder was very urgent. We had to cart with us six in number, and he had to leave us with the officer in charge of prisoners from the hospital taking their outside exercise ...

[Inspections]

While many of the prisoners are at work in the workshops those of the first stages [are] in the cells. Should the governor see anything irregular, such as unclean utensils, or untidiness, he draws the prisoner's attention to it, and the prisoner has to mend his ways or meet the consequences, which might be bread and water.

The same is found in the visits to the workshops, and warders are apt to keep themselves keen that they are not at fault. In large establishments there is sometimes a difficult time between the watching warders, the prisoners and the higher officials. A warder's lot is not always an easy one. Fear plays a large place in prison life in more ways than one.

Visiting magistrates inspect the whole of the buildings and halls, asking on every hand 'Any complaints?' The method of visiting is like the Governor's, usually the warder opens the door and announces 'Visiting magistrate.' Men are supposed to stand to attention. My usual method was to stand with elbows a little bent and to say 'No thank you.' The prison staff are generally kind and considerate in their duties, which are not always pleasant. I have no complaints to make. I do not appreciate prison life, but glad to know something of the life in these unfortunate places.

Should a complaint be on the lips of the prisoner, the Governor, his asssistant or the chief warder is on the rack of the visiting magistrate. Whilst in the prison the visiting magistrate may have offenders before them, and try them for breach of rules. Or a prisoner may prefer the magistrate's ruling in preference to the Governor's in case of the breach in question.

Inspector's visits are perhaps more thorough. He listens to any reports of the prisoner, and uses his judgement in either reporting the case, appeasing the individual, or in putting the prisoner's case right. The authorities are very careful, and watch for these complaints, and the inspector has the right to suggest a private interview with the prisoner if he feels justified.

The C. of E. chaplain often comes in with these visitors. Sometimes we could see humour arriving out of these visits. Complaints were put forward at times either imaginary or otherwise.

At Wormwood Scrubs the prison chaplain did not visit me, I saw him in the hall the day before I left, when he wished me good luck. When I had been in about six weeks, my wife wrote to me for enlightenment in money matters. A prisoner has the right to write an answer to problems of finance. This gave us the opportunity to write. The Governor gave me the right to answer the question. When written I put 'I am in good health, dear, and meeting with good treatment.' I asked the warder his advice, and he said that would be in order, and this is how my wife got through to me. When letters were received they were red-letter days. When our replies were due pen, ink and writing paper were put in our cells. Then they were read by the officials and duly sent out ...

The Governor's Goodbye

On my last day I was taken to the Governor and his assistant, a warder in attendance. They sat in a little recess, on the walls behind them were handcuffs, strait jackets, etc., which made a good background. I commenced conversation by asking 'If I had complaints to make I suppose this would be the time to make them?' The Governor said 'Yes,' and looked rather hard. 'Well, I have no complaints, but I have to thank you for the consideration given by the officials under you, and yourselves for that fairness shown in these unlovely places. I am pleased to have had the knowledge at first hand of men living under the eye of the law, and thanks ought to be pressed home as well as complaints. You have the opportunity of showing kindness, whilst doing your duty.' They looked at each other, then at me, and said 'That is very nice of you' ... I was with them about thirty minutes, and the interview was a pleasing one to both parties.[2] The following morning, leaving the cell in a clean order, I was conducted to the reception rooms. My clothing was in a cubicle, which I put on, leaving my prison clothing behind me. Breakfast, and at the escort presenting himself, my body was handed over to the military authorities, money, letters and some cakes my wife had sent in were waiting for me.

A Brief Respite

The gates opened, and my escort and self stepped out, where my dear wife and little daughter awaited me all smiles and true love; one of my sisters too, but my coming out of prison was a strain to her. She did not understand my views. She wanted to do right but was annoyed at my point of view.

We had breakfast, then our escort left us and we were to meet him at a set time. We sat quietly on some seats in London then went to some Italian restaurant for dinner. The food was tasty and a treat. I don't know when I enjoyed a meal so, and I don't know when a meal upset me so. We got on a train to Southampton, Margaret sat on my knee, but even that was too much. My sister added to my discomfort by pointing out to me my duty to the nation. I was wanting my wife and child to myself. She tried to make my escort press home my duties. She meant well, and it just proves that we can only be ourselves and cannot rightly judge for others. All the arguments of the usual war note were put forward, and how I stood it [I don't know] and the weakness of 112 days limited diet and the excess seasonings were telling on me. The steamer ride was a little better, a policeman asked us all our nationality, and then a train ride to Newport [Isle of Wight] and I was handed over ...

[Ewan was again back in an army guard room. Eventually he received a second court-martial, this time in Portsmouth.]

2nd Reading Out – A Two-Year Sentence

I was led out by a sergeant on to the square to be 'read out' before the whole of the soldiers paraded for that purpose, together with the officers. My second 'reading out.' A strange ceremony, and a lonely furrow we in our movement have met in our spiritual sense of joy and enthusiasm ...

We take our stand and the silent presence gives help, and we face the officer who reads the sentence of two-years hard labour. My hat had been rather roughly taken off my head, and my arm moved from a crooked position. I immediately wiped my nose, listened carefully, and felt the shock of the sentence. Six or twelve months had been in my mind. The 'reading out' was at the Duke of Clarence Barracks, and to that guard room I was taken. There I sat on a form, waiting whilst the order transferring my body over to prison authorities was filled in ... Then two officers came in and sat beside me. They had just arrived at the barrack, and knew I had been 'read out,' and with a sympathetic way asked how I had got on. I told them and they were very nice.

I was allowed to go back and taken to my old room. My old friend the corporal brought me my dinner. A very nice dinner and very nice pudding too. Such a big dinner the guard commented on it, and he put something from the cookhouse in his pocket for me together with an apple. I had to do justice to please him ...

To Portsmouth Prison

Then commenced my walk to Portsmouth prison, with two soldiers behind. I had left many peace magazines, etc. behind for distribution to the soldiers. For which I was pleased, and I prayed God's blessing upon them.

A pleasant walk. A great heavy door opens, and I am taken into a room. The documents passing over my body change hands, and a receipt is given for the exchange. I felt God had had a place for me in challenging the war machine, and I hoped there would be a place for me to witness for him alone, yet not alone. 'I will be with thee.'

To the reception cells, bath, change of clothing, pillow, slips, sheets, towel, etc. We entered into the prison which holds about 160 men, and 26 women. The women's portion being in a wing on its own. Tea was brought me at 5 p.m. Morning found me waiting to see the governor and also doctor. Both asked me questions as to what I should do if someone were doing-in my wife or children. I told them no one knows what they would do, but if we were living in the spirit of Christ a way would be made in which it would be almost impossible for evil to befall us or our loved ones. He said 'I would take up a chopper or the nearest thing I could lay my hands on.' The officer (with the doctor in attendance) said 'I'd like to shoot such men,' and I was passed out and entered my cell. They put me on sewing mailbags. There were about twenty-four C.O.'s here, and it was November dark days. I felt a real welcome in the smile of these friends, and there were two members of the Society of Friends there.

The Quaker chaplains were Robert Penny of Brighton and Charles Woodam of Southampton. The first Saturday I saw Charles Woodam who was a school teacher, and was very helpful. He sat on my stool and chatted on many things ...

The Quaker chaplain had a meeting for worship with us once a fortnight. The week we had no meeting we had a visit in our cells. They took turns in coming. Both Friends were quite different, but very nice. Robert Penny was more of a Quaker who took his place in the service of Friends, was always ready to listen to the things we were interested in, and quickly got some thought which was of real spiritual value. Charles Woodam [was] a younger man, interested and helpful and fully appreciated by all.

The meetings were always attended by an officer of the prison, and we felt that an opportunity was given us to make our meetings rich in spirit. We had the Fellowship Hymn book, usually had a hymn, the [Quaker] chaplain would read a portion, speak a minute or two, then the meeting would enter into silence, to be broken by one of us, and we do hope that Christ's spirit was felt.

Charles Woodam left the district and Robert Penny continued on his own. When he visited us I used to think out some spiritual problem that came before me, and we would talk it over. Then he would do the same. I used to sit on the floor or kneel, and he sitting on my stool. He always read a portion and never seemed in a hurry. Then after he always told me the news. I never asked for it. Many of the other CO's asked for the news he told me. Once he told me 'I'll have to come and see you last I think, as I find myself having to hurry my visits.' 'Oh! by all means and I will think and pray for you. I don't mind if you have to pass me by. These are mostly younger men than I and I want you to be doing what you can for them.'

Religion in Prison

Prison chaplains – Church of England, Roman Catholic, Wesleyan, Salvation Army, the Rabbi – are amongst those who can hold services, I believe, of their own peculiar way. Whilst I only saw the chaplain at the commencement and the end of my first sentence at Wormwood Scrubs, the way of prison life became more usual to me, and the method of getting in touch with the spritual adviser of His Majesty's Guest House – 'The Hotel Portsmouth.' When the warder came round in the morning to open the door after breakfast, we had the opportunity to ask for the doctor, the governor, or the chaplain. The chaplain if we required books of religious character, thus giving an opportunity to talk with the chaplain and also get books of an educational character.

There was an exchange of thoughts with some. One of the assistant chaplains told one CO it was a pity he was hiding behind prison walls, the reply was quick 'That's better than hiding behind a reversible collar.' He tried to close the cell door, but the CO placed his foot in, and continued the talk, giving his views on his stand.

I asked for several books at various times and always had one assistant coming to me first for my requests, then with the book. Thus we got some very nice talks in. As it happened this minister was not at his best form when in the pulpit. Preaching was not a good point. He was nervous and ill at ease. But his visits were helpful, his sympathy ready and very patient. One day he came, I had been taking round dinner, being a cleaner, and he stood talking for some time. As I had passed my door I had placed my dinner can in the recess where the lighting lights up the cell. When he went he naturally pulled the door to, my dinner being on the outside. I rang, and smilingly he opened the door, handing me my dinner. Once I told him his work lay not so much in the pulpit as amongst his congregation, in contact with his people, and he seemed pleased.

I had one visit from the chaplain. He came in very charming, and I said to myself 'You are my guest, how shall I entertain you?' The thought came 'see what he has to say and follow it up.' He went to the corner where the books were and picking first one up then the other he said 'Are you getting the books you require?' ... I said 'Yes, thank you' ... For about an hour we stood in the cell exchanging ideas. Our interests seemed of an understanding character. His interests seemed as keen as mine in the things upon which we spoke. He said it was not intended that anyone like myself should be placed in this condition, and he gave me credit for being there to my stand. I thanked him for the thought he had expressed in my sincerity, but in turn asked him what any governing body could do with anyone like myself, who in the case of conscription would not allow themselves to be conscripted. Should we be free, what would the other men say and do? ...

The Church of England service was held on Wednesdays about 8.30 a.m., when news was [read out] about the war, and a service of about half an hour took place, and ten a.m. Sunday and 2.30 in the afternoon. Sometimes we had a good talk. One could always see humour. In the chanting of the Lord's prayer one prisoner awaiting trial always used to sing out 'And lead us not into police station.' In the Wednesday talk we were once invited to vote for the next two weeks, either to have the Ten Commandments, or the Books of the Bible, and the Books of the Bible were voted for ... We had the Bishop of Winchester to speak to us once. Our chaplain got him to preach. He gave us an excellent address commencing with 'My dear brothers and sisters' ...

Part of my work was to help put up the altar for the Roman Catholics, and as we were returning the R.C. women prisoners would be marched in, and we would smile as we passed. In C. of E. the women were in the gallery. I succeeded the cleaner whose sentence had just expired. He had served six months for bigamy. Before he left I asked him if he was going back to his lawful wife. He said 'What do you think? I'm not.'

The Daily Round

My job gave me more freedom to roam the [block]. My work was to wash the WC's and landing daily, to put buckets and floor cloths into the various cells, so that all were kept clean, and to polish the rail surrounding the [landing] and stairs.

Cleaning the landing one day outside a cell occupied by a star man of about 60 years of age ('star men' are first offenders, and have red stars in the cap) he sat on his stool sewing. Knowing I was a Quaker, he said 'Who's the mother of Jesus' mother?' I was a bit at a loss at his question. I didn't smile, but said 'His grandmother, of course.' 'No! You know that chap in the cell next to you. He knows a lot about the Bible, ask him, he knows.' So I got up, carried my bucket round to this cell on the other side, down on my knees – the warder being on duty downstairs.

My neighbour [was] a Plymouth Brethren, a dark-eyed young man. 'Jim, lie down, I want to ask you a question.' My request adhered to, I said 'I've just been sent to you as an authority on the bible. Who's the mother of Jesus' mother? I said "his grand-mother" but I'm wrong I'm told.' Those dark eyes danced with fun. 'Mary and Elizabeth were cousins, were they not?' Now it was my turn to open my mouth. 'Yes!' I said. 'Well it was Elizabeth's aunt.' Back went bucket and self, down on my knees, another wet patch was made and wiped up while I gave the answer, which gave satisfaction.

We bath once a week in 9 inches of water prepared for us by another prisoner. You take your own soap and towel, and undress in a little cubicle. When ready go to the prepared bath. Quite a number are going, a warder in attendance. If he cared he has the oversight of all that is going on, both baths and lavatories have half-doors attached, so that nothing can be hidden away. On this day I saw an old man standing in his bath with his hat on as he splashed the water with his feet and prepared to get out. The warder said 'If you don't get down to it I'll bring the big bass broom in and scrub you well.' He got down and sat in his bath.

Porridge for the Governor

As cleaner it was my duty to carry the porridge round. It was a five-gallon can. First morning I went for my can to the cookhouse. My intention being to give the CO's a fair share, or over if possible. The warder at Portsmouth would open the door and you pour the porridge in each mug. I saw the other men take a stick or ladle and stir the can round. I picked up my can and had about six stairs to climb into the hall from the cookhouse. I had no idea that I was so weak. It took all my time to climb those stairs.

The governor always had a pint pot in a letter-tray, to see we were getting the right stuff. So I was told by the warder to fill the pot which was on a roll-topped desk. Up went the can, at first the porridge wouldn't come out, then all of a sudden it came gushing out. First the thick layer of crust on the top. (It then dawned on me why the men had stirred up their cans before leaving the cookhouse.) The pot was full, the letter-tray too, and a rich creamy substance was rolling down the desk and about two quarts were on the floor. Looking at the warder with a smile, I said 'There, I've given the governor his pint of porridge, what shall I do now? Shall I clean it up?' He said, 'No.' He thought the can a bit too heavy for me, and suggested the other fellow take it, much to my relief.

The governor that morning, on his usual visit round, had a merry twinkle in his eye, and I rather fancy it was to be seen in mine. That was all that was said.

The padded cell is padded all round the walls to about 6ft, so that no harm can follow any desperate act. The observation cell is one opened to the warders, having an iron door with bars from top to bottom, so that at any time the prisoner can be seen. To every cell is a spy hole to which the officer at any time may apply his eye. I have got right under the door at times, and it has taken quite a time to locate me. I feel sure he went away with a grin ...

It was my task to take bread to the front office for the warder, who bought it at cost. One morning a hot roll was thrown me (6oz. roll). The warder saw it and took no notice. I put it inside my coat. It was hot, and the steward had to smile at the lump he saw bulging there ...

[Ewan was released from Portsmouth prison on accepting work with the Home Office Scheme at Wakefield. But he soon came to feel this constituted a compromise he was unwilling to make. He with ten other CO's were returned, therefore, to complete their prison sentences. Ewan went back to Portsmouth.]

Back to Portsmouth

We all journeyed from Wakefield, splitting up at different points. The warders were in plain clothes, and very nice with us. We seemed a happy family. We were met in London by a member of our beloved

[Quaker] Society of Friends. We had refreshment at the station. When I offered to pay for tea for myself and my warder, the head warder said 'I shall charge this up, don't pay.' These warders welcomed the Friend, who placed himself at our disposal, crossed with us from one station to the other, mingling freely with us all, quite unfettered. Any questions asked and answered. When we all parted, the impression of our Friend left a marked feeling upon our guard. Just what I wanted.

We [arrived] at Portsmouth, my warder and I, late in the evening. In getting the taxi he could not make himself understood, and I made the man understand our destination. 'Drive us to gaol friend, will you,' and he did. I got out first on arrival, and gave the bell a pull. The gate opened, and the warder peering out could not see me, but I seeing him, put my hand in saying 'How do Mr. Robbins, awful nice to see you again.' He was equally pleased, and we all three walked into the reception room together. There he left us while he went to see Mr. Hall, the Governor, whose house was outside the wall. He said he would see me in the morning. 'Now, Mr. Robbins, my friend here should not have travelled to-day. He is heavy with cold. Can you see that he is in comfortable quarters for the night?' He assured me on that score. We had a little chat before I was taken and again had prison clothes on, and again locked in my cell. We were reduced to about six CO's now.

The Governor saw us in the morning. He was quite interested in all that had taken place at Wakefield ... He thought I had taken the right course, which was only natural. We had quite a long chat. Then the men I had left behind, in our taking exercise, wanted to know what had transpired. With them it was the wrong course I had taken. In the calmness of the quiet it seemed very easy. But in the turmoil and strife, with difficult conflict of thought, with all the shades of thought it was not easy having to come to an issue to find a way out.

I found myself in the store. This brought me almost all over the prison with my officer, cracked pots replaced – collected on the ward and exchanged by the department – hessian arriving in bales to be unloaded and kept in good condition, food stuffs, flour, oatmeal, salt, potatoes, etc., goods, utensils, etc. arriving from other prisons and checked over. Once a quantity of wearing apparel for Holloway [women's prison in London]. I was checking hairpins and ladies bonnets with my head covered. I went on with my counting, and the officer had to smile.

Often I came into contact with prisoners going to have fingerprints and photo taken ...

The last few months seemed to tell on one's nerves. Men come and go. Old hands you look to see back, and it's surprising how some seem to make prison almost their home.

Discharge ?? – At the Price of a Signature!!

I was sent for by the governor one morning, and he said 'Ewan, your discharge has come from your non-combatant corps. All you have to do is sign this card, which, when signed, I shall dispatch back. Then an order for your release will be issued. You will return to your unit, remain there a week or so and then be discharged.' 'Thank you Mr. Hall. I have as you full well know a marked respect for you, and for you personally I would do almost anything. But when you ask me to sign that card it is for the Military, and I must with every respect to you refuse to sign. As yet I have signed nothing, and do not intend to do so either.' His reply was quiet yet firm, 'I knew you would not,' and he then threw the card on one side.

'I would like to have sight of the card,' I said. With pleasure he handed it over. I saw it simply was a kind of discharge from prison to camp. We had a few minutes talk, and then I went back to my work.

On one occasion on the landing the Governor called across to me and said with a twinkle of the eye 'Remember I wear spectacles as well as you.' 'Well it's up to you to increase our writing paper to larger sheets.' 'No, not I.' 'Well Mr. Hall we'll have to continue as usual. You have got your wife and family here. We have only these letters to get to our homes and convey our thoughts; it's difficult to state, in letters that are read by all, the sacredness of heart and mind of husband and wife and to the children. Well, you know these letters are quite alright, but much the same sameness gets somewhat stale.'

On one occasion one of the sailor prisoners was cutting hair, and seeming to machine over the hills and dales of growth of the face. The officer in charge then was in the hall. The sailor was taking it out of the CO's. Mr. Robbins called me, and I occupied the stool. As my friend took charge of my head, stooping over my shoulder he said 'I can't understand you fellows, do you know every ounce of cheese and margarine that comes in has to be fought for by our navy?' 'Well I didn't ask them to fight for me; but if the fight is so real to you, what are you doing here? The navy is looking after your cheese too.' The officer smiled, and the sailor said nothing more ...

When I was a cleaner, when new men came onto the landing the officer would ask me to show the newcomer what was expected in our hotel de luxe. With the warder in the cell, usually I used to put out my hand and say 'Good morning, I am sorry to see you here, I'll just show you how we should go on.' One fellow answered 'Oh, alright, unfortunately I'm quite used to this life' ...

Release

The day of release was sudden. Nearly six months after the non-combatants had intended to release me. One dinner-time two of us were sent for, a Jew and myself, and after exchanging our clothes were shaking hands with officers and men. The officer said 'If Guv. had had his way all you [CO's] would be released.'

About three weeks before this an incident took place of marked interest. About six men were leaving. I went to the officer to ask if I could say goodbye, and the chief warder said 'They have just gone, but do you know what Brewer asked?' I said 'No!' 'He asked if he could stop and serve your sentence out, as he was single and you are married.' I felt his kindness I can assure you. (There were many things of interest one could spend much time recording. These thoughts are not taken in order, but just as they come, and are much disjointed.) We took a taxi out ... Wired 'Coming 10.15 Snowhill,' and what a funny thing, free to home and loved ones. What a wonderful thought, and the train could not move quickly enough.

Tired, but happy, I arrived at Snowhill. My dear wife was waiting for me, together with her closest friend (who is now my dear wife, my first wife having died several years ago). It was good to meet, to talk and to feel the sacred beauty of human life again. I expect I looked a bit grubby, for the chopper had been over my face early that morning. The devoted love and care, the suffering in silence the contempt of other women, all these things our dear ones underwent in their struggle with us for the victory of the spirit in freedom and love ...

My wife and I were convinced Friends, and their quiet worship had a real hold of us. Yet as members of the Society we felt a call. We felt the presence of God in our midst means having the Christ Spirit of Love, means following love, being misunderstood and taking a stand, facing odds, risking all natural things, liberty, friendship, separation ... We both felt Christianity was a [way of] life ... If we can portray anything of His love and character to point out to the war weary a new way of life, joy, peace and contentment in His love, we will not have passed the way of life in vain.

Notes

Source: 'Prison Memories of George Ewan: Being the Experiences of a Conscientious Objector in the First Word War,' typescript in the Archives of the Peace Pledge Union (London), pp. 9–13, 15, 16, 24–31, 33–7.

1 Around this time the eighteen-year-old CO Douglas Prichard, though the son of a (pacifist) Congregational minister and himself a member of the Battersea Free Church, did choose to attend the Church of England service while at the Scrubs. In a pamphlet he wrote shortly afterwards and published for family and friends, the boy described the Sunday service as follows: 'I had not been inside the chapel for two minutes before I got into trouble for looking round at the organ, which was at the rear of the building. A prisoner is not allowed to look to the left, right, or to the rear. The service is most formal. One loses the feeling of freedom of will which is essential to worship. To hear the clanging of the gates and the jingling of the keys as a warder locks the prisoners in the church, does not help to create a spiritual atmosphere. I remember in the middle of a prayer, one Sunday, a warder calling out to a prisoner who was not kneeling down. On another occasion, at the close of the saying of the Apostles' Creed, the [clergyman] remonstrated with the prisoners because nobody joined in the recitation. The hymns, however, were generally well sung. Just before the close of the afternoon service the chaplain told us his version of the news of the week. When he announced the collapse of the Italian army, and added that it would mean an addition of eighteen months, at least, to the duration of the war, a sigh, almost a groan, went up from the C.O.'s.' From D. Prichard, *My Case as a C.O.* (London: privately printed, n.d.), 18, 19.

2 Young Prichard, en route to the Home Office Centre at Knutsford, did not have such a happy conclusion to his stay at the Scrubs as Ewan did. He writes (ibid., 22): 'The last hours in prison were spent in receiving our "Scheme" clothes, the return of our own clothes and belongings. We [sixteen COs] were waiting to see the Governor when a warder discovered that one of the C.O.s had left a needle in the pocket of his coat, instead of in his cell. The warder exclaimed, "Whenever shall we be able to cure you fellows of your criminal tendencies." I doubt whether the C.O. concerned felt very guilty for having accidentally kept the needle.'

ROBERT PRICE

The role of the Churches of Christ in the CO movement in the First World War Britain has been overlooked. Neither Martin Ceadel in his study of that movement nor I, for instance, mentioned them when treating this period. The Restorationist denomination had originated as an offshoot of the Disciples of Christ founded in the United States by British-born Alexander Campbell in the antebellum era. It possessed from the beginning a strong pacifist tradition: the body had officially opposed the Boer War. However, 'the First World War shattered the pacifist consensus of the Churches.'[1] Most members of the denomination's middle-class congregations supported the war and accepted combatant service when conscripted, whereas the working-class congregations, particularly strong in Lancashire's Wigan coal-mines district and the coalfields of south Wales, as well as in the Glasgow area, opposed the war, the overwhelming majority of their young men opting for conscientious objection. The division between the west-end chapels and the back-street bethels[2] should not, of course, be treated too rigidly: the former produced some COs and the latter some combatant soldiers. The bethels remained in principle staunchly pacifist and pro-Labour into the interwar years, while clinging to a primitivist faith that rejected theological liberalism unreservedly.[3]

The Churches of Christ's pacifist primitivists displayed some of the shortcomings typical of British working-class radicalism before and since the Chartist movement of the 1830s and 1840s. For all their striving after self-education, their intellectual horizons were sometimes narrow; they were often intolerant of opinions differing from their own; and they did not always avoid self-righteousness. At the same time, their egalitarianism and hatred of Britain's class structure, their quest for social justice, and their abhorrence of war and the military spirit were all deeply felt impulses that they refused to abandon even at the cost of severe suffering. Take, for instance, the case of twenty-seven-year-old

Arthur Wilson, one of four brothers jailed as COs. He died in Strangeways Prison (Manchester) in December 1918 as a result of medical neglect after he had contracted influenza. Shortly before his death he had written home: 'I can say, after two years of imprisonment, that I would rather rot away for another ten years than compromise my faith, and my only regret would be that I would be separated from loved and loving ones.' After his death his father commented: 'I bless God for the honour of fatherhood to four such lads.' He thanked God, too, for giving him 'the grace ... to so train my lads from childhood to hate militarism that when the time of testing came they were ready to offer their lives rather than participate in the unholy cause.' This surely is the spirit, if not quite the message, of the seventeenth-century Scottish Covenanters.

At least seventy-seven members of the Churches of Christ were imprisoned as COs. And, writes Michael Casey, of these 'Robert Price was probably the most militant.'[4] Early in 1916 Robert, who was an elementary-school teacher and from the beginning extremely active on behalf of the Churches' COs, had applied, along with his brother Edward, for unconditional exemption, but the tribunal had rejected their applications. Robert would spend the rest of the war in one or another type of confinement, gaining release after the armistice only as a result of going on a hunger strike. In May 1918 he reported: 'I am getting quite used to courts-martial, guard-rooms, lock-ups and prisons. I have been in six police stations, ten guard-rooms, four prisons (one a military prison ...) – court-martialled three times, two terms of detention, thirteen and a half months' actual imprisonment. So you see I'm doing my bit!' 'I am now awaiting the promulgation of my [third] court-martial sentence. This, of course, will be two years at the least ... Now I am going to do, not a bit, but a lump.'[5]

Price's prison memoir, printed below, is brief but revealing. In contrast to the more gentle approach of the Quaker prisoner, Price's response to incarceration expresses his hatred of the harshness and cruelty of the contemporary British jail. He sees the prison system as part of an oppressive social order upheld by government, church, and army in an unholy alliance. For Price, Christian pacifism does not mean passivity but active protest against injustice. He writes passionately without any attempt at describing prison life with cold objectivity. True, he strives to be honest, but emotion eventually predominates. *J'accuse*, he (or his editor) cries out in the course of his narrative, indicting all three institutions of a criminal conspiracy to enslave 'the independent mind.'[6]

After vigorously protesting against my illegal arrest, trial by a Military Court, and being placed in a combatant regiment, whilst in possession of a non-combatant certificate – not, as I pointed out, that the latter mattered anything, for I had determined not to aid the war directly or indirectly, roundabout or square, at home or abroad – I was sentenced by a Military Court to six months' imprisonment.

I have never before so much as seen a prison, and looked forward to my new experience with great expectations. As a boy, I had read in my history books of the imprisonment of many reformers in the religious and political world. My father used to send my blood coursing warmly through my veins by stories of relatives, some of whom were either imprisoned or transported for taking part in the Chartist rising. These all contributed to sending me off on my new errand with buoyant spirits.

Any buoyance or enthusiasm I possessed was doomed to meet an early death, and something more solid and lasting was needed in its place. Prison was not what I expected it to be!

On my arrival at Wormwood Scrubs, I was surprised to find there were no quarries there. This surprise was expressed to me by others also.[7] Having entered, my first feeling was that of curiosity – a hasty glance round and a first impression. Then – of a sense of seclusion from the world without – for six long months!

I was soon introduced to my first cell. As I was marched by a warder along a corridor, there fell on my ears the rather uncanny sound of the warder's jingling keys and the tread of his heavy boots. Having passed into my cell, I was pierced through by the banging of the door and the turning of the key in the lock behind me. Thus began the two long years of my incarceration!

There was now no buoyancy left. The outlook was changed. One can wax warm when addressing his tens or his hundreds.[8] But under these circumstances one grows cold. No encouraging eye can be seen, no approving nod, no ringing cheers to stimulate, no criticism to call forth all one's energies in reply. No! all is the reverse! You are driven within yourself. You ask yourself: 'Is it worth the candle? Whatever has made me take this step? To where will your sufferings lead?' So I stood still; looked round, ruminated a little, realised my isolation and well-nigh choked with emotion, for I thought of home. I knew that somewhere in that same building was my only brother. I longed to speak to him; to signal that I was there, if only I could convey the word by telepathy! But

I hadn't faith in that. Could he be in the next cell? I tapped at the wall. There was no response. I tapped again. The only answer was the echo from the empty halls. How near was the next man? How far? Just then the corridors echoed with the tread of some unknown person. Who could it be? My cell door opened and the warder handed in my first prison meal, a pint of porridge and an eight ounce loaf of brown bread, but sans butter, sans sugar, sans tasty bits – and sans appetite also.

I then began to collect myself, and I realised that this was solitary confinement. In other words, I was deprived of my elementary rights, vouchsafed to all creation, of associating with my kind. I know no worse or more brutal form of punishment. I have seen men driven stark mad by it. On men with a highly strung nervous temperament it is disastrous. If a man has a moral weakness it drives his weakness within him and weakens what strong points he may have. It is no cure for criminality! It aggravates it. My varied experience of prison life amply bears out these statements.

The rigours of prison life are not confined to your cell, but extend over a much wider field. A most barbarous rule is the silence rule! Imagine yourself having to suffer the indignity of having your letters, which are already regulated in number and matter, postponed for a week, and you yourself placed on bread and water for a week, plus being kept in your cell for the same length of time – all because you were caught talking to a fellow prisoner. Or a similar punishment because you are caught looking through your cell window. Nothing dare be in your cell but by the warder's permission, and such things as are there are to be placed according to the idiosyncrasies of the Governor. This exactness re details serves only to make the prisoner concentrate his mind on obscure matters, which is the tendency of cell life itself, and harms him in concentrating on anything of moment. I have often found myself counting the number of bricks there were in the walls of my cell, or the number of knots in the floor, or else engaging in the most fantastic dreams. These things drive out clear thinking, and make sound judgment more difficult; whilst the strictness of the warders makes men cunning and crafty, aiming at all kinds of devices and petty deceptions.

I had, however, much chance for study, and read extensively. I read secular and sacred history, studied Latin, Greek, Euclid and Algebra, and when later we secured greater liberty, I taught logic to some fellow prisoners, whilst they tried to teach me Esperanto, etc., but without much success. I conversed much with Quakers, and read a number of their books, but ever failed to appreciate their standpoint. Whilst in Wandsworth prison, I addressed their meetings four times, with varied effects upon their members. They do not appreciate a New Testament stand.

My conclusion, after calmly studying my two years' experience, is that I fail to find anything that can be said in favour of our present prison system. It is no cure for crime, for it brings offenders together where they clandestinely compare notes. Rather than inducing them to look at their act with shame, it causes them to dwell unduly on the same. 'Familiarity breeds contempt' is a maxim which applies here also, and they become crime hardened. They realise they have lost their name, and they go on from crime to crime. I view with pity the juvenile offender, who is seldom cured by the system, but rather marked out by it to become a frequenter of these quarters.

The system requires to be uprooted and supplanted by another which shall rest not on force and punishment, but which shall give greater facilities for moral education and a persuasiveness to amend. At present, this side lacks fearfully. The predominant religious element is the Church of England, whose ministers have free access to every cell. They run three and four meetings a week, but the spirituality of these meetings and visits is, I regret to have to say, at a very low ebb. Nonconformity should rise to the occasion and demand an equal standing with the State Church, a free access to all cells, the same as these religious state hirelings. A system is required which will not drive a man within himself, but which will raise him up higher. There is a germ of good in the heart of every man if only we can find it, and it is so valuable it is worth the effort. A soul is at stake!

Brute force is the underlying principle of our prison system, whether civil or military. In the latter, you find it carried out to its utmost logical conclusion. My knowledge of this is based on a month's stay in France, the first fourteen days at Etaples, the remainder at Les Attaques No. 5 Military Prison. It was here I witnessed, and experienced, the most barbarous treatment. I will content myself by giving an extract from a letter written by me on my return to Wandsworth Prison.[9] 'On the "compound" at Etaples, we were horse-whipped, half-choked by sand-bags slung round our necks, and thrown into dark cells. Later, for an hour and a half, ten or twelve of the army's biggest bullies set about five of us, for refusing to obey the order to "double" – and we were whipped, struck and kicked, with fists and boots, thrown down, kicked whilst down, thrown against the railings, shaken as a dog would shake a rat, pushed and dragged about until totally exhausted, and we were all on the point of collapse. We were then transported to No. 5 Prison, Les Attaques. There, for refusing to unload a boat we were sentenced by another military tyrant to "fourteen days confinement to cell, fourteen days No. 1 Field Punishment, fourteen days No. 1 Diet." The field punishment consisted in being handcuffed twenty-four hours per day. During the daytime our hands were behind us, during the night they were fastened in front.'

I am told harrowing tales of men being doomed to death for small offences. But, not to rely on hearsay, I have seen men, or rather youths in their teens, beaten mercilessly with the buckle end of officers' belts, on head and face. At Les Attaques, I saw a youth chained hands and feet, stripped naked, doubled over an officer's knees, and then thrashed by two or three others with their metal mounted belts. The shrieks of agony, which lasted long after the incident was over, I shall never forget. Again, I heard the cries of a man who was shot whilst trying to escape. He was brought back, thrust into a cold cell, whipped with officers' belts, and allowed to bleed all night, if needs be to death.

J'accuse

There is no torture too severe, no punishment too harsh, if done to maintain the morale of the army. And these things were done with the full knowledge and consent of the authorities. I indict the Government of the day with knowing these things – for reports were made to them on the return to England of many who thus suffered – and permitting them to continue. And similar things are done in the military prisons in this country. I indict the Government with knowing these things and hypocritically howling down others for doing the self-same things. The independent mind which asserted itself in the army was thrust into prison, there to be bullied, starved and tortured till all love of independence was gone, and nought was left but a fearful slavish obedience, be he volunteer, conscript or conscientious objector – a man robbed of manhood. I indict them with soliciting my services to end such and yet applying it to me. I indict them with making such the foundation of the army. I indict the Church with defending a system which must have this as one of its integral parts. He must be more than a bold Christian who will justify this business.

I challenge contradiction of my statements and am prepared to prove them up to the hilt. These things happened in the sixth month of the year 1917, on the compound at Etaples and in No. 5 Prison, Les Attaques, Calais.

The following extract from a letter written at the time sets forth the spirit in which we were enabled to endure and become more than conquerors through Him that loved us: 'I shall no doubt come out of this crisis, by God's help, a vessel shaped more like the Divine image, made perfect through suffering.'

And the words of Robert Browning, as follows, will fittingly express what we desired and aimed to be in all our witness for Christ:

'One who never turned his back, but marched breast forward.'

Notes

Source: *For His Name's Sake: Being a Record of the Witness Given by Members of Churches of Christ in Great Britain against Militarism during the European War, 1914–1918* (Heanor, Derbyshire: W. Barker, 1921), 55–62. Available on the Internet: www.netcomuk.co.uk/-pdover/fhnsidx.htm.

1 Michael W. Casey, 'The Overlooked Pacifist Tradition of the Old Paths Churches of Christ,' pt. 1: 'The Great War and the Old Paths Division,' *Journal of the United Reformed Church History Society* 6, no. 6 (May 2000), 448.

2 These terms are found in the work of the English historian Peter Ackers, who, along with the American Casey, is responsible for re-exploring the history of the British Churches of Christ. See also note 3 below.

3 In 1924 the split became formal with the founding of the Old Paths Churches of Christ. The new sect continued, despite dwindling numbers, 'the tradition of labour activism, pacifism and general radicalism.' See Casey's article cited in note above, pt. 2: 'Labour and Pacifist Ties from the 1920s to the Present,' *Journal of the URCHS* 6, no. 7 (December 2000), 517–28.

4 Casey, ibid., pt. 1, 454–6.

5 His health damaged by his wartime prison experiences, Robert Price died in 1927.

6 It is worth noting that the future Communist general secretary of the National Union of Mineworkers, Arthur Horner (1894–1968), 'one of the icons of British labour history,' had been as a young adult a preacher in the Churches of Christ and was imprisoned during the war as a CO. He was, however, less consistently pacifist in his antiwarism than Price. At the end of 1916, though, 'Horner was still a strongly committed and high profile

sectarian Christian [pacifist], whatever doubts he then harboured' as he moved 'towards Marxism.' See P. Ackers and M.W. Casey, 'The Enigma of the Young Arthur Horner: From Churches of Christ Preacher to Communist Militant (1894–1920),' *Labour History Review* 66, no. 1 (Spring 2001), 3–23.

7 I presume that Price is referring here to the British stereotype of convict labour consisting chiefly of breaking stones in a quarry as then practised at the notorious Dartmoor Prison. Understandably, Price and his CO friends, coming from the north of England, might not be fully aware of what went on in London.

8 Price was used as an antiwar agitator to address public meetings in his district.

9 The Churches' newspaper (*Bible Advocate*) reported in the summer of 1917: 'Bro. Robert Price, after serving one sentence in Wormwood Scrubs for conscience's sake, and being returned to camp at Cleethorpes, where for fourteen days he was kept on bread and water, besides other cruel treatment, was on Friday, June 8th, forcibly taken across to France from Folkestone.' A little later he was returned to England – and 'twelve months hard labour' in London's Wandsworth Prison. Cited from P. Ackers, 'Who Speaks for the Christians? The Great War and Conscientious Objection in the Churches of Christ: A View from the Wigan Coalfield,' *Journal of the URCHS* 5, no. 3 (October 1993), 162.

Canada

JOHN EVANS

Canada introduced conscription in 1917 over strong opposition in Quebec. Provision was made for conscientious objection provided this was religiously motivated, though the terms were complex due to the fact that four pacifist groups – Mennonites, Hutterites, Brethren in Christ, and Dukhobors – possessed somewhat vague pre-war guarantees of exemption from military service if such a measure were to be imposed at a future date.[1] The position of other pacifist sects as well as of individual pacifists from non-pacifist denominations remained ambiguous at first. The Christadelphians, the small group to which the author of this document belonged, were among the pacifist religious groups that lacked 'any specific guarantees' until a central appeal court finally ruled that properly certified members of these bodies were eligible for exemption at least from combatant service.[2] Despite this clarification, abuses continued and 'scandalous mistreatment of conscientious objectors occurred,' especially during the winter of 1917–18. Jailings of objectors were not infrequent. Further mistreatment followed when some objectors, deemed to be soldiers, were shipped overseas. There they ended up in a military prison.[3] So far as I am aware, the Christadelphian objector John Evans (1894–1971) was the only one of these men to leave a memoir of his prison experiences.[4] He composed it in old age, stretching his memory back more than fifty years on a tape recorder provided by his son, who then reviewed it and arranged for its publication. His son notes of Evans senior: 'His knowledge of detail was remarkable ... Throughout my lifetime, I have heard him rehearse many elements of his experience many times. The story was always the same, it never varied nor did it suffer from exaggeration over the years. The memory of these events was indelibly written in his mind.'

At the time of his call-up Evans was working in his father's contracting business. His son writes: '[M]y father [had] endured a severe upbringing ... Army brutality when it came, was not a new experience for my father;

he had known similar treatment before' – at home! Evans, however, evidently at the same time possessed a sense of humour; he seems to have been popular among his fellow soldiers, who also respected his genuine, if narrow, religious faith. This helped him in the trials ahead of him.

His local tribunal had assigned Evans to non-combatant army service: a form of exemption that he, like most other Christadelphians, rejected. Early in January 1918, therefore, he was inducted into military service and taken under escort to the army camp at Niagara Falls. Here he was forcibly dressed in army uniform and severely manhandled by a sadistic sergeant. But he continued intermittent non-cooperation with the army through various vicissitudes that finally landed him overseas in an army camp in southern England. On 20 June 1918 he was sentenced to a spell in the 'Glass House,' i.e., the military division of London's Wands-worth Prison. The document that follows describes what he experienced in what he describes as a 'dreaded institution known for its reputation of having broken the most hardened offenders.'

Evans's sojourn there was brief. Release, though, returned him to the army and then inevitably to a formal court martial, since he continued to maintain his non-collaborative stance. He served his court-martial sentence now in a civilian jail, London's Pentonville Prison, where he was assigned to the mailbags workshop. Conditions were mild at Pentonville compared to those prevailing in the 'Glass House.' Evans summarized his impressions of his new jail as follows:

> The first day I entered the shop someone said, 'Hello, Canada, we've been expecting you.' Another said, 'Never mind, Canada, you'll be home for Christmas.' Some of the inmates were schoolteachers and were, like myself, conscientious objectors.
>
> Everything in prison was done to a certain routine. In the morning you arose, dressed and stood your bed up against the wall. Breakfast was followed by exercise, then cell or shop work and finally, after supper, reading time until 'lights out' at nine o'clock. Each cell was equipped with a stool and a small table over which hung an electric light. Between the time that night fell and until 'lights out' it was necessary to suspend a blanket across the cell window as an air raid precaution. Previous to my arrival, a bomb from a Zeppelin had fallen just at the side door of the prison, leaving a crater big enough to bury a truck.
>
> There was no inside sanitary plumbing facilities at Pentonville when I was there. The water closets were located in the prison yard, placed back

> to back in rows. The passage of time brought me a second chevron and more 'privileges.' For instance when we were on exercise in the yard, the guard, seeing my chevrons would call out my number and order me to check the toilets. When he called out, 'Sixty-eight, check the toilets,' I would go and flush all the toilets, see that no one was hiding, then returning to the exercise line and report as I passed, 'All correct, sir.' Thus the routine went on.

The young Christadelphian's ordeal came finally to an end when in mid-October he left Pentonville on his way back to Canada. His Discharge Certificate stated that 'No. 3314545 Private EVANS, John Henry Walter, enlisted in the 2nd Depot Battalion, 2nd. Central Ontario Regiment, CANADIAN EXPEDITIONARY FORCE at Niagara Falls, Ont. on the 19th. day of February 1918 ... served in Canada and England and is now discharged from the service by reason of DEMOBILIZATION.'

Evans's account of the Wandsworth 'Glass House' is, I think, valuable in the first place as a possibly unique eyewitness account of a First World War British military prison. Second, it represents an also seemingly unique Canadian contribution to the type of prison memoir represented in this book. Lastly, its provenance is interesting since it represents 'pacifism from unexpected quarters' (to use Theron F. Schlabach and Richard T. Hughes's phrase): in this case the primitivist restorationist Christadelphians, whose devoted adherent John Evans remained throughout his life.[5]

The Glass House[6]

The day finally arrived when I was to be taken to Wandsworth Military Prison in south London. It was the 25th of June and I was put in the custody of a young corporal to make the trip. I refused to carry my kit bag, which meant that the corporal was forced to carry it. He was a pretty good fellow and probably had a little sympathy with my stand, for he carried the kit bag without argument. When we arrived in London and found ourselves standing before the bars of the prison door, he handed me the kit bag and said, 'Well, Evans, from here on it will be between you and them.'

It was noon when I entered the prison, and thus before being actually registered, I was served lunch. This consisted of the head of a cod fish served in a tomato can. I am sure this was deliberately done as an indication of the treatment that I could expect, if I refused to obey orders. I simply set the can aside – they knew it was not fit to eat.

The prison was made up of several cell blocks enclosing a central hall. In the middle of this hall and located on a platform about five feet off the floor was a prison officer. I was given a card and ordered to take it to the officer on the platform 'on the double.' I started to walk toward the platform. Suddenly someone grabbed me by the seat of the pants and the scruff of the neck and I was forcibly doubled across the floor and up the platform steps to the officer. The officer looked at my papers and then assigned me to cell G.4.5 (Block G, Fourth floor, cell five).

As I was being escorted to this cell, I was threatened by a sergeant major from Edmonton who told me that I would be badly handled by the officers and abused if I continued to disobey orders. What he told me greatly discomforted me, so that I did not sleep. In the afternoon, when the soldiers came in off parade, the sergeant of the parade came in to see me. 'My, my,' he said, 'What have you been doing: You're up for office.' – meaning that I was being charged with an offence and would have to appear before the prison commander. 'I wouldn't know,' was my response. The sergeant then withdrew from my cell and I was left undisturbed until the morning.

My cell was furnished with a bed constructed from three nine-inch-wide planks raised up off the floor by batten strips which held the planks together. I was given three blankets and two sheets. The rest of my furniture consisted of a small stool and table.

When morning arrived, I was served a pint of oatmeal porridge without milk or sugar. This was my first and last breakfast during my sojourn in this prison. After breakfast, the same officer returned. He complimented me on the tidiness of my cell, objecting only to my tunic buttons being unpolished. He wanted to send me out on parade, but I refused to go; knowing that I would be in greater potential peril on a parade ground than I would be in my cell. Infuriated by my refusal, he began to curse and commence a violent physical attack. He struck both sides of my head simultaneously with his hands, attempting to produce pain by suddenly increasing the pressure on my ear drums. Then he banged my head against the brick wall, struck me in the stomach with his fist and continued battering me around the cell until he was exhausted. His object was to try to make me fight. If I had retaliated, he could have either accused me of being a traitor to my cause, or otherwise, depending upon his disposition, he could have called for reinforcements which may have cost me my life. I offered no resistance, although my actual urge to kill him was very great, and I could have done so had I yielded to the temptation. Nevertheless I did not yield nor did I complain. Thus, as was the experience of our Lord, my strength also was being perfected in weakness.

At about 9.00 a.m. I was paraded before the commanding officer of the prison and crimed [*sic*] because I had not run the previous day. The C.O. [Commanding Officer] sat with his head down and his eyes fastened upon his desk. He never looked up during my brief trial. 'Three days solitary confinement, punishment diet number 1; twenty-one days punishment diet number two,' was his sentence. Punishment diet number 1 consisted of six ounces of bread and a drink of water morning and evening. Punishment diet number two, in addition to that specified by diet number 1, provided one pint of thin porridge for breakfast and a pound of potatoes for dinner.

I was returned to my cell and spent the next three days in peace and quiet. Each morning and evening the guard would bring the little bun of bread, which he proceeded to drop at my doorway and kick it into my cell. It would roll across the floor and hit the far wall. Then I would go over like a dog and pick it up and eat it.

My cell was about twelve feet long and seven feet wide. The ceiling was an eight foot high brick arch. The floor was paved with asphalt. The toilet facilities consisted of one aluminum pot. Under solitary confinement conditions, all furniture, plank-bed, small table and stool were removed each morning and placed outside the cell. In order to guard against a prisoner attempting to commit suicide, all items such as suspenders, shoe laces and handkerchiefs were removed. Your options were either to walk about your cell holding your trousers up or sit on the floor.

On the fourth day, my punishment diet No. 1 having come to an end, they brought me a pound of boiled potatoes for dinner. They were the size of marbles; I counted twenty-one potatoes in the pound. I said to myself, 'I'm hungry, but I don't have to eat that.' So I sent them back. My forbearance did me no good, however. For when the two guards returned to gather up the dishes, they instantly devoured the pound of potatoes themselves, so that no one knew that I had refused to eat them.

This same day the officer returned to my cell giving me a military command, which I refused to obey. Once again I was subjected to the same violent treatment as before. He finally left my cell, being in a state of angry frustration and did not return again for another few days. I was then taken before the C.O. again, who on account of my continued refusal to obey orders, reinstated my punishment diet number 1 for another three days.

Once again, after three days, the same officer returned and once again gave me a military command. Upon my refusal, he attempted to strike me in the stomach with his fist, but I instinctively lifted my knee to fend off the blow, which resulted in his finger being hurt. This made him all the more furious and he left my cell, returning in a short time with other officers who dragged me from my cell, pressing my arms behind my back and wilfully pushed me headlong down a flight of winding stairs. I was able to save myself from serious permanent injury by leaning against the central steel pole which supported the staircase, as I stumbled round and round to the bottom.

When I landed at the bottom, another officer lugged me by the ear to a place where he wished me to go on parade. I still refused to take military commands and was hauled back to my cell by two officers, who twisted my arms behind my back like a butcher would twist a cow's tail going into a slaughter house. They left me in my cell – buttons torn off my clothes, my thumb badly wrenched, my arms and shoulders sore and my neck bleeding where they had dug their finger nails into it. All this was inflicted on me without cause whatsoever, inasmuch as I never attempted to resist or use violence in any form. Again I was re-sentenced to three more days of punishment diet No. 1.

On the ninth day of this starvation diet, the sergeant, along with two men entered my cell. He took my overcoat, placed it on the floor and had his two assistants, one at each end rolling it up bandolier fashion. 'Now you get down in the middle,' he said, 'and roll it up too, so that you'll see how it's done.' I said, 'No, that coat will do me just the way it is.' At this retort, the sergeant flew into a rage and began to belabor me with a heavy rope. Prisoners were often given cell tasks, one of which was the making of halter shanks. These were made from pieces of seven-eighths inch diameter brand new rope, as hard as a brick. With such an instrument, about three feet, six inches long, doubled in his hand to form a protruding loop, the sergeant went at me with all his might and flogged me mercilessly. There was no recourse but to endure the punishment. Retaliation was out, although the temptation to react violently was very strong. At that time the sergeant would have been no match for me had I taken the initiative. There was no way of escape, no place to hide – nothing to do but let him expend his sadistic energy.

Strange as it may seem, in the excitement and shock of the situation, I never really felt the rope. But after a few days, I began to feel the effects of my beating. At first I did not know what was troubling me. My back felt like it was made of boards. Why I did not instantly connect my strange feelings with the flogging, I do not know. Perhaps my bread and water diet was also having an effect. Suddenly, it came to me: 'The rope!' I turned my shirt down off my shoulders and looked. The sight of my back caused me great alarm. It was as green as grass. I looked like I had gangrene. I fell into a state of panic and frustration. Not knowing what to do, and being virtually beside myself, I began to walk up and down the cell like a caged animal, as hard as I could, until I walked it out of my mind. But I never complained.

One day a guard came into my cell and said, 'Look, Evans, they want you downstairs. If you will go peaceably, you'll help me. If you refuse to go, we will have to make you go. If we can't make you go, the prison officials will complain that we are not efficient. Come on,' he said, 'let's go and not have any monkey business.' He seemed to be a decent sort of fellow, so I said, 'All right, I'll go.'

We entered a room set up for a military law court, where I soon found out that I was to substantiate evidence concerning the abuse I had received by the barbaric sergeant at Niagara Falls.

They had the complete details on the case which they presented to me concerning which I affirmed was a true account of the incident. I was then taken back to my cell. After this, except for the continuation of my bread and water diet, I received no further brutal treatment. *It surely must have seemed ironical to some in that court room to hear a prisoner substantiating evidence concerning the preparation of a military legal charge against a malefactor in Canada, when far more atrocious acts were being committed against the same prisoner by the same body that was supposedly defending him, in the very building which housed the court.*[7]

Towards the end of my sojourn at Wandsworth, a doctor visited the cells, conducted by a sergeant. My case history was recorded on a card outside my cell. When the doctor read it, he exclaimed, 'My, my, that's an awful stretch! Is that man all right?' 'He seems to be,' said the sergeant. 'Well, you better let me see him,' said the doctor. As the cell door opened, I sprang to attention; not in a military sense, but rather to indicate to the doctor that by no means was I the worse for my punishment. The doctor looked me up and down and said, 'Are you all right?' 'Yes sir,' I said, 'I'm fine.' He went on, 'Do you mean to stand there and tell me that you feel fine?' 'Yes sir,' I said, 'I do.' 'Well,' he continued, 'It's not for me to argue with you, but I think you're awfully foolish. You know a lot of that prophecy that you believe in has already been fulfilled.' 'Yes,' I replied, 'I know. That's our assurance that the rest will be fulfilled.' With that the doctor departed.

During these last few days' imprisonment, at about four o'clock on a Sunday afternoon, six guards walked into my cell. At first I wondered if they were going to make an all-out offensive to make me come to heel. This, however, was not the case. The fact was that my behaviour had aroused the curiosity of virtually the whole prison. These men simply could not comprehend why a man should be willing to stand up to so much punishment as I had endured. They actually thought that in some way or other my motive was for money. They could not be satisfied until they found the answer for themselves.

We talked for about three-quarters of an hour and I explained my position to them as completely as I could in that length of time. Finally one fellow said, 'It's just about five o'clock – time for supper – we better get back.'

When they had all left my cell, the first one to leave returned and in the privacy of a moment he said, 'Well, Evans, I don't mind telling you, you are the best damn specimen of a man we ever had in the place.' Then he too bid me farewell.

Throughout the ordeal of my sentence at Wandsworth, my health remained in an excellent state. All my normal bodily functions operated without fail. I did suffer a considerable loss in weight to the extent that I could take the button hole on the front of my trousers, wrap my trousers around my waist and fasten the button hole over my suspender button at the back. Apart from this and a severe bruising, I was in good condition ...

It was Saturday afternoon, July 17, 1918 when I was released from Wandsworth. A sergeant and a corporal came to escort me back to Whitley in Surrey, the camp of the Eighth Reserve. We took the London District Electric Railroad from Wandsworth to Waterloo Station. From there we boarded a train which took us to the town of Godalming, a picturesque little town in Surrey. From Godalming we walked the seven miles to the Eighth Reserve at Whitley – up and down the hills of Surrey on the seventeenth of July, wearing a winter overcoat and carrying a kit bag.

'Give Evans a hand with the kit bag,' the sergeant said to the corporal. 'If we don't make time, we'll miss supper to-night.' We settled down to a steady walk – seven miles after four weeks on a starvation diet.

When we arrived at the camp, we proceeded to the orderly room where my escort said to the orderly sergeant, 'Evans hasn't eaten since Wednesday.' This was on Saturday evening. The orderly sergeant began searching for an order book. 'What are you looking for?' said another sergeant. 'An order blank,' said the first. 'Well,' said the other, 'you better watch what you're doing with an order blank, or you'll be in the Glass House yourself.' 'I don't care what they do with me,' said the first, 'Evans is going to eat.' He wrote out the order. No one actually realized that it was twenty-four days since I had eaten a proper meal, not just three days.

We went back to our hut and from there to the cook-house. I knew that it would be dangerous for me to eat very much after having been almost a month with virtually nothing to eat. I limited myself to a mere bite or two. I was afraid to eat any more.

At the Whitley camp it was customary to give the men an occasional evening lunch. It just so happened that my arrival coincided with one of those special nights. Along about eight o'clock, some of the boys told me, 'Evans, they're dishing out split pea soup to-night and it ought to be pretty good. Come and get your share.' I went to the kitchen, got my ration of soup and began to eat. I had eaten only three or four spoonfulls when I thought I must surely be going to die. I couldn't get my breath. I thought my end had come.

Acting almost instinctively, I began to run up and down between the huts until this strange reaction wore off. Presumably the heat and consistency of the soup reacting upon my empty and shrunken stomach, produced this terrible sensation.

It would seem that I was to have little rest this night. As the evening stretched on, the men began to return to the hut. They were happy to see me back – so happy in fact that they decided to celebrate. They took two or three of the hut's firepails, emptied out the water, took them up to the canteen and brought them back filled with beer. Then they blanketed the windows to prevent the light being visible in the event of a zeppelin raid and then settled down to a night of merriment.

Needless to say, after my recent experience in attempting to eat pea soup, I had very little of the refreshments supplied. The party continued all night long, interrupted only by the military policeman who shouted as he made his rounds, 'Pipe down, you fellows, you're making too much noise.'

When a man has served time in the 'Glass House,' military law demanded that he be given a four-day rest period before being required to do work. During this rest period, I gradually began to recuperate, but not without some difficulty.

At breakfast on Sunday morning, I ate a little more than I had the day before and at dinner time when they served cold Australian mutton, brussels sprouts and new potatoes, I had a little more and I really enjoyed it. However, on Monday when I undertook to write a letter, I began to shake so badly that I could not control either the pen or the paper. This spell also in due course subsided ...

Near the end of my rest period, I began to wonder what event was in store for me. Having served time in Wandsworth, I was now supposed to be a soldier. Therefore, lest there be any misunderstanding, I went to the office of the Provost Sergeant. His name was Miller, [a Canadian] formerly a member of the Hamilton Police Force. We were known to one another back home. I said to him, 'Now sergeant, I have no more intention of soldiering now than when I came here in the first place. So you might as well put me in the clink right now.' 'All right,' he said, 'You're in the guard room now.' The guard house was divided into three rooms: a waiting room, the office of the sergeant of the guard, and a cell block.

After a day or so in the cells, I was brought before the Commanding Officer. 'Well, Evans,' he said, 'word has come from Ottawa that you are to be given your choice of any job in any branch of the service you wish to serve.' 'Well, sir,' I said, 'I certainly appreciate the consideration, but if I have to continue to wear a uniform, I'll have so say no.'

Notes

Source: John H.W. Evans, *Test Case for Canada '3314545': The Experiences of a Christadelphian Conscientious Objector in World War I, 1914–1918*, ed. E.R. Evans (N.p.: privately printed, 1972), 53–61, 63.

1 See Thomas P. Socknat, *Witness against War: Pacifism in Canada, 1900–1945* (Toronto: University of Toronto Press, 1987), 74–88.

2 Ibid., 76.

3 Ibid., 82–6.

4 For further details of Christadelphians jailed in First World War Canada, see William A. Weir, *A Summary Report of the Work of the Canadian Christadelphian Standing Committee, 1920–1945* (n.p.: privately printed, n.d.), 18. The

names of fifteen men are listed, three of whom (including Evans) were 'shipped under guard to England.' The report was issued after the Second World War, primarily 'for educational purposes' within the Christadelphian church community.

5 See Charles H. Lippy, *The Christadelphians in North America* (Lewiston, Lampeter, Queenston: Edwin Mellen Press, 1989), 250–4, for a brief summary of the sect's attitude to war and military service. See also the booklet by John Evans's son, E.R. Evans, *'Ye Are Strangers and Sojourners with Me': A Sketch of the Christadelphian Teaching concerning a Christian's Relationship to the State* (Hamilton, ON: privately printed, 1990), esp. 1, 25, 28, 40, 41. (Mr Evans very kindly gave me a copy of his booklet.) There he explains why his co-religionists do not participate in politics 'at any level' or serve as soldiers, while at the same time not advocating conscientious objection to military service: to the world at large.' Unlike the ancient Israelites, he writes, Christadelphians today 'have no commandment of God to engage in physical warfare.' They will, however, 'fight under the banner of Christ when he returns.' Until that event, though, they remain 'sojourners' and 'strangers' on this earth, and any Christadelphian who becomes a combatant will be ipso facto cast 'into the category of the wicked' and excluded from the church for so long as he fails to express penitence for his action. Yet indeed 'it is not the taking of life that is absolutely forbidden by God.' The question, Evans writes, is 'whether or not we have been commanded by him to do so. Where there is no commandment there is no justification.' Though Christadelphian conscripts, in order to escape disfellowshipping, have been required to become COs, according to Lippy 'some diversity of opinion as to whether non-combatant service is acceptable' exists as well as 'much debate over what kinds of alternate service are appropriate for believers.' Nevertheless, we should note, almost all Christadelphian ecclesias (i.e., congregations) exclude non-combatant service in the army as a permissible alternative to actually bearing arms.

6 The section of Wandsworth Prison housing military defaulters was separate from the area housing civilian prisoners, including COs sentenced to a term in a civilian jail. John Hoare, for instance, was located at this time in the latter area; see his memoir above.

7 Italics in the original.

New Zealand

ARCHIBALD BAXTER

Archibald Baxter (1881–1970), the son of poor Scottish immigrants, began life as a farmhand. In 1914 he was working on the family farm. Forced to leave school early he was in fact largely self-educated. His antimilitarism began with his revulsion for the Boer War and developed during the subsequent years so that by 1914 he had become a committed pacifist. An unaffiliated Christian, Baxter based his case against war also on political grounds; and from its foundation onwards he was active in the New Zealand Labour Party, though he was to oppose its support of the Second World War. In his part of the country, he writes, in the early days 'I was without a single supporter, either in my pacifism or in the socialism which I looked on as a necessary part of it.' After conscription came into force at the end of 1916 he and his two brothers, Jack and Sandy, were arrested the next summer for refusing induction into the armed forces. Since they did not belong to a peace church, they were not legally entitled to any kind of exemption as COs; anyhow, they were unconditionalists by conviction. Detained first in an army barracks in Wellington, the three brothers were then sentenced to eighty-four days' hard labour in a civil prison. The extract below gives Baxter's account of his time in a New Zealand jail, at the end of which the three Baxter brothers were forcibly shipped to England on the *Waitemata* with eleven other COs.

Thus began Baxter's odyssey, which he has told in his memorable autobiography, *We Will Not Cease* (1939). The book was written in 1937 largely on the basis of notes which the author dictated to his wife soon after the First World War. After transferring him to France, the British army authorities by exceptionally brutal treatment did all they could to break Baxter's resistance and force him to undertake military service. But they were unsuccessful: in the end, he was shipped back to New Zealand as a 'mental case' and eventually discharged. After the war was over he farmed on his own for a time while continuing to be active in his country's fledgling pacifist movement. Baxter, his friends have pointed out, was an ordinary man, not an intellectual. Yet he followed unswervingly what he believed was right – in the face of intense hardship and the threat of death.

The Terrace Jail was a survival – and there are many such in the world – from the days when security, lack of light and lack of air, seemed to be the main things aimed at in building a prison. High outer walls successfully cutting off sunlight and view from the yards. Then more walls, still further preventing the admission of light to the small barred windows in the cells ...

We were marched in through the main gates to the reception office, where our escort formally delivered us over to the prison authorities. Several warders were present and one stern-looking individual in blue, the Chief Warder, an old army man.

'Are you men New Zealanders?' he asked us.

'We are,' I answered.

'Then I wonder you're not ashamed to look a New Zealander in the face.'

'I am not ashamed of looking anyone in the face,' I was beginning, when he silenced me with a roar of 'Shut your mouth! No back-chat from you!' and I had to submit. I had begun to realize that one need not expect to be treated as a human being here. Our particulars were taken. I said I did not belong to any organized Church and I did not notice at the time what they put down for me under the heading of religion. Next, an official seized me by the arm, and pulled me roughly over to a table. Holding my hand down, he pressed each finger with considerable force and weight, so that I felt as if the bones were being crushed, on to a sheet of some white substance. He did the same with the other hand and dusted the results with a black powder. Whereupon the finger-prints sprang clearly into view.

'By jove,' I said, 'that's pretty hot. They're actually taking our finger-prints!'

'Will you shut your mouth!' shouted the warder.

We were herded into an adjoining room where we were stripped to the skin. We were weighed and scrutinized for body marks, which were noted down where there were any. I believe that a prisoner on reception has usually to take a bath, but as we had come straight from another prison [i.e., Alexandra Detention Barracks in Wellington] our cleanliness was presumably taken for granted. Our own clothes were taken away, every object in the pockets being carefully examined, noted, and put away, to be returned to us intact when we went out. We then put on the prison clothing; woollen underclothing, quite good of its kind, and outer garments, shapeless, ill-fitting and badly patched in many places, consisting of a brownish coat and white trousers, plentifully bespattered with broad arrows. The boots, too, were shapeless and hardly to be recognized as boots. We wore, whenever we were outside our cells, a white cloth cap just as shapeless as the clothes and the boots. The others, especially Jack, who put on an air of ferocity befitting the occasion, looked typical criminals. I could not see myself, perhaps fortunately, for I don't doubt I looked even worse. It is astonishing the difference that clothes and a haircut can make. A few minutes before, we had been ordinary citizens, unnoticeable in any particular. Now anyone would have picked us as belonging unmistakably to the criminal class.

We were marched along, clumping in our clumsy boots, through corridors and doorways, till we came to a hall in the main building, flanked by cells on either side. Here we were each locked in a cell. I had had some experience of cells in the preceding month, but this was infinitely worse than anything I had known. To begin with, the door was always shut with a resounding slam and locked with a great clashing of keys, producing a sense of the inexorableness of the grasp in which one was held. The cell itself, narrow, dank and airless, gave me a feeling of physical oppression. The building was so large, the cell so small, that the walls seemed to be closing in upon one. The window, tiny, high up and closely barred, gave upon a wall; consequently so little light found its way into the cell that it was hardly possible to read at midday. It contained a straw mattress, up-ended against the wall, and blankets folded neatly, a pillow, a stool, a shelf, a tin basin, and a tin chamber-pot. I had not been long in the cell when the door was opened with more clashing of keys and dinner brought round by prisoner orderlies, escorted by a warder. It consisted of stew with vegetables and potatoes, quite wholesome. When we were taken out into the yard a little later, Jack whispered to me: 'Well, the dinner wasn't too bad, anyway. Perhaps things won't be so bad here, after all.'

The exercise yard was surrounded by high brick walls. On the roof was a pagoda-like structure, built to shelter the armed warder, who, from his position, could command the whole of the yard. For the first part of the exercise period the prisoners mingled together and talked indiscriminately amongst themselves; but on a given signal from the warder in charge, they formed into pairs and marched around and round the ring. At the side of the yard stood a row of w.c.'s. Anyone wishing to use them – and one was supposed to train oneself to do so at this time – shouted 'Rear!' An interchange of shouts with the warder generally followed, depending on whether there was an unoccupied cubicle or not. In time we became quite accustomed to this public performance.

We were brought back and locked in our cells again. Soon afterwards, tea was brought round. It consisted, invariably, of a twelve-ounce loaf of new bread which had to last till the same time the following day, and a cup of nauseating bluish liquid without milk. It was bitter stuff, but one got used to it in time to a certain extent, for it had the one advantage of being hot. Nothing else. It required a considerable exercise of self-control not to demolish the whole of the very moderately-sized loaf at one go and leave nothing for breakfast. I noticed that the knife with which we were provided was of soft tin. This and the prohibition of razors, was supposed to prevent the possibility of suicide. One could be shaved by the prison barber; but the experience of being shaved in cold water with a blunt razor, by a prisoner who didn't care how he did the job, was so unpleasant that I only went for a shave when I was compelled to. As was to be expected under the circumstances, the shave was not a clean one, the stubble showing as soon as one left the barber's hands.

The tea, so-called, though I got used to it later, I felt that first time I could not touch. So, my cell door having been left open, I ventured out into the hall to get some water from the tap. An angry warder caught me just as I was drinking the first mouthful. 'What are you doing out here? Get back to your cell!'

'I only came out for a drink of water. I don't like the tea.'

'Drink what you're given; you'll get nothing else, you understand that you don't come out of your cell unless you're told to.'

We were locked up for the night. One could read, if one had a book, which I at first had not, until lights were turned out at nine. Otherwise there was nothing to do but sit and think or pace up and down between the door and the end wall, three paces up, three down, until it was time to go to bed. Sometimes there was a click, and the spy-hole shutter, operated from the outside, would open. If all was in order, as it usually was, the shutter clicked back into place and the warder's slippered feet passed on. I have known him to look in upon me three or four times in one half-hour, sure that he would at last catch me in some breach of the regulations. One night, to create a little diversion in the wearing monotony of those long evening hours, when I heard my neighbour's shutter click, I placed myself up against the door where I was out of sight from the spy-hole.

'Where are you, Baxter?' shouted the warder and, hastily unlocking the door, he threw it open, appearing in the doorway in great agitation. He was plainly relieved at the sight of me. 'What do you mean, standing where I can't see you? don't you know you're not allowed to do that?'

'Is that another regulation?' I asked. 'I thought at least I had the freedom of the cell.'

'You'll get something you won't like,' he said, and slammed the door.

Those regulations! As every prisoner had to obey them it seemed only reasonable that there should be a copy in every cell. Far from it. We were not even allowed to read the copy pasted up in the hall. I tried to, but was driven away every time by the warder in charge. 'No loitering in the passages.' Finally, but starting every time where I had left off the time before, I managed to commit most of the printed form to memory. I don't know why there should be this objection to the prisoners knowing the regulations. Possibly because the warders are afraid of being held too strictly to them themselves.

That first night, when I started to go to bed, I found I had struck one of the worst things in my prison experience. No sheets, no pillowcase; only blankets, hard and brittle with age and much baking, and foul-smelling beyond belief. The pillow was a greasy, filthy bit of ticking, filled with small hard pellets of what appeared to be metal of some sort. I never found out what they were. The blankets were too old and hard to have much warmth in them. They were baked to destroy germs and lice, but the knowledge that the dirt and the odour were hygienic did not help me much that first night. In time I seemed to get accustomed to them. Or perhaps it was that I never struck anything quite so bad as those first ones.

Often during the night – and during all the nights I passed in prison – the silence was broken by horrible, long-drawn howls, expressive of pent-up misery, bitterness, hate. The warders rushed about, trying to locate the culprit. But they seldom succeeded. Such sounds echoing and re-echoing as they did were exceedingly difficult to trace to their source.

In the morning I was roused early, washed in the basin provided and emptied the dirty water into the chamber-pot. Shortly after, the door was unlocked, and I had to empty my slops into the tin brought round by the orderlies. The door was locked again, to be opened not long afterwards for breakfast.

A cupful of thin, watery porridge without milk or sugar and often without salt, the unappetizing tea, and whatever one had been able to preserve of the bread from the night before. Breakfast and tea never varied. For dinner one might sometimes have rice instead of potatoes. The entire absence of fat in the dietary resulted, on my part, in an abnormal craving for any kind of fat. At the same time the smell of the stuff that was used for greasing the boots made me sick, though I have known men to eat it. If the absence of fat in the diet had such an effect on me, what must it have had on men with long sentences? In some cases long-sentence men reached a stage when the prison allowance was more than they could eat, and I have seen bread lying uneaten in their cells after they had gone out. This implies, not an excessive allowance of food, but an unhealthy condition of body and mind. Most of the men who had been any length of time in the prison had a yellowish pallor as if they had been reared under a tub. There was no outdoor work in the Terrace. Breakfast over, a prisoner, brought in by the warder, gave me a demonstration of the proper way to fold my blankets, in a sort of symmetrical cascade, with the stripes running exactly in sequence. Then I had to do it in the same way, with the warder standing over me and shouting at me if I failed in any particular. Afterwards he gave me cloths and polish and told me to polish the steel of the stairway. I made what I considered a very fair job of it and went back to him.

'I've finished it. Have I done it all right?'

'Go on with your work,' He said.

'But I've finished all you told me to do.'

'What does that matter? Get on with your work and don't stand talking to me.'

'Do you mean to say that I've got to go on doing what I've already done?'

'That's part of the punishment,' he said.

That conversation has always remained in my mind as typifying the attitude of those who run our prison system. The authorities looked upon prison as punitive and still do, in spite of minor alterations for the better since that time, such as the abolition of broad arrows, the addition of golden syrup and a small quantity of dripping in the dietary (and I am told if you have golden syrup you can't have dripping and vice versa) and an increase in the amount of bread. Such being the system, it is impossible for the warders who carry it out to do anything but rule by fear and be ruled themselves by fear, fear of their charges and fear of spying and reporting which prevails among the staff.

On the second evening, I was put into another cell in a different part of the building. This cell had a drainpipe in a corner, covered with a grating, and a hammock instead of a mattress. Not being accustomed to hammocks, I put all the blankets on top of me as the night was cold. During the night I awoke with my back like a sheet of ice and found that the drainpipe was directing a shaft of cold air right onto it. I put blankets underneath, but, as it turned out, I was already too late. Towards the evening of the next day I felt hot and at the same time shivered, and my back ached. During the night I grew worse and in the morning when I tried to rise, I was too sick and giddy to stand and had to get back into the hammock. After a while the warder came in.

'Come on, you've got to get up.'

'I can't. I'm too ill.'

'Well, I don't know what to do about it,' he said. 'I'd better go and see.'

He returned with the information that he supposed I'd better stay there. Then he went out, slamming and locking the door behind him. For days I lay there without attention of any kind, wretchedly ill, in the extreme of physical and mental misery. I would see the walls closing in on me and fight them off desperately. They would melt away and I would swing right out into space. When my head was clear enough for me to be aware of my condition and surroundings, I was even worse off. The pain in my back was frightful. I was constantly sick, and I was forced at frequent intervals to pass, with excruciating pain, a small quantity of blood and pus. I was very thirsty, but there was only the tea to drink and that I could not touch. The ordinary prison meals were put in at regular intervals and removed untouched. Occasionally one of the warders came in and I asked for a doctor, but in vain. One of them looked at the contents of the tin.

'What's all this blood and stuff?' he asked.

'That's my urine.'

'By jove, you're in a bad way.'

But nothing was done for me.

After five or six days the fever left me, though the other symptoms remained, and I managed to take a little porridge. The warder came in and ordered me to get up and accompany him.

'You're going before the doctor,' he said.

I went with him, hardly able to keep on my legs from weakness, and bent with the pain in my back, but buoyed up with the hope that I should now get some treatment. In the office were the stern Chief Warder, a man in civilian clothes sitting at the other side of the room looking at papers, and the doctor who had examined me at the Barracks.

The Chief Warder followed me into the passage and shouted at me: 'Stand up straight and walk properly! None of that slouching! We don't allow it here!'

I was too utterly crushed to attempt to defend myself. Completely in the hands of men who were determined to show me neither justice nor mercy, I saw not one ray of hope. The warder took me back to the hall outside my cell and told me to scrub the floor.

'I can't,' I said. 'It's not that I'm not willing to. I really can't.'

'I know that,' he answered, 'but I can't let you off. I'll have to report you to the Governor for refusing to work.'

I wondered what would happen. I would be punished, I supposed, and how was I going to stand punishment in such a condition?

When he took me, later, back to the office, the doctor had gone; only the man in civilian clothes was there and with him the Chief Warder. The warder who had brought me made his report, and finished up with: 'He looks a pretty sick man to me, sir.'

'And to me too,' said the Governor. 'Give him a spell for a few days and then we can see.'

Only a few words, but they were spoken kindly, and they made all the difference to me. I went back to my cell a different being, with faith and hope and strength for the future springing up anew.

Health came slowly back and in those days of complete idleness I had plenty of opportunity for thinking matters over. What would happen to me I could not foretell, but that the path before me would not be an easy one, I had very little doubt. Come what might, I hoped I would be given the strength to go through with it.

It was Easter time. On the Sunday, a Catholic choir came into the prison and sang. The hymns of joy and aspiration floating through that abode of misery, seemed to me, lying in my cell, like angel voices, and my spirit was lifted up above pain and weakness to union with all the aspirations and ideals of man at one in God.

A few days later the warder asked me if I felt up to a little work.

'Do just as much as you like,' he said, 'and no matter how little it is, I won't say anything.'

After my illness most of the warders showed me what little kindness they could, which was not much, as the seniors spied on the juniors and the juniors on one another, and they all knew that the discovery of the slightest leniency towards a prisoner meant a report. Hence anything in the way of kindness or friendliness had to be clandestine.

It was very little I could do at first, but gradually my strength came back. The Governor, passing on his rounds, stopped and spoke to me. 'How are you getting on, Baxter? Feeling better?'

'I'm very much better, thank you.'

'You're not finding the work too hard?'

'No, not now.'

'I'm very pleased to see you better and getting on all right.' he said. 'You had a rough time, but I did my best for you and I hope you will soon be quite well.'

He spoke as man to man and not as jailer to prisoner. He made me feel an ordinary human being with an individuality again, a feeling one is apt to lose in the routine of prison. Moreover, seeing and talking to a man who was not in uniform was a relief to the eye and the mind.

I thoroughly served my apprenticeship in scrubbing and cleaning. I scrubbed cells, corridors, and halls. Every day I soaked and scrubbed the boards I had soaked and scrubbed the day before. The cells in that damp sunless place never got a chance to dry properly from one day to another. If by any chance the boards did look dry by the afternoon when the Chief Warder made his rounds, this was regarded as proving that they had not been properly cleaned, and I was told to use more water. I protested at the futility of it and the unwholesomeness, but of course fruitlessly.

Scrubbing out the next cell to mine I found it less damp and rather better lighted, owing to its position, than the one I inhabited. Moreover, it had a mattress instead of a hammock which I thought would be of an advantage to me with my sore back. As a matter of fact the mattress needed airing; lying as they did on the floors that were never quite dry, they were all more or less damp all the time. I approached the warder with a suggestion that I should move into it as it was empty. He looked in and agreed that it was better. 'Move in, and I'll say I told you to shift.'

When my card, giving my name and particulars, was shifted, I noticed that I was down as 'agnostic.' 'Who put that down?' I asked the warder indignantly.

'You must have given it in your particulars when you came in.'

'I said I didn't belong to any organized Church. That's not to say I'm an agnostic. I'm not, and you can take that down.'

To my surprise he did so. Evidently one had the freedom of one's religion in prison. I asked him what he thought agnostic meant, and he said: 'A man who doesn't believe in God or Devil.'

The space for religion remained a blank, but not for long. The following Sunday I was ordered to join the Catholic squad on its way to service.

'But I'm not a Catholic.'

'Yes, you are, it's on your card.' And it was. My predecessor in the cell had been a Catholic, and the hymn book and book of devotions he had used were still on the shelf. I had found them very interesting and had objected to giving them up. Seeing this, the prison authorities, greatly worried about the blank on my card, had thankfully put down 'Roman Catholic' ...

Once I was fit again I did not find the work very hard, but some of the casuals, usually in for fourteen days for drunkenness or the like offences, had a rough time. The warders were always hard on newcomers, shouted at them, bullied them, and harassed them until they had them thoroughly cowed and amenable to the discipline of the place. The casuals never got beyond that first stage. They were often in a poor state of health, recovering from a drunken bout, or 'without lawful means of support' because they had neither the mental nor the physical stamina to do steady work. I did my best to show them the right way of doing things, and they were very grateful for the assistance, but they found that they were still shouted at and bullied, no matter what they did or how hard they tried to do things the right way. There were some who took it quite calmly.

'Put some elbow grease into it,' a warder said to one of them.

'I'm doing my best,' he replied. 'A man can't do any more, can he?' ...

One poor old wreck roused my sympathy. He had got fourteen days for sleeping in a shed on his way into the country, having been warned to clear out of the town within twenty-four hours. He was manifestly unequal to the task he had to perform, and, having finished the job I was on, I offered to do it for him. He leaned against the wall, while I scrubbed, and we talked. Unfortunately we neglected to keep a look out and the warder caught us. He directed a stream of abuse at the old man, who seized his brush in terror. I explained that it was my fault, that I had offered to do it for him.

'He knows right enough what he's not allowed to do,' said the warder.

The last I saw of the old man, he was scrubbing for dear life under the eye of the angry warder ...

One day I was placed by the warder just round the corner from the bathroom, to await my turn in the bath. He went away for a moment and the man ahead of me called out: 'You can come in now; I'm ready.'

I went to the door and found him just finishing dressing. The warder came rushing back.

'What do you mean, going away from where I put you! Don't you know two men are not allowed in the bathroom together?'

'How can you expect me to obey the regulations when you won't let me read them?' I asked.

But he stormed on. 'I could put you up for this. Going into the bathroom when there's another man there is counted as being taken in the act.'

I was thoroughly sickened and disgusted.

'What's all this fuss about two men being together in the bathroom?' I asked the other prisoners.

'Just because there are one or two crazy men here,' they said, 'the rest of us decent chaps have to put up with treatment like that. That screw's had trouble when he's been in charge, so he's always on the look out for it.'

In the large majority of cases such precautions were not justified, and their application to everyone resulted in a lowering of self-respect.

We were always searched when we came in from exercise. The coat was handed to the warder, who looked through it, then ran his hands over one's body. One evening, as we came in, four names were called out in my section, my own amongst them. Each man of the four, as he came to his cell door, remained standing beside it instead of going in. When my turn came I stood in the doorway and removed my clothes until I was stark naked, throwing each article one by one to the warder waiting in the corridor. He went through them carefully. Then he came into the cell.

'Open your mouth. Raise your arms. That'll do. Now lean forward and spread your legs.'

He passed round behind me. When I realized what he was doing I said: 'That's a pretty disgusting thing to put on to a man.'

'Yes, it is,' he replied, unexpectedly, 'and I hate doing it to a man like you. I won't do it to you again if I can help it. Don't think that any of us like it. We all hate doing it.'

'I'm sure you do,' I said.

The next time my name was called he kept his word, and when he came into the cell, merely stood in front of me for a moment with a smile, then went out.

The senior warder in charge immediately shouted: 'You haven't searched that man properly! You haven't had time.'

He came into the cell. 'Did he search you properly?' he asked.

'Certainly,' I said.

'I don't believe either of you,' he remarked, with some justification. 'This time I'll let it pass, but you won't get away with it again.'

When the next time came I had to stand in the doorway of the cell while the warder examined me under the eyes of his superior.

'He beat you that time,' I remarked to him afterwards.

'No damn fear,' he said, 'I kept my eyes shut.'

Many of the prisoners complained of a lack of sex feeling. One would have thought this would have been an advantage, in a place where they saw no woman from year's end to year's end; but they strongly resented it and were unanimous in putting it down to dope in the tea. Nothing could shake this conviction. 'I know them,' they'd say, with the queer over-excitement characteristic of them, resulting, partly at least, from the constant repression, and certainly the strange appearance and taste of the tea lent some colour to the theory.

They were full of theories, always to do with prison life or police-court proceedings that were so closely connected with it ...

The interests of the men, naturally enough, centred round the petty gossip of the prison. They had nothing else to occupy their minds or to break the monotony of existence. Completely cut off from ordinary life and doing everything under orders and nothing that was not ordered, all initiative was slowly sapped, even in thought. Nothing was done to encourage them to organize amongst themselves for concerts or games. Now, I believe, interested people from outside give concerts and lectures at intervals, and others start men on suitable courses of study, providing the necessary books for them. But even now, I do not think there is any organization for recreation within the prison. Not in Mt. Eden [penitentiary] at any rate. When I was in the Terrace little or no interest was taken in the prisoners by the outside world, and of recreation they had absolutely none. Many of them were not readers and could not concentrate on a book for any length of time. They had no guidance in the choice of books. The library was a poor one and the librarian was chosen, not for his knowledge of books, but for his smartness in patching and re-covering them. It was small wonder that in the dreary monotony of their life the prisoners found amusement in childish and petty behaviour. The making of obscene noises was the favourite diversion, rendered all the more exciting by the notice the warders took of it. I attended the Anglican service one Sunday, after having extracted an assurance that I would not be compelled to attend it every Sunday thereafter if I did not wish to. An aged clergyman conducted the service, and preached a sermon as far removed from the needs and difficulties of his congregation as anything could well be. A loud, explosive noise was heard. The warders rushed at a man a few places from me and dragged him out of the chapel, amid loud shouts from him of 'I didn't do it, you've got the wrong man this time,' and answering shouts from them of 'Well, tell us who did it, then.' The aged clergyman took not the faintest notice and went serenely on with his sermon. It would have been better if the warders had done the same. We listened to the gradually receding bangs, thuds and shouts, which went on outside the door.

'And did they get the wrong man?' I asked the others afterwards.

'You bet they didn't; it was him all right. He's a champion at it!'

The same noise would also be heard after the men were locked in their cells for the night. It was not easy for the warders to trace it, and no doubt the champion got the blame, sometimes unjustly.[1]

I was told that punching and battering went on when men were being taken to the punishment cells. I never witnessed anything of the kind myself, but that is not to say it did not happen when men put up any resistance, as they sometimes did. To make a complaint against a warder was doomed to failure from the start. According to the regulations, which I did in the end manage to memorize, if a prisoner considered that an order given him by a warder was not justified, he was to obey the order immediately, but was allowed to make a complaint to the authorities. If he failed to substantiate his complaint, he was deemed to have made a frivolous complaint, and he was punished. In actual fact, no prisoner could make anything but a frivolous complaint, as his word was never taken against a warder's and the only witnesses he could bring were prisoners too. The only successful complaint that I ever heard of was when, a little while before I arrived in the prison, nearly all the prisoners combined to complain of the staleness of the bread. Stale bread, when it has to be eaten dry as the sole article of food at a meal, is not very attractive. The consequence of this most unusual solidarity was that when I was there the bread arrived for tea damp and smoking. As it was usually consumed then and there its effect on the digestions of men who ate it every night for years on end and remained in their cells for the night afterwards, can hardly have been good. In prison one can hardly ever get the men to stand together for anything and it is this characteristic that makes it easy to rule by fear.

One night I was awakened by blood-curdling yells. I leapt out of bed before I realized that if there was a tragedy I was prevented by the locked door from doing anything. It was a terrific uproar. Stentorian shouts at the top of a powerful voice, of: 'I am Jesus Christ, the Son of God!' Then more yells and scufflings and bumpings and shouts from the warders. By this time I had come to the conclusion, which was correct, that it was a drunk in the D.T.'s. The sounds continued for some time, then gradually died away.

Next morning the warder called me out. I followed him along to the padded cell. Instead of the usual spy-hole in the door, it had a hole nearly large enough to admit a man's head. The principal warder in charge approached his face to the opening. Immediately the fist of the occupant shot out, catching him between the eyes and laying him on the broad of his back. There was a rush of warders to the door and the man was dragged out attired only in his shirt, a mass of filth from head to foot. They handcuffed him and ran him down the passage to the bathroom. I went into his cell.

'Have I really got to clean this?' I asked the warder. 'Come and look.'

He stepped in. Walls, floor and even ceiling were plastered with filth. 'Isn't it something awful! But it's got to be cleaned so you'll have to get on with it. You can get it off the ceiling with a mop.'

Several days later, passing by, I saw the man standing in the door of the padded cell, completely naked, catching lice.

'Not enough light in there to see them,' he remarked to me.

He was a good physical specimen, tall and well-built. His nakedness was not obtrusive as he was covered from head to foot with a fell of reddish silky hair. The card over his door stated: 'Remanded for medical attention,' and beneath that, '4s. 6d.' I asked him: 'Have you seen the doctor?'

'No,' he said.

I asked some of the others about it.

They said, 'He may have had some dope shot into him the night he came in.'

The four and six, they told me, was the fee, at the rate of one and six a day. It would be added on to his fine when he went before the court. I have only his word and theirs for this ...

One day I saw clay on the floor of the passage I had lately scrubbed. This meant that someone had come over from Mt. Cook prison. The prisoners at the Terrace never had dirty boots. One of the other cleaners told me a man had just been brought over for punishment.

'He's in that cell.'

I went over and looked through the spy-hole. The man was like some trapped wild animal, his eyes glaring, his whole appearance expressing desperation and defiance. I rattled the spy-hole shutter and whispered: 'Got any tobacco?'

'No,' suspiciously.

'Like some?'

'Too right, I would.'

He came up to the door, human again, his face relaxed from his fierce revolt. I got him a piece of tobacco from the library where I knew the librarian had a store secreted, and pushed it through the hole.

A few days later one of the warders called me from my work. 'Come along; I've got a job for you; you're to come and talk to a man in the dummy [i.e., punishment cell or 'hole']. Wait a minute; I'd better search you; we don't want you to be taking him tobacco.'

The ceremony over, I asked him: 'Do you always do this when a man's in the dummy?'

'When he's in for fourteen days. We're not supposed to let him go the whole time without someone to talk to. He might go batty.'

We went down stairways until we were well below the level of the ground. The warder unlocked a door and we came into a small enclosed passage with a door opening into it.

'This is where he takes his exercise,' he said, unlocking the other door. 'You go in here; I'll be back for you after a while,' and he locked me in.

The punishment cell was a cement box, without a stick of furniture in it, nothing to sit on but the concrete floor. At night the inmate could get his blankets, but in the daytime he had nothing. There seemed to be no opening in it, but some sort of outlet to the passage there must have been, for there was sufficient light for me to make out the face of the occupant, who was the man I had given tobacco to a few days before. His defensive hostility melted almost immediately and he was soon pouring out all his bottled-up resentment against the injustice of his treatment. His sense of his wrongs prevented him from submitting quietly to jail discipline, and raised a whole host of new wrongs to fight against. He told me that he should not have been in jail at all. 'I've not done anything different from what thousands of men like me do every day and nobody thinks of putting them in jail and I'm here.'

He had gone, he said, to a picnic with a girl who had taken him and other men too, many times before. They had gone away from the others. Suddenly, people, strangers, had come upon them. To save the situation for herself the girl had screamed and there was a great uproar.

'Not that I blame the girl, mind you. She didn't mean to send me to jail, but once she'd told her story she had to stick to it. Up I went as high as a kite and got eighteen months for indecent assault.'

Coming to jail with a well-established grievance, the whole system had appeared to him as another grievance and he fought it all the time. He had had an argument with a warder at Mt. Cook.

'I was in the right and the screw knew it, but d'you think he'd say so? Not him, and his word was taken against mine, so I threw down my shovel and here I am.'

I admired his pluck, but it seemed pretty hopeless and I said so. Most men were done after fourteen days on bread and water in the dummy, though even in the short time I was at the Terrace I knew a man who was not. He got another fourteen days on top of it. He was done then.

We argued over the pros and cons of fighting jail authorities on one's own. I didn't see that he could help his case by making things hard for himself in prison. It went rather against the grain to advise him to act expediently rather than on principle, but it seemed the best way out for him, and hadn't I done it to a certain extent? I was obeying orders in prison and I had come there on a military sentence. My illness had come on me before I had thought the matter out.

We talked till the opening door showed that time was up.

'You've done me good,' he said. 'I'll think over what you said.'

Outside, the warder asked me: 'How did you get on?'

'All right; he seems a decent sort of chap.'

'I wouldn't be left alone with him for a good deal,' he said.

'And yet you'd lock me in with him!'

'That's quite different. He wouldn't touch you.'

They ruled by fear and were afraid of the men they ruled. And yet those men who fought against the system were not always the worst, by any means. There was often more hope of the man whom the authorities would call 'one of the worst men here' than of the 'good' prisoner, who was often subnormal and who, obedient and well-behaved under orders, was quite incapable of looking after himself in the normal life of the community.

There were a number of prisoners on remand at the Terrace. They did not exercise with us, but actually we had plenty of opportunity of mixing with them. Two boys, brothers, came in on a charge of stealing a sheep. The younger must have been fifteen, but he did not look more than twelve. In the daytime, when he was with his brother, he managed to stand up to it and keep a brave face to the world. But at night, locked up alone in his cell, his control gave way and he wailed and sobbed far into the night. The desolate sounds, echoing through the empty corridors, tore at the nerves of prisoners and warders alike.

'What's the matter?' a warder called through the door at the boy.

'Oh, my heart is broken.'

'Well, stop that noise or it'll be more than your heart'll be broken if I have to come in to you.'

He'd stop for a while and then break out again, uncontrollably.

Very different were three boys of about the same age, convicted of car conversion and on their way to Borstal. Bright-faced, high-spirited boys of a good type, they never allowed anyone to see them or hear them without the shield of pluck they held up, whatever lay behind it. The principal warder in our section read them a lecture, to which they listened respectfully. They were not to consider themselves criminals or to lose their self-respect. They were merely being sent to where they would be taught to behave. I wondered how they would fare in the Borstal. Would it be cells, warders and prison routine or would there really be a different system of development instead of repression? ...

I was not anxious for the change to Mt. Cook, which, I supposed, would come when someone, perhaps the Governor, considered me fit for the work there. I had become accustomed to the routine at the Terrace and knew the worst that could happen to me there. Whereas Mt. Cook I didn't know and I had heard lurid accounts from prisoners sent over to the Terrace for punishment of the hard work over there, of a brick kiln in which you were baked alive and the soles of your boots curled up with the heat. I thought that, not being up to my usual strength, I might find the work too hard.

However, what I thought on the matter was not likely to affect the course of events. In due time I found myself sitting on the back of a lorry on my way to Mt. Cook. It was pleasant, anyway, to be out in the fresh air again and see hills and the harbour down below me and hear the ordinary street sounds, after having been completely cut off from them for weeks, although I could not help being self-conscious in my conspicuous attire. The thought of escape did not pass through my mind, for the driver never turned his head, and I could easily have slipped off when the lorry was going slowly; but the broad arrows would have put it out of the question, even if I had had any real thoughts of escaping, and I had not. I had made up my mind on that matter long before.

The lorry ran up to the gates of the prison, passing a group of men shovelling out clay from the hillside with an armed guard over them. I recognized several of them, my brothers amongst them.

The warder who received me said I must have another pair of boots; the ones I had worn at the Terrace were not strong enough for outside work. I tried on a pair.

'No good. I'd go lame in five minutes in these.'

They brought me several pairs and I rejected them all. Finally, the warder took me up to the stores. Trying on all these boots had given me the illusion of being in a shoe shop, and it was with a distinct jar that I heard the warder say to the man in charge of the stores: 'Here's a prisoner can't get fitted for boots. See if you can fix him up with a pair.'

A prisoner! Well, I knew I was, but I never felt like one, and as it happened in the Terrace I had always been referred to as 'this man' or 'Baxter.'

I tried on pair after pair. Dreadful boots, impossible boots, all apparently made for men with feet as broad as they were long and mine are long and narrow. When I did get anything to fit in length there were inches to spare in width. Moreover, they were all out of shape and had bumps and ridges in the most unexpected places. At last they brought out a new pair and these I accepted in some triumph.

Next, I had an interview with Burrows, who was in charge of Mt. Cook. The two prisons were run in conjunction, under one superintendent.

Burrows was very reasonable. He asked me whether I looked on my sentence as military or civil. I said as it had been imposed by a court-martial, I would regard it as military.

'That's so, but once you are handed over to the civil authorities, you are entirely in our hands. The military authorities have nothing more to do with you as long as you are here. So you won't object to working as it won't be under military orders.'

I saw that he had probably had trouble with the others and wished I could have spoken with them first, but that, of course, was what he wanted to prevent. I said that as I had worked at the Terrace I did not see that I could refuse to work now. He seemed relieved. He always endeavoured to avoid trouble, often compromising when another man might have been unyielding, in order that things might go smoothly. Offences against discipline were fairly common at Mt. Cook, and men were often sent over to the Terrace for punishment, but I don't think it was due to greater leniency. Most of the prisoners at Mt. Cook were short-sentence men, who as a rule were less amenable to discipline than the men who had been in prison longer, having retained some spirit. They looked much healthier than the men in the Terrace.

I found a considerable difference between the two prisons. The work, for one thing, was nearly all in the open air. I worked in a gang with my mates. The cells, owing to the fact that the building was of lighter structure, were much airier, and admitted more light, especially where we were, on the upper landing, on which the cells had skylights instead of windows. We washed in the hall instead of our cells, and, consequently, never had time to wash properly as the warder's whistle always went before we could possibly have finished and we had to stop immediately and go back to our cells. The bread ration was larger, sixteen ounces instead of twelve, and so was the meat ration.

There was one warder at Mt. Cook who thought my pride needed taking down a peg – my overweening pride that was such a trouble to officers in the army. At least a dozen times, I am sure, in the six weeks, he made me strip naked for search. He succeeded in making me very angry, but not in taking down my pride. I very nearly revolted, but only refrained because I had so little time to go.

When I joined my friends in the clay-cutting gang I was heartily welcomed. No one seemed to have hit on illness as the reason I had been left behind at the Terrace, and as I was by now pretty well again I don't think they believed there had been much the matter with me. Many of these men I had known at the Barracks. Some of them I met for the first time. My new boots came in for admiration and envy. Did I think they could get new ones too? I thought it very unlikely, since they had put up for weeks with the ones they had.

As I had thought, my brothers ... had doubted when they first came over whether they should work in prison, but Burrows had explained to them carefully that they were entirely under civil control, and they had taken it on, though rather doubtfully.

The work was not hard for men accustomed to manual labour, and Jack and I, at least, soon found that we had to accommodate ourselves to a much slower pace than anything we had been accustomed to. Once we forgot ourselves and went on shovelling clay into the trucks with such vigour that the man who drove the trucks to the brick yard came back with a strongly worded message that we were to moderate our stroke; they couldn't keep up with what we were doing. Some of our lot, who were unused to work of that kind, didn't make a very good showing. One man, who had worked in a shop, used to get hold of a ridiculous little shovel that had somehow got amongst the others, which hardly lifted more than a spoonful of clay. The warder would say: 'There's Hugh got that shovel again,' and take it from him, but he nearly always managed to get it back.

I recognized several familiar faces amongst the civil prisoners. A Maori, who had been waiting his turn in the office when I had my memorable interview with the doctor, said to me with a friendly smile: 'Glad to see you well again. When I see you last you just one inch from the peg hole.'

One of our group told me hair-raising tales of the crimes he had heard of since he had come to prison – crimes he had never known existed. He pointed out the Maori as having committed a particularly bestial crime. I said I didn't believe it. He was not that sort, and anyway, I had heard something quite different about him.

'Who told you?'

'He did.'

'Did you ask him?'

He admitted he had. I said that that was what he could expect to get if he asked. They had feelings and would fire out that kind of thing as a sort of defence. But I don't think he believed me.

There were men there who had committed horrible crimes. There is a great deal of difference between crimes that are really horrible and crimes that are made to appear so by law. Words can hypnotize people. Nothing exemplifies this better than the phrase 'Habitual Criminal.' It conjures up a picture of incorrigible rascality and marks out the possessor of its brand as a being of a different species from his fellows. Even amongst the prisoners this was the case. I have had a man pointed out to me.

'Do you see that man? He's just been declared an habitual criminal.'

As if the man in question had suddenly become something entirely different from themselves. And what does it really mean? That a man, convicted of an indictable offence a certain number of times, has been declared by the judge who tried his case to be an habitual criminal under the Act, the Dog Act, as it was called in prison. Some judges would frequently make use of the act, others never at all. Having been declared an H.C., a man could be and often was, upon the expiry of his definite sentence, detained in prison until the Prisons Board, which as a general rule means the jail officials, saw fit to release him. And even then the brand is still upon the man, and the indefinite sentence can come into operation again if he is re-convicted, the judge of course being aware of it, and the jury too, in many cases, with the result that a conviction is certain on the sketchiest evidence. Men have no right of appeal against that sentence, no means of breaking out of the trap that holds them.

The habitual criminals I knew in prison were filled with bitterness and despair at the hopelessness of ever freeing themselves or being freed from the grasp of the Act. I was particularly sorry for one man. A kind-hearted, decent little chap, his trouble was drink, and he had frequent convictions for using obscene language when silly with it. For this he had been declared an H.C. and was being held for an indefinite period in prison ...

Often men worked themselves into a state of nervous excitement at the prospect of approaching release. One unfortunate man, who was to be released in three months' time, became so worked up about it that he could bear it no longer and, the opportunity offering, he escaped. We could see him for a long time running up the road that led to the hills, his clothes making him a conspicuous mark. Recapture was inevitable and in a short time he was back amongst us with a year to serve instead of three months.

All prisoners, at the conclusion of the first three months of their sentences, were allowed to smoke on exercise. But we, having only a three months' sentence to serve, were not allowed to smoke at all. Many of our gang were not smokers and the deprivation meant nothing to them. Though I was only a light smoker when I came to prison, I found the craving much stronger than it had ever been before and very hard to withstand. A tobacco allowance was sometimes put into my cell by mistake and as I couldn't smoke it I chewed it, as most of the other prisoners did, for their time for legitimate smoking was short. Sometimes I, and others too, risked smoking in my cell. It was a big risk, of course. One night I had just lit up, when there was a shout of 'Someone smoking!' in the passage. I hurriedly put it out, hid it and waited for my door to open. It did not, but some other unfortunate's did, and I heard him being removed from his cell with the usual accompanying din. But attempts at smoking were necessarily few and far between. I chewed and the habit called down many rebukes from my fellow-objectors. What filthy habits I had picked up in jail!

We talked together on exercise and we talked at work, too, within limits, and in my opinion we talked far too much on the everlasting subject of what would be done with us. Our business was to stand out against military service, come what might.

The time came when the sentences of ... my brothers and myself expired, and we were taken over to the Terrace ... When we were in the reception office getting back our clothes, Jack remarked: 'We're not going out; we've liked it so much here we're going to stay.'

The Chief Warder was there and several others ... They believed him.

'You can't stay here when your time is up,' boomed the Chief. 'We'll put you out.'

'Oh yes, we can,' I chipped in. 'We'll make a disturbance when we're put out and we'll be arrested and come straight back in here.'

It must have been with intense relief that they saw us depart with our military escort, making, in spite of our threats, no attempt to get back in again. We were marched to the Barracks at the other end of Wellington ... Arrived back at the Barracks ... through Wellington we found the same changed atmosphere.

'You chaps not taking on anything?' said the guards, and I am sure they would have been very disappointed if we had said we were. 'You'd like something to eat? It's late, but we'll manage to get you a cup of tea.'

There were many new faces. Teachers, clerks, farmers, workers, of all shades of opinion, united in their opposition to military service. I met many men that I should have liked to know better, but the opportunity was not given me.

Early, before the other prisoners were out of their cells, [my brothers] and I were taken down to the entrance and handed over to an escort of military police. Once again, and now for the last time, we were marched through the streets of Wellington. I came last ... and the guard walking behind me kept deliberately treading on my heels. At last I stopped.

'If you don't leave off doing that,' I said, 'I'll refuse to move a step.'

I had rightly concluded that they did not want a disturbance and he gave it up. I had a pretty good idea of our destination, and when we came to the entrance to the wharves I saw I had been right. As we turned down to the gates an individual leaning against the wall of the pub at the corner called out: 'Why did you wait till you've got to be taken?'

The transport *Waitemata* lay at one of the wharves and we were pushed up her gangway and down into the clink. It already had ten occupants. Seven we knew: they had been with us at Mt. Cook. Sanderson, a religious objector, had been brought from the Terrace, and two Irishmen, Maguire and Kirwan ... This made the number up to fourteen. We represented varying viewpoints. A member of the sect 'Testimony of Jesus,' a pacifist Catholic, a member of the Labour Party and an Irishman who wouldn't fight for the British because of what had lately happened in Ireland. These were a few examples of the different attitudes from which we came to our stand. One thing was noticeable about the experimental fourteen. Almost without exception we were drawn from the ranks of the proletariat, and the exceptions were known to be opponents of the Government. We were chosen for our obscurity, being thought unlikely ever to make our protests heard either personally or through our relatives.

The clink measured, roughly, twenty feet by ten. It had two tiers of bunks running round it and portholes on the outside. A small cabin opened out of it at one end with a porthole and a ventilator shaft leading into it from the deck above. The only entrance to the clink was through the isolation ward. No communication had been allowed with relatives or friends ...

The *Waitemata* sailed early in the afternoon.[2]

Notes

Source: Archibald Baxter, *We Will Not Cease* (2nd ed., Christchurch, NZ: The Caxton Press, 1968), 23–55. A North American edition of Baxter's book appeared recently (n.p., n.d.) under the imprint of the Eddie Tern Press. It includes a new preface by Michael King, some annotation, and an afterword summarizing the fate of the thirteen COs who had sailed with Baxter on the *Waitemata*. See pp. 35–70 for the passages reprinted here.

1 Sixty years after Baxter wrote his autobiography we find a criminologist taking a different view of this kind of behaviour when it occurred in an American prison. 'During one of my visits to a local jail,' he writes, 'I was told [by the inmates] that during count (when inmates report to their bed areas to be counted by guards) an occurrence that commonly takes place is what I will call "insubordinate farting." A standing rule exists stating all inmates must be silent until count is cleared ... During count the men sit or lie on their three-tier-high banks in silence while a guard walks up and down the dorm counting the bodies on the beds. With an expression that can be seen as nothing less than defiance, inmates will, once the guard has passed their bed area and is safe enough distance away to insure their anonymity, fart loudly. The resulting laughter obviously mocks the guard. It also, in a safe way, attacks the system. It ... allows the inmates to break the rules and reaffirm, at least for themselves, their own power.' From Charles

M. Terry, 'The Function of Humor for Prison Inmates,' *Journal of Contemporary Criminal Justice* 13, no. 1 (February 1977), 32.

2 For the First World War prison odyssey of a New Zealand Christadelphian CO, 'Brother James,' which may have intersected with the early stages of the Baxter brothers' odyssey, see Deborah Payne and Suzanne Beer, eds., *In Defence of Our Conscience: A History of Conscientious Objection among the New Zealand Ecclesias* (Torrens Park, SA: Christadelphian Christian Study Service, 1988), 81–136. I must thank Michael W. Casey for bringing my attention to this valuable – but rare – source. One of Brother James's fellow CO inmates during his incarceration in Paparua Prison Farm, situated just south of Christchurch, writes of 'Life at Paparua': 'At 6.30 a.m. the rising bell sounds, the prisoners get out of bed and fold their blankets in regulation manner, and tidy their cells. A warder then ... opens the [cell] doors so that the men can get their breakfast which consists of [milkless] porridge (good), mutton (tough) and very meagre, dry bread [and] black tea without milk. He is then shut up to eat it and get ready for work. From 8 till 12 the prisoners attend to their different departments when they are again shut in until 1 p.m. Then [after dinner,] from 1 until 5 work again, after which you [receive more porridge, dry bread and black tea and] are locked up in your "Peter" or cell until 6.30 a.m. next day, so that a prisoner does 16 of the 24 hours locked up and on Saturday and Sunday 19. There are no windows in the cells and one cannot see anything of the outside at all while locked in. Thank goodness they can't stop the larks from singing! It is a treat to lie and listen to them sometimes ... The cells are only 8 ft. ∞ 7 ft. ... We had no electric light during the winter months and it was very unpleasant and cold in our cells. We only had candles and the wind used to set the grease running all over the place. The snow used to come in through the skylights and drift against our [cell] doors. The five blankets we were allowed were not enough and we used to go to bed on straw mattresses on the floor half dressed, only to shiver all night ... The gaoler ... was wearing two suits of clothes [his wife told us] and had ten blankets on his bed – and still complained about the cold!' (ibid., 127, 128). However, 'in the busy lambing season,' Brother James, who was a farmer, 'was allowed out ... from 5 a.m. in the morning until 7 o'clock in the evening' (ibid., 113).

United States

ARTHUR DUNHAM

Evan Welling Thomas (1890–1974), brother of the socialist leader Norman Thomas, was working with the YMCA at the time of his call-up in the summer of 1918. Already a pacifist, as his brother Norman then was too, Evan was incarcerated, along with other COs, in the Fort Leavenworth (Kansas) Disciplinary Barracks. There he went on hunger strike and was placed in solitary confinement: his protest was against the harsh treatment meted out to COs who refused to work in the prison. He was released from prison in January 1919. After the war he trained as a doctor, seeing this as a way to give practical expression to the philosophy of pacifism, and was eventually appointed professor of clinical medicine at New York University. A passionate libertarian and anticonscriptionist, Evan Thomas, though religiously unaffiliated, remained an absolute pacifist until his death. Six feet seven inches tall, he was a striking figure who commanded respect by his forceful personality and transparent sincerity.

Immediately on regaining freedom in January 1919, Thomas composed a memoir revealing the atrocious conditions then prevailing at Fort Leavenworth, especially 'the unspeakable moral filth and vice to which one is constantly exposed' there. Entitled 'Disciplinary Barracks: The Experience of a Military Prisoner at Fort Leavenworth,' it appeared in *The Survey* (1 February 1919). I have, however, chosen for reproduction here another – hitherto unpublished – memoir by one of Thomas's fellow prisoners.

Among those COs confined, like Evan Thomas, in the Fort Leavenworth Disciplinary Barracks was Arthur Dunham (1893–1980). Dunham had been sentenced by court martial in November 1918 to twenty-five years' hard labour. His memoir gives a graphic account both of his own experiences and of the general conditions endured by military prisoners in that grim fortresslike army jail.[1] Dunham, when war was declared, had been a Presbyterian, but early in 1918 he resigned from the church in protest against its support of war. He now became, in his own words, 'an independent liberal Christian.' (After the war he and his wife joined the Quaker Society of Friends.)

In June 1917 Dunham registered as a conscientious objector; he had become a convinced pacifist several years earlier while a graduate student in political science at the University of Illinois. 'At length,' he writes, 'I felt that I had found a real basis for a vital Christianity in the principle of Love as the motive for every individual act and every group relationship. In religious social service work I had begun to try to work out some of the implications of this principle. Now the War challenged this principle ...'

Until drafted a year later, in July 1918, he continued in his job as a social worker. While he was not an absolutist and was ready to undertake alternative civilian service, he was unwilling to accept non-combatant duties in the army. In fact, he was not even eligible for that, since he did not belong to a pacifist church. Thus his conscript troubles now began, first in the tent camp at Fort Riley (Kansas), where he was interned with a number of other COs awaiting the army's decision as to how to deal with them. For Dunham, in effect, this decision came on 12 November – one day after the Armistice had been signed – with his court martial and twenty-five-year prison term.

Private William A. Dunham, Co. A., Casual Battalion, Fort Riley, and thirty-three other COs in the camp had then been charged with 'wilfully' refusing to obey 'a lawful command ... to assist in policing up [*sic*] the parade grounds.' In Dunham's case, specifically, the order was 'to pick up a rake' for this purpose; like his companions he considered that to be a form of the non-combatant military service they had all already rejected.

The sections of Dunham's narrative printed below begin with the massive iron gates of Fort Leavenworth Disciplinary Barracks (USDB) swinging open to receive a party of newly convicted COs, one of whom was Dunham (now to be known only as 15336).

After his release from Fort Leavenworth Dunham returned to his career as a social worker. Eventually, in 1935, he received an appointment as professor at the University of Michigan, where he taught community organization and social-welfare administration until his retirement in 1963.

Dunham describes the ordeal he went through with commendable restraint – and occasional humour. He tells us what happened and usually leaves it at that. He does not indulge in self-pity, and makes quite clear to the reader that the ill usage COs suffered in the DB was on the whole no worse than that inflicted on the ordinary military prisoners: 'Whitey' and 'Toledo Red' and 'Humpy' and the rest, with whom he succeeded in making friends. Moreover, in contrast to the fate that seemed most likely for the latter, he was confident that American democracy would not tolerate the incarceration of conscientious objectors for anything like the term to which they had been sentenced. They would probably be out, he believed, in a matter of months once peace had returned. Dunham, then, was a moderate, ready to concede that the authorities at Fort Leavenworth might sometimes have good intentions in their blundering way. This gives additional force to his indictment of the brutalities of American military prisons of that period.[2]

The great iron gates swung open. We passed in, between the two gates, under an archway that reminded one of a medieval castle. A young man – a strange-looking man in an ill-fitting brown suit and a visored cap – moved silently by with a lantern, sparing us just a glance. We turned to go into the little room to our right, and we faced a bulletin board. '*U.S.D.B. – POPULATION 3125*' ... We were prisoners, in the largest military prison in the United States – Fort Leavenworth.

A guard entered. We were rapidly and skillfully searched. Our money and jewelry, which had been given back to us upon our departure from the Guard House, were again taken, and placed 'on deposit.' Our hats, overcoats, and coats were left with our baggage in the little 'reception room,' and we crossed a large yard to a great brick building whose immense extending 'wings' loomed towards us out of the darkness. We crossed a footbridge of wooden planks; we traversed a gloomy half-finished and partly open rotunda; we descended a flight of steps; our guard paused before a barred door, which opened at his signal. 'Keep these fellows here in this wing tonight,' said our guard to another ... soldier, and he left us.

The room in which we found ourselves was the '6th Wing Basement.' It was a very large room with the inevitable concrete, bricks, and steel bars everywhere in evidence. In the middle of this room, back to back, were two tiers of small single cells ... each containing an iron cot, washbowl and toilet. Evidently the 'wing' was crowded, for in the corridor between the front of these barred cells and the wall were other cots, whose occupants seemed to be free to move about to any part of the wing. Our ... guard assigned each of us a cot in this corridor.

Just then we caught sight of a group of men at the other end of the corridor, and a thrill of joy went through me as I recognized the patriarchal beards of two of the Amish Mennonites who had been with us at [Fort] Riley. A moment later and there was a happy C.O. reunion ... Questions flew thick and fast. All our comrades had come to the D.B. 'Listen to this, man; there are about twenty-six men in the "hole" – that's what they call solitary – for refusing to work! ... Some of our men must have been in solitary for three or four weeks ... Of course they were receiving the treatment outlined for recalcitrant soldier-criminals who refused to work: solitary confinement, bread and water fourteen days at a time, and hand-cuffed to the bars of the cell nine hours a day. And one new addition – the "real" solitary cells were "boarded up" in front!'[3] ...

[To return to this first meeting of ours in the D.B.,] after a time the men who belonged in the cells were locked in, but the rest of us could still come and go about the 'Wing.' Finally a bell clanged. The men in the cells sprang forward to the doors and stood there silently, facing forward with folded arms. The other men stood just outside the cell doors, facing the same way, and in the same position. 'Fold your arms,' whispered a prisoner beside me.

The 'count' was taken by the Officer of the Day (for all things are conducted in military form in a military prison), then 'Lights out!' was called and almost simultaneously demonstrated, and I lay down for my first night's sleep in this strange place of bolts and bars and hard-voiced commands and curses and vulgarity – and withal, of friends ...

It seemed to me that I had scarcely fallen asleep when the rising bell clanged. I heard a tapping sound drawing nearer and nearer, and presently the cause was revealed. The room orderly, a prisoner, was passing rapidly around the wing. With the handle of a broom he rapped the bars of each cell and the iron foot-bar of each cot, to be sure that every man was awake. I began to dress immediately; but one man near me rolled over for another nap. In a few moments the room orderly appeared on a second round. Without a word to the man who was still asleep, he gave his cot a tremendous jerk. 'What the hell's the matter with you? Didn't you hear me say to get up?' he snarled. 'Aw, I'm go'n'a get up,' muttered the other pacifically.

This was my first acquaintance with prisoner room orderlies at the D.B., and it was typical. 'Don't ever trust a room orderly,' we were early told; 'they'll do anything to you to get in themselves with the "screw" [guard].' I think the room orderlies were often more brutal than the guards. A room orderly's position gave him opportunities to get a good many small favors and much petty graft. His tenure of office was dependent largely upon the pleasure of the guards in the wing. Two things usually resulted from this. In the first place the room-orderly became a 'hand-shaker' – he cringed and became subservient to his master, the guard. In the second place, he realized that his position depended largely upon helping the guards to preserve discipline in the wings. The room orderly proceeded to use the methods which were used throughout the prison, sharpened usually by bitterness over his own imprisonment.

After all, the brutal room orderly is only a logical part of Leavenworth, which is the personification of the theory upon which the military system is based ... There were dark stories ... ominous tales of the 'iron rule' of a few months before, more oppressive than even the present régime – stories of the man who hanged himself in his cell, and of the 'kid' who was clubbed into insensibility by two guards who threw away their weapons on the approach of the Chaplain and reported to him that the prisoner had attacked them. There was the fact that a man had been murdered by a group of prisoners a short time before; and a Mennonite told me that only a few days before our arrival riot had threatened in the mess hall, voices howled against one of the guards, 'Kill the ——!' and while a semblance of order was being restored, officers paced up and down the aisles with white faces. No one knew when the volcano would break forth.

When we asked the older prisoners about the food at the D.B. they generally shook their heads and replied, 'Pretty rotten.' The first breakfast was not quite as bad as I had expected. We marched into an immense mess hall with a capacity of some 1500 men. As this number was only about half of the inmates, there was an 'early mess' and 'general mess' for each meal. Our wing went to early mess for breakfast – 6 a.m. and still dark outside.

Inside the door of the immense mess hall was a small raised platform, with a chair and desk, for the Officer of the Day. About fifteen guards, armed only with small clubs, were scattered about the hall. All the prisoners sat facing the door. There were eight seats in a row between each two aisles. In front of these eight seats stretched a shelf-like 'table,' about a foot wide. 'Tables' and seats were of rough wood, the plates and cups were of more or less battered tin, and the knives, forks, and spoons were of some other discolored and unappetizing material. The waiters passed up and down the aisles, with large tin receptacles containing the food. 'Slum up!' was my introduction to the D.B. fare. Slum is a hybrid distantly related both to vegetable soup and to milk gravy, but most nearly allied to beef stew. When there is plenty of meat (or what passes for meat at the D.B.), carrots, and potatoes in it, and when the gravy is not burning with pepper, slum is edible. The main objection at the D.B. was that slum was practically the only dish at about six meals each week. The bread was about the best thing served. It was handed out by the waiters, five or six slices at a time, and passed from hand to hand until it reached the end of the row. Many if not most of the men who thus handled the bread had no opportunity to wash their hands before the noon meal; and I never heard of any sanitary instructions on the subject being given to the waiters or anyone else. I did hear, later, that at least one of the waiters who handed us our bread was suffering from a venereal disease ...

[There] was [a] stock menu with practically no change, for each meal of each day in the week. I often heard it charged by the prisoners that the fresh products of the prison farm, 'raised to feed the prisoners,' were sold at Kansas City; that 'somebody' pocketed most of the money, and that we were fed on the cheapest sort of food, purchased with the unstolen fraction of our food appropriation.

After breakfast the prisoners went out to work and we newcomers returned to the Wing. Seeing us idle, our ... guard ordered us to sweep up the floor. We did so, intending at the D.B. as elsewhere to keep our own quarters clean.

Soon we were taken out of the wing and in charge of a guard we started on the long process by which a man is degraded into a prisoner. At the office of the 'Yard Sergeant' we were allowed to take from our suitcases our bibles (but no other books) and such letters and photographs as we might desire ... Nothing came closer to my heart and nothing helped me more, while I was in the D.B., than the memories which were kept ever fresh by my photographs. And I believe it was the same with many there. One prisoner, who claimed that he had shot a man in a disreputable brawl, showed me a cheap photograph and said, with a softened look and a note of pride in his voice, 'That's my wife' ...

Soon after, we were lined up in the 'Executive Office,' located in one of the old front buildings of the D.B. and looking more like a stable than an office building.

Here Sergeant-Major M—— made out some sort of record cards for us. I happened to be first. 'What's the sentence – twenty-five?' said M——. 'Yes,' replied another soldier. A few moments later he handed me my 'little brown book' of rules[4] ...

I have since been asked how I felt when I knew that I was sentenced to twenty-five years' imprisonment. Frankly, the only sensation I remember was a slight paradoxical relief that my sentence was normally high! We had often said in the tent-camp, 'I'd rather get thirty years, like ——, than fifteen, if I'm going to the D.B. at all. And I *don't* want five years – a man *might* have to serve that!' I never for one moment considered it a possibility that an American C.O. would be left actually to serve an atrocious sentence of fifteen or twenty years or longer. I did feel that the length of the sentence was usually something of an index of the impression made upon the military by the C.O.'s stand. Evan Thomas was evidently considered a 'leader' (though no man ever refrained more carefully from influencing the action of his comrades); *his* court martial had sentenced him to *life* imprisonment ... But the normal sentence of a C.O. for refusing to shovel trash, cut weeds, or pick up a rake was twenty-five years; so I was glad that I received the military stamp of approval as a normally wicked C.O. We chaffed Ted unmercifully because his sentence was 'only' twenty years – and told him that he was no real C.O., and that he had 'pled for mercy.' The fact was, I think, that five years had been knocked off in recognition of the excellence of his court-martial statement! Since the day of my sentence I have learned more humility. 'What was your sentence?' asked Sam, long afterward. 'Twenty-five years,' I answered. 'Oh, man, man,' he said, 'you are no C.O. *I* was sentenced to be shot by musketry! But I was discharged, instead!'

After leaving the Executive office we set out upon a long series of travels which occupied the rest of the day and took us to nearly every administrative department of the D.B. Every piece of our own clothing was taken from us and was replaced by the 'grotesquely ugly' but warm and fairly comfortable nondescript black and brown prison suits, with our numbers painted in white figures about three inches high across the back of our overcoat, raincoat, coat, shirt, and working blouse and across each foreleg of our trousers and overalls. With our visored dog-eared caps, our ill-fitting suits, with their glaring numbers, and our great clumsy shoes, we were strange and wonderful figures, and we broke into laughter as we looked at each other ...

On this same day we had our first introduction to the D.B. 'barber shop.' We had been prepared for this institution by our Mennonite friends. 'You'll lose that mustache there,' one of them remarked to me. 'But you are wearing your beard,' I replied. 'I know,' he answered; 'that's on account of a special order that was obtained from Washington – that the religious sects who wear the full beards should be allowed to keep them. But if you shave at all, they'll shave it all off!' Which they did. The barber shop was a fearsome place. The barbers there did the quickest and worst work that I have ever experienced. I was always surprised when I was released from the chair with my throat still intact ...

Our meeting with the Chaplain of the institution was one of the greatest delights of the day. We six C.O.'s were going 'through the mill' with about a dozen other new military prisoners. All of us were seated on benches outside the Chaplain's office, and our guard – a long, awkward, decent sort of a fellow – happened to be standing with his hands in his pockets when the Chaplain suddenly appeared. 'I suppose if the Colonel himself came along, he'd find you in that position!' the Chaplain bellowed; and he followed this pastoral introduction by giving the poor guard the most merciless tongue lashing that I ever heard from any caste-swollen officer – and all because the private and his prisoners had not been standing 'at attention' when an *officer* had passed. 'Have these men stand up!' roared the Chaplain. 'Say the word, *"Attention!"*' 'Attention' repeated the guard docilely. We arose and folded our arms, as much from sympathy with our guard as for any other reason ... We were soon summoned inside to hear a stereotyped address delivered with a bored air by the Chaplain. 'This is not the place of lost hope – it is the place of another chance,' the speech began; but the Chaplain's actions of a few moments before were still sounding so loud in my own ears that I heard the words but faintly.

At the end of the day we found ourselves again in the Executive Office, this time to be addressed by a stout, good-natured-looking lieutenant, the Assistant Executive Officer. He explained to us that there were three grades of prisoners: first-class, wearing 'white numbers'; second-class, wearing 'red numbers'; and third-class, having 'yellow numbers.'[5] 'You are beginning in the highest class – first-class prisoners with "white numbers," – you are now entitled to *all the privileges of the institution!*' said the Lieutenant with wholly unconscious humor ...

When the Lieutenant finished describing the grades of prisoners, he began to tell us about work at the D.B. Most of the work – farm-gangs, shops, kitchen, laundry, hospital, offices, etc. – was primarily or entirely for the support of the institution and so was military only in the sense that it was performed under military orders of military officers and that the institution itself was a military prison.

The Lieutenant began to question us as to our previous employments and as to our preference for work at the D.B. One great heavy-set man, whom I had thought might be a prize fighter or a bricklayer, turned out to be a university man, a former reporter, and a relative of a prominent political leader. I think he had been convicted of having immoral relations with an officer's wife, and he was sentenced to five years. Five years for adultery – twenty-five years for refusing to pick up a rake!

At length, the Lieutenant came to a tall solemn-faced negro. 'What work would you like to do here?' he asked. *'De Lawd my God commands dat I shall not do any wuhk here!'* came the unexpected reply. A thrill went through us at the calm fearlessness of this colored brother – one of the religious absolutists, belonging, I think, to 'the Church of God and the Saints of Christ.'[6] The Lieutenant had evidently met plenty of C.O.'s before, and he took it philosophically, as part of the day's work. In a matter-of-fact tone he explained the punishment for refusal to work and then told the colored boy he would be assigned to work with [the first] Gang, and if he refused he would be 'tried' by the Executive Officer and put into solitary ...

Our six C.O.'s were the last to be questioned, and I happened to be the first of the six. 'What work did you formerly do?' asked the Lieutenant. 'I was a social worker.' 'What work would you like to do here?' 'I cannot conscientiously do any work here.' Ted, Jake, Ray, and Ezra gave the same answer. Robert, the Plymouth Brother, had believed from the beginning that he ought to work in the D.B., and of course none of us questioned his sincerity nor sought to change his views. The Lieutenant made no comment, and we were sent back to our cells in the Wing that night. Our comrades there told us that our 'work test' would probably not come until Monday.

Our separate decisions not to work had come during our travels about the prison, on Friday. There was no bravado about it. We realized perfectly well that it was extremely serious to defy one of the fundamental rules of a military prison. Yet what else could we do if we were to be consistent? 'Shall we give in on the first really hard test we have had?' said Ted. I frankly admit that I made my decision reluctantly. I was not afraid of solitary, but I was far from anxious to break my health and to cause what I knew would be almost unbearable worry on the part of my loved ones at home.

On Saturday morning, after breakfast, we new prisoners were ordered to 'wait at the water tower' in the prison yard, for a guard who would, presumably, take us through the rest of the process of removing us from normal humanity and dehumanizing us into prisoners. Somehow or other, the guard did not come, and suddenly we heard the Yard Corporal saying, 'All right, you fellows come with me.' He led us straight to the tool room ... We were face to face with the work test.

The Corporal handed out several brooms to the soldier-prisoners. Then he remarked to me, 'Come on, step up and grab a broom; don't be bashful!' I answered, 'I explained to the Executive Officer yesterday that I intended to refuse to work here; I'll take the penalty.' The Yard Corporal took it as calmly as the Executive Officer. 'All right – stand over there against the wall.' Ted, Ray, Jake and Ezra were soon beside me. The rest of the prisoners were put to work cleaning the yard, and we were taken into the general Executive Office. We were of course the subject of considerable curiosity and comment. Sergeant-Major M—— remarked, as the inevitable papers were being made out for us, 'I wish they'd let me go through this place with a shot gun!'

One by one we were taken in before the Executive Officer ... Captain B—— looked up and, in a business-like tone, said, 'You are charged with refusing to do any work at all. Is that right?' 'Yes, sir,' I replied; 'I explained to the Assistant Executive Officer yesterday that I couldn't conscientiously work here.' 'All right, that's all,' said the Captain, signing my 'punishment slip,' and I went out marvelling as to why they called this process an 'executive *trial*' ...

A short time before we came to Leavenworth, it had been decided that, as an additional punishment for refusal to work, the recalcitrants should be put into 'yellow numbers' as third class (especially dangerous) prisoners. Accordingly we were again conducted to the clothing room, where our white numbers were painted yellow, to the accompaniment of curses from the painter, a prisoner who was being caused 'a hell of a lot of trouble by you damn slackers,' and of dire tales by the guard of 'that water-cell in Alcatraz – I've been a guard there myself!' The guard called us all the names he could conveniently think of ... and he finally summed up the matter by saying, 'Well, if I ever meet a C.O. in civil life, either he'll get beat up or I will!'

We returned to our cells and bundled up our belongings, then we descended a flight of stairs into the 7th Wing Sub-Basement, where the solitary cells were located. As the corporal of the solitaries was unlocking the gate, Ray peered around the corner and then whispered, 'Say, these are the *real* solitaries, – *boarded up*.' We had doubted whether we should be put into these boarded cells; there had been so many C.O.'s who had refused to work that there had not been enough boarded cells for them ...

Our sentences by the Executive Officer were, technically, fourteen days in solitary confinement, on full diet if we worked on the rockpile, or on bread and water, hand-cuffed to the bars nine hours a day if we refused to work on the rock pile. Of course, we refused to work on the rock pile, as that did not differ materially from other work done at the D.B.

Five cell doors were opened. I was ordered into one. The barred door was locked. I placed my hands through the bars of the door, and for the first time the steel handcuffs closed over my wrists. For a moment I caught a glimpse of a guard grinning malevolently at us; then the wooden door was closed, shutting off most of the light and deadening all sounds. I was alone in the Hole.

After a few moments I began to whistle softly to myself. And the air that I whistled – wholly unthinkingly – was '*The Marseillaise*.' The flaming hymn of revolutionary France was the natural psychological reaction to the Hole of Leavenworth. Ray, who was musically inclined, soon began to sing and whistle aloud. 'Shut up!' I heard a guard roar; 'do you think this is a playhouse? If you don't shut up I'll handcuff you this afternoon, too.' It was Saturday morning, and we had entered the Hole about ten o'clock. The handcuffs were taken off at noon, and we were handed our 'meal' through the bars, three slices of bread and a cup of water. I ate sparingly (my interest in bread waned after a few meals), chewed the bread very thoroughly, and lived on the crusts as much as possible. From the warning of other prisoners, we were afraid that the soft center of the bread might clog up our stomachs, inducing constipation or other digestive disorders.

During that first Saturday afternoon and Sunday, I had plenty of opportunity to observe the surroundings which the government counted upon to reform my character and restore me to a normal condition of mind. My cell was about 8 ∞ 5 feet and perhaps 8 feet high. The walls were of brick; the floor of concrete. The front was, of course, barred. About six inches in front of the steel bars was a wooden partition, shutting out the light and air, except what came through two pieces of screen at the top and bottom of the narrow wooden door. These pieces of screen were about six inches wide and fourteen inches long. Within the cell were a washbowl, toilet, three blankets (dirty, I need not say), and a tin cup of whose former possible history I dared not think.

Late Saturday night, after five separate requests of different guards, I received the remaining article of furniture which was allowed to the solitary prisoner. This was a board about eighteen inches wide and not quite six feet long, constituting my bed ... (I had not realized that a short time before we came to Leavenworth the men in solitary slept on the concrete floors of the cells!)

There was one advantage to the darkness of the solitary – one could not see so plainly the bedbugs which crawled in and out of their holes between the bricks. Some of the men were greatly troubled by these vermin, though, in fact, some of the upstairs cells were more alive with them than the solitaries. I remember opening my eyes one time in an upstairs cell to see three of them crawling up the wall within three or four inches of my face.

On Monday the 'real thing' began. We were awakened at six, swept out our cells, ate 'breakfast,' and were handcuffed to the bars at seven. I had not been standing there very long before I heard Jake call, 'Hello, Arthur!' 'Hello, Jake, what is it?' I replied. 'What century is this we're living in?' queried Jake.

From twelve to twelve-thirty we were freed from the handcuffs (though one lazy guard left mine hanging to one wrist) for 'lunch'; then from twelve-thirty to four-thirty we were 'strung up' again. My hands were at about the level of my breast; I could move them in a limited number of positions, and could also lean against the wall as I stood. The position of my hands was not particularly painful in itself, though the steel on my wrists was rather cold and the arms of a smaller man would have been slanted up in a manner to induce coldness through the stopping of the circulation.

Sometimes windows were opened in the corridor, making it cold in the cell. We were allowed no extra clothing – only the one suit of prison clothes, including the cap. I used to sleep in my clothing, with my coat doubled up for a pillow. One morning, feeling chilly, I put on my cap. A peculiarly obnoxious little red-headed guard, after handcuffing me, silently took off my cap and pitched it on the floor. However, I had plenty of time to pick it up with my foot, transfer it to my hand, and put it back on my head after he had closed and locked the door.

We were allowed our toilet articles, but no reading matter, not even our Bibles. For that matter, there was no light to read by, except when the cells were open at meals or, at the pleasure of the guard, in the evenings. Usually, we were allowed to talk from cell to cell, but it was difficult to make one's self heard when the wooden doors were closed.

One evening, when the doors were open, we were having an interesting historical discussion of some of Napoleon's campaigns, when suddenly our red-headed guard burst into the corridor, cursing at us for 'talking socialism,' and noisily closing both the doors and the discussion.

There were a number of other C.O.'s in the same line of cells with us ... Besides this there were a number of ordinary prisoners, most of them working on the rockpile. One of these boys, 'Toledo Red,' a generous-hearted Irish lad, twice slipped into my cell contraband articles of food which he had abstracted from his own 'full diet' portion. Out of pure generosity, this 'criminal' risked punishment to do a good turn to a despised C.O.

We were constantly being 'inspected' by various officers of the prison staff. The Executive Officer or his Assistant came through, I think, almost daily; the Officer of the Day came through each night for count; and at various times we saw the Assistant Commandant, the Chaplain, ... and others. One day several ladies, said to be officers' wives, came through. They appeared to have the same interest in us that the Roman matrons had shown in the gladiatorial games.

Sometimes the officers would question us. 'How long is your sentence?' the Assistant Commandant asked me. 'Twenty-five years.' 'Well,' he said, 'You're apt to get pretty tired standing there that long, and I guess that's what you'll do if you won't work.' We were frequently asked whether we were ready to work yet; and we understood that we should probably be taken out of solitary at once if we agreed.

On one of Captain C——'s visits, he began a conversation with Clark [Getts, another CO]. I heard Clark laughing as he answered; he was always full of good humor, anyway. A few hours later, Clark was taken out of solitary. We later learned that Captain C—— had placed him in the 'nut ward' of the hospital for observation. We always considered this a mere subterfuge, and believed that Clark had been sent to the 'nut ward' purely for punishment. He was held there for weeks without any mental examination, and he was subjected to the association of imbeciles and sex degenerates until he actually feared for his own life or reason. Finally, in response, I believe, to a protest from without, he was declared mentally normal and was put back to work among the other prisoners ...

In the ordinary course of events, a solitary prisoner might never leave his cell from one Saturday to the next. On Saturday afternoons the cells were cleaned, and all the solitary prisoners went to the washroom for a bath and shave, the only one during the week.

It happened, however, that we were taken out several times during the week. On Monday, Ray, Jake, and Ted completed their trip 'through the mill'; and the next day Ezra and I followed. We both came out of our cells blinking at the light and feeling a trifle weak; and besides, Ezra was really ill. We were taken to the Medical Examiner's, where we were put through a superficial medical examination, specimens of our blood were taken for the Wassermann test ... and our finger prints were taken once more. Profile and full face pictures were taken of each of us in our prison garb, with our numbers across our chest.

Finally we came to the Sociological and Psychiatric department, where a non-com or his prisoner assistant filled out a long 'first interview' blank with dozens of items of information. A pleasant young prisoner filled out my blank. 'What's your sentence?' he asked. 'Twenty-five years.' 'What were you charged with?' 'Refusing to pick up a rake.' 'That's D.D. – direct disobedience of orders. Gee, I don't know how many times I have heard that!' he exclaimed ... Finally, I was informally examined by a pleasant young lieutenant in the same department. He looked over my interview blank and asked me a number of questions about my C.O. stand. What would have happened to Belgium if she had refused to fight when Germany crossed her borders? Did I think the Draft Law was unconstitutional? I replied that I did, so far as it affected religious C.O.'s, and I referred him to the First Amendment to the Constitution. He looked interested, but did not argue the matter. My respect for him increased considerably when he did not ask me the old stock question about 'the Ruffian' [attacking my mother or sister]. I used to gauge the intellect of my questioners partly by the place 'The Ruffian' occupied in their questions! Finally, after asking why I had refused to work, the Lieutenant dismissed me with the advice, 'You'd better think it over and decide to work.'

We were [then] taken back to the cells ...

No doubt it is a mark of immaturity of character, but I must confess that two or three times that week the conditions of the solitary were so far psychologically effective as to produce the blackest fits of mental depression that I have ever experienced. Personally, I always felt that this mental effect was the most real torture of the Hole. No doubt the other men had similar experiences; we did not discuss such symptoms, but always alleged that we were 'getting along fine,' in answer to shouted questions from each other.

In the end, we agreed to work. On Saturday, December 7th we began to discuss the matter. To prevent the guard from catching the drift of the discussion, I talked French (distinctly 'after the school of Stratford-atte-

Bowe') to Ted, and he relayed it on in German to Jake, who understood Yiddish!

We recognized that in agreeing to work we were compromising the strict logic of our position. But we felt that there were certain circumstances which more or less justified the compromise. In the first place, the War was over. By working we should be helping keep the military machine in shape for the *next* war, but we should not actually be aiding in any *present* war.

Then, too, we believed that staying in the closed solitary cells meant definitely breaking our health. I had found myself rather exhausted at the end of Thursday and Friday and I believed that I should go to the hospital within the next week, if I stayed in the Hole. Was it worth the price, this late in the day, we asked? Should we not rather preserve our health for ... service when we should be released – perhaps within a few months or even weeks? More unselfishly, we all probably thought of the worry and anxiety which our confinement in solitary must be causing our friends and relatives if they knew of it.

I believe now that my reasoning was fallacious. I believe that it would have been braver, more logical, and more consistent to have persisted in my refusal to work and to have remained in solitary. I regret the weakness which caused me to compromise, and I doubly honor those who refused to compromise. But, unfortunately, a week in the Hole does not increase normality of thought or clarity of reasoning. So I failed to 'stick it out.'

We finally decided to agree to work, providing that light work was given us at first, until we gained our normal strength. We were all agreed that we would stay in the Hole rather than go to the rockpile, or even to the 'First Gang' (a gang of the roughest men doing the roughest manual work), at first.

We told the Corporal of our decision, and confirmed it to an officer on Sunday. Immediately things were 'loosened up.' The Hole is intended, as one officer is reported to have said, 'to break men in body and soul.' In harmony with this typically military aim, the guards had made the confinement as rigorous as possible, by every means in their power short of actual violence ... Upon our confirming once more the fact that we were willing to do work which we were physically able to do, Captain B——— ordered that we be 'promoted' into 'red numbers,' as second-class prisoners; and he also agreed to our request that we receive a medical examination ...

Altogether, Ted, Jake and I had been in the Hole nine days, from

November 30 to December 9; during about six days we had been 'strung up.' Our experience was, of course, nothing compared to that of the men who 'stuck out' the solitary for six or seven weeks; but, rightly or wrongly, we always were glad that we had made even this much protest before we worked ...[7]

After the week of 'light duty,' we were transferred to the 'First Gang.' The First Gang was intended to include the most dangerous men and to do the hardest work in the prison. All 'red' and 'yellow' number men were in it, as well as a large number of first-class prisoners, some of them recent graduates from 'red numbers.' The First Gang did various sorts of manual work in and near a stockade about a mile and a half, I think, from the prison. When I worked on the First Gang, the Gang still marched to and from work in the 'lockstep.' The lockstep is a remnant of the old-line prison savagery. At Leavenworth it was retained only for the First Gang; and a few weeks after I left the gang it was abolished there ...

In the lockstep as we practiced it, each man marched so close that his body almost touched the body of the man in front of him. Our hands hung at our sides until the line halted, when we were supposed to fold our arms. Men who had been in the First Gang a long time or who had 'done time' in other penitentiaries where the lockstep was used assured me that I should soon get used to it so that it would become purely automatic. In the close marching order which the lockstep involves, if one man gets out of step, a general tangle of feet, stumbling, cursing and kicking of shins usually results.

I never felt a more bitter hatred of the whole military and prison system than the first evening that I returned from work on the First Gang. Our part of the Gang had been shoveling dirt and carting it off in 'buggies' (wheelbarrows), all day. We were more or less tired, and as we tried to keep the cadence of that damnable lockstep, our feet slipped in the soft mud that covered the roads. Men cursed under their breath, as their fellows fell against them or stepped on their feet; the guards constantly snarled, 'Close up, there, '35! Close up!' or 'Get that grin off your face, '39!' For the first time, during that march, I felt a fundamental understanding of the point of view of [Victor] Hugo's Jean Valjean, released from the galleys with his heart turned to gall against prisons and the society which maintained them. I felt an all but irresistible desire to break loose and smash something – anything to express my hatred against this organized idiocy that called itself a military prison.

Returning to my cell in this frame of mind, I found that all the cells in the Wing had been 'shaken down' or 'searched' that day, – my bed was torn up and everything lying together in a heap. Many of the men ... complained that tobacco had been stolen from their cells during the search. But there was no redress. Rule 57 provided that, 'Your cell is subject to search at all times. If articles are found that might be used to injure or destroy or promote escape in any way, you will be dealt with as attempting to escape.'

We were, of course, allowed no 'sharp-pointed instruments.' It was always a problem how to keep one's finger-nails clean, as no provision seemed to have been made for this anywhere in the system, even in connection with the barber shop. I finally took to using the somewhat sharp point of the handle of my tooth-brush. 'How do you trim your finger-nails?' I asked one of the older C.O. prisoners. 'Bite 'em off,' he replied, laconically. 'When a man comes in here, he doesn't bite his nails; when he leaves, he does.' Even this procedure did not solve the problem of toe-nails; as some one observed, 'they're too tough!'

In the 7th Wing Basement all the 'red number' men occupied locked cells; but the cots in the corridor were occupied by 'white number' men. The crowd in this basement was supposed to be about the roughest in the D.B. Horse-play and general 'rough-house' were the common order of events; and fights were probably more frequent here than even in the rest of the prison. At one time, our room orderly appeared with his head bandaged as the result of some fray; again I saw a hot-headed Southern prisoner knock down a little inoffensive fellow, with a terrible blow under the eye, upon some trivial provocation.

But by far the worst thing connected with the whole D.B. was the unutterable filth of the moral and conversational atmosphere. Nothing else was quite so horrible. The foulest words in the language – the most hideously depraved conceptions of sex degeneracy – were bandied about every hour of the day, as the commonplaces of speech and thought. To live from day to day amidst this vileness was like shuddering through some slimy nightmare. I was much amazed one day, when some prisoners had been swearing and using vile epithets for some time, to hear a guard shout, 'Cut out that cursing!' It was the first and last time that I ever heard that order given by a guard. Usually the guards' conversation was not noticeably different from that of the prisoners.

There were of course sex degenerates in the prison, some of them sentenced there for abnormal sexual crimes. It was common talk among the prisoners that sodomy was frequently practiced by some of the men ...

[A] group of men in the Sub-Basement cells was rather admired, though little envied, by a good many of the prisoners. There were thirteen men held in 'isolation' awaiting the issue of their trial for the murder of another prisoner a short time before. We used to hear 'the murderers' (as they were called) occasionally shouting a lusty ragtime chorus from their cells.

It was an interesting group of men that were with us while we were in red and yellow numbers – 'Whitey,' the room orderly, who labeled me 'Gyp the Blood'; 'Monty,' 'Toledo Red,' 'Mickey,' and 'Humpy' ... Then there was Joe, a dark-haired, mysterious young man who confided to Ted and me that he was an Indian and had been a jockey, winning his races by daringly maiming the other horses, until he was discovered and driven from the turf. 'Whitey' apparently had some doubt as to the literal accuracy of this story. 'Indian?' he observed, – 'that damned wop.'

Most of these men were not depraved degenerates, – usually they simply had not had a fair chance. 'Red' told me he had been shuttled in and out of a 'reformatory' from an age when he was still needing 'mothering.' By nature he was bright, quick-witted, and generous. But society had probably first choked him in a slum environment, then poisoned him with inhuman penal institutions; now he openly admired and imitated criminals. There was another shifty-eyed boy who got hold of some paint and painted his yellow numbers white. 'I'm as crooked as they make 'em,' he told me. Then, in another tone, 'Well, I ain't never had much chance. When I was just a little kid I was taken' – but someone interrupted and I never heard the rest of his story. But because he 'never had much chance' he was behind the bars at Leavenworth, a felon, becoming more hardened every day in crookedness, brutality and crime.

They were perfectly human, these boys, and at times flashes of deeper feeling showed even through the customary profanity ...

The D.B. is a vast, grinding, deadening complex of rules. From the rising bell to 'Lights out,' the prisoner is beset and weighted down with minute regulations. The men who published the Rule Book knew that there were so many orders that they would inevitably fall foul of each other. So they provided for the contingency in Rule 20: 'When orders conflict, obey the last one given you, first stating what other orders you have received' ...

Sometimes the oppressive weight of these innumerable rules, the snarling and pettiness of the guards, and the moral filth of our environment made us almost regret that we had ever left solitary.

Ted was talking one day with one of the 'Israelites' – small-sect objectors braiding their hair in an attempt literally to follow an injunction of Leviticus against 'rounding the corner of the head.'[8] Ted was getting an idea of the Israelite's theology, and he asked, 'What do you think hell is like?' The Israelite looked around at the prison walls about them. 'This is hell,' he answered.

[At last, either by 'accident or design,' '15336,' now again a 'white number,' received 'a soft job as a messenger' in the office of the Chief Clerk of the prison. He worked there until his release by a special government order on 27 January 1919.]

Notes

Source: [William] Arthur Dunham, 'The Narrative of a Conscientious Objector, [1921],' unpublished MS, Bentley Historical Library, University of Michigan, Ann Arbor, pp. 5, 27, 76, 97, 115–18, 120–3, 125–9, 131–3, 135–46, 151–8, 160.

1 For another, but much briefer, account by a CO of roughly the same experience in the Fort Leavenworth Disciplinary Barracks as Dunham's, see the autobiography of the humanist pacifist Howard W. Moore, *Plowing My Own Furrow* (New York: W.W. Norton, 1985), 130–42. In contrast to Dunham, however, Moore received 'extra punishment' when he failed to stand to attention during the officer of the day's inspection. Enraged by such disrespect, the latter, Moore relates, 'ordered the guards to enter my cell and teach me a lesson. They proceeded to beat me with their clubs' until he lost consciousness (pp. 131, 132). Thomas's memoir has been reprinted as *The Radical 'No': The Correspondence and Writings of Evan Thomas on War*, ed. Charles Chatfield (New York and London: Garland Publishing, 1974), 253–9. See also Michael Casey, 'New Information on Conscientious Objectors of World War I and the Churches of Christ,' *Restoration Quarterly* 34, no. 2 (1992), 83–96. This includes a short autobiographical account of his incarceration in Fort Leavenworth by Charles Terrell Clay from Granite, Oklahoma, one of seventeen Churches of Christ COs (including one black) imprisoned there.

2 'It was standard practice in military prisons at the time to manacle prisoners to the bars or grating of their cells for eight hours in every twenty-four.' David M. Kennedy, *Over Here: The First World War and American Society* (New York and London: Oxford University Press, 1980), 165.

3 Dunham adds here: 'By far the greater number of C.O.'s in the D.B. were

working.' Many, like the Plymouth Brethren, had no objections to doing so. 'Were they not prisoners now, convicted by the recognized military laws of the land? Was not work a part of the "punishment," legally, if not justly pronounced upon them?' There were, though, some among the COs accepting work, who considered they had compromised by doing so because '*any* work done to support the D.B. was indirectly aiding the upkeep of the military machine ... but they did not believe that the compromise was great enough to justify or demand their refusal to work.' Dunham divided those refusing work into three categories: (1) 'radical anticonscriptionists'; (2) 'religious absolutists, whose deepest ... convictions forbade them to work anywhere under military direction'; and (3) men like Evan Thomas 'who had started to work, but ... had later begun a "sympathy strike" with the Molokans.' They were determined 'that if they could not end the punishment of the Russians, they would at least share it.'

4 On a preliminary page Dunham saw inscribed after his name (the army always called him William A. Dunham): 'Your total sentence is 25 years ... Your allowance of good time is 8 years, 2 months. You can lose all or part of it by misconduct. It is not yours unless you earn it by constant good behavior ... You are convicted of: Disobedience of orders ... You will be eligible to apply for release on home parole 5/25/1931.'

5 'You will be known by number while here,' the Rule Book informed prisoners.

6 The Church of God and Saints *in* Christ was one of several largely black pentecostal sects, which at that time espoused pacifism as well as conscientious objection when the draft came. See Theodore Kornweibel, Jr, 'Race and Conscientious Objection in World War I: The Story of the Church of God in Christ,' in Theron F. Schlabach and Richard T. Hughes, eds., *Proclaim Peace: Christian Pacifism from Unexpected Quarters* (Urbana and Chicago: University of Illinois Press, 1997), 70.

7 In his typescript 'Experiences of a C.O. in World War I' (II-MS-26 ['World War I Conscientious Objectors Private Papers'], Eastern Mennonite University Archives, Harrisonburg, VA), 9–11, the Virginia Mennonite Ernest H. Miller (1887–1973) confirms Dunham's narrative in its most dramatic phase. Miller had been drafted in June 1918 while farming in Kansas. After a few months a court martial sentenced him to twenty-five years in prison. On 8 December he was taken to the U.S. Disciplinary Barracks at Fort Leavenworth, where Dunham was then incarcerated. Miller writes: 'In prison you did not have a name, only a large number on the front and back of your clothes. My number was 15505. In Leavenworth Prison, I saw C.O.'s in solitary confinement, handcuffed to the bars of their cells nine hours each

working day. They slept on a cement floor with insufficient clothing or blankets to keep warm, and were given bread and water to eat because they had refused to work even in Leavenworth. They regarded Leavenworth Prison a part of the military machine. This scene I never will forget ... I am happy to say [because such conditions became known to the public they were] changed; handcuffs were removed, a board was given ... to sleep on, and an extra blanket. Soon afterwards [the men] were transferred to outside barracks under better conditions ... It has occurred to me since starting this account of my experiences that I probably was the only C.O. to see these men in their solitary confinement in Leavenworth Prison, besides those of their own group. The prison was overcrowded and there was a wide space or hall-way in front of the cells where the men were in solitary confinement. In this space I and others had cots. In this way I became acquainted with some of these men and witnessed their condition and treatment ... The C.O.'s were only a small minority of the men in the ... prison. Many of the men in prison were hardened criminals or serious offenders, while there were others [besides the COs] that you would not regard as criminals.' In fact, in contrast to his fellow Mennonite Albert Voth's year in the USDB at Fort Leavenworth [see below], Miller only remained in jail for nineteen days, receiving 'an honorable discharge' on 26 December: 'a nice Christmas gift indeed, although a day late' (p. 13).

8 The Israelite House of David was founded by Benjamin and Mary Purnell at the beginning of the twentieth century. A communitarian – and sometimes controversial – sect, its colony at Benton Harbor, Michigan, numbered around 400 members in 1918. Like some other millenarian groups, the Israelites espoused pacifism. When war came in 1917, 35 young men from the colony were drafted. Supported by Benjamin Purnell they claimed conscientious-objector status, but agreed to do non-combatant military service. 'Four were sent to Leavenworth, however, after they refused to handle dead animal carcasses, since [they believed] the Israelite injunction against the "dead burying the dead" still applied.' See Robert S. Fogarty, *The Righteous Remnant: The House of David* (Kent, OH: Kent State University Press, 1981), 101, 102.

ALBERT VOTH

A young Mennonite from Kansas named Albert Voth was Dunham's fellow prisoner at the Fort Leavenworth Disciplinary Barracks (USDB). Voth's father[1] had emigrated from Russia in the early 1870s when compulsory forestry service was imposed on the country's Mennonite draftees: Mennonite young men hitherto had been exempt from any state service. After the war was over, Voth junior attended college and became a schoolteacher: at that time the number of Mennonite college graduates was not large. The account of his experiences as a conscientious objector was written around 1937.

Voth tells us that, then aged twenty-one, he was among the first to be drafted after the United States entered the war in 1917. Among the motives leading him to become a CO were not only the non-resistant teaching of his forefathers' church but also his memories of 'the gentle-mannered smiling Hopi [tribesmen] and ... the mild Hopi children' with whom, as a young boy on the Hopi Indian reservation where his father had been a missionary, he had played – having learned to converse with them in their own language. After call-up the young man had been despatched to an army camp in southern Texas. 'I had left my parental home,' he writes, 'with the one expressed guide of conduct, namely, whatever befell me, I would not kill anyone.' In camp COs were segregated. Although at first Voth had been prepared to undertake non-combatant duties in the army, he became increasingly determined to resist mounting pressure to perform some kind of military service. As a result, he was eventually court-martialled and sentenced to life imprisonment, subsequently reduced to twenty-five years.

The brief narrative printed below covers his transfer from southern Texas to the USDB at Fort Leavenworth and the twelve months he then spent in that institution.[2] Like Dunham, the Mennonite resented *inter alia* the grotesque prison garb as well as the bedbugs, which seem to have been more aggressive in the ordinary prison cell occupied by Voth than in the isolation unit where Dunham did part of his time. Voth presents a lively reconstruction of what it felt like for a Mennonite farm boy to find himself in a military prison along with dangerous criminals as well as some more harmless characters. Unfortunately, his narrative is totally lacking in precise dates.[3]

[The] lieutenant in charge came daily to give us rigorous physical exercises. He stated he was getting us ready for what was to come. This was the extent of his information. After a week or so of this had passed, regulation army uniforms were reissued to us with orders that each of us appear the following morning in full uniform of the depot brigade for roll call. This, all of us believed meant a final effort toward induction into some form of military service. Questions arose as to what to do. It was agreed among ourselves that each would make his own private decision regarding the order. The following morning five or six appeared in uniform, the rest in the fatigue clothes we had been wearing. After roll was called the men in uniform were asked what branch of service they henceforth accepted. Having voiced their choice, they were taken to camp. The rest of us, forty-five in number, were informed that we would be court-martialed for disobeying military orders. We were given the choice of a civilian defense attorney. Since we, however, declined any form of legal defense an army lieutenant was assigned the task. The newspapers gave the case front page prominence, with unfavorable designations and verbiage, to say the least. The trial was held earlier than the announced date. The court tried to prove conspiracy, the defense claiming no conspiracy to be involved. To our best knowledge each of us had acted individually and according to his own convictions. Whatever was proven or disproven at the trial, we were each given a life sentence of imprisonment which in review was reduced to twenty five years.

Immediately after the trial we were taken to the camp stockade as prisoners. Watches, razors, knives, money, etc. were taken from us, to be placed on deposit. Other excess personal possessions were shipped home. We were held in the stockade a little over a week on the south side of a building under the open sky. Just enough ground was allowed us for the forty five of us to spread our bedding for the night. During the day the hot southern Texas sun scorched us. The ever-present guards were constantly shouting threats of a dungeon whenever someone moved a little too close to the edge of our assigned ground. Obviously no escape was possible because of the high barbed-wire stockade fence. One night during a heavy rain we were herded into a small building where there was little more than sitting or standing room for the remainder of the night. Before we were finally removed from the stockade several high-ranking officers from camp officially apprised us of the exact nature of our sentence, namely, twenty five years' imprisonment in the United States disciplinary barracks at Fort Leavenworth. The offer was made to commute the sentence for anyone who would accept service in the army. No one accepted. The day for our shipment to Leavenworth came soon after this. We were handcuffed in pairs and the rumor was that we were to be marched through camp as a spectacle. Fortunately, just as we left the stockade a terrific rain storm came up and continued throughout the nearly two mile tramp to the depot. We embarked and then dried at leisure, for we remained handcuffed and under guard for the remainder of the trip. At Denison, Texas we were marched around on the depot platform for a short time to stretch our legs. A sizeable group of the city's citizens was out to view us. A few remarks about slackers were shouted but otherwise everything was peaceful.

Paradoxical as it may seem, my first impression on entering the prison gates at Leavenworth was one of genuine relief. Others in our group concurred in this. The mental pressure of uncertainty and countercurrent events in camp had become so increasingly severe that at times one's rationality seemed in question. Here suddenly the atmosphere was changed. Prisoners were simply dressed and clean in appearance. The white walls seemed peaceful, and above all there was a certain attitude of natural ease in evidence around us which we so badly needed. Certain it was to us that a different, non-military, chapter lay ahead of us. We were 'checked in' according to regular prison procedure, and were happily relieved of an uncomfortable beard stubble of ten days' standing. Clothes were numbered on the back of each upper garment and across the front of each pants leg. Henceforth each man was known only by this number.

After the tidying process of this first day was over, we, with a few other military prisoners who had come from camp with us, were led into the presence of the prison chaplain. He acquainted us briefly with prison rules and gave us each a printed pamphlet setting forth our prison status. He also informed us of his willingness to act as the prisoners' friend as far as prison rules would permit. Then, drawing himself up into an air of severity, he went on to say 'but those among you, and you know whom I mean, who have refused to participate in this most holy of holy wars – well, I will refrain from saying what I would like to say – that is all.' We were lead into a basement cell house where we were assigned our bunks in an open corridor for the first night. Here with gloomy, massive walls on one side and locked cells on the opposite hand we had time for reflection. Our first thoughts centered around the dire meaning of the chaplain's remarks. Were we to be made the objects of a further sweating process even in this place? Was the mental pressure never to cease? We read our pamphlets. Our sentences of twenty five years could be reduced, through good behavior, to approximately fifteen years. Under the circumstances the difference between fifteen and twenty five years was amazingly meaningless. In any event a sort of mental panic was the only answer one could find in contemplating the future. I left my bunk to explore the immediate premises, expecting at any moment to be shouted at for overstepping some unknown restriction. Since no one, however, stopped me I became inwardly more liberated. I talked to a few prisoners who were locked in individual cells. Some of them were deserters, some had been insubordinate to their officers, and one was a young Jewish boy whose incarceration had produced what seemed to border on an unbalanced emotionality. With late afternoon we were marched in file to the mess hall, where about fifteen hundred were already seated. Since we had to go to the back end of the hall I had a good opportunity of getting my first view of a whole body of prisoners. I had expected to see hardened sullen men. Instead, I was impressed with the many intelligent normal faces all around me. This dispelled my sense of depression more than anything that had happened thus far. A feeling of kinship with these men began to take possession in me – maybe even here life was not entirely hopeless and impossible. That night I slept well. A few of our group complained of having experienced sleeplessness. The next day we were scattered throughout the prison in various cell blocks, some with open cells, others with individual locked cells. I shared an open cell with five other prisoners, strangers to me. For all of us prison work had begun. We were assigned to various gangs under guard. I became a member of a group of six men (all COs) who under shot gun surveillance worked daily in the prison truck fields.

For brevity's sake many of the details of prison life cannot here be recounted. Suffice it that accounts of prison practices and behavior reported in sociological treatises seem to represent universal norms wherever men are incarcerated in large numbers. Food was bad to the point of frequent worms in the stew. 'Crimping' or punishment for petty infractions of minor rules was amply applied. Overcrowded conditions of a serious nature prevailed, which in part led to dangerous mass disorders and finally to an extensive strike. Sexual perversion, fights, and favoritisms were well known among the prisoners. The cardinal virtue was to keep one's mouth shut. To my knowledge none of the five or six hundred COs ever became involved in any underground difficulties. Instead they were generally treated with respect and good will by the rest of prisoners. Among those who were generally referred to as COs were also some who held more to ideas of a political complexion, mainly Socialism. Some of these men were well educated, several holding Ph.D. degrees. These men were actively instrumental in bringing about an amicable and humane settlement of the strike [see below]. Food and living conditions were greatly improved, order quickly restored, and sentences reviewed as a result of this settlement.

After having worked on the truck farming gang for three months I was unexpectedly offered the job of library assistant under the supervision of the chaplain. In addition I was given the task of taking summary histories of each new prisoner for the chaplain's files, histories showing surprisingly heavy sentences for the general run of military offenses. It thus happened that the chaplain and I frequently drifted into informal conversations, sometimes to the extent of giving the CO issue an airing. This association with the chaplain eventuated in a friendship of mutual regard and understanding which entirely obliterated the effects of his terse remarks on that first day of our arrival.

With the passing of a few months nearly all COs had been given the regular so-called star parole. This enabled us to go outside the prison wall unguarded during the day in line of duty, and for strolls on Sunday. Quite a number of the COs were milkers at the dairy and had their living quarters there. Also at about this time the influenza epidemic broke out. Four of my immediate group from the Texas camp died. Bad hospital facilities took a heavy toll in the general population. At the height of the epidemic there were eight hundred patients. I had recovered from my siege of flue early and so temporarily fell heir to carrying daily mail to the epidemic quarters. This also was handled through the chaplain's office. Through the disorganization and confusion caused by the epidemic, patients freshly released from the hospitals were placed wherever room happened to be. I had the misfortune of getting an old single locked cell. During the day I was at my job in the library, but the nights were miserable. The cold October winds blew in through a broken north window opposite my cell, and to top it all off the place was infested, literally, by thousands of bed bugs. To the request for some insect spray or powder it was suggested that I kill the bugs by hand as best I could. I did my best! After a week or so I was transferred to parole quarters, but I could not readily forget the men who were still among the bugs.

After the war had ended, the continued acute over-crowded conditions demanded review and reduction of sentences. Subsequently prisoners were released in relatively large groups. With the release of some COs, however, some of the prominent newspapers created such a furor that for awhile discharge of COs was discontinued. My release came at the end of a year's sentence. I gained my knowledge of the impending freedom in an at-random manner from various prisoners a number of days before I received official notice. Such knowledge came through 'grapevine' channels, which by the way represents one of the most amazing phenomena of prison life. The strike, for instance, both in its execution and termination was handled nearly entirely by the grapevine method without benefit of mass meetings.

During the long slowly moving winter months that had passed I had often looked out across the distant wooded hills with feelings of gloom and nostalgia. The future on such occasions seemed a never-changing, never-ending thing. I gradually found myself renouncing the outside world as something entirely apart, and possibly even unfriendly. During Sunday strolls I had been in the surrounding hills and little post village, but this had been only an extended portion of the prison, the world outside still lay beyond all this. When I heard of my coming release I tried mentally to reestablish connections with the outside but without much success. After all, I was about to enter a society again which had so heartlessly and enthusiastically executed a war with meat-grinder efficiency.

On the day of departure I received many handshakes and well-wishes, many from men whom I had learned to know through the work in the library. No one was ever begrudged his liberty by other prisoners. In possession of a railroad ticket, a five-dollar bill, a cheap blue serge suit, and tan army shoes, all furnished by the prison, I, with several other COs, was lead through the front gate and bade 'good luck.' This was a bewildering experience. We stood there awhile to look around and collect our senses. Finally we ambled down to the interurban station to catch a car for Kansas City. We hardly felt certain that we had the freedom and right to do so. We were still mentally looking for some directing authority. In Kansas City we were quickly accosted by pawnshop men to exchange our telltale prison garb. We did not bother about this. I myself had had my clothes sent to the home of a friend in Kansas City where I made my change. It was not until that night on the train that I regained some semblance of being a private human being in his own right. The private home in which I slept the first night after leaving the train seemed so entirely like a toy play house; it seemed to have the comfortable quaintness of the little sugar-cookie house of childhood fairy tales.[4]

Notes

Source: Albert C. Voth, 'The Experiences of a War Objector in World War I,' typescript in the Mennonite Library and Archives, Bethel College, North Newton, KS, pp. 19–28.

1 See John F. Schmidt, 'Henry R. Voth,' *The Mennonite Encyclopedia* (Scottdale, PA: Mennonite Publishing House), vol. 4 (1959), 858–9. Voth's father belonged to his church's 'intelligentsia.' In the course of his missionary activities among the Hopi Indians in Arizona, he had become a pioneer cultural anthropologist, whose writings were published by the Field Columbian Museum in Chicago. One wonders if this small tribe's pacifist impulse, which emerged during the wars of the twentieth century, may have been first aroused by Voth and his fellow missionaries from the General Conference branch of the Mennonite Church. The latter succeeded in producing a translation of the New Testament into the Hopi language, knowledge of which may have fused with pacifistic elements in the tribe's indigenous tradition. For Mennonite work among the Hopi, see *ME*, vol. 2 (1956), 810.

2 'To my firsthand knowledge,' writes Voth in his typescript 'Experiences' (Addendum, p. 31), 'the majority of Mennonites I knew in prison, most of them farmers, would have gladly accepted farm furloughs had they been given the opportunity.' But release usually came before this opportunity offered.

3 Albert Voth certainly does not fit into the stereotype of a Mennonite objector in the minds of the three-member Board of Inquiry, set up by the Secretary of War on 1 July 1918 to deal with COs. In an article entitled 'The Conscientious Objector,' *Columbia University Quarterly* 21, no. 4 (October 1919), 253–72, sometimes considered to be 'a classic in the defense of nonconformity,'

one of its members, the learned law professor Harlan F. Stone, recalled his preference for the generally lively and articulate socialist objectors over the tongue-tied, stolid, and 'bovine' Mennonite (and Brethren) COs, who patiently waited their turn to appear before the board. The board periodically visited the USDB at Fort Leavenworth to hear the cases of men it had remanded there. But apparently, since they had received a prison sentence, neither Voth nor Dunham qualified for a board hearing.

4 John Neufeld's 'Diary,' a rather laconic document jotted down on the spot as opportunity allowed, supplements Voth's account of incarceration in the Fort Leavenworth Disciplinary Barracks and its preliminaries. It is printed in Melanie Springer Mock, *Writing Peace: The Unheard Voices of Great War Mennonite Objectors*, Studies in Anabaptist and Mennonite History, no. 40 (Telford, PA: Pandora Press U.S., 2003), 215–20. Neufeld's impressions of the daily routine at the DB were by no means entirely negative. Like most of the COs, he too got on well with 'prisoners ... of the criminal kind.' 'The reason,' he thought, 'perhaps was that we shared their fate with them and were not given any privileges whatsoever.' For all its shortcomings, Neufeld's diary possesses a specially valuable quality, its immediacy and directness: it presents a voice recorded at the time of the events taking place. Only very rarely did prison regulations give COs such an opportunity. Cf. the diaries of Hassler and Osborne below. See also *Diary Kept by Noah H. Leatherman While in Camp during World War I* (new ed., Rosenort, MB: PrairieView Press, [1968?]), 33–44, for the time this Holdeman Mennonite from Kansas spent in the Fort Leavenworth DB (November 1918–January 1919).

PHILIP GROSSER

Philip Grosser (1890–1933) was one of the obscure who have always made up the vast majority of humankind. Anarchist by conviction, Jewish by birth, Grosser, as all who knew him testified, was a man of unswerving principle, certainly a man of peace if not an unconditional pacifist. The famous Russian anarchist Alexander Berkman, in his foreword to Grosser's posthumously published prison memoir, wrote of this document: 'The story is powerful, sincere and strongly written.' Grosser, a single man haunted by loneliness and a sense of failure and feeling increasingly alienated in the America of his day, committed suicide in 1933. To quote Berkman again: 'This [pamphlet] is the story of a heretic ... His heresy – in 1917 the heresy – consisted of a passionate belief that the common people of all lands were brothers, and that it was wrong to have any traffic with the business of slaughtering them. (A quaint idea, nineteen centuries old.)' Berkman went on to describe Grosser as 'a shabbily dressed working man, who [spoke] in foreign accent and idiom, but in a vocabulary enriched by reading good literature.' Asked how he had managed to endure the atrocious treatment he received in Alcatraz, Grosser had replied: 'Well, ... I figure that there are times and occasions when a man either has to show down or show up.'

I was never a soldier, yet I spent three years of my life in military prisons. After I registered for the draft as an objector to war on political grounds, I refused to submit to a physical examination for military purposes and refused to sign an enlistment and assignment card. Instead of being tried for violation of the war-time conscription act, which was a Federal civil offence, I was turned over to the military and was subjected to all forms of punishment as an erring soldier, not as a civilian who refused to participate in a war waged 'to make the world safe for democracy.'

My name was called among the first five per cent of the draft quota in August, 1917. The military machine was not quite ready at that time, and the local Draft Board did not know what to do with me when I reported to them and told them that I was opposed to war and that I would not participate in military life; that to be examined physically for military purposes was to me the same as a military order and that I refused to submit to it. Chairman Burroughs of Local No. 5 Draft Board, Boston, told me that my case would be turned over to the Federal District Attorney. A few days later I reported to the Federal District Attorney and submitted to arrest for violation of the conscription act. I was released on a five hundred dollar bond to await the action of the Federal Grand Jury. Provost Marshal General Crowder, however, defined the draft act so that a man could be automatically indicted into the 'selective' army, and in December, 1917, I was notified to report for military service, that I was a soldier under the automatic ruling of General Crowder, that failure to report according to notification received constituted desertion, and desertion in time of war was punishable by death. I still refused to obey the military call and surrendered to the Federal District Attorney. He in turn notified the military, and a soldier from the Irvington Street Armory, Boston, with fixed bayonet on a rifle, was sent to the Federal Building to bring me in as a deserter.

The desertion charge was not pressed, and I was transferred to Ft. Banks, Boston Harbor. Arriving at the harbor fort the guard took me to the guard house, yelled out, 'Corporal of the guard, one prisoner.' A Corporal came out and answered 'Turn him in.' Next morning I refused to obey military orders and was put in solitary confinement on bread and water diet and tried by a special court-martial. Before being sentenced, however, I was transferred, not as a prisoner, to Ft. Andrews, Boston Harbor, where my objections to the military were to be overcome with kindness. Lt. Stanley G. Barker, the officer of tact, was to take charge of me. After being in the guard house at Andrews, not as a prisoner, the officer of tact decided that the situation was impossible. I refused to don the uniform of a soldier, refused to stand in military formation and behaved in general as a civilian in a military post in time of war. I was not a very good example to other drafted men. An agent provocateur, posing as a Conscientious Objector, was placed with me in the guard house. He talked about blowing up the place, running away from the Island and other silly stuff. I was not taken in on that and the so-called C.O. (Conscientious Objector) suddenly disappeared. Immediately thereafter Lt. Barker and Post Adjutant Lt. Chase came to the guard house, searched me, took away all my letters, newspaper clippings, the book 'Under Fire' by Henri Barbusse,[1] and placed me under arrest by order of the Northeastern Department without preferring specific charges against me. All the prisoners in the guard house were ordered not to talk with me, and the order on the guard report was that I shouldn't be allowed to leave my cell unless a non-commissioned officer accompanied me. So to be taken from my solitary cell to the wash room in the same building a Corporal or Sergeant had to be my valet. For about ten weeks I underwent all forms of torture. I was dragged with a rope around my neck to the Quartermaster's Office to be given a pair of government shoes. I was beaten with a rifle butt. A couple of soldiers used to carry me out to stand in military formations, and when the soldiers were not holding on to me, I used to sit down on the parade ground and spoil the whole show. I was chained by my hands to the bars of my cell. My arms were stretched upward till I had to stand on tiptoe. The blood was pushed back into my muscles and shoulders. Besides the twisters were tightened so that I could not move. For nineteen hours I was not even allowed to go to the toilet. At intervals the Officer of the Day, Lt. Carpenter, came to ask me whether I'd submit to military authority, and upon my refusal he would order the Sergeant to leave me in my misery. After the first nineteen hours in chains, the Commandant, Lt.-Col. Ayers, ordered that the chaining to the bars should be three hours off and three hours on, day and night. All my belongings were removed from the cell, the straw sack taken out and the three hours I was off the chains I had to rest on the iron bunk with nothing to lie on and no blankets to cover up with. Between the cold and the chaining up, I did not sleep for nights.

On April 25, 1918, I was taken before a court-martial, charged and found guilty of the following military crimes:

'Refusing to obey a lawful command of Lt. Stanley G. Barker to go to work.

Saying in the presence of officers and enlisted men that I would not obey any military orders.

Refusing to stand at attention when ordered to do so by Lt. Carpenter.

Attempting to create mutiny in the United States Army, by writing letters to other objectors, and urging them to stand fast, and not to submit to military authority.'

My punishment, according to Court-Martial Order No. 152, Northeastern Department, Boston, was: 'To be dishonorably discharged from the service, to forfeit all pay and allowances due and to become due, and to be confined at hard labor for *Thirty Years* at such place as the reviewing authorities may direct.'

The place of confinement was designated at Ft. Jay, Governor's Island, New York. On June 11, 1918, chained to another prisoner, who was found guilty of desertion and of throwing a live cat into a hot furnace and whose punishment was four years' imprisonment, I was brought to 'Castle Bill,' as the military prison at Ft. Jay is known in the army. My stay here was not of long duration. The place getting overcrowded, one hundred fifty of us were put 'in irons' and, after a three-day-and-night travel being chained, we arrived at Ft. Leavenworth military prison.

The mistreatment of the C.O.'s and the abuse of all other military prisoners at Leavenworth, with the resulting 'prisoners' general strike' of February, 1919, is a story by itself. The Commandant blamed the revolt of the general prisoners on the Objectors, and soon after the strike all Objectors were removed to a stockade which was connected with the prison. We were practically left to do as we damned pleased, so on May 1, 1919, some of us even celebrated the International Workers' Holiday. The lining of our prison caps was red, so we turned our caps inside out, and carrying a few magazine photographs of Lenin and Trotsky and singing revolutionary songs, we went round and round the stockade enclosure. The guards notified the Commandant and he came running with a dozen officers, and told us not to be parading. We promised, and that was that.

Some of the boys imprisoned had newspaper experience. Many of them had office work assigned to them by the prison authorities and had access to typewriters, and spontaneously a crude sheet appeared for general distribution among the prisoners. It was called *'Wire City Weekly,'* one of the numerous underground Bolshevik weeklies in America, circulation subterranean, printed in the United States Disciplinary Barracks, Ft. Leavenworth, Kansas. Somehow the Department of Justice got hold of a copy and immediately an agent came to [the] fort, with full power to unearth the printing press. Of course they couldn't find a press because there wasn't any. The *'Wire City Weekly'* was made almost in the commandant's office, on government paper and on typewriters owned by the United States Army Quartermaster

Corps. Col. Rice, Commandant of Leavenworth military prison, got good and sore and decided that he had about enough of the slackers. Officers were heard to say with great sincerity that they cursed the day that Conscientious Objectors were ever sent to them. Col. Rice obtained permission from the War Department to get rid of all the undesirable prisoners. In June, 1919, thirty one prisoners and myself were transferred from the disciplinary barracks to the post guard house, and at two o'clock the following morning we were called out and some of us were chained in pairs by the wrists and others were in addition shackled in twos by the ankles. We were taken to a side track where a couple [of] cars were ready for us. The commissioned and non-commissioned officers accompanying us wouldn't tell us our destination. 'Sealed orders,' they claimed. To outside inquirers, however, they gave the information that we were a gang of German prisoners being transferred to a concentration camp. We were in 'irons' all the time, confined in the cars from the morning we were placed at Leavenworth until we reached Oakland, California, where we were taken to Ft. Mason docks, and placed aboard a government boat to sail to 'Uncle Sam's Own Devil's Island.' At all stations, windows and doors of our cars were locked, and guards were posted to watch us. At railway junctions, where transfer to other lines had to be made, our cars were shifted to make the proper connections. Four train seats were allotted to each pair of convicts, and by having two vacant seats facing us we managed to fix up a 'comfortable' sleeping place. If my partner, who happened to be an Oxford University graduate, forgot in his sleep that he was Uncle Sam's passenger and wanted to turn in his sleep he had to drag me along. The first day of our journey I suffered from diarrhea, and my partner had to go along with me quite often, for the bracelets were not taken off for any purpose whatsoever. The trip from Leavenworth to Alcatraz took us three days and three nights.

Alcatraz Island is a 12 acre rock at the mouth of the Golden Gate, capped with a white 'house of silence.' The fascination of the horrible clings about the misty Gibraltar whose history reaches back to the time when it was a military post in the day of Spanish domain. The Island is reached by government boats only, and the visitor must obtain a pass from the Commandant. The place is known as 'The Rock,' and sometimes as 'Uncle Sam's Own Devil's Island.'

On my arrival at Alcatraz I refused to work or to stand [in] military formations. I was taken before Executive Officer, Lt. J.J. Meskill. He gave me the formal military order to go to work at once, and when I refused he sentenced me to 14 days' solitary confinement in the 'hole' and a bread and water diet. He said, 'If Jesus Christ were to come to this Island and refuse to work, I would put him in the dungeon and keep him there.'

Sergeant Cole, overseer in charge, switched on the electric light and took me down a flight of stairs to the basement, hollowed out of the rock under the prison. He ordered me to take up a bucket, and when I wasn't quick enough he lifted his club and yelled, 'I'll knock your God damn brains out!' He showed me into a cell, locked the iron barred door behind me, and I heard his footsteps going up the stairs as I was left alone in the dungeon. Then he switched off the lights and I found myself in complete darkness. I tried to investigate the place which was to be my abode for the next fourteen days. Attempting to walk through the cell I bumped my head against the ceiling. Feeling my way, I found that the cell roof was arched and lower at the sides than a man's height, so that it wasn't safe to walk around in the dark. I sat on the door-sill waiting for something to happen.

After a while the lights were turned on and a guard came down with a few slices of bread and a pitcher of water. Trying to have a good look at my cell while the lights were still on I found that there was no furniture or toilet facilities, the only things that were to be seen were the pitcher of water, the few slices of bread, and the 'old wooden bucket' which the guard told me would be emptied only once every twenty-four hours. The dungeon cells were under the prison, situated so that not a ray of daylight ever penetrated them. The air in the cell was stagnant, the walls were wet and slimy, the bars of the cell door were rusty with the dampness, and the darkness was so complete that I could not make out my hand a few inches before my face. It seemed eternity until the officer of the day and a guard came about nine o'clock in the evening. The cell door opened and the guard threw in a pair of lousy army blankets, wholly insufficient, as was evidenced by the fact that four blankets were provided for the warmer and drier cells upstairs. The prison officer had to put a searchlight on me to note that I was 'present and accounted for.' The light was switched off, and as no other prisoners were at that particular time confined in the dungeon I was left alone with the rats for company. The water and sewer systems of the jails were located in the center of the underground dungeon in front of the cells and in case of accident, as the bursting of a pipe, a prisoner could have been drowned like a rat before anyone in the jail proper could have noticed it. I took off my shoes and coat and used them as a pillow, wrapped myself in the two blankets, and with the concrete floor as a mattress made myself a nice comfortable bed.

Next morning, a guard took me up to the wash room to empty my bucket. Behind the guard's back I managed to beg some of the prisoners around to give me some tobacco. A few minutes later I was back in the 'hole,' searched by the guard and locked in safely again. I planted a part of the bootleg tobacco under a loose brick in the wall and 'rolled my own.' As soon as I lit my cigarette, however, the guard returned, searched me and confiscated the tobacco. The part that I had hidden in my cell he did not get, and I managed to have smokes for the next twenty-four hours in spite of the unexpected raid.

The things hardest to endure in the dungeon were the complete darkness, the sitting and sleeping on the damp concrete floor, and the lack of sight or sound of any human being. The eighteen ounces of bread was quite sufficient for the first few days, and towards the last I had some of the bread left over. The rats were quite peaceful and friendly. The fact that the dungeon was made a store house for the 'ball and chain,' straightjacket, wrist chains and other implements of medieval torture was not very pleasant.

After serving fourteen days in the rat-infested dungeon I was taken out in a weakened condition to the prison hospital. The prison doctor thought that eating too much bread was the cause of my sickness. I knew better. To place any human being in the 'hole' for fourteen days, even if one were given a chicken diet, was enough to weaken him. It felt good to be given a soft hospital bed after the concrete floor as a sleeping place. The food, which was quite good in the hospital, was also a treat compared with the eighteen ounces of bread. Then the daylight and the association with human beings again made me feel as if I were on a holiday.

After a two-day stay in the hospital the Doctor transferred me back to the cell-house and I was assigned to 'make little ones out of big ones' on the rockpile. I did not refuse to file out with the workers, but I refused to accept tools or to perform any labor when I got there. Under military regulations no prisoner can be kept in solitary for more than 14 consecutive days, and must have at least 14 days in the regular cell on normal diet before he can be returned to solitary. Being unable, therefore, to send me back to the 'hole' at once, the authorities placed a special sentry over me and I was forced to parade around the windiest side of the Island for eight hours a day, while the other prisoners worked. At the end of 14 days of grace I again disobeyed a formal order to work and was returned to the dungeon. During my interval out of solitary, a charge of disobeying a military command, under the 96th article of war (not of peace) was preferred against me. The specific offence was that I did not obey Lt. J.J. Meskill's order to go to work. I was also placed in 'yellow numbers' (3rd class prisoner), which meant being segregated with the degenerates in the cell block and being seated in the mess-hall at the same table with them. For one offence I was subjected to three-fold punishment: 14 days in the 'hole,' court-martial under the 96th article of war and 'yellow numbers.' On being called for trial I refused to plead or to say anything to the military judge. He (his honor, the judge) was quite perplexed. Then he said, 'The prisoner stands mute.' I was found guilty and three more months of hard labor were added to my original thirty-year sentence.

Visitors were allowed to see prisoners on Sunday provided they procured a pass from the Commandant. Men in the 'hole' were not entitled to have visitors. The first visitors to the Island were Anna Coggins and Margaret Stanislowsky of Oakland, Cal. They came to see Clark Getts, underground postman of Leavenworth fame, who had informed the outside world of the torture and chaining to cell bars of Objectors in that prison, and was punished with solitary for fourteen days when found out. Capt. Chambers, psychiatrist at Leavenworth, confined him in a cell with the violently insane after his fourteen days solitary was served. It was only the news smuggled out that procured his release from the 'nut' factory. At Alcatraz, Getts again started the underground ball rolling, and the Commandant, Col. Jos. Garrard, started to receive protests against the use of the dungeon from all over the country. My brother and other friends in Boston, and the Civil Liberties Union of New York protested to President Wilson and Secretary of War Baker. Friends in California tried to obtain a pass to visit me, but the Commandant, abiding by the rule that no prisoner in solitary confinement was entitled to a visitor, refused passes. Alice Park, of Palo Alto, wired to Senators, to Newton D. Baker, and to the President of the United States until Col. Garrard allowed her and two other friends, Robert Whitaker and Marion Alderton, to visit me although I was in solitary. On the second term of my fourteen days solitary I was treated to the most unusual thing, a visit of three friends. I was taken up to the library by an old soldier who was to listen in, and my visitors talked with me for about three hours, or rather, I talked and they listened. After one is denied the privilege of talking, as at Alcatraz, where the silence system prevailed, when one is given the opportunity, one talks a mile a minute. The old soldier became rather tired and snoozed a little. That gave my visitors a chance to take notes.

In a letter to my brother David, Lt. J.J. Meskill, Executive Officer of Alcatraz prison, states: 'Your brother Philip has assumed the role (*sic*) of a Conscientious Objector and when given an order by me to go to work he persistently refused. He also refused to recognize military authority. For his persistent refusal, he was placed in solitary confinement for 14 days on a bread and water diet. When not in solitary your brother has the freedom of the air and sunshine, notwithstanding the fact that he persistently refused to work and bores his fellow inmates, who labor arduously while he stands looking on.'

On account of the protests of the Civil Liberties Union and others the War Department ordered an investigation and assigned Col. Phillips to investigate the doings of Col. Garrard. The Alcatraz authorities got wind that an investigation was contemplated and prepared for it. Other Objectors and I, who were serving time in the dungeon, were transferred to solitary dark cells on the ground floor of the prison. These are ordinary cells with no bed to sleep on and the barred cell door boarded up to shut out the light. Through the cracks of the boarded door I could see prisoners carrying cement bags and beds with iron springs to the dungeon. I did not know the reason. It seemed, however, that the authorities of the jail knew the reason. At the same time the Colonel allowed four blankets for men in solitary. A few days later the investigator arrived. Everything was nicely prepared, the dungeons were floored with concrete smoothly polished, all rat-holes were blocked up, the iron springs and beds arranged. A plate of freshly grated cheese was placed in one of the cells over night to prove that there were no rats. Col. Phillips had an army stenographer with him and all those in solitary that were previously confined in the dungeon were called before the investigator. I told Col. Phillips that there was no bed in the dungeon cell where I served my 14 day stretch in, also that the concrete floor polishing was done in anticipation of his arrival, and though all my testimony was taken down by the stenographer not a word of it was reported to the Secretary of War who ordered the investigation. Col. Phillips, the military man, could hardly be expected to be dissatisfied with Col. Garrard's methods of handling men who refused to recognize military authority and who according to army regulation were justly punished. The dungeon was not officially condemned, but on the investigator's departure the dungeon, so far as Objectors were concerned, was done away with.

On completing the third term of solitary, which was served in the dark cells, I was chased out again on the rock piles. The number of non-working C.O.'s increased to nine and all of us at that time were out of solitary. We were assigned to work on the rock pile, but refused to accept tools or to perform labor. The sentry paraded our army of the unemployed right near the quarry laborers, until one day we simply struck on the guard, refused to obey his orders to parade, sat down and did as we damned please. After numerous threats of bodily violence, the guard turned us to the Executive Officer. He, not being able to place us again in solitary until our fourteen days of grace was over, locked us in the cells and did not order us out to the quarry any more.

A group of young men and women in Oakland and San Francisco organized regular visiting parties to the Island. Many of the civilian visitors were penalized for their sympathy with the slackers ... Others who were recognized by the guards as undesirables even disguised themselves in order to get to the Island.

Liberal, radical, even 'bolshevik' literature was received by us underground regularly. A few tricks of the trade. We had some one in New York insert a two-sheet I.W.W.[2] paper in a N.Y. Sunday Times, and the censor was fooled. Some of our papers were mailed to a Sergeant on the Island, and a trusted prisoner who was not suspected of radicalism and who worked for this non-com got hold of the papers ahead of the Sergeant and brought them in to us. A copy of the Communist Manifesto was bound in the covers of the Holy Bible, etc. Why, when the right and left wing controversy in the Socialist Party culminated in the forming of the Communist Party, some of us even signed the roll and joined the Communist Party in jail.

A change of administration at Alcatraz. Brigadier General James B. McDonald was appointed Commandant in place of Col. Garrard. Major Johnson became Executive Officer to replace Lt. Meskill. Old Col. Garrard was about 80 years and in his second childhood. He had been retired long before the war began. On declaration of war, however, he was called back to service and appointed Commandant of the Pacific Branch United States Disciplinary Barracks, and the destinies of hundreds of young Americans were placed in the hands of an old, deaf Southern Gentleman, who was physically unable to handle the situation. The result was that Alcatraz Prison was mismanaged by Col. Garrard's subordinates. The notoriety and publicity Alcatraz received after the arrival of the war Objectors may have been the cause of Col. Garrard's going back into retirement.

Executive Officer, Maj. Johnson, and the newly appointed Commandant thought that the army regulations for the punishment of military prisoners were too mild when applied to Objectors. The chaining up of prisoners to cell doors had been abolished by Sec. Baker in 1918, as a result of the undue attention attracted by the publicity given that practice by the C.O. prisoners at Leavenworth. The War Department News Bureau release No. 9, Dec. 6, 1918, read:

'The Secretary of War authorizes the following statement: Disciplinary regulations in force in military prisons have been modified by the War Department order. Fastening of prisoners to the bars of cells will no more be used as a mode of punishment. This and milder devices have been effective in the past in breaking the wilful or stubborn opposition of prisoners of the usual military type, who would not submit to work requirement of disciplinary barracks. Instead of being allowed to lie in the bunks while others worked, they were compelled to choose between working or standing in discomfort during working hours. Practically, under usual conditions, this has been more of a threat than an actuality, and as such it has been effective, but during recent months with the influx of political prisoners to the disciplinary barracks, particularly Fort Leavenworth, Kansas, extremity of attitude on the part of this new type of prisoner has at times led to extremity of discipline, as provided by military regulations. These clearly were not formulated with the political type of prisoner in mind, and their effectiveness as deterrents has been questionable. Men have returned for repeated experiences of the severest form of discipline. The most extreme of these is discarded and the order is comprehensive. It applies to not merely political prisoners, but to every other type.'

Not being able to chain us up, therefore, McDonald and Johnson conceived the idea of building 'Iron Cages,' which they afterwards named 'vestibule doors,' in which to confine men who still refused to work after repeatedly enduring dungeon and solitary punishment. These 'coffin cages' were 23 inches wide and 12 inches deep. Each cage was made of iron bars bolted to the doors of the cells. The prisoner stands upright, with an adjustable board at his back to reduce the depth to about nine inches so as to make a tight fit, – a veritable iron straight jacket. A religious Objector named Simmons and I were placed in the 'Iron Maiden' for eight hours a day, alternated by sixteen hours of solitary confinement in dark cells on a bread and water diet.

By that time our underground news traveled fast, and the American Civil Liberties Union managed to have the news of the cages on the Associated Press wired the first day they were used at the Island. The cage form of punishment for Objectors to war was introduced about a year and a half after the war for democracy was fought and won, and many of our liberals thought that it was safe to protest against this form of cruel and unusual punishment. Newspaper reporters came to the Island and the authorities had to find a way to explain the torture chambers to the War Department and to the press. Commandant McDonald's explanation was as follows: 'In other prisons they chain prisoners to the cell doors when they refuse to work. We place them in those standing cages, 'vestibule doors,' and compel them to remain in an upright position during working hours only.' All along the war, Objectors had puzzled the authorities. Col. Garrard had complained to a reporter, 'I have had more trouble with the C.O.'s, I.W.W.'s, than with any other prisoners. I came here from West Point in '77 and had many prisoner soldiers under my charge, but the C.O.'s I cannot understand. They refuse to work, some of them even refuse to eat. Now what are you going to do when you are faced with a situation like that? ... These so called C.O.'s are yellow men not white men, and as yellow men, sir, we are so treating them when they seek to break the rules of this institution.'

The undue attention or publicity was, however, successful to the limited extent that the cage punishment was not thereafter given in combination with solitary, and we who were 'caged' and put in an ordinary cell, were allowed regular rations, and were placed in the torture chambers only for eight hours every day. I endured it for about two months, until I saw my reason going, and realized that brain and body could stand no more. I had made my protest – I gave in and agreed to work and was taken out of the torture cage.

Adjutant General Harris sanctioned the use of the Iron Cages. In a letter to Beatrice Kinkhead, of Palo Alto, Cal., dated April 27, 1920, he says that the cage punishment was 'not cruel or unusual.' The Iron Maidens are still at Alcatraz, though they have not been used of late. Adjutant General Lutz Wahl, at Washington, replied to an inquirer about the cages under date of Nov. 1928:

'The arrangement of the "double cell door" as a punishment for the military prisoners at Alcatraz, was discontinued shortly after 1920, not because punishment was believed to be severe, but rather because of the undue attention attracted to it by misrepresentation as to its severity.'

Though it may be true that no one has been confined in the cages recently, I have reliable information, as late as 1929, that the 'Iron Maidens' four steel cages erected in Alcatraz military prison in January, 1920, are still in their proper places as before, ready for use.

Time and again my friends were advised that if I'd ask for clemency my release might have been granted. I never asked for mercy. On November 23, 1920, Wilson and Baker were magnanimous enough to release all Objectors. My release also was signed and forwarded to Alcatraz.

On Dec. 2, 1920, the authorities of Alcatraz Island, San Francisco, California, were ordered by the War Department to set me free. They put me in solitary confinement for refusing to sign [the] soldier's release papers which stated that I was a recruit unassigned not eligible for re-enlistment, had no previous enlistment, no horsemanship, no markmanship, etc. My answer was that I never consented to obey the draft act, that I did not recognize the government's right to make me a soldier automatically, that I did not sign any papers to get into military jails and that I would not sign any papers to get out. A wire was sent to the War Department to have my release cancelled and to have me court-martialed again for disobedience to military orders. Evidently the War Department did not care to keep me any longer, for an order was given to let me go free without my signature. So I was inducted into the service of the United States Army automatically and was released from the service also automatically, after being transferred from one military prison to another, without serving a single day in a military barracks.

The government gave me a new prison-made suit of clothes, a Dishonorable Discharge and a 'donation' of $10. I was free to face the world and the American Legion.

Notes

Source: Philip Grosser, *Uncle Sam's Devil's Island: Experiences of a Conscientious Objector in America during the World War* (Boston: Excelsior Press, 1933), 3–26.

1 Barbusse's famous antiwar novel, *Le Feu*, had first appeared in 1916.

2 I.e., International Workers of the World, known familiarly as the 'Wobblies.'

PART TWO: THE GOOD WAR

In one way it was easier in English-speaking countries to be a conscientious objector in the Second World War than it had been during the previous world conflict. At least in Britain public opinion was less hostile than earlier, and legislative provision for COs was more generous everywhere. In another way, however, COs might find it more difficult to maintain their pacifism, for this was a war against Nazism and Fascism, against the powers that suppressed freedom and savagely persecuted minorities and dissidents. This was, or seemed to be, a 'good war' (as the Second World War is often known today), which even sincere peace lovers found it difficult to oppose. Pacifism appeared to lose political relevance; most often, it had become even for its adherents a faith alone.

In May 1939, when war with Hitler's Germany seemed to be almost inevitable, Britain returned to conscription although hostilities had not yet broken out. In its CO clauses, the subsequent National Service (Armed Forces) Act of 3 September 1939 marked an advance on the legislation of the Great War dealing with the subject. As Constance Braithwaite remarks: 'The tribunals under the National Service Act were concerned only with decisions as to the exemption of conscientious objectors; they had no functions with regard to other kinds of exemption dealt with by the tribunals of the First [World] War ... and there was no army representative – to present the case against exemption ... [T]he tribunals, in general treated those applying for exemption as conscientious objectors more judicially and more efficiently than did their predecessors.' By 1939, she adds, 'the public were more familiar with the views of conscientious objectors than the public' had been in the Great War. 'Both Parliament and the administrators of the law were concerned to fit objectors into useful work which they could conscientiously perform and to minimise the occasions for law-breaking. A much larger proportion of objectors was exempted without being involved in any breach of the law.' In the Second World War there were over 48,000 COs (including some women COs) – roughly three times more than in the Great War.[1] CO tribunals could choose from three categories for applicants they considered sincere: unconditional exemption, exemption conditional on performing alternative civilian service, and non-combatant service in the army. The law, moreover, did not restrict exemption to religious pacifists: even 'selective objectors' were included, at least in theory.

Nevertheless, despite the positive factors outlined above, there *were* law-breaking COs in Second World War Britain who spent time in jail.[2] First came men sentenced to army detention by court martial; these men were in the army usually because, after being unsuccessful at their tribunals, they had then submitted to medical examination and afterwards reported to an army unit. In such cases a sentence of three months or more gave the right of appeal to a CO Appellate Tribunal. And most were eventually to gain their discharge from military detention through this channel.[3] Second, there were those COs – 'the largest group of law-breaking objectors' – who, after failing to receive any exemption or being assigned non-combatant duties, which they were unwilling to accept, had then refused medical examination, even when taken for that purpose to an army medical board under police escort. Force, however, was never applied to make them submit, but a prison sentence normally followed such refusal. Sentences usually varied between three and twelve months. 'Only one objector is known to have been sentenced to the maximum period of imprisonment of two years (which he served with the usual one-third remission).'[4] At first these men were subject to reimprisonment after serving their first sentence: 'cat-and-mouse procedure,' as in the Great War. But a clause in the National Service (No. 2) Act of 1941, passed at the end of that year, gave the right to another appeal to jailed COs sentenced to three months or more. If the Appeals Tribunal then exempted them, they were released from prison without delay. Appeal Tribunals began hearing such cases in March 1942.

This of course did not end the jailing of COs. Henceforward, however, those who spent a prolonged period in prison belonged to the third category of conscientious lawbreakers: 'those who had received from tribunals exemption conditional on performing civilian work of a type specified by the tribunal, and who did not comply with their conditions of exemption.'[5] Women COs who were jailed fell into this category; not many women were in fact imprisoned, since courts were reluctant to 'criminalize' respectable girls for this offence. Absolutists, male and female, made up the majority in this category; tribunals, as in the Great War, often found difficulty in understanding the motivations of these persons, though they were sometimes ready to concede their sincerity.

In addition to objectors to military service, Home Guard objectors – all of them men – and objectors to compulsory firewatching duties or to industrial conscription – among these there were a few women – might also find themselves behind bars for a short period.[6]

On the whole, wartime Britain, both public and government, had shown a surprising degree of tolerance of the country's pacifist minority. Despite the intensity of the struggle and the magnitude of the losses suffered through air raids or in battle overseas, COs had been treated with remarkable fairness even if there had been occasional lapses or inequities. Pacifists had responded for the most part positively, and this facilitated coexistence between the dissident minority and the overwhelming majority of the population who supported the war.

In New Zealand, however, the situation was different. In that country there were indeed barely 3000 objectors. Though the government was in the hands of the Labour Party, which had been antiwar in the previous world conflict, official policy towards COs was marked by a severity absent in other English-speaking lands. The Armed Forces Appeals Boards, set up by the New Zealand government, dealt not only with conscientious objection but with applications for exemption from military service based on 'private hardship and public interest': an arrangement that had proved very unsatisfactory in First World War Britain. COs considered to be 'genuine' were assigned to civilian work on soldier's pay or to non-combatant service in the armed forces. The definition of a CO was, moreover, a narrow one: normally only those who belonged to a pacifist denomination[7] or had been brought up in a pacifist household qualified for exemption. There was no provision for unconditional exemption or for the exemption of non-religious 'humanitarian' objectors, however sincere – or even for those COs belonging to the small but vigorous Christian Pacifist Society if they were not affiliated to a peace sect. (In fact, most of these men were Methodists.) And of course almost all Jehovah's Witnesses (JWs) ended up in jail.

Those COs who refused to conform were after a spell in prison confined under semi-penal conditions in defaulters' camps for the duration of the war. 'By 1945, 803 men had been sent to the camps.' Those 'defaulters' who refused to report for camp duty were jailed for the duration, as were those who, like Ian Hamilton (extracts from whose memoir are printed below) had refused to cooperate after reporting for duty in camp. But there were only about sixty of these intransigents. 'Unlike Britain,' J.E. Cookson writes, 'New Zealand failed dismally to produce a satisfied, generally cooperative CO population ... Ultimately perhaps New Zealand's intolerance represented the insecurities of a small [and at that date] remarkably homogenous society ... [G]overnment and pacifists diverted a lot of energy into the CO issue for little positive result.'[8]

In Second World War Australia or Canada, apart from JWs, few COs were jailed. On the other hand, by 1946 the figure for the United States amounted to over 6000.[9] Yet Congress and the administration, on the one hand, and the three historic peace churches and other pacifist organizations, on the other, had started off, when conscription was reintroduced with the Selective Training and Service Act of 16 September 1940, with high hopes that both conscience and wartime requirements could be reconciled as they had never been before.[10] The optimism continued after the shooting war began with Pearl Harbor on 7 December 1941. For those objectors unwilling to accept non-combatant army service, Civilian Public Service (CPS) camps were set up: their financing and day-to-day arrangements were in the hands of the three historic peace churches – Quakers, Mennonites, and Brethren – under the supervision of the Selective Service administration, whose director was appointed by the president. The three peace churches agreed to accept exempted COs who did not belong to their fellowship, though eventually government-run camps were established for those COs who did not wish to serve in a church-sponsored camp. Eventually, too, CPS men were permitted to serve in 'detached' units – in mental hospitals, for instance, or among the deprived in Puerto Rico. They could not, however, serve outside home territory, unlike the British or Canadian COs in the Friends Ambulance Unit, which worked during the war in Finland, North Africa, and China. For the slow undermining of what had seemed to be a vision of pacifist service incarnated in wartime CPS, I must refer readers to Sibley and Jacob's fine study of the problem.

The prisons, meanwhile, filled up with JWs because of the draft boards' inability to accept their claim to be full-time ministers of religion and therefore exempt on that score. In contrast to the British CO law, there was no provision in U.S. draft legislation for absolutist objectors. In respect to nonreligious humanitarian objectors, moreover, the position was ambiguous; despite the decisions of the United States Circuit Court of Appeals in the Kauten and Phillips cases, on 8 February and 7 May 1943 respectively, many draft boards failed to regard philosophical and ethical grounds of objection to military service as valid. They still interpreted 'religious training and belief' (the terms used in the act) narrowly so as to exclude humanist objectors.

Among the remaining almost 2000 non-Witness jailed objectors, therefore, apart from some 160 Black Muslims, religious absolutists as well as humanists and political objectors (who might also be absolutists of course) figured most prominently.

Thus, though 'the act of 1940 [was] an improvement over the law of 1917,' yet it was 'in many ways harsh and illogical.'[11]

Prison sentences on COs were fairly severe, usually ranging from a year and a day to five years. After arrest a CO was taken to a county jail, where he awaited trial – as a federal prisoner – unless released on bail. If his term was a year or less he would probably serve its entirety in a county jail 'approved for the housing of Federal prisoners,' which, for all its shortcomings when compared to conditions in federal penal institutions, was probably superior to the country's remaining three-quarters in that prison category. Those receiving sentences ranging from a year and a day to five years, and in two cases over five years, would soon be transferred to one or another type of federal prison – penitentiary, correctional institution, reformatory, prison camp, hospital prison – where they were to do their time. (Some COs, if actually drafted into the military, found themselves in an army guardhouse or disciplinary barracks where brutality was rife.) In contrast to Second World War Britain the lengthy incarceration endured by most American prison COs at least formed a favourable milieu for the production of prison memoirs, which help to illuminate the various aspects of jail life in that period. I can indeed only take a sampling here from a fairly extensive literature.

In conclusion, I may note that Second World War America's prison COs, like those in First World War Britain, succeeded in making 'a significant impact on prison life, especially with regard to racial segregation.' At various times and in various prisons, they initiated and engaged collectively in protest action, including both hunger and work strikes, against such 'prison practices [as] "Jim Crow" ... segregation, censorship of prison mail, parole practices, regimentation, and the excessive use of force.' COs also engaged as individuals in a number of largely symbolic acts of protest against what they saw as injustices in the penal system.[12] Some of these collective and individual protest actions are reflected in the narratives printed below.

To readers who would like to dip further into the CO-produced prison literature of Second World War America, I may recommend the anthology of ten brief memoirs edited by Larry Gara and Lenna Mae Gara, *A Few Small Candles: War Resisters of World War II Tell Their Stories* (Kent, OH: Kent State University Press, 1999). 'Each contributor,' write the editors in their preface, 'was asked to relate his reasons for opposing the war, what happened to him as a result of that opposition, and how he feels about the experience today.'[13]

Notes

1 Constance Braithwaite, *Conscientious Objection to Various Compulsions under British Law* (York, UK: William Sessions, 1995), 172.

2 See ibid., 203–13 ('The Law-Breakers and the Law concerning Them'). Edward Smithies, in his *Crime in Wartime: A Social History of Crime in*

World War II (London: George Allen & Unwin, 1982), 18, 19, notes: 'Refusal to perform military service [on the part of conscientious objectors] caused [a] wave of prosecutions,' especially as the number of men called up increased.

3 Stanley Hilton became a *cause célèbre.* A Jehovah's Witness (JW), Hilton spent three years and three months either in civilian prison or in military detention before gaining release from an Appellate Tribunal. See Denis Hayes, *Challenge of Conscience: The Story of the Conscientious Objectors of 1939–1949* (London: George Allen and Unwin, 1949), 108–11.

4 Braithwaite, *Conscientious Objection*, 208. This man was Ernest E. Beavor, also a JW; Hayes, *Challenge of Conscience*, 162.

5 Braithwaite, *Conscientious Objection*, 210.

6 Ibid., 213, 257–63.

7 The largest group here were the fundamentalist Christian Assemblies.

8 See J.E. Cookson, 'Pacifism and Conscientious Objection in New Zealand,' in Peter Brock and Thomas P. Socknat, eds., *Challenge to Mars: Essays on Pacifism from 1918 to 1945* (Toronto: University of Toronto Press, 1999), 292–311.

9 Of these, 4441 were JWs! Stephen M. Kohn, *Jailed for Peace: The History of American Draft Law Violators, 1658–1985* (Westport, CT: Greenwood Press, 1986), 47. JWs, in addition, usually received excessively severe sentences when compared to those imposed on 'confirmed criminals.'

10 The classic account of conscientious objection in Second World War America, not likely to be replaced as an overall survey for a long time, is Mulford Q. Sibley and Philip E. Jacob, *Conscription of Conscience: The American State and the Conscientious Objector, 1940–1947* (Ithaca, NY: Cornell University Press, 1952). The scholarly co-authors were both Quaker pacifists, but they write without a trace of sectarian bias.

11 Harry Elmer Barnes, 'Conscientious Objectors as a Correctional Problem in the Second World War,' *The Prison World* 6, no. 4 (July–August 1944), 27, 28. A sensible comment indeed. However, Barnes's comments on the Murphy-Taylor [Krawczyk] case on page 30 seem to me to be entirely unacceptable, as do many of his comments in his article 'Here Is the Truth about Springfield,' *The Prison World* 6, no. 3 (May–June 1944), 4, 5, 21, 23–5. (In protest against various abuses of the prison system Stanley Murphy and Louis Taylor had gone on hunger strike and been forcibly fed. The prison authorities attempted – unsuccessfully – to have them declared insane! Prolonged brutality failed to break the men's spirit. In the end they became almost cult figures among radical pacifists in the United States.) See also Ralph T. Templin, *Democracy and Nonviolence: The*

Role of the Individual in World Crisis (Boston: Porter Sargent Publishers, 1966), 56, 57: 'Regarding conscientious assertion (in its negative form of conscientious objection), we began as a nation by claiming the democratic right of rebellion against arbitrary authority ... We [however] were not prepared to give to conscientious assertion of the human spirit – the basic psychological democracy – a recognized place and dignity in our laws.'

12 Kohn, *Jailed for Peace*, 55–7.

13 Contributors to the volume were Bronson P. Clark, David Dellinger, Ralph DiGia, Arthur A. Dole, Larry Gara, John H. Griffith, George M. Houser, William P. Roberts, Jr, Lawrence Templin, and George Yamada. We may note that, in its statistics at least, the Bureau of Prisons distinguished between conscientious objectors and Jehovah's Witnesses, who formed the majority of COs inside American jails. However, even if the character of the offence they had committed 'differed in a fundamental way from that of other Federal offenders' (e.g., theft, fraud, forgery, trafficking in narcotic drugs, etc.), the Bureau rejected the idea that members of either group were 'political prisoners.' Its policy, therefore, was 'to deal with them – and think of them – merely as another group of convicted offenders, for whose custody and, if possible, rehabilitation, we are responsible.' While the JWs – 'a strange people' – had generally 'proven tractable prisoners,' obeying the regulations and working 'satisfactorily,' the Bureau lamented the trouble which chiefly 'absolutist' objectors of various kinds had caused the prison authorities: 'work strikes, destruction of Government property, hunger strikes which ... necessitated forced feeding, attempts to smuggle out propaganda statements, and [sometimes] complete noncooperation.' These people, the Bureau complained, 'continued to fight everything except the war.' Although most jailed war resisters had been able to adjust to 'the prison program,' the prison authorities admitted to often having had a problem in dealing with the families and friends of imprisoned objectors protesting against, as the Report put it, 'some real or fancied grievance.' Then 'the mildest pacifist [mother] sometimes becomes the fiercest lioness fighting for her cub.' 'To explain to parents and friends, who feel sure such rules are unnecessary in dealing with their boys, the reason for many rules and regulations which have been found essential in dealing with criminals, is a painstaking job.' See *Federal Prisons* (Washington: U.S. Department of Justice, Bureau of Prisons), *1943* (1944), 10, 11; *1944* (1945), 6, 7; *1946* (1947), 10, 12–15.

ALEXANDER BRYAN

Members of British tribunals for conscientious objectors, however good their intentions may have been, often found it difficult to comprehend the motives of the young men, particularly those in their late teens or early twenties, who appeared before them as applicants for exemption as COs. Understandably they sometimes made mistakes. And clearly they did so in the case of Alexander (Alex) Bryan, whom his tribunal summarily rejected, directing instead 'that his name shall, without qualification, be removed from the register of conscientious objectors.' Though his Appeal Tribunal allowed him non-combatant duties, this did not satisfy Bryan.

Aged twenty and a student at the University of Sheffield, Bryan had registered as a CO early in 1940. Perhaps superficially his credentials as a pacifist were not particularly good. He did not come from a pacifist background. He had signed the Peace Pledge Union's antiwar pledge only in 1939, not long before war broke out, and he had not subsequently been active in any of its many groups. It was as late as the beginning of the war when he began to attend Quaker meetings for worship, though he was soon to find that his spiritual home was there and not in the Methodist church in which he had been brought up. Still, his story is typical of many young British COs who had to face difficult decisions at an age when in other, more happy times they and their peers would be enjoying the carefree existence of youth.

Part of Bryan's story, that part which brought him to know three English prisons from the inside, appears in the passages printed below from the pamphlet he wrote four decades later for young Quakers of a later generation who had not experienced military conscription at first hand. During the war years conditions in British jails differed from one prison to another and from one year to another. Bryan's narrative may be compared with the other accounts in this volume of prison life in Second World War Britain.

The Imperial War Museum also interviewed Bryan for its oral-history recordings, but no transcript has so far been made of this interview. See *The Anti-War Movement, 1914–1945* (London: Imperial War Museum Dept. of Sound Recordings, n.d.), 11, 12.

... Early in the new year [1940] I returned ... to the University, and at the beginning of February the law finally caught up with me. I received a summons to appear in court for not submitting for medical examination as the first step to complying with the order of the Appellate Tribunal, before which I had appeared almost a year earlier. I pleaded guilty and was fined £5 and given a week in which to pay it. Failure to do so would mean a month's imprisonment, I was told. Then I was taken for medical examination, but I refused to undergo this. There was no attempt at coercion and I was then transported back to the police station, where I was handed the possessions, such as my watch and a bunch of keys, which had earlier been taken from me, and finally released.

Of course, I had no intention of paying the fine, and as I found it impossible to discover when I should be arrested for this, the old uncertainty and suspense settled upon me once again.

Then on March 7, 1941, the eve of my twenty-first birthday, I returned from the University to the hall of residence early in the afternoon, to be met on all sides by eager informers bursting to tell me that my arrival had long been awaited by someone who wanted to see me on an urgent matter of business. Even as I approached the steps to my corridor, I caught sight of my 'visitor.' He was standing in the main entrance looking anything but friendly. When I spoke to him he said, 'Well, have you got that money?' I shook my head and he continued: 'Then you'll have to come along with me.' I asked if he could wait until I'd had my lunch. 'Sorry,' was his reply. 'I've waited long enough already. You'll get a meal down there.' He was referring to the police station, for he was a plain clothes policeman who had been sent to collect my fine. He then gave me ten minutes to lock my possessions up in my room, I scribbled a hasty note for a friend, telling the news of my arrest, and dashed downstairs again to my escort. Then we walked together to the nearest tram stop, talking as we went. We might have been two lifelong friends, or father and son.

'I can't understand you blokes,' said the policeman. 'You all seem to know exactly what you are going to do next. Everything seems planned.

Who tells you what to say and do?' I told him that every pacifist was free to act according to the light as he saw it and that there was no question of discipline from a high authority. The discussion ended with a warning from my inquisitor of what lay immediately in front of me – a night in a prison cell prior to yet another appearance in court.

When my turn came to appear before the magistrates I declared my guilt and re-stated my refusal to pay the fine. 'Is there anything you want to say?' I was asked. 'No thank you,' I replied, 'Twenty-eight days imprisonment,' said the chairman. 'All right, get down,' he continued, after which I was led back to my cell to wait for the next move.

At 2 o'clock, along with another prisoner, I was ushered into a Black Maria and taken to Strangeways Prison in Manchester. Once inside there, my clothes were taken from me, and after having a warm bath I received in exchange a complete, but ill-fitting suit of grey and a painful pair of shoes, two sizes too small. Then I was provided with half a pint of cocoa and six ounces of bread, and while I ate that I was questioned by a harsh-faced Principal Officer, who took down particulars regarding my age, religion, home address, and so on. The stable-like appearance of the reception hall added to the grimness of the place. Everywhere was quiet: the atmosphere was faintly mysterious.

At half past seven in the evening the day's new arrivals filed into the central hall and waited to be conducted one by one to a reception cell. The prison wings, four storeys high, radiated from the centre like the spokes of a wheel. The stone flags, the iron staircases and the dim light gave the appearance of cold bareness. Library books, Bibles and prayer books were distributed to each of us, and I was eventually locked up in my temporary cell and told to go to bed. I was glad of the chance and quickly had my wooden board and mattress down on the floor. I undressed and snuggled between the clean sheets, pulled the top one well over my ears, for the blankets had been slept in before, and tried to sleep. Somebody paced up and down in the cell above me, a voice called good-night from a nearby window, and an answering call came from another wing. Then silence and I fell asleep.

At 6 o'clock the next morning the prison bell woke me. Doors were unlocked; blankets had to be folded, and we hurried to slop out and get cold water for washing from the latrines on each landing. The doors were locked again and we were given a few minutes to wash. Then breakfast was handed in to us – a plate of porridge, a mug of tea, six ounces of bread and a little pat of margarine. I ate slowly to kill time. After that I washed my cell floor and sat down to wait for the next move.

At nine o'clock, I think it was, my door was unlocked again and I was told to pack up all my possessions – sheets, comb, hairbrush, toothbrush and towel – and wait with them at the end of A Wing. By dinner time I had been before the chaplain and the deputy governor and I was settled in cell 39 on landing C3 for young offenders on remand. I was the only senior prisoner there.

To begin with I was put to work in the mailbag shop sewing bags for use by the GPO, but I had only been there for a couple of days when it was decided that I should be promoted to the position of landing cleaner. From then on I washed the slate slabs on the landing each morning and dusted the iron railings that ran along one side. It was a privileged position, but I did not fully appreciate it. In fact, I hated the job – it seemed such a waste of time.

The discipline was strict. Talking was forbidden almost everywhere – even on exercise, which consisted of walking round and round a square yard in single file several yards apart.[1]

Day after day the same things happened at exactly the same time. Always the same routine, always the same wasting of time. At 4.30 pm we were locked up for the night. I used to be the last one to be shut in, for I carried round to each cell the ration of bread for tea under the watchful eye of a prison officer. Sometimes there would be a spare ration, which he would allow me to have in addition to my own. That I *did* appreciate, for I never seemed able to satisfy my hunger on the usual rations.[2] Once inside my cell I would kick off my uncomfortable shoes, put on my cloth slippers, cover my knees with a mail bag or two for warmth – we had to sew these during the evening – and settle down slowly to eat my tea while reading a library book, spinning out this enjoyment as long as possible.

Usually I tried to get to sleep early: time seemed to pass more quickly in sleep. Five nights in succession during my imprisonment I was disturbed by the wail of air raid sirens. I had experienced air raids before, but never had I felt so afraid as I did in prison. At the first sound of the warning the officers could be heard switching off all the lights in the wings outside our cells. Then followed complete silence until the first burst of gun-fire. Outside, the moon shone brightly. The drone of aeroplanes, the explosion of bombs and the roar of the guns intensified as the raid increased in violence. For a few minutes all was noise and terror. Then silence until the next wave of enemy planes reached the city. And all the while I lay enclosed in my cell with the heavy iron door locked and double locked. Through the little high window, the moon beams cast a pale light, and from my bed I could see the outside wall of the adjoining wing and nothing more. I did not get up. I lay waiting in the darkness – for what I knew not. I could not tell how near the prison was to the danger zone. I could only listen, and wait, and imagine. Then after a longer silence the all-clear would sound, and shortly afterwards the pad-pad of the duty officer's feet would be heard on the landing outside, as he made his tour of inspection, stopped to peer through the spy glass in each cell door to make sure that all the inmates were still there.

Those five nights of suspense were for me the most trying part of my time in prison. Many people, I know, endured more air raids than I did, but relatively few had to go through them locked up in a tiny dark room three storeys high. There was one consolation, however: the prison escaped harm.

During the long hours in my cell, or as I washed the floor outside, I used to review my position as a CO with a view to settling upon the right course for me once I regained my freedom. I gave up thoughts of completing my University studies and decided to take up some sort of emergency work at the earliest possible opportunity. Practically all the students of my year had by this time been drafted into HM Forces, and I did not like the idea of taking advantage of my position as a CO to finish my studies. Apart from that, although I was within two months of taking my final exams, I had lost a valuable month of lectures and reading. Moreover, I had no idea how long it might be before I should be in prison again, for I had no intention of altering my pacifist stance. So I wrote a formal letter to the Vice-chancellor, informing him that I had decided to break my study course for the duration of the war and, as it turned out, I thus severed my connections with the University as a student in training once and for all.

[On 8 April 1942, Bryan was tried a second time for refusing to undergo medical examination prior to induction into the army.]

The court hearing was quite short and I got the sentence I was expecting – twelve months. As a second offender I was despatched to Wandsworth Prison, where I had a gloomy cell that always had to be lit artificially. To add to the air of despondence that pervaded the prison, a hanging was carried out on the site during my stay there. Though the inmates saw nothing of this, they were well aware that it was going to take place, and until it was over it seemed to generate in most of them a tacit feeling of bitter resentment and despair. To my surprise, I had not been there long when I was informed that I was to be transferred to Wormwood Scrubs Prison, which was for first offenders. Apparently, I had been sent to Wandsworth in error, for it had been officially agreed that no matter how many times a CO received a prison sentence for refusing military service he should be treated as a first offender.

Whereas in Wandsworth I was almost the only CO, in Wormwood Scrubs there must have been several hundred. At any rate, the large workshop where I sewed mailbags for several hours each day was full of them, and we were even allowed to talk to each other – a rare concession. But most of our waking hours were spent in solitary confinement. We had access to library books and we were allowed to write and receive one letter a fortnight. Visits from friends and relations were very restricted, but a Quaker 'prison chaplain' used to look me up in my cell fairly regularly, and on his initiative a Quaker meeting was held on Sundays, which I used to attend along with a number of other COs.

Almost seven weeks elapsed before I was informed of the date for my second appearance before the Appellate Tribunal. [The tribunal exempted Bryan so that he could continue as a social worker, and he was released from prison after serving nearly eight weeks of his sentence. After the war he worked with Quaker relief in the British zone of West Germany.]

Notes

Source: Alex Bryan, *'Bloody Conchies ...!' A Conscientious Objector Looks Back to World War Two* (London: Young People's Committee of Quaker Home Service, 1986), 16–20, 26.

1 Alan Litherland confirms this for Strangeways Prison: 'We weren't allowed to talk.' From Felicity Goodall, *A Question of Conscience: Conscientious Objection in the Two World Wars* (Stroud, UK: Sutton Publishing, 1997), 160. But in other prisons, for example London's Wandsworth and Wormwood Scrubs, by now this silence rule was not usually imposed.

2 In Maidstone Prison Ernest Lenderyou reports often waking 'up at night from vivid dreams of unlimited eating.' While working there on the garden party he was able to benefit from 'additional food' consisting 'mostly of raw carrots and parsnips, which we cleaned of as much dirt as possible and ate squatting behind the potting shed. We even tried raw potatoes, but most of

us found them quite unedible, even in our ravenous condition.' He was sometimes also able to obtain on the job 'uneaten porridge,' left over from remand prisoners' breakfasts. 'We intercepted [this] when we could and ate from flower pots, using bits of broken pot as spoons. The porridge was cold, congealed, lumpy, unsweetened and generally pretty awful. But it filled a gap.' From Goodall, *A Question of Conscience*, 160, 161.

PETER BROCK

In contrast to the First World War the Second World War produced very few British CO prison memoirs. Yet over 4500 objectors were sent to jail during this period, the majority of whom were convicted for refusal of medical examination under the two National Service Acts of 1939 and 1941.[1] In addition, wartime conscription was now in force in Britain for a more extended period of time than during the earlier conflict or in Second World War America. But COs in Second World War Britain, when they went to jail, went for a comparatively short time in contrast to most of their American counterparts, while conditions in British jails, though far from perfect (if perfection is ever to be found in a jail), registered a considerable improvement over those prevailing during the First World War on either side of the Atlantic.[2] Thus, there really seemed to be less to write about – at any rate less of significance.

When, however, I recently attempted systematically to recall my own experiences as a jail-CO in Second World War Britain, I found plenty to write about. True, I did not possess any letters, notes, or other documentary materials from that period. I never thought, then or long long after, of writing memoirs of any kind: I had my whole life before me, after all. And today I know I have not achieved 'total recall' through the process of 'memory retrieval.' Not surprisingly, since almost sixty years had elapsed since my incarceration. At the same time, I was indeed surprised, as were some of my friends, at how much I was able to salvage from the past, how many memories now surfaced of my prison life – incidents I had thought long forgotten, faces (though not always names) and sequences of events seemingly obliterated. I cannot, of course, guarantee that memory has not tripped me up over one or another detail.

In composing my memoir the main difficulty I had to face was to know if what, sixty years after, I thought I then thought, felt, and observed was really what I then thought, felt, and observed. But this is a problem all memoir writers inevitably face. My prison memoir was unrepentedly subjective, a personal account – without, I fear, much sociological value – and limited to two London local jails, Wandsworth Prison and Wormwood Scrubs Prison, over a time span of only four months.[3]

Aged twenty, I had been drafted in the early summer of 1940 while a second-year history student at the University of Oxford, and I was subsequently assigned to non-combatant army service through the Military Service Act's tribunal procedure. But I was unwilling to become a soldier, even if not required actually to handle a weapon. After some delay I received a court summons. Then, about a week before Christmas 1941 I had been sentenced to six months' imprisonment for refusing induction into the British armed forces; I was released from prison towards the end of April 1942, a third of my sentence being remitted for good conduct while in jail.

When, nearly sixty years later, I wrote my account, I issued it at first only in thirty-five copies, 'for private circulation' – primarily for friends and family.[4] At that date I had not yet thought of compiling the present anthology. I have printed below seven extracts from my narrative that runs to about 38,000 words. In view of the paucity of British prison memoirs from this period, I hope these pages will help fill a gap.

Early Morning Slopping-Out

Slopping-out, as this early morning ritual was called, was decidely unpleasant, though one got used to it. Every prison memoirist who has experienced slopping-out comments on it with distaste, often with expressions of repulsion. Cells in the antique jails of Britain had been built without toilets; and the landings on which the cells were located had been provided with very few toilets. As a result of this inadequacy of lavatory facilities outside and inside, when prisoners were locked in their cells after work for over fourteen hours (as they were during my spell in jail), they had no alternative except to use the chamber pot – the 'jerry,' as in Britain those now vanished domestic utensils were affectionately called – for their human wastes. A man might be suffering from diarrhea, a not infrequent concomitant of the prison diet, but he had virtually no chance of being taken out by the 'screw' (i.e., prison guard) to use one of the landing toilets, even though he might bang on his cell door and ring his cell bell for this purpose.

Every morning, after the screw on night duty had opened the cell doors prisoners emerged and lined up to pour the contents of their chamber pots into the toilet in the recess nearest their cells. I never felt my jerry was properly clean. A perfunctory swilling with cold water from the tap in the recess, where the landing toilets were located, was all that one was able to manage. Screws saw to it that prisoners did not dawdle outside their cells. Often the toilet became blocked as a result of several dozen overnight loads of excreta and toilet paper being poured rapidly – and with inadequate flushing – into one lavatory bowl; with dire results unless the landing cleaner succeeded in unblocking it. In any case even when the lavatory was not blocked, the water with which to swill the pot after its contents – but probably not all its contents – had been hurriedly deposited into the lavatory bowl had still to be drawn from the tap (where incidentally one also filled one's water jug for the cell). It was tempting, therefore, to do the whole job at the sink where the tap was located. And, it is true, there was danger of overspill if one took the pot back to the lavatory bowl and swilled it there. At the Scrubs my landing cleaner was a cheerful Jehovah's Witness (JW), always smiling and seemingly oblivious to the early morning stench. With respect to slopping-out, the person most to be pitied was probably the screw, the prison officer who guarded the prisoners' line; freshly arrived on duty that morning from an orderly suburban home, he was condemned to a lifetime of periodic supervision of this noisome procedure.

Since prisoners were required to return to their cells as soon as possible (lingering outside usually led one to get a yelling from one of the screws), at most two or three out of some twenty to thirty inmates per recess could use the recess lavatory – provided of course it wasn't blocked – for purposes of defecation before or after breakfast or other mealtime, when cell doors were briefly open. Moreover, the operation would have to be done in full view. Thus few inmates chose this way; I never did.

At the Scrubs in each landing recess there was a narrow window, slit-like, about two feet broad and perhaps five feet from top to bottom. From outside it blended into the jail's medieval defensive aspect. (One might imgine an archer standing there, poised with bow and arrow to decimate an enemy assailing the cell block.) A thick lateral and horizontal iron bar prevented egress should any exceptionally slender prisoner have tried to exit that way. Such windows were positioned beside the recess water tap and basin and constituted the only way fresh air could penetrate directly into the fetid cell block interior. Most mornings, having emptied and swilled my chamber pot, I liked, if I could, just for a moment – half a minute or so – to stand by the window and breathe the fresh air. The early morning chill was delightful, the predawn darkness almost romantic. The moment, though, passed only too quickly. Back then to the stink and the hectoring screws ... And of course breakfast, too.

Breakfast indeed was always welcome. Even though the meal consisted only of a plateful of lumpy porridge, a small loaf of bread with a pat of butter, and a mugful of tea, the prisoner had last received food around 4 p.m. the previous day and was now ravenous. The screw, assisted by a prisoner, handed the various items quickly through the open cell door, which was then at once locked. Why the rush, why the hurry? I always wondered. Or was there a reason for this hurry and rush not apparent to me from my prisoner's cell?

The Lavatorial Problem

Physical functions loom more prominently in prison cell life than they normally do outside. Their position in the life of a hospital patient is perhaps the nearest equivalent to their position in the life of a prisoner undergoing the kind of régime prevailing in my time in Wandsworth and at the Scrubs. That the mind constantly returned to the thought of food I have already said. Naturally alcoholic drink was not permitted in prison (in those days drugs were not yet an issue). Deprivation of alcohol could, of course, cause problems for a prisoner who was an alcoholic. But my financial situation outside alone precluded my drinking much alcohol. In fact, I never craved for drink although I had liked an occasional cider or shandy.

The chamber pot and its contents was, however, another question. I don't think I became obsessed with excretion and urination. (At any rate I was never a match for Dean Swift in those matters.) But one could not, I think, help being concerned – more than was normal outside – with the lavatorial question, as happens, say, when one is suffering from dysentery on a journey. Locked in a cell without access to the toilet, how could this be avoided? I was too inhibited in those days to discuss such questions with fellow prisoners but I suspect they responded in much the same way as I did.

There was one aspect of the prison lavatorial problem I shall never be able to forget. It was wartime, I know; outside, toilet rolls were rationed. So, I agree, prisoners could not be permitted unlimited access to such an essential item of civilized life. But for some screws this scarcity seems to have opened up the possibility of a little covert sadism, gave an opportunity to humiliate. A screw came round the cells every few days and handed out to each prisoner a few sheets of thin toilet paper. It was seldom sufficient, especially if one was suffering from diarrhea. One had then to go out onto the landing and ask a screw for more paper. If he was decent, he would give it discreetly after one had stated one's need. A certain screw on my landing, however, reacted quite differently to my request. Why did I need more bumf? he asked and went on to make further comments on my situation that fortunately I have managed to forget. I was stupid to be so sensitive; I am no longer so in such matters. Yet it still rankles ...

I read later of wartime prisoners tearing pages out of their cell Bible to replace the missing toilet paper. But I never contemplated doing this, not indeed from religious scruples but simply because I lacked the inventive spirit. I do not recall anyone suggesting this resolution of the problem, although it may be that my memory has let me down here.

Exercise

In Wandsworth exercise was taken in two stints: half an hour after breakfast and half an hour after midday dinner, in each case prior to the work period. At the Scrubs the exercise period was normally concentrated in one shift in the morning before work. In both prisons the exercise routine was roughly the same. As prisoners emerged from the cell block they were formed into threes. At the block doorway a screw stood to see the prisoner did not stray. If he seemed about to do so, he was at once yelled at; indeed he was often yelled at even though he kept on a straight path. At intervals screws were positioned around the prison yard facing the prisoners. Some of these were ready to converse – even to joke – with the latter as they were awaiting the order to start walking; other screws were unwilling to do this. One soon learnt to distinguish between the two types. Once set in motion, the prisoners continued to perambulate around the yard until the end of exercise time. Talking was permitted provided one kept in one's line and did not shout to prisoners in other lines.[5] Handicapped prisoners walked at their own pace alongside the revolving lines of prisoners in threes. At the Scrubs one of these was a CO with a club-foot. Obviously he would have been exempted on medical grounds if he had chosen this easy way out. Instead he chose to take his stand as a CO and, for reasons I could never figure out, had failed to gain exemption. And here he was in jail, limping along with his club-foot. Not only his fellow COs but the 'crimmos' (to use the New Zealander Ian Hamilton's apt term) admired him for his courage. I noticed a certain bitterness in his attitude to his fellow humans. But then, I don't have a club-foot.

The view from a prison exercise yard is not inspiring: on one side the serried rows of barred windows on the cell blocks and bars aplenty screening the windows of the other prison buildings. In the other direction, the high prison walls (only with the imagination could one picture what was going on on the other side), with broken glass embedded in cement at the top to prevent escapes.

My spell in jail stretched from early winter to spring: I did not experience the heat of summer, which must bring its own trials for the prisoner. The cold of January and February, in particular, could be trying, though. I recall at exercise each naked hand tucked into the opposite jacket sleeve so that each jacket cuff met the other, hopefully covering gloveless flesh. When rain or snow prevented outdoor exercise we circled in single file round and round the block landing on which our cells were located – a pretty lugubrious procession. There was usually a lot of shouting from the screws since it was more difficult for them to control the necessarily single lines in a more tightly compressed space than out of doors. For us it meant conversation was more difficult, if not impossible. I was always glad when indoor exercise came to an end.

A curious, but of course essential, feature of the prison exercise yard were the latrines. A screw was positioned to observe what went on there. I don't suppose he particularly enjoyed this but it was his job. Users of the urinals were thus exposed to full view and the wooden water-closets were little more private. Still, one soon got used to all this. In fact, I look back to the daily outdoors exercise, monotonous though it was and located in dismal surroundings (the march by the urinals might have been a not inappropriate name for it) as an enjoyable episode in the otherwise cheerless routine of prison life.

I recall that there was one way to relieve the monotony of the daily exercise. In my time the prison yards at the Scrubs had concreted surfaces from one end to the other. When spring came we saw no flowers or blossoms in that area. But in our yard at any rate several large flattish rocks remained at the side. Decent screws allowed prisoners briefly to sit on the rocks during the exercise period (the 'bastards,' though, if they were near by, did not and yelled at them to get moving double-quick). Though accustomed outside to vigorous walking and long distance hikes, prison exercise often tired me – a result, I suspect, of the meagre diet, since we were not required to overexert ourselves physically. So I took the opportunity to rest now and again on one of these stones – having made certain that a 'yeller' was not in the vicinity.

The monotonous parade around the cemented prison yard that separated the long, forbidding exterior of the Scrubs's C Hall from the equally forbidding, indeed exactly similar, exterior of D Hall might also be brightened up, as I discovered one day, by a stop at the Part-worn Store situated opposite the lateral entrance to C Hall. The Store was located in a small edifice. Its windows were, of course, heavily barred. But its door almost always stood hospitably open and often the screw in charge could be seen standing in the doorway. He was a portly man in his forties, usually smiling, and exuding an air of benevolence. As we passed by, we most days saw him talking to the guard who watched us from the entrance to C Hall. The two men obviously liked to chat together thus relieving their boredom. We filed between them in our rows of three but did not interrupt their conversation.

Prisoners, whose clothes or shoes needed repair, could exchange them at the Store – not for new garments, but for 'part-worn,' but clean, items of apparel. After several months of constant use my shoes began to cause me pain. At first I did nothing about the problem. Prison induces apathy. But the nail that was at the root of my trouble did not go away. So one day I decided to trade my shoes in at the Part-worn Store as soon as I came on exercise. As I approached the Store I saw that the Store door was open but neither of the screws was visible. I had no wish to be yelled at for intruding where I was not supposed to go. And I really did not know if, for all his promising exterior, that store screw might not be 'a bastard' at heart. But I decided to enter through the open door.[6]

When I had penetrated inside, I saw the screw, alone and seemingly with nothing to do, sitting on a chair with a wooden bench in front of him. Advancing, I said: 'I would like to get another pair of shoes, sir: there's a nail in the pair I'm wearing.' I stood waiting for his reply. He told me politely to sit down on the bench and, getting up from his chair, went to a nearby cupboard and took out several pairs of shoes. 'These should be more or less your size,' he said, 'try them on.' I did so. One pair seemed to fit me. 'Walk around in them a bit,' said the screw. Yes, they fitted. I then presented my old pair to the screw, who exclaimed brightly: 'I'll give them to the shoe-repair shop and they'll be as good as new again in no time' – for use by someone else, of course.

I left the Store with regret. How pleasant it was for a prisoner in a British wartime jail to be treated with such politeness by a screw. I would like to have lingered – and to have returned another day on a different pretext. However, my prison uniform, although it came to look increasingly worn, stubbornly resisted tear. As for my second pair of shoes, they saw me out. So alas, I really had no excuse to go back again to the Store.

Weekends

On Saturday afternoons at the Scrubs prisoners were allowed an extra period of exercise. (In my day there was no weekday afternoon exercise there.) But as the prison was short staffed, we were returned earlier than usual to our cells so that screws could return home to begin what I am sure was a well earned weekend rest, leaving a skeleton staff on duty for the holiday period. The only trouble – for us – was that at least one hour was added to the wearisome count between afternoon lock-up and our release from cells next morning. I must confess to sometimes feeling depressed on those Saturday afternoon exercises (unless brightened by a visit as they occasionally were); the grey English winter weather increased the gloom. On one such afternoon I was on my way back to my cell. Inside the block as I reached the staircase going up to the third landing where my cell was located, the line of prisoners paused as the men began to mount the stairway. A screw, whom I did not recall seeing before, was standing on guard at the foot of the staircase. He smiled at me and said more or less the following: 'It's not much fun being here, is it lad? It's much better, I know at home.' What a nice man that is, I thought. By the time I reached my cell my depression had dissipated and, having finished my bread and cocoa, I picked up the book I was reading and sank down contentedly into it, leaving the prison world far behind.

Whether in Wandsworth or at the Scrubs weekends dragged. Locked up I missed the companionship to be found in the workshop, though naturally not the mailbags I was required to patch in Wandsworth or the mattresses I attempted to stuff at the Scrubs. I might even have been glad to hear a screw's hollering, especially if he were yelling at someone else. In both prisons, from Saturday midday until Monday morning only two exercises, two slopping-outs, chapel – and your locked cell. The sounding silence of a cell block filled with prisoners in their locked cells is impossible to forget, even if it is difficult to convey to those who have not heard that silence. The stone walls of the iron-barred edifice are deadening. Yet the place is alive with faint sounds: tappings, suppressed murmurs and rustlings. You listen for the soft padding of the screw's slippers as he moves around the block on his tours of inspection. Is he at my cell door? No, that faint noise had some other source, and the spyhole in my door remains unopened.

I have to confess, however, that, for me, the weekends locked in my cell were, like the long weekday evenings, not wholly unpleasant. I at any rate had my book to immerse myself in. But for the average 'crimmo' it must have been an extremely difficult period to get through.

Visits and Letters

Prisoners in my time were allowed one visit a month of half an hour's duration. Visitors had to be near relatives or 'respectable' friends; the maximum number of visitors was, I think, three. I had been at the Scrubs several weeks before I got my first visit. It was a rather painful affair. This first visit always took place in a long cubicle. At the far end of the part occupied by the prisoner, a pane of glass intervened between the prisoner and his visitors. Communication had to be carried on, with the prisoner standing, through a wire mesh on either side of the glass pane; the glass barrier gave the impression one was suffering from a contagious disease against which the outside world needed to be shielded. Seating was provided on the other side of the glass for the visitors. But when seated they had difficulty in communicating with the prisoner. When my mother arrived accompanied by my aunt she received a shock. There was her son standing behind the glass partition in grey prison uniform. Everything was painful; my mother obviously remained distressed to the end, to the moment when a screw came up behind me and, tapping me on the shoulder, told me time was up.

I am glad to say that subsequent visits took place in a more congenial atmosphere than that first one. I knew several jailed COs, who had told their relatives not to come to see them because they did not want to subject them to the unpleasantness of that first visit. But there was no way to jump it. Those were the rules and they could not be circumvented. From the second visit onwards, however, prisoner and visitor met in a large room – with barred windows, it is true, but at the Scrubs, apart I suppose from the Governor's residence which was prisoner-free, every window without exception had its bars. A screw was of course present, perched on a high seat to the side of the room. Prison officers almost invariably tried to make themselves inconspicuous; they pretended not to hear the conversations going on below them – perhaps indeed they didn't hear them. There was no privacy of course. A row of wide tables (at the Scrubs this visiting room had formerly been the schoolroom) stretched the length of the room. Each prisoner and his visitor(s) occupied a separate table, which was closely adjacent to the next, with prisoner on one side of the table and his visitor(s) on the other. A wooden partition under the table prevented the prisoner from receiving undercover any articles from the outside. Prisoners were supposed to keep their hands on the table but I don't think screws enforced that rule. My mother did not at first take to the new environment. No other persons except us had been present in the cubicle where the first visit had taken place. But here what one said could be heard without difficulty by those seated at the tables on each side. True, there was probably little eavesdropping, since both prisoners and visitors were eager to make the most of their brief time together. After all, half an hour is over almost before it has begun. But I don't think anyone felt really at ease under such conditions – not even the presiding screw. My mother did get more or less accustomed to these conditions. But prison visits inevitably remained a source of unhappiness to her as they have been to countless others before and since.

At my last visit, however, which took place a week or two before my release, three colleagues from the social center where I was working at the time of my incarceration came to see me in place of my mother. We sat this time in a small circle on low chairs instead of facing each other across a table in close proximity to other prisoners and their visitors. Barred windows, locked doors and discreetly placed guard remained, and as before the half hour was gone in no time. But this was obviously an improvement.

The other means of communication between prisoners and their families was the monthly letter. On arrival in prison the prisoner was allowed to send out a brief message stating in which jail he was commencing his sentence and informing the addressee that he was in good health. Then the prisoner had to wait at least a month before he could apply to his landing officer for the form letter prisoners were required to use. The prison regulations concerning letter writing were printed on its first page, along with the address of the prison. The screw filled in the prisoner's name and prison number – in my case 182 Brock Peter.

All that left only about three smallish pages for the letter itself. Still, it was sometimes hard to know how to fill up these pages. And if I, a fairly well educated man, had difficulties here, how much harder it must have been for a less educated person, not to speak of someone who was illiterate like 'Jim' in the Bedmaking shop, my Scrubs location.

A major difficulty was that there was so much one could *not* say. One could not breathe a word of criticism of the prison régime even if the potatoes were rotten (as they frequently were at the Scrubs), or the heating system did not work properly, or you did not like the way the screws yelled at you. It was forbidden, too, to mention the name of another prisoner. This was not unreasonable since imprisonment brought with it the stigma of criminality; it left a stain on a man's good name and knowledge of it could be used for the purposes of blackmail. Still, the ban limited the scope of your correspondence. I remember once in my letter home inadvertently mentioning that I had met so-and-so, a CO I had known outside, a few days previously at exercise. My letter was returned to me with instructions to write a new one omitting the name of my acquaintance. Letters from outside were similarly censored (by whom I was never quite sure); and they were rationed, of course, to one a month – to the person to whom the prisoner had written his letter out. But what a joy they were to receive. I read my mother's letters, with their news of my friends that she had managed to gather, time after time.

Guards

Prison officers – 'screws' in the ubiquitous prison slang – encompassed the life of the inmate at all times and on every side. A screw woke him in the morning as he switched the cell light on. A screw was standing at the recess to guard the sloppers-out. When cell doors were open, screws circulated around the landings and a screw was usually positioned in a look-out niche on the bridges connecting one side of the landing with the other. 'Get back into your cell, you over there,' was a frequent sound at these times of the day. Outside the cell block, a prisoner, who wanted to pee or shit, had to ask a screw's permission, and not infrequently a screw was there to see him do it. Locked in his cell, when he needed to perform these natural functions he had to take precautions to be sure he would not be viewed by a screw. For the latter, unexpectedly flipping the door's spyhole open, might easily catch him at it. During a visit the screw's presence could always be felt, however unobtrusive the latter tried to be. If a believer, a prisoner would attend Sunday service in order to worship, if an unbeliever to escape the monotony of his cell. Believer and unbeliever were both subjected to the overview of screws perched above them; both felt they might at any moment hear a screw harshly reprimanding them. In the bathhouse, like the chapel regarded by many prisoners as a place of social relaxation, each cubicle had a swing door, which covered only a small portion of the aperture. A screw looked in from time to time to see that the naked figure in the tub had not taken too much hot water or perhaps to hand out clean clothing. And of course if you have broken some prison regulation he doesn't hesitate to bawl at you. There was in fact no getting away from the screws, even on the chamber pot or in the bathtub.

Of course screws surrounded prisoners at exercise and guarded their every step as they filed through the prison grounds. When prisoners were taken for some purpose outside the prison, for instance to attend a court hearing or do some job in a screw's home beyond the prison walls, he went under escort – sometimes handcuffed (and, I must in fairness add, usually in civilian clothes or overalls covering the conspicuous prison garb). I never went on any of these excursions but they were not infrequent occurrences. In fact, from the moment the Black Maria, bringing him to prison after his conviction in the court-room, had deposited him inside, the prisoner was constantly the *object* of a guard's attention – from that first frisking onward, through countless bodycounts and possibly other friskings until the day of release came.

Throughout his sentence, the prisoner was entirely dependent on the turning of the screw's key wherever he moved – was moved – within the prison. Then, if the governor passed, the screw called out, 'one on, sir – five on, sir – ten on, sir,' depending on the number of prisoners he was escorting. Back in his block and locked in his cell, the prisoner, as we have seen, was still under the screw's eye. The screw could see him, although he could not see the screw. At the end of the day the screw came without warning and, standing outside, turned the light out, plunging the cell suddenly in darkness. True, for the rest of the night, he was not likely to disturb the prisoner, but, hopefully, the latter would be sound asleep almost all that time. Finally, it was a screw who opened the gate to return the prisoner to freedom.

No wonder new prisoners, unfamiliar with prison slang, soon learn the word 'screw' – and never forget it!

Eventually I came to realize that these prison officers' working lives were not altogether enviable, even from a convict's point of view. This struck me forcibly when at the Scrubs on a number of occasions I watched our blue-uniformed screws marching (two abreast was it or in threes?) in much the same way as they marched us. This usually happened in the late afternoon. The sight seemed to me curious, and I began to understand that the quasi-military regimen to which we were subjected encompassed our guards as well. Perhaps indeed they did not mind this kind of thing since for them, after all, there were many compensations. But we, of course, disliked it – most of us, I am sure, intensely.

Release

The day at last arrived when I had to say farewell to my cell. I had to leave the screws, the 'bastards' and the 'nice guys,' to their careers within prison walls, and I had also to leave behind bolts and bars my fellow convicts, who, whether conchies or crimmos, would sooner or later follow me into freedom. I was glad to leave; in fact, I had become heartily sick of prison. I have often speculated what it can be like to serve a long sentence in a British jail (or indeed in a prison in any other part of the world). My mind boggles at the thought!

On the morning of my release after receiving breakfast, which I was too excited to eat though I had eaten every scrap of food after my first morning in jail, a screw came to collect me and, together with other prisoners being released, I was marched down to 'reception.' There a prisoner, looking a little envious, brought me my civilian clothes. My suit had been freshly pressed: a nice gesture, I thought, on the part of the prison authorities. I waited alone. Prisoners were released one by one at intervals; hopefully in this way they could be prevented from linking up with undesirable prison pals.

I began to get restless. But at last a senior officer arrived and led me down a passage to a small side-door to the prison, which he proceeded to unlock. I went out into freedom as the officer said: 'Let's not see you here again, lad.' I could only silently agree with him.

I guess every prisoner reacts in his own way to freedom regained. I celebrated my release in a rather tame way by taking a bus to Marble Arch and ordering the most elaborate of the English breakfasts offered on the menu of the near-by Cumberland Hotel.

I had not boarded the bus at the bus-stop immediately opposite the main gates of the prison. I imagined that everyone would know I was a recent inmate of that institution: although in one way I was rather proud of that status, at the same time I was a rather timid sort (as I fear I have remained), and I was not entirely sure I wanted to be stared at as an ex-convict. In fact, no one was about as I emerged from jail: it was still early in the morning. Arrived at the Cumberland Hotel I looked around and wondered if the other guests knew I had just come out of prison. True, the waiter was exceedingly polite. I enjoyed his politeness, such a contrast to being constantly yelled at by screws. But was he sincere? Of course he was, and I eventually outgrew that silly sensitivity to what strangers might think of my prison past.

In jail, like other COs I had been informally exempted from only two standard procedures applied to the convicted prisoner: photographing for criminal record and finger-printing. (Ironically, the only occasion on which I have been finger-printed occurred when much later I applied for an American residence permit in connection with my appointment as a visiting lecturer in history at Smith College in Massachusetts.) I think, therefore, my jail experiences were typical for convicts in 'my' two London prisons at that particular time.

Let me conclude by citing some light but lively verse that appeared in the samizdat journal circulated among COs at the Scrubs.

The title its anonymous author (I wish I knew his name) gave to his composition was 'The Convict's Lament,' and he adds the instruction: 'To be sung ... mournfully and with deep feeling.' The text runs as follows:

To think I ne'er again shall see
White, Gosling, Steve, McBane and Leigh:
Time marches unrelenting on.
To-morrow's dawn will find me gone.
It fairly breaks my bloomin' heart
To think for ever we must part.
Alas, no more to hear the call
Of Harris shouting in D-Hall.
No more to stand in line again
In frost and snow and wind and rain.
To say the least, it's worse than rough
To think that I'll get no more duff.[7]
I've asked the Guv'ner to be kind
And please let me remain behind,

But his consent could not be won,
There's only one thing to be done:
I'll have to make the utmost haste –
And get me well and truly 'cased!'[8]

Notes

1 Denis Hayes, *Challenge of Conscience: The Story of the Conscientious Objectors of 1939–1949* (London: George Allen and Unwin, 1949), 388, 389. Figures given on these two pages are of 'cases known to the Central Board for Conscientious Objectors ... up to December 31st, 1948.' One has, however, to extrapolate a total figure for wartime jailed COs from the diverse array of statistics assembled there. I think Hayes presents the most accurate record available.

2 'The evils of the wartime prison were partly due to ... black-out, bombing, shortage of staff ... and many improvements have been made since 1945,' writes Mark Benney in his comprehensive report prepared for the Howard League for Prison Reform, *Gaol Delivery* (London: Longman, Green and Co., 1948), v. The report was based on replies to a questionnaire sent out to 95 wartime ex-prisoners, 'almost all' of whom were COs. 'Their [responses] covered four years of wartime administration and twenty-two [penal] establishments' (p. 28). The evidence, as summarized by Benney (28–104), gives the most reliable presentation available of conditions in British prisons during the war years 1940–4. Benney incidentally was author of that classic of the London underworld, *Low Company: Describing the Evolution of a Burglar* (1936), written before he turned from crime to criminology.

3 The Governor of Wandsworth Prison during my sojourn there was Major B.D. Grew, though I do not recall him at all clearly as a person. In his autobiography, *Prison Governor* (London: Herbert Jenkins, 1958), 124–5, Grew writes sympathetically about the majority of COs in his charge. 'They had made their formal protest in court and had been sent to prison for their principles, and having made their stand against compulsory service were prepared to accept the consequences, and they got on with their sentence in a proper manner.' But he was less appreciative of the small minority of COs who refused to work or obey prison officers' orders, condemning 'their attitude of defiance' and lack of cooperation. I must thank Dr Philip Priestley for helping me to locate this source.

4 Peter Brock, *From Wandsworth to Wormwood Scrubs: One Man's View of Prison*

(Toronto: privately printed, 2000). A revised edition has appeared under the title *The Black Flower: One Man's Memory of Prison Sixty Years After* (William Sessions Ltd: York, 2001).

5 Cf. Benney, *Goal Delivery*, 50, 51: 'Until recent years ... exercise ... was ... in silence.' Benney, though, is mistaken in dating the change to the summer of 1942, since talking at exercise (and in workshops) was permitted in Wandsworth and at the Scrubs while I was there in late 1941 and early 1942. But it is true that in some other prisons the silence rule continued for a little longer. Of course, Benney is absolutely right when he states: 'prisoners *will* talk, whether you forbid them to or not, and ... prisoners *will* form friendships, however much you discourage the practice.'

6 Cf. the comment of 'Matthew (C-42893),' the imprisoned American Vietnam War resister: 'Sometimes, simple little things [are hard] like going in and asking for a new pair of shoes – my old pair wore out. It takes me a long time, sometimes, to get the courage to go in and say, "Look, my old shoes wore out, fell apart, and I need a new pair." I don't know why it is. I don't like getting into these kinds of situations, hat in hand, where they can turn me and twist me and ask questions.' From Willard Gaylin, *In the Service of Their Country: War Resisters in Prison* (New York: Viking Press, 1970), 67.

7 'Boiled pudding (PLUM *duff*).' *The Concise Oxford Dictionary of Current English* (1982 ed.), 298.

8 *The Flowery, 1942–4: The Scrubs 'Conchie' Review* (London: Central Board for Conscientious Objectors, 1945), 47; originally published in the January 1943 issue. At least five of the six men named were principal officers (POs) at the Scrubs at this time: not particularly agreeable characters, as I recall – at least viewed prisoner-wise. Not only 'Harris of D. Hall' was an accomplished shouter. (*To case:* to put prisoner 'on report' to the governor, dietary punishment with solitary confinement being at that time the usual consequence of the screw's report.) Cf. the negative verdict of Peter Ure on life at the Scrubs. On leaving that prison in May 1942 after a second Appellate Tribunal had given him a satisfactory condition of exemption, he expressed his relief that at last the mailbag sewing, 'the shouting, the lining up in threes, banging of doors, the cindery exercise yard, the intolerable clothes, had gone.' Quoted in the memoir by Frank Kermode, 'Peter Ure, 1919–1969,' in C.J. Rawson, ed., *Yeats and Anglo-Irish Literature: Critical Essays by Peter Ure* (Liverpool: Liverpool University Press, 1974), 11. Though at the beginning 'religionless' (that had not helped him at his earlier tribunals), Ure later joined the Friends Ambulance Unit; after the war he became a well-known literary scholar.

ROBERT L. HOCKLEY

Robert (Bob) Hockley was a young pacifist active in the Peace Pledge Union in the late thirties. After being called up for military service at the age of twenty-eight, he received a prison sentence on 19 September 1942 for refusing his army medical examination. He was at this time gravitating towards Quakerism; and, coming from a working-class background, he has been a socialist and a Labour Party supporter throughout his life. (His pacifism always had a keen social thrust to it.) In 1940 he had worked as a carpenter first at an army camp and then at a military airport. 'Not a very wise move,' Hockley commented later when he attributed to this experience his successive rejection by local and appellate CO tribunals. He had evidently not yet thought out his position as a CO with sufficient care, and he was to pay for it with a spell in jail.

Hockley served almost the whole of the first part of his sentence in Dorchester Prison. Of his time in that jail he retained, on the whole, 'happy recollections.'[1] His experience at the Scrubs was less idyllic, but even there he records that the days 'ticked over' nicely. Hockley indeed was a skilled handyman. An inmate of this sort was useful in a prison and might be reasonably certain he would be employed in connection with his craft. As he tells us in his memoirs, when employed at the Scrubs 'repairing prison plants' he was, for most of the time, left alone in the workshop by the screw in charge – and 'actually I made several items' for him. And, he writes, in the electrician shop, where he sometimes worked, he succeeded in making 'items not always connected with the prison.' (But what exactly these were he does not tell us.) Hockley, though, was a special kind of craftsman, for he was an amateur violinist who played in quartets and he also composed verse! His musical talents were displayed in the concert held at the Scrubs on Christmas Day 1942. Thus, because of his unusual qualifications he brings something special to his description of his 'six months hard' jail term.

Announcing the decision of the Bench the chairman said 'Six months hard labour.' The magistrates were very sorry, but they were simply concerned with the order for medical examination 'which defendant had refused.' My father was the last to see me at the police station and brought cakes and chocolate ... [I was now] placed in a ... cell with a merchant seaman charged with (according to him) stealing electric torches. His fears were mainly due to 101 other convictions that might tell against him. A week's remand had been given. A little after 2 p.m. we were taken to a 'state-car' and the journey to Winchester Gaol began.

As one can imagine, my thoughts, whilst the car containing two policemen as well as the sailor and myself sped through the town, was when should I see it again? Brilliant sunshine made the journey ... quite pleasant. I think the sailor enjoyed the cigarettes given him by the driver and my chocolate went down well. The large green doors were the first view of a prison for me and it was only a matter of minutes before we were 'inside.' Passing through the inner barred door of the 'gate' (a feature of all prisons) the four of us passed down to the 'reception' underground. This moving from place to place was accompanied by a jangle of keys, for needless to say all doors were locked.

Preliminaries of warrants and all property taken, even the Youth Hostel badge I was wearing, the reception officer gave me an illustrated magazine and put me in a reception cell. A small 'slit window,' with external bars, gave a poor light to the small cell, whose only furniture was a table and chair. The quiet atmosphere was the first thing which impressed one; except for the muffled sounds of passers-by nothing else was heard. A short time elapsed and then I was taken to the reception office, height and weight being taken. The next item was to place all my clothes in a bag and proceed to the bathroom. Whilst bathing, my prison outfit, which consisted of a white striped shirt and gaberdine tie, flannel coat (1 breast pocket only), gaberdine trousers (no pockets), black socks (with a red stripe around the ankle) and leather shoes, was hung on the door by a prisoner. Another wait in the reception cell and tea or supper was handed in. A pint mug (minus handle) of cocoa accompanied by a piece of bread (8 ozs?) and small pat of butter did not take long to consume. Before leaving the cell the gas-light was turned on and with five others I was taken into the main part of the prison and lined up grasping our pillow slip which contained 2 sheets, 1 towel, 1 handkerchief and a tooth brush. Calling out our names and asking if we had been in prison before, an officer then proceeded to state several rules including one regarding making application to see the chaplain, doctor, Governor or even the King!

The main block of Winchester Prison is built on the same style as most H.M. Prisons, being in the form of a hub with blocks of landings going out like spokes, one line of cells at the bottom with three landings on top reached by a metal spiral staircase and metal balusters.[2] Stretched across from side to side of the first landing is coarse wire netting. At the end of the block was a window the height of the building. In the middle of each landing a recess with a W.C., two wash basins, a water tap and a large sink (for slops) was used by the occupants of the ten cells.

To return to the next part of the proceedings which was the issuing of books, ... I received the following: a Bible and prayer book, one fiction and one non-fiction. We were then given our cell numbers and I found myself looking for B.4.84. This cell which was on the top landing was one away from the end window. The librarian spoke words of encouragement and showed me the right landing, and an officer coming along escorted me to the cell and finding I had 'hard labour' took the mattress away, remarking that 14 days would soon pass. This deprivation of mattress is the only distinction between imprisonment and 'hard labour.' As soon as the gas jet, which was in a foot square opening with no glass, was lighted (from outside, by removing the covering strip of tin), [I undertook] a detailed examination ... Two small tables, one square and the other triangle, a 6 ft. by 2 ft. bedboard, one washbowl, ewer and chamber, three blankets, one bedrug, a mirror on the wall and a chair completed the outfit. Cell measurements were approximately 12 ft. long, 6 ft. wide, 10 ft. high with a curved ceiling; window 7 ft. from floor, 3 ft. 6 ins. by 2 ft. with 21 panes. The floor was black [stone]. Walls were stone, coloured part from floor to a black dado about 4 ft. high and white distemper the rest.

Having so much to take note of, the hour or so till the light was turned out soon passed, and my first night in prison began. Going to bed at 9 o'clock found me awake sometime after 6 o'clock and this was to be a regular habit. 7 o'clock the unlocking of doors began and I followed the rest to the recess to 'empty out.' Breakfast, consisting of thin porridge in a not too clean tin, with two thick slices of bread and a 'pat' i.e. said to be margarine and butter mixed, was brought round the landings by prison orderlies supervised by officers. Being Sunday, there was no labour, and after strolling round [the exercise yard] in pairs for a short time we re-entered the prison to attend the Church of England service. One of the first points I noticed was the barred windows; it seemed so wrong and contradictory to the 'way' as taught by Jesus. The Chapel was similar to any small parish church, having organ on left of altar a pulpit on right. I well remember the lesson and sermon being taken from Daniel. (The lesson was read by a Salvation Army officer) ... The men's singing during hymns did not synchronize with the organ and a medley of sound was heard after the first line.

Greens and potatoes is all I remember of dinner. Rain in the afternoon did not permit the exercise to be taken outside so we walked around the landings instead. Supper at 4 o'clock concluded the day. I think my feelings after that first day were of general satisfaction that prison was not so bad as I imagined and [that] it could have been a lot worse.

Monday morning after breakfast my name was called (or perhaps yelled would be more accurate) along with several others, and we lined up to see the doctor. A very brief 'look over' and a question or two regarding former illnesses and the examination was over. Next item the Governor (or was it the Chief Officer?) ... I was then told that I was going to Dorchester ... which ... made me extremely happy remembering [some good things] I had been told of this prison. These two interviews with long waits in the intervals (another feature of prison, time has no meaning it seems) took nearly all the morning. But before dinner myself and another C.O., who was likewise bound for Dorchester, were taken into a workshop and started winding into large balls skeins of rope. Labour and exercise filled the afternoon. On Tuesday morning a razor was passed into the cell and the preparations for the journey began. Leaving the cell as I had found it and saying goodbye to several I had spoken to, the transfers were paraded in the Hall. Books, sheets and oddments were collected and our [civilian] clothes were given us and we quickly changed. While waiting for the conveyance handcuffs were brought out and I found myself [joined] siamese-twin fashion to an ex-policeman [now a prisoner]. The number of times we assembled and were checked over seemed farcical. A private char-a-banc stood waiting by the gate and once again a check was made when we were safely inside. Passing through the gate into the world again so soon seemed almost a miracle and with the pleasant sunshine to gladden our journey at least one heart was content. Cigarettes were given by the two officers who accompanied us, and my 'other half' received mine, 8 in all ... We had left Winchester at 11 o'clock and at 1 o'clock Dorchester was reached. The gardens right outside the 'gate' and general prim look of well-being contrasted well with the dreary fortress just left behind.

A Spiritualist, and a Roman Catholic with the other C.O. shared the cell, and dinner commenced. After the meals at Winchester this one looked a feast; a large tin of corn-beef, mash with bread and cheese followed by a new bun and jam. Then followed a lengthy discussion [led] mainly by the Spiritualist, who rather upset the Biblical C.O. whose faith was mostly quotations from the Scriptures. A mug of cocoa and a good lump of bread and 'fat' with about ° oz. of demerara sugar came at 4.30 p.m. Clothes were exchanged and sheets etc. being given, we filed into the main prison to hear the 6 o'clock news on the prison radio. [Dorchester Prison was] built with landings like Winchester but with only two wings and a small office in the centre. [I was assigned to] B.4.14 ... and to this cell I went just as the gas was lighted. My fellow C.O. was next door. The following extract from [my] first letter [home] may be interesting: 'As you may observe by the new address I am now spending my days close to the Dorset countryside. A pleasant "coach" ride brought us safely here. The conditions and staff here – not forgetting the building – is "streets ahead" of the last "habitual domicile." Today has been the first work-day of my prison life and it has seen me busy making a mail bag ... Radio by courtesy of the Governor is the next and last item to-day. By the way I obtained permission from the last named to receive the [Quaker] *Friend* weekly, it may help to keep a closer touch with the outside affairs of mice and men, so please forward like steamship luggage wanted on voyage!!'

One of the happy recollections of Dorchester is the exercise circle with the flowers and rose trees in the centre and the vegetables on the outside. The good portions of food in clean utensils made mealtimes something to be looked forward to. I do not remember a cold or poorly-cooked meal. The first week was spent sewing mail bags, not a difficult or hard task, but monotonous. However, it was with feelings of joy that I departed from the Governor after being told I was to be 'carpenter red-band.' This implied liberty to walk without always having an officer and gave one quite a status.

The same afternoon instead of exercise we (the carpenter whose place I was taking and the plumber red-band) went into the prison workshop and, overalls donned, the works officer, Mr. T., the carpenter and myself passed out of the gate heading for the officer's house. The officer's house was one of a terrace adjacent to the prison, and our job was re-decorating. A cup of tea and cakes went down well in the middle of the afternoon ...

Perhaps at this point a few details of the average day would help to form a mental picture of a day in Dorchester. The first sound that broke the morning silence was the rising hand-bell at 6.50 a.m., 7 o'clock heard the jangle of the officers' (known to all as 'Screws') keys unlocking doors. By this time I had washed, and my door being opened, I joined the procession to the recess to 'empty-up.' Returning to cell and closing door, blankets and sheets were folded and a look round the view from the window, standing of course, on the chair. I formed a daily habit of reading a chapter of the Old Testament, and this utilized the interval until 7.30 when breakfast was served by three prison orderlies and the screw following to slam the door. One pint of porridge – made with oatmeal I understand – one pint of tea, rather too strong for me, but weak for most others, six ozs. of bread and [a] small round of butter-margarine. I found this sufficient and managed to save a portion of bread. After breakfast till 9 o'clock I worked on the cell task, generally completing a mail bag. Sewing the seams of mail bags becomes quite easy after a little practice, the most difficult being the rope edging around the top. 9 o'clock the door being opened again, we filed down to the exercise circle outside. I being in the Works Dept. went straight to the workshop and prepared for the day's job. Those on exercise walked in pairs a few paces apart, much earnest conversation being carried on. Overalls donned, the works officer and myself passed through the gate and outside to the officer's house where we were decorating. Front bedroom, stairs, parlour and hall were painted and papered throughout. At 10 o'clock approx. a cup of tea or cocoa with cakes or sandwiches was greatly enjoyed. We returned to the workshop to wash (hot water from kitchen) at 11.45, and at 12 o'clock took our dinner off the table in the Hall. The Kitchen screw supervised the handing out. Dinner consisted of 22 ozs. of food including 2 ozs. of bread, and there were a number of types [of meal served]. Vegetable hot-pot with potatoes and suet pudding. Meat stew with potatoes and greens and treacle pudding. Bacon and beans with potatoes and jam bun. Corned beef, potatoes and greens and rice and prunes. Cold meat, potatoes and greens and jam bun. The meals were always hot and nicely cooked. The Chief Prison Officer told me they were lucky in having a good cook who [took] an interest in his job. Like breakfast it was sufficient, and on three days one oz. of cheese was added. I saved mine for tea.

Another mail bag and perhaps a little reading filled the time till 2 o'clock. My window overlooked the gate and clock so I always had the time.

2 o'clock, and the same procedure followed as at 9 o'clock, and the

afternoon was spent as happy as the morning, including the break for tea and cakes at 3 o'clock. Returning just after 4 p.m. we washed and chatted till 4.30 as the tea or supper (?) was being taken round. One pint of thick cocoa (said to be ship's cocoa which if left till cold a layer of white fat formed on top), 8 ozs. of bread, one round of fat (butter-margarine) about the size of a penny ... and two tablespoons of demerara sugar, was the last meal of the day. Finishing the cell task, which was sometimes two and sometimes three whole bags a day, quickly brought the time to 6 o'clock when the doors were opened to allow us to hear the news, the sound of the music being heard several minutes before this. Unless one has been entirely cut off from all other channels of news, one cannot appreciate what a boon the 6 o'clock news was, besides being an opportunity for conversation with the other prisoners. The news over and the doors slammed the books next received attention, the only disturbance was the 7.30 p.m. chance to 'empty up.' As the light faded the gas was lighted by my fellow 'works red-band,' the plumber. Just before 9 o'clock the bell was rung and at the hour the lights turned out. It was my habit to be in bed before lights out, and the day concluded with a chapter from the Bible. Several nights I heard the 9 o'clock news coming from the officer's wireless in the Gate. Firewatch was needless to say done by the officers ...

One quickly got into the routine, and for those confined to sewing mail bags all day it must have seemed very monotonous, but the days spent decorating soon passed. A weekly change of underclothes, shirt, handkerchief and towel was effected during the bath. The Works' bath-day was Friday ...

The prospect of a journey to London, a change of prison and an early release [because of another Appelate Tribunal there on October 21st] made the remaining days at Dorchester very happy indeed. Easier contact with officers on account of my 'red-band' made conversation possible, and many interesting discussions were enjoyed ... Sunday Oct. 11th stands out above the rest for it was on this last Sunday at Dorchester that a large table in the prison laundry collapsed, and after the morning service I spent my time repairing it. The other Works 'red-band' assisted me and several officers came in to watch progress including the Chief who remarked amidst other matters how handy I was to them, and how seldom they get a carpenter there, in fact they could use me quite a lot.

However, everything ends with time and on Thursday 15th, after a very pleasant 3 weeks, I said 'Au revoir' to my job of decorating, to the officers in the Works Dept. and the prison in general (as far as possible) and prepared to leave. A walk to see the doctor, and being asked if I was 'all right' walked out again which finished that part. A glance at me fully dressed had seemed sufficient! After tea I packed the pillow slip with sheets and the other personal items, and was taken to the reception cells near the Gate. A naval rating, also leaving in the morning, was in the next cell. Undressing and throwing the prison clothes outside the door I entered the cell and dressed again, this time into my own clothes. A copy of Shakespeare's works I kept to read, the other books were handed in. It was not unnatural, I suppose, that a great deal of speculation went on in my mind as to the future, but whether the Appeal was to be successful or otherwise a journey to London with a change of prison was something that was not forthcoming every day.

At sometime after 6 a.m. the next day I was called and the light put on. I arose and had my last porridge and bread. As I was waiting the officer (P.O.), who travelled with me, arrived and the only part that betrayed his identity was his cap, otherwise his dark mac and dark blue trousers gave no sign of his connection with H.M. Prison. Whilst waiting for the car to take us to the station an escort took the young naval rating away. The 7.20 train to Waterloo was punctual and I found myself in a reserved compartment much to the annoyance of other travellers who subsequently joined the train and wanted a seat. It was not long before an earnest and frank discussion on various subjects, including, of course, pacifism and socialism, and the officer's views on these subjects were very close to my own. He mentioned how his father had been on the 'Gate' at Wormwood Scrubs for 20 years, and it was during the railways' amalgamation and he getting dismissed from a railway office, started with the prison service as a clerk. Eventually he donned the uniform and had risen to Principal Officer in 15 years, but his opinion was such that if it was not for a pension he would not stay. During the journey he gave me chocolate and several egg sandwiches, which was greatly appreciated. Handcuffs were not used, the P.O. remarking he knew who to trust.

Waterloo and the usual hustle and bustle of a large London terminus, but on this occasion instead of dashing for tube or bus we entered a waiting car and were quickly speeding through the traffic ... My first view of Wormwood Scrubs was a 20 ft. wall a short distance from the road ... behind the officers' houses. Other tradesmen's vehicles were in front of us, and as only one at a time was admitted between the double doors, we waited several minutes. Entering the prison one sees the Chapel with its Spanish columns and flower beds in front and the ends of the Halls on either side ...

[After Hockley's application to the Appellate Tribunal for exemption from army service was turned down he remained at the Scrubs, where he served the rest of his sentence. His memoirs include his impressions of that prison, which in general resemble those given in Peter Brock's memoir, though they are of a slightly later date.]

All prospects of an early release now gone I quickly settled down and began to make full use of time ... The days were 'ticking over' nicely now ... [As he wrote home,] 'I again find myself in the privileged position of carpenter in the Engineering Department of H.M. Prisons. Mentioning my trade to the booking clerk in the Mailbag shop (to which I had been first assigned) he forthwith spoke on my behalf to the P.O. concerned. Last Tuesday during exercise I saw him myself and within two hours was engaged in erecting a partition. Quick work!!'

The high-light of [my time at the Scrubs] was the presence of charismatic prison journalist Herbert Moore in the next cell [and it] transformed the rest of my time in prison; we shared all we had, even intimate matters of our lives outside.[3] From the first introduction till waving good bye on the way out, anything that would be done to ease the burdens he did cheerfully, and I endeavoured to reciprocate. Perhaps the finest witness he made during his 8 months' stay was that of a voluntary fast of 21 days to give support to Ron Smith who was fasting as a protest against a second sentence of 12 months for refusal of medical examination. These two stalwarts, who were joined by a third for a short while, lived on a pound of bread daily and steadfastly refused anything else, although every meal was a temptation and testing time. Apart from a natural loss of weight there were no after effects, in fact Herbert stoutly asserted it cleared his head extremely well ...

Undoubtedly the deepest impression [of prison life] was the taking away of one's individuality and treating one as a unit with a number. Apart from first offenders being star-men, there is no segregation between the various criminals. Homosexuals, [those committing] petty and grand larceny, thieves and housebreakers, murderers and others who had used violence on their fellow men, in fact, wrongdoers of all types are herded together ... The [odd] part about all these anti-socials is that few portray the characteristics which are associated with those who have strayed from the normal path.

Notes

Source: Robert L. Hockley, 'Prison Memoirs,' typescript in the Archives of the Peace Pledge Union (London), pp. 3–19. Another, not greatly different, version of these memoirs has appeared in Hockley's privately printed autobiography *Beyond the Next Hill: My Story*, ed. Hilary Clark (Wolverhampton: The Model Printers, 1998), 58–94, under the title 'My Witness [pts.] 1–3.'

1 A First World War Quaker CO, Wilfrid E. Littleboy, has also recorded happy recollections of his sojourn in H.M. Prison, Dorchester in 1917–19. 'I spent almost exactly two years at Dorchester,' he writes, 'one of the least unpleasant of H.M. Prisons, and the experiences of those of us at Dorchester were, on the whole, easier than those in many of the bigger gaols. Dorchester is built on a hill overlooking the Frome valley, of which we could get occasional glimpses. Thrushes and blackbirds sang in the governor's garden, curlews sometimes called at night. The prison was small and we [COs] formed the majority of its inhabitants. The warders found there were some advantages in having to deal with us rather than with their usual charges, and as they were mostly good fellows we got on with them comfortably enough.' See his article in the *Friend* (21 September 1934), 869. Littleboy almost seems to have found his two years in Dorchester Prison a relief after his '112 days' hard labour' at the Scrubs!

But compare the Dorchester jail experiences in the Second World War of Tom Burke, a working-class CO who ultimately became a Quaker. There Burke found himself 'in a cell with two other men. The only thing they had in common was their chamber pots.' In addition, 'Tom had the unfortunate experience of being in Dorchester when there was to be an execution. Executions took place at eight o'clock in the morning. As this hour approached, the prison fell quiet ... Then, as the local church clock struck eight, the prison erupted into a frenzy of sound – a wailing, hopeless sound. All hell was let loose as the prisoners banged, shouted and screamed.' In fact, however, the condemned man had been reprieved at the last moment, life imprisonment replacing capital punishment. See Audrey Pitchforth, ed., *Faith into Action: Recollections* (Hemel Hempstead, UK: Preparative Meeting of the Religious Society of Friends, [1999]), 28.

2 I can confirm from my own experience in Wandsworth Prison and at the Scrubs the bleak and cheerless appearance in this period of the interiors of British prisons. In fairness, however, I should quote from a letter from the Quaker prison visitor at Durham Prison, dated 12 March 1942. He writes of 'something about the prison ... which is ... much to its credit ... In the main

hall of the prison itself there are pleasant pictures on the wall, giving a cheerful appearance to the building.' He notes, too, that from the cell window of the Quaker inmate whom he had been visiting 'there is a glorious view of the magnificent cathedral of Durham.' 'This inspiring view,' he was sure, would help the young man in his ordeal and to some extent offset his otherwise grim surroundings. The latter, we may add, was indeed lucky not only in possessing such a prison outlook but also in being permitted by the authorities to look out without fear of punishment, for in most prisons it was an offence for a prisoner to do this from his cell window, placed as it usually was high up in the wall. (From Archives of Friends Home Service Committee: Prison Minister's Sub-committee, Correspondence 1942, Library of the Religious Society of Friends, London.) Over half a century later Gilbert Rigg told friends how he spent the long evenings after having been locked in his cell in Liverpool's Walton Prison already in the late afternoon. He made the meagre evening meal last as long as he could. Then he got up. 'There was a window, very high up. If [he] stood on the back of his chair, leaning his body against the wall to balance, he could just see out of the window. He could see and hear some lads playing football and he would watch as long as he could manage to stay on the chair.' See Pitchford, *Faith into Action* (note 1 above), 10.

3 According to Fenner Brockway in his introduction to *The Flowery ... The Scrubs 'Conchie' Review*, 4, 'Herbert F. Moore ... largely originated *The Flowery* and was responsible for its first five issues.' And Moore's prison friend, Bob Hockley, wrote *inter alia* concerning Moore: 'We are next to each other in the cells and on the table' for meals in association. 'He cannot go without a smile when with others ... There is no sign of prison on his face.'

ERNEST SPRING

Most prisoners, conscientious or otherwise, serve their sentences in a civil jail or penitentiary.[1] The number of those detained in military prisons, though, is likely to rise in wartime, especially when conscription is in force. Since at least the 1880s COs have occasionally found themselves in these uncongenial surroundings, whether in the form of a tsarist penal battalion, an American or British detention barracks, or an army prison elsewhere. In such institutions military discipline is combined with penal conditions to create a regime of unusual harshness matched in few civil prisons.

In British-army slang, military detention barracks became known as 'glass-houses.' In one of these places (a category of jail distinct from the section of London's Wandsworth Prison in which the Canadian Christadelphian John Evans had been lodged in the Great War) Ernest Spring found himself briefly during the Second World War. He later wrote an account of his experiences there that is, I believe, unique in CO prison literature.

Spring, a law-court reporter before being called up, had been working part-time in civil defence during the London Blitz when, in September 1941, having previously registered as a CO, he was summoned to appear before a tribunal. There, he tells us, 'I ... expressed my willingness, in a non-combatant capacity, to co-operate in supplying the soldier with his needs as a human being. It was enough. Without resorting to any cross-examination, the Tribunal exempted me from combatant military service.' Private Spring, no. 97005910, served first with the Pioneer Corps and then in a unit of the Non-Combatant Corps (NCC) until demobbed in November 1945 after the war was over. For a time he had worked as a volunteer in a bomb-disposal squad, certainly a dangerous occupation.

On several occasions Spring clashed on a matter of principle with the army: for instance, when he insisted on his right as a non-combatant to refuse construction work connected with an ammunition dump. Labour of that kind, he told his commanding officer, was 'incompatible with true non-combatancy.' He felt it would be 'the thin end of the wedge,' though he was prepared in a spirit of compromise to work as a dining-room orderly in the workers' camp, indeed in any army camp. Neither the threat of an eighteen-month jail sentence nor (to his 'surprise') the readiness of the majority in his NCC unit to continue working at the dump succeeded in moving him. The compliance of the latter in engaging in what was clearly war work he charitably assigns either to their being family men afraid on that account to risk the possible consequences of refusal or to their membership in the Plymouth Brethren (either 'Open' Brethren or the still more rigid 'Exclusive' Brethren), who believed in obeying the powers that be, according to the Pauline injunction. On this account, indeed, the Brethren were strongly represented in the NCC. There they obeyed all orders except any to shoulder a rifle.

What brought Spring a twenty-eight-day sentence in the glass-house was a comparatively minor affair: refusal to perform physical exercises he thought the medical officer had excused him from on health grounds. 'I was,' he relates, 'a prisoner in the guard room for several days while arrangements were made for my admission to the detention barracks. The guards were decent, even friendly, to me. With me in the lock-up were three other sentenced men, each waiting to serve 21 days ... I maintained a buoyant spirit, resolved to meet my misfortunes without repining.'

In The Glass-House

The bleak hills above Chorley in Lancashire were powdered with snow as I came to the Detention Barracks, via Manchester. During the rail journey ... I puffed philosophically at my pipe, knowing I would have to part with it 'inside.' An escort of four NCOs had charge of the three unfortunates of whom I was one. They kept watchful eyes on us from the very moment of our setting out ... On the train they raised their voices in song – perhaps to impart a little cheer to those soon to be 'in durance vile.' In contrasting our respective lots they must have found it easy to resort to light-heartedness.

Chorley's notorious place of detention was formerly a bleaching mill, at the foot of an incline on the fringe of the town.

The party entered the precincts at a slow pace as though to defer the inevitable farewell to freedom for the time being, then lined up for a few words of 'welcome' from the RSM [regimental sergeant major]. A heavily built, ramrod-backed man with a flushed face, his speech was pungent and emphatic. 'Obey orders and keep your mouths shut,' was what it amounted to. It ended: 'I got no friends here, and I don't want none.'

Passing through the main door of the barracks (unlocked after the ringing of a bell), we marched into a room labelled 'Receptions,' and were curtly commanded to strip. Every article of clothing, every item of equipment, was carefully searched for cigarettes, tobacco, matches and/or razor blades. Valuables were deposited with a sergeant, who entered particulars in a ledger. I stood there wearing only PT shorts and shoes, everything else being heaped on the floor. Things to use in detention were chucked on to an outspread blanket. After a shower bath, I re-dressed.

Outside, squads of prisoners carrying rifles tramped heavily on the iron-plated floor of a long corridor. The mechanical precision of their movements as they marked time or went forward at the behest of frosty-faced 'screws' made sounds which fell ominously on my ears.

I was given a number (155) and put in 'B' company; and with my bedding and possessions tied up in a blanket (minus those confiscated) I passed along the corridor and up flights of stone steps to the company's quarters. Here some 150 men were domiciled. This section of the barracks was in three divisions, each caged-off from a landing by strong wire mesh and having its own door. By a small bare room for the use of the company commander stood a trestle table and a bench for the staff sergeants. Set off from the landing were rows of troughs and taps for ablutions.

Getting to my bunk, I was surrounded by prisoners all apparently anxious to assist in sorting out my bundle. When I became more familiar with goings-on, I tumbled to the import of these attentions. My tunic, trousers and greatcoat were whisked away to be brushed for possible specks of tobacco dust for secret indulgence of the craving for a whiff. Smoking was most strictly forbidden, but this did not deter men making wretched 'gaspers' from a mixture of tobacco grounds, obtained in the manner described, and residue tea leaves smuggled from the kitchen. The method of lighting the fags was extremely ingenious. A tiny heap of powder would be scraped from the bone handle of a toothbrush and converted into a red glow by means of sparks induced by striking a safety razor blade on a minute flint embedded in a bootbrush. When lit, the fag would be shared between three or four men, who of course had to keep a sharp look out for 'screws.' None of the three rooms had a window, but daylight came in through the glass roof, under which wire netting was spread. Every man had a large washing bowl and a three-legged stool by his bed. Meals were eaten out of a tin basin or tin plate with the aid of a spoon, knives and forks being prohibited. Kits were arranged with meticulous exactitude, and all metal articles shone like silver. Even dustbins, buckets and hurricane lamps were thus polished, and the pair of planks on each bunk scrubbed almost white. Spare clothing was neatly folded and stacked on a shelf running the length of the room, and underneath this hung service equipment such as respirators, packs and water-bottles. Rifles were placed in racks outside on the landing. Not possessing a combatant's equipment, I had less cleaning and polishing to do than my companions. I believe I was the only non-combatant in Chorley at the time. The total number of prisoners was about 500.

My first sight of the Commandant was on the afternoon of my admission. All the new arrivals paraded in the gymnasium, in a corner of which the Commandant had his office, and were marched in batches into the office by the RSM. The Commandant had a few stern words to say to each man after glancing at the documents before him. When my turn came, the following dialogue ensued:

COMMANDANT (appraising me with gimlet eyes): You were sentenced to 28 days for refusing to obey an order and for using a highly improper remark to a warrant officer.

MYSELF: Yes, sir.

COMMANDANT: Were you drunk?

MYSELF: No, sir. I am in effect a teetotaller.

COMMANDANT: Then why did you not comply with the order?

MYSELF: Because, sir, it required me to perform physical exercises for which I was unfitted and from which I had been exempted by a medical officer.

COMMANDANT (raising his eyebrows): Hm; if you want to appeal against this you can do so from here. Have you considered the question of appealing?

MYSELF: Yes, sir, and I have decided the more sensible course is for me to serve my sentence. I'm not in for a long time, and it will be an interesting experience.

COMMANDANT: Very well. I see you are in the NCC. Are you a conscientious objector?

MYSELF: Yes, sir.

COMMANDANT: On what grounds?

MYSELF: On religious and humanitarian grounds.

COMMANDANT: Humanitarian! (This with a note of asperity.) Are you willing then that little children should be murdered?

MYSELF: I am unable to discuss this with you, sir. (I had almost brought myself to ask 'Are you referring, sir, to the obliteration bombing of Berlin, Hamburg and other German towns?' but prudence curbed my tongue!)

The day started at 6 am when the night duty screw bawled, 'Come on, let's 'ave yer.' Within a minute or so one had to be out of bed or risk a report to the company commander.

Procedure on rising was first to fold blankets and then to scrub or wash planks and stool and the floor under and around the two-tier bunk. It was obligatory to remove shirt and vest for ablutions, and the allotted time for shaving was five minutes. All razors were kept in the stores and had to be handed in after use. Pulled up once for 'blueness about the gills,' I was asked whether I had shaved that day. I stated that I had. 'What with?' was the next question. My name and number were taken, but nothing ensued. Before breakfast there was scrubbing to do, on the landing or downstairs in the corridor, which was sometimes filthy with spillings from the latrine buckets carried along there early each morning.

At meal parades no wearing of tunics was permitted and sleeves had to be rolled to the elbow. Talking was against orders. Every ten yards or so all the way to the kitchen a screw was stationed to detect any infringement of the regulations. When the main body had mustered in the long shed-like structure which adjoined the kitchen, a screw was sure to be seen stealthily approaching behind the backs of the men in the manner of a cat stalking pigeons.

The daily menu was this:

Breakfast: Porridge, two slices of bread, a pat of butter and cocoa.

Dinner: Potatoes (cooked in their jackets and unsalted), meat, soup, peas (or swedes or cabbage), rice without milk, and half a slice of bread.

Tea: Two slices of bread and margarine; small piece of cheese and tea.

Supper: Cocoa only.

The tea was never sweetened, neither was the porridge or cocoa. Porridge had no milk, or precious little of it, and resembled a thin gruel. Dinner was the one satisfying meal, but rendered less appetizing by partly bad potatoes and the mean deprivation of salt. Furthermore, as the last meal of the day was at 4 pm nourishment as well as drink was needed by 7 pm. The food was dished out in old, battered tins, and consumed in that part of the building where one was quartered.

My room-mates included two soldiers in for two years for desertion. Another was doing 12 months for smuggling articles from America over a period of two years. He was caught in the act as a result of a warning to customs officials that Merchant Navy men were suspected of peddling dope, and must therefore be closely searched on coming ashore.

The bulk of the prisoners with whom I had contact were absentees from their respective units and displayed no desire to be in the firing line. Not a few of them wanted to be out of the war altogether, and declared they would dodge service again as soon as they were clear of Chorley. A brawny artilleryman regaled me with lurid tales of various detention barracks he had sampled in the past ten years. 'I've seen,' he said, 'a nigger knock out eight screws at Aldershot, where there was a riot because of harsh treatment.' Two years ago, he averred, Chorley was the worst of the DBs [detention barracks]. Conditions eased up after the Government Commission issued its report on detention barracks throughout the country, following the manslaughter of a prisoner at Chatham. 'Paddy,' a volatile and voluble Irishman, who occupied a bunk near mine, was extremely lewd and foul-tongued, yet he preserved such a lively sense of humour that I could not dislike him. He was fond of giving me sly digs, and our relationship, at first unpromising, became amicable. At the start of our acquaintance he called me unpretty names for being a Conchie, and when I inadvertently stepped on a blanket he was folding on the floor, he abused me with all the richness of the language at his command. 'Paddy,' I said, 'I offer you my apologies. If there's anything I can do for you ...' Paddy grinned, and thereafter addressed me as 'Charlie boy' and never lost his temper with me.

A Pioneer who refused his food went on 'hunger-strike' as a protest against his 'wrongful' imprisonment. He kept this up for seven days but on the eighth day accepted liquid nourishment, followed up by a bowl of skilly. His fast was brought to the notice of the Commandant, who promised to forward an appeal on his behalf. Later, the hunger-striker angrily told a screw, 'Don't talk to me like a dog.' Men were overheard to say 'Hear, hear.' The screw summoned a colleague and shouted, 'Men here have been making cat-calls.' He announced through the wire mesh: 'The whole company will be on a report. In future you all stand when a staff sergeant enters the room and remain standing until he has left.'

We were in the middle of breakfast and the screw came in, thus compelling every man to rise from his stool. He walked slowly round as we continued our meal on our feet, and there were plenty of ugly looks behind his back. To a 'stretch' (long sentence man) he said, 'I broke the spirit of one bloody company and I'm going to do the same to this ——— lot.' Standing Orders, with which prisoners were familiarized on admission, laid down that staff NCOs must be addressed as 'Staff,' and that when speaking to or spoken to by an NCO a prisoner must stand to attention.

With one or two exceptions, the screws were a hectoring and sadistic type, and classed as 'bastards.' Rumour had it that no warder dare show himself alone in the streets of Chorley at night, so unsavoury was the reputation of the barracks staff in the town. A Cockney was the most human of the staff sergeants. With a knowledge of glass-house life obtained from a 56 days' sentence earlier in the war (he himself confessed it), he naturally had something of a fellow-feeling towards the inmates. I was once or twice in a squad he drilled on 'the square.' He put everyone in good humour with his (rather crude) witticisms, and if no officer was in the offing he would, instead of drilling us, pass the time with familiarities, which provoked immoderate guffaws. Heaven knows there wasn't much else to fetch a laugh.

Foot drill and saluting on the march figured in the programme most mornings and afternoons, and there was also PT, ... rifle drill, bren gun and grenade-throwing instruction. The MO [medical officer] exempted me from PT but I voluntarily joined in light exercises with a special squad. The alternative was to link up with the Industrial Section, members of which performed various menial, dull and dirty tasks, principally inside the barracks. I preferred the activities on the square, which at least enabled me to get into the open air. I was a passive listener at the arms 'lectures,' at which bored NCOs filled in the time by desultory questions or invitations to men in the class to demonstrate what they knew of the subject.

Two incidents at one of these lectures tickled the fancy of the class but did not amuse the humourless instructor. A youth who had paid scant attention to the proceedings (a gun was being assembled) was noticed by the sergeant. 'Come out 'ere, you,' he yelled. The youth ambled forward listlessly. 'Tell us what you remember of what I've been telling you of.' With a devil-may-care air, the youth said 'I'm not interested.' A look of incredulity spread over the face of the screw, and the class pricked up its ears. 'You're not interested, eh?' spluttered the instructor. ''Owzat?' A hush of expectancy, then 'It just don't interest me.' Said the youth, 'I should never 'ave bin called up. I never 'ad a proper medical.' The only thing for the screw to do, was to write down the youth's name and number, and hint darkly at a report.

In the same class a prisoner was invited to display his knowledge (or lack of it) of the subject in hand. 'I don't know nowt,' he said, but his professed ignorance struck me as a pose – a prelude to taking a rise out of the instructor. 'What's up with you?' he was asked. The answer was, 'I'm in the "Q" Pioneers; I'm mentally deficient, I am.' In the ripple of sniggering, the screw could do nothing but order the dumb one back to his place.

Newspapers never came the way of prisoners; the only substitute was the bulletin which could be heard on the tannoy in some sections of the barracks. One's proximity to the loudspeaker was important if anything was to be heard, not to mention the disposition of the warder on duty, who might disregard pleas of 'Make it a bit louder, Staff' ...

On Sundays three separate services were held simultaneously for the C of Es, the RCs and the Free Church adherents. The latter were all lumped together as 'Wesleyans' ... Apart from this break, Sunday was a wearisome day, polishing and scrubbing forming the principal activity. No matter how burnished utensils might be, the rubbing with cloth and brickdust had to go on, or one was liable to incur a fatigue job outside the cage. Conversation in groups was 'verboten,' the one permissible recreation being reading books from the library between 8 and 9 pm. The library, stocked with a few dozen volumes ... was looked after by a 'stretch' man. At 9 o'clock the lights were dimmed, but by now most of the unhappy souls were quiescent on their bunks.

Once around midnight I was awakened by a prisoner singing 'Shine through my dreams.' His voice was melodious and he completed two verses, yet he was asleep! I had heard of somnambulists, but this was the first time I knew that anyone could actually sing in his sleep. In the morning I enquired of the man whether he realized he had sung 'Shine through my dreams' and he thought I was joking.

An eagerly awaited event was the distribution of mail – our one tangible link with the world outside. All incoming and outgoing letters were censored. Letter-writing day was Saturday, when each man received a single sheet of paper and could borrow a one-inch long stub of pencil. A miniature envelope was issued as well. Any article that arrived was kept for the recipient in the office until his release. The office was dusty and disordered; piles of documents and oddments littered the shelves and tables, and I heard a sergeant exclaim, 'This place is run by a set of nitwits.'

Scrounging was prevalent. My own losses were a towel, a bootbrush and a toothbrush – the latter no doubt purloined on account of its bone handle, indispensable for the dodge of lighting fag ends. A missing towel was recovered by a screw from underneath my blankets after its owner had notified the loss. This looked rather bad for me, but I was able to satisfy the screw I was not to blame. Patently the towel was planted on me by the scrounger in a moment of panic.

A missing regimental badge led to the entire company having to line up while two sergeants searched all pockets, but they soon tired of the business or concluded that the culprit had rid himself of the badge.

Regularly on Friday afternoons a route march took place for prisoners not serving long sentences. The ban had its *raison d'être* in the stronger incentive they had to 'do a bunk,' though one gauged the chance of escape as nil. The marchers wore full equipment and carried rifles, and covered six or seven miles over hilly roads away from built-up areas. I would have gone on the march, but not having a combatant's equipment was excluded from the chance of getting out of the barracks, albeit for a short spell.

The building was surrounded by formidable barbed-wire fencing in addition to other obstacles to unauthorized egress or ingress. A breakaway was attempted by one prisoner, but his freedom was nominal.

A screw on a bicycle accompanied the marchers, who were naturally kept under close scrutiny by their escorts. 'There was no dog-ends where we went,' lamented an acquaintance of mine. He amusingly pictured the avidity with which everybody tried to spot discarded cigarette ends along the route. 'Even if we saw any,' he said, 'we were bound to have been nabbed by a screw.'

Not less than once a week, every inmate had to submit to a hair crop, heads being shorn of all they grew below the crown. Bread and water diet was the penalty for a man who refused to have the scissors applied twice in a week. Prisoners had the right to bring a grievance to the Commandant and to the Visiting Officer if desired. This official came every seven days, the entire complement of men parading before him on the square. Anyone with a complaint had to advance at the double. I saw two prisoners leave the ranks to acquaint the Visiting Officer with their complaints. They were taken to the guard room. One was charged with approaching the officer without first notifying the commandant, as laid down in the rules. He was awarded 'Number one diet' (bread and water).

Lavatory arrangements were primitive, and in some respects deplorable. Bunks stood less than 6 ft from buckets in constant use throughout the night and ineffectively screened. Sanitary men emptied them in a drain by the parade ground.

From his sanctum at the entrance to the barracks, the RSM put over the tannoy announcements to each company. These generally related to suspensions of sentence, interviews with the commandant and such matters. A man with several months yet to serve dramatically heard during a 6.30 am broadcast that he was to be ready for release at 7 am. A remission of this kind was in consequence of a prisoner's unit being on the eve of departure for active service abroad and subject to his willingness to rejoin the unit.

Nearing the completion of his time, a man might be selected for the privileged task of working in the Sergeants' Mess, beyond the main gate.

'Going sick' involved the familiar inanity of donning full kit as for field manoeuvres (minus the rifle). The army authorities have an ingrained scepticism concerning soldiers who report sick. It can't be said that this is never justified, and he who parades for the medical officer is not encouraged to repeat the move. For a genuinely sick man to be compelled to burden himself substantially with all the accoutrements of soldiering is fat-headed, especially when he may have to march some distance with his paraphernalia and wait maybe for hours until the medico is ready to examine him.

The MO's panacea for numerous ills was the 'milk diet' – watered-down tinned milk and bread (two slices) – which a patient might have for breakfast, dinner and tea. There was no escaping the MO's prescription, for the names of the milk-dieters were passed on to the screws, who saw that all diets were doled out before meals were served to the rest of the inmates. Such commiserating remarks as 'Hard luck, mate' could be heard as the diet men passed the waiting queues. The food, unpalatable to me at first, I soon ate greedily and my weight increased. This added poundage, however, was due to the fact that on admission to the barracks I was weighed in my pants, while at the finish I stood on the weighing machine wearing heavy boots and full uniform!

The Commandant was not much in evidence except when disciplinary matters called for attention. He was not sadistic or sullen or officious like so many of the staff. Having recalled to him the title of my unit and the nature of my offence, he smiled and said he supposed I would come there again. I assured him I had no desire to sample Chorley a second time.

At meal times a whistle was blown. We stood in line, and on the blast being repeated we briskly stepped forward half a pace in unison (rather was it a jump to the front). The whistle sounded again, and we then turned with a double stamp to the right or left, as the case might be.

After the gate at the top of the stairs had been locked, anyone wishing to enter the company's quarters indicated his presence by flickering the electric light by means of a switch at hand. On seeing the light flicker, prisoners shouted 'Gate, Staff,' in case the screw on duty was unaware that a person was seeking admission. This obliging gesture significantly ceased during the duty period of a screw who was beastly to us.

I greeted the passing of each day with thankfulness. I apprehended that conditions could have been worse, notwithstanding which I loathed the lack of privacy (of which there was absolutely none), the utter denial of the normal freedoms, the punitive restraints, the snarling posture of those in authority over the transgressors. Yet existence was not altogether unrelieved by humour and the humanities, else it would have been degrading and desolating. I came across soldiers under sentence to whom Chorley was 'a piece of cake,' but these were oldtimers in detention with rankling memories of other glass-houses. A minor annoyance was the nightly 'chug-chugging' of the overhead pipe connected to the boiler house, but one gradually became inured to its monotonous rhythm. I felt the cold outside only when doing PT in shorts in a draughty shed used in wet weather. Exercises in the open air were performed with jackets off and sleeves rolled; and it was near to refined torture to be compelled to keep one's cold palms pressed down on rough cinders and to engage in 'wheelbarrow' races.

Approach of the discharge date allowed me the privilege of tidying up, cleaning the floor and peeling potatoes in the sergeants' quarters. Back in the cage, I was besieged by men wanting to know how much 'snout' I had managed to spot and secrete on my person. I hadn't any. The mess had been given the once-over by the sergeants. Not even under the piano nor in the grate was there the tiniest fag end. Those sergeants knew more than a thing or two about soldiers under sentence! The maximum number of marks obtainable in a day was eight. A register stated the total needed for remission. An NCO was empowered to dock marks for infringements of standing orders. By the skin of my teeth, I escaped a loss of marks on account of hairs left in my shaving mug. I was able to get my shaving water warmed by a pal filling his water bottle overnight and tying it to the heating pipe which ran the length of the room at a height of ten feet. The screw who detected my 'serious crime' (his own words) let me off with a caution.

With other 'releases' I lined up to receive my kit bag and its detained contents. One by one we were called to a desk to sign for the deposited articles. On signing the register we were not handed anything, and I demurred at giving a receipt before ensuring that belongings were intact. An NCO instructed an orderly to fetch the belongings from the store. 'I hope you'll now believe we're not thieves and vagabonds,' remarked the man at the desk tartly.

In the midst of silently intoning a song in my heart on this last day in detention, I had a nasty jolt. While the check-over was in progress, the supervising screw enquired whether any man was short of any item. I mentioned my loss of a towel, toothbrush and hairbrush (which had been scrounged), and was dismayed to hear I would have to be on a report. Three fellow releases were in the same boat, but as the screw bustled round concentrating on affairs of the moment, he forgot the matter of the shortages. I saw no reason to remind him or mind when he called for the names of those whose kits were incomplete.

Chorley had a tradition that a man due for discharge bequeathed his last breakfast porridge to someone remaining. My own skilly had been booked a week previously, it being pointed out that I would soon be enjoying a square meal.

At 8 am I shook hands with a number of mates in the cage and, with a letter I was asked to post secreted in my kit bag, I went down the steps for the last time. What was left to do was to make a final appearance before the Commandant. There were some 20 releases in all. We were marched into the office. The Commandant addressed each man tersely. Obviously the occasion was generally regarded as one for the maxim 'The least said the better.' Here is what the Commandant said, and the replies.

To No. 1: I see you have had detention no less than six times. Let me warn you that if you commit an offence again you will be in for a much longer time. – Yessir.

To No. 2: How is it that you got into this trouble? – Don't know, sir.

Have you got a home? – No sir.

No father? – No sir.
No mother? – No sir.
H'm – well, pull yourself together in future. – Yessir.
To No. 3: Have you done with this nonsense now? – Yessir.
You really mean that? – Yessir.
To No. 4: Have you learned your lesson? – Yessir.
To No. 5: And you? – Yessir.

I was number 6. The Commandant reminded himself of my case by consulting documents on his table. 'You are one of those men who think too much of their own opinions and talk too much.' I smiled – just a ghost of a smile. The Commandant was drawing a bow at a venture. He jerked his head and regarded me coldly. I gazed at him fixedly. Raising his voice he said I could still lose my remission. Did I understand that? He did not see what there was to laugh at. 'Take that smile off your face instantly.' I was ordered to stand to one side until the men at the end of the line had been disposed of.

Two minutes later I was alone with the Commandant and the RSM. I half-feared that my exit from Chorley was fated to be postponed. I said, 'I smiled at what you said to me, sir, because you do not really know me.' The Commandant then questioned me about my pre-Service occupation, and after I had supplied him with some details his manner underwent a change. He was no longer abrupt and frigid. He was even amiable. I had a notion he thought I would be writing a newspaper article on Chorley. He wanted my impressions of the barracks and enquired whether I had read Mr Justice Uthwatt's Report on DB Administration in this country. He advised me to get a copy and study it. Perhaps it was to correct any unfavourable impressions I had formed in Chorley – as though my experience of it could be refuted by any whitewashing findings! Dismissing me from his presence, the Commandant, to my astonishment, directed the RSM to show me anything I cared to see. He mentioned the instruction centre where classes were held periodically for prisoners training as drivers of motor vehicles. The RSM, somewhat taken aback by this request, I think, dutifully complied with it, and imparted all the information I sought. He stressed that the Commandant had initiated several improvements at the barracks and that one under way related to the sanitary system.

A corporal from Hereford came as an escort for me. The Commandant had said I should not regard an escort as an indignity, but agreed that in my case it was perhaps unnecessary. Some conscientious objectors, he said, declined to sign their release papers, and as thereby they gave no undertaking to return to their unit, it was customary to send for escorts for all non-combatants leaving Chorley.

As the gates of the barracks closed behind me, I encountered four soldiers, glum of mien, heading for them. Passing by, I shouted, 'Good luck – it's not too bad inside.'[2] My escort was a companionable fellow and soon calling me by my Christian name.

How sweet on the train were the puffs at my old cherrywood as I gazed at the flying landscape and ruminated on the events of the past!

That night I rejoined the 12th NCC Company at Hereford ... In my kitbag was a brand new pair of boots. How they got there was a mystery. I liked to think that a kindly screw at Chorley could have supplied the answer!

Notes

Source: Ernest Spring, *'Conchie': The Wartime Experiences of a Conscientious Objector* (London: Leo Cooper, 1975), 2, 68–86, 95.

1 In Britain during the Second World War a few very young COs were incarcerated briefly in a special boy's prison or Borstal institution, where they sometimes received rough treatment. This happened, for instance, to an eighteen-year-old Jehovah's Witness, William Heard, early in the war at the boys' prison at Feltham (Middlesex). While prison officers turned a blind eye to what was going on, throughout the seven weeks he spent there in mid-1940 inmate gangs harrassed young Heard, at first the only C.O. at Feltham. His front teeth were knocked out; at night the sanitary bucket of his dormitory was emptied over his head, while scalding cocoa was poured over his head in the canteen. Understandably, Heard took a dim view of the juvenile delinquents who were his constant companions at Feltham. (He narrowly missed meeting the sixteen-year-old Brendan Behan, who had spent a month at Feltham earlier that year before being assigned to an open Borstal; see the famous Irish playwright's classic prison memoir, *Borstal Boy* [1958]).

Three years later another JW, Douglas Beavor (son of Ernest Beavor, see above p. 178) served two sentences at Feltham, amounting in all to ten months. However, in contrast to the 'rough time' juvenile COs had had there earlier, Beavor describes his own treatment as 'quite fair' and most of the prison officers as 'quite understanding.' At this date COs mixed with other inmates only at exercise and work. I am grateful to the Imperial War Museum (London) Sound Archive for providing me with tapes of hitherto untranscribed interviews with D.E. Beavor (no. 4788/1), E.E. Beavor (no. 4787/2), and W.H.R. Heard (no. 4760/4). All three men had – unsuccessfully – claimed unconditional exemption as full-time 'ministers of religion,' the usual JW practice in a conflict in which they considered themselves to be 'neutrals.' This stance often angered the authorities. Sentencing Ernest Beavor to an unprecedented two years in prison, the magistrate declared: 'I think you're the worst of your kind.' Inadvertently, he had given Beavor the opportunity to read the whole Bible consecutively from Genesis to Revelation as well as convert several of the warders to his faith! See also Keith Thompson, 'Inside a Boys' Prison: Five Weeks in "Free Association" with Others,' *C.B.C.O. Bulletin* (London), no. 33 (November 1942), 13–14, for a non-Witness CO's impressions of Feltham Prison. 'After the official preliminaries at the Receptions,' writes Thompson, 'I found myself dressed in Borstal uniform, with brown [jacket], short trousers and studded boots.' In the South House, where Thompson was now sent to begin a three-months' sentence, he found 'eighty prisoners comprising house-breakers, male prostitutes, forgers, Black market dealers, frauds, and [young] men convicted of assault – and, to his relief, three fellow 'conchies.' Most of the crimos were illiterate. 'We soon made friends with our immediate neighbours, and so as to enjoy a fuller intercourse with them I compiled and learned four pages of their slang. We taught two lads to read and we read stories to those unwilling to learn. Writing [a] letter home for those unable to write was oftern amusing ...' Sanitation, alas, was 'exceptionally poor.' 'One W.C. had to suffice for eight of us, and even that allowed us no privacy. Sometimes we would have to wait half an hour to use it, and there was always a fear of [venereal] disease. In the dormitories, with twenty beds in each, an uncovered bucket was placed in the middle for all purposes. In the hot nights of June this was distinctly unpleasant.' Eventual transfer to Wormwood Scrubs proved a relief 'though to leave what we considered a good work among other youthful delinquents cause[s] us some pangs.'

2 The *C.B.C.O. Bulletin* published two brief accounts by COs of their experiences in military detention barracks around this time that were considerably less favourable than Spring's: John A. Lindsay, 'I Was in Detention Barracks' (no. 28, June 1942: 3–6) and Robert Foster, 'An Open Letter to *Picture Post* ... on Detention Barracks' (no. 29, July 1942: 13, 14). See Denis Hayes, *Challenge of Conscience: The Story of the Conscientious Objectors of*

1939–1949 (London: George Allen and Unwin, 1949), 103–6, who writes: 'Many C.O.s had little difficulty in Dentention Barracks [and military prisons], but there were a few notorious exceptions, some of which came to light when the Oliver Committee was holding its Enquiry into Detention Barracks in 1943.' Both Lindsay and Foster in their accounts revealed the prevalence of brutality in at least some army detention barracks.

KATHLEEN LONSDALE

Second World War Britain was the first English-speaking country to conscript women into one of its women's wartime services (though without compulsion to handle a 'lethal weapon' unless the woman consented). Britain, therefore, was the first such country to produce women COs. A few of them, absolutists and JWs, were jailed. Unfortunately, none of these women, so far as I am aware, produced a prison memoir. They were indeed mostly working class and, therefore, not usually trained to undertake such a task.

One woman pacifist who went to jail was the distinguished Quaker scientist Kathleen Lonsdale.[1] She spent a month in London's Holloway Prison for Women for refusing compulsory fire-watching duties against incendiary bombs from enemy planes. These duties were obligatory for women between August 1942 and September 1944, and no provision existed for conscientious objection in the case of either men or women. However, Lonsdale, if she had wished, could have obtained exemption as the mother of three children under the age of fourteen. But she chose, instead, prosecution and prison – not because she objected to the duties themselves but because she felt that both a connection with war-making and a wartime civil-liberties issue were involved.

Soon afterwards she wrote an account of prison life, printed below, that is factual and balanced, with an emphasis on medical problems since it was published by the Prison Medical Reform Council. Though brief, Lonsdale's memoir is worth reading, not only on account of the intellectual credentials of the writer, but also because of the scarcity from this period of prison memoirs by women prisoners, whether conscientious or otherwise.

I left Uxbridge Police Court in the police van at about 1.30 p.m. on 22nd January, 1943, and was taken first to Rochester Row Police

Station, where we were all put into another police van and taken to Holloway Prison. Here we were locked into separate reception cells. I remained in this cell for about 3° hours. There was no printed card in the cell giving any sort of information as to procedure, nor was there any bell. I gathered, by listening, that the only way of attracting attention (for example, if one wished to use the W.C.) was to shout. The W.C. in the reception wing was used by all prisoners, healthy or diseased, since no one had had a medical examination. As most of us had had a lengthy journey, nearly everyone had to use it. There was no alternative.

Some prisoners had their bath before the doctor arrived. I listened with interest to the patient, and finally successful, efforts of the bathwomen to persuade an old prisoner whom they addressed as 'Granny' to enter the bath. After some time I was taken into a little cubicle, where a nurse examined my hair and asked me if I had any fits or varicose veins, and if my periods were regular. I told her that I had had a hysterectomy, and she enquired when. She asked if I had any children and how old they were. I replied 'Three; now 13, 11 and 8,' whereupon she said that I had done my duty to the country in that respect. This was perhaps the most comprehensive medical examination I had. I then returned to my tiny cell and was shut in again. From remarks shouted outside I gathered that we now had to wait for the doctor. When she eventually came I was fully dressed, wearing a high-necked blouse and tie. 'These women should have had their blouses undone,' she called to the reception officer. When I began to take off my tie – 'No, it doesn't matter,' she said, 'leave it!'; and placed the stethoscope to my *throat* for a second or two. 'Any fits or varicose veins?' she asked. I said, 'No.' The question 'Periods all right?' was again answered by a reference to my hysterectomy, which apparently did not interest her. That concluded the medical examination proper, from beginning to end of which I was fully dressed. On the basis of this examination I was passed as fit for any work and allocated to B4 landing. I fully agreed with other prisoners who afterwards remarked to me that this examination could not distinguish those women who were suffering from V.D. or those who for various reasons were unfit to carry heavy loads or to do the harder forms of work. A woman who wished to conceal a state of pregnancy could also do so quite easily in the earlier stages. My later enquiries showed that this brief examination was the usual thing. Only those prisoners whose previous history was such that the doctor had very good cause for suspicion, or who had admitted to symptoms which were suspicious in themselves, were set aside for a later and more comprehensive survey.

That it was fully recognized that some forms of contagious disease could be overlooked at the reception examination was proved by the fact that prisoners sent to work in the kitchens *or in the officers' quarters* were given a second and more rigorous examination.

After the doctor had seen me I was again locked into the reception cell, from which I was finally brought to strip and change into prison clothes. I suppose it would have been possible for the officer then on duty to notice whether my body was covered with sores (a thing that the doctor certainly could not have seen) but she was fully occupied and did not appear to be observing me. I was weighed (in a cotton wrap only, at the end of an exhausting day during which I had had very little food. The next routine weighing took place some two or three weeks later, just after the mid-day meal, and with the prisoners fully dressed except for shoes. I probably showed a very satisfactory rise). Then my belongings were checked over, and I was allowed to keep my wedding ring, spectacles, spectacle-case and two hair-slides. I was not warned to keep my pocket-comb, and it did not occur to me to ask if I might do so. I did ask if I might keep a large clean handkerchief, as I needed one; but I was told that this was not allowed, and that I would be given one in my 'bundle.' So, in fact, I was; but I afterwards found that there were not nearly enough to go round; that many women had none at all and that it was hopeless to expect a change when the first was soiled. Indeed, when I was due for discharge a kindly officer advised me not to put my handkerchief into my bundle of dirty clothes, *but to give it to a woman who had not had one!*

When I went into the bath cubicle for my 'reception bath' the prisoner in attendance said to me, 'The water is quite cold. I wouldn't have a bath if I were you.' As I had had a hot bath the same morning I gratefully agreed to skip the bath and dressed straight away. If I had been filthy it would, I suppose, have been the same choice – a cold bath or none at all. My prison clothes (in mid-winter) consisted of cotton vest and knickers – voluminous enough to have spared material for half a dozen handkerchiefs and still fitted – a cotton frock lined half way down the back, black woollen stockings and shoes. In my cell I found a dark blue serge cloak (the temporary property of a series of my predecessors) which I was expected to wear on outdoor exercise. It was greasy with dirt all round the neck, so I scrubbed it all over and shivered until it dried. After a day or two a kindly officer, seeing a group of us sitting shivering outside the Governor's office, cried, 'Oh, good gracious, you girls *must* be cold,' and fetched us all little sleeveless woollen coatees. With this and the work-apron that I was given still later, I managed to keep reasonably warm.

My shoes had to be selected (in a hurry, for I was the last, and the officers and women were tired and irritable) from a pile which were not even arranged in pairs. I suppose that they had been tumbled about by previous prisoners. In my anxiety to choose a pair that did not pinch I chose badly. One shoe soon developed a habit of slipping its fastening; both were like hedgehogs inside after a couple of days. However, I was at first so deadened to feeling of all kind that I did not even notice the nails until I found that both my feet were bleeding from small punctures. (They were not properly healed until nearly a month after my discharge.) Bandages are not legitimately obtainable except by the procedure known as 'booking for the M.O.' I did not feel inclined to miss the day's exercise in order to do this, so I used a few scraps of new flannel left in my cell by the previous occupant to pack my shoes until they were endurable; and put two of my scanty sheets of toilet paper inside my stockings to keep the black dye away from the sores. These shoes had been repaired in the prison workshop. It seems a pity that when women are taught to do a useful job, such as cobbling, they should not be taught to do it properly. The prison shoes were a disgrace; no woman could hope to walk comfortably or gracefully in them; for women with 'difficult' feet they must have been sheer misery. The discomfort was increased by the fact that the woollen stockings given to me had holes in them nearly large enough to put my fist through, nor had I any means of mending them or of keeping them up. A kindly prisoner, seeing that I was reduced, when on exercise, to clutching one stocking with each hand, presented me with a pair of garters, for which I was grateful and about which I asked no questions.

Apart from vest, knickers, dress and stockings, my 'reception bundle' contained two sheets, a pillowslip, nightdress (identical in length with the vest; both came just below my knees), towel, handkerchief, facecloth and toothbrush. In my cell I found a tiny piece of soap, not more than 1 in. ∞ 1 in. ∞ ˇ in. in size (which had to last me for all purposes for over a week) and a very slimy rag, both left by the previous occupant. The slimy rag was a floorcloth and was the only one I could get, though later on a neighbour employed in the 'workroom' gave me a piece of cloth which I kept for my enamelware, furniture and windowpanes. Unfortunately, the rag and the soap were not the only things that my predecessor had left behind her. On the shelf were a dried piece of bread and some crusts; on the floor were dried faeces; under the mattress were some grimy hair-curling rags, and on the floor, furniture and all the utensils was a layer of dirt and grease. One of my neighbours told me that I was unlucky; my predecessor had been a 'very dirty girl.' It was quite evident that no attempt had been made to clean or disinfect the cell after she had left it. It was impossible to do anything about it that first evening; the next day I borrowed one of the few scrubbing-brushes on the landing and effected what transformation I could with the minimum of soap. I was thankful to find no vermin.

While waiting in my cell the first morning I read with interest the 'Notes for the Guidance of Prisoners – Women,' of which I had two copies. Rule 4 said: 'You are required to keep yourself clean and neat ... You will have a bath once a week ... You should ask your Landing Officer for any toilet articles with which you have not been supplied ...' As I had been given neither hairbrush nor comb, I took the first opportunity of asking the landing officer for either or both. She smiled: 'My dear woman,' she said, 'I can't give you a comb; we haven't got any.' (Brushes were apparently unheard-of luxuries.) I visualized the state of my curly locks after a month of no attention and asked *how* I could get one. 'I don't know,' she said. 'Didn't you have one in your handbag when you came?' I agreed that I had, but pointed out that it had been put away with the rest of my belongings. 'You'll have to apply to the doctor to have it taken out,' she advised, 'but to-day is Saturday. You can't book for the M.O. until Monday, except for something *really* serious.' I booked on Monday, therefore (meanwhile borrowing the comb of a clean and very obliging neighbour) and obtained my own comb on Tuesday, four days after entry. On Thursday a small, bent, dirty prison comb appeared on my cell table. I don't know who put it there, but it was immediately begged from me by a prisoner who had been in a week and had no means at all of doing her hair. I was warned by an officer to carry my own comb about with me, as if I left it in my cell it would certainly be stolen by some unfortunate prisoner who had none. Three weeks after my entry there was a hair-drill. In view of the absence of hair-brushes and the impossibility of washing the hair properly with the small portion of coarse soap provided, it is not surprising that the officer examining my hair told me severely that my scalp was full of dandruff.

I learned, by advice from other prisoners, that I could obtain my own corsets, which have been a necessity ever since my operation, by applying to the M.O. This I did, but it would have been far more sensible if the doctor who saw me on reception, and who was then informed of the hysterectomy, had told me at once that I could, if I wished, have permission to keep the corsets. A first offender is naturally wary of asking for anything until she knows the ropes.

I had no separate tea-towel for drying food utensils, nor had any other prisoner whom I questioned. I gathered that one used the bath-towel or left them wet. It was only after my discharge that I found that a separate tea-towel should have been part of the normal equipment. I expected to find a slate and pencil in my cell, but no one had these. A few prisoners had small mirrors; I was not one of them. Toilet paper was in very short supply; pages from the Bible or from library books were used as a substitute ('Use Moses,' was the laconic advice given by a neighbour). Enamel-ware was also scarce; 'You can have a chamber-pot or a pail, but not both,' I was told by a landing officer, when I pointed out that my pail had been 'borrowed' in my absence and that I now had neither. The shortage of handkerchiefs and floorcloths was, to a certain extent, remedied by the destruction of clothing. One vest that I was given had a square patch on the back where a 'handkerchief' had been removed. Dresses frequently had sleeves torn out for use as floorcloths before they were put on the laundry pile in the recess. One felt that it would have been more economical in the long run for the smaller necessities to have been supplied.

The statement 'You will have a bath once a week' turned out to be a little over-optimistic. On the Sunday after my reception I had a warm bath while the majority of the prisoners were at the afternoon C. of E. service; the next week none at all; the following week a quite cold one; and the week after that a very good hot bath which I greatly appreciated. A number of women, however, refused to use the prison baths for fear of infection, preferring to wash themselves down in their own cells as best they could. I watched the bath-woman cleaning the baths, and asked her what she used. 'Just bath-brick,' she said. There was certainly no disinfection of the baths between one prisoner and the next, although she managed to keep them very clean. The method of arranging for baths seemed to be very haphazard. A landing officer would shout from below, 'I can take six women for baths from B4,' and then wait until she had the requisite number. The names and locations of those who had baths were inscribed in a book. Whether a check was kept to see that all women had an occasional bath I do not know; I can hardly imagine that anyone could be so clever as to get more than the prescribed 'once-a-week.' One very small piece of common soap was the monthly allowance for one's personal use and for cleaning the cell. The rest went to the laundry and to the prison cleaners. But it did not always last out the month: 'We had no soap to scrub with to-day,' my neighbour (a laundry girl) told me, 'the clothes just had to be boiled without.' It was quite obvious that the underwear and nightgown with which I was supplied had never seen the soap: they were stained from the previous wearer's menstruation and streaked with the dirt of ages.

I was directed to work in the officers' quarters, but when I presented myself the officer in charge told me that I must first be given another medical examination. 'That's because they are not going to risk having any V.D. women *over there*,' my neighbour told me. 'It doesn't matter about *us*,' she added; 'everybody knows that that woman in No. — has gonorrhea,' and she nodded to an opposite cell. I accepted this statement with reserve; 'what everybody knows' is not evidence; but it was quite true that an uneasy suspicion of their neighbours was felt by many prisoners, a suspicion which was based on the superficiality of the reception medical examination ... Incidentally, I was myself ordered out of the very large kitchen in which I was working, by an officer, whose exact words were: 'Get out of here. I want to make myself a cup of tea.' If this feeling persisted *among the officers* after a *second* medical examination, is it any wonder that the prisoners shared it in respect of those who had never had the more careful test, and who nevertheless had to share the same baths, W.C.s and even clothes as themselves?

I soon found that I was quite incapable of doing some of the work that was required of me. I was taken down to the kitchen and given a large container of cocoa, holding some 2–3 gallons, to carry up to B4 landing. I managed to get it up two flights of stairs. The second flight I had to struggle up step by step, slopping the cocoa over my feet and the stairs on the way; but at the bottom of the third flight I collapsed and another prisoner ran down and rescued the cocoa. This heavy container had to be lifted to table height at each cell for the cocoa to be poured into each mug. Only a very strong woman could do it.

In the course of my work in quarters I was told to fill all the coal-scuttles (from a heap some 20 yards or so from the front door, in the pouring rain) and then to carry them to the respective rooms. I managed to fill sixteen of them and to bring them to the hall, but I simply could not lift them upstairs. 'How was it that you were passed as fit for carrying?' the officer in charge asked me. 'You had better see the M.O. again and tell her that you can't do it.' So once more I booked for the doctor. Each booking means the loss of the day's fresh air exercise and part, at least, of the day's work, while the prisoner sits locked in her cell waiting for the doctor to come. The doctor questioned me a little, said 'You look rather frail,' endorsed my card to show that I was 'excused carrying,' and prescribed me a tonic. It is on the basis of the *preliminary* examination that prisoners are supposed to be classified for work. It should not be necessary for a willing, but physically weak woman to strain herself severely before it is recognized that some tasks are beyond her powers. The medical officer who saw me in my cell was very kind; I heard her spoken of most appreciatively by other prisoners. But the impossibility of getting the smallest thing in the way of medicine, dressings or advice without the cumbersome machinery involved in 'booking for the M.O.' is stupid and infuriating. I contracted a severe cold during my second week in prison and, after struggling against it for some days, I decided that as I had recently had pneumonia and did not want a repeat performance, I had better 'book.' I had an obvious temperature (although it was not taken) and the doctor said that she would send me in some medicine. I went to my work in quarters and when I returned at dinner-time my cell door was locked. The officer who came to open it for me remarked, 'I see you've got some medicine. They have to shut the door or some other woman would come in and drink it.' (This was a way of obtaining medicine without consulting the doctor that had never occurred to me.) I had indeed got some medicine. On my table were two pills and four little jars – two containing a dark red fluid (my tonic), two containing a colourless liquid smelling strongly of ether. I looked at the officer and said helplessly, 'Have you any idea what *order* I take these in?' 'I haven't,' she replied; 'you'd better not take any of them just yet.' And then she added kindly; 'If I see the nurse I'll ask her.' At tea-time she came and gave me precise instructions, for which I was very grateful. Many of the officers were exceedingly kind in these little ways, going beyond their duty to supply the deficiencies of the system; others were not so helpful. During the course of my cold my nose became very sore, and I longed for a little ointment to put on it. I asked the nurse for some, but found that there was no way of obtaining it except by 'booking' and missing exercise. The same thing applied when my hands became so sore and chapped that they began to bleed from innumerable cracks. Here again, however, an officer came to the rescue by suggesting that the grease from the top of the cocoa, rubbed well in, was an excellent remedy for chapped hands. So it was; I skimmed it off on to a plate and applied it just as it began to set.

The ringing of bells was a continual bone of contention between officers and prisoners. I never tried mine, but on several occasions I heard the officer on duty call out, 'Oh, *stop* ringing that bell,' when a bell had rung intermittently, without attention, for a very long time. From 4.30 p.m. to 7 a.m. is a long time for a woman to be locked in one room, when the only sanitary convenience is a partly-covered pail, and when the onset of menstruation may take place suddenly and perhaps unexpectedly. Pregnant women, also, were locked in for the same hours, a refinement of cruelty that one can only ascribe to lack of imagination on the part of those who are responsible for it. Some of the bells did not ring at all, or only made a feeble clicking sound, and in any case a prisoner who urgently required help may be quite incapable of answering the question so often shouted, 'Who is ringing that bell?' Sanitary towels of normal quality were supplied, one at a time as required, on application to the landing officer. Only once did I hear an officer refuse to supply a (new) prisoner, because she had asked at an inconvenient time, but later she relented and brought two.

Rule 5 of the 'Notes' hung upon my wall stated that 'Clean underclothing is issued once a week, and if you do not receive any article of underclothing or if you specially want to change any article of underclothing earlier, you should ask your landing officer.' This sounded fine, so I asked my neighbours when the weekly issue took place. They smiled at my innocence. 'We haven't had a change here for over three weeks,' I was told; 'if you can get round a laundry girl she may be able to get you some when you want it.' However, I preferred to try legitimate means. After eight days I asked for clean underclothing, but was told by the landing officer that she could not issue it until there was enough to go all round. The next day I washed out my towel, apron, stockings and knickers, and dried them as well as I could in my cell. (On the whole, it is not surprising that I caught a chill, but they were *very* dirty, even when I was given them, and more so after my coal-heaving activities.) Sometimes a prisoner on exercise, on a bitterly cold day, would whisper that she hadn't any knickers on; she had washed them and they were not dry. The shortage of soap and lack of *all* other cleaning materials, such as soda, impeded the efficiency of this kind of 'home laundry.' When I had had my original towel (the one and only) for nearly a month, the officer taking me for my final bath was so appalled at the colour of my towel that she fetched me a clean one then and there. I was grateful, but I would have been more grateful still to have had it a fortnight sooner. When the prisoners did get a change, particularly of stockings, they were apt to risk punishment by concealing the discarded garments and washing them out, so that they could retain their own 'kit' and have a change when they required it. (I am referring, of course, to the short-term prisoners with whom I mostly mixed. Long-term prisoners had their own marked kit and did get it laundered regularly. I could see it distributed to the 'penal women' each week.) In this way, no doubt, the shortage was aggravated, but the temptation was great. Quite a number of young prisoners refused to wear the black woollen stockings altogether, and went bare-legged. Such heroism, in January, was too great for me, but I appreciated it. The shortage would have been even greater if it had not been for them. There was only one distribution of clean clothes on B4 landing during the whole month I was there, and no issue of clean towels. I found later, however, that the prisoners who worked in the officers' quarters were more fortunate than others in this respect; the officer in charge made it her business to see that 'her women' had fairly regular changes of clothing, and a bath once a week if possible.

I seldom found any evidence of the use of disinfectant within the prison. On the contrary, the stench from the W.C.s in the mornings, when everyone was emptying 14° hours' slops, and many women were discarding soiled sanitary towels into and over an uncovered pail, was often almost unbearable. Hot water, if any was available, could only be obtained from a sink just between the two W.C.s, and I was daily sickened as I stood in the queue waiting my turn at the tap. The water supply from the W.C. cisterns, even when they were not out of order (which they frequently were) was hopelessly inadequate. Even in the officers' quarters I was given no disinfectant to use, although the cleaning of baths, sinks and W.C.s was my special job.

Finally, I must mention the medical examination on discharge. The purpose of this examination is to assure the fitness of the prisoner for her journey home. The actual procedure was that about half a dozen of us were lined up in a row, with our dresses undone at the neck. the doctor moved down the line with her stethoscope, asked each prisoner in turn, 'Are you all right?' and received an affirmative reply. The whole examination of all of us was completed in about half a minute.

In concluding this statement I think I should say that I realized that, in common with other institutions, Holloway Prison was bound to suffer from [wartime] shortage of equipment that would normally have been supplied. What I was not prepared for was the general insanity of an administrative system in which lip-service is paid to the idea of segregation and the ideal of reform, when in practice the opportunities for contamination and infection are innumerable, and those of re-education for responsible citizenship practically nil; which is so rigid that it goes on exhorting women prisoners to keep themselves neat and clean, when they ask for nothing better than the opportunity of doing so, of which they have been deprived; which goes on telling them to ask their landing officer for supplies that are unobtainable; which allows prisoners no responsibilities at all except the relatively enormous one of deciding for themselves whether they shall answer the questions put to them by the doctor truthfully or not; which, if they are unfortunate enough to require the services of the medical officer, deprives them of the only hour of exercise and fresh air that they can hope for during the long day; which treats short-term prisoners with less consideration than long-term ones in a variety of little ways, presumably because they are less guilty; and which expects repentant women to derive hope and inspiration from Bibles which they are compelled to use as substitute toilet-rolls.

Notes

Source: Kathleen Lonsdale et al., *Some Account of Life in Holloway Prison for Women* (Chislehurst, Kent: Prison Medical Reform Council, 1943), 6–16.

1 Dame Kathleen Lonsdale (1903–1971) had joined the Quakers in 1935 and remained active in the Society of Friends until her death. Specializing in crystallography she was appointed after the war to a chair in chemistry at University College, London. Understandably peace and prison reform were prominent among the numerous causes to which she gave her support.

KATHLEEN WIGHAM

Kathleen Wigham, *née* Derbyshire, was not a prominent scientist like Kathleen Lonsdale but a twenty-two-year-old working girl from the English midlands. Her parents were pacifists, though, and she herself had begun to attend Quaker meetings. She later joined the Society of Friends. In July 1942, as an unmarried woman she received 'a direction to do hospital work' under the wartime legislation imposing industrial conscription on women. Declaring herself a CO at her local labour exchange where the industrial tribunal sat, she explained that she was refusing to comply with the direction 'because I object to doing any work which will relieve anyone else to do military service.' Her present work in a health food store in Blackburn was, she felt, unconnected with the war effort. In the narrative that follows she tells the story of what happened to her after that.

I have extrapolated the passages printed below from a transcript of the interview with her conducted by the Imperial War Museum in London. Therefore, this is the spoken word and not formal writing designed for print. Wigham's account is sometimes clumsy and repetitive. But it has a freshness and vivacity often lacking in more polished narratives. It represents, too, one of the few views of prison life by a woman CO.[1]

And a few months passed and then I received a summons for five pounds for having refused industrial conscription, and I was given ten days to pay it. Of course I did nothing about it, didn't reply or anything, I just did nothing about it at all. Then after the end of ten days I received a second summons asking me to appear before the court at the session house ... in Blackburn to give my reasons why I had refused to pay this fine. And I was given a date to go and I went and stated my views against war and the reason why I'd refused to be conscripted into industrial work. And they actually did their best to persuade me to pay the fine; they said 'We don't want to send people like you to prison, can you pay your fine?' So I said 'I can pay it but I'm not prepared to.' 'Well, would you pay it if we said five shillings a week?' I said 'No, it isn't a question of hardship. I've half a dozen people wanting to pay the fine for me but I just refuse to take their offers. I have ... a conscientious objection to doing this sort of work.' So it was left in abeyance until they contacted my employer to see whether he would pay it. Well, he was very willing to pay it because he'd already had one son directed to war work, and one son with a prison sentence [as a CO], only one son remaining in the shop; and he was well prepared to pay my fine to keep me working in the shop. But I said 'No, if you pay the fine within a month there'll be another summons and it'll happen all over again.' So he wrote to the magistrates and said that, although he was prepared to pay the fine, he understood my reasons for [objecting] and he was not prepared to go against my wishes.

So on the 2nd of July 1942 I was summonsed to appear in the sessions house ... [when I again stated] my reasons for refusing to pay the five pound fine ... And, scratching his head, the chairman says 'Well, there's nothing more we can do only to send you to prison, and we're giving you the shortest period of sentence that we can possibly give anyone. We hope that this will help you to change your mind. Fourteen days in Strangeways. If at any time during the sentence you change your mind all you have to do is let the governess know that you'll pay your fine and you'll be released immediately.' They were almost begging me to pay the fine, they couldn't have been more earnest really in trying to persuade me that I was doing the wrong thing. However I managed to assure them I wanted to do this, that I knew exactly what I was letting myself in for and I was told to stand down, and ... a prison wardress came and took me down to the cells.

And I was allowed to see my mother and one more friend, a Quaker friend, for about half an hour ... [After] they went away ... I had to ... sit there on my own for most of the afternoon until there was a prison car ready to take me to Strangeways in Manchester. And I travelled in the police car with a policeman driving, a policeman sat at the side of him and a policewoman at the back. And the three of them did nothing but try to persuade me all the way that they didn't want to take me; I only had to say the word and we would turn back. So it was really very difficult to keep to your convictions when you were being persuaded all the time not to go ... [They were indeed] very kind. They said 'Prison's not for a girl like you, you're too sensitive, it'll break you. Do pay your fine, all you have to do is say you'll pay your fine, we'll take you back. We don't want to take people like you to prison. And just say the word and we'll go back, it doesn't matter.' Even when they got to the gates of the prison they stopped and they said 'Oh, have we to ring the bell?' And I said 'Yes, please.'

Well, I felt calm somehow ... I just felt this was the right thing to do ... And ... many of the COs from the Blackburn Pacifist Fellowship ... had more or less prepared and told me what to expect, but even with all that they said it was far harder than what I had anticipated ... But [going to prison] is one of those things, I think, that, however much it's described to you and however much you're told about it, until you have the experience it's very difficult to grasp exactly what it means. I had the feeling in my mind that I knew all these other COs; and I felt that if they'd gone through it, and also with longer sentences than what I'd got, I could certainly get through it. But I have to admit that I did find it difficult.

What happened to me in Strangeways? Well, the door opens; there's a huge studded door and you obviously know that when you go through that ... you're cut off from the outside world. It's a huge, heavy oak, ... an iron barred door, and once you get through that there's another door almost within the length of the police car, a sort of a second door that you go through as well, and then there was a sort of a short drive to the building itself. And even when we got to the building and the police officers got out and the policewoman said 'It's your last chance' I said 'I'll go ahead.' And she took me in, and that's all; you don't see them again. Immediately you're handed over, the police car and the police lady and what you might term your kind friends have all gone.

And you enter in there and the voices immediately are harsh, and shouting; there's no one soft spoken, or so it seemed. And you go to a reception desk and there's a prison warden behind that – or wardress I should say; they're all females on the female side – and they want your age, your name and address, whether you're pregnant, various particulars about you. She didn't say 'Why are you in?' or anything like that, didn't ask anything like that. And I'd been told that ... at the reception desk ... I must tell them that I was a vegetarian and then I could get the vegetarian meals ... So I said to the lady 'Would you mind putting down that I'm a vegetarian?' And she just said 'You'll be treated like the other ones here, you haven't come to a convalescent home.' And after that I didn't dare say anything else. I didn't say 'Well, I do know that you do provide vegetarian diet.' I was just shut up ...

And then she said 'Go in that cubicle and undress and put this round you, undress to your waist and put this round you,' and what she threw at me was a grey cloak of very heavy, coarse material. So I stripped. And the cubicle is no bigger than just a toilet with a wood board across and a door; they didn't close the door, and opposite's a row of toilets; and I sat there for quite a while and then someone did come along and close the door but it wasn't locked, and this is to stop you from talking to incoming prisoners. You sit there and all the other people are coming in. And I stripped and then they said 'Push your clothes out under the door.' So although I'd taken the trouble to fold them up and put them in a neat pile they were just sort of kicked away with a foot and picked up and taken away. And a note is supposed to be made of your belongings, if you've taken anything in with you (I took very little really).

And then you hear a shuffling and a clanging, wherever you go you're aware of the clanging of keys. They seem to all have a belt with a huge number of keys on and you hear keys and you think 'Oh, someone's coming.' And the doors were opened and we were given our tea for that afternoon, and there was a piece of white bread; and I'm not telling a ... lie when I say it was an inch thick, and it was spread with margarine. You know, just a dollop in the middle and just spread out, all the edges not touched, and a grey cup, like an ... enamel tin, of cocoa with no milk or sugar. It was terribly hard to get down. I didn't feel particularly hungry anyway but thought 'Well, perhaps it'll be a long time to breakfast' – this was probably about half past four – 'so I'd better try and eat some of it,' and I did try.

After what seemed about half an hour or so, again there was movement and voices and quite a bit of noise and we were filed up outside the doctor's room to have a medical examination. Well, there's a male doctor and a nurse there and he could only just say 'Have you had any operations?' 'No.' 'Any recent serious illness?' 'No.' 'Right.' Look through your hair, look into your eyes, and then you're past. And I thought 'Well, I've never had such a scanty medical examination.' And it was obvious if there were any venereal disease, or any contagious diseases of any sort, they couldn't possibly have found them out unless it came from the person themselves, if they were honest enough to say.

Then you go to another room, and there are prisoners in charge and they give you your prison dress. This consisted of a calico vest, very harsh material, which you could wear as a slip ... you could have worn it as a slip, you know an underslip, and a pair of knickers obviously made on the large size so that they fit all individuals (I mean I could quite easily get two pairs out of mine), and a blue prison dress. And you're given nothing else, you ferret around in a cupboard to try and find a pair of shoes, if you find a pair that match you're lucky. You're looking for a pair that match and then you might find that there's a nail in one of them ... I wasn't given any stockings, so it was just the shoes. Then you're given blankets and sheets and a pillow-case, and you're marched in file across the yard to the main part of the prison. ... [And here] you meet ... a [new] prison wardress. She was allocated about half a dozen [prisoners] and she marches you all off to your cells. And it's very strange because you want to look round ... and you're really not given any time to look round to see what it's all like; it's only after a few days that you can absorb what the surroundings are like. And I can only describe the place as being like a huge circle, like a cartwheel. The centre circle is the core of the place and is all the officers' rooms, and then all the various spokes of the cartwheel are rows of cells. And there's several floors, in fact four floors, and you go up to the one where your cell's going to be. And each landing from side to side, or from corner to corner, is covered with wire netting. This is to prevent suicides ... And the corridors and the landings they seem to be of steel ... so that footsteps echo along, and of course with the clanging of keys it all sort of throws echoes about – it's weird really. I was taken to a cell and it was right at the end of the landing, which would mean that I was on an outside wall on one side. I would have a neighbour on one side but not on the other, so I'd probably have two outside walls because the cell window looked out into the open air and then, as it was the last one on the landing, there was obviously no one on that side.

Now the cell ... It had a flagged floor, and there were squares of black and orange and fawn. And the bottom half of the wall was painted green and the top half and the ceiling were white, a grey-ey white sort of whitewash. As you open the cell door at the back there was a wood fitment of a triangular shape of three shelves and on the top shelf you normally would have your utensils for having your meals, which consisted of a tin plate, a tin mug and a knife and fork – the knife not being very sharp. Underneath you had a bowl and a scrubbing brush and a pail, this was for cleaning your cell. And underneath all that your sanitary utensils, which should have consisted of a sanitary pail, with lid, and a chamberpot. And when I say that it should have consisted of these things I had no pail of any sort at all to bring water to the cell and the chamberpot leaked. I had a bowl for washing myself in and a tiny piece of soap, which I was told would have to last a week and that was for washing yourself and for scrubbing your cell and all the utensils and so on; everything had to be done with that one piece of soap. Although you weren't given a cloth, you had a floorcloth and I suppose that was to do everything else with. I'd no handkerchief, I'd no comb, I'd no brush – and I had been told that if anything was missing from your cell when you were opened up in the morning you asked for it. To whoever opened the door you said 'So and so's missing from my cell; [for example] please could I have a comb?' But you couldn't ask for a comb and a brush and a pail and a handkerchief; you could only ask for one thing. So it depended on what things you had for priority. Of course my first priority was the chamberpot, getting something that didn't leak, and I managed to get something the next day. But I didn't get a pail. And considering that you're fourteen and a half hours locked up in your cell, from when you've finished your work to being opened up next morning when you walk along the corridor with your chamberpot ... for what they call slopping out, to empty the slops, it's very difficult. And of course the stench is unbelievable. And whilst you're there you're supposed to get a pail of water to come back and scrub your cell out, and all I had was the bowl that I was expected to wash myself in. So it's very difficult trying to carry a chamberpot and a bowl without spilling something; and coming back of course carrying a bowl of hot water and everybody looking at you because you'd got the wrong utensil. But you know you just have to put up with all these sorts of inconveniences.

Also there should have been on the wall a list of prison regulations which tells you what your duties are while you're there. But there was nothing like that in my cell. And so on the second day when the wardress opened the cell door I said 'I haven't seen any prison regulations,' and she said 'Oh, the previous person [using] your cell was a night wardress, so of course there's a lot of things missing because she didn't require these things.' [Another problem was that] I wasn't getting vegetarian diet, and so every day I was putting my dinner out of my cell door ... putting the dish of meat and gravy outside the cell door to show them that I didn't eat it. And after about the fourth day it was only then that the wardress said 'Why don't you eat your meat and gravy?' And I said 'I'm a vegetarian, I asked to be registered as a vegetarian and no one's taken any notice up to now.' And she says 'Oh well, you're not supposed to keep returning your dinners, you return them once but after that they make enquiries.' Anyway she took it away. My first dinner had consisted of potatoes, meat and gravy, and the potatoes not only cooked in their jackets – which I appreciated – but with soil and tails and eyes all in as well; you had to pick and choose what you could eat, and you could hardly cut it out because the knife is so blunt. So I was virtually only having potatoes so that I was of course getting weaker and weaker and faint because of not having sufficient of the minerals and vitamins that I should have been having from the substitute meats, or cheese, or something else.

As to breakfast, you didn't get a cereal at all you usually just had bread, and for some reason or other they would bring you a tiny little pot, not much bigger than a thimble, of brown sugar to have with your ... porridge ... The porridge was very lumpy and thick and almost grey in colour; it may have looked like that because the utensils were so dull and dark that it may have been like a reflection shining on the food. But you got no milk, you got only this tiny thimbleful of sugar and a mug of tea ... and a slice of bread, thick bread very much like you had for tea. That was for your breakfast. And then your tea is the same: a very thick slice of bread with margarine dolloped in the middle and cocoa, and the only way you could have sugar in your cocoa was if you could spare some from your breakfast, ... which I could do because I didn't take sugar in tea anyway ... I saved it for the evening drink. But then again you had to be careful where you hid this little pot because, when you went out to do your work, other prisoners who perhaps weren't in the workshop would go round the cells to see what they could pick up. And thus you would lose some of the things that you had ... I did not have a comb but if you had one, or anything that they thought they could make use of, it would disappear so you carried it round with you as much as you could. [Derbyshire, in fact, did not have a comb at any time during her fortnight in Strangeways and was unable either to comb her hair or wash it while in prison.]

I only had one bath and that's all I wanted to have there. I'd had a bath on the morning before being taken to prison and then, on entering prison, you have a bath ... And the baths are ... I suppose they're like the slipper baths that you have in these old wash places, I don't think there are many available to-day ... They have very low walls and rows and rows of baths, the taps on the outside of the wall and long term prisoners in charge of them. Prisoners aren't supposed to talk to one another. There's a wardress in charge; she sort of stands aloof at the door well away from everybody. And as the door was opened for me to go in the water was already in the bath. But it didn't look very clean. However I stepped into it to bath, after telling the girl I'd already had a bath that morning. She said 'Well, it's my duty that you've all to have a bath, you've got to get in the water anyway,' more or less pushed you in you see. And then as I [got] out they were putting another girl in! In the same water, just adding a little bit more to it. Very little water, it would hardly cover your thighs. The water was not hot, only lukewarm. But they *were* adding more water, and then of course the girl coming in probably thought this is a fresh bath of water. But the prisoners were whispering to one another and the girl that had been in charge of my bath said to the girl in charge of the bath next door 'This is the third I've had in this water,' as though it was something clever to have done to have managed to get three girls in one bath. I don't know why they did that, whether they were saving the time, or they were in a hurry, ... or whether there was a shortage of water ... I don't know why they did it but it was very unpleasant ...

So I had no comb, no hair-brush, and certainly no other bath. And I had no toothbrush either. And no handkerchief until my fifth day when I was transferred to the prison hospital. The fact that you can't groom yourself makes you feel terribly depressed really, and it makes you almost have second thoughts as to whether you have done the right thing. You know within yourself that you have and you know that time is passing but it's terribly hard to live through it, it is really. I just hope that conditions are better now, I believe that they are to some extent better now that the war isn't on.

Another gruelling factor was that this was the time when Liverpool was being badly bombed each evening – Liverpool and Manchester, all the dock areas – and at night when you'd finished your work in the workshop – mine was sewing mail-bags – you came back and at four o'clock you were back in your cell for tea, and eight o'clock it was lights out so there was obviously nothing to do only to lie down whether you went to sleep or not. And you virtually just stared up at the window and of course everything was in darkness because of the blackout. And then you'd hear the sirens going, and hear gunfire and bombs dropping, and then this would aggravate the girls; you know there would be terrible tension. And you'd hear a girl shouting on the landing 'Let me out, let me out, take us to the air-raid shelters.' And nothing, no nothing happened; you heard no comforting voices, no one saying 'Shut up' or anything [just] to let you know that there was someone about; you heard nothing at all. And it gave the impression that all the officers and wardresses must have gone to their safety shelters and we were just left. I don't know if that was so but it gave you that impression. And sometimes I would perhaps shout and say 'We'll be all right you know, we're being watched over,' try to say a sentence. But you were very often sworn at back; it stopped you from even saying a prayer for them because they would tell you to bugger off and so on (and the language was pretty foul really). So I just said my own prayers and tried to sleep. But it was just hysteria. And I was told the next morning by one of the wardresses that you're not let out. They don't take the girls, they don't evacuate the building unless there's a bomb very close to the prison; otherwise you're just left. All night you were left hearing and knowing that you're trapped, knowing you can't get out, you can't possibly ... you had no escape. I mean even if they're not moved they don't open the cell doors so that you can get to safety yourself, so it's real mental torture there's no other description for it. You just said your prayers and hoped that you would be kept safe. And of course I had this link with my home ... I knew that the friends at home were saying prayers and holding me in their thoughts, and in this way I was uplifted and helped really to face up to it although it was so terrible really ...

What happened if I had a period in the prison? Could you get ... sanitary towels from the warders when you wanted them? No, not when you wanted. If you began a period during the day it was next morning, when your cell was opened, when you got your sanitary towel and you were only issued with one; whether it was the first day of your period and your period was heavy you were issued with one sanitary towel, that's all. And of course again the difficulty was getting rid of the sanitary towels, when you went to slop out in the morning you could only then get rid of your sanitary towel. We had separate pails for them by the side of the toilets, and obviously they were always full and overflowing and they were lying on the floor. And the chamberpots – it's awful to say this – the chamberpots were overflowing and they were being slopped out anywhere. The toilets weren't flushing because there was so much going down them at once, when you're in a crocodile file – as quick as that you see – and queueing up and getting your water to wash your cell floor. It was just awful. It was degrading to think that your fellow human beings could treat you like that, it's almost too horrible to describe because you can't really believe that conditions could exist like that in 1942 ...

[To return to my vegetarian food problem.] An appointment was made for me to see the doctor and a nurse came to my cell and said 'You haven't to go to the workshop this morning, the doctor's coming in and he wants to see you. And what's all this business about you returning your meat, you can't have what you want in here you know.' And so I said 'I agree with that but I do know that on the male side there are vegetarians and they're getting vegetarian food.' 'We have nothing to do with the male side, you're in the female side of the prison.' So I said 'Well, I don't see why if it happens there it can't happen here. You're certainly going to have to cater for them because I may be the first one but I won't be the only one.' 'Don't be so saucy.' So I had to wait in my cell doing nothing at all and hearing everybody else go off to work, and you're of course locked in.

And then naturally the clanging of the keys along the corridor, with little sharp footsteps and followed by a heavier footstep – obviously a man's. The door was open and there stands the doctor, he comes in. 'What's all this about refusing your meat?' 'Well, doctor, I'm a vegetarian and I don't eat meat, I haven't eaten meat for a number of years' – six years by that time – 'and I know if I eat meat I'm going to be ill. And I did ask ...' I said. 'The authorities know that I'm a vegetarian.' ... And he just pulled the eyes down – you know how they pull the cheek down – and looked in the eyes with a flashlight and turned to the wardress and said 'You can find her a bed in the hospital, she's barmy.' And I was very close to tears because I felt that his visit had been unnecessary and for what he did for me was certainly more unnecessary, and his remark was extremely rude. And he went, he picked his case up and he went, and ... apart from just saying those words he was in the room less than two or three minutes.

And he went out and then the wardress started on me and she didn't half give me a dressing down. She said to me: 'Our men are out fighting for sluts like you. Fold your blankets and you carry them down to the laundry,' 'I don't know what the country would do ... If I had my way you'd certainly be hanging from the end of a rope,' and all sorts of things [like that]. And prodding me all the time, ... giving me not just a prod, a nudge almost knocking me over, when I was wrapping the blankets up. And I just said nothing, I just found it difficult to talk. A lump was in my throat and I was very close to tears; I probably was crying. And I folded the blankets up and she took me down the stairs and I'd to put these in the laundry.

And then she took me across to the hospital part, and she took me to a ward and said to the sister 'She's had to come over from the prison side and she's one of those bloody conchies.' And I can remember the matron just sort of tapping me on the shoulder and pushing me on, just sort of saying 'Go in there.' I think she knew that this person had a foul tongue, she knew that I'd taken enough and she just touched me on the shoulder and said 'Go along and sit in there' and I just went through a room. I was in a ward and I just sat on the first chair that I came to and I was heartbroken. I realised then I was in a hospital ward and all the prisoners were ... Some sat on their beds, and I looked at them and I thought 'Good Heavens above, this is almost like being in a mental ward.' There were patients shaking; there was one woman with her tongue lolling backwards and forwards on her mouth, and there was another girl screaming and making noises and pulling her hair out. I looked round ... some were just sitting quietly. And I waited in there and this person spoke to the matron and then she went. The matron came and spoke to me and said 'You're going to be all right here, don't worry.' So I thanked her very much. And she was the first person since leaving the police officers that had spoken in what I call a soft tone; so it was like music to my ears. And she said 'Have you any special interests?' I said 'Well, what do you mean?' She said 'Is there anything special that you'd like to do while you're in here?' So I said 'I'm willing to do anything; I'll just be glad to do something because you just feel like you're wasting your time.' And she says 'Are you any good at sewing?' So I said 'Yes.' And she says 'Oh well, we can find you plenty of that to do.' So I said 'Well, I'll be very, very grateful.' And for the rest of the time I was mending nurses' aprons, mending torn pockets and sewing on sashes and things like that, and doing buttonholes and sewing on buttons.

And then the sister said to me 'Would you like to come round with me tonight; I'm going round with the trolley of medicines and we go through the maternity ward?' And I said 'I'd never thought of a maternity ward in a prison.' She says 'Oh yes, if a prisoner comes in that's expecting a baby, if it's near to the end of the pregnancy they are released early, but if it happens that it's not the end of the prison sentence they have the babies in prison. But they do try to get them out if possible.' So with that she allowed me to push her trolley round. I know she could do it on her own, but it was an interest for me to do, for it took about an hour and a half every evening, going round and taking the medicines to the various wards in the hospital. It was a different atmosphere of course; it was pleasanter for one thing. These wards had beds with a locker at each side; you were able to keep your things in a locker much more easily somehow. The patients weren't the same; they weren't looking round to see what they could take. They often, though, came round to beg; they would ask you if you had something different to what they had and, if they admired something that you had, they admired it in such a way that they expected you to give it to them ...

During the second week they allowed me a Quaker visitor. He was George Sutherland, the principal of Dalton Hall which was a university college in Manchester. And they allowed him to come and visit me because they'd got to know from the male side that I'd been moved from the prison to the prison hospital so they were concerned that I wasn't well. [They felt] it was important that somebody gets in to visit this person ... And I was taken to matron's office by one of the nurses and he came in and as he came towards me – there was a long table you see and I was told to sit at one end – and as he came in he was coming towards me, because Quakers always shake hands on meeting, and he was stopped by the nurse who said 'You sit over there.' And he says 'Oh, but I want to greet my friend,' and she said 'You're not allowed to shake hands.' And this is because they're suspicious that he might have handed me something that I wasn't allowed to have. You see they don't trust anybody at all.

So he sat down at the table and ... he talked to me for half an hour. 'Why have you been moved?' [he asked]. And I said 'I think it's because of my weak condition because I haven't been getting vegetarian food.' And he said 'Has that been changed now?' And I said 'No, it hasn't been changed. But we sit round a table having our meals. There's about ten of us in the ward, and we sit at the table and I have persuaded two of the prisoners to share my meat and in return they give me some of their greens and potatoes.' So I was getting a little extra potatoes from one, and they're cooked better, served on a white plate; it's more respectable anyway and more appetising, and they of course liked to have my extra meat and this is how we've managed. It's very strange, but I never got vegetarian food all the time I was in ...

[Sutherland and the Manchester Quakers obtained permission from the prison authorities for Derbyshire to attend the next Sunday morning the Quaker meeting, which was held on the male side for imprisoned COs.]

On the Sunday a prison wardress came to me and said 'You're going to the male side of the prison for this Quaker meeting.' So I said, 'Oh, that's very nice; I'm very very pleased about that and thank you very much, or thank whoever's responsible for it.' 'Well,' she said, 'you can't go without stockings.' So I said 'Oh, Quakers don't bother, it doesn't matter how you dress.' 'Oh, you can't go to the male prison without stockings.' So I was given a pair of black woollen stockings to put on and nothing to hold them up with. So I had to walk across this prison yard, hobbling along under my cloak grabbing hold of my stockings ... and wondering what would happen when I was required to shake hands. So it was an uncomfortable experience from that point of view. But that really didn't matter; I wasn't worried about that. As we went across the prison yard this wardress was asking me questions all the time about the Quakers, and I gathered she was really a little bit nervous. She wasn't quite sure what to expect; I did try to say that she would be one of us. And she said 'We mustn't shake hands, we mustn't touch anything, and we're not sitting near the men' ... And when we got there there was Doctor Vipont Brown, a well-known Quaker in Manchester, and Edgar Upperton, who were both Quaker visitors to the male side of the prison.

[As we arrived] there the wardress pushed herself in front of me and was going firmly to walk right past in her official way. But Edgar Upperton just stopped her and said 'Just a minute, Friend, we shake hands, we welcome each other. You're very welcome to this meeting; you can forget your prison uniform, you're one of us.' And she was so surprised that she just managed to smile. And Vipont Brown shook hands with her; they shook hands with me and we went and sat right on the very back row and all these seats were set out at the front. And within about five minutes the doors opened and the male prisoners began to come through, and of course again they were shaken by the hand of Doctor Vipont Brown and Edgar Upperton and, before any of them went to their seats, they walked right across to the back row and came and shook hands with both of us. And she never said a word; she didn't say it wasn't allowed but she just let them. And of course fortunately I was sitting down so it didn't matter about the stockings. And I shook hands with them all. And of course I met [my friend,] Stan Iveson, who gave me a wink, and Fred Barton too – a man I greatly admired. And we sat down to begin the service. A Quaker service is based on silence. But first of all Doctor Vipont Brown spoke to us, and he was able to give one or two messages from various homes ... And he also said 'This morning meeting is a very important one historically; this is the first religious meeting in a prison where the females have been allowed to join the males without a screen in between them. It's the first but we hope it won't be the last, we hope there will be many more to come although next Sunday we won't have our comrade, Kathleen Derbyshire, with us.' Then the Quaker meeting began ... [And at the end] of course the men left first and they shook hands with us again [as did] Doctor Vipont Brown and Edgar Upperton. And we went back, and all the way back the wardress said how much she had enjoyed it and felt moved by it, and asked quite a lot about how she could find out more about it. So you know perhaps a seed had been sown.

This meeting was very important indeed [to me], for one thing I had been looking forward to it very much having missed the Quaker meeting the previous Sunday, although I had tried to put my thought into a Quaker meeting then on my own in my cell. But it meant a great deal because of the suffering that I'd experienced on having to be transferred from the prison to the hospital. It was just a great comfort to me ... when I had been feeling down and wondering whether I had done the right thing; it gave me hope and the spirit to go on ...

How about the maternity ward? Did it upset me at all seeing small babies in prison? It did and it didn't. It shocked me ... that the authorities were so hard that they could allow a woman to have her baby in prison, because you think that the child is doomed for life with a birth certificate which says where it was born. And I believe now the tendency is to get them out as soon as possible; even if they have to go back to serve their sentence they get them out for the birth of the child. But I was rather pleased in a way that there was this extra little task to do. And it was so nice to get to a cot; and you know how you talk to a child and chuck it under its chin. And on occasions I've said 'Can I hold it?' because it's such a lovely feeling to hold a baby in your arms. And on occasions I [was] allowed to hold them and nurse them and see the delight on the other's face that someone else was taking an interest in their baby. I think it helped them, you know that. Things are so harsh in prison; you go a long, long way to see a kind face or hear a loving word.

On the prison side I was not able to learn too much about [the other prisoners]; you weren't really allowed to talk. You had exercise for about half an hour in the afternoon and you walked round in groups. And then, if it was fairly warm – and this was July, it was fairly warm – you were allowed to just sit in small groups and talk quietly. Well, people would whisper 'What are you in for?' And if you said conscientious objection, I don't really think they understood. And they'd [say] 'Oh, I'm in for stealing' or 'I robbed my employer' or things like that, they were nearly all robberies and shoplifting and things like that. You only sort of passed sentences; you really felt that you were all in the same boat. There was no good or bad amongst you. You were all evil;

because you'd done wrong you were in there. But as far as regarding it as a place of correction that couldn't be further from the truth ... One or two people I did speak to said 'Wait [until] I get out I'm going to have him.' You know this [would be] her employer; she was going to get her own back. So when they had gone out they were going to do something far worse than what they'd done to get in. 'I'll make it worthwhile next time I come in, I will do something proper, I'll murder him' ... And I believe the catch phrase of the Governess when most of the prisoners are going out, although she didn't say it to me, was 'You'll come back, they all do. We'll see you again, they all come back and you will too' – but she didn't say it to me.

Did I have any hostility from the prisoners when I was in the prison itself? No, I don't think they really understood. There weren't enough opportunities given to say that you were in there because you objected to war. I think ... they're a bit annoyed because they've been caught and sent to prison and feel sorry for themselves [so] that they don't really concern themselves with anyone else. The hostility I received was from the wardresses. And there was only one really, the one who came to see me with the doctor (perhaps if I'd had someone else then I would have had a very different impression) – apart from the reception, the remark in the reception when I asked to be registered as a vegetarian.

[As for the wardresses in general], I'm just surprised that anyone should ever want to do that sort of work. I think I would rather starve than be a wardress in a prison ... Most of them are very hard and strict ... [But] I was only frightened of the one who was there when I was folding up my blankets to be transferred, I'd visions that she was going to trip me up going down the steps because she was constantly pushing me; she couldn't leave me alone because she was so ashamed of me. I should imagine ... she may have had brothers or even sons perhaps in the war and a person like that would certainly consider me a coward. You'd think that I'd no right to be alive [because] I wasn't prepared to fight for the country. I think she was rather bitter; she must have had people in the war, so I can perhaps understand [her] ...

What was my mental state in prison? Were my nerves affected by it? I'm quite sure they were. I believe I must have been fairly highly strung and very, very close to tears. I cried an awful lot – on my own I cried a lot. I came to ask myself whether I shouldn't pay my fine and then realised that I couldn't; there was something stopping me from doing that. And I was very, very grateful that it was only going to be two weeks, because I felt sure that I wouldn't have lasted any longer than that without possibly going mental myself. You really felt on the verge of a breakdown, and I think the only thing that kept me sane was remembering messages that I'd had from friends [and family] ...

I was in the hospital wing for eight days and in prison for six ... In the main prison I went to the general workshop where most of it was sewing mail-bags for the post offices. And other prisoners were doing sort of things like domestic work. If you were a long term prisoner you might get cleaning out one of the wardresses' offices or rooms, and the girls rather liked doing that because there was always the odd cigarette given to them or extra bar of chocolate or something like that, things that you don't normally get [in prison]. But I went to the workshop and I was given mail-bags. But I didn't go there very long because I went in on the Thursday and the Thursday was all taken up with settling down in your cell. Friday you've got to see the Governess and lots of other administrative work. But you're hanging around in your cell quite a lot on your own; you go to the Governess and you may only be there for ten minutes, and then you've missed the workshop period so you go back to your cell. And you're only in the workshop in the mornings; in the afternoons it was exercise, which was walking round in groups of two or three and then sitting in clusters on the ground on your cloak while the wardresses talked and chattered in a corner. And of course then some of the girls were very crude and shouting out remarks [like] 'Look at them lot, what they're short of is a man; ... that's what they want.' And when we were walking round in groups I remember being a little shocked with one of the prisoners, who was a very coarse girl; she used to lift up her dress and say 'The tip of my tongue and the back of my arse to you.' And she would keep repeating it, but I didn't know whether she knew what she was saying or whether she was making a remark that she knew would offend [others]. And then of course they would turn round and threaten her with the fist, and she would be quiet for a little while and then she would repeat it again. Which makes you think afterwards that perhaps it was something that she'd learnt and it was sort of ingrained on her brain and she repeated it whether it meant anything or not. But it would set the other girls giggling and laughing and there would be uproar. And then we would all be silenced and told to stop talking. So ... her ill manners affected us all; we were stopped from talking and we all had to suffer [on account of] her. So the girls weren't always so pleased with her ...

What was really the worst thing about prison for myself? I think the sirens, the sirens and hearing the bombs and knowing that you were a prisoner and couldn't get out. It's a feeling of being chained, not being able to help yourself if danger came, or to help anyone else. And almost a bitterness really. I'm not a person that likes to dwell on bitterness. But you almost felt bitter towards your fellow [humans] that they could treat anybody like that, be so insensitive to anyone's feelings.

Notes

Source: The Imperial War Museum (London) Sound Archive, Accession no. A-004761/07, pp. 24–47, 49, 50.

1 See *The Anti-War Movement, 1914–1945* (London: Imperial War Museum Department of Sound Records, n.d.), 44, 45. The Imperial War Museum (London) Sound Archive also holds the typescript of an interview with the staunchly pacifist working-class housewife and volunteer CO adviser Mrs Nora Page, in which she describes the two weeks she spent in Holloway Prison for refusing to register for fire-watching duties. Her fellow prisoner there was Kathleen Lonsdale: both women give a roughly similar picture of prison life. See Accession no. 004 659/07, pp. 35–54. The *C.B.C.O. Bulletin* published two accounts of less than a page each of women COs' prison experiences: 'We interview Constance Bolam ... the First Woman C.O. gaoled' (no. 25, March 1942, p. 5) and Ivy Watson, 'This happened in Holloway' (no. 49, March 1944, p. 7). Bolam, a 21-year-old Newcastle-on-Tyne housemaid, had adopted an absolutist position: her refusal to pay a small fine for failure to carry out the condition of her tribunal exemption thus led to her being sent to prison for a month. In Holloway Prison Watson found the lack of toilet paper very trying. 'For the first few days,' she writes, 'I kept asking for paper but was ignored. This was most awkward when I was suffering from an attack of diarrhoea. I had to do what others seemed to do – tear up the Bible. When I say that I am a Christian and believe the Bible to be the inspired Word of God, perhaps you can understand how I felt at having to do such a thing.' 'Using Moses,' as Kathleen Londsdale had been advised to do by a fellow prisoner (see above), was obviously not a pleasant task for this deeply religious girl.

New Zealand

IAN HAMILTON

'Till human voices wake us, and we drown.' Ian Hamilton has taken the title of his striking prison memoir from the first half of this line by the poet T.S. Eliot. I would like to reprint all 233 pages since Hamilton's book, for all its high literary quality, is little known outside New Zealand. But of course this is not possible. I have included here as many pages of what I judge to be a fair sampling of his work; I trust some readers may even wish for more. Hamilton's memoir is 'a highly personalized record' of his jail experience, marked by 'an uncompromising attitude towards everything physically or spiritually confining.' The author 'rages, hectors, lectures, and often drenches the reader with bitterness ... [His] righteous indignation seldom falters.'[1] His stance here contrasts indeed with that of Archibald Baxter's classic account of his formidable CO experiences in the First World War, *We Will Not Cease*[2] (title taken this time from the eighteenth-century English poet William Blake), for Baxter writes throughout dispassionately and with quiet dignity, unlike Hamilton's tempestuous prose.

The son of a distinguished English surgeon and an ex–public school boy, Hamilton at the age of twenty-four had emigrated to New Zealand, where he became a sheep farmer. In his spare time he began to write plays, several of which were successfully performed during the 1930s. By 1939 he had become a convinced pacifist, on humanist not religious grounds, and a critical supporter of the country's Labour party. As in Baxter's case, his pacifism and his socialism were inextricably interwoven. Called up for military service after the outbreak of war, Hamilton refused to accept assignment to a government-run defaulters' camp for COs. Thus he joined the 'approximately sixty of the 800 confined men [who] utterly refused to co-operate and went to prison for the duration of the war.' He then did time in three jails: first in Hautu detention camp, then in Waikune prison (called in the narrative Wenukai), and finally in the penitentiary-style Mount Eden prison, situated 'on the hill.' The 'boorish cruelties' he encountered in these jails of his 'adopted country' proved a sad disappointment to Hamilton, but they provided the materials for one of the most telling denunciations of the modern prison.

'In confinement he had kept notes for a book about his experiences.' A couple of years after the end of the war he got down to writing it, and it was eventually published in 1953. The delay was due to the danger of criminal libel proceedings if the book were to appear as Hamilton had written it. In the end, 'for legal reasons ... the identity of many people and places ... was disguised.' Since, even so, no commercial publisher could be found to undertake it, the book was published 'by private subscription' in a run of only 750 copies, the money being put up by a number of Hamilton's friends and admirers.

In the postwar decades Hamilton became a market gardener and recycling expert; he also engaged in part-time journalism and writing. Moreover, he retained the 'intransigently' radical stance that we perceive in his prison memoir.

After some introductory paragraphs the extract below opens with Hamilton's transfer from the ordinary defaulters' camp to the Hautu camp, generally known as 'the Bad Boys' Camp' since COs were interned there as punishment for an infraction of camp rules.

I was going to say that long afterwards I got used to the locked door but that would be a lie. You never get used to it. You can, after innumerable repetitions, become temporarily unaware of its full implications. But every now and then, caught off guard as it were, all the horror and degradation of prison life comes home to you and they're symbolised by the crash of the heavy door, the turning of the key in the lock, the rattle of the keys and the receding footsteps, leaving you alone to face your own blankness. Later on, yes, when your cell becomes your fortress, you may even be glad of it. Nevertheless it is the most soul-shaking fact in prison, the moment you realise, I don't know why, that you're no better than an animal. Is it because you return to some early period when you were helpless and dependent and some hated person in authority shut you in a room by yourself? But the sensation is so overpowering that it seems to go further back than that, back and back to some dim memory of death and the absolute loss of individuality.

Why no better than an animal, you ask?

Well maybe I didn't mean that, maybe I meant a body. That's what you mean to do when you put a man in jail, cut off the head of the

Sphinx. Make a man aware only of his body, but a helpless, snuffling, debilitated body, deprived of sun, deprived of sex, deprived almost of senses. They left the cover of the spyhole open in the lockup and I remember seeing some small insect flying aimlessly round on the other side of the glass, and thinking even that insect was better off than all the miserable creatures who had been thrown into this cell. Then you start making resolutions like you'll never chain up a dog or visit a zoo. The desperation and the viciousness of the trapped thing swirl up inside you and if ever there was hate in your heart, it's for the owner of those receding footsteps. Who thought it all out, anyway? How could any magistrate or judge have experienced it? And if he had, how could he hand out a sentence of one hour, let alone a day, a year, seven years, life? Will the prison reformers realise one day, that the first reform, the reform from which all others come, is the abolition of the locked door, the ultimate insult to the soul of civilised man or any other kind of man? Long after I was released, I attacked a friendly copper in my district about it.

If you knew, I said, what you do to a man when you lock him up, you'd never turn a key again.

He agreed with me too. We always think of that with the young chaps, he said.

But he didn't know anything about it really, he'd always had the keys in his hands and that makes all the difference. If you really want to see a little of its effect on a human being, talk to a Maori just after he's been locked up for the first time. To a certain extent we're used to the idea. We've seen it on the films, we've read about it in books and newspapers, so we think we know. We think we have a hell of an advantage over a Maori because we've just about succeeded in killing the feeling by means of the intellect. But the Maori knows what cruelty is. He knows that the business of the locked door is infinitely more cruel than cutting a man's throat. Cutting a man's throat is done under emotional stress, but the locked door has nothing to do with emotions or the flesh. It's a cold-blooded, sadistic horror ...

[The Bad Boys' Camp]

One night [in our defaulters' camp] we had a meeting in a hut belonging to a fairly active resister called Jack, with a few men who were on the verge of nonco-operation. We kept a very careful look-out, but the next day at breakfast Mike [who had just arrived from Mount Eden prison after two and half years in jail for subversive pamphlets] and I and Jack were told to pack our things, we were being shifted. Some screw had been earwigging, I like to think, though there were quite a few toppers and crawlers at that camp. We had only an hour to pack up, but it didn't take Mike five minutes to find out we were being taken to the bad boys' camp which was about sixty miles further into the back of beyond, behind one of the prison camps.

I was glad I had Mike and Jack with me when I landed there, two old-timers in resistance. Jack hadn't decided to go to jail then, but he was responsible for many subversive moves and an enormous amount of information reaching the outer. Even the screws liked Jack. He was a big strong chap and one of those rare people in a resistance movement who can keep the admiration of all but the very worst of their enemies, without any loss of their own dignity or integrity or self-respect. The camp might have been a tourist's delight, but no tourist penetrated within miles; you have to go through prison property to get to it. The bush-covered hills enclosed it all round and there was a mountain river, full of trout, running round one side of the camp. In the morning you could hear tuis and bellbirds in the bush. There were about sixty men there and, as I learned afterwards, one screw to two and a half men. There was a barbed wire fence, ten feet high with a verandah all round the camp, then a patrol track and then another ten-foot fence. There were searchlights and sentry boxes on the hills and the whole camp was floodlit every night. Most of the inmates were escapees or men who had tried resistance in one way or another. The camp was divided into three compounds, each separately wired and each having its own gate which was locked from eight o'clock at night. The Red Compound was there with six men held in huts with bars on, and windows that opened only five inches at the bottom. There was a hell of an atmosphere in the place. It was the first time I'd really had anything to do with men who had tried resistance and been broken, and it gave me the jitters. To come straight in from the outer to this was really something.

I think the floodlights and searchlights at night put the whole thing, for me, over the edge and into the realm of nightmare. Looking out of my hut the first night, at the glaring lights and the wire fences with the bush vaguely discernible as a black mass in the background, I started thinking. Here were sixty men, most of whom were professed pacifists, many of them university students, school teachers, members of religious bodies like the Christian Pacifist Society – caged in like tigers escaped from the zoo. And this in New Zealand, two or three thousand miles away from any war zone. God Almighty, I thought, what would they do about something really dangerous?

Disintegration had set in badly amongst the inmates; it was so bad that some of them cursed the six men in the Red Compound, mainly on account of a sense of guilt, because most of them did quite a lot to help the unfortunate six. Since then, I've become used to all kinds of methods in jail communication, but when I first saw a hut with the window nearly closed and heard a voice issuing from lips pressed close to the bars, I got a shock that will last me all my life.

I'll tell you more about the camps as I go on. I'd decided to join the six men within a week. One of them had been in a hut alone over ninety days – all through the winter. But I wrote first to the Minister of Justice, telling him what I thought of him and his government. By this time, though, the outer was really getting to work, a little publicity had scared the government, and I'd been down there only a few days when the six men were moved. They were charged in court and received jail for the duration. Mike had been trying to rouse up a few men to go with me, and Mike was a most persuasive talker but it was no good; the paralysis that always attacks men confined for long had done most of its work, and the camp was as dead as mutton.

So a fortnight after I'd landed, I told the screw I wasn't working any more for the National Service Department and went and sat in my hut. About an hour later I was taken down to the Gauleiter. I'll tell you about this man one day. Of all the creatures I met in the camps and the jails, I'd say he was the worst. A Scotchman, with reddish hair and a blotchy skin and a big pitted nose and hair on the backs of his hands. I don't know just how far he would go if he had his way in a camp, but Jesus Christ, I wouldn't like to be there.

He was stupid, of course, but a little more on the spot than most of the gauleiters and screws. He harangued me for nearly an hour and even pretended to be nice about it, which was a silly thing to do. He could talk for hours in that grating Scotch voice and he'd actually managed to persuade a few chaps off nonco-operation by just going on talking till they got tired. It couldn't have been any other reason because he never gave expression to anything but banalities. Actually, in such matters as nonco-operation I knew he had no power and that he would have to ring up the city to find out whether they'd send me to jail or try and break me in the Red Compound. That was what I was waiting to find out, so I hardly bothered to listen to his persuasions or his veiled threats. When he saw he wasn't having any effect, he told a screw to take me up to the Red Compound and lock me up in a hut there. I was five days in a hut alone, and though this time I'd prepared for it, it was pretty tough. You weren't allowed tobacco, of course, and I had decided to try and give it up, which made it a lot tougher. After two days, Mike managed to slip in a whole fig and matches and papers, so I gave up trying to give it up. You could smoke only when the screws weren't around, and the first smoke I had, I was reeling round the hut as if I'd been half-shikker. They took your boots away, except when you were let out for exercise, and it took about an hour every morning, jumping up and down in your socks, to get the circulation going. The Gauleiter came up on inspection most days. A couple of months later, when I came back from my first two months in jail, I spent over three weeks in the Red Compound and became acquainted with the peculiarities of this particular brand of sadism, but luckily he didn't have a great deal of power over a man who had decided on absolute noncooperation with the camps. I contented myself this time with making a number of protests every time I saw him. He liked it and it improved my morale. As long as I can keep them from imagining that I'll take anything lying down, I thought, I'll still be on the surface.

The rest of the screws were downtrodden bums, most of whom would have been sympathetic, only they were scared. I used to try to argue with some of them about their jobs at first, but I soon dropped it. You can't do anything, at the time at least, with a man who's decided to dump his self-respect overboard.

Some of them were manpowered there and some of them took the job to get out of the war. Windy was the word. Imagine anyone taking a job as a screw in a detention camp in New Zealand. It used to beat me how they found them, but if there was one thing a concentration camp proved to me, it was that you'll always be able to find God knows how many yesmen who literally don't care what they're ordered to do, so long as they feel psychologically safe. The *âme damnée* of the human race, the cats-paw, the slave, the hanger-on, the flunkey, the mercenary, the stooge. He regrets doing everything he does, of course, but them's his orders. Do I make myself clear? When, at the last of thirteen appearances in front of the beaks, I said that I had seen plenty of screws who were capable of doing anything that was done at Belsen, the prosecutor threw up his hands in horror and the newspapers headlined it, as typical of the crazy statements of the crazy conchies. But the dumbest boobhead'll tell you it's true.[3] When modern man dumps his self-respect, there's nothing you won't be able to push on to him in the end.

When the screws weren't around, Mike used to get behind a hut in the next compound and shout a few words. On the fifth evening he called me up and told me I was going to court the next day. I hugged myself and jumped up and down in the hut. Christ, what a relief. Sure enough, the next morning while it was still dark, I was fetched out of my hut and, after changing into ordinary clothes, I was taken about eighty miles in the back of the gauleiter's car. All the way, I had the wind up about which jail I'd land up in. Wenukai was about the toughest, they said, and I asked God to make it one of the others my first time. Either He wasn't listening or He saw a lot further ahead than I did, because it was there all right. I heard one of the coppers talking Wenukai before I went into the court. They didn't even take the trouble to disguise the fact they knew I'd be convicted, whatever I said. The magistrate – well, almost all of the recalcitrants from the camps passed through his hands and I often wondered what was his real opinion about the camps, though it wouldn't have mattered anyway. They're ordered to do it and they do it, just like the screws. This time, he allowed me to have my say and I said quite a lot about the camps and for some reason or other, quite a bit got into the newspapers. The next time I came in front of him, he jumped on me smartly as soon as I started giving things away. I felt a good deal better in court than I had done the first time, and I felt better and better as time went on. Towards the end I almost liked coming up in front of these traitors to common justice.

Two months, I received that time. The usual periods were three months the first time up, and the duration of the war, the second. But a fair amount of publicity had arisen about conchies going to jail and the government was getting a bit windy. I don't know why really, because they could twist regulations round in almost unbelievable fashion. Right at the beginning, they'd done something in the emergency regulations that was a prime piece of British hypocrisy. When you disagreed with the concentration camps, you were 'transferred' to a jail, in which you were treated exactly as if you were a hard labour boobhead. But if any question arose as to whether you should or should not be there, or whether you should be transferred to another jail, you were then considered to be in a detention camp. In plain language, if you protested against being put in jail, they could and did reply that you weren't in no such place. On the other hand, when you landed in the boob and kicked up a dust about conditions, you were told you were a hard labour prisoner, and those were the hard labour rules and one more word from you, my boy, it'll be bread and water and the pound. In other words, as far as the conchies were concerned, they had deliberately suspended the writ of Habeas Corpus, and just as deliberately concealed it from the public. No, no, the defaulters weren't really in jail, they were just transferred there for their own good and the good of the camps.

I think it was this that tore away the last shreds of the umbilical cord attaching me to the British race. *Perfide Albion* was far too limited for me. I can stand a chap pulling a fast one on me, but when he struts around forever after, insisting it was for my own and everyone else's good, then I do feel like spitting in his eye. Some people might say that you can't expect things like Habeas Corpus in a total war. Refugees don't, do they? Habeas Corpus merely means that any person, at any time, can ask the authorities their reason for keeping him in jail. But we couldn't do that, because officially, and for that purpose, we weren't in jail. You shouldn't be surprised we kicked up a dust. If ever there was a dirty bit of hypocrisy, it was that. Do you want to get a man jumping mad? Well, try that. Try putting him in the white trousers, sending him out to crack stones at sixpence a day, locking him up alone for seventeen hours each day, poisoning him with maggotty meat. And then, when he starts frothing at the mouth, tell him he's not there at all really, he's just having a bad dream ...

['Wenukai' Prison]

I arrived at Wenukai in a snowstorm.

Back in detention, in my brief stay, I'd come to know Dave. Dave had done three months at Wenukai, for some protest or other, and it was he who told me what a cow of a place it was.

One of the worst things, he said, was the weather, nearly always snow, rain or sleet and if not, then a fair dinkum old-man frost. It's a tough place, Dave had said, when he heard I was nonco-operating, I hope you don't land there.

But of course I did land there, and of course it was night-time and there was a snowstorm on. It was September, and up there you can look forward to crook weather till the end of December at least. I thought the detention camp was cold enough, some mornings you found ice on the water in your mug, with the window closed all night. But from there we'd gone on climbing past one of the prison camps, and it was colder and colder and then the snow started, and the driver had to stop the truck about every half mile and scrape the snow off the windscreen.

I'm beginning to think it's always like this up here, he said, or else I'm unlucky.

There was a screw in charge of me they called Windy. He was rather a pathetic figure, he had an ulcerated stomach and was scared stiff of everything. Most of the men at the camp couldn't stick him at any price and I know that screws who are exceptionally scared of authority are a bit of a headache. But I can't get steamed up about obvious windiness, even in a screw; and besides, they're always in a jam trying to keep on everybody's right side.

Gawd, Windy kept saying to me all the way over, why do you want to do these things? Go to these horrible places?

Then I'd ask him if he thought the bad boys' camp was just a home from home.

It is, compared with this, he'd say, it is, compared with this.

I was in the clothes I'd brought from the North, silly clothes for this climate, and I was beginning to feel properly crook. It wasn't much after sunset but it was pitch dark. Suddenly another truck loomed up in front of us. It was going at a fair speed and we only just got by and as we passed, I caught a glimpse of what looked like a sheep-crate with some white figures. For something to say, I asked why they were carting sheep in that Godforsaken spot at this time of night.

Sheep, said the driver, that's not sheep, that's prisoners. Had a breakdown, I suppose.

The sight of those ghost figures wasn't too good when you knew they weren't sheep. I felt Windy's arm begin to shake and he started off on another moan. We went on climbing, and then we got to what seemed like a plateau because we were going on the level.

How high up is Wenukai, I asked?

Two thousand six hundred feet and right under the mountains, Windy answered.

I broke out a bit then. Jesus, I said, why do they want to put a prison in a place like that?

But if I didn't know the answer then, I know it now. It's all part of the punishment, the standard boobhead answer. Don't worry, sport, it's all part of the punishment. During the course of the next fifteen months, I used to get bored and irritated by it. Maggots in the meat? It's all part of the punishment. Standing naked in a queue on a bitter Saturday afternoon, waiting for a shower. Lights so low you can't read, or failing altogether. Damp clothes in the morning and damp, six-by-eight huts at night. And then the senseless, preventable things, like not being able to choose a library book and finding the one left in your cell with a quarter of the pages missing. Only one letter a fortnight to friends, and the same with visits. Not allowed this, not allowed that. To be treated every day, every hour, like a half-witted child.

But God Almighty, why? I used to say.

And back came the ironical answer, don't worry sport, it's all part of the punishment.

But it's not a satisfactory answer, even in New Zealand. I don't believe that if you asked the maninthestreet, he would say he really wanted to treat people like that, even if they were criminals.

So later on, I started to find out for myself and one of the first questions that had to be answered was why they should put the prison camps in those particular places. The answer is, to a certain extent, the answer to a problem peculiar to New Zealand ... Progressive Social Legislation ... We'll get the bad boys out of the cities ... teach them things like farming ... So came the prison camps.

Set down in about the coldest part of the island, right up against the great snow-capped mountains, the camps shiver through the long winter in what is the nearest approach to a desert in the island, two of them to blossom forth as socalled farms in the short summer of about three months, and Wenukai working quarries with a farm attached. The climate at the first two is passably dry in winter but the other side of the mountains seems to catch all the snow, rain and sleet that falls there. The farming, of course, is just a joke, or it would be a joke if it weren't so excruciatingly cold. As it is, the stock on the farms is a walking indictment of the government and also the jails. Day after day, riding to the quarries in canopies on the backs of trucks, we passed the herd of cows staggering out to bare pastures and day after day I never ceased to wonder how many of them had managed to survive the winter. You could have cut your hand on their backbones and counted every rib. And yet, incredible as it may seem, they managed to drag enough milk out of them to supply, not only sixty boobheads with their miserable quarter pint a day, but at least some of the milk up at an asylum ten miles away.

So here was my first question and, with the answer, the way would be opened to a lot of others. Why did they put the camps in this Godforsaken part of New Zealand where farming was virtually impossible unless, of course, you consider that farming is underfeeding with superphosphate and hay? Why? ...

Reactionary heads of the Prisons' Department never go beyond the idea of punishment. You could explain till you're black in the face that there are other ideas, floating around or actually being put into practice in other countries, about how to deal with prisoners. You wouldn't get anywhere. And the reason is that it's not just slackness, there's a purpose. Over the years they've grown to like it. After all, to be able to inflict punishment on grown men is a great sop to sadism. Yes, they like it, in time they grow to love it, to fatten on it like a tick fattening on its host. But at the same time, they have a sort of feeling that it isn't done in a Progressive Social country, a wish to hide their little sadisms under a bushel, or anything else that's handy. Keep them out of the public eye and we're set, is the idea. Along comes the respectable New Zealander who wants to shut his eyes tight at the possibility of a criminal in God's Own Country, and the result is a foregone conclusion. Out go the camps to the back of beyond where there are no prying eyes.

If you happen to be a reactionary and a bit of a sadist, the scheme is right up your alley. Naturally, the thing has to be done with a certain amount of care, but the odds are overwhelming in your favour. You're dealing with outcasts from society and that gives you an enormous advantage at the start. From that point on, you just have to be careful to pick yesmen, of whom there are countless numbers in New Zealand. Yesmen superintendents, yesmen doctors, yesmen ministers of religion and yesmen Justices of the Peace. Even at that, you wouldn't think it was so easy. But it is, believe me. I've been there.

I got out of the truck, stiff with cold, and a voice coming from a lighted doorway, shouted to bring him over here. Windy was beside me and as we walked towards the light he was moaning in a frightened voice, what a ghastly place it was. A thin, pale, darkhaired young man in a khaki uniform was standing by the door and I was told to wait inside. There was a desk in the middle of the room. I stood by it, too cold to think.

After a bit of a palaver outside, I heard the truck drive away into the night. My last link, I thought, but I wasn't thinking of detention, it was Windy with his moans and groans and his sympathy through fear. There wouldn't be anything like Windy at Wenukai, I was willing to bet. After a while the pale young man came in and sat down at the desk. He had a mouth like a codfish. He was suave and polite and efficient and, rising above my misery, I felt a growing dislike for his white codfish face.

There's something malign about a screw that's polite, you can bet your life on it. If they're irritable or fussy or roar at you or merely ignore you, it means they still have a conscience working somewhere. But I must tell you that, as far as my experience of boob goes, politeness is out.

This bird started asking me questions and writing down my answers in a large book. Where-was-I-born, was-I-married, had-I-any-children, what-was-my-mother's-maiden-name, all the usual stuff that goes down in those files that one day, I thought, when the second Christ sets them alight, will change the world for a brief space into heaven's brightest star.

While I was answering these questions the door opened, letting in an icy wind, and an enormous figure walked in and stood by the desk. He must have been six foot four at the least, and he wore an oilskin buttoned up to the neck, but with the arms hanging loose, and a blue-uniformed paunch bulging from the lower, unbuttoned part of the oilskin. The melting snow dripped from his hat on to the floor. So this was it, I thought, Obie Dowell. Dave had told me about him.

One of the other big disadvantages at Wenukai, Dave said, is the Super. A big slob of an Irishman named Obie Dowell. Seventeen stone of Irish ignorance, a conchie had called him, Dave said, and he'd received a back-hander for his temerity.

Obie will say to you – I am Obadiah Dowell and they call me King of this county, but to you, my bhoy, I shall be MISTER Dowell.

But he didn't say anything to me, he didn't even look at me. He just stood there, enormous, rocking backwards and forwards on his heels and breathing heavily through his nose. I'm under average height and this wordless performance made me nervous so I went on answering the questions as if I didn't give a damn.

But the huge presence was distracting. Years ago, at the time of the Irish troubles, I remembered seeing Punch's cartoons of the Irish rebel, the dirty Sinn Feiner, a short, sturdy, low-browed peasant with a shillelagh in one hand. The low brow, the button nose, the small pig eyes, and the colossal jaw under the tightclosed, trap mouth. Here they all were but on the body of a giant. Jesus Christ, I thought, where do they get hold of such specimens? How do they dig them up? What do they look for in a jail superintendent? At that time I didn't think they would deliberately pick such a monstrosity, even if there were a sort of unconscious purpose in their minds. It seemed to me inconsequent somehow, in a country full of Progressive Social Legislation, to choose an obvious anachronism like Obadiah Dowell to run a prison.

Much later, I was to look back on Obie with a feeling that approached benevolence, in comparison with some of the people I saw. Judgment is only relative and if you want to prove that one, take a trip through the New Zealand prison system as a boobhead. The man you'd ordinarily walk across the street to avoid becomes, simply by comparison with still greater horrors, someone quite tolerable.

Yes, you'd say to a short-termer who's indignant about one of Obadiah's blatant injustices. Yes, but you wait until you meet soandso and soandso.

The office was bare and cold and I wondered what was the matter with them that they didn't seem to feel it. But they'd probably gotten used to it. Everything looked slightly dilapidated, even the part of Obie Dowell's uniform that bulged out of the oilskin. I had been driven ninety miles to the court and about a hundred and twenty miles back to Wenukai and all I wanted to do then, was to get between the blankets.

Another youngish screw with a perpetual scowl on his face, blew in with the icy wind. He barked at the codfish, have you finished with him and then said to me, through here. I followed him under an archway and into a sort of quadrangle, a bare shingled yard surrounded by small huts, placed close together. Dimly I saw this through the driving sleet. Some of the huts had oblong lighted windows, but they looked very small and the lights were dull. We walked down a covered concrete way which ran down the fourth side of the quadrangle and the man with the perpetual scowl unlocked a heavy door. I walked into what looked like a small grain store, but with bags of manure piled all down one side and bars on the windows. A small fireplace without a fire grinned hopelessly at me, from one end of the store. The door was slammed and locked behind me and as usual the footsteps receded into the distance.

I walked up and down, wishing to God they'd come and put me in a cell. Every year as I grow older, it seems I feel the cold more and more. Who was it said everyone, in the end, dies from cold? Within reason, the hotter it is the more energetic I feel but, unlike most Nordics, the approach of winter doesn't stimulate me into brisk preparations for murder in the spring. All I want to do is get in a deep hole and close the entrance until the warmth of the earth above tells me the sun's on his way back.

So this was Wenukai. What a senseless mess I'd landed myself in, to come from the winterless north into this Godforsaken icehouse in the wasteland. I am, on the whole, an anticipator. If I'm going through hell, I like to go through it first in my mind. In a general way, though it may have its disadvantages, this is a useful, and moderately efficient defence mechanism. Things aren't usually so bad as you imagined they were going to be, or perhaps they're bad in a different way. But occasionally you strike up against a situation that looks to be every bit as bad. Then you begin to have senseless regrets. Here was I, nearly forty, a moderately successful farmer, with no personal enemies that I knew of. Critical of, but not actively hostile to the society around me. Here was I, stuck in a situation like this, simply because I'd refused to compromise. Looking back, it would have been so easy to avoid going even to a detention camp. They call it a socialist country but don't make any mistake about that; if a man with a bit of money wanted to get out of fighting for it in this war, he didn't have to look far to find a way.

So, in this cold, cheerless room I suffered from senseless regrets. Senseless because I knew quite well I would behave in the same way if I had another chance, or a million chances. There's no greater unhappiness than running away from your own tail. But the experiences in the court and the lockup, the long cold drive in the truck, the feeling of being pushed around like a sack of grain; and then the codfish and curt questions and orders, the man with the perpetual scowl and that paunchy monstrosity, Obadiah Dowell; these had got me down and somehow this room where, I guessed, the prisoners were congregated on wet weekends, finished the business. I sat down on a bag of manure and bloody near wept.

But if there's one thing prison life teaches you, it's how to wait. After what seemed an age they brought me the prison clothes, meticulously accounting for all my things as they took them away from me. Very careful the jails are, about that. Most boobheads don't arrive with much in the way of gear, but it's all carefully entered up in the book until you're due to return to the world. You read about it and it's called the honesty of the British official. I know it's all very correct but it seemed to me, the boobhead, kind of ridiculous, like wearing evening dress in the jungle or fiddling while Rome burns.

What would they do if they didn't keep a check, you say?

Ah, I don't know. I think I'd say, keep the lot, my boys, and anything else that belongs to me. And then let me out into the street, naked, unashamed, and without a razoo.

Altogether I was in Wenukai nearly eight months. During that time I was sent back to detention in the hope that I had reformed my ways, but the hope wasn't realised and I nonco-operated again. This time it was jail for the duration of the war and, as nobody had defined the end of the war, it was a case of trying to escape or settling down and wondering what you should do about it. Some of this settling and wondering process took place in Wenukai, so I'd like to tell you a little story entitled a day in the life of a lag, Wenukai style.

You wake up to the clanging of a hammer on the discarded iron truck-brakedrum which is hanging in the corner of the yard. In the winter it's dark and they'll switch your light on from outside in a minute. It always seemed to me typical of Wenukai, the hammer and brakedrum outfit, just as the harsh note of the bell at The Hill was typical of conditions in that hygienic hell. On the first morning I couldn't take my eyes off the clothes I was to put on, which were hanging up behind the door. God stiffen the crows, I thought, even the lowest swagger on the bum would spit in your eye if you offered him clothes like that. The coat was ripped from elbow to cuff and the ripped piece hung down a foot below the sleeve. The dirty grey sweater was more holes than wool and the famous white trousers weren't white at all, they were a sort of greyish-brown colour and patched from arsehole to breakfast time. I lay and contemplated these threadbare garments for a while and then heaved myself up, but the floor of the hut was wringing wet and cold, so I decided to do what I did most of the time at Wenukai – dress on the bunk.

The rattle of keys starts down the line and suddenly reaches your hut and the door's pushed open. You bend down, seize your pisspot and a tin dipper for water, and walk across the yard. Your pisspot's nearly always full, the cold weather and the stuff called cocoa you get at night, are great kidney stimulators. You never know, too, you may have been taken short during the night and the pisspot has to hold everything. There are two open lavatory pans the other side of the yard, and that's where you're making for, trying maybe, but always failing to stop the contents of the pisspot slopping over. When you reach one of the pans you pour everything in and move away as quickly as you can. No plugs are pulled until the contents of sixty boobhead's bowels and bladders are reposing in the pans or somewhere down the pipe. If the pot's really dirty, you scrape a bit of shingle or sand from the yard, whirl it round in the pot and throw the shingle back in the yard. The washhouse door's nearly always kept locked, but by this time, a screw's unlocked it and you stand waiting in a queue for your turn at one of the basins. You won't have much of a wash in winter if you've got any sense.

Back in your hut, you comb your hair if you feel like it, and then there's another hammer-clanging and you move over to another queue by the kitchen slide. You collect two flat tins, about six inches in diameter, and take them back to your hut in which you're locked up again. One tin contains porridge and the other hash. You put some of your quarter pint of milk on your porridge and a little sugar, sir, to taste. Most times the porridge will be burnt but you don't mind about that, it's a bowel-opener and it counteracts the taste of varnish in the hash which is usually what's left over from the night before. At least once a week in the summer the hash is really bad and then there'll be a roar, and it'll be alright again for a week. I don't know where the taste of varnish comes from but that's always there.

These things don't matter so much as people make out. Boobheads don't eat, they shovel down their food. Why not? They know it's only about once in a blue moon you get food in which you could possibly take any interest, let alone pleasure. Having shovelled it down, you may have time to read a few pages of a book, unless, as so often happens, the water supply has broken down and you've had to be mustered by a screw to wash in the river.

Before you're unlocked again you put some things in a small linen bag. A knife, some bread, butter, if you have any left, cheese ditto, and a small bottle containing syrup or, if you've been lucky, Borstal honey which is a mixture of syrup and animal fat pinched from the cookhouse. It's a pretty foul mixture, but it replaces butter, which is always short in jail. When you're unlocked, you stand around for about five minutes, or wait in your hut if it's raining. Then the brakedrum clangs again and you form up in front of the offices, in the gang you were in the day before. There are usually four gangs, two quarry, one farm, and one small road gang. Each one forms up in line, with a screw at the end, and Obie stands in front and slightly to the side, colossal jaw stuck in the air, scrutinising his crowd of derelicts. The screw with the perpetual scowl whom they call The Dog, stands next to him with a pad, ready to take down changes in the gangs. While they're counting and checking, you wonder if you look as bad as the rest. There's no doubt about it they look a pretty crook crowd. The prison hat makes them look like clowns and the clothes like swaggers and – my God, you think, what a collection.

It's typical of the prison system that the clothes at The Hill, where there are plenty of visitors, are passable, and you'll even get in trouble up there for not reporting a tear in your coat. This is Obie's moment though, and the more downandout the boobheads look, the more highfalutin' becomes his voice.

Boswell, move to Mr. Doolan's par-tay.

Then a pause while the little pig eyes travel along the lines, never looking at you, but in which gang your body is.

R-r-romwell to Mr. Hoggin's par-tay.

It's a play, and you get to enjoy it after a while. None of the boobheads ever look at Obie or The Dog, they look in front of them but they don't stand at attention. You'll never get a crimmo to stand at attention just as you'll never get him to do anything but shuffle along when he's walking in line. Some Supers have tried to smarten their jails, but they've always come up against a wall, tougher than the stones of The Hill, a kind of deep, passive resistance. You can keep a man behind bars, you can drive him out to work, but you can never compel him to be smart or to do more than the absolute minimum quantity of work. For a little while, maybe. But Hitlers come and go, and jails go on forever and it's there, above all places, you realise the truth that compulsion never does anything but put a light to the slow fire of undying hostility. Hardly any jail Supers have the faintest conscious realisation of this, but most of them know instinctively that, when it comes to a sustained effort, passive resistance always has the wood on compulsion.

So, the boobhead parades for work, hostile, not at attention, not at ease. So he shuffles off to his job. So, he gets through the day with the minimum amount of effort required. You don't blame him, do you? It's his only way of showing his independence, unless he wants to go through a living hell.

When Obie's finished his daily comedy you go out, by gangs, through the prison gate to the trucks. Number One party, shouts the screw, Left-turn-break-off-for-labour-quick-march, and the response is what I said, a slow turn and a shambling clatter of boots along the concrete. It always used to give me a bit of a kick, that response. Between the idea and the reality falls the shadow of the boobhead's innate, unconquerable, stubborn, unending resistance to all forms of military discipline.

Outside the gate, the trucks are backed up to the canopies and each quarry gang lifts its canopy on to the truck and gets inside. The canopy is really a sort of movable hut with seats down each side, but there were usually too many in the gang for the seats and you just piled in on top of each other and sat anywhere, with some, especially the Maoris, clinging to the back and sides like dogs with their heads into the wind.

Shouts of let 'er go Charlie, and it was this part of jail life at Wenukai that used to get me down. I've driven a car or a truck for years and I'm as nervous as a cat when anyone else is driving. The nearest quarry was about six miles and the furthest ten miles. Most of the trucks were in a hell of a bad state of repair, and most of the boobhead drivers went for the lick of their lives. Prisoners don't care, is true. But I did. Up on the side of the banks, hitting bridges, the steering gear breaking near the top of the road up the mountain. Jesus, it was purgatory as far as I was concerned. Several times I've jumped off the truck at the quarry and told the screw I'd refuse to get on again, unless something was done about the truck. Luckily, you could usually rely on support for any complaint, even though boobheads don't care. One day the traffic cop who used to roam the district in a black V8, stopped us and tore into the screw about overloading.

It's only a few miles, the screw said.

But the traffic cop was wild. I don't care if it's a hundred yards, he said, one of these days there'll be an accident and ten or twelve men will be killed.

The screw grinned. They're only prisoners, he said.

Most of the trucks had overturned or been in serious trouble at one time or another, and it was the usual jail luck that nobody was killed. I wasn't going to take any more chances than I could help. To take risks of being killed or maimed by a crazy truck driver in jail, without any purpose whatsoever, always seemed to me to be the height of imbecility.

After they'd dropped the gangs at the quarries or on the roads, the trucks went off on errands for the rest of the day, in between carting metal out of the quarry. Up to the asylum to deliver the milk, to the station to pick up goods, or on some other errand for the prison. Truck drivers were 'staff men' and nearly always toppers and crawlers. There were plenty of perks; each driver was supposed, officially, to have a screw with him wherever he went, but this was hardly ever done. A lot of skull-duggery went on, nearly all the houses within miles of the prison had been done over, goods, particularly booze, pinched from the station. If the police came along Obie had to allow them interviews, but in some subtle way he'd let the boobheads know they were under his jurisdiction. It's a stone certainty he wouldn't give the police any help because Obie didn't like the police.

What you did when you got to the quarry depended on the screw. Some were crook and chased you around, but most of them were fairly easy. Obie was such a dictator that two or three of the screws were almost as keen to put one over him as a boobhead. The only thing was, you couldn't trust any of them. Not one. Still, it made for a very much better atmosphere than in the city jails.

Two of the quarries were in fair situations but the third was a fair cow, it was almost at the bottom of the great gorge and you hardly saw the sun all day. Many a boobhead's health had been undermined down there. If you offended Obie, but not so as he could put bread and water on to you, you'd find yourself wading about in icy slush at the bottom of the gorge for a long spell. Some chaps didn't mind quarry work but I'd almost take a staff job to avoid it. There's nothing more cold and dead than stone, unless, I suppose, you're a sculptor or a builder with an idea in your mind. You can't have a great idea in spawling stones with a hammer or shovelling the bits on to an iron-lined truck. There must be something superlatively Nordic about a man who likes it. The icy-mountain type. If I could work it I used to get the job of stripping, taking the earth off the top of the pit. With a shovel in my hands and earth to put it in I could imagine, sometimes, I was digging a garden.

For lunch, or when it was wet, you repaired to a shelter made from sheets of corrugated iron. One of the boobheads would build a fire which filled the shelter with smoke but most days in that part of the world, you were only too glad to get in there as close to the fire as you could, even though the water dripping down your neck from holes in the roof just about balanced the effect of the fire. There you listened to the interminable boob stories, jobs done or jobs contemplated, fights with coppers or demons, and smut.

Well, Lofty would say after a pause in the talk, time for the sexo hour.

Or maybe it was food or booze or how much longer someone had to go. Release, food, booze, sex. The four things were uppermost in the mind, in that order. They didn't talk so much about release when there was a conchie there; we were on indefinite sentence and every boobhead knows what that means.

Between four-thirty and five p.m. the truck turned up again if it hadn't broken down, and you'd earned sixpence for the day. If you got into any trouble you'd nearly always be fined ten shillings as well as bread and water and the pound, so that would be twenty days it would take you to start again from scratch. The drive, back, for me, was much worse than the drive over because the majority wanted to get home, like horses. (They call it home, Obie said to a visitor, I've heard 'em.) It seems funny somehow, that a man should want to be locked in with a tin of food that, nine times out of ten, is as crook as hell. But it isn't that, really. Between about six and nine o'clock you can choose, within the narrow limits of your cell, what to do. Read a book or magazine, write one of the two letters to your family for the week, go to sleep. That's why you want to get back.

When you do get back, you're lined up and counted by the screw who took you out, and the count's checked by the screw in charge of the office. Then the washhouse is unlocked and you stand in another queue for a basin, after which you go back to your hut which, once a week, you'll find has been done over by a screw in your absence. You're just back in your hut when the brakedrum clangs and you go over to the queue by the kitchen slide and collect your tin of food and as you cross the yard, you raise the lid to find out if the meat's short or bad. Sometimes you don't have to raise the lid and then you prepare yourself for a complaint to Obadiah, which certainly won't do any good and will probably land you down in the gorge for a few weeks.

In summer you're let out for an hour in the shingle yard after the meal, but in winter it's dark and you're locked up for the night just after five o'clock. If you're wise you'll hit the cot smartly. You're probably wet and it's just as well to get warm. They give you two coarse canvas sheets but you never use those, you put as many thicknesses of blanket over you as you can arrange and then tuck the canvas sheets round your feet to keep the draught out. Though I like fresh air, I'm no fresh-air fiend and some nights I had no hesitation in closing the little window down tight. It would open only a bare four inches anyway, with wire netting and expanding metal in front of that.

On nice evenings the boobheads would shout to each other for a while if there was an easy screw around, and it's an uncanny performance when you first hear it. Somehow you always expect to see people, when you hear them talking and shouting close at hand. It used to start off at quite a rate, with some shouting to a hut the other side of the yard and others, in lower tones, to the huts nearer at hand. Then it gradually dies down, like birds going to sleep in a tree, until there are only two voices left talking, with an occasional pause as a screw walks out of the office. About my third evening there the weather had cleared and it was much warmer. Conversation had practically ceased, it was just after dusk, when a voice sounded not far from my cell.

What a beautiful evening, it said.

There was no reply in the jail, but a dog barked in the distance somewhere and I heard a train whistle further away. Jesus Christ, I thought, so this is what it's going to be like ...

[Later:] I sentence you to three days solitary confinement on a diet of bread and water ... it's the V.J. [Visiting Justice] speaking, and I'm confronting him across the table, with fear in my heart and probably an expression of stout determination and pugnacity on my face. He used to spit those words out as if he'd like to do a lot more to you.

I didn't allow myself to hold a personal hatred against many of the riff-raff that go to make up the New Zealand prison system, but if ever I came near to hating a man it was this one. I admit that I tried to humiliate him in a lot of ways. It was hard enough, anyway, because they hold all the cards. There's only one thing, especially with a man like this, you know you're a goner before you walk into the court, the only question being how many charges they can cook up against you. If he's alone, a J.P. can give you only three days on each charge. Needless to say, they can soon find another yesman to form a magistrate's court and give you fourteen days, if they want to. They did it with us twice. The procedure is simple. The two beaks sit in the office and as you walk in, Obadiah comes to the door and announces to the desert around Wenukai that the District Court is now open. But if they don't do that, they'll often cook up several charges on one offence and give you three days on each charge. The inevitability of the law. Most experienced boobheads don't even bother to put up a defence. With this joker I used to sentence myself first, and then try and make him feel guilty about his damned Visiting Justice job.

I often wondered why he was so vicious. Justices of the Peace are usually appointed because they've achieved some standing in the community. In a semi-capitalist, decadent society, this usually means that some horrible pieces of work get the job and I have a shrewd suspicion that anywhere near the jails, the J.P. is selected by the prison authorities ... This one was so personally vindictive in his manner that I suspected some childhood trouble behind all this, probably unnecessary whippings by a sadistic father.

Anyway you asked me about solitary confinement and that's how it starts, with a bloke sticking out his underlip at you and repeating those words ... in as nasty a way as possible. Then you're led off by a screw and locked up in your own cell until they're ready to begin the torture. For one thing the doctor has to examine you before you do bread and water. A mere formality of course, nowadays. A dab at your heart with the stethoscope and a question: do you feel alright? I always used to reply to this with a nonchalant yes: I don't know why really? I felt like saying No, you so and so, what do you expect? But I never got around to it. It's best to save your energies in jail and what's the use of arguing, anyway, especially with a screw doctor? The sooner they get on with it the better.

The first thing that strikes you about these preliminaries is the extreme inhumanity of the whole business. You can understand an enormous amount of cruelty on the spur of the moment. You can even understand the personal pleasures of the Comte de Sade. It's when order creeps in that it becomes, in some way, inhuman and almost unreal. With the conchies in jail, this inhumanity was more than ever noticeable, because they nearly always went out on some protest against injustice. The jail authorities, the V.J., the screws and the doctor all knew this. Some of them thought the conchies were crazy but none of them could actually think they were guilty of a crime. And yet the inhuman routine was carried on just the same. It never did any good, even from their point of view. True, they tried to break them with bread and water but they must have known you can't do that with such men, particularly men who are acting on a principle. Solitary confinement's hell, but it boosts your morale. If you went on long enough with it, you'd undoubtedly be crazy but that wouldn't have suited the authorities either. If they'd been wise they'd never have given a conchie bread and water, they'd have treated them soft. That's the way to break a man surer than anything. Keep him behind the bars, leave him to his own devices and treat him soft. Inside a few months he'll be a jelly. A sort of assupwards argument for Pacifism, I suppose. But one of the things that struck me very forcibly about the authorities was their rank stupidity. They couldn't have thought that one out in a month of Sundays. Thank God they didn't, for the sake of our characters. You'd have thought they might have been pushed into treating us soft by the publicity and protests on our behalf. But no. Put another nickel in the machine and the band plays on. The routine must be adhered to, until the jail walls collapse. Till Doomsday.

My first three days solitary were a hell, literally. As far as I'm concerned that goes for all solitary, but this one was particularly bad. Chiefly on account of the temperature which, during those three days, was about as low as you can get, even at Wenukai. It was September and the first night there was a snowstorm. The pound is a real punishment at all times and there are few crimmos who go looking for it. I've seen some pretty tough men come out of it like wet rags. It's the psychological factor, of course, like everything in jail. The strain. But intense cold makes it a great deal harder. Three days bread and water. It doesn't sound much said quickly like that. And after you've done a long stretch like fifty-nine days as we did, it doesn't sound anything at all. When we'd finished our resistance effort I used to laugh at other boobheads worrying about getting three days. That's where I was wrong. There's something about bread and water. No matter how much you've done of it, you've only got to do a spell of a month or two of ordinary jail life, and it's just as hard to take. That's one of the things I learnt. It was one of the things the authorities knew, that I didn't.

The rules are you're allowed three blankets and no mattress. Most jail blankets are pretty thin and in the daytime these are taken away and your clothes put in. You're left with nothing but the Bible, a mug of water and a small loaf of bread. No stool. You might get gay with it and start smashing up. The eternal pisspot, of course, in which you do everything you can. At The Hill there's a wooden slab let into the floor, but in the prison camps there's an ordinary wooden bunk. You can ask for what they call a text-book but I didn't bother usually. Nearly all the books they keep for the dummy[4] are unreadable even under the best conditions. I did kick up a dust once.

Why the religious stuff? I said to the screw.

The screw looked indignant.

You don't expect anything else when you're on punishment, surely now? he said.

But in any case, one of the things you soon discover in solitary is that you can't read. Or very little. You get no exercise until the third day and often not then, depending on the Super. From the third day on, you're allowed exercise for an hour a day, usually. If you're doing a longer stretch than three days, you're supposed to have a break between each three day period, of one day on No. 2 ration. That's what they call humanitarian. In other words, they don't want you to die on their hands. They have charge of your body. When it comes to your soul you can rot in hell, but the body must be kept living at all costs. Or half alive.

To realise what three days bread and water means, you have to go through it yourself under the conditions obtaining in a jail. There's no other way unless you're gifted with a superlative imagination. Many people couldn't be really alone for three days without going crazy but most of them imagine they could. In fact, most people talk as if they'd like to spend some time on their own. Time to think things out they say; only somehow they never get around to it. As for the bread and water, well a fast does you good, doesn't it? Correct. All I can say is, if you go to jail, don't start boasting to yourself about how much bread and water you could take ... It's a good idea not to boast about such things until you've tried.

I remember seeing some idiot writing in the paper saying that bread and water couldn't be hard to take, he'd spent three days lost in the bush with only bread and not much of that, and he felt fine. It's only after you've been in jail some time that you just grin when these Knowallnonothings come out with that sort of stuff. Physical conditions mean a lot in jail but it's the psychological factor that finally weighs the balance down. Cold and hunger are hard to take, especially cold, but when they're forced on you by a hostile authority, in ninety per cent of cases unjustly, they are incomparably more difficult ... The one factor people leave out when they try to describe life in jail, is the pain that is always covering your mind like a black curtain, blotting out all the pleasures you once had in the outside ...

Well, you're locked up for three days and the footsteps die away in the distance. You sit there on the hard wooden bunk for a while, thinking what kind of people they are to do this sort of thing to you. Who invented locking up, anyway? You can imagine the one-eyed lunatic who invented the door with the lock only on the outside, looking at his handiwork, patting himself on the back at the sight of the blank unassailable expanse of the lockless door. Like most scientists, it would never occur to him to think about the feelings of the human beings involved. Prison, Prison, PRISON. A word in daily use only after the coming of Christ. Christianity and prisons born together. Was it Christ who made people feel like this? But no, that wasn't the story. Just about at that time, they were beginning to invent the more refined tortures. People in the western world discovered they had minds and that the way to get at a person was through his mind. You're in the dummy, down in the pound, the digger, whatever you like to call it. You've started doing three days solitary confinement on bread and water only. There's the bread, there's the water. Well, what about a bit of bread? But no, you'd better not start yet. There's an interminable time to go. Interminable seconds, minutes, hours, days, to go ticking away into oblivion. Slowly. Slower and slower the hungrier you get. Better keep the bread for a while and then just a finger, so's you'll be able to space it out.

You get up and start going over the cell inch by inch. Some kind boobhead may have left a smoke tucked away for the next man. I've never found one yet, in a dummy cell, but there's always the chance. You draw a blank, as usual. Well then, what about the smokes you've hidden in the lapels of your coat. You can't smoke now, a screw might smell it. You can't smoke until after nightfall, but you've got to get the smokes out of your coat before they take your clothes away. Hell, why didn't you think of it before? There's all the time in the world in front of you, but feverishly you begin to get the smokes out of the seams, feverishly search for hiding places. You've tied cotton to a few of them and these you hang through the ventilator. The same with the striker and a few split matches. Then one above the door, one in some crack by the window, or in the loaf of bread. You hear a footstep outside and hide everything, keeping your eye on the spy-hole. But it passes on. After you've done all this, you sit down and start thinking again. God Almighty, to what a state they've reduced you already, exactly one hour out of the seventy-two hours bread and water. That's one of the worst features. Your hearing and observation become so acute within the confined limits of the jail, particularly in solitary confinement, that you know, almost to a minute, what time it is ... Oh then, there's the Bible. Why not make up your mind to start reading it from beginning to end? Or make a study of one book? The book of Job? The Lord gave and the Lord hath taken away. Blessed be the name of the Lord. But Job wasn't in solitary confinement. Good God, he wasn't even in prison, the lucky soandso.

You start reading, but you find you can't concentrate. Your mind wanders away to the people outside. I suppose the V.J. is looking forward to sitting down to a nice lunch. Meat and white bread and pastry, I'll bet. I hope it ties knots in his guts. Jesus Maria. How did you ever let yourself get in this position? ...

Outside, in the world which you left behind you ages ago, there are people actually walking about the streets wondering what they'll have for lunch, worrying about some silly business problem, thinking what a time they're going to have that night with some girl. Girls, my God. While you squat here, like some bloody animal in the half-dark.

Or in the country. Actually in the country near birds and trees. Grumbling about having to milk cows. It's almost unbelievable. They ought to throw their arms round the cows' necks and hug them for the privilege of being free to milk them. Of being free to touch them. Of being free ...

Sixteen months of experience in New Zealand jails, with about ninety days in solitary confinement, have convinced me that most human beings are capable of adjusting themselves to anything. Some crack up, of course, but only a few. I mean that they are capable of adjusting themselves at the time ...

The adjustment in solitary confinement consists of simply finding something to do to fill the time. Different people have different methods. Some men manage to sleep, and I knew one man who could sleep nearly eighteen hours a day. The punishment does vary a little with different personalities. One of the reasons why I found the dummy so tough was that for years I've slept only for five hours a night, and that was when I was taking plenty of physical exercise. In the pound I didn't average three, at first. But whatever resistances you have, dummy'll get you where you live, in the long run ...

Eventually I found two methods of adjustment. One was the usual method of spacing the day out into as many different activities as possible, and the other was a sort of Proustian technique of reviving the memory. The first, in various forms, is adopted by most men doing dummy. You get up, you walk around, you sit down, you lie down, you read the Bible, you eat a bit of bread, you sit on the pisspot, you take a sip of water, you do some exercises, you try to sleep. All this at fairly regular intervals. The band plays on, but you don't know it's there. Momentarily you're deaf to the madness of reality, and blind too. You're simply concerned with regular things at regular intervals. That isn't to say that you can forget the pain. It's always there, the black curtain that may one day blot out everything and drive you insane. But meanwhile we'll eat a bit of bread or walk forty-six times round the wooden slab, or do Mr. Benjamin's naturopath exercises, or sit on the pisspot and try to evacuate.

The Proustian method was something quite different. It was a God-send and when I'd really got into it, I almost forgot the black curtain for a while. Almost, and for a while. In effect it was simple. To find some way of reviving memories that had long been in abeyance, to see how far back you could go, and how vivid the memory would become. They don't supply you with cups of tea and madeleines in the pound, but I did it by means of tunes. Mostly popular tunes, some of them dated a long way back. It was astonishing how far back and how vivid the memories were. In the end I found I could relive a scene from child-hood as if I were once again a living, active participant of the scene. By the time I had done this several times, the personalities of the people who were in it gradually became so clear I could hear the slightest difference in the intonation of their voices, remember the way they moved their mouths and hands, even found a sort of fresh insight into their characters. The comparatively irrelevant things became most vivid. The exact shade of someone's hair, the glint of a few strands of it just above the temple when the sun shone on it. A word dropped casually by some long forgotten friend. The particular mixture of scents that came from a patch of gorse and broom growing on the cliff below the house where I spent the first nine years of my life. Maybe I came to realise that the flick of an eyelash can give you as much psychological insight as two volumes of theory by Mr. Butterlugs, M.D., Associate Psychiatrist at such-and-such an institute. Whatever it did to me it was a marvellous anodyne in the dummy. Nostalgia par excellence. It was even a sort of gateway to contemplation. After I had practised for a long period, I could sometimes dispense with the memories. I'd start off by humming my little tune, go back to a room in the big house on the cliff and talk to the people I hadn't thought of for years. If you can go to this point, you've achieved a certain feeling, the feeling of nostalgia. And after a while the tune and the house and the room and the people will fade away and you'll be left with the feeling itself. And so you can go on sitting for hours on a hard wooden bunk, staring in front of you, thinking nothing, not moving, without a sound or a picture in your brain.

I discovered this process in those first three bad days at Wenukai, but it wasn't really successful until much later. Even then though, it made me forget the cold for a while and after you've made one of these projections into the past, you feel as if you've done something of value. Getting in touch with the unconscious self, I suppose you'd call it. Nevertheless, those three days had me scared of dummy, so scared, I think it made any future bread and water harder to take. Like a horse that's belted in its first race. It's the memory of the first trials that persists as a living entity in the mind ...

I did a lot of that long spell [i.e., dummy] in Wenukai, and it would have been much harder if the crimmos hadn't rallied round and helped. But this always happens in jail. As soon as a man goes into the pound there's always someone who'll organise a system of getting smokes and bits of food into the cell. It's one of the best things you see in jail, and if only some of the diehards, or even some of the more reasonable people who are frightened of the crimmos, could really get an insight into this mutual aid, they wouldn't be so hearty in their condemnation of the derelicts. Some of them will go short of rations or tobacco, they'll steal, they'll run the risk of pound themselves, in order to help the animal that's caged up a bit closer than they are. Their ingenuity is terrific. Of course, when it comes to smuggling things in, the boobhead always has one advantage over the screw. Numbers. Twenty or thirty pairs of eyes to one, and always on the watch. Sooner or later the screw is bound to turn his back on one mob, and boobheads have the patience of Dingoes waiting for a Kangaroo to come out of the water. Why shouldn't they? Their whole damn life is spent in waiting.

They're not all like this of course, but it's a pretty rare specimen who won't do anything for a man in the pound. A lot of responsibility rests with the cleaners. You'd have to have an army of screws to watch the cleaners at all their jobs, and the cleaners know exactly where the screw is, each moment of the day. When you're in the dummy you're not allowed out of the cell, so a basin is brought to you to wash in, the bread is brought to you, your pisspot taken away. All by the cleaner, screws aren't allowed to dirty their hands with such things. A few of the cleaners are scared but they have to be very scared to resist the pressure put on them by the rest of the boobheads. If they are too scared, then another way will be found ...

[The Prison on the Hill][5]

The Hill [is] a grim place, a true penitentiary, and the tough ones and the lifers all finish up there. The actual buildings are modelled on one of the big English jails, I forget which, yet it has an atmosphere of its own. With the prison farms there was a certain latitude of pattern which would allow a man to use his initiative in control, but The Hill is fixed by those twenty-foot surrounding walls, by that dark grey stone, by those clanging iron doors ...

Many days and weeks I spent wandering round [the prison] yards or sitting talking to other boobheads. Draughts and chess were allowed, but no cards. The Maoris enlivened things a bit with their own made-up games and their cheerfulness. I got blisters on my feet walking round in heavy boots on the concrete. The shortage of screws made this yard-common-room routine the daily routine of many of the prisoners and there were quite a number who'd spent months in these yards and were due to spend years more. Mostly the tough ones who weren't allowed out in the quarry without a screw on every bridge. The tough ones were the best and easily the most intelligent. Whenever I found a chap who was interesting he almost always turned out to be [one of these] or doing about five years.

There's a hopelessness about these yards with the high grey walls, the iron-barred gates and the plot of grass in the centre. Once I was sitting with a young Maori boy who'd just come in. He was only doing a short term but the first few weeks are bad, particularly for the Maoris. A gull flew up from the grass plot and over the wall and away. The Maori watched it circle slowly round one of the square, grey towers and then shoot off into the blue.

Gee, he said, I wish I had those wings.

Theme song for boobheads all over the world. Oh for the wings, for the wings of a dove. Or a seagull or a sparrow.

Maoris have their feelings there, on the surface, where you can almost touch them. Free white men have them under the surface, when the cast iron pattern of their lives hasn't squashed them out of recognition. But crimmos have driven them down into the depths and if the man's got character, that's when he becomes dangerous. The more intelligence they have the more dangerous they are. They're not natural, crimmos; they can't afford to be. If they were, after months and years in these yards, they'd go down and buy a gun with as many rounds of ammunition as they could carry and then they'd walk down the street shooting.

That's for you, and bang, that's for you. Because you don't understand and you don't want to understand.

And the penalty for being natural would be another dose of those walls for life.

You'll hear Controller and Minister spouting about the twenty-seven different trades you can learn in jail. In the words of the Aussie that's politics; there are only two lessons to learn in The Hill. Learn to do nothing, and to stop yourself from getting out of control. And in jail these are the hardest lessons anyone can learn. Unless you're a phenomenon, you've got to kill the life that's in you. With most lessons there's some sense of achievement in the mastery of the technique, but not in that one. Learning to kill the creative instinct in you doesn't achieve anything. Abandon hope all ye who enter here ... And yet they come back. Over and over again they come back, and good God, what do you expect: You can't kill creation like that and leave a vacuum. Destruction comes rushing in to take its place. And what then? Do you expect a man to come out after five years and switch everything round? You'd be crazy if you did, and ignorant. It doesn't take a psychiatrist to tell you that things don't work that way.

Those walls ... There's the outer grey wall at the Hill, twenty feet high, topped with broken glass, spikes, barbed wire, in any place where it would be possible for a miracle man to climb over. Then there are the inner walls dividing the place up into many different yards. And overlooking all this are the dark grey walls of the prison itself, with the little barred windows and the towers square against the grey sky.

They say the prisoners built the thing in the early days and I bet some of them did it at the end of a cat o' nine tails. It would take a lot of bread and water to make me put one stone on top of another ...

You [if you are a CO] can walk inside those outer walls if you want to, and if you happen to know a boobhead inside. You can walk in, escorted by a warder, as far as the visitors' room. But not the prison, not those inner sanctum yards. Those are reserved for the privilege of the boobheads. If you're a conchie, you might have some highflying ideas about yourself until you get into the yards. But half a day in there'll knock the stuffing out of you. You're a boobhead same as the rest, and for the same reason. You couldn't get on with society. Don't run away with the idea the average crimmo thinks he's guilty: he doesn't. It's society's done him wrong. And a few months in these yards will strengthen his belief into certainty.

If you go through the double doors and the iron gates past the offices and visitors' room, then you're in the Dome. The Dome has iron gates all round it, and on three sides the triple-tiered wings stretch away into the distance. It gets its name from the glass-dome top four stories up. The dome's the assembling point for all boobheads. When you're in the Dome you know you're in jail unless you happen to be a dodderer or an M.P. with a special pass. The iron gates surrounding the Dome have automatic locks and all day, if you like that sort of noise, you'll be enlivened by the sound of clanging gates and rattling keys.

Take him up to the Dome and leave him there.

That's what the screws say, when they haven't decided what to do with this crimmo, this sack of grain. Leave it in the Dome, someone'll collect it later. It waits in the Dome when it's going in to see the V.J. for bread and water. It waits there when it has a visitor. It waits there for a bath. It waits there when it comes in and it waits there when it goes out. It waits in the Dome.

The triple-tiered wings with their steel-railed platforms and lines of red, iron-doored cells stretch away from the Dome on three sides, but I won't go on about those. You've seen them on the movies, I expect. You've seen almost everything on the movies ...

The Hill was an exact replica of an English penitentiary, down to the very last detail. One of the worst points about official New Zealand is its lack of originality. I used to think that American capitalists who imported English cottages and set them down in the American scene were pretty crazy, but to import a whole jail seems to me just a bit over the odds. Even down to the tins you eat your food out of. Those tins, never quite clean, and always giving the food that peculiar taint you remember ever after. And porridge in the morning and porridge at night, and the stewed apple once a week in season. Stewed and flavoured with tin.

But don't let me weary you over details like that. I'd hate you to think you could fix The Hill by doing away with the tins from which you eat your food in your cell alone. I'd hate you to think that these things counted. They don't. Just a drop in the bucket, that's all.

The air of hopelessness you feel in the yards is thick all over The Hill. It's the same with all the jails, you say? You're telling me, but The Hill is worse than most. Human beings carry their aura around with them, but they also leave bits of it behind. The dummy yard, where they hanged and flogged, was thick with the atmosphere of acute pain, of society's official, sadistic orgies and over the prison itself hangs a cloud of boredom and hopelessness ...

When I landed in The Hill the first thing I heard was that a chap had died from swallowing his fork. Jack told me about it. Jack was a conchie who had done the best part of two years in The Hill and he was used to queer goings-on, but he said it gave him the shudders to see this fellow wandering about doing a bit of cleaning in the wings, and knowing all the time he had a fork in his guts. He was wasting away and the authorities knew he'd swallowed the fork but there was some hitch about yanking it out. After a few weeks he collapsed and they took him up to the hospital for an operation, but he died. Then there was Cedric and his cutlery swallowing, and later on, a chap in a cell just below me cut his wrist open. He didn't have a knife or he wouldn't use it, so he smashed some of the panes of glass in his window and dug his wrists down into the broken parts. It made a noise though, and he hit the padded cell for a few days ...

Imprisonment for life. One of the factors at the back of that overwhelming atmosphere of depression in The Hill, is the presence of the lifers. There are nearly twenty of them there, most of them are in for some sudden fit of violence, usually directed against their wives. People often ask me about the lifers as if there's something about them, but they're just the same and just as different as any other group of twenty, taken from different parts of the country.

A man who's capable of committing murder, must be different in some way, you say?

But every man's capable of committing murder; you don't have to have a war to know that. It's only when you come in contact with lifers every day, and know them as individuals, some pleasant, some unpleasant, some easy to get on with, some irritable and short-tempered, some extroverts, some introverts, some thinkers and some feelers, that you achieve a full realisation of the truth, that every man has murder in his heart. You've been lucky, that's what. You've never struck up against that precise combination of circumstances, the nerves shaken beyond bearing, the brainstorm of jealousy or hate, the room apart or the lonely place and the knife or gun in your hand.

There are certain things you couldn't do under any circumstances, you say?

Well, some of the lifers are like that; I've met several who were the kindliest persons in the jail, they wouldn't hurt a fly.

Nevertheless there's one common factor amongst the lifers when they get behind the bars, they're all facing a possible twenty-one years of jail life, and the big struggle for them comes after the excitement of the trial and conviction has died down. If you don't become violently insane during that period you'll probably survive, though you'll certainly never be a human being again. Even to a lifer, the jail must always remain a temporary unreality; if you thought of it as anything else, you really would go crazy. But the lifer has to make such enormous adjustments compared with the man on a short term, that he deprives himself of the greater part of his humanity, which means his hope in life. If jail contained a creative side, it would be different. But The Hill is a house of negativity. Try facing up to nothing-doing for twenty-one years and see what you feel like.

After you've been there for a while, the inevitable effect of the presence of the lifers is one of intermittent horror. You talk to one of them and he makes some ordinary joke and you both laugh and then he walks away, and you think Jesus Christ Almighty. It's intermittent because, you're in there confronted with them day after day, [it] just doesn't bear thinking of. Not that the lifers go round with long faces moaning about their lot, I've only once heard a lifer mention his sentence and that was when I dropped a terrible brick and asked one of them how long he was doing. Most of them complain hardly at all, and if they do it's only about little things or about their job in the jail. No, it's really connected with the black curtain of pain which never leaves you while you are in jail, which almost nobody can realise till they've been there, which is impossible to describe unless it's in a poem that's never been written. It's the Alpha and Omega of jail life and yet you never talk about it, even to your cobbers. And you know the lifers don't talk about it either. When you're doing one or two years it's hard enough to struggle against the unmentionable thing that's hanging over your brain, but when you try to think of a man facing twenty-one years of it, the mind boggles and refuses to function.

To imprison a man for life is the high point of civilised sadism ...

Life imprisonment, [the intellect] will say, why that's nothing. Think of what they used to do, hanging, flogging, burnings, chain-gangs, red hot needles under the finger nails. Why the New Zealand jails are hospitals compared with what they were.

You may crawl away beaten when you hear that, lots of people do. But if you've ever been in jail you won't. You'll shrug your shoulders, you'll hitch up your pants and you'll go looking for the nearest point from which you can start that swim for the Islands of the Blessed ...

As I put my things into a bag and tied some books into a parcel in the office of The Hill, ... the chief warder was watching me with his mouth hanging open and the usual half-daft expression on his face.

You can ring up for a taxi if you like, he said.

I looked up at him and that was the moment it first hit me; I was free ...

You can ring up for a taxi if you like, he said.

It was that 'if you like' that nearly deprived me of the use of my legs. The first time for sixteen long months it wasn't just a question of do-this-or-else, but if I liked.

So we go out through the great double doors and there's the taxi waiting and everybody's merry and bright. Almost shaking hands. The soandsoes. The stupid morons that they should think they could get away with that. And going out in the taxi past the final barbed wire fence I thought – no you don't my boys, not so easily. You don't make me forget with a few jokes and smiles. Not if you go down on your knees, not if you offer to lick my boots, not if you give me a million pounds. There's an expression they use, and I looked at the taxi man and said it aloud.

How long have you been in the boob? he asked.

About sixteen months, I said, and it's just sixteen months too long.

Then he asked me what for, and I had another of those shocks. In jail you never asked a man what he was in for, like that; you waited or found it out from someone else. I told him I was a conchie.

Jesus Christ, he said, they shouldn't have done that to you chaps.

Well they did, I said, and a lot more besides; and I told him.

What's it like in there? he said. I've heard some nasty tales.

Well I told him some of that too, to the best of my ability, but I couldn't really talk properly. Have you ever heard people talking after they've been on a long jag? Well it was like that. Words come tumbling out in jittery fashion and the mind seems to leap from one subject to another without any visible connection. You have millions of things to say and no time to say them in. That's one of the first things you realise when you come out of jail, the lack of time. The whole thing's turned bottom upwards if you see what I mean. In jail nothing happens and time drags along, minutes like hours, but when you look back on it a month seems like a day. Out of jail, countless things seem to be happening all at once and time scatters past at such a rate that you feel you'll never catch up. And then you look back and a day seems like a year. You don't have to read Proust or study relativity to get a line on time. Just get yourself a spell in the boob and you'll know that time can't be measured in seconds, minutes, hours, days. It's what happens that counts.

So I tried to give the old taximan an idea of what it was like in there, but I didn't succeed. You can't convey what it's like on the wrong side of those grey walls by telling a few tales. He seemed impressed, and maybe it was the excitement in my voice that did it. But it wouldn't last long. In the evening he'd go back and repeat the tales to his wife and, after due reflection, she'd say, maybe, but think what those buzzards would do to us if they were free ... Confronted with the usual hopeless contradictions of existence, he'd say to himself: ... it doesn't bear thinking about.

But I couldn't say much anyway. All the time I was looking at the trees and the shops and the people and the houses and the gardens. At a crowded part I wanted him to stop so's I could get out and buttonhole the people.

Look, I'd say, look at me. I'm free. I can get into a tramcar or walk into a shop or throw myself into the sea if I want to. I can actually climb a fence without three whistles, pandemonium, and everyone back to the cells. Don't you realise what it's like after sixteen months behind a blank steel door. If you don't you're dumb; even dumber than you look, you numbskulls. But it was just as well I didn't stop the taxi at that moment; I might have finished up weeping on the pavement and been taken up to the wow, because I had a lot of things to learn.

The taxi stopped at my friend's house and I walked up the path carrying a small case and my ragged parcel of books. I knocked on the door and his wife opened it; you know what she's like, one of those real, friendly Irish girls you don't often meet in New Zealand.

She stared at me for a moment and then she said, My God, it's Ian.

And that's what you get when you come out of the boob, from your friends and even acquaintances.

My God, it's Ian.

'I am Lazarus, back from the dead, come back to tell you all, I shall tell you all' ...

Notes

Source: Ian Hamilton, *Till Human Voices Wake Us* (Auckland: Auckland University Press and Oxford University Press, 1984), 14, 15, 22–41, 60–9, 71, 72, 88, 101–3, 142–4, 149, 223–5.

1 The citations I have made here are taken from the introduction by Tony Reid to the 1984 edition of Hamilton's *Till Human Voices Wake Us*.
2 See extract from Baxter's autobiography, above.
3 *Boobhead*, convict.
4 I.e., punishment cells.
5 Where Hamilton was eventually transferred from 'Wenukai.'

Australia

PHIL HANCOX

New Zealand's 'strange criminal,' the rumbustious freethinker Ian Hamilton, contrasts in almost every respect with the prison memoirist we have from Second World War Australia, Phil Hancox.[1] For instance, Hancox was theologically an avowedly conservative Baptist; he became a lay preacher at eighteen, launching at this early age on the Evangelical circuit. (That circuit once included preaching in a prison: little did Hancox then guess he would ever attend the prison chapel as an inmate.) Again, while Hamilton was an ex–English public school boy, Hancox had left school by the age of fifteen to work as a junior clerk in the office of the Brick and Pottery Works situated in a Brisbane suburb. His parents, both committed Baptists (though not pacifists), were lower middle class. An avid reader, Hancox was largely self-educated. His conversion to Christian pacifism came in his mid-twenties; a young man in his church had been responsible for this turn in his religious development by a passing remark to Hancox as to 'the stupidity of war.' Hitherto, relates the latter, 'I had never given any thought as to whether war was stupid or not,' even less as to whether a Christian might participate in war. His wife, Helena, whom he married in March 1940, came to share his pacifist views.

Compared at any rate to New Zealand, Australia has had a fairly good, though by no means impeccable, record with respect to its treatment of the tiny minority who became COs when wartime conscription was introduced.[2] Hancox received a call-up notice in May 1942 when his age group, the twenty-eight year olds, was conscripted. Since he took up a rather intransigent position he failed to gain exemption as a CO, and on 15 February he was given the maximum sentence of six months for refusing induction into the army. On release, having lost his job at the brickworks he fortunately succeeded in gaining employment with a construction company while continuing his off-duty circuit preaching.[3] During the Cold War Hancox, unlike most other Evangelicals, took part in the anti-nuclear movement. He was also vocal in his opposition to Australia's participation in the Vietnam War. His advocacy of pacifism, however, did not prevent his election in 1972 as president of the Baptist Union of Queensland.

In the introduction to his autobiography Hancox tells us: 'The title 'Cavalry or Calvary,' represents the choice I had to face at the age of twenty-eight, shortly after the war began. The horse (Cavalry) is, in the Biblical setting, the symbol of war, while the Cross (Calvary) is the symbol of peace and sacrifice.'[4]

Hancox's prison experience shows that in his time Australia's prisons varied considerably in character. Whereas the State Prison Farm at Palen Creek, his final destination, was run on relatively enlightened lines, the regime prevailing at the Boggo Road jail where he had first been lodged was harsh and, like New Zealand's Mount Eden, the prison on the Hill, was reminiscent of the standard mid-Victorian penal institution with its guiding principle of 'a just measure of pain.'

GAOL FOR REFUSAL TO TAKE SERVICE OATH

Joseph Phillip Hancox, 28, Welbeck Street Alderley, who claimed he was a Baptist lay preacher and preached in about 25 Baptist churches in Brisbane, was sentenced to six months' imprisonment yesterday for refusal to take the oath or make an affirmation for service in defence forces.

Hancox said that his religious beliefs would not permit him to undertake either combatant or non-combatant military duties.

Mr. G.A. Cameron [the Magistrate] told Hancox he was a very misguided young man. 'This is God's war for the freedom of the world and to wipe out the tyranny of our oppressors,' he said.[5]

'And They Led Him Away' (Luke 23:26)

The hand of a nearby police officer fastened on my arm. I was escorted down to the Watch-House, and locked in a cell. As the key turned, an uncanny feeling came over me, and I wondered what the next move would be. Within a few minutes my two friends [who had accompanied me to court] arrived. They had been given permission to enter my cell and spend a short time with me. Such an experience leaves a deep impression on one's mind and heart. Who could forget the prayers they offered for me and the members of our family?

When they had left, I was transferred into a large cell with ten to fifteen other men. Most were alcoholics 'picked up' the previous night. One tall thin fellow had worked out that this was his fifty-ninth appearance. Some men found relief from their 'hangovers' by marching up and down the cell. One man in the cell above was in the 'horrors' – loudly proclaiming in regular bursts the superiority of *his* children over the ones next door. There were no seats in our cell, so some men stood, while others sat on the concrete floor.

The scene was most depressing. I began to understand the feeling of Ezekiel the prophet as he came to dwell for a while among the captives at the River Chebar. 'I sat where they sat, and remained there astonished' (Ezek. 3:15) ...

Numbered with the Transgressors (Isaiah 53:12)

The rattling of keys heralded the approach of the prison officers. As we walked out of the cell one by one, one end of a pair of handcuffs was fastened on the wrist of every second man, the other end clasped on the wrist of the man following. Chained together in this way, any ideas a prisoner may have had of escaping were soon forgotten.

Out of the prison cell into the courtyard we marched. Then, like Noah's unclean animals entering the ark, we stepped up into 'Black Maria' – the armoured van used to transport criminals and suspected criminals.

We crossed the Brisbane River and arrived at His Majesty's Prison in Annerley [Boggo Road]. The huge iron gates swung open and were closed again the moment our van was safely within the walls.

The usual formalities were completed and we were taken to our respective cells. These 'units' were approximately three metres long by two metres wide with one small aperture near the top of the cell wall and another above the door providing the only ventilation. The extreme temperatures in summer and winter made life most uncomfortable. Seventeen out of the twenty-four hours each day were spent in these cells.

Other 'amenities' included a plain wooden table, a water jug with a tin mug, a canvas hammock and blanket, but no sheets. A library book was obtainable on request. A low powered electric light bulb provided the only lighting and was switched off at 10.00 p.m. The convenience can in the corner completed the furnishings.

Clothing consisted of well worn flannel shirts and dungaree trousers, rock-hard boots (but no socks), and an old digger-type hat.

To the unbiased observer, the sole object of the prison system in those days was to punish the guilty, and in some cases, to break a man's spirit. Rehabilitation was unthought of, while today, efforts are made to combine rehabilitation with punishment.

Prison Regulations and Discipline

Maintaining discipline in any prison invariably presents problems. At Boggo Road, these problems were caused partly by the way the prison rules were presented to the inmates. One soon learned not to walk on to the parade ground without first saluting the officer in charge even though this instruction had not been communicated to you. Nevertheless in his eyes you were guilty of showing disrespect. You were therefore ordered to stand over against the wall, where later you received a severe lecture for your misbehaviour.

When two prison officers burst into your room at night to check whether you were concealing any illicit objects, you quickly learned never to say, 'Good evening, officers.' That would bring down their wrath upon your head immediately. You must spring quickly to your feet, step over and face the wall until they are gone, otherwise you would be subjected to threatening abuse. This is the way you discovered the rules and how they operated. These and many other lessons I had yet to learn the hard way.

On that first morning, just before midday, I was called into the superintendent's office. I was informed that later that day I would be going to the State Prison Farm at Palen Creek. My first thought was, 'anything must be better than this place.' The wide open spaces of that area near the border of New South Wales had a special appeal to me.

After sounding a few warning notes, the superintendent handed me over to the next-in-charge to arrange my transfer to the farm. That afternoon I stood at the appointed spot waiting to be called to 'get on board.' When two hours had passed, an officer suddenly realised that the truck must have left without me. Back to the cell I went ...

All Things Working Together for Good

Naturally, it was somewhat disappointing to learn that I would remain at Boggo Road for another seven days – the truck left every Monday for Palen Creek but in these circumstances, our Heavenly Father takes over, and works all things together for our good. How true that was for me.

Two things happened that week to make me glad I had been kept in Brisbane. First, Helena [Hancox's wife] learned I was still in Boggo Road jail and so arranged to visit me. This was, for me, an unexpected bonus. On Thursday afternoon we faced each other. Two sets of iron gates separated us. The initial shock of seeing her husband in prison garb unsettled Helena for a while, but soon she rallied. We covered a wide field of interests during the next fifteen minutes. What a pleasant interlude that was – a beam of light shining in darkness. As we separated, I wondered when we would meet again.

Next morning found me working in the vegetable garden outside the walls, on the southern side of the prison. As the morning wore on, the effects of our meagre food ration began to tell (my dog would be offended if I were to offer him the quantity and type of food on which we were expected to subsist).

The Cup of 'Cold Water'

Earlier, I noticed a fellow working on the roof of a new block being constructed in the women's section, about sixty yards away. He looked remarkably like an ex-employee of the Albion Brick and Pottery Works, named Clarie Holland. To make sure it was he, and hoping I wasn't breaking prison regulations, I took the liberty of waving to him. He responded enthusiastically.

Later in the morning, I saw him walking slowly in my direction, carrying a black billy. He placed it on the ground about twenty yards from where I was working, pointed to it, and then retraced his steps. I looked around, and watched my opportunity to step across and pick up that billy. It didn't seem that an opportunity would come. I would have to make one.

Pacing up and down near the tower on the top of the wall was a prison officer on sentry duty. A .303 rifle hung on his shoulder. With one eye on him and the other on the billy, I strode over quickly and picked it up. It was tea all right, true 'Billy-tea.' I drank as much as I could as quickly as I could, then back to the garden to work with renewed vigour.

By this time, Clarie was again on the roof. I waved to him and gave a nod in gratitude. A little later, he retrieved the billy ...

The Sunday Morning Church Service

The second thing that was 'working together for good' became evident on the Sunday morning.

Two officers from the Salvation Army arrived to conduct a Church service. A good percentage of inmates turned up, though not all motivated by an impulse to worship. Any type of get-together, be it church service or entertainment, provided a complete break from the dull routine of prison life.

A problem soon rose. Neither officer could play the organ. This was a disappointment to the gathering. Strange though it may seem, prisoners do love to sing, especially the better known hymms. Although I could never claim to be a celebrity among church organists, I had on occasions played for services in our own church. I quickly dropped a hint to the fellows around me and after some delay in obtaining permission from the acting-superintendent, I was seated at the organ.

The service proceeded. My mind went back some six years to a Sunday afternoon in that same room. There were three of us there then – Major Pratt of the West End Corps (Salvation Army), Cecil Sweetman [a friend] and I, plus a congregation of thirty prisoners. My part was to speak for ten minutes. I chose as my subject, 'Time.' The idea was to draw a contrast between life inside and outside of prison, to remind them of the hustle and bustle of life outside, especially when time is at a premium. All went well until I added, 'Sometimes I envy you your time.' This brought a laugh. I was not aware that the word 'time' in prison parlance was synonymous with 'length of sentence.' In that case they were not to be envied, but would willingly have exchanged their time for mine. It was quite evident to them I was a novice in prison circles.

However, it had been a privilege for me to speak to those men about the love of Jesus, and to show how, in the quietness and solitude of their cells, they could spend time in prayer and communion with the risen Lord and Saviour, Jesus Christ.

On that Sunday, I had stood near where they sat.

On this Sunday, 'I sat where they sat,' enjoying the experience of worshipping the Lord within the walls of a prison, as well as being privileged to assist in the service.

A Convicted Criminal

'There is no difference, for all have sinned.' How many times had I heard those words? How often had I repeated them? Now once more I was about to be reminded that in the eyes of the Lord all men are in the same category – sinners. There are variations in the *degree* of sinfulness, but the category remains the same – sinners.

It was Monday morning again, seven days after I had stood for two hours waiting for the call that didn't come. This was to be the day of my transfer to the Prison Farm.

My cell door swung open. I was escorted downstairs to the room adjacent to the superintendent's office. I was introduced to a professional-looking man – a partner in a business firm specializing in fingerprinting and photography. In a business-like and friendly way he attended to the various details, explaining the procedure as we went along. My thumbs and forefingers were pressed on to a black-inked stamp pad and then placed gently but firmly on to a sheet of white paper. A number was assigned to me. Now, with photographs, fingerprints and number complete, I had all the evidence to prove that I was a convicted criminal. I should have said, '*They* had.'

My photos and fingerprints would be circulated to every capital city in Australia. This was the information supplied voluntarily to me by the gentleman who had just completed his specialized service.

Sure, I hadn't committed murder, rape, or any of those other serious crimes, but in the eyes of the law I was in the same category – a criminal. My treatment while in jail was no different from that of any other criminal. Such an experience served to illustrate that great truth in God's Word: 'There is no difference, for all have sinned and come short of the glory of God' (Romans 3:23).

'Down on the Farm'

There was no chance of my being forgotten this time! As I arrived at the same spot, I met three new arrivals. They had been sentenced a few days earlier for a crime similar to my own.

The driver of the truck, Paddy Donavan, had, during the morning, collected all the stores for the Palen Creek Farm and was ready to depart. The four of us climbed onto the truck and within a few minutes had passed through the iron gates and were off on the 110 kilometre journey. It seemed strange that a week before we had arrived in an armoured van, handcuffed and under strict security. Now we were in an open-sided truck, apparently no one caring whether we escaped or not. In fact, when we stopped for a while half way to the farm, Paddy quite casually said to us: 'If any of you fellows get any ideas of escaping, you just go right ahead. I won't be chasing you, but I think, if you're wise, you'll stay put.'

The men he had on the truck that day were not likely to act so foolishly. Prisoners sent to Prison Farms are carefully selected. For that reason it rarely happens that anyone attempts to escape, even though there are no locks on the hut doors.

The sun was just setting when we arrived at the gate of the Prison Farm. Two hundred metres up a slight rise, we could see the main buildings, and the wooden huts on either side. These looked far more inviting than the concrete and iron cells.

As we approached, we could see over on our right that stately mountain named Lindesay, one of the highest of the mountains grouped in the McPherson Range. The rays of the sun were still falling on the mountain peak. The sight presented a scene of great beauty and gave a sense of peace.

Mt. Lindesay is one of nature's landmarks. It can be seen clearly from many of the hills in the Brisbane region and from many vantage points over a wide area. It is readily recognisable by its unusual dome-shaped summit ...

The brakes squealed and the truck stopped with a jerk. We jumped down to mother earth and were conscious that we were stepping into the unknown. The thought uppermost in all our minds was, 'It would have to be better than Boggo Road.'

We were directed into the dining hall. In the kitchen adjoining, the evening meal had been prepared. I had just taken a seat when a man about thirty came strolling in, took one look at me, and almost went into convulsions.

'No!' he said. 'It can't be! I know you. Now where have I seen you?'

I kept silent and just smiled. I had already recognised him and remembered his name. He was Herb Samson, a former employee of the Albion Brick and Pottery Works. I hadn't seen Herb for more than four years. He had been found guilty of rape and sentenced to seven years' imprisonment.

'You're the last person in this world I'd expect to see here,' he continued. The shock of seeing me had certainly disorientated him. His behaviour provided some unexpected humour, as he turned around, paced up and down, desperately trying to resolve the problem. After the pantomime had continued for a few minutes, I told him who I was and the reason for my 'visit.'

This was my introduction to a group of men, all convicted criminals like myself, yet so much like the average man one passes in our city streets. After our evening meal we were shown our individual huts. These certainly were a vast improvement on the cells at Boggo Road.

We had a wooden bed and a pillow. The blankets consisted of chaff bags, but at least we would keep warm.

The first morning, twenty of us were taken by the yard foreman, Mr. Ringelstein, to the sorghum paddock. Here with cane knives, we hacked our way through a large area of tall stalks and later stacked them in the huge hayshed. This procedure continued for a week. The manager of the Prison Farm, Mr. Rinke, said that never before had the hayshed been as full as it was at the end of that week. He further commented in my presence, 'I don't mind how many conscientious objectors they send me' ...

The People You Meet

Let me introduce you to a few of the men with whom I shared prison life at Palen Creek during 1943.

Eric Smith: He was the prison carpenter but his name was never on the pay-roll. Although he was 72, his job was still permanent. He had spent the last fifteen years of his life at Palen Creek, apart from the week's leave he took after each sentence had expired.

Eric could hardly be called a 'habitual criminal,' although he had been sentenced to imprisonment more than twenty times during those fifteen years. He loved the place. It was his home. His hut was painted inside and out and no one occupied that hut even during his absence.

The authorities knew that at the end of the following week Eric would be back. His little lark was to make out a cash cheque for $100. When it 'bounced,' the police knew where they could locate the culprit. Within days he was back at Palen Creek to serve a further sentence of three, six, or twelve months.

Eric was quite uncommunicative and, sad to say, there seemed no way of reaching him with the gospel ...

Time would fail me to tell of Bobbie Roberts, who shot his fiancée's father because he wouldn't consent to Bobbie's marrying his daughter.

Wally Jones was a solicitor who embezzled a large amount of money entrusted to him. Wally found great delight in reminding the conscientious objectors that they were no better than he. They were 'criminals like himself.'

What shall I say of Bob Edmonds from Townsville, who was arrested for being A.W.L. [absent without leave]? He came from a highly respected family and his father was a medical practitioner. Bob had enlisted in the A.I.F. [Australian Imperial Force] and in the months following was in the thick of the fighting against Rommel's Forces in North Africa. After experiencing days and nights of shelling, his nerves could not stand any more, so he and a friend decided to quit. Three days later the Military Police caught up with him and he was court-martialled and sentenced to two years' imprisonment. The stories Bob told of the treatment they had been subjected to by 'Courtney's Screws' suggested that the inmates of that prison would willingly have changed places with their mates in the Changi Prison in Singapore.

Swanie Evans was a born comedian. He loved to refer to himself as the 'Goondiwindi Anzac.' In a drunken brawl in the main street of Roma (a town 450 kilometres west of Brisbane) he punched another soldier so hard he fell over backwards, his head landing on a concrete kerb. Within a few hours he was dead. Swanie at this time was serving a seven year sentence. Along with a number of other soldiers, he was transferred from the Military Prison to the State Prison.

Swanie and I became good mates. Every morning we would walk down to the prison gate to collect the mail-bag. In between his frivolous but witty remarks I endeavoured to present some aspects of the gospel to him. He listened, but always with a degree of scepticism and without any visible response. I tried to draw a picture of him wielding a good influence over the lives of young lads, how they would regard him as their hero, and how that hero-worship could be transferred to Jesus Christ.

'Me, Swanie? Whatever would my buddies say if they saw me teaching a bunch of kids?'

'That's not the *important* question, Swanie,' I quietly interposed. 'What would Jesus say? That's what really matters.'

Harry Attwell: To me, Harry [a CO] was the most colourful personality at Palen Creek. A Pentecostal preacher, about 30, he was appointed kitchen-hand. His main job was to chop the wood and keep the oven-fire burning.

Harry and I had more in common than either of us had with the other prisoners. His main concern was the amount of time he was wasting in jail when he should have been out preaching the gospel. When discussions or arguments arose between Jehovah's Witnesses or Christadelphians and ourselves, I would quote a relevant Scriptural verse in support of our contention, but Harry would invariably know the book, chapter and verse which supported me.

After a number of informal encounters, there were no further serious discussions on points of doctrine where we were at variance with the other groups. The relationship among these men with such a variety of beliefs and convictions was most harmonious. Mr. Rinke seemed happy with the way the farm was functioning during that particular period.

Prisoners Conduct Church Services

One Sunday morning, Harry and I were having a time of fellowship. The conversation suddenly switched again to the subject that was troubling him most.

'You know, Phillip,' he began, 'we shouldn't be here wasting our time. I feel guilty sitting here when I should be out preaching' ...

'Harry, you don't have to wait until you get out of here before you begin preaching. What about the thirty or more fellows here? Many of them need to hear the gospel.'

'Say, that gives me an idea,' said Harry thoughtfully, 'How about we conduct a service in the amenities hall tonight?'

'You'd have to get permission from Rinke.'

'If we asked him, he'd have to say "No." After all, we do have the Scriptures to back us. Remember what it says in Acts 4, verse 18: "The Jewish authorities commanded Peter and John not to speak at all, nor teach in the name of Jesus, otherwise they would be put back in prison, but they answered, "We cannot but speak the things which we have seen and heard."' There is a time, Phillip, when you must proclaim the gospel and be prepared to take the consequences, just as they did.'

'Well, I'm willing if you are, Harry. Let's go!'

During that Lord's Day, Harry and I approached every prisoner in Palen Creek – Jehovah's Witnesses, Christadelphians, Salvation Army, soldiers and those without 'labels.'

That evening, after dinner, we were dressed as neatly as possible – white shirts and all. We stood at the top of the stairs leading into the amenities room, waiting for the promised congregation. Slowly they began arriving, none wishing to be among the first arrivals to the 'Church.'

When the appointed time came, twenty men were seated in the front, close to the platform. A few more came later.

As we expected, someone had informed Mr. Rinke of our plan. We were therefore not surprised when he arrived. However, instead of coming into the hall, he and Mr. Ringelstein seated themselves on the elevated ground outside the building. From here, they were able to watch proceedings through one of the side windows without the congregation being aware of their presence.

There were no hymn books, no organ or piano. Harry had prepared the sermon, while my role was to conduct the 'preliminaries.' Having had some experience in leading community singing, I began the service by introducing the well known and popular hymn, 'Onward Christian Soldiers, Marching As to War.' The enthusiastic participation of the group surprised us. The sound of their voices rang out through the still night air, ensuring that everyone on the farm property heard the joyful sound. We paused after each verse, while from memory I quoted the words of the next verse. This procedure was followed with another hymn, 'What a Friend We Have in Jesus.'

The order of service, prayer, Bible reading, etc., was similar to the usual pattern apart from the taking up of the offering. Then came the sermon. Harry presented the 'unadulterated gospel,' covering a wide area of the Bible. He spoke for about twenty-five minutes, earnestly and sincerely, in the style of preacher speaking to a vast audience. The service closed with the singing of the hymn, 'I Need Thee Every Hour,' followed by the Benediction ...

Next morning, Mr. Rinke called us aside and in his fatherly way informed us that although he personally had no objection to what we had done, it was definitely contrary to prison rules. An assembly of prisoners, no matter for what purpose or objective, was strictly forbidden. In that case there was no point in 'bucking the system,' so we agreed to confine our efforts in evangelism to the personal approach.

Battling on the Home Front

In many ways life was quite pleasant on the farm. To the single man with no family obligations or without any ambition, a year or two on a prison farm presented few hardships. For those of us who had families, the conversation often turned to the difficulties some were facing. It was therefore a thrill for us when we learned that our wives would be visiting us the following Sunday. We would then be able to discover at first hand the true state of our families' affairs. The men concerned would make special preparations for the event. Washing, ironing, haircuts and shaves were the order of the day.

Due to the kindness of the parents of one of the prisoners, Helena arrived on the Sunday afternoon with our two-year old daughter. Such reunions mean much to married couples. At the same time, they create a sadness among the remainder of husbands. Their wives, for various reasons, are not able or willing to visit them ...

The saddest moment comes when a couple have to part [after the allotted hour]. Then follow the moments of reflection and self-examination. 'Did I do the right thing in bringing all this trouble and disorganisation to so many other people? Am I really as sincere in my announced convictions as I claim to be?' There may come a feeling of depression at that time. Some of the hard things that have been said will be recalled: the newspaper report where the magistrate is supposed to have said, 'Mr. Hancox, you are a misguided young man.' Was he right? ...

I thought [then] of those young fellows I had known three years before in the Windsor Road [Baptist] Church. Where were they now? Practically all were in the Defence Forces. Some, I knew, were in New Guinea in the Milne Bay area. My prayers were for their safety.

For my part, I believed I was bearing the reproach of Christ who suffered shame, humiliation and separation. Compare that with what my young friends were suffering: sleeping in rain-sodden jungles – no roof over their heads, nor knowing when an enemy bullet would claim one of them, no regular meals, no household amenities, many privations which only those who experienced life in such conditions would be able to describe ... The yoke I accepted seemed as though it would be rather awkward, but it proved to be comparatively easy and the burden surprisingly light ...

Counting the Days to Freedom

Four months had now passed since Magistrate Cameron had shouted 'Six Months.' However, prison rules provide that where a prisoner has a record of good behaviour, he may be recommended to have his sentence reduced. This reduction is referred to as 'remission.' Seeing that I had no visible 'black marks' against me, one quarter of the original sentence of six months would be remitted. This meant that in two weeks I would be released ...

The calendar told me we had reached the shortest day of the year, but every day to me seemed to be getting longer. Wednesday, June 30th was the day three of us were to be released, and Paddy Donavan was sent down specially on the Monday to take us back to Boggo Road Prison. There was a ring of sadness when saying 'farewell' to the fellows we had come to know and in many cases to appreciate. However, this was more than compensated for in the expectation of being back in 'circulation' in a couple of days and the joy of being reunited to home and loved ones.

The New Day Is About to Dawn

Boggo Road hadn't changed. Rigid discipline was still the order of the day, but having had previous experience, I was more conversant with the routine.

The night was extremely cold. It was impossible to sleep for any length of time. How I longed for some of those Palen Creek corn sacks. Next morning I was taken into an office and introduced to an army chaplain. As he began to speak to me, I noticed his hand trembling. His voice was kind and subdued. I did feel sorry for him because I sensed it was the type of job he would have preferred not to do.

He began, 'Mr. Hancox, you'll be pleased to know you are not going to be asked to take the Oath of Service today.' I heard a voice within me saying, 'Praise the Lord,' but then he went on to say, 'However, I would like you to think very carefully about the attitude you have adopted. I believe there is a place you could fill in the service of your country in our Defence Forces. I'll leave it with you.'

I thanked him sincerely, but made no further comment. (Jehovah's Witnesses were not treated in this way. Some of them found themselves back in jail within two days of their release, since Jehovah's Witnesses were regarded by the government at this time as a subversive organisation.)

Later that day I was introduced to a prison official who handed me my discharge form and pay-slip. He asked me to sign for the wages I had earned – one pound, nineteen shillings and seven pence ... . This was the total payment I received for over four months solid work on the Palen Creek Farm, but after all I *was* there to be punished, not to be rewarded for service.

One more night! Between intense cold and excitement, I again had little sleep ... The prison bell tolled. It was 6.30 a.m. The big iron gate swung open. There, a few yards in front of me stood my faithful friend, Cecil Sweetman. What a thrill! ... When we arrived at Alderley, Helena had prepared breakfast ... A weight seemed to lift from her shoulders ... 'Bless the Lord, O my soul, and forget not all his benefits' (Psalm 103:2).[6]

Notes

Source: Phil Hancox, *Cavalry or Calvary? The Christian's Dilemma – An Autobiography* (West End, Queensland: Christians for Peace, 1984), 47–67, see also p. 6.

1 Neither Hancox nor his book are mentioned in the two overall studies of conscientious objection in Australia during the Second World War: Bobbie Oliver, *Peacemongers: Conscientious Objectors to Military Service in Australia, 1911–1945* (South Fremantle: Fremantle Arts Centre Press, 1997), 76–144, and Peter Brock and Malcolm Saunders, 'Pacifists as Conscientious Objectors in Australia,' 272–91 in P. Brock and Thomas P. Socknat, eds., *Challenge to Mars: Essays on Pacifism from 1918 to 1945* (Toronto: University of Toronto Press, 1999).

2 'Australia's Defence Act of 1903,' which provided for conscription in wartime or if war threatened, 'was the first national legislation to grant total exemption from military service on [religious] grounds.' In 1910 exemption was extended so as 'to cover all grounds of conscience.' But of course this was only the beginning of the story. See Hugh Smith, 'Conscience, Law and the State: Australia's Approach to Conscientious Objection since 1901,' *Australian Journal of Politics and History* 35, no. 1 (1989), 13–16, 25.

3 After he came out of prison, Hancox writes, 'it soon became clear to me that I should be willing to do for the soldier what I was prepared to do for the civilian – the only qualification being that I would not join the Defence Forces to do it. If I were given a job in a bakery, and all the bread manufactured was supplied to the army, I would have no conscience worries about that. A soldier has the same right to eat as a civilian. However, if I were required to work in a munitions factory, I would refuse. I would not supply weapons of destruction to a civilian, therefore I would not be prepared to supply weapons to soldiers for the purpose of destroying others.'

4 Phil Hancox, *Cavalry or Calvary? The Christian's Dilemma* (West End, Qld.: Christians for Peace, 1984), Introduction.

5 *Courier Mail*, 16 February 1943.

6 Leslie Hoey has sent me the following note from Kenmore Hills, Queensland: 'My application to be registered as a conscientious objector, shortly before my twentieth birthday, had been refused. I was not a member of a recognized church or organization, though I had firm religious and moral beliefs, and, already before the outbreak of war, had crystalized a determination not to join the army. An independent away from a support group like the Quakers, I was, however, fortunate in having supportive parents. I admit that it was difficult for me then to articulate my pacifist position

with clarity. I applied for registration as a CO more at the instigation of my family than through my own motivation. I did not see why I should have to prove that I was genuine, and I did not put a lot of effort into giving an account of myself. It is understandable, therefore, that my application was rejected. The magistrate thought that I was a misguided young man and that being in the Army would "make a man of me." At that time I was working on a farm just outside Brisbane with some Quaker friends. Not long after the court finding I received a call-up notice to report to Army barracks. I ignored this as I believed myself to be a genuine CO. In a matter of days a policeman arrived on a motorcycle with sidecar with a warrant for my arrest. I had been sentenced in my absence to six months' imprisonment and was taken directly to Boggo Road jail. This was in early May 1941 and I had therefore completed my sentence before Phil Hancox commenced his. My experiences at Boggo Road and later at Palen Creek Prison Farm closely parallelled his.

'Boggo Road was a nasty, brutal place, but I only spent about a week there before transfer to Palen Creek. This place was a relatively benign operation, and as I was accustomed to country work I probably fitted into it easier than some others. I was assigned to work in the dairy, milking, separating, preparing feed for the cows, and otherwise doing miscellaneous farm work. It was not a lot different from some of the work I had been doing outside, except that there were some prison guards; you had to work according to the rules, though the operation functioned largely on an honour system. Unlike Phil Hancox, whom I did not know until after his release from jail, I was not concerned with proselytizing, and my attitude to organized religion was certainly different from his. As I found out later, he was fundamentalist in his beliefs and seemed to consider it the greatest good to convert non-believers to accepting Jesus Christ as their Lord and Saviour.'

United States

ROGER W. AXFORD

Roger Axford, a radical pacifist and Methodist minister, wrote the satirical article printed below after a brief sojourn in a county jail, a type of American prison where conditions were notoriously bad. COs were usually sentenced to at least one year and a day, so that they did almost all their time in a federal correctional institution or penitentiary, where standards of cleanliness at least were considerably higher than in a county jail. A few COs, though, received a prison term of a year or less; these unfortunate individuals served out their sentence in the county jail. But COs with longer sentences often spent a few weeks in the latter type of penal institution, too. And some CO prison memoirists have included – uniformly unflattering – descriptions of what they encountered there.

As a CO Axford became a non-cooperator in jail: he eventually served twenty-seven months (plus twenty-seven days) in prison. For further light on his prison career, see Roger W. Axford, *A Peace of My Mind: The Unrepentant Peacenik* (Tempe, AZ: Enlightenment Press, 2001), 21–6, 88, 89. After the war Axford became a professor of adult education at Arizona State University and eventually, attracted by their church's social activism, he joined the Unitarian-Universalists.

In the second-largest city of the empire of Japan, the secret police entered my office one afternoon in midwinter. After a short talk I was informed that I was under arrest. The following is a true account of my experiences in jail, written with care lest it occasion retaliation on those who remain behind. For that reason I shall not use names.

After being taken to the largest and most modern jail in the city, the Kangoku, I found myself in a cell of the block that is known as the 'hole.' Many of the men were in solitary confinement. The Americans next to me were on bread and water. Some had not had food for two days, but only water. Each had refused on some point to cooperate with the guards, most of whom I was soon to learn had sadistic tendencies. The jail routine required these guards to take six fingerprints of each hand. During this process the guard badly wrenched and twisted my arm. Then pictures were taken, and I was put into line with other prisoners. Each was stripped to the waist. Everything was taken from me but my clothes – my keys, postcards, pen, chain, watch, my one precious book. All money was confiscated and checked except for the equivalent of three dollars in American money, and we were told we could draw this out from time to time, which I found was true. Many prisoners did not have any money.

Medical Treatment

We were lined up for medical inspection. While in the medical line I found that many of my fellow prisoners had been working in munition plants but had violated some rule and were now in prison. Many of them did not know why they were there. Such was Japanese justice. Many should have been in hospitals. The man in front of me had a bad rupture, greatly enlarged. The doctor said, 'Think you're going to die?' Submissively the reply was, 'Don't know.' The medic retorted, 'I don't think so either; move along.' I was next. He looked me over and barked: 'T.B.? Syphilis? Gonorrhea? Smoke? Drink? Take dope?' When each answer was no, he laughed and said I must be a Christian.

We were then told by the warden to read the rules that were given us. I noted especially Number 7 which read: 'No food of any kind is allowed to be brought in to you.' Number 16 said: 'Any letters that you write ... *must be left unsealed.* On the back flap of the envelope, write block, tier and cell number.' All letters are censored, of course. I was to learn that letters I sent out were delayed many days although I paid extra for early delivery.

When we were asked if we had any requests, I asked for the book that had been confiscated. The warden said he would get it for me or have a guard get it. I never saw the book.

In the small space known as the 'bull pen' we prisoners got acquainted. One Irishman (a citizen of a neutral nation), who could not speak Japanese except for a few words, stared at the wall day in and day out. He had been there for some weeks. He thought it was for violation of a military order, but was not sure. He was psychotic and should have been in a mental hospital. The men said I was the first person he had spoken to for weeks.

One man was blind. I saw them release him. He had beaten his wife, a prisoner said, but it seemed unlikely, for he was as helpless as a child. Another foreigner to whom I could speak in his native tongue had been there for two weeks but had not been able to get word out to his wife for lack of the price of postage, which is equivalent to two cents American money. When I gave him this he was very grateful, as he believed he could be released in a few days once those outside learned where he was.

Pacifists and Murderers

Another prisoner, who had already served one year, upon 'hitting the ground' (being released) was immediately rearrested by the tokkoka (FBI) for not keeping his military board informed as to his address. He was willing to go into the army but was thrust into prison. He will probably get a sentence of from three to five years for violation of this technicality. Surprisingly, three prisoners were in jail as Christians who would not take part in war. One said he had learned that Christ commanded us to 'love our enemies.' Another had been sentenced to three years because he had said and preached that 'God is love' and believed that 'thou shalt not kill.' Two of the other prisoners were being held for murder. One of these said to me, 'I'm in prison because I killed a man. But that man is in prison because he refuses to kill!'

Eighteen of us were put in the bull pen. It measures about twenty by thirty feet. The long way it is exactly eleven steps from one end to the other. I must have walked it thousands of times. After a short time one becomes like a lion in a cage. Back and forth, back and forth we all walked, until I thought I would go mad. This happens so often that 'stir crazy' is the name given to this form of insanity. Prisoners frequently crack up, beating the walls and bars of their cells at night or of the bull pen in the day and screaming until they fall exhausted. Twelve hours of the day we spent in this bull pen, locked out of our cells. There were men in our pen who had not seen the sun for over six months. Their skin was flabby and pale. No one has ever seen out of the high, opaque windows of this prison.

Locked in Cells

Then at night from seven to seven we were locked into cells about eight by five feet. Since this was a modern prison, cells are electrically locked. Inside these three steel walls, with a fourth made of bars, was our equipment. I had luxury furnishings: a hard steel bed with straw mattress, a hard pillow, one sheet, two blankets and a wash basin. The wash basin must serve *all* purposes, because the cell is electrically locked and one must buzz a bell to get to a toilet during the twelve night hours. Often one rings for hours and no response. The straw mattress fairly crawls. Bugs, bugs, bugs. The prisoners call them livestock. Their biting and the prison clamor make sleep almost impossible. The man in the cell next to mine was slowly going crazy. Over and over his monotone droned: 'Someone open the door. Someone open the door.' Some beat the walls and scream. In this purgatory personality quickly disintegrates. One is no longer a person, but an animal, then a number and at last a cipher.

In searching my clothes I found that the police had overlooked a small prayer book that a friend had given me. I was reading when a cellmate asked to see it. He read it half aloud over and over. As a boy he had gone to a Christian mission for a few weeks, so I gave him the book. He was pleased and grateful for a moment, then the prison gripped his mind and he growled, 'By God, I'll kill anyone that touches this.'

Food Unfit for Humans

As with other former prisoners of the Japanese, my most revolting memory is the prison food. 'Food' is too dignified a word for it; 'slop' is more accurate. Much of it cannot be eaten, even though many prisoners are half-starved. Prisoners try to eat it because they must do so or starve, but much of it went down the toilet when the guards were looking the other way. Even when it was eaten, it often could not be retained. Prisoners say they haven't seen greens for months. On holy days (Sunday for us) we get rice for dessert, a wonderful treat. The American government pays through a neutral agency for adequate food for such prisoners as me, but the money is grafted away. Somebody is making a huge profit on this food. Just before I was released a prisoner died. The authorities attributed his death to 'high blood pressure,' but the prisoners know it was the food.

Twice a day the prison pushcart 'store' comes around. Since it is impossible to get food from the outside, one must buy from this profiteer if one has the money. An orange or an apple costs, in our money, fifteen cents. Small bars of candy sell for ten to twenty cents. Paper and stamps are sold at exorbitant prices. The store of course is run by the prison administration. An inmate told me that for weeks there was no store because two prison officials were fighting over who should get the concession. There is a special menu that you can get meals from if you have the money. It's a good business – and starving the prisoners makes it doubly profitable. In this way whatever funds one may have on entering the prison are used up. The prison gets your money if you stay long enough. Many of the men have no money.

Prison Humor [and Other Little Things]

When I entered the jail, a man who had been in one prison or another for nine years said to me, 'I see you've never been in before.' I pleaded guilty to the indictment. He laughed and said, 'I knew that, or you wouldn't have that tie on. You don't see any others, do you?' I agreed that I didn't. He retorted, 'You can't trust yourself after a while. A tie makes too good a noose. You better get rid of it.'

Little things assume an enormous importance in prison. One is fresh air. When the small window in the outside wall of the jail is opened men crowd around it to snatch a breath of fresh air. The toilets are in the same room, and the smell is always stifling except for this respite.

All mail is censored. When I was arrested my sister was dangerously ill, and so I tried to get word to her. I sent four special delivery letters to different friends the day I entered. They were held for days before being sent. When I asked the guard about censorship he said, 'I get off early. I forget all about the prison and I go right by the mailbox.' Whether the crossing of the palm of the guard with *kane* (cash) really eliminated censorship I do not know, but it was tried.

Effects of Prison Life

In prison the first thing one learns is that he has no rights. Even getting out of the cell into the bull pen is a privilege, which need not be granted. You learn this vividly from 'solitary' or the 'hole.' No one knows, you feel, what happens to you, and you soon begin to wonder if anyone cares. So you walk, eleven steps, back and forth. You take them a thousand times, back and forth. You wonder if you too are going stir crazy. Back and forth, even paces, now alone, now six at a time. Back and forth. You've got to walk or you can't sleep at night. Back and forth. The walls press in on you. You know they are going to crush you if you don't keep moving. Back and forth ...

I often thought of Kagawa[1] while I was in prison. He had been there. Now he was out and was influential. But he had not been able to reform these prisons. The one I was in, which was a 'model,' was run by the local political machine. The guards, who have the prisoners at their mercy, are the appointees of politicians and cannot be touched. But the community as a whole cannot evade its responsibility for these conditions. Kagawa, I reflected, ought to have done more to reform them. At least he might have remembered that Jesus blessed those who visit the prisoners.

But this isn't Kagawa's problem. It is ours. The above events happened in Chicago, not in Tokyo. Because they happened when the country was being deluged with stories of atrocities in Japanese prisons, I decided to use this device to tell of my experiences in the Cook County jail in early February 1944. To make the above story completely true in every detail, substitute the word American for Japanese, our comparable institutions for theirs, and your own name for that of Kagawa. The narrator, who is a minister and a conscientious objector to war, was released on bail but is yet to stand trial.[2]

Notes

Source: Roger W. Axford, 'This Happened to Me in Prison,' *The Christian Century* (Chicago), 22 March 1944: 367, 368.

1 A social activist, Toyohiko Kagawa (1888–1960) was Japan's most prominent Christian pacifist, for long active in the Fellowship of Reconciliation and much admired in the West.

2 Axford was to continue his uncompromising CO stand; see introductory text above.

ALFRED HASSLER

In his foreword to the *Diary of a Self-Made Convict*, the distinguished penologist Harry Elmer Barnes (not himself a pacifist) wrote: 'The book is surely one of the most illuminating and instructive volumes ever written dealing with the impact of prison life on all types of inmates, from delinquents with a long record of crime to high-minded intellectuals not guilty of any conventional crime.' He stressed its author's 'well-trained mind, sensitive personality and acute perception.' Alfred Hassler, after serving his sentence in the federal penitentiary at Lewisburg, Pennsylvania, from June 1944 until he was paroled in March 1945, went on to a long career in the service of the Fellowship of Reconciliation, acting for a time as its general secretary and editing its journal, *Fellowship*. A man of strict principle, in his pacifism Hassler was always a moderate. Thus, during the Vietnam War he was to clash on occasion with some of the more fiery radical war resisters concerning the proper stance that pacifists should take vis-à-vis the Communist 'enemy.'

Hassler's *Diary* was put together some years later 'from the 70,000-word journal,' camouflaged to escape confiscation by the Federal Bureau of Prisons, as well as from letters written out legally and materials smuggled out of jail – and 'memories ... carefully put on paper' immediately on release. The *Diary* contains 182 printed pages. Thus, it is impossible to present here more than a small sampling of its entries. But the whole book is worth study. I hope some readers may decide to read it from cover to cover.

There have been many books written about prison and the men who are their involuntary inhabitants. Wardens, penologists, and psychiatrists have all in their own ways tried to tell what makes a criminal and how society attempts to punish or reclaim him. I can presume to add to the number of such books not because I am an expert, but precisely because I am not. This is not the story of one who has studied convicts, but of one who, with few preconceptions, has found himself living with them twenty-four hours a day for month after month. It is the story of ... the bootleggers, ... the confidence men, the murderers, the white-slavers, the robbers and hijackers and extortioners and dope-peddlers and draftdodgers who slept in the same dormitory or cell-block with me, ate at the same table, washed in the same block of showers, and shared the same feelings of fright and bitterness and anger ...

In the very first days of the draft, before the United States was in the war, I registered my position as a conscientious objector. Had the order for my induction come then, or almost any time in the next two years, I would almost certainly have obeyed it and served out the war doing 'work of national importance' in a Civilian Public Service camp as the law permitted. In the intervening time, however, evidence of the kind of 'made work' that characterized the camps had bolstered a growing conviction that resistance to war must include resistance to conscription as a part of the system of modern war.

[27 June 1944] [T]he most impressive example of [a convict's] kindness came a few days ago [very early in my sentence]. A young Jehovah's Witness, barely eighteen years old, was brought in with a three-year sentence for refusal to accept the draft. Just a boy, probably brought up in a kind, decent, middle-class home and totally unprepared for anything like this, the youngster simply could not take it. He shrinks from everyone, can hardly talk, and seems on the verge of complete mental collapse. With the instinctive cruelty of unhappy, frightened men who find someone in an even worse state than themselves, some of the inmates have tormented him pretty badly.

Newcomers usually spend at least the first night on the second floor, but the authorities assigned him directly to the third, apparently hoping that the relatively quieter atmosphere there would help. When it did not the lieutenant went to Harry and his cellmates for help. The result was that the young JW was moved in with the three desperadoes – an act that on the surface would seem completely irrational. But the lieutenant knew his men. The three desperate criminals could not be kinder to the boy if they were his brothers. They actually come close to hovering over him, and when they talk to him, as Harry does frequently, they are as compassionate as his own parents could be. Under their influence, and in the protection of the constantly locked cell, the boy is beginning to respond a little, and today I saw him smile briefly at one of Harry's sallies. It would be funny if it were not so touching. Any time I am tempted to categorize *anyone* as unrelievedly bad, I shall remember Harry and the young JW.

On the way out to the penitentiary, a marshal told three of us that Harry Beach was a 'killin' ----.' He said the authorities knew for a certainty that he had killed at least fourteen men, but never had been able to pin it on him. When they finally got a conviction on a bank robbery, he explained, the judge 'threw the book' at him – that is, gave him the maximum possible sentence.

[Arriving at Lewisburg penitentiary in Pennsylvania, from Manhattan's West Street Detention Center, Hassler now becomes federal convict number 13847-NE.]

[6 July 1944] [A] few minutes later the marshals parked their car with some others outside the twenty-foot wall of the penitentiary.

Except for an impression of a mass of brick buildings with red-tile roofs, I didn't really get much of a look at my new home from the outside. I was too busy concentrating on that high gray wall and the barred gate: the highest, meanest, most positive-looking wall and gate I had ever seen in my life. We had been chatting on a pretty friendly basis ever since the doughnuts and coffee, and the marshals went right on with their light-hearted babble up to the gate, but the three of us fell quiet, and I think we all felt as though we should hunch up our shoulders and get ready for something pretty unpleasant.

It's odd how easy it is to take barred windows and high walls for granted. I suppose I have driven past institutions sporting these signs of involuntary residence dozens of times without giving them a second thought, or sparing any compassion for the people confined behind them. Never again for this cookie, though! Walls and barred windows suddenly become the most important thing in the world when you know you are going to have to live behind them for endless stretching months or years. It will be a long time before I can pass a prison without a cold feeling at the pit of my stomach, I feel sure.

The gate turned out to be the entrance to a sally-port, guarded by a man posted out of sight and reach up in the tower. We were frisked by an electric eye and then paraded impersonally and briskly inside and into the 'quarantine' wing of the prison. There we stripped, bathed, had a cursory examination evidently designed to ascertain that we had the full complement of arms and legs, and got a set of khaki clothes and a pair of prison-made shoes – large, bulky, and about as chic as a couple of cardboard cartons. Then we had a short preliminary interview with a young parole officer and some supper, and were led away to our cells.

Nothing much has happened since. We paraded down to breakfast under the watchful eyes of the guards early this morning, where we ate over at one side of a large, impressively gothic dining-room with stone arches and heavy, Spanish Mission refectory tables, for all the world like a monastery. While we ate we stared at the endless tables of most unmonkish blue-clad men over in what I find is called 'population.'

Later a nice young fellow – an Army prisoner, he told me, with fifteen years – showed me how to make my bed the approved way in the quickest possible manner, and told me a few things about the prison. He didn't know too much himself, though, since he has been here only a few days. Since then I have just been sitting here. The cell is locked, and I have nothing either to read or write. The suspicion grows on me that time may drag for a while.

FRIDAY, July 7 – Still dragging. I figured out that I spent 22˘ hours in the cell yesterday. That's a long time with nothing to do, and today seems to be going the same way. It is mid-afternoon now. We have been out for two meals – about twenty minutes each, I would guess – and then had a half-hour in 'stockade,' which is the outdoor recreation area.

SATURDAY, July 8 – I am beginning to regret never having gone in seriously for contemplation, or Yogi-ism, or something. What a place this would be for someone who really wanted to meditate at length! The same thing has happened today as yesterday, only more of it. The only chance one has to talk is at meals and during stockade, and the meals have to go so quickly that it's dangerous to spend much time talking. Aside from the likelihood of having to go back to your cell hungry, there is some unspecified but horrid punishment promised to anyone who does not eat everything on his tray. Probably he gets sent to bed without his supper.

Of course, there is always someone to enjoy even the least attractive situation. One chap here, a draft dodger, illiterate and slightly soft-headed but pleasant, has 'found a home' as the boys say. I sat next to him today at lunch and asked him what he did to kill the time. He looked at me with mild surprise.

'I sleep,' he said, and went on to document it. He gets up in the morning, dresses and shaves, has breakfast, and goes back to bed. Lunch interrupts his nap briefly, as does stockade, but as soon as he gets back in his cell he curls up again. After dinner, he said, he 'sits around for a while' before going to bed, but he's nicely tucked in long before lights out at nine-thirty! In here you can almost envy a guy like that ...

SATURDAY, July 15 – Well, I am out of 'solitary,' and already I wish I were back in. Yesterday I got moved out of my cell and into the quarantine dormitory, a room about sixty feet long by twenty wide, presently occupied by eleven other men and myself. The change evidently is supposed to be a boon, since only men expected not to start riots or fights get the chance to live in the dormitory, but they can have it back for my money.

I never met such a bunch in my life, and I don't *think* I have led an especially sheltered life. The largest bloc are Army prisoners with sentences of from ten to forty years; the second largest group are draft dodgers; and besides these there are a white-slaver, an absconder, and I. Most of the Army men come from the Southern mountains, and the rest of the men are mostly slum-raised, virtually illiterate characters. A couple of them I knew upstairs as nice guys, but here they have been engulfed by a hard core of leaders who set the tone for all the talk and activities.

Some of the time they brag about their criminal exploits in the past, and these are childishly naive and lead one to wonder how they ever managed to stay out of jail at all, but most of the time the talk is of sex, which they explore over and over, painstakingly and in incredible detail, and on a level I have never heard or imagined before. The language, of course, is continuously obscene, and with all of us in the one room it is physically impossible to get away from it – ever. I never wanted to do anything as much as I want to ask to be put back in cell, but I have resolved to stick it out as long as I can. After all, I wanted to see what prison was really like! ...

I find myself prone to self-pity to a disturbing degree. The whole experience is so totally different from anything I have ever known before, and life outside was so richly satisfying, that it is a great temptation to indulge in orgies of feeling sorry for myself. It troubles me, because I had thought myself better able to stand adversity, particularly in a time when so many millions of people are undergoing much worse physical hardships. I think that what contributes to one's sense of depression in here is not so much the intensity of the experience as its omnipresence. In the dormitory here ... there is literally no escape from the reality of prison, no chance to be alone even for a minute. For twenty-four hours a day, seven days a week, one is smothered in the sights and sounds of prison and of one's fellow inmates.

[My wife] Dot wrote the other day, as others have done, that this can be a tremendously 'creative' experience. I know what they mean, because I have had the same notion myself, but have come to doubt it greatly. Instructive, yes; creative, no! I believe now that the experience of prison tends to be degrading and disintegrating, and if too prolonged will almost certainly result in serious psychic injury. Not merely the fact of imprisonment, though that is bad enough, but the throwing together of inmates of widely varying moral development, and the common tendency of men to adjust to the lowest common level – a tendency that is strengthened here, of course, by the prevailing cynicism and despair.

I have not changed my feeling about going to prison when that is the one way open to protest effectively something one feels to be wrong. But to believe that such an experience will 'deepen one's spiritual life,' or something of the sort, seems to me as unreasonable as to believe that a man can be strengthened physically by being denied all nourishing food ...

I am cooped up here with eleven other men, with whom I have practically nothing in common but humanity, and I doubt even that sometimes. That sounds hysterical or insufferably snobbish, but it is neither. Morally, these men are degenerates. Association with them for twenty-four hours a day deepens one's compassion for men whose lives never budge above the level of animal existence, but even compassion is frustrated here, with no way of implementing it. Of course, I am still in the early, and perhaps worst, days of this thing, so that I may change my feelings considerably later on. As of now, though, prison looks like something one endures while trying to conserve what one can, rather than as an opportunity for growth.

As you walk along the main corridor of Lewisburg from the hospital at one end, you pass on either side the entrance to five cellblocks and three dormitories that are the heart of the prison proper. These are the only homes Lewisburg's inmates have, some for a year, some for two or three times that long, many for decades or even for the rest of their lives.

FRIDAY, August 4 – Well, the novitiate has ended – I am now a full-fledged inmate. Yesterday, clutching my blanket-wrapped little bundle of possessions to my breast, I preceded a guard down the long corridor that leads from quarantine to 'population.'

Acting on the advice of some of the other COs, plus my own experience in Quarantine, I had put in a request for assignment to a cell, rather than a dormitory. The assistant warden sent back a note that the prison needs its cells for long-termers, psychopaths, and homosexuals, and that such relatively well-behaved characters as I must get along in dormitories.

So here I am, unhappily bedded down in H-2, the home away from home for some forty-eight of Uncle Sam's involuntary guests. H-2 is a second-floor dormitory, roughly a hundred feet long by thirty-five wide. Rows of beds line both side walls, and two other rows stand back to back down the middle. Between each two beds is a tin cabinet-desk for our possessions.

My bed is the first in one of the center rows. Two big tables adjoining it provide the space on which the men play interminable games of dominoes and checkers, which makes my own location even noisier, if that is possible, than the rest of the room.

From what I have seen so far, H-2, whatever its other virtues and shortcomings, is definitely not the ideal location in which to develop the contemplative life ... [T]he noise is incessant, although of a different quality. I suppose whenever forty-eight men spend all but their working and eating hours in one room the result is certain to be a pretty high level of noise.

The men are of widely varying types ...

[SUNDAY, August 6] Considering what we have learned about sex, it is hard to reconcile this compulsory celibacy with the assertions of the penologists about the use of modern psychological insights in treating criminal behavior. One is in prison only a very short while before the extent of homosexual activity makes itself known. The prison officialdom frowns on any overt relationships between the men, of course, and punishes severely any that it discovers, but the relationships go on nonetheless. The men are amazingly skilled at carrying on their complicated courtships without discovery, and an undertone of excited speculation and rivalry runs through the prison with the arrival of any unusually youthful or effeminate looking offender.

Masturbation, of course, is widely – almost universally – practiced. One of my friends tells me that the prison psychologist, in a special class on 'learning to live with yourself,' commended the practice to the men as a realistic method of reducing the prison-induced tension. Be that as it may, it is commonplace to walk into the washroom and find one or more men masturbating into the urinals.

Another psychologist with experience in penal institutions also is widely quoted as having said that after one year's imprisonment, 80 per cent of the inmates have 'homosexual tendencies' and 10 per cent gratify them. The 80 per cent sounds high to me, but I suppose the definition of 'tendencies' has something to do with it ...

FRIDAY, September 15 – It is almost ridiculous the way one's scale of values can be upended here. Take what happened today. The parole and educational offices [where Hassler then worked] went out to commissary this morning. (For the record, we get to commissary once a week, to buy fruit, candy, razor blades, and so on, to a maximum of $10 a month.) Usually, we return from commissary to our cells, where we leave our little store of goodies and either go back to work or, if it is late, get ready for supper. This afternoon, however, they sent us right back to the offices. The result was that when I trudged back to D-3 after work, I carried in my hand a paper bag full of my little purchases.

The guard who stands at the entrance to the cell-block is a young chap named Holland. He is a pleasant young fellow, and I have stopped to talk to him several times. He is doing some studying at night – at Bucknell [University], I think – and hopes to get a more respectable job after a while. In the meanwhile, though, he can't see anything wrong with this one, a point that I have discussed with him several times. He understands my position, though he does not sympathize with it, and thinks it is silly to put COs in prison.

We smiled at each other as I came down the corridor today, and I stopped to say good evening. He asked me what I had in the bag, and I told him. Then he demanded that I show him – and a wave of resentment flooded over me that I had a hard time not to show. As it was, I showed him the open bag, meanwhile pointing out to him how the nature of his job was getting to him, so that, though he knew I would not lie to him, he still must look in the bag for himself.

It sounds ridiculous to get angry about something like that, but it would be a mistake to underestimate the incident. It is this kind of thing, in itself an almost insignificant part of the whole organization of humiliation, but magnified out of all proportion against the trivia of our days, that characterizes our emotional reactions to prison. And exaggerated or not, it is the cumulative effect of this cycle of humiliation-resentment that guarantees that prison will not do any real good for the men confined within its walls ...

[SUNDAY, October 1] – [Very] impressive is the almost universal delicacy when it comes to inquiring into another man's misdeeds, and the refusal to determine one's relations with another convict on the basis of his record. This does not mean that to a criminal all crimes look alike. On the contrary. There are categories of crime rigidly defined though somewhat different from those recognized by the 'law-abiding citizens' outside.

The occasional political bigwig, ... of course, is regarded with awe and the wistful hope that the great man will remember his friends when he comes once again into his kingdom.

Men who attempt armed robbery of banks or post offices or the like, are highly respected for their courage. They 'put it on the line.' They take the big chance when they go out for crime.

Bootleggers, like my friend Tony, regard themselves and are regarded as respectable business men who have suffered a temporary reverse. Absconding bankers, who usually were the pillars of church and community, are looked on with a mixture of awe for their former positions and a human delight at their collapse. At the bottom of the list are white-slavers (the professional, not the amateur 'one-woman' operator), rapists, kidnappers, dope smugglers.

But these are still all categories, and most of the time do not affect an individual's actual standing in the prison community. That is determined by the man himself – his personality, attitudes, and so on. This morning I ate breakfast with two men whose crimes were atrocious and are generally known. One, a Greek boy in his twenties, an Army prisoner, killed a taxi driver by bludgeoning him to death with a tire iron rather than pay a fifty-cent fare. He is a cheerful, handsome, fairly stupid boy who seems to be troubled neither by a bad conscience over his crime nor by worry about his life sentence. Before his brief life in the Army he worked as a pimp for a New York bawdy house, and frequently regales us with stories of that unbelievably sordid life ... But though Benny's crimes and character are widely known and deplored, Benny himself is moderately popular – a friendly, cheerful, 'good guy.'

Next to Benny today sat a twenty-year-old boy with a seventy-seven-year sentence. For sheer, cold-blooded brutality, his offense ranks with Benny's. He hitched a ride with a motorist, knocked him out, beat him very badly, and stuffed him into his own trunk, from which he was rescued two days later by a suspicious state cop. The victim lived, though minus the sight of one eye and badly crippled. Tom, then only eighteen, drew a sentence of seventy-five years, subsequently increased by two years when he attempted to escape. He is sullen and uncommunicative; around him there eddies an aura of sudden violence. The other prisoners detest and avoid him, but only because of his present attitude, not because of his violent crimes.

Benny is not liked because of his crime, nor is Tom detested because of his. Most of the men here disapprove of violence about as much as the average person outside. Consequently, they would disapprove strongly of the behavior of both men. But this disapproval does not determine the degree or nature of their acceptance by the prison society; only their present behavior and attitudes do that. It is a significant and perhaps promising sign ...

[13 October 1944] – Time continues to go pretty swiftly now, except when I look ahead. Then the months seem terribly long, and nostalgia floods over me. But when I keep my eyes on the days immediately ahead and the job or the person at hand, I find I haven't enough time to do everything I want.

The unvarying routine is about the worst part, I suppose. We get up at six, to the unholy screeching of the factory whistle and the whistles of the guards. In the dormitories the lights go on, too, which means really getting shocked awake in a hurry. In the cell, a man can grope around in the dark for a while, giving his eyes a chance to become accustomed to being open before turning on the light.

A few minutes later the guard makes his 'count,' at which time each man is supposed to be standing, fully dressed, at his door. Since the hack simply glances in at the window, however, it is a simple enough matter to slip one's shirt on and, by standing close to the door, give the desired impression.

At 6.30, to the accompaniment of more whistles, we line up and march into the huge dining-hall, which I would guess is about 200 feet square, done in a Spanish mission style. In the dormitory, I was part of the group that went in last and out first, and I had considerable difficulty adapting myself to the consequent need to complete a meal in about twelve minutes! Now, as [once again] a resident of a cell, I go in with the first and out with the last, giving me enough leisure to eat in the way the Lord intended. Even so, we are out of the dining-hall and back in our cells before seven!

The next hour we spend cleaning up, shaving, etc., and I usually make my entries in this journal. At eight we go to work, until eleven: at eleven-thirty we go to 'dinner,' and at twelve back to work again until four-fifteen. The return to my cell then is the high spot of the day, since that is when the mail, if any, has been distributed.

After supper – 4.45 to 5.15 – there is 'inside stockade' for those who want it and have no school or other evening engagements. Stockade is a long, relatively narrow room where the men talk and play cards to the unending accompaniment of a high-pitched radio that no one ever takes the trouble to tune. The racket is such that I go very seldom, usually choosing instead to sit on my bed reading until lights out.

Library comes twice a week: for me Thursday evening and Sunday morning. The prison has an excellent library. To go to it – as everywhere else – we line up and march under the vigilant eye of the hack. Sunday also we drowse lazily in bed until 6.30, and have outside stockade morning and afternoon, with church service at 5.45 and movies at seven. At 5.20 and 9.20 p.m. daily we have count, again, standing at the cell doors, and periodically through the night the guard flashes his light in on us to make sure no ungrateful wretch has attempted either escape or suicide. At ten the lights go out and we, perforce, go to sleep.

I am fortunate in many ways. Our office looks out over the front wall to a vista of rolling farmland and wooded hillside. These days the leaves are gorgeous in their autumn colors, and I always stand at the window for a few moments in the morning, seeing the mist rise from the little valleys, and the steam from a distant train, and a herd of cattle grazing peacefully on a soft, still-green hillside. So many of the men get no chance for such restoring glimpses of another world!

I was thinking, yesterday, though, of how strange it will seem to be free again: not to have to line up for everything one does, not to be ruled by whistles and shouted commands, and to be cast once again on one's own initiative. I can understand how fearful and reluctant to leave some men become after really long periods in prison. When one has had one's whole life completely ordered down to the minutest detail, it becomes a fearsome thing to face the prospect of freedom and responsibility again. This, of course, lies at the heart of the total inability of the prison to accomplish the thing it is supposed to do. For men who need, almost more than anything else, training in self-discipline, it provides a complete system of rigid discipline externally applied. The result, of course, is to make the man even less capable of coping with the problems and temptations that come to him than he was to begin with. And the men who 'adjust' to this unreal kind of life – who, in other words, are able to submerge completely their individual personalities in order to fit the prison-envisaged stereotype – are assumed to be those most ready to return to society, and therefore most suitable for parole! ...

SUNDAY, December 31 ... I am acquainted with the prison now: my life has settled down into the sterile routine that is the worst curse of this kind of life. Up at six, breakfast at seven, work at eight, lunch, supper, inside stockade or choir or library and bed – these make up my life, with the mail from outside and the precious monthly visits from Dot.

This is prison – an endless round of petty routine overlaying the ever-present fear and hostility. Work, school movies, stockade, library – they are all attempts to help the men kill time, nothing more. For the overwhelming majority of men in this first-class, modern prison there is nothing whatever to challenge or improve them. Time is their enemy whom they must overcome. Time here is wasted, useless, the bitterness inflicted on them by a reasonless, unaware, impersonal monster outside called society. Some men stay in perpetual rebellion, becoming more cynical, more hostile, more dangerous every day they stay. Some become adept at the art of dissembling, making the gestures of the 'adjustment' to which the authorities do obeisance, and which promises them an early parole. Some simply sink into a lassitude that drags them further and further down from the level of the reasoning human being.

Once in a thousand convicts a man rises above the prison, and by the sheer force of his own will achieves the miracle of reconstruction in his own personality. But these ... 'do it in spite of prison, not because of it.'

... The immediate and overwhelming impression of prison, and one that continued through my sentence and beyond, was the feeling of humiliation. This is the reality of prison, more even than the all-too-frequent physical brutality, the occasional sadism of prison personnel, or the hopeful but frustrated system of rehabilitation. More than anything else, I think, the convict is infuriated and discouraged by the planned indignities and degradation that are his lot from the moment he gets into the hands of the prison authorities. Totalitarianism always is characterized by this disregard of ... the individual human personality ...

Prison – even an American prison – is fashioned on equally totalitarian lines, and the results in terms of its expressed aims are no less predictably dismal. The prisoner has no rights, but only privileges which may be taken away at the whim of the authorities. In every way the prison authorities can contrive he is deprived of his individuality. He stands in line to get the same drab clothes every other convict wears, which are handed out to him with a minimum of regard for size and condition. His cell must conform to every other cell in its complete sterility; his letters are read, his belongings pawed through every day or so, his movements regulated through the day by bells and whistles and observed by night by a flashlight-carrying guard who periodically peeks through the 'judas-window' in his cell door. That some convicts still manage to evade this all-seeing observation long enough for the final contemptuous gesture of suicide must stand as a tribute to the indomitable ingenuity of man.

At several important points I did not have to endure the same kind of humiliation as most convicted felons. Partly this was because many of the men in authority with whom I came in contact recognized a deviation from the normal criminal personality, while a few even expressed a sneaking agreement. More important, probably, was the fact that considerable numbers of respected and influential people 'outside,' pacifists and nonpacifists alike, were indignant that conscientious objectors should be imprisoned at all and were alert and vocal about any attempts to add to their difficulties in prison ... Moreover, as a federal prisoner, and especially as a federal prisoner in the Southern District of New York, I escaped some of the more inhuman experiences of the men who do their time in the filthy, germ-ridden holes that so frequently serve as the municipal, county and state prisons of our country.

Yet in spite of this relatively easier time, I found myself sometimes shaken with rage at the insensitivity of those who had become the keepers of the keys of my life. Within days after my incarceration I found my sympathies heavily with the convicts and against the authorities, even though my natural inclinations were to support a law-abiding society and its rules.

It was to become clear to me in the months that followed how crucial this matter is, and how completely it nullifies all the really excellent intentions and insights that many professional penologists bring to their jobs.

The best of prisons does not reform or rehabilitate. It punishes, but punishment neither eradicates the original misdeed nor reforms the criminal ...

The institution of prison does take a few criminals out of circulation for varying periods of time, which some people like to call 'protecting society.' But since in most cases the criminal eventually is released again, equipped with some new prison-acquired skills and motivated by prison-enforced resentment, such 'protection' is of doubtful value at best. The stark truth is that if the fundamental consideration is the protection of society against criminals, then the proper treatment is either life imprisonment or execution for every convicted criminal. Since both humanitarian and practical considerations of space and equipment make such a program impracticable, we come back to our original thesis that prison actually serves no useful purpose ...

Source: Alfred Hassler, *Diary of a Self-Made Convict* (Chicago: Henry Regnery Co., 1954), 2–4, 32, 41–3, 47–50, 58, 59, 63, 64, 98, 99, 116–18, 123–5, 158, 159, 177–80.

MALCOLM PARKER

Malcolm (Max) Parker was one of the most original characters I have ever met. A brilliant mathematician and a fine violinist, he was at the same time a skilled mechanic who could open a locked safe with a piece of wire or mould a key that would unlock a jail gate. (I should interpose here, he landed in jail of course as a CO and not as a crook!) With his hair rarely combed and his clothes tattered and invariably in disarray – though at the same time always clean – women found him attractive; he got on well, too, with his male peers. His father had been a university professor, and he could easily have followed in his footsteps had he elected to do so. Instead, when the war was over he chose to pursue at first a service career with the Quakers in Poland (where I got to know him) and then in India; after that he settled in a remote area of British Columbia and, with wife and children, followed a lifestyle close to nature until his untimely death.

The prison memoir, extracts from which are printed below, was composed nearly forty years after the events it describes. Therefore, as Parker explains in a note, 'there are inevitably some factual inaccuracies, albeit minor ones ... There are undoubtedly a few embellishments – they have a way of creeping in. But again [hopefully they are] only minor ones. With rare exceptions, the dialogue is, of course, no longer verbatim, although it pretty well reflects the mood and spirit of the moment. The chronology of events is somewhat mixed up, but where this has happened, it is only because the sequence is unimportant anyway. What is important is that the basic story really did happen.'

Parker 2501-SS tells his story and that of the other 'strange criminals' who shared his incarceration in Sandstone Correctional Institution with balance and with humour (occasionally slipping into a facetiousness, illustrated by the memoir's subtitle *A Light-hearted Romp through Durance Vile*, that I find inappropriate in an essentially serious theme). And his racy colloquial style carries the reader along until the day of Max's final release from Sandstone.

Parker's memoir, since it was privately printed and only a limited number of copies were distributed, is, I think, not so well known as it should be either to students of penology or to those interested in the history of war resistance.

Appreciation

The one factor that stands out above all others in making this story possible is the well-nigh unbelievable tolerance and restraint shown toward us by the staff of the Federal Correctional Institution at Sandstone, Minnesota, in the face of what at times amounted to extreme provocation.

Although I feel sure the main policies regarding our treatment originated in Washington, there is considerable latitude possible in the interpretation and implementation of these policies at the local level.

It was certainly not an easy situation for the guards and officials dealing with us, and I just wonder if I would have acquitted myself equally well had I been in their shoes. Although I have no love for prisons or the basic philosophy behind them, I take off my hat to the men who are trying to run them with decency and respect under difficult and degrading conditions ...

Quarantine

When a prisoner first gets to a federal prison, he is put into a separate group called quarantine. This doesn't mean quarantine in the medical sense, as there are new arrivals constantly coming into the group and others constantly leaving it for the main prison population. It is more of a social quarantine. They are kept in a separate cell block, have a separate and closely supervised yard time, have a separate line and eating area in the mess hall, and so forth.

During this quarantine period, which usually lasts about a month, the prisoners are given physical examinations, IQ, psychological and aptitude tests, as well as interviews with psychologists, chaplains, education officers, vocational counselors, etc. All of this is ostensibly to find out what each inmate's needs are, how he can be helped to rehabilitate himself and where he will best fit into the prison system.

During my stay in quarantine, two things came up which seemed fairly unimportant and insignificant at the time, but which later had unexpected repercussions.

One of these arose during my physical examination, when the doctor discovered that I had a rather erratic heart beat. When I am at rest, my heart will occasionally skip a beat or two, or even more. When any demands are made on it, then it will settle down to a nice even beat. I had known about this for a long time, and had been told that it was nothing to worry about – in fact, it was beneficial in that my heart was getting extra rest. Apparently, though, this was the first time this doctor had encountered this condition, for he got quite concerned about it. He hooked me up to his electrocardiograph and ran a bunch of tests on me to see what his machine would make of it. He wasn't able to give me an immediate verdict on this – he had to 'interpret the results.' When I heard nothing from him, I supposed he had decided there was nothing to it. Or maybe it was just that he had wanted to play with his new electrocardiograph machine. Anyway, I soon forgot all about it.

The other item was a small contretemps in the mess hall. The quarantine group was always the last group to go through the mess line, and one day I happened to be the last man in the line. That noon we were being served grilled cheese sandwiches, and as I held my tray out the guy flipped a sandwich onto it, laid down his spatula, turned around and walked off. There were four or five sandwiches left lying there and no one else to come, so I picked up an extra one and walked back to our assigned eating area.

Very shortly a guard appeared and relieved me of the extra sandwich. We were then informed that as a result of my misdemeanor, the whole quarantine group would be kept locked up in their cells that afternoon instead of being allowed their usual yard period. Theoretically this method of making the group suffer for the sins of the individual is a fairly effective way of using group pressure to keep people in line, but in this case it didn't work out that way. Most of the guys supported me, saying that they'd probably have done the same thing if they'd had the chance. I thought this missed yard period would be the end of this incident, but it proved to have greater importance than I realized.

At some point during quarantine, one is given an opportunity to express a preference for his work assignment.

I thought that with my natural predisposition for things mechanical, I might learn more and have more fun in the machine shop. Although at this particular institution it had been the standard practice to assign anybody who scored above 120 on the IQ test to the prison library, I felt there was a fair chance I might get the machine shop, since the library already had more inmates assigned to it than it could profitably use.

Among the aptitude tests that we were given was one for mechanical ability, in which we were given an old-fashioned door lock, completely disassembled. Without telling us what it was or what we were to make of it, we were told to put it together. I recognized what it was, so was able to assemble it fairly rapidly without having to puzzle it out. Since I completed it in considerably less than the allotted time, I felt that should be a plus factor in my getting the machine shop assignment. So when I was given the opportunity to express a preference, I said that since I felt I was best able to do work of a mechanical nature, I would like to go to the machine shop.

On the last day of his stay in quarantine, each inmate is called before a panel of the prison staff who have reviewed his record, and he is given his work assignment. When it was my turn, the warden told me that my 'claim to being able to do work of a mechanical nature was not borne out' and so I was being assigned to Labor 2 – the dirty job pick and shovel crew.

The only reason I can figure out for my not being assigned to the library – the hitherto automatic placement – or the machine shop – my expressed preference – was the blot on my otherwise unsullied escutcheon caused by that extra grilled cheese sandwich.

From Population to the Hole

It was on the day that I left quarantine for the main population that I found out what the doctor's verdict was on my electrocardiograph tests. As I lined up with the Labor 2 crew for the first time, the associate warden came by and called me up to the head of the line where the regular guard for this crew was, and said, 'Parker, what's this I hear about your having a heart condition?' I was a bit taken aback, never having considered it as a 'condition' and so I mumbled something about yes, I did have a certain systolic irregularity. He went on, 'Well, we don't want to give you any trouble with that. We're not here to aggravate your physical problems. So I'm telling you now, here in front of Mr. Godwin, and I'll write it down on your record, that any time you feel like resting, I'm giving you full authority to do so. Just don't overdo it, now. OK?' I averred as how that was OK and went back to the line-up.

The job that Labor 2 was engaged in at that particular time was obviously something to keep us busy – digging a ditch for a drain line from the dairy barn that a backhoe could have dug in a couple of days. Labor 2 was a sort of semi-punitive assignment – they did all the hard, dirty, unpleasant jobs like shovelling snow or coal or dirt or manure.

However, I had had a couple of months' inactivity in county jail while awaiting my assignment and transfer to a federal prison, and then another month of relative inactivity in quarantine, so I was glad for the opportunity for some exercise. It was fall, and it really felt good to stretch my muscles in the brisk autumn air.

The ditch we were working on was being dug in twenty-foot sections, with three-foot dikes being left between sections to keep the walls from collapsing, as they had a tendency to do in the sandy soil there. The ditch was about eight to ten feet deep, and the dikes were tunnelled through at the bottom for running the pipe. However, every section of trench that I worked on, instead of turning out to be a nice 3' ∞ 20' rectangle, ended up as a nearly circular twenty foot crater. Somehow, the side walls kept caving in. Sometimes I'd have to move a shovelful of dirt four or five times to get it up to the top of the trench, and then when the wall would collapse, I'd have it all to do over again. To say nothing of the new dirt that had falled in. Musta been sumpin' I was doing wrong. But at least it fitted in with their made-work program.

Godwin, our regular guard, was one of the more tolerant ones, and would considerately look the other way when one of the crew would slip into an adjoining field and come back with half a dozen ears of corn. These would then be poked into the coals of the fire we had going to help keep our hands warm. Ten or fifteen minutes later, there would be a small epidemic of chilled hands, and we would all crowd around the fire. Even without the butter and salt one might have wished for, that roasted corn was a mouth-watering delight. All in all, it wasn't a bad go.

There were times, however, when it wasn't quite so pleasant. One time when it was Godwin's day off, we had a relief officer who must have been fresh out of training school for prison guards. He certainly went out of his way to emphasize the fact that we were prisoners and he was Authority. If anyone stopped for a breather, about the second breath he'd get would be that of the guard, breathing down his neck and exhorting him to keep that shovel swinging and the dirt moving, reminding him that this wasn't a vacation at a country club, etc., etc.

Needless to say, there was no roast corn that day. In fact, there wasn't even a hand-warmer fire. If we complained of the cold, we were informed that we weren't working hard enough. All in all, he was rapidly getting to be a very large and noticeable pain in the neck, and everyone was getting thoroughly fed up with him.

Suddenly I remembered my cardiac dispensation, which I'd not had any occasion to use, and which would, no doubt, be well buried in my file. Surely a relief guard would not have bothered to read through the file of every man on the crew. So with studied nonchalance I folded my hands on the top of my shovel handle, rested my chin on my hands and waited for the wrath to come. Nor did I have long to wait.

'Hey, you there! These shovels aren't handed out for head props. Get that dirt moving!'

'Naw! I don't think I will.'

'WHAT? Why you – you ...' The effrontery of it left him momentarily speechless – but only momentarily. 'I don't give a damn what you think! You aren't here to think, you're here to do what you're told! Get shovelling!'

'I don't feel like it.'

'OK, you bastard! You asked for it! What's your number?' He grabbed me by my shoulder and whirled me around so he could read the number stencilled on my clothes. Whipping out a pencil and notepad, he wrote it down and went storming off to the nearest phone presumably to get someone to escort me to the hole – the traditional prison punishment cell. Fellow crew members, who didn't know about my 'delicate condition' were aghast at my temerity, and were gloomily predicting everything from a month in the hole to the remainder of my three-year sentence there. I didn't explain, but went back to work, since I was warmer shovelling than standing around yakking.

Very shortly the guard returned, with noticeably less bluster than when he had left. As soon as he got fairly close, I very deliberately leaned on my shovel and smiled sweetly at him. He got very red and flustered, and suddenly found an absorbing interest in some birds in the sky.

My fellow crew members looked at me with a mixture of awe and amusement, wondering what sort of pull I had with the front office that I could get away with such insubordination. I think the guard must have gotten a chewing out for walking off and leaving us the way he did, as he was noticeably quieter, less arrogant, and more tolerant the rest of the day. All in all, a very satisfying experience.

After about a month of Labor 2, though, the situation began to pall. The exercise, instead of being a pleasure, was getting to be a drag. The program of made work was making less and less sense. For me, personally, this was aggravated by the rankle of the front office's seeming arbitrariness in disregarding my expressed preference for my work assignment. Then, too, the idea of helping to run the institution that was keeping us imprisoned was becoming less and less palatable.

Various of these views were shared by other CO's, and ideas of strike action of one sort or another were bruited freely about. When it finally came down to the nitty-gritty of it, though, there were only five of us who were able to talk ourselves into actually doing something about it. These were Walter Gormly, who, of the five of us, had been here at Sandstone the longest; Glen Hutchinson; Ed Adamowicz; Chuck Worley, and I, the newest of the bunch. Worley and I both worked on Labor 2, resigning from which certainly carried the greatest appeal. The other three all worked at different jobs. Our reasons for joining in this strike action were as varied as our reasons for being CO's in the first place.

We set ourselves a deadline of October first. In keeping with the terminology of the times, with D-day, V-E and V-J days, we referred to our deadline as O-1 ...

A couple of weeks before our deadline, we informed the front office of our intentions, so they'd have time to get used to the idea and decide what they wanted to do about it. We tried to emphasize that we were doing this as a matter of principle, and not just to make their custodial jobs more difficult. We stated that we would not recognize their authority to order us around, and that except as we were physically constrained from it, we would do as we wished.

Prison, of course, is not the ideal place to issue any sort of declaration of independence, as the physical constraints imposed by the system are fairly ubiquitous. However, there were various places where we could assert our independence. We could refuse to work at our assigned tasks, refuse to stand up in the proper manner when the whistle was blown for count (five or six times a day), not keep our cells in the conditions called for by their regulations, and so on. Certainly nothing that would shake the system to its foundations.

According to enlightened penology – which is how federal prisons are run – the granting or withholding of privileges is a much more effective means of keeping prisoners in line than physically coercive punishments and restraints. Consequently, one has simple privileges – like the yard privilege that was denied [in] quarantine the day of the grilled cheese sandwich episode, or the Saturday movie privilege, or the privilege of checking out two books per week from the prison library – which might be denied for minor infractions. More serious offenses called for withdrawal of the privilege of sending or receiving mail, or perhaps of having visitors. Really major misconduct would result in the withdrawl of most amenities by sentencing to the hole. Of course, if one got very many disciplinary infractions – 'shots' in the local slang – on his record, he would jeopardize the most valuable privilege of all – the possibility of release on 'good time' (statutory time off one's sentence for good behavior) or parole.

In taking our position of non-cooperation we were in effect thumbing our noses at their whole system of privileges. While we thought it unlikely, there was the very real possibility that we might spend the rest of our sentences in the hole – where one's privileges are minimal – a rather unappealing prospect, at best.

In rejecting the system's hierarchy of values, we substituted our own so that now we had the 'work privilege' which we were relinquishing. For hearings before the disciplinary court we had 'court privilege,' which always resulted in our getting the 'hole privilege.' Lockup in solitary confinement was 'privacy privilege,' and so.

By treating these normally dreaded punishments as privileges, even if only verbally, we went a long way toward reducing their negative impact on us.

When our O-1 deadline rolled around, they took our action very calmly and matter-of-factly, with no apparent hard feelings about it. This was in striking contrast to some other prisons where CO's had gone on work strikes or other forms of non-cooperation with a great deal of resultant rancor and bitterness. But whether there were hard feelings or not, the net result was that we got our court and hole privileges with promptitude, if not alacrity.

The hole in this prison, unlike most prisons, was simply a group of six regular cells on the second floor at one end of a cell block. They were blocked off from the rest of the cells by a brick wall, and had the added distinction of having the windows covered by a secondary screening of ˘" hardware cloth to prevent things from being smuggled in to hole habitants. Aside from that, they were just like ordinary cells except that there was no furniture – just the bare concrete cell. It had the standard cell plumbing – a wash basin and toilet – and a ceiling light. As holes go, it was a very homey hole. One was allowed a mattress and blanket from 11 p.m. to 5 a.m. – again, a nice homey touch.

The meals were not quite up to the usual standard for home cooking, however. A typical meal might consist of a wad of half-cooked potatoes and a few limp leaves of overcooked cabbage. Breakfast might likely be a gooey mess of very over-cooked, over-stirred oatmeal. With, of course, no seasoning for any of the meals. Really not what one could call haute cuisine.

The Prison Itself

It might help in visualizing this story to have a general idea of what this particular prison is like to provide a basic framework to fit the various incidents into. Although some of the following descriptions may seem overly detailed, most of these details are relevant to the story at one place or another. Relevant, but not essential to the narrative, so it's not necessary to try to remember them all.

This prison, known as a Federal Correctional Institution, was a medium security prison. There was none of the traditional tier after tier of barred cells and iron catwalks so beloved for movie and TV scenarios. Neither were there the often pictured machine gun turrets and patrol dogs. Most of the prisoners lived in dormitories rather than cells, although there were two two-story cell blocks.

The main prison building was in the shape of a huge hollow square, two stories high and about four or five hundred feet on a side. This building contained all the administrative offices, the kitchen and mess hall, the auditorium, the dormitories for the inmates, the library, the hospital, and so forth. Projecting toward the inside of the square from one wall were the two cell blocks, about 25' ∞ 100'.

Since most of the action of this story takes place in cell blocks, I'll describe one in some detail. Each floor of each cell block had the same basic pattern – an eight-foot-wide corridor running most of the length of the block with cells on each side. There was a stairwell at each end, and at the end projecting into the yard there was a common room, called a day room, which went the full width of the block and was about 10 or 12 feet deep. This was separated from the corridor by an iron barred grill with a gate of similar construction set into it.

There were ten cells on one side, with two less on the other to allow for a stairwell. Each cell was roughly a 6' ∞ 10' rectangle with one corner taken up by the plumbing shaft. There was a basin with hot and cold running water and a flush toilet. Just above the toilet there was a grill leading into the plumbing shaft which was in turn connected to the forced suction ventilation system. Adjacent cells were mirror images of each other so they could share a common plumbing and ventilation shaft. Access to these shafts was from the corridor through a 2' ∞ 4' opening covered over with a 3/16" steel plate fastened on with Allen head cap screws.

The outside wall of each cell had a steel framed window about 40 inches square, made up of 8" ∞ 10" panes. The center section – two panes high by three wide – was hinged at the bottom so it could swing inward with an arrangement to keep it from opening more than about 30°. The openable section had a screen removable from the inside.

The doors to the cells were of ˘" steel plate mounted on a frame of 2" ∞ 2" ∞ ˘" angle iron. Each door had a 'Judas hole' – a 4" ∞ 8" window of heavy reinforced glass set into it about at eye level. The locking arrangement for the doors was rather elaborate. The doors themselves, even when unlocked, were held closed by regular hydraulic door closers. Each door had a pin tumbler lock which shot a bolt into the steel door jamb. The strike for this lock was controlled from the day room by racking levers, one for each side of the corridor. These were in steel boxes, which were kept locked at all times. Each racking lever had three positions: In the open position, the strike was lifted up so that there was nothing for the bolt of the lock to catch against, and the cell door could be opened, even though the lock was in its locked position. In the intermediate position, the strikes would drop down for all the cells on that side, so each one could be locked or unlocked individually. In the final, or deadbolt, position a bar would slip down into notches in the bolts of all locked cells, preventing them from being unlocked even with a key. The standard practice was to keep these levers in the intermediate position during the day and put them in the deadbolt position at night.

At the end of the corridor near the day room there was, on one side, a storeroom in which extra blankets, pillows, bed linens, etc. were kept, as well as an insecticide spray gun in the event of unauthorized arthropodous visitors. On the other side there was the shower room, and adjoining it, a mop closet about three feet square. In it there was a large mop sink as well as mops, brooms, soap powder, cleanser, etc. – everything needed to keep the cell block not only spic but even slightly span.

The gate and grille separating the day room from the rest of the cell block were massively built. There were vertical bars of 1" diameter steel with case-hardened inserts to discourage saws and files. These were placed about three inches apart, and held in place by horizontal flat steel bars °" thick and 2" wide with holes cut through to take the round bars. It was all welded together to make a sturdy, if not particularly aesthetic, barrier.

The day room was a fairly pleasant place. It had windows on three sides, and while the view was primarily of the prison courtyard, it gave a feeling of openness that was in pleasant contrast to our cells. There were benches and tables, so the inmates could gather there to socialize, play games, write letters, or even just sit and listen to the music over the centrally controlled loudspeaker system – usually tuned to radio programs as chosen by the inmate council, but also available for general announcements.

For furniture, in addition to the tables and benches in the day room, there was in the corridor a wooden box, divided into two compartments – one for clean socks and the other for dirty ones. This arrangement enabled inmates to change socks as needed without having to be taken care of individually. (Other clothing was assigned to the individual, had his number stencilled on it and was kept in his cell.) The furniture in each cell was all steel and consisted of a bed with a sliding drawer underneath for clothes, papers, etc., a chair and a small table. There was a single unshaded light bulb in the ceiling. Positively luxurious compared to county jail accommodations – really quite a comfortable home away from home.

Administrative Segregation

Our hole privilege continued for a month. We were all continuing in good spirits and no one showed any sign of weakening or giving up. Suddenly we were all transferred to other quarters – the remainder of the cell block from which the hole had been partitioned off – the second floor of cell block C. One likes to think that this transfer from the hole was in recognition of our Steadfastness in the Face of Adversity, but more likely it was simply that they needed the hole for other guys and we were kind of monopolizing the place. Be that as it may, we weren't about to complain, whatever the reason. We were now in regular furnished cells and on a main line diet. We even got our library and mail privileges back. Not only that, we got a new name. Although strictly speaking, the name was for the conditions of our lock up, it got to be attached to us: Administrative Segregation. Though our condition was very considerably ameliorated, we were still kept locked up in separate cells 22 hours out of the day. We had one hour's exercise in the cell corridor each morning and one hour's outdoor exercise by ourselves in a 50' ∞ 100' yard area each afternoon.

As other CO's found out that we were not going to be kept in the hole indefinitely, they began, one by one, to take similar positions of non-cooperation. It got so that they were simply being sent to Administrative Segregation without getting their hole privilege at all.

As with the original five of us, the reasons for others joining our group were varied. Some came as a matter of principle tempered by expediency, others came as a matter of expediency tempered by principle, and others came simply as a matter of expediency – because we had a better go in Administrative Segregation than in population. I don't remember the order in which they joined us, but the other members of our group were Igal Roodenko, Jack Taylor, Henry Dyer, Agard Bailey, Dick Zumwinkle, Dave Jensen, Bill Taber and John Hampton. All but Hampton, as I remember, came to us from population; he was the last one and came to us direct from quarantine. We had heard about him through the grapevine as a non-cooperator even in quarantine. He was a small, slightly built fellow with wavy dark brown hair, about 25 years old, and with a slow, soft speech in which there always seemed to be a trace of sardonic humor hovering in the background.

Since our section of C-2 had only 12 cells, it was completely filled before Hampton joined us. So when it came time for him to leave quarantine, the administration moved us all over to the E Cell Block, where we had the full 18-cell second floor – E-2 – to ourselves.

As they were moving us into E-2, several of us began inactivating the door closers on the cell doors by tripping the ratchets on them. This way, the doors would not automatically close so that they could all be locked by one motion of the racking lever, but would have to be dealt with individually. Others of us started taking the threaded rods off the closers. These were especially desirable, as the rod, with the two nuts that came with it, made a very acceptable adjustable open end wrench. Don't ask me what we wanted an adjustable open end wrench for – we had no immediate use for it in mind – it was just a nice illegal something to have. When we started tripping the ratchets, the guards ran around after us, trying to re-engage them, but then when they found the closers were beginning to disintegrate, they quickly locked us all up and then removed the closers altogether. But not before we had liberated a couple of wrenches.

Another thing they took away shortly after we moved in was the loudspeaker in the day room. We never did find out whether this was because, since we were still on a semi-punitive status, the loudspeaker privilege, like the Saturday movie privilege, was one we weren't supposed to have, or whether it was simply to save their loudspeaker. They couldn't have known that for us and our tastes, it would have been far more punitive for us to have to listen to the inmate council's choice of programs than to do without. Cruel and unusual punishment, I think they call it. In all honesty, I have to admit that if they'd left the speaker there, we'd undoubtedly have inactivated it within a week.

The meals were served to us in our cells. They had a special metal box made which would hold all the trays, silverware, and food containers. Each mealtime this box would be loaded up in the kitchen and brought up to the day room. There the guard would ladle out the food onto the trays, carry them one by one to each cell, unlock the door, hand the tray in, lock back up again, and so on to the next one. When there got to be a dozen of us, it became quite a chore, and when we began making such a point of our room-service privilege, they decided the time had come to make a change in the arrangements.

Instead of serving the trays, they would simply set the food box on a table in the day room, unlock our cells and the gate to the day room and let us fend for ourselves. It was much more pleasant for us and a lot less trouble for them, so everybody benefitted. After about an hour they would come and lock us back in our cells and take away the remains.

I guess that finally the bother of unlocking and relocking each separate cell five or more times a day got to be a bit of a drag for them, because eventually they just left the cells unlocked all day long, locking them up only at night. They did, however, keep the gate between the corridor and the day room locked except at mealtimes. But at least we had the run of the corridor and could visit back and forth in our cells, which made life more friendly and sociable ...

And the Waters Prevailed,
And They Increased Greatly

Hampton and I seemed to have an unfortunate affinity for the hole. Not infrequently we got our hole privilege at the same time, although not always for the same reasons. Only in the Case of the Broken Toilet did the reason have any relevance to developments there – otherwise one reason was as good as another. As I remarked about the ditch when I was on Labor 2, it musta been sumpin' we were doing wrong!

One time, shortly after our arrival at the hole, Hampton told me that he intended to flood the place that night, so if I didn't want my mattress soaked up I'd better put it up on the toilet when he started.

Sure enough, about midnight, halfway between visits by the circulating night guard, he warned me he was about to begin. He ripped an arm off his coveralls, jammed it in the toilet and then started flushing. These toilets were the power flush kind – you press a button and get a five second gush of water under full line pressure. Hampton just kept tripping it every five seconds or so, and soon the entire hole area was awash. The hole was on the second floor, above the quarantine area, and soon the water was pouring down the stairs and spreading out down there. After fifteen minutes or so we began to hear a few cries from below. As more and more guys woke up, the uproar grew in volume. The guard must have been at the far side of the building complex, or else enjoying a midnight cup of coffee, because it was another fifteen minutes before he appeared. He followed the cataract up to its origin, splashing and slipping up the stairs.

When he found out what was wrong, he bellowed at Hampton, 'What the hell are you doing there?' I don't know what sort of answer he expected – one would think it was fairly obvious.

Hampton smiled at him. 'I'm trying to flush this toilet, but it seems to be stopped up.' Then he pushed the button again. The guard knew it was useless to tell Hampton to stop, and he also seemed not to have the slightest idea of where to turn off the water to the toilet. He dithered about a bit, and all the while Hampton was standing there, smiling at him and pushing the button, and the flood was steadily increasing in volume.

Finally the guard seemed to realize that even though he might not know what to do, unless he sounded the alarm, things were going to get worse instead of better. He pulled himself together, turned around and sploshed and slid down the stairs, and we saw him no more. He must have pushed the right panic button, because in about another ten minutes the spring ran dry. The problem with this was that the only way they could turn off Hampton's water was to turn off the water for the entire cell block, so that now quarantine was without water – running water, that is. They had plenty of the other kind.

The next morning a crew of inmates – Labor 2, perhaps? I never thought to ask – came with mops and squeegees and dried us, and presumably quarantine, out a bit. Later on the maintenance crew came and put separate shut off valves in Hampton's water lines so the water could be turned on again for quarantine. The stockpile of mattresses in an adjacent cell, from which we were allowed to take ours at night, were, of course, thoroughly soaked and had to be taken out to dry. As soon as the source of the flood was cut off, the water in the hole mostly drained down to quarantine, but there was enough on the floors of our cells so that the mattresses we had used after the waters had receded were pretty wet, too, and also had to be dried. From the sound of things down below, it took the better part of the day to restore order out of the chaos Hampton had created.

When one of the guards was giving Hampton a hard time about all the extra trouble he was making for others, Hampton told them that as long as they tried to use the hole to coerce him, he would use the hole as a weapon against them. If they didn't like what he was doing, all they had to do was to let him out of the hole, and he'd stop making that sort of trouble.

His position had a degree of logical justice to it ...

[The Master–Slave Relationship]

One of the principles of prisons is that the master–slave relationship must always be maintained, that fraternization with the inmates leads to a breakdown of authority and all that. However, we had put ourselves outside this authority framework, and quite a few of the guards felt free to talk with us, sometimes at considerable length. Also I think that many of them were thoroughly fed up with the pettiness of the whole prison bureaucracy, and were glad to see it get pushed around a bit.

Some of the guards even got quite friendly with us. There was one guard in particular who was only a year or two from retirement who almost seemed to be on our side. One time he was fumbling with his bunch of keys, trying to find the proper one for the storeroom so he could get another blanket for one of the guys. I happened to be standing near by, and knowing from previous experience that the lock was ridiculously easy to pick, I said, 'Here, Mr. Norlin – let me.' I picked up a paper clip from the typewriter table nearby, jiggled it in the lock for about a second and opened the door with a deep bow. His eyes got big and he said, 'I didn't see a thing – *not a thing!*' and marched in to get the blanket ...

Strikes within Strikes within Strikes

Even before we went on our non-cooperation strike the war had already ended. Many people, including several public figures, felt that now that the war was over, all Selective Service prisoners should be released – that it was pointless to continue with the trouble and expense of keeping them locked up. Needless to say, we tended to concur with this view.

When six months had passed and there had been no appreciable speed-up in the release of draft cases, some of us felt moved to take action. Several of us – about seven or eight, as I remember – announced that we were going to go on a hunger strike to protest the situation. We launched a big publicity campaign, asking our personal correspondents to spread the word, and deluging public officials with a steady barrage of mail, asking for the unconditional release of all Selective Service cases.

The only immediate response by the administration to our strike was to improve the quality of the food they sent up to us. I think they must have been supplying us from the officers' mess in the hope that we could be lured out of our strike action.

When a couple of weeks had passed with no change, they took action of their own. They arrived in force – the doctor, a couple of orderlies and a couple of extra guards in case they might be needed. Then, one at a time, they'd force us onto our beds, pry our mouths open, slide what they admitted was simply an enema tube down our throats and then pour about a quart of goop down the tube. The goop really wasn't bad stuff – basically milk, eggs, and orange juice, with added vitamins, oil and malt. Of course, when it was going down one couldn't taste it, but when they pulled the tube out there would be a taste on the end, and it also had a slight tendency to repeat on one.

We told the doctor that since this hunger strike was simply for publicity purposes, we would not actually resist being fed – we simply wouldn't do it ourselves or cooperate with it – so they wouldn't need the extra reinforcements they had brought with them. This considerably simplified the feeding process, as for some of us they would simply tip our heads back, open our mouths and pour the stuff down. Others of us stuck to the tube routine. In neither case was the process actually unpleasant, although hardly what one would choose if all options were available.

This continued for about three or four months, and it did seem as though the process of releasing draft cases was being speeded up with a relaxing of the conditions of release, so we felt we were accomplishing something and that it was worthwhile continuing.

Shortly after we had started our hunger strikes, a couple of Jehovah's Witnesses, whom some of us had known from our days in population, took the same position of non-cooperation that we had taken. This time, though, the administration, instead of sending them directly to Administrative Segregation, as they had done with the last five or six non-cooperators, threw them in the hole. I guess they felt it would be easier to break these JW's since they didn't have the backing of their group. There is a verse in the Bible that tells people to submit to governmental authority, which would rule out such tactics as a non-cooperation strike. The JW's generally do not consider themselves as CO's, since the basis for their imprisonment is that they didn't get the ministerial deferment they felt they should. Since they spend a certain amount of time each week going around preaching the Word, they felt they should have a preacher's classification. The administration probably felt that with not only the absence of support from their fellow JW's, but with their active disapproval, the two JW's should fold easily. One thing they overlooked is that JW's glory in suffering for their cause. At any rate, they were made of sterner stuff than the administration had counted on, as they continued in the hole in good spirits. We felt they were getting a raw deal, but then, the original five of our group had had a month in the hole, so it wasn't entirely unfair. However, when a month had passed and they were still there, we felt some sort of protest action was called for.

Now, however, we were faced with a problem. When we took our position of non-cooperation the administration lost much of their hold on us. They could withdraw various of our privileges or throw us in the hole, and we'd just laugh at them. However, it was a two-edged proposition. They had lost their hold on us, true, but at the same time we had lost our hold on the administration. Already on a hunger strike, we could hardly non-cooperate much further than we were doing.

There seemed to be only one point left where there was any semblance of cooperation. So in protest at the discriminatory treatment these two JW's were getting Hampton and I announced that until they got the same conditions of imprisonment that we had, we would forcibly resist our feedings. The doctor came around the next day and said that he appreciated that we weren't doing this to make his job more difficult, and that he'd try to be equally considerate and not make things any more difficult or unpleasant for us than necessary. He said that he'd keep an eye on our condition and wouldn't start force feeding until such time as we showed clinical signs of malnutrition.

This time they let us go for 28 days before they resumed feeding. I have since heard that this is the Public Health Service's statutory limit for letting people go before starting force feeding. The show of force they put on for this was really amusing. They came in with six burly guards – none under about 6'2" and 200 pounds – along with the doctor and orderly. By way of contrast, Hampton and I had had no nourishment for 28 days, and had each lost some 35 or 40 pounds of weight.

They got to me first. While I didn't quite qualify as a 97 pound weakling, I sure wasn't any 97 pound strongling, either. Any one of those guards could have thrown me around like handbills.

They grabbed me as I was walking around in the corridor, frog marched me to my bed and threw me down on it. Then, with a guard holding each arm, and another one on each leg, and a fifth one holding my head, with a sixth hovering nearby in case I should overpower one of the others, they tried to force my jaws open to shove the tube down my throat. However, when one is determined, it is almost impossible to force his jaws apart short of using some mechanical pry. So then they shoved the tube – not a nasal catheter but the same sort of small enema tube they'd been using before – up my nose and so down into my stomach and then poured in the goop.

And then on to Hampton, where the show of force was even more laughable. Hampton was a much lighter build than I and had much less reserves for his body to draw on. The last week of the fast he had spent mostly just sitting in the day room huddled under a blanket or else lying on his bed. He really was a 97 pound weakling, but he got the same sort of overkill I'd received.

This kept on for a week or ten days. The tubes they were using, being rather large and stiff, were really tearing up the backs of our nasal passages and getting to be very uncomfortable. This just tended to make us more resistant than ever to our tube feedings. On one occasion Hampton secreted a razor blade, and when they had the tube down his nose he wrenched an arm free and cut off the tube. Another time he simply overturned the big bowl of goop onto the floor.

The way the impasse was finally resolved was to transfer the JW's to another prison where they would be outside our ken. A neat way of settling the issue without anybody losing face, I thought ...

Goodbye to Prison

As our hunger strike began generating publicity, pressure was being brought to bear on both Washington and our prison for our release.

When the officials came to us with some tentative parole propositions, we turned them down. To be released on parole one has to agree to a lot of conditions and supervision, and we weren't having any of either. We felt better able to supervise our lives than some overworked parole officer, and we certainly weren't going to sign or agree to anything.

This threw them for a loop. If we wouldn't even apply for parole or good time or agree to the conditions of them, then, they moaned, how were they going to get rid of us? 'Easy,' we replied. 'Just open the gate and say go.' In fact, they wouldn't even have to say go. They replied that their rules and regulations wouldn't let them do that, however much they might like to.

Finally, through contacting our correspondents and friends of our correspondents and friends of these friends, they located different people who were willing to report to the prison system what they might ascertain, even in a very casual and haphazard way, as to what our locations and activities were once we were released. It seemed they had to have in their books some sort of monthly report on releases. That was all right with us. If someone else wanted to stooge for the prison system, that was their worry, not ours. So it was on that basis that the releases for many of us in Administrative Segregation were arranged.

... [T]he day for my release drew near ...

Source: Malcolm Parker, *Prison Privilege!* (Kaslo, BC: KLC Publications, 1984), ii, 5–28, 58–61, 73, 74, 81–8.

LOWELL NAEVE

Lowell Naeve, after a short period in New York's West Street Detention Center in Manhattan, did most of his time in the federal prison at Danbury (Connecticut) where he took a leading part in the COs' prolonged strike against racial segregation – 'Jim Crow.' An account of this strike is given in the extracts from his prison memoir printed below. But he was also an inmate of several other penal institutions. His descriptions of prison life are both forceful and insightful. Once again, one can only recommend a reading of the whole book, of all its 231 pages (with a special commendation of the numerous drawings it contains by Naeve himself). A graduate student at Indiana University reported recently that Naeve's memoir 'had not been checked out [of the university library] in at least twenty years.' It is indeed time the work became better known.

Naeve was a non-registrant CO: as a non-violent anarchist he had an intense hatred of all forms of regimentation. On leaving school without completing his high-school education, he had taken on various odd jobs while spending all his spare time on his work as an artist. After the war he published several volumes of drawings, of which *The Phantasies of a Prisoner* (1958), a haunting evocation of his wartime experiences in jail,[1] is perhaps the most compelling. A young scholar (Philip Metres) has written of his unexpected 'discovery' of Naeve's considerable 'artistic output' reflecting his jail journey: 'The drawings delineate the existential loneliness of prison, the way in which it infiltrates the minds of inmates and guards alike. Frequently superimposing human figures against prison architecture, Naeve invokes the internalization of punishment and the diminishment of the individual.'

June, 1941

Danbury is supposed to be for short-timers, some of the men at West Street had said. 'Not like here, where ya got killers, pimps and every-

Illustration by Lowell Naeve

thing else. It's only sixty miles north of New York. It's a new place, it's supposed to be a pretty good can.'

The government car rolled steadily forward. Two pistol-hipped marshals sat in front. We three prisoners sat in the rear, handcuffed together. The prisoner next to me wanted to smoke. I was glad to oblige him by moving my hand up and down with his.

Trees were exceptionally green. The hills in the distance were a vibrant deep blue. The white strip of highway. What would Danbury be like?

Three miles beyond the city of Danbury, Connecticut, high on a hill overlooking the countryside, the government Chevrolet came to a stop. The rear doors were opened. We stepped out.

One of the marshals pointed to a shack where we could see a guard holding a machine gun. 'It's hard to believe,' he said confidingly, 'but that guy up there is an awfully good shot – he can hit sparrows.'

The front of the prison was shiny, streamlined, new-looking, a light cream in color. There was nothing to suggest bars, cells or cages. Danbury did not look like a prison.

We were being led toward a small green door. I felt a rising excitement, my curiosity reached a nervous peak. A Danbury guard opened the door, we were ushered in. The green door was locked, our handcuffs were removed. The guard, as if on a time-schedule: 'Take off your clothes. Lay them on the counter.' The three of us reluctantly took off our clothes.

'Want them sent home or burned?' I stared at my trousers, shirt, shoes. Sent home or burned? The words stood up before me like a flash on a movie screen. I couldn't imagine myself getting out of prison. My release date, June 16, 1942, felt like it was many years away. 'Sent home or burned?' stopped my mind, it seemed impossible to proceed beyond 'burned.' 'You'd just as well burn them.'

An impatient doctor arrived, put blue ointment under our arms and legs, to kill the crabs. We were handed blue-grey coveralls, brown shoes, white socks; a toothbrush, a small tinny metal comb. The coveralls were baggy and ragged, hung limply on us. The three of us looked at each other dejectedly, said nothing.

The guard standing in a doorway motioned with his hand, 'In here.' Disinterestedly we moved ahead. The curiosity, excitement we had experienced before the green door had given place to despondency.

In the adjoining record office we were finger-printed, our numbers given us, our pictures very carefully taken by a Mr. Kunkel.

While we waited somewhat impatiently for each process, I followed with my eyes the sunspots on the cement floor. The sun shone into the cold sterile room from an outside window. It was hard to believe that the sun could and did shine into the prison. The sunspots busied themselves with changing positions on the cold grey floor. At times there was a brilliant gay gem-like glitter, the spots glittered, the spots sparkled and danced.

Shortly, like dogs on a leash, we were following a guard down a very narrow corridor toward a large green door marked 'Quarantine.' The door was unlocked, we were led in. Quarantine cell block was a big hollow place with two tiers of cells on each side. Some fifty prisoners were moving about on the ground floor. They wore baggy ragged blue-grey coveralls like our own. I recognized some of the men as prisoners I had seen at West Street.

We were turned over to the quarantine officer. 'Here's what's expected of you during your stay. You are always to address an officer as "sir" – answer "Yes, sir."' (It soon proved that when he spoke to me he just growled out 'Hey you over there'; if I hesitated to respond: 'Naeve, hey Naeve 786.') 'You are always to make your bed in the same way, one of the boys will show you how it is done.' 'You get up at six o'clock, lights out at ten. You are given the privilege of writing two letters a week. In your letters you are not permitted to say anything about the prison.'

We had to fill out papers, cards, report to the guard in charge several times. It was evening before I got a chance to talk to some of the men. They were quick to relate: 'They've got about a dozen guys that believe like you out in the regular part of the prison.'

At 9:30 when we were told 'It's lockup for the count' we went to our assigned cells, the guard to 'the lock box.' We could hear him adjusting the levers that closed the doors. He yelled: 'Keep your fingers out of the doors. Keep your heads in.' The solid steel doors, one row at a time, slammed shut in unison – CRASHED. The crash echoed throughout the building. It emphasized the hollow space between the opposite tiers of cells. I glanced out of my small cell-door window. I felt oddly separated from the man across the way.

The crash of the doors made me, as it probably did most men, go to the window at the other end of the cell, peer out. The crash of the doors, peering out, made me feel that Danbury, where I now was, was a *very very* strange place ...

When I turned from the window ... I inhaled, the smell of fresh concrete seemed to penetrate – saturate me.

I wondered what the rest of the prison was like. I wondered if the men in the other cells were looking out like myself.

I undressed, went to bed. I thought of many things, kept turning over in my mind the impressions of the outside. I lay and lay, so it seemed, just thinking and thinking.

It was a long while before I could go to sleep.

July, 1941

The days in quarantine – the first, the second, the rest – went very much the same.

The first thing we heard in the morning was a bugle sharply calling out reveille. (I envisioned a row of army tents, a row of soldiers, disgruntedly standing at attention.) Next there were sounds of keys – a key opening the quarantine door. There were sounds of a guard shuffling about inside the cell block, laying his brief case and keys on a table, hanging up his coat.

We stayed in our bunks, waited. We heard more jangling of keys, then a key turning the lock of a lever box. The door squeaked as it opened. I imagined the guard peering into the box to see that all the dials and levers were 'just right.' He took ahold of a lever; the long steel arms above our doors scraped, fell into place. The moment was near.

A shrilling piercing whistle. It entered every cell, filled the void between the opposite tiers. The echoes of the shrill died out, leaving the cell block cold and hollow. A curt command: EVERYBODY UP! Our cell doors slid open simultaneously. Like everyone else I looked through my open door at the tiers of cells across the way. Everyone was getting up.

We didn't want to get up, but we did. Why? We didn't know. We just got up. Behind me and behind every man hung one vague doubt: if we didn't do what we were told, what would they do to us? There was the 'hole'; various stories and descriptions of it were going the rounds. If the authorities put us in the hole, in solitary, for a couple of months, would we be able to take it?

There was this big question mark. So – everyone got up, everyone did as he was told.

When the guard said, 'O.K., boys, let's mop up,' we mopped up. If the guard said, 'Let's clean the brass,' we cleaned the brass; it made no difference if the brass was clean and we felt it could be made no cleaner. If the guard said 'O.K., line up,' we lined up. That's all there was to it. Dictatorially prisons are run; by threat the men are ruled.

The only thing that kept each individual, including myself, from feeling completely stupid and ridiculous was that he saw everyone doing the same and obeying the same as he did ...

I went, said nothing. Inside me was a rising feeling I could hardly suppress. With some other prisoners I followed the guard across the yard. I was completely disgusted with myself for obeying. I knew as I followed the guard that sooner or later I would have to balk at being dictated to.

I looked ahead at the walk. Twenty feet forward was a spot. I looked at the spot, and I knew I was going to stop. I grew warm all over. I felt a gathering of my loose emotions. I reached the spot, stopped.

The guard and the other prisoners reached the green door they were headed for. The guard turned, counted his men. He noticed me standing in the walk about forty feet back.

'Hey, you!' he yelled, 'Come on!' I said nothing. 'Hey!' he yelled, 'What's the matter?' He waited a bit, then walked towards me. 'What's the matter?'

'I can't go any farther.'

'What do you mean?'

'I won't go any farther.'

He broke in: 'You mean you refuse to work?'

'You can call it whatever you want, I don't care. It's just – I want to have some say how my own life is to be run. I'm tired of being dictated to.'

He acted as though he didn't hear me. 'Are you coming along?'

'No.'

'Well, we'll see about that.'

He took me over to a cell house in the corner of the yard. I wondered what was going to happen, but I didn't particularly care. With another guard, he marched me up past three tiers of barred cells, locked me in a top cell.

The burning growl inside of me was gone. I had opposed what I thought wrong. For the first time in a month I felt sure and collected.

In a few minutes a young prisoner came to the front of my cell. He rested his elbows on the bars, and in a very friendly voice said: 'You're Naeve, the new war objector?' I said yes. He enthusiastically extended his hand through the bars: 'I'm one, too; Schoenfeldt's the name.'

In a soft voice he asked me what had happened. We talked awhile. He left, saying: 'I'll be back. If there's anything you need, tell me. I'll get it for you.'

An hour passed. Then a guard marched me over to the prison hospital, locked me up in an observation cell. There was nothing in the cell but a bed, nothing to read or occupy my time.

The thought came vividly to mind: They were trying to frighten me with being put in the hole or being shipped to Springfield, Missouri. 'Springfield' was, I heard, the federal prison-hospital where prisoners were often intimidated and roughed up. If you are sent there, it implies you are crazy.

How long would they keep me in the cell? How long could I stand it? I walked up and down. From time to time I noticed faces peering in through the cell-door's small shatterproof window.

The large window opposite the cell door had no vent. The July sun shone in. By 10:30 the cell was stifling hot.

At twelve o'clock the cell door was opened and a tray of food set in. Then from time to time in the afternoon there would be a knock at my cell door. A prisoner would motion in the little glass window, then talk to me through the crack between the door and the door-jamb. They all said pretty much the same. 'Take it easy kid. You're right to buck'em, but you can't beat the system.' Then in a friendly way: 'Why don't you give it up? Why don't you do like everybody else? You're doing it the hard way.'

I contrasted their feelings with mine. They were depressed and disgusted with themselves, pulling hard time for doing what they didn't want to do. I felt comparatively free.

Two days passed, I took to walking back and forth, to facilitate my thinking. Doing nothing but thinking was, I discovered, amazingly enjoyable. I thought a good deal of Madeline, those I knew back home. I thought a good deal about equality – that I, as a human being, had a right, an inalienable right, to equality. No man was above me, no man was below me. I thought about the right to run my own life. I had occasionally thought of these things when free. Now I thought of them a good deal.

The third day – nothing happened.

On the fourth day at 7 p.m. I heard a key in my door. Surprised, I looked up. A short pear-shaped man in carefree tennis slacks walked briskly into the cell. He smiled, made motions he wanted to shake my hand. We shook hands. 'Hello, Naeve, I'm Warden Gerlach.'

He paused, grinned. 'How are you getting along?' He moved over to the low cell-window, sat on the window-ledge, adjusted his dark-rimmed glasses. In a serious tone: 'What's the matter, Naeve, what's the matter?'

'I think I ought to have some say about how my own life is to be run. I want to do some physical work three or four hours a day to keep in good shape. But the rest of the time I want to study and paint. I'd just like to be left alone to paint my own things.'

He looked out of the window awhile. 'I think that can be arranged. We can probably set aside a fund of fifty dollars or so for art materials.'

I didn't want to feel obligated to Mr. Gerlach. I told him that I preferred to have paints sent in from the outside, pay for them myself. He agreed.

'Would you be willing to go back to quarantine and stay there till your paints arrived?' I said I would, 'Is there anything else you want?'

'I'd like to get out of jail.'

He laughed, the conversation shifted. After twenty minutes of casual talk, he left. He seemed pleased with the visit and the bargain he'd made.

The next day, back in quarantine, I began thinking about the warden's $50 proposal. It puzzled me. Most of the men in quarantine didn't even have socks to wear. The warden's cry was, the institution didn't have funds.

In the remaining three weeks of quarantine I came to know many of the prisoners. Two were new war objectors, one of whom, Gene Garst, was a tall sharp-featured merchant seaman from Philadelphia. Gene, in a long speech in court, had advocated everyone leaving the army, to curb the trend toward war. For this he was given the limit – five years.

The other objector, 'Scotty,' was a very cheerful insurance salesman, married just a short while. His wife was expecting a baby.

A month passed. For some of us, the quarantine period was over. We were given regular prison clothes – white undershirt and shorts, white socks, one pair of light-blue trousers, an army belt, one light-blue shirt. 'You'll get a change of clothes once a week' ...

July–August, 1941

I was moved to close-custody (75 cells), the largest cell house in the prison. I was put on the second-tier. On the top tier, above me, in a screened-off section, was 'the bing' – 'the hole.' The 'bing' cells had no windows. At their entrances were regular barred gates plus solid steel doors. When the doors were closed, the cells were dark.

The cell house was used to house the 'trouble-makers' and the men who were most likely to try to escape.

It became clearly visible that the prison had distinct divisions. One cell block housed a crew of German sailors who with their captain had scuttled their ship at the outbreak of the war in '39. Another housed a crew of Italians who with their captain had done the same. Negroes were kept in a Jim Crow cell house. One cell block was pretty well filled with bootleggers. The rest of the cell houses held letter carriers, car-theft cases, check-writers, border-jumpers, army sodomy cases, income-tax violators.

The only other sizeable group was the war objectors, some thirteen or fourteen men who were very popular with the other prisoners. One, Don Benedict,[2] pitched expert softball. He set several strikeout records against visiting outside teams. He was by far the best known prisoner.

Eight of the war objectors were divinity students, of various denominations, who had refused to register. This group went on strike every now and then, operated together. It appeared they were the only section of prisoners not afraid to protest an act of the authorities.

The other war objectors included one fundamentalist; two men not attached to anything; and two Socialist Party members. These were the first Socialists I'd ever met.

These fourteen men were the first I'd known who held what I'd call genuine anti-war ideas. I enjoyed talking with them.

They spoke of James V. Bennett, the head of the Bureau of Prisons. Several had met him – 'a very slick and evasive politician.' They talked of Scotty, the cheerful war objector I had met in quarantine. He had suddenly become very melancholy. He had no more than entered the prison when his wife's new-born baby died and she became very ill. Scotty began to look worried and gaunt. He was beginning to stay pretty much to himself ...

If a man was thrown in 'the hole' or had been banged around, I wrote my parents that I felt it was inhuman and barbaric. On these occasions I was called down to the front office to explain. On one such trip the censor read my letter aloud to me: 'But – how can you say such things – !'

I told him flatly: 'It's all true and you know it.'

A pained look on his face asked that I not accuse *him* of anything. 'But we can't let you send anything like this out. Why don't you take it back, write the letter over – ' pleadingly – 'omit the objectionable parts, so we can send it on to your parents.'

I told him I would not change the letter. They filed it away – refused to send it out ...

In the middle of February, after 97 days in the cell, just as I was looking forward to warmer days, a guard much to my surprise opened my cell gate, informed me: 'You're going to be moved [i.e., to another part of the prison]. Get your mattress.'

I never hesitated to leave, as it was nearly certain I would go to a warmer place, that the change would be for the better.

February–June, 1942

The Segregation cells of Danbury prison are located on the second floor of a two-story cell house projecting out into the prison yard. As the guard led me through the segregation door on the first floor, and we ascended the dusty stairway to the second floor, our each step echoed.[3]

The guard led me down a short corridor, showed me into a cell, closed its solid steel door, left.

I stood motionless for a minute, listened ... It was very quiet ... I was alone ...

The first month of segregation went slowly, evenly, uneventfully. In the middle of March, the snow of winter began to thaw. Signs of the war began to appear. War planes en route to Europe were flying over the prison. Frequently we would see Warden Gerlach in the company of army visitors. Air-raid tests and blackouts were held frequently. The prison's lights would go out, the prison's escape siren would wail at an earsplitting pitch.

In the latter part of March, I'd finished nine months ... I began to wonder what would happen when my 'good-time release' date came.

The federal law reads that if a prisoner has done his time in 'good conduct' he is entitled to 72 days a year off his original sentence. If a prisoner smuggles something illegal, beats an officer, etc., he loses the 72 days 'good time'; otherwise he automatically gets it. The terms of good-time release are very similar to the terms of parole. You have to report to a probation officer (an outside prison-official) once a month. You have to ask the probation officer for permission to travel out of his district, get his O.K. before you can take a job. You have to ask him for permission to marry, etc. Re-imprisonment is his threat. To wit – you are being dictated to.

On April first I was told I could go home if I would accept a conditional release. My answer was no, I didn't want to live under a dictatorship on the outside ...

The desire to get away from Danbury was too persistent; soon again I was looking forward to release. The days filled with plans for the first, the second, the third days in Vermont, etc. ...

By May, the days became sunny, the cell house warmer. Prisoners were beginning to walk in the yard after work hours in large numbers again. The new war objectors now and then stopped at the bottom of the segregation building, when hacks weren't around, to talk up.

As it grew warmer I wanted very badly to get out into the fresh air and sun.

... The last two weeks. I nervously anticipated my release date. What was the outside like now that the war had begun? I had heard stories of World War I hysteria. Would it be the same in this war? How long would I be left free?

Seven days. I could hardly wait. Each day seemed endless. The past year of 'time,' the 97 days in the cold cell, shrank to unreality, the whole prison was already on the way to becoming an image in the past. It seemed at times I was already out ...

[Having completed his first sentence, Naeve was rearrested in May 1943, again incarcerated in the West Street Manhattan Detention Center where he went on hunger strike. He was removed to the neighboring Bellevue Hospital and forcibly tube-fed there. Then he was given a three-year prison sentence.]

July–December, 1943

It feels strange, entering a prison where you've done time before. I spent the first night wondering – would I ever be put in Danbury for a third sentence? Would I have to do time in the place in the next war?

These thoughts haunted my mind for the first week, then I began to seek the new ins and outs of the prison.

There were two hundred objectors instead of fifteen, and a new warden. There were the same yellow cell houses, the same regimented routine, the same black-uniformed guards. There was, I heard, an objector who refused to take orders from the prison authorities. He was kept in segregation.

I had decided to take orders for a while. I was tired of argument, just wanted to be doing as everyone else was doing.

To accentuate the feeling of sameness, war objector Gene Garst was still in Danbury – had three years yet to do. I met several others I had known in my first sentence. One said: 'I thought you were still up there in segregation. I didn't even know you were gone.' After a few days it was hard to believe I had ever left.

Each day as I went with the other quarantine prisoners to the mess hall to eat, I looked toward segregation. Several times I caught a glimpse of a dark figure standing before segregation's windows. Usually I saw little, but on one occasion the man in segregation waved. I felt a sudden excitement, waved enthusiastically back. The striker's name was George Kingsley. I felt uncomfortable about his being on strike alone. I debated when I should quit work and join him.

A month passed – George went off strike. He was let out into the rest of the prison. One evening during yard period George was pointed out to me. He was sitting on a bench on the south side of the yard.

George was around twenty-eight, large and muscular, his face roughly hewn, his hair unruly (he had his large left hand on it, holding it down). George was looking reflectively at his broken-down prison shoes. As I approached he looked up quizzically, smiled boyishly. After a while we were talking.

'How come you went off strike?' George nodded toward segregation: 'There's not much sense to settin' up there alone.' He paused a moment, then went on: 'I came down here to see what was goin' on. There's some talk about a strike. Maybe something will shape up. There's a lot of objectors in the place. We ought to be able to do something.' Then in measured slowness: 'There's not much been doin' though. There's been a lot of talk of striking, but nothing's happening.'

From George I gathered that Jim Peck and three or four others were the only ones who weren't afraid to protest an act of the authorities and be put in the hole. Every few days I heard objectors mention Jim Peck. I began to ask about him.

Jim came from a family of considerable wealth. He had left home, gone to work as a merchant seaman. After a few years at sea Jim took a job as a labor news reporter, writing stories in support of strikes. He came to believe in organized labor and direct action by workers to obtain a larger share of corporation earnings. Jim sounded interesting. I wanted to meet him – but he was in the hole ... I sent him a note, told him I'd like to see him when he got out.

A few days later a hunched-over sandy-haired thin man of thirty approached me, shook my hand, said abruptly: 'Hello, I'm Jim Peck.' Jim said little after his initial gesture, kept going straight to the point with short quip-like comments, here and there a sharp observation. Somehow, though we didn't say much to each other, we hit it off, got together occasionally.

From Jim, George and Mat Kauten (who had also been put in Danbury) I learned that Danbury prison was in several ways far different than in my first sentence. There was a grumble among the objectors – a growing resentment for prison officials promising parole releases that never came through – a resentment for prison confinement, prison regimentation. Nearly everyone was sorely angry at being numbered and dictated to. They wanted to strike back and protest, but didn't know how. Release seemed an unobtainable goal. The men began to look at the other issues that agitated them.

In July, just before my entry to Danbury, the racist policy fostered by the prison authorities had come to the forefront of the conversations. There was Jim Crow in most of the cell houses. Negroes were generally given the worst jobs. Blacks and whites were made to eat separately in the mess hall. Most of the objectors believed, like myself, that no matter what his color, one man's as good as another. Some of the men began to feel that there was a chance of winning a strike for racial equality. But there was so much bitter argument over what to do that I was sure a strike would never come off.

In a few weeks there was talk 'Let's work-strike, end the Jim Crow in the mess hall.' The objectors elected a committee of five to represent them. Mat Kauten and George Kingsley were elected representatives, Jim an alternate. I was just getting my second-sentence bearings; then all at once I was swept into watching the committee and following each new development. The committee went to see the new warden, Alexander, about abolishing the racist policy. He answered with double-talk. The committee asked the warden several more times to change things, but nothing happened.

Then there was a gap – everyone began to ask – What should we do next? There was so much argument among the forty or fifty of us interested, it appeared there could be no strike. I began making my own plans. I notified the warden I was going to quit work as in my first sentence.

Immediately after, the committee took the initiative to plan a strike to end the racial segregation in the mess hall. I had never been on a group strike in my life, but I decided to join. Somehow, the enthusiasm of Jim, George, Kauten and the others swept me into wanting to go. I saw little hope of winning the strike, but like some of the others I believed if you try there is some hope, if you don't there is none.

The night of August 10th the committee passed out strike instructions. We were to meet at the yard's baseball backstop the next morning – refuse to go to work.

The next morning, amid much nervous excitement and speculation, eighteen of us gathered at the baseball backstop. Most of the men I knew only by sight. When the other prisoners were off to work, and the yard cleared, the eighteen of us were herded into segregation where Harry and I had been.

When we reached the top of the segregation stairs, there was a feeling – *we were actually on strike.* To the tune of Glory, Glory Hallelujah, some of the men began singing, shouting out – Sol-i-dar-i-ty For-ever, Sol-i-dar-i-ty For-ever, THE UNION MAKES US STRONG. The song boomed out several times over the prison yard to notify the other prisoners a strike had begun. The authorities sent up a guard to stop the singing, but we paid no attention.

Shortly several guards were sent up. Segregation had been enlarged to include the entire floor of the cell house, eighteen cells. Each of us was put in a cell, the cells locked.

The first night was quiet. We all wondered what the strike would lead to. Winning the strike seemed impossible, much more impossible than it ever seemed before.

At daybreak the second day, segregation was alive with stifled activity. I noticed Jim Peck's head appear in the cell window directly across the corridor. George I learned was in the cell next to me, Kauten possibly nearby also.

There was an excited yell. 'Hey, there's a one-inch crack under each door.' The corridor acoustics were fine; we soon learned we could yell under the door, be heard by all.

Several of the men had carried magazines on strike. We could, if we took careful aim, slide a magazine out our one-inch crack, across the corridor – flip – it would go into the cell across the way!

The conversations in the empty corridor rose to a din. – 'Hey – Hey – the light-plug plate on the side of my cell comes off.' Soon we were all removing our light-plug plates. There was a duct through the wall to the next cell. We could speak through the duct, 'the phone,' talk to the man in the next cell!

Hands, minds, were feverishly working – maybe – Hey DiGia, got a little string – maybe –

Every new measure we had to take to contact one another emphasized the fact we were sitting on the top floor of a cell house, locked into two rows of cells with solid fronts – each cell a grey concrete box.

By mid-day the time began to go more slowly.

Second day: We were all familiar with the small court outside our rear windows; there were four small trees, a square of ground, enclosed by a walk and buildings. The guard on duty notified us we would soon be given books, pencils and some paper.

The confines of the cells began to weigh. George frequently grumbled over 'the phone': 'We've got to get the cell doors open so we can walk in the corridor, get some exercise. We've got to get the same food as the men out in population. Why the guys up here are hesitating to take action on this stuff, I don't know.' I felt much the same. We exchanged growls. Others were beginning to do the same.

Occasionally the growling entered into the group meetings. 'We've been here now a week. I propose we go without eating a few days to show them we mean business about the food.' Another voice: 'Take it easy!' emphatically 'Let's stick to the strike issue.'

Jim and some of the others with strike experience avoided the arguments, kept the strike going. Jim, when asked his opinion, would briefly give it, follow with: 'That's what I'm for but I'll go along with the majority.'

When things became too quiet Jim would, as if by instinct, stir things up. 'Hey Mecartney!' We all knew what was to follow. 'How are ya doin'? Readin' the beard book?' (the bible). Mecartney would wait, as if loading his guns. The beard-anti-beard argument would begin. God had been labeled by atheist Peck 'the man with the beard.' Mecartney would try and hang a beard on atheist Peck, Peck would try to 'shave' Mecartney.

This would go on for some time. Subtly they would approach the vital question:

'Explain to me, Mecartney, how can I believe in something that I can't detect with the five senses and the aid of science?'

Mecartney would chuckle, then call out from under his locked door: 'Peck, answer me this. Where did the world come from? It couldn't come out of nothing.' We'd all laugh.

There was kidding and razzing. But the days in the cells – the frictions among us over strike policy – our grumbles – grew, multiplied. Here and there one of the men would propose a group hunger-strike. We were bitter, resentful, felt stifled. Once we embarked on a hunger-strike, but after a few meals we gave it up.

Frustration

Frustrations

I would call to George: 'I wish I'd never joined this strike.' A moan, a growl: 'Yea, same for me, same for me.'

Two weeks, three weeks, the eighteen of us in the cells.

One month, month and a half. Slowly surely the minutes of each day ticked by. We more or less forgot about the strike issue. We began to think in terms of the two and three years left in our sentences.

From the yard below a prisoner yelled up to our cell windows – 'Italy surrendered!'

There was a momentary interest in the war.

Sixty days passed. We heard nothing from the local officials. James V. Bennett, the head of the Bureau of Prisons, had been quoted as saying: Race segregation always had been a bureau policy and always would be. The pull of the strike – futile. We were accomplishing nothing. Each day of the sixty days had been a distinct, separate chunk of time. Each day was one of thinking – how many more days would the strike last?

How could we win? *Nothing has happened so far. It's easy for them to just let us sit. We should have never started on this issue anyhow.* During one meeting in despondency over the way things were going we voted to go off strike. Off strike!! Actually? *Off strike?* That afternoon and evening the cell house quieted, nothing was said, nothing heard. Others like myself must have walked to their outside windows, looked into the small court below. We had voted to go off strike, yet none of us wanted to leave.

In a few hours we decided to keep going, stick together.

The eighteen of us, cold-storage like so many eggs in an egg crate. Seventy days. Eighty days. November. The heat in the radiators came on. There were no control valves. At times the heat was so extreme we had to put our mattresses, blankets over the radiators, lie on the floor where it was not so hot. Sometimes there was no heat, the cells very cold.

Our hopes and interest in the strike slightly lifted. Articles supporting the strike, blasting the Bureau of Prisons for its racist policy, appeared in two papers. In a few weeks more, several other papers backed us up, ran stories of the strike. Our first chances of winning the strike appeared.

To make for a change, two men went off strike, two new men came on. One of the new men, Dave Wieck, was locked into the cell directly across from me. Dave smoked a long, low, curious, crooked-stem pipe. His hair was long, very wavy, his face thin; he was a little younger than myself, medium height and build. Dave had a quiet way. He talked to Jim as though he knew all about the labor movement. Jim and others who knew labor history immediately accepted him. He spoke with a slightly idealistic slant on things. When he did, I liked to listen.

Ninety, one hundred days. Every day was still one of taking aim, shuttling magazines, papers, from cell to cell, spending a lot of time on the phone talking to the man in the next cell, lying on our stomachs listening to conversations out in the empty corridor. We kept grumbling, thinking about the time ahead ...

Some of the men began to take on various projects of writing, etc. I started a little daily cartoon paper, labeled by Peck 'The Clink.'[4] We obtained the paper for it by washing the ink off Life magazines. The Clink grew rapidly, soon nearly everyone was contributing. It contained articles, drawings, poetry, numbered at times as many as twenty pages. We whisked it from cell to cell.

The fourth month. The strike was dragging hopelessly, hopelessly on. Feuds – Why don't we do this, Let's stick to the issue – widened the differences. Some of us were contemplating – waiting for a chance – to leave the strike – or hoping it would again actually come to a vote and be voted over.

The publicity boosting the strike appeared again in several papers. The American Civil Liberties Union and other organizations were beginning to criticize the Bureau of Prisons for its racist policy. Our hopes lifted – lifted toward what? The eighteen of us in our cells, the strike, proceeded slowly toward Christmas.

As usual, we heard that Warden Alexander had hinted that if we went off strike he might abolish the segregation policy. As usual we paid no attention, the strike would go on and on. We had come to fix our minds to one thing – one feeling – the strike couldn't be won. Most of us were convinced it would be best to end it in one month – at most in two months (the six-month mark).

On December 22nd, on the 144th day, we were let out of our cells, told to go to the end room – the warden wanted to speak to us! What! They were surely going to con us directly, tell us to face the facts!

Tired, nervous, skeptical, we doggedly left our cells. Warden Alexander, dressed in a well-tailored civilian suit, stood at one end of the end-room table, waiting. We slowly gathered, sat down on the table's benches.

When things quieted down and it was obvious something should begin, our chosen spokesman began to speak. The warden motioned with his hand that it wasn't necessary. The room quieted to a hush.

The warden began very slowly – 'I've been having family troubles' 'My wife has been ill' 'I haven't been feeling well' – in an effort to be casual he spoke of many things. Finally he approached the topic: the strike. Very shortly, seemingly out of nowhere, he proposed to end the racial policy in the mess hall if we would go off strike before Christmas!

There was a look from one striker to another – a swift, tired, bewildered look. Was the strike over? Were the authorities actually going to meet our demands? It was true. There was a feeling it couldn't be. Thoughts seemed to be racing wildly in each striker's mind, trying to find a new and stable position. Thoughts like words seemed to flash from one man to another. It was actually over.

The warden asked if we had any questions. He told us to let him know our decision. There were no questions. He walked out of segregation – was gone.

A little later, amid wild excitement and unbelief that the strike had actually come to an end, we voted to go off strike. Our action, a few newspaper stories to back our point of view, had forced the Bureau of Prisons to back down. We could hardly believe it. 'It's over, it's over, we've smashed 'em,' Jim exuberantly exclaimed. The strike was over. The strike had been a success.[5]

December, 1943, to December, 1944

The day the race strike ended, as planned, five of us – Joe Czarniecki, Ernie Smith, George Kingsley, Dave Wieck and myself – notified the warden that we would not submit to the prison's regimentation or work under the dictatorship of the prison authorities.

Christmas Eve the other men went off strike into the regular parts of the prison. The warden ordered the five of us to move into the old section of five cells ...

August, 1945

The prison work-gangs did not go to work. Segregation was left open for a two-day V-J holiday. The moment the segregation door was unlocked, we went to meet the other war objectors, the prisoners we knew. We walked excitedly about in what seemed a vast, boundless area – the prison yard.

As we talked jerkily, uncomfortably, to the other prisoners, we found that the two years' close confinement of segregation had made us nervous, very high strung. It was hard to find the balance between saying nothing and saying too much.

We walked around and around the prison yard like second-hands on a clock. Being able to walk in the prison yard gave the impression we were free. We walked, our legs began to ache, we continued walking.

Most Danbury prisoners had never seen the inside of segregation. Most were curious to have a look at it and those of us in it. They streamed in and out. They asked what had we done in the two years we had been locked up. We told them of ... the reading and studying we'd done. I showed them my paintings, the water colors, the mache globe, the guitar of oatmeal and ground-up newspapers. Most prisoners were amazed at how profitably we had used our time. One commented: 'You have a lot to show for your time. We have nothing.'

[Ashland Penitentiary, Kentucky, where Naeve had been transferred]

May 18th, 1946. Just four more days to do. It's hard to believe. I can hear a radio playing up the hall. The music makes me think of the outside, makes me feel I am already out ... It's a strange feeling to be so short.[6] Other prisoners keep coming into the cell and watching while I paint, ask: 'You're gettin' kinda short, aren't you?' And I tell them: 'Ya, just four more days counting today.'

It's hard to believe. I've been in prison now going on my fifth year. A lot has happened. It seems I have learned so many things. I've learned the way of prisons, the way of prison officials, the way of prisoners who have to do time. I've learned what government means. Government is the instrument of the rich, who sit behind the four and five billion dollar corporations, the steel, munitions, radio and newspaper empires. Government is kept clothed in sanctity. It is the instrument through which the crime of imprisonment can be committed wholesale. The machine is so set up that no one official carries the burden of full responsibility. It is so set up that each official who has a part in the crime hardly knows it, and he can go home with a clear conscience, or nearly so. Government, to the individual of contrary opinion, means brute force. It's a gigantic, brutal, feelingless thing that can wriggle a pen and crush him.

Note: (May 19th is last entry, as I had to make arrangements to get this and other writings smuggled out.)

May 19, 1946. It is a little after noon. Very clear, sunshiny day outside. A little smoke is rising out of the smokestack.

This morning, painted a little and worked out a composition for a painting of a prison gate, with a released prisoner standing before it. The gate behind him has not yet been closed; he's paused for a moment. In front of him are two walks; one leads to the left, one to the right. He's confronted with the problem of which way to go. The idea not being whether to steal or not to steal – it's just simply he has no friends, no nothing. He's wondering which way should he go to find the simple things – a place to work, a place to sleep.

Wonder how the guys hunger-striking at Danbury and elsewhere are getting along. Dave [Wieck] gets out in fifty days. By then I should have a place to stay and a few dollars. If everything goes as planned, we should be able to pull the story together in six months or so. Then comes the big adventure – taking it around to the publishers.

Then in ten months, in February, I plan to exhibit the paintings I made at Danbury and the ones I've been planning to do when I get out. I think there's a good chance of success. I've seen but one prison painting in my life. Prison paintings are a little different from the regular run.

In long-range plans, in eight or ten months after my first exhibit I plan to go somewhere else ...

Well, anyway I plan to go out. I've dreamt and planned for an exhibit of my paintings. I've dreamt and planned with Dave that we should try to get this [memoir] published. I hope it all works out that way ...

In the meantime I plan to paint – the thing I know best, the thing I've had most of my experiences with – prisons, prison scenes.

The music is playing just now, down the way. The sun is shining out, it is a very beautiful day.

Notes

Source: Lowell Naeve in collaboration with David Wieck, *A Field of Broken Stones* (Denver: Alan Swallow, 1959), 33–40, 42–9, 77, 83, 84, 87, 133–44, 169, 228–31. First published by Libertarian Press, 1950.

1 His prison experiences included forcible tube-feeding (a brutal procedure he has depicted in one of his drawings). This happened to him in May 1943. Seventeen years later a young mathematician, given 'a six-month prison term for having refused to testify about his political beliefs and associations before the House Un-American Activities Committee' when he pleaded the First Amendment, reports the following dialogue he had with a kindly but unimaginative – and perhaps not very intelligent – prison officer. '"You know, Davis, we had hundreds of those conscientious objectors in here during the war." "Yes sir." "Those guys aren't sincere, they don't mean that about conscience." "Oh, really?" "Naw. Or those that are sincere are crazy." "Oh, really?" "Yeah, I mean they're always going on hunger strikes. Now what's the point of that? We just force-feed them." "Yes sir."' Quoted from

Chandler Davis, 'So You're Going to Prison! Some Tips from a Political Prisoner,' *The Nation,* 3 December 1960: 435, 436.

2 Benedict was one of the Union Eight who refused to register for the draft in 1940. See his memoir later in this section.

3 Naeve had been kept in segregation because of his non-cooperative stance.

4 'Bureau of Prisons confiscated all copies' – Lowell Naeve.

5 Other accounts of this Danbury strike against prison racial segregation, organized by CO radicals, include Jim (James) Peck, *We Who Would Not Kill* (New York: Lyle Stuart, 1958), 101–30, and his *Underdogs Vs Upperdogs* (Canterbury, NH: Greenleaf Books, [1969]), 41–53; Howard Schoenfeld,' The Danbury Story,' in Holley Cantine and Dachine Rainer, eds., *Prison Etiquette: The Convict's Compendium of Useful Information* (Bearsville, NY: Retort Press, 1950), 12–26 – reprinted in Peter Mayer, ed., *The Pacifist Conscience* (New York, Chicago, San Francisco: Holt Rinehart and Winston, 1966), 332–44. See also Peck's brief prison memoir, 'The Ship That Never Hit Port,' in *Prison Etiquette,* 46–69. A facsimile reprint of *Prison Etiquette* appeared recently (Carbondale and Edwardville: Southern Illinois University Press, 2001), with a 20-page foreword by Philip Metres entitled 'War Resistance and Radical Pacifism in the 1940s.' See also Metres's revisionist essay centring on the poet Robert Lowell's antiwarism, 'Confusing a Naive Robert Lowell and Lowell Naeve: "Lost Connections" in 1940s War Resistance at West Street Jail and Danbury Prison,' *Contemporary Literature* 41, no. 4 (Winter 2000), 661–92.

6 'So short' means so near release from prison.

DONALD BENEDICT

On 14 November 1940, eight students at Union Theological Seminary in New York made the newspaper headlines when, having refused to register for the draft, they were arrested and jailed for a year and a day. They saw their act as a protest against military conscription by the state. If they had applied for exemption as COs, there is little doubt all eight would have been allowed to perform alternative civilian service. At the Seminary the well-known theologian Reinhold Niebuhr (himself a pacifist a decade earlier), while expressing his 'appreciation for the integrity of our eight young men,' accused them of courting 'martyrdom' and of espousing 'essentially anarchistic philosophies of government.' For others, especially in the pacifist community, they appeared as champions of liberty of conscience. In fact, the Union Eight became 'the catalysts and leaders of a new radical pacifist movement that was forged during World War II.'[1]

Donald Benedict, among the eight, differed from his seven colleagues in two important respects. First, he was a champion softball player, for which accomplishment he earned wide popularity among the convict population,[2] and, secondly, after serving two prison sentences he decided to reject pacifism and enlist in the army.

Benedict came from a Midwest rural background; his mother was a devout Methodist. After four years at Albion College (Michigan), where he became an enthusiastic pacifist, he entered Union Theological Seminary. Never an academically brilliant student, he was drawn at once to social activism. Under the influence of another Union student, David Dellinger, he now found what would be his life work in combating urban poverty and racism – first in Newark, New Jersey, and then in Cleveland, Chicago, and New York City. Jail had put an end for the time being to his plans to become a minister of religion (after the war he became a United Church of Christ clergyman).

It was after his release from his first prison sentence in September 1941 that Benedict began to have doubts about the rightness of his pacifist stance. Awaiting a second call-up notice and renewed incarceration, he went to Detroit in the spring of 1942 and worked there in a depressed black area of that city. Race rioting later developed. As a result law and order temporarily broke down and was only restored by the National Guard. 'Ironically' in view of his pacifism, writes Benedict, 'it was with great relief that I [now] watched trucks rolling by with grim-faced soldiers in position behind machine guns, in patrol of city streets.' His gladness at the sight of armed soldiers entering the riot-torn districts of the city worried him. 'Why did I feel so guilty at my joy in seeing that army? My joy in seeing those machine guns? Was I following the pacifist line merely out of intellectual or emotional habit?'

Thus, when eventually he was put back in jail, he did not enjoy the inner peace he had felt during his first bout of imprisonment. Instead, as we see in the extracts from his memoir printed below, he was tortured by doubts and assailed by questions as to his motives for resisting conscription. He sought – and obtained – parole but the doubts and questions continued. 'I felt guilty about forsaking the nonviolent stand I had held for years in order to go out and kill somebody. I felt guilty about going into the war, and guilty about staying out of it.' A counselor at Chicago Theological Seminary, where he had enrolled as a part-time student, helped him to resolve his agonizing dilemma. 'Drop out of school and join the army' was the advice Benedict received. Once he had decided to become a combatant soldier, his trial was over. 'No longer did I torture myself,' he writes, 'with the old perplexing questions ... My doubts had quieted, and I was prepared to be ordered to shoot.'

In fact Benedict, as he tells us, 'never had to shoot a man.' He was eventually promoted to the rank of sergeant and was discharged from the army in November 1946. On 16 October 1990, half a century after the Union Eight had 'non-registered,' Union Theological Seminary, under the sponsorship of its then president, Donald Shriver, held an anniversary reunion commemorating that event. Two of the eight were unable to attend, while one had in the meantime died. But Benedict was among the five present along with Dave Dellinger and George Houser, one of the founders of CORE. Summing up, Shriver called the Union Eight's act of fifty years before part of 'a vital strand of Union tradition.'

Congress passed the draft registration law in July 1940. Apart from my nonviolent philosophy, how could I ever serve in a segregated army? We talked in Newark about the draft, and in September five of us decided to go on living there, continuing to work with children and identifying ourselves with workers and lay people. We rented a house and lived in Christian Ashram style, having prayers together; working at [house] painting, washing windows, and various odd jobs; putting the earnings into a common pot. Each of us took a dollar a week to spend. We decided to attend classes half-time at Union.

The draft issue quickly involved practically everyone at the seminary, where we discussed it in relation to the Christian faith. There was a minimal recognition of the legitimacy of pacifism for conscientious objectors (COs). The crux of the matter for us was that while draft registration was mandatory, seminarians were automatically exempt from military service. Certainly we did not want to be drafted into the fighting army, but neither did we want to be excused because we were different from other people or because we were members of a special class. We felt we should face the draft like anyone else, and as pacifists, we resisted involvement in the process of war.

Dal [Meredith Dallas], Dave [Dellinger] and I, living together in Newark, knew that the only consistent attitude for us was to decline to register, thereby refusing to be classed as an elite. We would be doing the same thing we did when we moved out of the seminary. Ministers, we had said, are not better than others; they are the servants. We were being protected unjustifiably. If the government's stand was based on an assumption of our pacifist beliefs, that was in error; not all seminarians were pacifists.

Another consideration was my calling to preach the gospel. I believed that it was the incarnation – the good news that God had sent his only Son, incarnate as a human being – that was central to the gospel. This identification of Jesus with all humanity made rebirth and liberation possible. Could I, as a clergyman, preaching this gospel, ever separate myself from other persons? Could I accept any kind of exemption, any favored position solely because I had indicated my intention to become a follower of Jesus? That would be ridiculous.

Finally, twenty-two of us prepared a signed statement as a public announcement of our intention to refuse to register. *The Christian Century* printed our statement; newspapers picked it up, and intense pressure was exerted – especially by our families – to get us to rescind our decision. My mother wrote that she and my father hoped I would reconsider but that they would stand by whatever decision I reached in good conscience. Their reaction was quite different from that of most others. Dave's father [a wealthy Bostonian] actually threatened suicide.

It did not change Dave's mind, but other students began, one by one, to succumb to the pressure. We expected opposition from 'Uncle Henry' [i.e., Henry Sloane Coffin, president of Union], but we were surprised to have well-known pacifists like Harry Emerson Fosdick and Ralph Sockman, the nationally known radio preacher, come to talk to us and counsel us to register. Norman Thomas came. His brother, Evan, had been in Leavenworth during World War I for the same offense. Even the American Friends Service Committee tried to dissuade us, holding that alternative service was preferable to jail.

Many people misunderstood our direct purpose of course, but it was clear to me that, aside from the specific point we intended to make, the refusal to register was the most effective and concrete thing we could have done as seminary students to make public our opposition to the war and the war system.

By the time the draft law was signed – October 14, 1940 – fourteen students had dropped out of our group. Some had decided to register as COs, which meant they could eventually go into Civilian Public Service (CPS). On the day we refused to register, Roger Shin left school and enlisted. He agreed with us that he ought not to have this exemption, but he thought if he believed in the war he should enlist like anyone else.

The night before the national registration day the seminary community held a public worship service as an expression of solidarity even though many students held opposing views. On the day of registration eight of us appeared before the draft board set up at the seminary and presented a signed letter stating the reasons why we, in good conscience, could not register. To our amazement, the man who took our communication was a United States district attorney. He immediately served a subpoena calling for our appearance the next day before a New York County grand jury. They handed down indictments charging us with failure to register for the draft. We pleaded guilty.

The eight of us were Dave, Dal, Howard Spragg, George Houser, Bill Lovell, Joe Bevilacqua, Dick Wichlei, and me. Ted Walsh, our lawyer, was a prominent corporation counsel who had volunteered his services. He pointed out something that had not occurred to any of us. Our joint signing of the letter indicating our intentions opened us to a possible conspiracy charge that carried a maximum sentence of forty-three years, rather than the five years maximum for draft violation. For the next month national publicity was intense. Letters came from all over the country, supporting or condemning us.

On the day of sentencing we were allowed to make a final statement to the court. Mine implied that anyone who was a Christian could take no other course. As I look back, I see that my attitude was terribly self-righteous, but at the time I was sure I was acting rightly. The judge sentenced us to a year and a day, with the stipulation that at any time we decided to register for the draft we would be immediately released. All we had to do was register, but we had found this impossible to do.

We were led out of the courtroom, handcuffed together, taken down the back elevator, and put into the paddy wagon single file. Reporters and photographers were waiting, and an Associated Press photo of the eight seminary students being taken to the federal jail at West Street was front-page news in the evening papers. Our one-week stay at West Street was an introduction to the prison system. Six of us were put in one room together and two on another floor. We were told we could write two letters during that week.

If our sole concern had been our exemption, then our logical behavior was to become model prisoners, serve the minimum term, and get out. But as pacifists, even in prison we could demonstrate against violence and racism. I tried falling into the food line for blacks only and was promptly jerked away by a guard and placed with my 'own people.' That night, lying awake, I heard white guards talking to prisoners, calling them 'black nigger bastards.'

The second day at West Street I wrote reassuringly to my mother. I had decided that stopping the war system was going to take years of hard work and long suffering, so I suggested she read up on the pacifist movement and its full implications. I told her we were kept busy doing maintenance work, but I didn't tell her what the maintenance work had been that day. Howard and I had been ordered to clean out a cell that housed drug addicts. They were men under the torture of being forced to shake their habit cold turkey. If the officials thought seminarians were squeamish, they were wrong. We would not try to avoid trouble or suffering.

There were other efforts to get us to change our minds. 'Uncle Henry' visited us and reiterated his argument that we were being foolish. The warden called us to the front office and spoke about the terrible ordeal we faced. The only thing he was specific about was that we would not be called Mr. but addressed by our last names. This became a standing joke among us.

Two days later I wrote again to my mother. I kept thinking of how she and my father must feel – good, substantial, conservative, church-going people, bewildered by the sudden transference of their only son from seminary to prison. I assured her that I found prison life enjoyable. This was true. There was time for rest and study, and I made some interesting new friends.

Finally, one evening we were taken to the Danbury Federal Correctional Institution under personal escort of the warden. During the drive to Connecticut he said he had a new, young Protestant chaplain and was concerned about the effect we would have on his ministry. We reassured him but privately felt we would not relish the job of preaching to eight theological students. Warden Edgar Gerlach wore horn-rimmed glasses that made him look like a Ph.D. He was, in fact, a criminologist from the University of Michigan whose reputation had convinced the authorities that he could run the model institution at Danbury. The combination of his solemn self-importance and fussy mannerisms made him, for us, somewhat comic. We arrived at Danbury at 3:00 a.m., and when the guard slammed and locked the cell door behind me and I found myself alone, I felt for the first time that I was really in jail.

For most of the day the doors were open so that we could use a common recreation room. We read or talked to other prisoners between a series of tests and interviews. Following this period I was assigned to the library.

All of us were kept busy writing and reading letters for inmates or counseling them day and night. Most of the time it was just listening to their problems. Men in jail have terrible family troubles. There are usually wives and children on the outside left without support. Each prisoner was allowed to have seven certified correspondents. I could send out two letters a week, but there was no limit on the number I received. My weekly letters were to my parents. The best religious discussions I had ever had were going on here, I told them. If it were not for the forced separation from family and friends, I felt I could stay here and work with these men for the rest of my life, for there was plenty to be done.

Danbury was known as the country club of the prison system. It boasted no walls; none were needed because it was built as a quadrangle. To get out, an inmate would need to climb over a two-story building. Beginning in January I was out in the cold all day on a pick-and-shovel team and felt in fine condition. One day while out with the work crew, digging not far from the main gate, I saw a civilian walking toward us, escorted by one of the men. He stopped and shook hands with Dal, and after talking with him for a short time I heard him say, 'Which one is Benedict?' He was the alumni secretary at Albion [College], paying Dal and me a visit. He had tried to see us through official channels and had been refused, but walking out to his car, he had spotted Dal. The obvious alarm of the armed guard in the tower did not deter him. Over he came for a chat with us. Not every college can boast so persistent and dedicated an alumni secretary.

All through my prison term I planned to return to Union and live in Newark. But in early April the seminary sent us the terms for our reentry. We would be expected to refrain from active opposition to the draft. Returning to Union, therefore, was not to be considered. After that I wasn't sure what I would do.

Many others were in prison for draft law violation, and about twenty of us decided to celebrate International Student Peace Day in April by fasting and refusing to work. We informed the warden, and he reacted typically. Calling us together, he gave a little speech about our 'positive' relationship. Then he informed us we had ten minutes to talk things over and change our minds, and left the room. In precisely ten minutes he was back. 'You know, fellows,' he said, dusting off his knees, 'I'm not a very religious man but I've been downstairs praying that you will see this thing my way.' Stunned for a moment by this display of piety, we reiterated our intention. Instantly his manner changed, and we were ordered back to our cells.

Our demonstration was set for the following Tuesday. On Monday the warden called all the prisoners into the yard and made a speech – something he loved to do. Pointing to our group, he explained that he had tried to ease our stay in prison. He had been good to us. We had been given better treatment than the others.

'And now,' he continued, 'these men propose to strike not only against the Federal Bureau of Prisons, but also against our beloved President, Franklin D. Roosevelt. They propose to refuse to work tomorrow. If they carry out this threat I will be forced to take away all yard privileges for inmates – also Ping-Pong, softball, movies, and library privileges.'

The men began to stir. It was clearly an invitation for the prisoners to mob us. Then a distinctly nonpacifist inmate called out, 'Warden, we've heard your side of the story, now let's hear theirs.'

'To the mess hall for chow!' the warden shouted back.

Because of the warden's threat, we had to get our story to the men. We arranged to sit at different tables to tell our side of the case. The warden stayed in the mess hall, pacing the aisles. Whenever he noticed a discussion going on he would call out comments like, 'You think I'm a phony, but I'm not!' and this of course helped us in our argument. It was never difficult to enlist support from prisoners in any disagreement with the warden. A prisoner always takes the word of another inmate.

The evening before Peace Day, after the buzzer rang indicating all inmates present and accounted for, the lights did not go out as usual in our block. No one knew what to expect. There was an air of unrest. After about an hour the guards called me out with two other COs housed in the block. We were led to the warden's office, where one by one we were taken in. When my turn came I found the warden wearing a smoking jacket, with a pipe in his mouth and a book in his hand. He politely offered me a chair and then in a friendly tone asked if I intended to work the next day. No, I said, nor did I intend to eat. He repeated the same question and I repeated my answer. Obviously, he was recording our conversation. The record would be evidence if any trouble developed later. After this I was taken to one of the new quarantine cell blocks and locked up. All twenty of us were put into this segregated block after the questioning. On Tuesday we were offered no food, although we would not have eaten it anyway. Our belongings and some books were brought to our cells, and we settled down to spend the day reading.

Wednesday at 5:30 a.m. we were awakened and ordered out for breakfast, apart from the inmate population. As we came through the cafeteria line we noticed that behind each man who was serving stood a guard. The men had been ordered not to speak to us, but they would smile or wink as we passed. The waiter who poured our coffee did so with a decided air of hospitality. 'Officer's mess!' he whispered as he handed us our cups. It seemed to me the best I had ever tasted – real coffee rather than the bitter brew of chicory we had been getting. Our segregation went on until Friday, when we were taken to the Disciplinary Committee, a body made up of the captain, the psychiatrist and the prison social worker. The men called it the Kangaroo Court, because an inmate had no chance whatsoever. Each of us appeared and was told individually that we would be continued in the present cell block, allowed out to eat and work, but the rest of the time locked in our separate cells. By the time the committee finished with us the prison population had filed around the quad and into the mess hall. The twenty of us were led to the hall and released for chow. This was our first appearance among the men since Monday night. Standing in the center of the mess hall was the warden, evidently there to observe our reception. As we came through the door unattended, the inmates began to clap and shout. They stamped their feet and roared approval. A few stood up cheering, and the warden quickly left. Afterward we were again locked in our cells.

I had been playing on the prison softball team for some time and had pitched a one-hitter on the previous Saturday against the best team in the town. Another game was scheduled for Thursday of the following week. On this day the prisoners gathered at the softball diamond in the center of the yard. The warden was there, and the game started, but when the inmates saw that I was not with the team a few of them called out my name. The warden paid no attention. The prison team was doing well, and early in the game they were out in front by three runs. Then a group that was getting out in a few days asked the warden to send for me. The men said they wanted to see me pitch again before they left. The warden sent a guard to my cell. I refused to go unless the other men were also released, and the guard pleaded that he was under orders and might lose his job if he failed to bring me along. I consulted a few of the others through closed doors, and they decided I should go out and pitch. I realized that their counsel had a purpose. I pitched three innings, struck out nine batters, and then walked back to my cell.

The next day three of us asked to see the captain of the guard. I acted as spokesman. 'We are wondering what is happening,' I said. 'All of us were ordered confined to our cells for thirty days, yet I was released to pitch a softball game. Just what *is* our status?' He said he would find out from the warden.

We heard nothing more until the following Saturday, when another softball game was scheduled on the grounds. Half an hour before the game all twenty of us were let out and informed we were free to go back into the prison population.

I have never regretted a day that I spent in jail. The men in my dormitory were great teachers. They poured out their troubles. Hardly a man among them had any relationship with a church or minister or priest. They attended services because there wasn't much else to do at that time on Sunday or because it would count in their bids for parole.

In September, after ten months, we were released from prison, with time off for good behavior. It did not mean that we were excused from registering for the draft. If we did not register, we could be picked up again at any time. The eight of us were released together. We assumed we would be met by a paddy wagon and sentenced again. Nothing of the sort happened. We walked out.

I went back to Newark ...

... [In 1943] I went home to visit my mother and father ... The next morning ... I was stopped by two FBI agents who asked my name. When I replied they said they were taking me into custody. 'On what charge?' I asked. 'Failure to register for the draft' was the reply.

I explained that I had business to transact, and they agreed to pick me up later at home ... I went home and packed a few belongings. The FBI agents appeared on schedule, taking me to the Wayne County jail. I was ordered to appear at the federal court in Newark. Just before Christmas, after pleading guilty as I had two years before, I was sentenced by a Newark judge to three years in prison. Again the judge left the term open. I would be released at any time I was willing to register and return to the seminary or accept alternative service.

I was returned to Danbury, and I walked in feeling again that I was doing the right thing, but there was no exhilaration this time. Nor did I have eight boon companions. The experience of the [Detroit] riot had affected me. The attack on Pearl Harbor. The reality of war.

Many of the old guards remembered me and their welcome was cordial. 'Now we'll have a winning softball team,' they said. I heard that the former warden had left the prison system. The new warden was a younger man, thought to be competent and likable. I learned, too, that there were more than two hundred COs in the prison and that a large group of pacifists had been on a work strike in protest against the segregation policy. They had been locked in their cell blocks for almost three months but were due to come out soon. Three days later the entire mess hall was opened up so that prisoners could sit at any tables they chose. I had the honor of being the first person to sit with blacks, because quarantine units were always the first to go to the mess hall. The housing units remained segregated ...

I began to think about my pacifism as I [started to] read Reinhold Niebuhr's *The Nature and Destiny of Man* ... My pacifism was not a rigid philosophy in the sense of rules, nor was it a hierarchy of options. I simply had a strong feeling against violence all my life. I had always tried to break down the case for force. But when it came to acting I thought I would be ruled by my feeling at the time.

It seemed to me now that to kill in a crisis of self-defense was to strike directly at evil. This was permitted. But no matter how evil their cause, to invoke the name of justice and strike at other people when they might be brought to reason was surely wrong. To use force against misguided persons would be only an indirect blow. And how can one avoid striking through others to get at the center of evil?

Suddenly, a thought struck me, preventing me from going on. Here I was, a deep-rooted pacifist, actually trying to figure out a way to use force justly. Nazism was at the back of my mind. Was there such a thing as a just war? Were the Jews only absorbing aggression? This might be a just war but whom would I have to kill? And if it was a just war, what was my attitude saying? OK, it's a just war, but I won't fight – let someone else do it? I had to abandon that line of thinking temporarily, but I realized I would have to give more thought to my own pacifism. What was my stand? What was I going to do?

Coming out of quarantine as a known pacifist serving my second term, I was approached by a man called Chick who had been a United Mine Workers organizer. After being put in jail for failure to register, he had tried to get out by registering as a CO but was refused because he was not religious. He wanted me to help in another demonstration against prison as part of the war system. I agreed, and we recruited sixteen pacifists who would refuse to work for the rest of our terms. One man was to quit work each Wednesday so that the warden would have no way of knowing how widespread the strike was. Chick and I would be the last. We would go together, signalizing the end of the line.

When the day came, we stopped work and were immediately put into solitary confinement. This was my second time, but it was not to be like the first. I had no suspicion that this time it would break me down, that I would face a terrible crisis. At first I was elated. I was glad I had stopped reading Niebuhr's book and that I had joined the work strike. It was the right thing to do. I might have held back, overindulging in self-examination. I was glad that I hadn't wavered. I had been true to myself. And for my belief I had now gone all the way to the wall. But by the end of the next day I was wondering how long they would keep me in solitary. Probably just a few days, then back to a lock-in in the cell. I could understand why men in solitary spent their days waiting for the only events in their lives – the rattle of the lock, the swish of the door opening, and the sound of the food tray in the slot.

By the seventh night I no longer felt I was in solitary because of this last work strike. I was there because of my entire past life, and the question that faced me was not whether I could continue in solitary for the term of my sentence but for the rest of my life. There was no way to follow Jesus and mitigate the suffering. There was no way without, in the end, facing crucifixion. I knew that and I had always been prepared for it. I would go out from jail into a system I would resist and I would be sent back. In prison, too, I would continue to follow my convictions, and that meant solitary. There is no way to compromise when one follows the perfect One.

But was I strong enough? Always before I had thought I was, but now I was racked by doubt. From boyhood, I had believed violence was wrong. Now I faced a direct contradiction. The mere demonstration of the power of force in the Detroit streets had stopped the riots. I had to face that fact. Here was the one case that disproved my convictions. Not only could force bring order and peace; it had to be a superior force. This was hard for me to accept. Violence ought not to be stopped by violence. Where would it end? Nevertheless, my belief in pacifism as an absolute was shaken. How could I stay in solitary if I was unsure that what I was doing was right? What if I were wrong? No answer came. All day and through the night I was repeating a litany:

I have refused to fight. *Lord, hear me.*

I have tried to love everyone. *Lord, hear me.*

I have tried to be like Jesus, the perfect One, and the more I have tried the more impossible it becomes. *Lord, hear me.*

Midge Miller, shortstop. *Shot down over Germany!*

Lou Krueger, first base. *Killed at Anzio! ...*

Maybe it makes a difference who wins the war. *Lord, hear me.*

I have never compromised. *Lord, hear me.*

I have followed my conscience. *Lord, hear me.*

I have striven for perfection and I have become only self-righteous. *Lord, hear me.*

I have given up all sources of income except the bare necessities. *Lord, hear me.*

When I lose count of the trays will I know day from night? *Lord, hear me.*

I am entirely removed from the world. *Lord, hear me.*

I am utterly alone. *Lord, hear me.*

God, God, are you hearing me? What good can I do here? Does it make a difference? How can I get out? How can I get out of here when I talked the others into striking? Is pacifism the only choice? There is nothing here. There is nothing ahead. How can I go on? There is no ground, no place to step. I don't have enough faith. Why am I thinking these things? Am I thinking these things trying to make myself guilty for staying in solitary? Selfish for going to prison? Am I thinking these things because I am losing my mind? I don't know what I believe. Only that I believe in you. You are my faith. And yet how can I go on? Into nothingness? Or have I already made the step?

I fell on the mattress, lying there, tossing from side to side. Gradually, the sense of the terrible silence changed to a feeling of quiet, then of peace. I thought it must be almost morning. I was exhausted and seemed to be falling asleep. I closed my eyes and began to drift, and then the words came, not a voice speaking, only the words, clear, in my mind: *You are my beloved.* This was the word of God to all people who have faith. For the first time I realized that word was also meant for me. I, myself, was loved by God – loved with all my guilt and imperfections; I felt surrounded and supported by love. And I slept.

I slept for an hour. When I awoke I knew I was going to get out. Not just go back on work detail and get out of solitary; I was going to get out of prison. But by the time the guard came and I asked for the razor I was shattered and shaking again. That hour of calm had left me ...

The guard reached through the bars to hand me the razor. I was twenty-six years old, and I had been in prison long enough to know what was going through his mind: 'This guy is a religious nut. He won't try anything.' Nevertheless, rules were rules: he had to stay. But when he saw how my hand shook he probably added, 'You never know what solitary will do to a man' and decided to keep his eye on me. The shaking was residue – the aftermath of the night.

It is not true that one can think in solitary. Or, rather, one cannot trust one's thinking here, which is far worse. There is nothing to hear or look at, and the emptiness seems to swallow up deliberate thought. I had intended to stick it out. I had come in to prison of my own free will during World War II refusing to register for the draft. But I could not make the monumental decision I had to make until I was physically free. Yet the decision was partly made when I made up my mind I had to get out. This was the obsessive thought that made my night so wretched, tossing on the mattress, or on my knees in prayer, or trying to walk in the confined space – a few steps; turning, bumping, and scraping the walls; grazing the bars like a caged animal. I told myself the resolve to get out was not a premeditated decision I must justify, and walking out would not be an action but a reaction. I told myself I could come back again to jail. But I had to get out in order to think. I knew that people sometimes went mad in solitary. I had seen some taken out in straitjackets. Could this happen to me? I thought I still knew right from wrong. How long could I hold on to this certainty?

The cell was six by eight feet, with concrete walls and floor, literally bare except for the toilet and sink. There was no window – only a dim recessed light high in the corner – and nothing to sit on but the john. The mattress was brought in at night and laid on the floor. No reading material was allowed and no outside exercise except going down the hall for a shower twice a week. The heavy door outside the barred door was opened only to push meals through the slot. The cells were built in tiers, with walkways along the rows of doors. It wasn't so terrible at first, and I started out feeling pretty good, even self-possessed and self-reliant, because I had a reason for being there. Solitary was the ultimate, and I was defending my principles, demonstrating support for a cause in which I believed. But the cell got to me. As a boy I could never follow the others into a cave or crawl through a tunnel without having an awful fear that I might not get out. This feeling came back in the cell.

This was my second term in prison, and I was facing two and a half years. Would most of this time be in solitary? Being an inmate for ten months hadn't bothered me. But now, after only seven days in isolation, I was wrestling with the idea of reconsidering my whole philosophy of life and accusing myself of giving up my convictions. I still believed war was wrong. Violence and killing were wrong. As a pacifist, I would not kill or cooperate in any systematic support of war. Was I capitulating now just to get out of jail? I still wasn't sure, but this morning I was going to see the warden. I was going to shave. It was a gesture of propriety – possibly of conformity – but also of stubborn pride. I wanted to look neat but also to muster at least the appearance of being unaffected and unbeaten, even though I was going to say the word and sign the papers that would get me out. Getting out didn't mean going into the fighting army. I would be paroled for the purpose of going back to seminary. As a seminarian, I would be exempt and later if drafted could choose alternative service. But this would be capitulation. How was I going to decide? Did I know what I was doing?

I finished shaving, wiped off the razor with the towel, and handed it through the bars. The clang of the massive door cut off distant sounds. I began to pray that when I went through the door I might find a new direction for my life ...

I put on my shirt, and as the door opened I was thinking that when I got to the warden's office I would write a note to the other pacifists. I felt I owed them an explanation.

It was the morning of the eighth day, and I stood in the doorway, blinking. A draft of fresh air came through, and a shaft of sunlight fell across the floor. The light almost hurt my eyes. I turned to look back into that cold, dim cell and felt for a moment intense sadness. Something fine was being left behind. Also certitude. Also my youth. I knew I would never come back ...

Out of jail on parole I found myself in the state of doubt that is paralyzing. To be thrown into such a state after being so certain, so sure of my own motives, was terrible. I still had my faith in God, and I was clinging to this, but in every other way I was at sea. I could not reason away my doubt. I knew what I ought to do, but I could not bring back the old feeling of certitude that had stayed with me so long.

Notes

Source: Don Benedict, *Born Again Radical* (New York: Pilgrim Press, 1982), 1–3, 30–8, 44–8.

1 For the 'Union Eight,' see James Tracy, *Direct Action: Radical Pacifism from the Union Eight to the Chicago Seven* (Chicago and London: University of Chicago Press, 1996), 1–6, 10–12, 16–18, 155. David Dellinger was generally acknowledged to be the leading figure in the group. Their joint statement *Why We Refused to Register*, slightly abbreviated, is to be found in Staughton Lynd and Alice Lynd, eds., *Nonviolence in America: A Documentary History* (Maryknoll, NY: Orbis Books, 1995), 161–3; see above, p. 379.

2 Cf. an analogous situation around this time at England's Feltham Prison for juvenile delinquents, when skill at sports gained prestige and liking for 'conchies' among an otherwise sometimes hostile convict population. One of the young COs who did time at Feltham describes an incident that took place during compulsory physical training: all but four of those participating were 'crimmos.' 'A team relay race to a wall and back was organized in which one of the C.O.s managed to outstrip his opposite number in the opposing team, and thus gave his [own] team an advantage ... [S]everal fellows were heard to remark "Cor! Can't old conch run!" From Keith Thompson, 'Inside a Boy's Prison ...,' *C.B.C.O. Bulletin* (London), no. 33 (November 1942), 13.

DONALD WETZEL

An unconventional – and unaffiliated – Christian pacifist, the future author of note Donald Wetzel had been exempted by his local draft board on condition that he entered the Quaker-run Civilian Public Service (CPS) camp at Big Flats, New York. While 'not particularly religious,' he writes of himself in the early years of the war, 'I liked the Quakers, the genuineness of their concerns beyond themselves, their true gentleness, and beneath it, their strength.' Nevertheless, after a little he resolved to 'walk-out' of camp: now an absolutist, he felt he must refuse on grounds of conscience 'to cooperate ... with the draft, the selective service law.'

His memoir *inter alia* tells the story of his jail journey. His first prison was the Manhattan West Street Detention Center, where he met Louis Lepke, a Jewish gangster awaiting execution for murder. (Other COs, whose initiation into the prison world took place in this detention centre, including the poet Robert Lowell, had conversations with Lepke and made the contrast between the man of blood and the men of peace together in the same jail.) Wetzel was then transferred in succession to federal prisons in Rochester (New York), Chillicothe (Ohio), and Ashland (Kentucky). His account, highly personal, reflects an original personality with its own individual view of prison.

Prison

With shocking abruptness all official amenities ceased with my entrance into New York City's West Street Federal House of Detention. The official papers told the uniformed prison personnel who I was and why I was there. The papers were consulted, studied; I was taken away, stripped, showered, brought naked before other officials, where again the papers were consulted. Words were spoken among the men; I was glanced at. I was led away to another place where other disinterested dark-uniformed men moved here and there about me on silent business of their own. Not yet in a cell, but in view of cells on every hand, still naked, I was told to stand and wait.

I stood and waited.

Behind me, unseen, a guard spoke, his voice a command; 'Bend and spread your cheeks.' An incomprehensible command. What cheeks?[1] Then I bent, understanding, awkwardly reaching back, clutching my buttocks, trying to hold my head erect, not to look down. Then the voice again, impatient; 'Bend, spread them,' and in psychic shock, unbelieving, I bent low and tugged and looked back between my legs and saw the guard there, crouched, staring with seeming wonder into my sightless Cyclops anal eye. Within which blind orifice he expected to find ... what? A file? A gun? Bombs? But I was breaking into prison, as surely must have been noted somewhere in the official papers. Or then, forth from which orifice he expected to emerge, perhaps ... a dove?

Still upside down and holding my ass, I laughed.

God knows the sight of the guard's face, framed by my trembling legs, was not at all funny. He might as well have been candling eggs. But at that point something in my nervous system was shorting out. I laughed. It helped. I straightened, turned, and saw a quite readable, sane, understandable human expression on the guard's face; anger. I could have shaken his hand.

I learned later that what the poor bastard had been looking for was dope. I don't think it would have made much difference if I had known this beforehand. It was still a senseless indignity for both of us. How much dope can a man really bring into prison packed up his ass?

I didn't object when the prison clothes finally issued to me all proved to be too large, particularly the shoes ...

Clothed as a clown, still I was at least clothed. Clown I would not be; my wrists not yet broken, my heart not yet dead. Handed a broom and told to sweep the cell to which I had been assigned, I handed it back. The startled guard took it. I would not cooperate, assist at my own imprisonment. Nor would I say sir.

Quickly, then, I was removed from my cell and segregated from the general prison population, placed in a cell with five other variously 'special' prisoners. Two were men who had turned state's evidence and were isolated for their own protection; another was an incredibly filthy-mouthed character ... [T]he fourth was a pathologically promiscuous homosexual who was also isolated for his own protection, and the fifth was a tall, thin, smiling man from the west, a cowboy it was believed, quite out of his gourd, who paced the floor like a polar bear, endlessly, and who now and then stopped to lift his head and to bellow, with amazing volume and verisimilitude, like a cow in heat. It was rumored that he had written a threatening letter to the president. He stayed with us only a few days. I was considered also probably bananas. All pacifists were ...

Prison: from West Street to Rochester ...

The trip to Rochester was ridiculous, sitting alone in the back seat of a Ford Sedan in need of a new set of points and plugs, my manacled wrists in my lap, the car laboring slowly through sights and sounds of the free world unseen by me for weeks, with the marshal's young teenage nephew, along for the ride, leaning over the back of the front seat and playing inquisitor. He would prove me heretic, wring from me confessions of cowardice and error. He kept trying, until finally I said, 'Look, kid, I'm tired of your fucking stupid questions.'

The kid told his uncle that I didn't sound like much of a pacifist to him.

On arrival in Rochester I was interned with a minimum of ceremony in what I believe was a county jail, where I remained some ten or twelve weeks awaiting trial. The jail was a kind of small brick box, ancient and filthy, the chief feature of which was the central exercise area, or bull pen, a walled windowless enclosure that stank continuously of old urine and windless air.

I'd never seen a bull pen before; a dark arena, a kind of desolate one-ring circus where the clowns in rags were for real – coughs and curses, belches and farts to prove it – and the spectators, ghosts.

In no time at all I came to know it well. A worn, uneven wooden floor supported a random scattering of chairs and benches. At its center was a large linoleum-topped table upon the surface of which had accumulated a rich collection of penciled art – breasts burgeoning to the point of bursting; nipples like daggers; penises attached to neat round balls; central and large, spread thighs, and a vagina dropping great pearl-shaped drops of passion, a sketch, in its biological simplicity, reminiscent of certain church art renderings of the bleeding heart of Christ. And an endless variety of messages of scribbled hope or despair, directed to no one in particular, or occasionally to God. *Goddamn this fucking place and this fucking food and you stupid fucks that read this. I have died and gone to hell like Mama said. Christ died for my sins but here I am anyhow.* Or the more literate: *Thirty days hath September; I hath sixty.*

Around the bull pen on all four sides were the cells, small, low-ceilinged, dark; cages, in truth, which we entered, only as we must, at night.

After West Street, I found the place more or less homey.

By and large my fellow inmates had known earlier a condition in the free world, in regard to the day's rewards and the morrow's prospects, not all that different from their present condition. If their imprisonment marked a fall, it hadn't been much of a fall. Generally they didn't care to discuss the specific misadventure that had led to their current predicament, their shame being at its very pettiness. They were, at first nod, a bunch of bums.

They weren't too damn impressed with me, either.

Most of them didn't know what a conscientious objector was, and when informed, implied with a shrug, or said directly, that it sounded to them like a bunch of shit. A draft dodger, and what the hell; they had problems of their own ...

Prison: Rochester

I trimmed my hair with a safety razor on the morning of the day of my trial.

The trial was a church-like ritual in an empty court-room, a kind of responsive reading, but with teeth in it. I remember the high ceiling, the faded pale, green walls, the indifferent minor officials coming and going throughout the proceedings, like altar boys, and the always-to-me suspect solemnity of cathedral echoes and men dressed in robes. I pleaded nono contendere – no contest, indeed – and was sentenced to two and a half years.

I had planned to make a statement to the court, but it seemed bootless. Had I tried, most likely I would have botched it. I was nervous; my hands would have shaken. Possibly my head would have shaken.

My aunt had written wanting to know what I considered to be the positive social value of my going to jail. The positive social value, I finally decided, if there was any at all, was statistical. I increased the numerical strength of the absolutist pacifist movement by one.

I'm not sure how long I remained at Chillicothe [Ohio] – a few months at most – before I was transferred to the federal prison at Ashland, Kentucky.

At Chillicothe, as at most federal prisons where conscientious objectors were being held, objectors tended to be employed, along with embezzlers and other white collar criminals, in the administrative office of the prison, so that we objectors often knew what was going on in the prison and in the prison system itself well before many of the prison civilian employees did. So it was that I knew in advance that I was to be transferred to Ashland, and transferred there as an agitator.

This last came as quite some surprise, as it had seemed prudent to me – upon entering the general prison population and after looking around and listening about – to remain as modestly inconspicuous as possible without being obviously chicken. My fellow non-pacifist inmates, whatever their other social failings, were virtuously, even violently, patriotic. They were young, conventionally red-blooded; when denied all access to the sexual or criminal outlets of their choosing, patriotism did indeed become their last refuge. They were hardly those among whom a thoughtful worker for social justice and world peace would seek to win converts. There were, of course, a few pacifists who tried, but I, fresh from the psycho ward or not, was not among them.

(I would guess, as a matter of fact, that a more patriotic group cannot be found in any nation during wartime than in its prisons and reformatories. And I would suggest that this tells us something at least about one of the reasons why men are willing to go to war in the first place; not so much that they are all that hot to defend what they have and what they are, as they are to escape it.)

And while that may not have been an observation first made by me – as to what can persuade a man to put down his welding torch or pocket calculator and to pick up the real or symbolic gun and go off to kill or get killed instead – it was for certain an observation brought home to me at first hand, and most forcibly, as it was to other objectors, with a fist in the mouth or a knee in the groin, as this or that imprisoned patriot would have it.

We cowards numbered, I'm sure, not more than fifty; probably less, in a population of many hundreds. With such odds, it was remarkable that although we were most of us more than once beaten, none of us, at Chillicothe, were actually beaten to death.

Friday nights, I remember, were movie nights, and the movies more often than not were war movies. And so on weekends, with nothing else for the general prison population to do, it was open season on conscientious objectors. We joked about it among ourselves; couldn't the administration at least show the bloodier movies on week nights?

Steve was a socialist, a scholar, a New Englander; precise in speech, deliberate, logical, often devastating in debate. He had that sort of detached intelligence – a respect for clear thinking in and of itself – that could not easily remain silent in the face of aggressive and otherwise unchallenged stupidity. At the time I met him, he had, as well, discovered that it lessened the impact of a blow to the head if one moved one's head with the blow. Steve asked me about it during our first meeting. Was it, he wanted to know – was moving one's head with the blow – in my opinion, a compromise of the principle of non-violent resistance?

I told him I thought not.

I also pointed out to him that by leaning forward toward a blow to the head – most of which blows your average brawler throws in a round-house fashion – the blow will wrap harmlessly around the neck, or better yet, bruise or bust some knuckles on the bastard's hand as it comes up against the harder part of one's skull. Make them, for God's sake, hit your head, not your face, I told him. At that first meeting his face was a bruised and lacerated mess.

We became friends. Steve was impressed, if somewhat taken aback, by my occasional gutter vocabulary and my familiarity with the skills involved in fighting with one's fists. He confessed that he found me a rather unconventional fellow member of the Fellowship of Reconciliation ...

I remember him telling me one day, quite thoughtfully, that he supposed it must be extremely difficult for one of my background and so earthly an orientation just to stand there and take it.

You have no fucking idea how difficult it is, I said. But I think he did.

I ducked, went around all such confrontations, avoided all such 'taking of it' as decently I could.

Steve, I'm sure, understood. But for himself, he stayed and contended, and rolled with the blows as best he could.

He was no kind of an athlete at all.

Many of the pacifists and war resisters I met in prison were from the traditional peace churches; they were brave in the strength of their traditions and their faiths. Others, like Steve, were men only of principle, without faith or illusion; they were simply brave.

During the months I was at Chillicothe I worked in the shop where prison uniforms were made and shoes were repaired. My job was to polish the shoes as they were finished. I sat on a box and listened to prison talk and waited for shoes.

Racial segregation was practiced in federal prisons at that time in all areas except work assignments. I spoke out against it in the shop, even though in the shop I spoke mostly only when spoken to, which wasn't too often. The one black who worked in the shop took me aside and told me, with indifferent concern, that that kind of talk could get my ass killed.

Remarks or questions directed to me more often than not identified me as a nigger lover or a draft dodger, or a nigger-loving draft dodger. Those with whom I worked did not similarly identify their distinguishing eccentricities, but they were variously car thieves, burglars, armed robbers, white slavers, rapists, embezzlers or bootleggers. I liked the bootleggers. They were like caged animals, they missed the woods and their freedom so. While the others were not all of them stupid or hostile, the majority were.

I did not build good time at Chillicothe.

For the trip to Ashland, a small group – some six or eight of us, as I remember it – were linked together in pairs, joined at wrist and ankle by handcuff and leg-iron. I was paired with an enormously large and tall Negro who was in transit from another federal prison and was being sent to the penitentiary in Atlanta.

I had not anticipated leg-irons. Their use somehow amazed me, that it was still being done, a practice that seemed to me to belong to the time of dungeons, of iron rings in stone walls to which prisoners were attached with chains. So much so did this amaze me that the absurdity of being chained leg and arm to a giant was only slowly brought home to me, even though his briefest movement tended to fling my attached leg or arm about in the manner of a ball at the end of a string.

I hadn't really taken note of the man except to note that he was large. I remember that it was only later, after we had been chained in pairs and maneuvered into line, that I thought to wonder just who it was to whom I was chained, looking up to find, incredibly high above me, a black, god-like face gazing blankly earthward, shocking, heroic in its total sadness. If the stricken man saw me at all I must have seemed as foreign to him as a small white bird. As we entered the van he moved slowly, carefully, so as if not to destroy me.

He had no interest in conversation; I learned only that he was being transferred – a punishment (for what he didn't say) – to close custody confinement in Atlanta where he was sentenced to remain for the following eight years.

Midway to Ashland, the prison van stopped at a roadside rest area. One pair at a time, we were allowed to enter the restroom and make use of the toilet facilities, in tandem, with whatever awkwardness or unpleasantness this might happen to entail. The giant and I were the last to go. The path led up a low hill. Down the hill's other side was a wood. We stopped and looked at it. I recall this so well, how we cleared the hilltop, and there below us was the forest, the animal woods, which we stopped and silently observed, chained animals, before we turned and went into the restroom and in silent and terrible brotherhood, urinated.

The prison van was a modified carry-all, with windows all around and a partitioned-off section at the rear where an armed guard sat. We were in prison blues; obviously prisoners in a federal prison van. In the cities and small towns through which we passed, as we paused at stop signs or waited at traffic lights, the passers-by looked in at us, quickly, the way people glance in through the half-curtained windows of a hearse.

(It was strange to be so looked in at, to be so looked in at while looking out, while not yet cold or even dying, while still quite alive, not dead as a mackerel at all; this indeed was to be The Stranger, and is well remembered as troublingly strange.)

We moved through the flat empty plains around Chillicothe, south, to the rolling hills of northeastern Kentucky. The drive took only a matter of hours, most of it through open country. Again to see green fields, hardwood trees in leaf, rolling hills, brought tears to my eyes.

The prison at Ashland, as at Chillicothe, had the same stark barrack type buildings and cell blocks, and fence, the guard towers; but it was smaller and stood among hills. It seemed more my kind of a prison.[2]

To quarantine again.

The isolation, the silence, didn't trouble me at all this time. I welcomed it. I watched autumn come to the Kentucky hills. It was beautiful.

While in quarantine I read a biography, or an autobiography, of Jawaharlal Nehru. (At Ashland we were permitted reading material while in quarantine.) Nehru, I learned, had spent seven years in various ... prisons, non-violently contending with the British, where, as an aid to circulation and clear thinking, and apparently just to have something to do, he often stood on his head. He would do this for considerable periods of time. I tried it, and found that it did, in fact, seem to have a beneficial effect, similar to that achieved through calisthenics. It seemed silly, but no sillier, in a small silent cell, than knee bends and push-ups.

We were counted several times a day. When the whistle was blown at the entrance to our cellblock, we had to stand at the barred cell door and wait to be counted. I tried it once standing on my head. The guard always looked at our feet when he counted. When he saw my face where my feet were supposed to be, it startled the hell out of him. Stopped him cold as a matter of fact. I think he believed for a moment that I'd done something wildly morbid, strangely harmful to myself. He was an old and kindly man. Don't ever do that again, he said, and I didn't.

Quarantine done, I was assigned to a dormitory and to a work detail on the prison farm.

I was deeply disappointed at my being assigned to a dormitory – I preferred a cell of my own – but, on the other hand, I was much pleased at having been assigned to work on the farm.

Most of all, I was surprised at how deeply disappointed I was, on the one hand, and how very pleased, on the other. It shocked me. Prison, I realized, was beginning to have its way with me. I was adjusting to its small closed world; I was beginning truly to care about its few and wretched options.

It appalled me.

Even so – as I remember it – even as it was happening and I was aware of it happening, it happened. It came to matter much to me that the breakfast eggs be scrambled soft, not hard; that the vegetable at the evening meal be green beans, rather than peas; that my prison blues come back from the laundry with a decent crease in the pant legs, I cared. I tried not to care, but I did.

And I was not alone. I remember one day looking down from my cell window at a small group gathered in the yard, at the center of which a conscientious objector was holding forth – one of our heavier thinkers, a leader of sorts – gesturing with clenched fist, face twisted with passion. Later, asking about it of one who had been among them, I learned that what that clenched fist and circle of nodding heads had been about was a description, from memory, of a tossed green salad with blue cheese dressing.

(I have thought since about all this, and to this conclusion, briefly:

Prison life, as with chronic illness, tends to foster an increasingly petty self-involvement. The prisoner, as with the invalid, largely because he must, turns inward. How else to fit decently within the limits of so shrunken a world? He becomes small, so that small things may seem large. In time, all sorts of little things come to matter greatly. He seizes at straws, not that he may be made whole or free again, but only that this day, this hour at hand, might have some meaning. He comes to nibble at life like a mouse.

And this disgusts him.

It is this about prisons, I think, that so surely erodes and destroys, that so outrages; which so defeats, from the start, the notion, the hope, that some good may come of it. It is as though we asked of the invalid that his illness make him well.)

Reluctantly, I moved into a dormitory.

My first work assignment on the farm was to operate a jack hammer at a construction site there. This, without apology or explanation, I refused to do.

I refused, one, because I believe sincerely that a machine which deafens a man and will roll his eyes about in his head like marbles if he holds the thing wrong is a machine to which any man has an absolute right to say no. And I refused, two, because I knew that if I refused I'd most likely be transferred immediately into cellblock.

Which is what happened. I was also removed from the farm detail and assigned, again, to work in the prison shoe repair shop.

At Ashland, the shoe shop was a two man operation. I worked with a short-heavy, tough-minded black man whom I'll call Gregg. Gregg had been addicted to heroin. The insides of both arms looked like the Milky Way; needle tracks like stars.

He had kicked his addiction cold turkey and alone. He went clean with an absoluteness that I sensed, in time, as having to do with even the flesh itself, the great strength of his arms, the power of his back. There was a guarded ease about Gregg when I knew him, but no slack.

I remember one of our first conversations.

So you're a conscientious objector to war?

Yes.

Are you afraid?

Of war? No.

Why not? Gregg said.

I remember that he faced me and waited, a beetle-browed black convict, who was not, to my not-so-unprejudiced calculations, supposed to be that real or that smart.

I don't recall an answer; I think possibly I shrugged. Gregg turned away. Shit, he said, a man's not afraid of war, he's stupid or crazy.

It took time, but we became friends. I had to watch it; Gregg had no tolerance for the bullshit at all. I think it seemed to him as deadly as dope ...

The work pace in the shoe shop was slow. We spent long idle hours sharpening tools, cleaning and oiling the machinery, shooting flies with rubber bands. At one point Gregg made a set of darts fashioned from large needles used in leather work and wooden shafts carved from chair rungs. We used a wall calendar backed with cardboard for a target, and played keenly competitive dart games for about a week straight, continuously, until the guard caught us and confiscated the darts.

We slipped reading material into the shop with us and talked about what we read. For a time it was organic gardening. We read everything we could find on it, became knowledgeable about mulch and compost and the values of various kinds of shit. (It was, I imagine, the first time either of us used the word that regularly in speech while actually referring to shit.) We also talked a lot about worms.

The big thing with Gregg, I remember, was tomatoes. He meant someday to grow, organically, incontrovertibly real tomatoes.

Then we happened onto some material on the construction of houses – homes – made of rammed earth. We approached it cautiously. I recall clearly our initial skepticism. Rammed earth?

We became obsessed with it. For days on end we talked of little else but the problems and possibilities of the construction of human habitations, this side of the grave, made simply of dirt. We drew floor plans, made sketches; house, trees, sky and all. We schemed. We would do it, each of us, build a house of earth itself, a home – simply, as a beaver gnaws down a tree, a woodchuck burrows – when we were free.

In the meantime, we built time.

The shoe shop occupied a corner room at the front of the building that housed the prison laundry. In a small room to itself, between the laundry and the shoe shop, was the large vault-like tank in which the shoes to be repaired were first treated under pressure with formaldehyde. This treatment left the shoes reasonably clear of fungi and infectious bacteria, and stinking of formaldehyde rather than feet. It was my job to run the cooker, as it was called.

Behind the tank, in a welter of pipes and conduit, wine was being made. The wine makings were in several glass jars, and consisted of sugar, raisins and water. (Raisins were often served as a breakfast fruit.) At certain stages of the wine making process the brew actually put off an odor identifiable as that of fermenting fruit. During such times I operated the cooker with a frequency that I was certain would alert the guard, but which never did. By opening the tank door before the pressure gauge had quite returned to zero, I could be sure – while burning my eyes and lungs – that the acrid mortuary odor of formaldehyde would obliterate, for hours, the winey-sweet odor of fermenting fruit.

In return for my cooperation I was entitled to share in the finished product. It was sorry stuff. I drank it on occasion, chiefly to be companionable, and with a salute to prison, to war; it tasted like formaldehyde.

Notes

Source: Donald Wetzel, *Pacifist: Or, My War and Louis Lepke* (Sag Harbor, NY: Permanent Press, 1886), 48, 49, 65, 99–101, 109, 139–43, 147–9, 155–61.

1 Another CO who did not understand the order to spread his cheeks was Lawrence Templin. He had responded by putting 'two fingers in his mouth' and stretching it! See L. Templin, 'How the War Changed My Life,' in Larry Gara and Lenna Mae Gara, eds., *A Few Small Candles: War Resisters of World War II Tell Their Stories* (Kent, OH: Kent State University Press, 1999), 185. The Garas also include memoirs by two of the Union Eight: David Dellinger (pp. 20–37) and George M. Houser (130–51).

2 The penitentiary at Ashland was the scene of a non-violent protest by COs against racial segregation in American prisons. The action revolved around a black Quaker objector, Bayard Rustin (1912–1987). The COs found it intolerable that Rustin 'had to live in a segregated cell block and in the dining hall ... had to eat at tables set aside for African American inmates.' And so, writes Larry Gara (in *A Few Small Candles*, 87), 'we began organizing for nonviolent action ... But the night before it was implemented Bayard was placed in the Hole' for 'homosexual activity.' The accomplished and charming, indeed charismatic, Rustin was to play a prominent role in the civil rights movement and as an advocate of war resistance and social democracy – and eventually as a protagonist of the gay rights cause.

In the Second World War Rustin spent over 27 months (28 February 1944–11 June 1946) in prison as a CO. See Jervis Anderson, *Bayard Rustin: Troubles I've Seen – A Biography* (New York: HarperCollins, 1997), 99–110, 369, 370, for his CO career; also Daniel Levine, *Bayard Rustin and the Civil Rights Movement* (New Bunswick, NJ, and London: Rutgers University Press,

2000), 1, 2, 40–8, 258–60, and John D'Emilio, *Lost Prophet: The Life and Times of Bayard Rustin* (New York: Free Press, 2003), 72–124, 505–8. Of his time in prison Rustin later wrote: 'By some prison officials we [COs] were considered the worst scum on the earth, because we had refused to fight for country ... [But] we were there by virtue of a commitment we had made to a moral position; and that gave us a psychological attribute the average prisoner did not have ... that made us respond to prison conditions without fear [and] with considerable sensitivity to human rights. We thought we were making a contribution to society, in the same way that Gandhi, who was our hero, had said to a British judge: "It is your moral duty to put me in jail." That was our feeling. It was by going to jail that we called the people's attention to the horrors of war.' Quoted in Anderson, *Rustin*, 108, 109. *Time on Two Crosses: The Collected Writings of Bayard Rustin*, ed. Devon W. Carbado and Donald Weise (San Francisco: Cleis Preis, 2003), 11–13, prints the letter Rustin sent to his draft board in November 1943, explaining why he refused to undergo medical examination. 'I regret that I must break the law of the State,' he wrote. But 'I am prepared for whatever may follow.'

Sadly, at any rate in my view, during the last two decades of his life Rustin moved steadily to the right, virtually abandoning his earlier pacifism. As flamboyant as ever, the dashing college drop-out, jailed in the early fifties 'for public lewdness,' now received the plaudits of the political and academic establishments. Rustin the vibrant and intreprid antiwar activist belonged to the past.

Donald Wetzel, who came to Ashland several months before Rustin's arrival there has – like others – recorded how deeply he was moved by the sweetness of Rustin's singing, in this case of 'Negro folk songs' at a show put on for their fellow prisoners by Ashland's COs. See Wetzel's memoir, *Pacifist*, 172–4. Wetzel also pays tribute to Rustin's 'intellectual and moral commitment to non-violence,' to 'his very considerable abilities and ... his great personal courage' (174).

PART THREE: COLD-WAR AMERICA

In Britain military conscription was phased out during the decade and a half following 1945. In the United States selective service continued, to be reinvigorated as American intervention in Vietnam mounted in the course of the sixties. Meanwhile, over the whole globe hung the shadow of the atom bomb: nuclear war remained a possibility – hopefully remote – even after the fall of communism and the ending of the Cold War at the beginning of the 1990s. By that time many European countries had begun to abandon conscription, considering it no longer necessary for effective defence, though compulsory military service remained in force in most Asian, African, and South American states.

In June 1948 in the United States a new draft law had replaced that of 1940; it continued in force throughout the Korean War of 1950–3 and the subsequent Vietnam War, terminating only in 1973 when selective military service fell into abeyance. Even though 'the costs of becoming a C.O. declined significantly between the declaration of World War I and the conclusion of the War in Vietnam,'[1] after 1948 COs had continued to be jailed; there was 'an unbroken witness,' even though the numbers imprisoned rapidly declined to only a small percentage of those imprisoned between 1941 and 1948.

Opposition to America's involvement in Vietnam embraced many non-pacifists, especially those on the left. Young men, when drafted, often chose to become 'draft exiles,' leaving the United States for Canada or western Europe. Others applied for conscientious-objector status. If this were refused they went to jail, as did non-registrants and those who, like the 'Catholic Worker' David Miller, burned their draft cards in protest against the war. Certainly the U.S. Supreme Court's (admittedly rather complex and imprecisely worded) decision in 1965 in the case of Daniel Seeger marked an advance over the situation hitherto. It had ruled that a 'sincere and meaningful' lifestyle on the part of a conscientious objector could substitute for an 'orthodox belief in God' in justifying his exemption from military service. But draft boards did not always take the hint! 'Between 1965 and 1972, some ... 4,000 [young men] were imprisoned' for draft-law violations.[2]

While the prison community contained only a few COs from the historic peace churches – these men usually received an acceptable form of exemption from their draft boards – the boards rarely exempted selective objectors; and non-registrants and absolutists, by the very nature of their war resistance, automatically became draft-law violators and paid the penalty for this. They usually spent several years behind bars. What they then witnessed comes out in the narratives printed below. As the unhappy conflict drew to a close 'stiff prison terms' became less frequent,[3] while parole boards often reduced the terms of draft resisters to less than half of what had originally been imposed, so that they sometimes spent only six to twelve months in prison. However, 'there were exceptions: Richard Duvall of New Orleans, for instance, was imprisoned for four years, most of it in maximum security at Terre Haute.'[4]

In the United States (and elsewhere) during the Cold War era, war resisters, women as well as men, went to jail for various forms of radical antiwar protest, even though they were not liable for military service. The Catholic Plowshares activists are a good example of this; their leading protagonist, Philip Berrigan, spent eleven years in prison for his antiwar 'actions.' Some of these people have written about their experiences in jail. I have not, however, included any of these accounts here. Their authors (in my view at any rate) are certainly prisoners of conscience, who have witnessed to their abhorrence of modern war sometimes in ways that most pacifists would not have the courage even to contemplate. But it has seemed wiser, for the sake of consistency alone, to restrict this volume to memoirs by COs to military service (more or less *sensu stricto*).[5]

On the other side of the 'Iron Curtain,' in Communist-dominated Eastern Europe, only one state granted a very limited measure of exemption to – religious – conscientious objectors. This was the German Democratic Republic (DDR). In 1964, in response to pressure from the Evangelical Church, which was not a pacifist body but contained a number of pacifists, especially among its members of draft age, the government set up non-combatant 'construction units (*Baueinheiten*)' within the East German army.[6]

Naturally such conditions of service proved unacceptable to many COs, even to some who would have accepted alternative civilian service of the kind offered COs, for instance, in West Germany (BRD). For JWs, of course, the construction units provided no solution and, as in Hitler's Germany, they continued to receive severe jail terms for their refusal to serve in the army.[7] There were also unconditionalists (Totalverweigerer), like the Evangelical Church member Michael Frenzel, whose brief prison memoir was published in 1990.[8] Very likely Frenzel would not have been jailed if CO legislation existing in Britain during the two world wars had been introduced in Communist East Germany.

Notes

1 Margaret Levi, *Consent, Dissent, and Patriotism* (Cambridge: Cambridge University Press, 1997), 173.

2 Charles C. Moskos and John Whiteclay Chambers II, eds., *The New Conscientious Objection: From Sacred to Secular Resistance* (New York: Oxford University Press, 1993), 41 (from essay by Chambers). Not all these men became draft-law violators on grounds of conscience; it is not always easy, though, to distinguish between the conscientious and the others. It is interesting to note that Australia, which had abolished conscription at the end of the Second World War, re-enacted it from 1951 to 1959 and again, during the Vietnam era, from 1964 to 1972. During the Vietnam War several hundred draft resisters, mostly selective COs, were jailed there – despite their 'obvious sincerity.' For those Vietnam War COs in the United States, who were given either alternative civilian service (1-W) or non-combatant army duties (1-A-0) by Selective Service, see Jean A. Mansavage, '"A Sincere and Meaningful Belief": Legal Conscientious Objection during the Vietnam War' (unpublished PhD dissertation, Texas A & M University, 2000). I am most grateful to Dr Mansavage for giving me a copy of her extensively researched study now awaiting publi-cation.

3 Moskos and Chambers, eds., *New Conscientions Objection*, 41.

4 Lawrence M. Baskir and William A. Strauss, *Chance and Circumstance: The Draft, the War, and the Vietnam Generation* (New York: Alfred A. Knopf, 1978), 103–5.

5 On the edge of the memoir category are the lengthy interviews with six imprisoned Vietnam War COs (i.e., Selective Service violators, printed along with extended commentary by the psychiatrist Willard Gaylin in his book *In the Service of Their Country: War Resisters in Prison* (New York: Viking Press, 1970)). Most of the men interviewed by Gaylin, including his six major *dramatis personae*, were non-religious, some of them selective objectors of one kind or another (and several were black). Gaylin chose two federal correction institutions for his investigations, carried out over eighteen months with the cooperation of both the prison authorities and 'the gentle felons,' whose confidence he won by his sympathy and understanding for their stance. At the beginning of his book Gaylin notes that, in the prevailing war climate, he had felt obliged to 'protect the anonymity of the prisoners' interviewed, though changes made for this purpose had been only minor ones. The book remains a valuable contribution to prison literature as well as to the history of American war resistance during the Vietnam

War. A non-CO prisoner once pointed out to Gaylin (ibid., 34–7) that the COs in jail, predominantly middle class, enjoyed 'one great advantage that they don't seem to recognize or appreciate.' They were, on the whole, very much better educated and considerably more articulate than the average prisoner. 'If only,' he said, 'these boys would open up.' And it is indeed surprising that so few of them have produced accounts of their incarceration, usually for a fairly stiff term.

6 For the establishment of these construction units, see Peter Schicketanz, 'Die Einrichtung von Baueinheiten innerhalb der Nationalen Volksarmee der DDR,' *Kirchliche Zeitgeschichte* 10, no. 1 (1997), 189–205. See also Lawrence Klippenstein, 'Conscientious Objection in Eastern Europe: The Quest for Free Choice and Alternative Service,' in Sabrina Petra Ramet, ed., *Protestantism and Politics in Eastern Europe and Russia: The Communist and Postcommunist Eras* (Durham and London: Duke University Press, 1992), 280–3, 395, 396. Construction soldiers (*Bausoldaten*) did not carry weapons as other conscripts were required to do. But their work remained closely connected with the military and was administered by the army. Abundant materials concerning the construction units must lie, hitherto unexploited, in German government archives. But a useful collection of documents has appeared: Uwe Kock and Stephan Eschler, eds., *Zähne hoch – Kopf zusammenbeissen: Dokumente zur Kriegsdienstverweigerung in der DDR 1962–1990* (Kückenshagen: Scheunen-Verlag, 1994). The editors are former COs from East Germany's Evangelical Church but, unlike Frenzel, not 'total resisters.'

7 Since 1945 'countries that have imposed stern punishment on Witness draft resisters have been Turkey, [South] Korea, Egypt, Cuba, and the communist republics of Eastern Europe,' including the Soviet Union, as well as Greece and Franco's Spain. See M. James Penton, *Apocalypse Delayed: The Story of Jehovah's Witnesses*, 2nd ed. (Toronto: University of Toronto Press, 1997), 142, 143. The social scientist Jésus Jimenéz, in *Los objetores de consciencia en España* (Madrid: Editorial Cuadernos para el Dialogo, 1973), 218–52, lists 264 JWs jailed between 1962 and 1973, i.e., two years before Franco's death. Some of these men spent up to ten years behind bars: one of them was in prison without a break for more than eleven years.

8 In Heinz Janning et al., eds., *Kriegs-/Ersatzdienst-Verweigerung in Ost unde West* (Essen: Klartext Verlag, 1990), 255–61. A translation of this memoir is printed as an appendix below (pp. 492–9). We can read there the experiences of a CO jailed during the Cold War – on the other side of the Iron Curtain.

BRADFORD LYTTLE

In 1954 a twenty-six-year-old pacifist and draft-law violator, Bradford Lyttle, spent from 7 to 24 June in Chicago's notorious Cook County Jail before being transferred to the Medical Center for Federal Prisoners at Springfield, Missouri, to complete the remainder of a nine months' sentence.[1] After gaining a B.A. from Earlham College in philosophy (1949) and an M.A. from the University of Chicago in English literature (1959), he had worked as one of the American Friends Service Committee's Associate Peace Secretaries, first in Des Moines and then in Chicago. (Since his student days Lyttle has been close to Quakers of the Universalist persuasion.) In the tumultuous sixties and seventies, while remaining faithful to Gandhian non-violence he played a prominent role in the antinuclear and anti–Vietnam War movements, participating in a series of antiwar demonstrations and marches, including several transnational 'walks for peace,' as well as in acts of civil disobedience at home. He also authored a number of books and articles on peace and international affairs. In 1983 Lyttle founded the United States Pacifist Party and subsequently ran for president on that party's ticket, a protest action with no chance, of course, of a successful outcome. A sympathetic political analyst has described Lyttle as 'a thoughtful, compassionate soul whose prime goal is the wellbeing of the human race.' Increasing years have not slowed the pace of his antiwar activities.

Lyttle's objective in writing about Cook County Jail had been to help COs and jailed non-violent direct actionists, whose numbers he rightly predicted were on the rise in Cold War America. What he had to say would, he believed, make it easier for such people to face the experience of incarceration in a local prison, the first port of call on their jail journey.

Few things seem to have changed at Cook County Jail since another CO, Roger Axford, spent time there a decade earlier (see his document above). True, there were no longer bedbugs to give prisoners sleepless nights, and improvements were promised with regard to food and medical treatment. But the daily routine and the generally sterile atmosphere as well as the countless humiliations suffered by inmates remained roughly the same. Moreover, overcrowding had already become a serious problem. At the same time, with regard to other problems like the spread of narcotics in U.S. prisons and the danger of rape, Lyttle's account of Cook County Jail contrasts with later prison memoirists, whether 'conchies' like David Miller (1970), printed below, or non-COs like Victor Hassine (1999), who all paint a more sombre picture of prison conditions.

Lyttle's *Guide to Cook County Jail,* with its twenty-three typescript pages stapled together along the spine in lieu of a more regular binding, appears to have had a limited circulation. Anyhow, the pamphlet is not easy to access today. I am grateful to the Peace Collection, Swarthmore College, for supplying me with a xerox of their non-circulating copy. I have selected a few sections of the *Guide* that usefully supplement Axford's earlier account.

Introduction

In Chicago, most federal prisoners who are waiting for transfer to a federal penitentiary, or are not free on bond pending their trials, are housed in Cook County Jail. The Jail, reputed to be the largest county jail in the United States, was designed for 1300 inmates and has a current population of between 1900 and 2100 prisoners. It is located on the south west side of Chicago at 26th and California, just behind the monolithic Cook County Court House building.

The ultimate administrative responsibility for the Jail is in the hands of the Sheriff of Cook County, while routine administration is the duty of the Jail's warden. The United States government pays the County a stipulated daily sum for the housing of federal prisoners. Most of Cook County Jail's personnel requirements are filled on the basis of political patronage, and for this reason the Jail is often in the news. An occasional riot and more or less continuous reports of the bad food, vermin and unhealthy conditions which exist there have built its reputation to fabulous proportions.

A conscientious objector who is convicted and sentenced in a Chicago District Court for violation of the Selective Service Act may be held in the Jail for a period of from one to forty days before he is transferred to a federal penitentiary ...

Admission

Usually, federal prisoners are brought to Cook County Jail from the Federal Court House at Clark and Jackson in a paddy wagon. They are handcuffed in pairs for the trip and closely guarded. Upon arrival at the Jail they are herded thru a massive steel door into an ante-room where registration and classification begin. Every prisoner is fingerprinted, searched, and his clothes are examined for hidden weapons, narcotics or other contraband. All of his belongings are taken from him and scrutinized, those being returned which the prison officers believe he should be allowed to keep.

The confiscated possessions are listed and a receipt for them is given to the prisoner. They are held at the Jail until they can be picked up at the 'Bundle Cage' (see below) by friends or relatives of the prisoner. The prisoner is then photographed, assigned quarters, and receives an identification card which carries his picture, registration number, and tier number. He is given linen, in the summer time one sheet, a pillow-case and a towel, and, since most transfers from the Court House occur in the late afternoon, he will have supper in a large open cell or 'bull pen' with a throng of other transferred prisoners.

After supper the prisoners are taken by a guard to their respective tiers. In all but a few cases federal prisoners are housed in tiers A-3 or B-3. Upon arriving they will find themselves in a steel cage about fifty feet long and thirty feet wide.

Tier Organization

While the federal courts are in session there may be between 20 and 55 prisoners in each of the federal tiers. A person who had never been imprisoned before might expect that amongst this population there would be no government whatsoever. This is not the case. The tier must be kept clean, and arrangements must be made for the distribution of food and the assignment of new prisoners to cells and benches. These responsibilities are placed by the prison administration upon one mature and husky inmate who is called the 'barn boss.' The barn boss may be serving a short sentence on the tier. The new prisoners will be introduced to him as part of the routine customary for all new inmates, and from the barn boss he will learn where he is to sleep and what his maintenance and sanitary duties are. Any questions which he may have about tier routine or rules should be directed to the barn boss.

A 'kitchen boy' has responsibility for distributing the food after it has arrived by the dumb waiter and to count and return to the guard the spoons which are distributed before each meal.

In addition to the organization which is sponsored by the Jail administration it is likely that the inmates themselves unconsciously will have set up a hierarchy of respect and responsibility. There will be one or two older inmates who will attempt to prevent fights from breaking out. These influential men may be experienced convicts who have earned respect because of their records and are 'con wise,' that is, understand how to get along with other inmates and with prison officials. These 'old cons' are often kindly and tolerant and they are a source of information about prison life which the novice may find useful ...

[Jail Routine]

Prisoners who are going to court or who are being shipped to a federal penitentiary usually leave the tier in the morning before the other inmates have been released from their cells, although often the time when a prisoner is shipped to a federal penitentiary cannot be determined. New prisoners generally arrive in the late afternoon or in the evening after the other inmates are in their cells. The shout 'On the new!' heralds a contingent of new prisoners. Inmates who are waiting shipment do not know when or where they will go. Naturally, rumors concerning shipments abound, but the reliability of these rumors is unpredictable and one of the surest ways to do hard time in Cook County Jail is to believe them and set your hopes on being transferred at a given time.

Every Tuesday, right after breakfast, the benches, tables, toilets, washbowls, cells, bars, and day room floor are scrubbed, squeegeed, dusted, or mopped. Each week a different contingent of prisoners will be assigned to do some part of the general cleaning.

Provision is made for personal hygiene when the shower bath is opened once a week (usually on Tuesdays). At other times inmates are limited to the facilities of a washbasin and tub.

On Thursdays a movie is shown. A screen is passed thru the bars and hung from a girder in the day room. The tables and benches are arranged to form a gallery and the film is projected thru the bars of the cage. The films the author saw were filled with violence but also carried a strong moral lesson.

Sunday morning the Catholic and Protestant services are broadcast to the tiers, and later evangelists invade the prison and exhort the inmates thru the bars. A prisoner in this situation can be called a captive audience.

This routine is unvaried. It is mechanical, designed as part of an efficient institution.

Food

The author finds it difficult to describe adequately the food he ate at Cook County Jail. He was interested in determining the nutritional sufficiency of the diet and therefore limited himself to only that food which was served by the prison. In 17 days he lost 17 pounds. This experience was not unique for a Jehovah's Witness, who was incarcerated at the same time, reported losing 15 pounds in ten days ...

The diet may be augmented from the travelling Commissary (cart, wagon, or store) from which [sweet] rolls, fruit, ice cream and candy may be purchased. The Commissary arrives once each day and its approach will be heralded by the cry 'On the store!,' or 'On the hot!' There is some cynicism among the inmates about the food sold thru the Commissary and this sentiment may be reflected in the often heard quip that the 'hot wagon' brings 'cold coffee and hot pop' ...

Shaving and Barbering Facilities

One razor and one blade are made available each day to the entire tier. Since a blade may be dull after the 38th shave it is wise to contact the barn boss one or two days in advance in order to establish first rights to its use. Blades may be sharpened on a leather belt or on your forearm (if you are dexterous). Mirrors are contraband, but shaving without a mirror is a valuable skill to learn and occasionaly a contraband mirror of minuscule proportions will seep into the tier. The barn boss will know where it is.

Laundry

Each inmate is expected to do his own washing unless he can find another inmate who will accept this job out of friendship or for a small reward. Clotheslines can be improvised from torn strips of discarded clothing stretched between the bars. There is a sink, a washboard and soap in the washroom.

On Tuesdays soiled linen is exchanged for clean. Each inmate receives a clean sheet, pillow case and towel ...

Sexual Aberrations

The author did not encounter sexual aberrations while he was on A-3. Other C.O.'s have reported that these practices do exist on the federal tiers. Close custody and a shifting population tend to discourage the development of homosexual relationships. The question 'Are you married, son?', which might mean the first move in a courtship, has no way to be developed there. The sexual instincts and imaginations of the men burst forth in the raging sea of profanity which sweeps up and down the day room during the day and calms down gradually in the cell block at night ...

Books and Writing Materials

Books are one of the finest ways to 'do time' discovered by convicts, and the author advises that a C.O. take a three weeks supply of books and writing materials with him to the Jail. A committee has been established there to censor all books which the prisoner may have brought with him or may have been sent to him by friends or relatives. While previously only books with 'religious' contents were admitted, it is reported that now almost all books and magazines will be passed with no restriction on number.

When an inmate is transferred to a federal penitentiary his books go with him.

Visiting

Visiting days for the federal tiers are the first and third Wednesdays of each month. Visiting is carried on by means of shouting thru a barrier of half an inch of plate glass. No privacy is provided and two inmates may be forced to share the same visiting 'booth.' A guard may be present thruout the visit. The circumstances associated with visiting at Cook County are so undignified and harsh that the author advises that as few visits as possible be made.

Separate, private facilities are provided for visits from attorneys ...

Recreation

The main activities of the inmates are talking, smoking, walking, card, chess and domino playing, reading, letter writing, and sleeping. Any legitimate method for killing time seems to be accepted.

There is no yard period and no facilities for exercise are provided, although it is reported that the administration is attempting to set up some recreational programs for those inmates who are serving their sentences at the Jail. The author found running up and down the cell block corridor before breakfast invigorating, and, of course, calisthenics may be performed in the cells.

A loudspeaker secured above the cage blares music, news and sports in the morning and afternoon. The distortion in this instrument sometimes makes its message unintelligible ...

[County Jail and] Federal Penitentiary

Cook County Jail is the initiation which prepares a C.O. for the federal prison system. In one respect the Jail is like all prisons, that is, it is a cage in which men are locked, and as such will offer the valuable experience of physical incarceration. But in comparison with a federal prison the Jail is a-typical and it may be of help to know some of the ways in which these institutions differ.

The food in the Jail may be inadequate and unpalatably prepared. In a federal institution the food will be nutritionally adequate and, at first, it will taste delicious.

While Cook County Jail is not filthy, neither is it as clean as a penitentiary, and in the penitentiary there will be ample facilities and opportunities to bathe and shave. In addition, clean (if sometimes ragged) clothing is provided in a federal institution.

No exercise facilities or yard period are provided in the Jail. At a penitentiary there will be time each day for some kind of exercise or physical activity.

The penitentiary will offer periods of quiet and solitude.

It is likely that after undergoing the orientation program of the penitentiary the C.O. will never be locked in an individual cell but only on a ward whose facilities will be open to his use at all times.

In one respect the penitentiary will be a more difficult place in which to live than the Jail and that is in the social relations which the C.O. will have with other prisoners. In Cook County Jail a rapidly shifting population and close confinement in one crowded room depersonalize all relations. A penitentiary, on the other hand, is more like a college dormitory, and there is time and opportunity for the prisoners to come to know each other and to enter into emotional relationships. The C.O. will have the chance to make friends while in the penitentiary but he should be careful that he does not make enemies as well. Further, it is important that he consider the problem of homosexuality and prepare beforehand an idea of how he should conduct himself in the presence of individuals whose sexual preoccupations are aggressively homosexual.

The Medical Center for Federal Prisoners, at Springfield, Missouri, the institution at which the author served his time, has besides its function as a medical and psychiatric hospital, that of a control unit to which all the homosexual inmates who are unmanageable at other federal institutions are sent. As a result, this psychological phenomenon reaches incredible proportions there. To image it properly the reader should consider that in a prison homosexuality comes to take the place of the heterosexuality which is normal in the 'free world,' and the kinds of problems which are raised are similar in kind to heterosexual problems.

The obvious truth is often stated by 'old cons' that it takes two to make a homosexual relationship. There is no reason, therefore, why any C.O. should be 'debauched' or perverted sexually while in a federal institution. If he is secure in his standards of sexual morality he can look forward to handling successfully any problem of homosexuality which may be forced upon him.

Responsibilities after Release

No one who experiences our local prisons or federal penitentiaries can fail to come to the strong feeling that drastic changes must be made if these institutions are to be humanized. Most men deliberately forget the days or years they passed in prison as they would a nightmare, but a sensitive few will try not to forget and will undertake, as a personal responsibility, however slight, the reform of the prison system. The author will not make an attempt here to appraise his own reactions or offer his penological theories. He only wishes to say that he believes every person who goes to prison and who bears a concern for the problem of crime should think carefully about the nature of a prison, the experiences which make governments believe them necessary, and the philosophy which is used to justify their existence. He did not find these simple matters. In regard to reforming the prison system he found the administrators of the institutions in which he stayed sensitive to: 1) political pressure 2) the courts 3) public opinion 4) moral argument. He believes, therefore, that reform of the prison system is a political, judicial and legislative matter, and that moral concern will be the most effective if it is channelled so as to motivate people on these levels. He does not see how significant changes can be brought about thru a direct moral appeal to the administrators of a given prison, although he does not doubt that these people are open and responsive to humanitarian and religious concern. When men are conscious that just and noble action is expected of them they tend to react this way, but there are limitations imposed upon even the finest intentions by the system within which they must be expressed.

Notes

Source: Bradford Lyttle, *Conscientious Objectors' Guide to Cook County Jail* (Chicago: Chicago Regional Office of the American Friends Service Committee, [1955]), 6–8, 10, 12,15, 16, 20–2.

1 Bradford Lyttle kindly sent me a xerox copy of the chapter of his so far unpublished 'Autobiography' dealing with the Medical Center for Federal Prisoners at Springfield (pp. 78–86). He describes the prisoners he met there as 'the most interesting part of my experience.' The majority of them, he adds, 'I never would have met in the course of my "normal" life' (81). 'Most prisoners came from poor families and had terrible backgrounds.' Yet many remained 'humane and reasonable ... despite these handicaps' (85). On the whole, Lyttle compared the conditions he had encountered in Cook County jail adversely to those he found while at the Medical Center at Springfield.

JEFFREY PORTEOUS

Jeffrey Porteous was one of those drafted into the military during the years when the United States' involvement in the war in Vietnam was deepening. But already by the time he had graduated from high school the war, as Porteous recalled, 'had been in the papers for years.' At the age of eighteen, though still feeling his way into the world and with only vague ideas as to what being a conscientious objector entailed, he knew he was unwilling to carry a weapon in a conflict that seemed to him – and many others – clearly wrong. His amorphous objections to fighting were humanitarian rather than strictly religious. On induction he declared his wish to be a medic. The recruiter told him to make this known at 'boot camp,' the duty station at Fort Lewis, Washington, to which he would be sent. This was in November 1967.

Basic training he soon found did include weapons handling. And, since Porteous had failed to register as a conscientious objector and become exempt from this obligation as a I-A-O medic, he was forced to conform while at the same time making his position on the war clear. 'I was the CO, the guy against the war.' Later he described himself at that time as 'eighteen, intellectually arrogant, confused, inarticulate, and up against the United States Army. I had no framework of formal religious training.' Eventually the breaking point came. He left and went off into the mountains. Guilty of being 'absent without leave [AWOL, i.e., for less than thirty days],' he had been joined by his girlfriend; they got married. He now decided, on the advice of a lawyer, to 'file for discharge as a conscientious objector' after having rejected such alternatives as becoming a draft exile in Canada or his original intention of enlisting as a I-A-O medic. He gave himself in before his thirty days were up (after which he would have been classified as a deserter) and received a ninety-day sentence for being AWOL, which was suspended on his agreeing to continue basic training at Fort Lewis. On completing this he was sent for a course of Advanced Infantry Training (AIT) to the NCO Leadership Preparation School at Fort Polk, Louisiana, with Vietnam as his final destination.

Though Porteous, throughout, seems to have been a model trainee, he had made up his mind as to his future course of action. 'I continued to train as an infantryman, but I told them that I wasn't going anywhere. I said, "You can train me, but I'm not going to Vietnam, I'm going to prison."' Later he puzzled over his failure to realize that he might in fact have won his discharge as a conscientious objector without having to go to prison. 'Even then,' he notes, 'I had made the conscious decision to go to prison.' The climax of Porteous's odyssey came when, on completion of AIT, he was transferred from Fort Polk back to Fort Lewis, where he had orders to report to its Overseas Replacement Center. Arrived there, he discovered that the army authorities had not yet got around to processing his application for CO status! For the time being they put him in a holding company. As he relates:

> At some point during my stay at the holding company I did something I shouldn't have done, or didn't do something I was supposed to do, whatever, the result was a revocation of my suspended sentence for AWOL. I had to do my ninety days. I felt angry and hurt about going to the stockade; but I also felt proud and self-righteous. I was convinced I was doing the right thing.[1]

The stockade at Fort Lewis proved to be a preliminary stage on Porteous's road to the U.S. Disciplinary Barracks at Fort Leavenworth. Some fifteen years later he described his time at Leavenworth to a fellow Vietnam war resister (and Vietnam veteran of an unusual character) named Gerald Gioglio, with whom he had become acquainted in the antiwar movement of that era. They renewed contact in connection with the 'oral history of conscientious objectors in the military during the Vietnam War,' which Gioglio was preparing.

The reader may wish to compare Porteous's experiences behind the walls of the Fort Leavenworth penitentiary with those of the Quaker-to-be, Arthur Dunham, half a century earlier. Some things had certainly changed for the better; on the other hand, there were dark aspects, like the sexual harassment of young prisoners,[2] not present – at least to the same degree – in Dunham's time. And much remained unaltered. The 'Hole,' of course, still loomed large in the vision of the inmates, and the high crenellated walls and the bars and the guards and the rigid military discipline all continued in place to haunt the mind of Jeffrey Porteous – and the others – for the rest of their lives in all likelihood.

When escorted into Fort Lewis stockade you are locked in, then unhandcuffed, then issued a mattress and led back into the body of the prison, into 'C' block which is a caged bay of two-tiered bunkbeds ...

My days in the stockade were filled with routine. One of the tricks of prison is that you begin to understand and appreciate the value of routine. Routine is the agent that makes your days endurable, because it hides time, makes it invisible, each day running into the next, each week indistinguishable from the last; until it all becomes a kind of dream.

There were no trades in the stockade, it being a holding pen. There was just a lot of laying around in that compound. I was very fortunate, though, to have my wife nearby, I could see her for a few hours on Sunday. We would talk until the last moment, and then she would leave me with books ... And I met many fine, fine men.

I was also thrown into the hole for being a smart-ass, for lipping off to one of the guard officers, a lieutenant from the margins of Texas someplace. To look at his face was to know that no member of his family had ever been made an officer and a gentleman before, and he'd had to bust his hump to get there. The problem being that 'there' was behind barbed wire in the stockade with the rest of us. But he was going to make it. You could just tell that.

There was another officer whose job it was to inspect us first thing each morning. He'd step from prisoner to prisoner, regarding the shine on the toes of our shoes. One morning I asked why he always looked at our shoes, why he didn't look in our eyes? There was no guile in the question, rather it was an attempt to cut through. I mean, look at it, if recruits were almost invisible to the caste system of the service, you can imagine how prisoners in the stockade were viewed, something on the order of inventory, something to be kicked, counted and fed.

When I got out of the stockade I was assigned to another holding company, where I met several other COs. There were Buddhists, Jehovah's Witnesses, Seventh-day Adventists, radical Catholics, politicos. Most were very fine young men, some were extraordinary. Amongst them all I found a circle of friends, friends I grew very close to ... There was an acute intelligence in this group, a certain kind of energy that I could identify with. We were all fighting the same thing, in twenty different ways, all saying, 'This is wrong. This I will not do ...'

During this time, my application came back disapproved. I sent it in again, again it came back to me disapproved. The night of its final disapproval I was given an order by my company commander to report to the Overseas Replacement Center. I knew this was coming and had talked to my lawyer about it. So, I saluted the company commander and said, 'Sir, for reasons of conscience, I respectfully decline to obey your order.' I was then taken to an office, kept under guard and sent back to the stockade the next morning. I was there three months awaiting my general court-martial.

I felt a bit like a spectator during the court-martial ... The whole trial had a kind of queer, dreamy atmosphere to it. I couldn't see any of it for one thing. My military lawyer had advised me to take off my glasses, they were wire framed eyeglasses – hippie glasses at the time – he thought they might get me another year. So, I didn't wear them, I couldn't even see the faces of the men who sent me to prison ...

My civilian lawyer managed to get in a long and eloquent brief about the war. Then, I was called to the stand. The prosecutor asked if I had disobeyed my company commander's orders, I told him I had. He had no other questions. Then my civilian defense lawyer asked [about] my opposition to the war. My heart was a knot, my tongue tied even tighter, though I finally managed to say what I could, simply that the war in Vietnam was wrong and I didn't want to be part of that wrongness. I wanted to separate myself from them and it, and I felt morally impelled to do so.

We were then excused while the officers conferred. When called back a few moments later, I was ordered to stand in front of the room, where I saluted the front table and was sentenced to three years hard labor and a dishonorable discharge. The last thing the presiding officer said, before I was led back to the stockade, was that the trousers of my uniform were too short. For the next trial, the colonel advised, the guards should get the prisoner a pair of pants that fit. This seemed to have upset him a good deal. A real martinet, I guessed. Though I could never tell. I only got my glasses back after I'd been taken out the door.

I went back to my friends in the stockade, happy to be back among the living. There were eight or nine COs in the stockade at the time; we supported each other a lot, before and after our trials. Some guys got short sentences and did their time in the stockade; but the majority went to Fort Leavenworth ...

The army's stockade at Fort Lewis was a relatively new building, less than twenty years old. But it had been filled for so long, by emotions so intense, that the place seemed gutted, ugly, filled with ghosts. I saw men being harassed, fucked with, driven to suicide attempts, insanity, and to odd acts of beauty and kindness. I heard men being beaten, heard them screaming through the walls of 'B' block at night.

B block was maximum security, the stockade's 'hole.' The whole inside was painted gloss black. It had a steel pallet, no mattress, a sink, a lidless commode, and an overhead light that never went off. The cell was fronted by a row of black bars and beyond that by an iron door with a peep hole in it. You could reach out and touch both walls. I was thrown into the hole twice, spent a couple of weeks in there. Once I was put on 'rabbit food,' which was dried bread and dried corn flakes, three meals a day, with water, because you had your sink. I had a buddy who was down there too, and we'd meditate – we'd do these long chants until we got pretty high. I took mescaline there once, a friend who brought my food smuggled it in to me. He also brought some funny papers. I remember thinking they were the saddest damn funnies I'd ever seen.

Late that summer they formed a line of us inside the stockade compound, handcuffed us, and took us all to the Seattle-Tacoma airport. We flew out that morning, arriving in Kansas City in the afternoon. We then took a prison bus the twenty or thirty miles to the base.

If you get into trouble in the Army or the Air Force, bad enough trouble that you're given a general court, then Leavenworth is your eventual destination. The penitentiary is old, built ... in the last century. High sandstone walls and red-roofed guard towers surround the main cell blocks, which are housed in a massive central building dubbed 'the castle.' Entrance to the castle is through a steel door set in a windowless, red brick wall rising ten or more stories above your head. Here we were ushered in, then herded through a central rotunda, vacant except for a single guard shack, then more steel doors, and the first sight of cell blocks rising eight stories above us. We were lined up, stripped, searched, photographed and finger-printed. It was all relatively benign, but I didn't know that then ... All of a sudden I was there, *in prison.* I remember standing real quiet, waiting, keeping a real steady eye on everything.

Each day we would be let out of our cells to go to breakfast, then back to be counted, to work, back for count, lunch, then count, work, dinner and evening recreation, and about four more counts. It took a couple of weeks for the routine to assert itself, before time began to pass unnoticed.

During recreation time we would carry on long group conversations, comparing notes, a kind of on-going critique of the system that put us there. There were robbers and murderers and thieves – I knew a fellow who had shot his entire chain of command. Several had real strong feelings about the correctness of the U.S. being in Vietnam, so we'd engage with them. Of course, much of the population at Leavenworth had already been converted – they'd seen it, they'd been there ... I was very tight with a Special Forces guy named Harris. He did two tours in Vietnam and just quit. They tried to send him back for another tour and he said, 'No, I'm not going back there.'

The population shook itself out into three broad categories, 'the brothers,' 'the heads' and 'the cowboys.' But within these categories were represented every kind of story. For awhile, I worked next to a country kid, a cowboy, who happened to be a small-time thief. He was also quite harmless.

But the other end of the scale was represented too. In my wing there was a big, bug-eyed dude named 'Frog.' Frog was in for murder, and in Leavenworth for life. For entertainment in the evening he liked to check out the white boys in the showers. One night, after dinner, he had a buddy filch my towel from outside the showers. So I borrowed someone else's, to wear up to my cell, until I could get one back to him. Then, later that evening I ran into Frog up on the catwalks – and I said something to him. Frog looked down at the kid standing before him, and asked what in the world was I talking about, a smile all over his bug-eyed face. He was huge, and we were above tree-line in the tiers; he could have made a human airplane out of me. One toss. But he never bothered me after that.[3]

In the evenings, we would all listen to music on the radio. Each one-man cell had a headset and three jacks, and each jack played a different kind of music; rhythm and blues, country and rock'n'roll. And since we had all segregated ourselves according to our respective inclinations, there being just three of them, this worked out fine ...

And, of course, there were friends. All the general court martialed COs from around the country were there, maybe 25–30 of us. We hung out talking, reading, arguing, proselytizing, celebrating birthdays and Christmases, making plans for when we'd all get out. It was a time in my life, perhaps the only one, in which I knew exactly what I was doing – and why.

On Sunday, a protestant clergyman would come to the prison to minister to the COs. We'd sit in a circle and talk about our feelings and our different beliefs.[4] It was wonderful, it helped you remember you had a positive emotional muscle in your body and that you could use it. Also, come Christmas 1969, the COs got cards from people all over the country. Somehow, our names had been put on lists and we got cards wishing us Christmas cheer and telling us to persevere, that there was a commonality of concern with us and with what we were doing. We posted them on the walls where we worked and the guards would rip them down; we'd put them back up and the guards would rip them down again ...

One day, after I had been there fifteen months, I was sent to the Administration Building, then ushered into an office. There were shades on the lights, and I was told to sit on a chair with a cushion. A corpulent young captain who sat behind a big wooden desk said, 'How'd you like to get out of jail today ...? It seems like your orders came through about five days ago, I don't know what the fuck-up is, but we can let you out right now – today,' he said, smoothing out a piece of paper on his desk, 'if you'll just sign this waiver.' It was a form saying I'd drop all rights to sue the Army for any damages, past or future. I had never even thought of that before, though once he'd brought it up, I didn't want to do it. I told him I'd think it over. But I wanted out. I walked around, saying goodbye to the guys still in medium security with me, then I went back to my cell and wrote a poem in pencil on the concrete wall. It read something like, 'I've been here before you, and I've done this, and I've kept faith. I keep faith with you who are to follow.' Then I went back and signed their piece of paper.

They cut me loose and I walked the whole twenty miles right on into Kansas City. It was summer, and it was sunny. I walked in one perfect, uninterrupted direction for hour after hour, caressing the warm bricks on the building sides as I passed through their towns. I stood still to watch the manifold miracle of women simply walking by, of children playing in the parks, of dogs running free ... In prison we were all guards, no matter what we thought. But once out, you could let it all down, and the whole warm world rushed in at you at once.

I had gotten out of penitentiary five days before my twenty-second birthday. The whole decade had changed, it was 1970 and I was out. I was free.

When I had got out of the Army's prison I was as tight as a drum. I'd been run through the drill and it would take years before I would be able to say that I finally walked out of prison. I was on the edge for years. I was an angry man. That rage also traded over to people in suits and ties, to the establishment and to my country. That experience split my life apart in a way that made me feel like I had a life before the Army and a life afterwards – like I was two different people.

I don't know what it means to people when they see the flag go by, but I have a hunch it doesn't mean the same thing to me. I am a veteran of the Army's bootcamps, its infantry schools, stockades and Leavenworth penitentiary. I am a United States veteran who invested a little over three years of my young life in their institutions. But I cannot forget those other veterans, for I'll always remember I was not seeing the worst the military had to offer. They were putting that little show on ten thousand miles away, on the other side of the world ...

To be an American, and to declare yourself a conscientious objector, is to enter into a life-long meditation upon good and evil; upon what is strength, and what is weakness; what is cowardice, and what is heroism? Each has to answer for himself, and then live with the answer.

Did I do the honorable thing by refusing to fight in Vietnam? There have been times I thought suicide the only honorable act left me. At times I've been hugely proud of what I was able to do as a very young man. Let me put it this way, given the same circumstances would I do it again? Yes, I would, over and over and over again. And my dreams have never told me I am wrong. Not once.

Ultimately, conscientious objectors are as common as dirt, and as old as time. Conscientious objectors are the young men who have simply said, 'no,' to the old men's war. No to the sterile blandishments of: *Dulce et decorum est pro patria mori.* (It is sweet and seemly to die for one's country.) And yes to love, yes and yes and yes again to love. Hell, I think we are all conscientious objectors – until we are swindled out of it.

Notes

Source: Gerald R. Gioglio, ed., *Days of Decision: An Oral History of Conscientious Objectors in the Military during the Vietnam War* (Trenton, NJ: Broken Rifle Press, 1989), 169–78, 263, 264.

1 Another CO in the holding company, Howard Koby, recalled his reaction to Porteous being removed to the stockade: 'That was a sad day. When they loaded Jeff on a truck to take him to the stockade, I told him how badly I

felt that he had to go to jail. He looked back at me and said, "Don't worry about it Koby, I'm free now." I'll never forget that.' Koby was of Jewish working-class background and had been brought up in Brooklyn, NY. But he was by then a Buddhist pacifist. Inducted into the U.S. Army in 1968, he eventually gained CO status and the next year was released from the forces, where he had found training to be simply 'instruction in premeditated murder.' See Gerald R. Gioglio, ed., *Days of Decision: An Oral History of Conscientious Objectors in the Military during the Vietnam War* (Trenton, NJ: Broken Rifle Press, 1989), 207–12.

2 This theme runs ever more insistently through American prison writing in the second half of the twentieth century. When towards the end of 1968 Arlo Tatum and Joseph S. Tuchinsky compiled their *Guide to the Draft* (Boston: Beacon Press, 1969), they had this to say on the subject of draft resisters who were contemplating prison: 'Many of the stories one hears about homosexual activity in jails and prisons are true. But forced sexual activity is less common in federal prisons than in the city and county jails and state prisons. It is true that virtually any draft-age prisoner will be "propositioned" repeatedly, but physical assaults are rare. The vast majority of men, in prison or out, have a strong preference for willing sex partners, even though they may use aggressive methods to determine whether someone who appeals to them might be willing if they "play their cards right." If you are able to convey an active dislike for the prospect of a sexual relationship with another prisoner, you can be reasonably certain his threat of attack will remain verbal. Perhaps that is the most one can ask of a sexually starved artificial community. Certainly the armed forces have similar problems' (265, 266).

3 David Brown, who was in the Fort Leavenworth DB as a CO around the same time as Porteous, told Gioglio: 'For me, Leavenworth was a pretty low-key place. The majority of the prisoners were there for AWOL and desertion. It wasn't a heavy scene, but you had to be careful. Everyone, especially if you were not real big, went through a sort of testing to see if you were going to allow yourself to be used sexually. I had to do some fending off and did. But, that soon stopped.' Before his call-up Brown, whose family was 'religious' and 'middle class,' had been a student at Yale University; eventually he would become a Methodist minister. A month of basic training had convinced Brown that he 'could not let the government turn me into a killer.' He knew he must somehow obtain discharge as a CO. From then on his career followed roughly the same pattern as Porteous's had done, concluding with the stockade and penitentiary from which he was released in July 1968 after a year in jail. His response to Fort

Leavenworth, though, differed somewhat from Porteous's. As he recalls: 'Prison time is blank, dead, nothing happening time. The routine is set and things happen to you; you don't make them happen. I read a lot. Before going to prison, I loved to read, but I came to hate it.' But, then, Brown seems to have been more of a social activist than his younger jail mate, Porteous, who described himself as 'not a joiner' and as yet reluctant to get involved in antiwar activity, in fact 'a pretty shy kid.' See Gioglio, ed., *Days of Decision*, 100–4, 232–7, 297.

4 According to Brown, who was naturally more aware than Porteous of denominational distinctions, this Protestant clergyman was a Unitarian minister. He described the Sunday meeting as a discussion group. 'A lot of the political people attended this.' Whereas the COs in the penitentiary 'tended to be religious individualists,' 'political prisoners there [were] people who had refused orders because of opposition to the war in Vietnam ... The COs were putting in their time, the political prisoners were into gaming the system.' Unlike Porteous and the politicos, Brown, who had been working with the Salvation Army immediately prior to his induction into the U.S. Army, obviously did not get much out of these Unitarian-inspired Sunday discussions. Ibid., 237.

J.K. OSBORNE

In June 1968 J.K. Osborne, a twenty-seven-year-old Seattle school-teacher, was sent to prison for four years as a Selective Service violator. An unaffiliated Christian pacifist, Osborne received one of the more heavy sentences imposed on COs during the Vietnam War. During the eighteen months he spent in jail he kept a diary in which he noted down his observations of prison life and his reflections during that period on life in general. His narrative forms the most detailed CO prison memoir of the Vietnam era so far published. Though perhaps not strikingly original, it is insightful and often infused with poetic feeling as well as a sensitivity to the plight of the convicts whose captivity he shared that is striking.

Osborne's style is leisurely; after all, he had plenty of time to do (and not too much of importance to do in it). That, however, does not make the anthologist's task easy, for too rigorous abridgment may destroy the memoir's special quality.[1]

June 7, 1968
At last I have something to write with. At last I can put my thoughts in concrete form to save myself from going mad. The end of my first day in prison, and I am desolate, ready to die; wanting, almost, to die.

After I was sentenced I was handed over to a U.S. marshal who brought me to the county jail. I was again fingerprinted and photographed. My possessions were taken from me and I was given a pair of coveralls to wear. I will wait here in this jail until transferred to the Federal Penitentiary on McNeil Island, which will probably be within two weeks.

Now that I am actually in jail, facing a four-year sentence, I am very close to weeping. The safest thing is to try to keep my mind completely blank, for when I think, all that I think about concerns either freedom or some happy memory of a time before everything went bad. That is when the tears well up, and the throat contracts, and you feel like you're going to be very sick. I suppose the feeling will come often to me until I get used to what has actually happened to me.

This prison is a terrible place. Thank God I am here for only a few days! There are twenty men in this cell, or 'Tank Two.' On both sides of the 20' ∞ 25' tank are bunks – twenty-four of them, in twelve small cells immediately outside the larger one. Besides the two metal bunks, one on top of the other, there is a toilet and washstand in each cell. We are not allowed to be in our sleeping cells during the day but must remain in the tank. In this receiving cell we are fed twice daily, at 11 a.m. and at 5 p.m. The food is quite bad, but one gets used to that also. What one doesn't get used to is remaining in the tank all day long, with no radio, books, television, cards, or any activity that would break the boredom. The men pace the floor, or sleep, or smoke, or sometimes even talk. Throughout, there is a pervading aura of waste and futility. Boredom seems to be the accepted way of daily life here; total, complete boredom. Some who have been in before tell me you get so bored you aren't even interested in killing yourself anymore, which is one of the chief thoughts in your mind for the first days. The only place that I have seen which resembles this is a room for paranoid schizophrenics in a state mental institution. We sit and stare, just as they do, at the walls, the floor, our hands, nothing in particular. Some have even begun to rock back and forth, and to take strange positions. The tragic difference is that here, and in all prisons, the waste is ordered by society, sanctioned by the general public, and forgotten by everyone.

The second day. I've been moved to another cell, the first one being apparently a receiving tank. Those who have never experienced incarceration have no idea at all what it is like. Movies and television have done nothing toward giving the 'straight' world (I am learning the jargon) a true concept of prison life; if anything, they have made it seem romantically ineffectual.

This is the county jail of King County, Washington, a large, metropolitan area. There are hundreds of jails like it throughout the country, few any better, most even worse. I am in tank C-1 with thirty-six other prisoners. Most of us are under thirty years of age, with this our first or perhaps second experience with jails: the crimes we've committed are considered minor by policemen – assault, breaking and entering, drunk driving, trespassing, breaking the peace, possession of marihuana, and so on. There is one bond that unites everyone in this cell – aside from the fact that we're here – and that is the fact that *none* of us is from a middle-class background. There are two Indians, one Oriental, eight Negroes, and twenty-five Caucasians. Of course, there is no racial tension here for two reasons, I would guess: we're all in the same fix, and we're all young, adaptable, changeable, more open to anything than are older people who have settled into patterns of behavior and prejudice.

The routine is deadly simple. Bells ring at 6:30 a.m. to signal us to rise, dress, and make up our beds. Thirty minutes later the bells ring again, the doors of the small cells, which hold four, open by remote control, and we go to the tank, or 'day room' as it is called by officials, until nine thirty at night when the bells again ring. There are no clocks or watches allowed and nothing marks time except the changing programs on the television, which this tank has. (We are also allowed to play card games, although only two decks of cards are allowed in the tank.) Prisoners may mail out two letters on Thursday or Friday, and must supply their own stationery and postage. There are regulations against keeping diaries or journals, so perhaps if this scrap of brown bag I am writing on is taken from me, I will one day have to rewrite this part of my record. It won't be a difficult thing to do since every part of this terrible place will be forever in my memory. (I don't know what will happen if I'm caught. There really is not much chance of it since guards are rarely seen in the halls surrounding the tank and never actually come inside it. But I must take the chance of being caught since to keep my sanity I must use my mind, and write, and think – but not too much and not about certain things.)

I am gratified and hopeful, seeing the strength of the human spirit. How easily it can be crushed under circumstances like these, but how gloriously it resists crushing! With only two meals to break the monotony of the day (for cards and television soon lose their effectiveness), I am surprised that so few of the men break down emotionally. It seems that the whole system of incarceration is to break one's spirit, beginning with the process of booking.

All possessions are taken from you; you are given a pair of prison overalls (which are changed weekly) and you are fingerprinted and photographed. You pick up a small, hard mattress for your metal bunk, along with a towel, sheet, and blanket, take them to your sleeping cell, and go to the central tank. You are allowed no personal possessions except paper, pencil, cigarettes, and candy. These must all be purchased from the prison commissary and cannot be mailed to you or brought in by friends. A daily newspaper is occasionally given us by a trusty, although it is technically against regulations since it is first supposed to be censored. All of us share the same single toilet and shaver, both of which are rusty and odorous. You are given a metal cup, tray, and spoon which you keep between meals but return to a trusty after the five o'clock meal. They are seldom washed but merely rinsed with hot water before being turned in.

The food is served from large metal buckets, and you must eat fast if you want a second helping, since there is little left. At first you don't want anything, since the food is quite bad. Hunger soon overcomes this. No provisions are made for you to clean your teeth – you may buy a toothbrush from the commissary cart but toothpaste is not allowed. On certain days you are permitted to shave, with a razor provided by a guard, while a trusty keeps watch over you. There have been some attempts made in the past at suicide. Absolutely nothing can be done in privacy, for privacy does not exist in a prison and it is a constant battle to retain a sense of personal identity. But still the spirit resists ...

Chapel this [Sunday] afternoon. I expected to attend but learned instead of more prison routine. There are now thirty-eight men in this tank. Only five from each tank are allowed to go to chapel. It breaks the boredom, so is cherished by those lucky enough to go. Sunday mornings a list is passed around, purely for sake of show, for those wishing to go to chapel to sign. The guardians of the list are the trusties, of which there are three. Naturally, their names go first, followed by those whom they favor. The guard later calls off the first five names on the list and these are the ones allowed to attend chapel. If one of the five decides not to go, no one is allowed to replace him. Some Sundays there is no service at all since the prison does not hire a regular chaplain and depends on a volunteer priest or minister. Some Sundays apparently every priest, rabbi, and minister in this county of nearly a million is too busy to come down to the county jail and hold a service. Little wonder that there are few conversions among prisoners. Rather, the opposite is what happens.

An extremely depressing day. The sun was shining, and, although I could not see the sky, I could see spots of sunlight, coming from somewhere, on the floor of the hallway outside the tank. I looked at the sunlight on the brown floor and could not keep myself from crying, although I was able to hide my tears from the others. There are many here who have not seen the sun or the sky or trees or grass for two hundred days, and will not see them for nearly another two hundred. Any sentence longer than a year is served at a state institution. One year. To persons 'on the streets' who have never experienced imprisonment, it is almost nothing. To us in this cell with nothing to see but green bars and green walls, a brown floor and ceiling, that year is ten, each week a month, each day endless. What in the name of justice have you done to us? ...

June 11, 1968
Thank God! Federal marshals are here, waiting to transfer me to McNeil Island. I wonder – Will it be worse than this hell? ...

June 15, 1968
Two hours from Seattle to McNeil Island, in the back of a small panel truck with ten others, packed like the proverbial sardines. We sat on our haunches, stooped over because of the low roof, so we were stiff and aching by the time we arrived at the boat that would take us to the prison island. Were it not for the fact that we were on the final leg of our journey to a prison, it would have been an enjoyable boat cruise, taking slightly more than thirty minutes. One man was already gauging the time it would take to swim from the island to the mainland, marking what seemed the shortest points from one island to another. He had been sentenced to life imprisonment, so had nothing to lose by trying. He is a young man, just twenty-three, and I wondered what the circumstances of his crime had been that he should receive that harsher-than-death punishment.

On arrival we began the two-week arrival-orientation program – basic training in prison life. Again the skin search, accompanied this time by a medical officer's scrutiny to ensure against obvious spread of diseases, lice or fleas, open sores. We showered and proceeded to our quarters, a sixty-bunk room in the basement of one of the buildings. From there we repeated the rounds of fingerprinting, photographing, and filling out of endless forms. Down to another part of the building where we were issued shoes, socks, trousers, shirt, underclothing, sheets, blankets, and towels. Everything is provided here and we were not allowed to enter with anything from 'the streets.' Through a great deal of persuasion, the arrival officer allowed me to keep the record book in which this is being written; however, he kept it for a day in order to inspect it. I had entered nothing in it yet (there being three separate journals for the three parts to this record), so he allowed me to keep it.

The orientation program will be finished within two or three weeks. In that time, we go through complete medical, dental, and psychological examinations. We learn through a series of lectures what we can expect and what is expected of us. Our backgrounds are thoroughly investigated in order to give us a suitable work classification. (I asked to work in the farm, the yards, or the fisheries in order to be outside as much as possible. But I imagine everyone else asks for the same thing, with the same motives.)

The routine here is basically simple, but it is filled with activities. That is to say, each man's day is taken up with a routine of work, recreation, meals, study time, and sleep, so that – in sharp contrast to the human waste evident in most city and county jails – he does not tend to decay inwardly. I will go into this routine in greater depth after I become more familiar with it.

The prison is a self-contained society, much like a monastery. Most of the food is provided by the farm, fisheries, orchards, dairies, and bakeries located on the island and maintained by the prison population. All clothing, shoes, and bedding are manufactured here or in another prison. There is much that can be done with a work force of eleven hundred men. Schooling is provided in a near-normal classroom setting. There is a library, commissary, hospital, gymnasium, sports field, and chapel.

The sixty of us are confined to two rooms, the large bunk area, 35' × 50', and the smaller television and card room, one fourth the size of the sleeping area. We file to and from meals at six and eleven thirty in the morning and four thirty in the afternoon. For the rest of the time, except filing to the hospital for various examinations, we are here in these two rooms.

Today we had a surprise. We were allowed thirty minutes on the sports field before going to lunch. It was a beautiful day, broad expanse of blue sky with clouds on all distant horizons. Water on the Sound very calm: the tide was at its height. Green, green, green everywhere. So beautiful it almost hurt to look at it. How hard it was to go inside. But there was much in that short thirty minutes to be thankful for.

First impressions. Relief that I was being taken away from the horror of King County Jail. Humiliation at being handcuffed to a chain of eleven men, herded to, stuffed in, a small, dirty, closed truck. Depression so acute that tears were impossible, at the feeling of loss and departure: loss of personal freedom, loss of one's place in the mainstream of society, departure from the city one loves, in spite of the betrayal that city has at times wrought. I was at the rear of the truck, and could look out the wired rear window at persons driving their cars along the highway. How free they seemed! I could see the homes on the sides of hills south of Seattle, and wanted, right then, to be safely in one of those homes, wanted, protected, needed. I had traveled that highway many, many times, and occasions would be remembered: the first time I came to Seattle. The times I left, the times I returned ...

When we boarded the ferry that would take us to the prison, there were the glances and outright stares of the townspeople near the dock. Everyone looked, except three children: two girls about eighteen and a boy of ten or so, all hurried and full of school vacation excitement, readying their boat just a few yards away from ours, for a dash to some favorite sunning spot. How fitting that the last free people I see were children, out of school for the summer.

The coldness and drabness of the huge gray and yellow buildings making up the prison compound. The stone marker above the metal doors in the administration building – FEDERAL PENITENTIARY, MCNEIL ISLAND, WASHINGTON – ironically prefaced with the words, UNITED STATES DEPARTMENT OF JUSTICE.

Resignation. I am committed to prison. I am no longer a citizen, but a subject. Failure to obey all orders means extension of my prison term. I am no longer part of society, I am an outcast. Within me, I fervently pray for strength. It is now the most important thing.

Sunday evening, June 16, 1968

Eat. Sleep. Eat. Sleep. Read. Sleep. Write. Sleep. Eat. Sleep. Deadly. I wonder if perhaps one of the reasons we are kept by ourselves, without activity, for so long is that when once given a program of activities, we appreciate it. What a devastating way to make one enjoy his undoing!

My bunk, on the top tier, is in the corner of the room, beside an open, but barred, window. Kneeling on the bunk, and leaning over to the wall, I can look out the window, smell the fresh air from the water, see across the sound to the town, Steilacoom, on the other side. The grass was cut and watered yesterday, and the smell is quite fragrant. Robins hop around right outside the building. Last evening some songbird was there, singing beautifully. A slight breeze rustles the rosebushes on the other side of the lawn, against a building about fifteen feet away from my window. I ache to be free when I look out. Perhaps it would be better if I didn't torture myself by thinking of pleasant things.

The business of 'adjusting' has given me some concern. One must adjust to conditions, of course, if one is to survive. By adjusting to physical conditions, though, does not one's mind come to accept the causes of those conditions? What I mean is this: I do not want to be merely a species of animal which, to survive for a few years, adjusts to a foreign environment, *at the expense of his knowledge of what he is.* I do not want to become something other than what I should be, simply because I must change in order to live ... an open-ended proposition. But this captivity must be used in order to make even this part of my life meaningful.

June 19, 1968

How devastating inaction becomes! I have been imprisoned only twelve days, yet the forced inaction has become almost unbearable. Every magazine in this room has been read; letters have been written; additions made to this record; still, the waiting, waiting, waiting. It will be at least another three weeks before I get a work assignment, before I will be able to move about from room to room at various times of the day. I find myself thinking too much of my situation, feeling too lonely, too cut off from the outside, too hopeless. I am merely waiting. Most of the past two or three days has been spent in a semisleep, for there is too much noise and activity to sleep soundly, especially for someone like myself who has spent his life living alone, or at least with a private bedroom. I [lie] on my bunk between meals and force myself to drift off in fantasy, to keep the reality of imprisonment from winning my soul over to total and permanent despondency ...

Why am I so fearful? I cannot remember another time in my life when each day was filled with so much fear, hesitation, anxiety. One would think a prisoner would have fewer fears than most: he is in prison, his every physical need is being met, he has nothing left from which to run. In fact, as I observe those around me, they seem to be able to accept their situation, and they are already beginning to gather about them creature comforts or suitable substitutions. They are beginning to *settle into* the situation, to make the most of it, to live, as it were. And me? I retreat, I withdraw, I turn inward. Perhaps that is my way of 'adjusting' to the situation – I have no way of knowing, since I've never before been imprisoned. Were I not here by choice I would be spending my days planning escape.

Perhaps, after I get a work assignment and get out of the confinement of these two rooms (now filled with sixty-six men), my withdrawal will cease. I feel it *must*. I cannot concentrate on anything around me for more than a few minutes. I can write this only a few sentences at a time, otherwise I ramble into obscurity. I am looking for something reasonable, something logical, to grasp onto, but I find only illusions, mirages, glimmering, then fading, becoming an indistinct part of the conflagration of undisciplined imagination. God help me keep intact!

If only I could cease dreaming – at night – the day would be easier. I dream of things *as they were*, only to wake to the stifling reality of the present.

Being merely human, I am subject to the human condition. I love and, I suppose, hate. I desire. I need. Now, where I am and why I am here, and how long I will be here, makes sorrow an oppressive factor in my daily life.

Perhaps the cruelest thing about imprisonment is the forced separation from those you love.

... We prisoners are allowed one visit every two weeks, and up to three people may visit a prisoner at one time ...

A visit from a loved one makes a tremendous difference in the outlook of a prisoner. We have something to look forward to, we have something to expect, we have the knowledge that someone does care about us. Continuous visits, I imagine, can make the difference between madness and sanity in a situation like this. What a difference it has made in me already! I am filled once again with hope, with faith, with strength. All my mind can say is thank you, thank you, thank you!

Out of orientation, finally. A good temporary assignment also – surveying for a new sewage disposal system ... I have applied for a permanent farm job, feeling that work with the earth will stimulate contemplation and bring me closer to God.

I am in custody in the main cellblock. It is quite an imposing sight, one I would do well to forget but doubt I ever will. There are five tiers of cells, rising from ground level to the ceiling seventy feet above. There are forty-five cells back to back for a total of ninety cells in this block. Each holds ten men. Nine hundred men in this huge steel and iron and concrete honeycomb.

In the cell are five double bunks, one man below and one above on each bunk. I am the youngest man in this cell; the oldest is sixty-three. Each of us has a stool-type locker with about one cubic foot of storage space, and two wall pegs for our clothing. The toilet and a double sink are at one end of the cell, enclosed on two sides by a four-foot-high metal screen. There is a small wooden desk in the center of the cell. The bunks line two walls and the barred front of the cell, except for the two-foot space in front of the cell doorway.

August 15, 1968

Some weeks have passed since I was permanently classified. I will not be transferring to the prison farm, but will remain in this cell, where I was first assigned ... My seven cell mates are all good men, in the sense that they are not the self-centered, immature persons who comprise a certain percentage of any prison population. All are glad that I was not transferred to the farm, since now I will be able to give them some help with their educational work (those who are enrolled in studies) and afford them the entertainment usually found in someone unfamiliar with prison life. As one of them said to me: 'It's refreshing to talk with someone who's naïve to the world of crime. And we get some views we otherwise wouldn't get.'

My permanent job assignment is also satisfactory. I am a clerk in the mechanical services department, which is responsible for maintenance, new construction, and repair of all facilities on the island. My job involves no more than several hours each day in filing, answering the telephone, typing memos and letters, and regular office procedures. For the remainder of the eight hours a day I am permitted to write, or read, or just sit, as long as I don't leave the building. Those who work there are escorted to lunch by guards, since the mechanical services building is about two hundred yards distant from the dining hall.

In the evenings (I am finished with dinner and a shower by six thirty), I go outside to the play field, where I usually play tennis, handball, softball, or basketball for an hour. Then I just sit in a quiet spot on the lawn or in the bleachers south of the play field for another hour, watching the clouds move overhead, the boats skimming back and forth over the water, and the cars on the highway on the mainland three miles away. It gives me a strange, detached feeling to see the activities of free men all around the island, and not be able to be a part of that constant activity. We are called in from the yard shortly before sunset, and I then usually spend an hour in the library reading recent issues of news and literary magazines. I spend the time remaining until lights are shut off writing letters or helping my cell mates with their studies.

Weekends go slower, since I don't have sixteen hours accounted for, but I usually fill up nearly all of my free time with writing and reading and visiting with friends I have made among the prisoners. There are many good people here, people who would never have been in prison if it had not been for matters of simple fate, or destiny.

So time is not passing as slowly and laboriously as I first thought it would. I have been here two months now, and it seems only a short time, in retrospect, although simultaneously I feel like I have been here much longer. Perhaps that is what they mean when they speak of 'adjusting.' Time has lost its meaning, while its impact on the individual has become greater than it normally would.

... The first thing one feels after losing one's initial shock and bitterness at being imprisoned is an ever-growing feeling of frustration. It appears that 'the system' of incarceration, the 'administration' of the prison itself, fosters this feeling and institutes procedures that maintain its existence. This may sound unbelievable, and only those who have ever been in prison can appreciate what I say, but I will give a few specifics to prove my claim. One thing must be remembered: as a prisoner, a man is a ward of the Federal Government. He has no rights – constitutional, human, or divine. Those persons acting as agents of the Federal Government who ensure his imprisonment have the right (indeed, the duty, as they see it) to impose any arbitrary decision upon the prisoner that they may feel is in the least justified. If a person makes any physical attempt to escape from prison, they are duty bound to prevent his escape even if this means shooting him down. A man in prison for thirty days is treated no differently from a man sentenced for life, and the man who has committed a murder has no greater chance of being killed while escaping than the man who fudged on his income tax or smoked a marihuana joint.

Now, a few specifics. There is a 'self-improvement' club for the inmates, in addition to a 'welfare committee,' made up of inmates and staff members. Men are urged to join these organizations, since they are the only outlets for personal gripes. (Which is not to say that anything will be done about them.) These meetings, about five out of six times, are scheduled at suppertime. Thus, you have to make a choice: the meeting or the food. Also, the men are allowed to take showers only between five and six in the afternoon, the same time that supper is served.

The day is divided into 'periods,' much like a school day, with each period beginning five minutes after the hour and lasting fifty minutes. The population is allowed to move from one room or building to the next only in the ten minutes between periods. However, if a man goes to his cell for any reason, he is not allowed to leave it until the next period change. I learned to take everything I might need with me during the day in a paper briefcase, as the first month I was here I wasted many hours waiting in my cell for a period change, having run back to get some forgotten item.

On entering, the new prisoner gets no instructions or printed regulations. Instead, he is left guessing as to what are the rules pertaining to any particular matter: showers, period changes, passes, meetings, etc. He picks up what he can from the fellow inmates, but for the most part he learns simply by breaking a rule he didn't know existed and then being reprimanded for it. To complicate things still further, any change in old regulations is not communicated to the population. The guards and other prison employees get a written notice of a change, say, in library hours, but no one else does. Consequently, whoever is caught in the library at any other time outside of the newly 'approved' hours (which he didn't know had changed) is punished.

The most fundamental right of man is the right to privacy – which is nonexistent in prison. Since I came, there has not been a time when I have been alone in a room, not even for as much as five seconds. Worse yet, we are not even allowed the privacy of conversation. There are microphones placed in cells of characters whose conversations might be interesting to prison officials or law enforcement people; in some places in the institution there are placed closed-circuit television cameras, high up in a corner of the ceiling. But the final, always intolerable gesture of mockery by prison officials is the invasion of one's mental privacy. All letters and written correspondence of any kind are closely censored by a staff of mail readers, whether that mail is incoming or outgoing. Poetry, stories, writing of all kinds, may not be submitted for publication until first sent to the prison bureau headquarters in the nation's capital and approved by the staff there, in writing. Periodically, shakedowns occur, wherein individual cells are entered by inspecting guards, and all possessions of the prisoners are thoroughly gone through, including letters, all personally written material, newspaper clippings, and photographs. If, in the judgment of one of the inspectors, any of the material in the possession of an inmate is considered detrimental to the prison's reputation, or to any of its inmates or employees, that material may be destroyed and the individual possessing it liable to punishment.

So the frustrations first felt on being put behind bars grow and grow, and every day there is one time or another when the individual feels himself suspended by a thread above a vast and deep abyss, as in a bad dream. Sometimes the thread breaks, and you fall, but, as in the dream, you never land. You only wake, to find yourself at the end of another thread, and you don't know whether the last was the dream and this the reality, or this the dream, and reality something never to be found.

... My parole hearing took exactly four minutes. I entered the room and sat down across the desk from the parole officer.

'Do you feel the same way about your beliefs concerning the Armed Forces, today, as you did before you came to prison?' he asked.

'Yes.'

'How do you feel, now that you've experienced imprisonment?' The question confused me, and I took a moment to put my answer together.

'Defeated, in a sense, yet strengthened by the defeat. Down, temporarily I suppose, but by no means out. And useless, to a certain degree. I am doing no *good*, where I am, although it's really impossible to say that with any real certitude. Perhaps I am doing *some* good.'

'In what way?'

'In making friends here. Friendship is always a good thing.'

The officer grunted, and passed on to another subject.

'What do you intend to do when you leave here?'

'Resume my profession, if that's possible. I realize the extent of my choices will be somewhat limited due to my having been in prison.'

'Um-humpgh. Do you have anything you want to say?' He sat back in his chair, pushed the tape recorder mike closer to me. This is the question that usually elicits long and fervent statements by the prisoners. I looked directly at him.

'No. It was all said two thousand years ago, but no one seems to have listened.'

A moment of silence. Then, grunting again, he dismissed me ...

Parole denied. Another year must go by before I can again receive a hearing. I will live each day of it without thinking of what comes the next, for what comes is always the same as what has passed. By the end of the next year, I will be on the leeward side anyway, and regardless of the outcome of that hearing I will at least know I have only one year remaining, unless I get into 'mischief' and am refused a year's 'meritorious good time.' But for the present I will ignore the upward climb. It is easier for one who has found peace, who has no quarrel with things ...

... For many months after I came to prison, I was confident in my ability to withstand all sorts of pressures, hardships, and conflicts; I felt that in whatever trials I was forced to endure, the strength of my convictions would see me through. I had then, and I have now, a belief – among the hierarchy of my beliefs, one of the highest – in the efficacy of nonviolence to overcome all hatred. I believed myself, at that time, to be incapable of resorting to violence as a personal measure to ensure my safety, or someone else's, or as a means to an end, however good that end might appear. This belief is put to the test often in the course of a peaceful man's life. My own is no exception.

I have been importuned, on a number of occasions, to participate in activities among other prisoners which were personally distasteful to me, although I cannot condemn the practice of such activities where it is entirely voluntary. Demands were made by a particular convict that I be used as his sexual outlet. I had time and time again refused, but apologetically, as is my habit. The man would not be put off.

One day I was sitting alone at a table in the dining room having lunch. The fellow, whose friendship I had hoped to cultivate while not giving in to his sexual desires, approached the table, greeted me, and sat down. He put his hand on my knee. I moved away. He grabbed my wrist tightly in his hands – he was a large man while I am slightly smaller than the average – and, turning my wrist, snarled in my face: 'You meet me in the library lounge tonight at third period, and this time no excuses. I'm going to get what I want from you one way or another.'

An unfamiliar feeling took hold of me. My whole body tightened and my head rang as if filled with giant gongs. For a few seconds I lost sight of everything except his face; all around it everything was black, and filled with strange movements of color, as if I had been struck nearly unconscious by a blow on the head. My free hand felt for the fork beside my tray, and I clenched it tightly. Raising it up slowly to the level of my chest, I began unwillingly to rise from my chair. My ears were still ringing, louder than before. In that instant that we stood glaring at each other, our brotherhood was confirmed. He released his grip, and with a wry smile said, 'Remember, third period.' He turned and walked away.

I sat down at my place. I don't know how long I sat there, fork tight in my hand, my blood pounding as if to burst all its vessels and arteries and the heart itself. My full sight returned, the ringing stopped, and I gradually resumed my normal composure. But for quite a while afterward I felt a chill.

What was it that I had experienced? What had I undergone? I gave much thought to this episode for a long time after it had passed. It has left me with a little understanding of myself, and perhaps also of man. Was it fear I had experienced? Perhaps to some degree fear was present in it. Fear itself is not new to me, although it is an emotion I do not usually find myself burdened with. What it was that had caused me to grab my fork and [rise] up out of my chair, what had caused my head to ring and impaired my sight was, I believe, hatred. Pure and solitary hatred. At that moment, I had been seized with what man has been striving to overcome for all his turbulent centuries; I had been seized, and very nearly moved to become anti-man, by hatred.

I did not meet the fellow later nor, in fact, did I ever consequently have anything more than a nodding relationship with him. What had caused him to discontinue his advances is unknown to me, although there are those who will see in this episode a justification for violence. But since that incident in the lunchroom, I have seen the whole question of pacifism in a clearer light.

I know now that I, as a fallible human, am capable of surrendering to hatred and fear and striking out at another being. I am even ready to admit my capability to kill another man. I can see, too, where this instinct lies in every man, in man's nature. I also see that it is *because* we are all capable of murder that it is imperative to the survival of man that we purify ourselves of this unholy and satanic failing. A century ago, it may not have been as urgent as it is today.

But it must be recognized that, since we now possess the means of destroying all of mankind and of throwing nature itself off balance, the question of whether or not we must change the nature of man from an aggressive one to a peaceful one can no longer be debated, delayed, or doubted. It is quite simply a matter of deciding whether or not we want man to continue his existence on this earth ...

[December 1968]

Several days ago there was an escape from this prison. I was sitting in the library, reading Gide, when I thought I heard a muffled popping. Minutes later, the bells rang and all of us were summoned back to our cells for lockup, the usual procedure while the island is on 'escape status.' It was snowing, and has since been snowing, but there has been no trace of the escapee. He is a young man of twenty-seven, and just may be strong and healthy enough to make it. I hope so.

We remain in our cells, day and night, except to go to meals. All prison guards and employees are summoned immediately after an escape to form search parties. The island is about seven square miles of mostly timberland. One could hide in the woods easily enough for a few days, perhaps even weeks or months. But during the winter there is no food to be had, unless the fugitive – what an ugly word that is! – took the chances of being caught while breaking into one of the storehouses, or one of the employees' homes on the island. I am told that several years ago, a prisoner escaped detection for over a week while hiding in the house of the associate warden, who was at the time out searching for him.

The greatest barrier to cross is a natural one – the waters of Puget Sound which surround the island. In December they are near freezing.

Christmas Eve. Snow is still falling. As I write, two guards are going from cell to cell, handing to each man a brown sack containing two packs of cigarettes, a box of cookies, a cellophane bag filled with nuts and hard candies, an orange, and a piece of fruitcake. But tonight there is little sadness or sentimentality. The minds of fourteen hundred convicts are concentrated on one hope: that the man who went over the fence will succeed ...

January, 1969

A new year, and the beginning of a new life. I will be transferred out of my cell this month and taken to the prison farm, where I will live until my sentence is over or until I'm paroled. For some reason, I can't really believe I'm leaving all this, this penitentiary and its guards and gun towers, to go to a dormitory where there are no fences or walls, no guns, very few guards, open fields, trees, flowers, grass, birds, cattle, pigs, chickens – my God! is it really happening? I shiver in anticipation. My teeth chatter and I tremble at the thought of touching a tree, holding a kitten or a calf. What if they changed their minds? What if they decided to keep me here a while longer? What if I go, only to have something happen and be transferred inside again? What if ...?

Whatever comes, I've got to be solid, I've got to steel myself for anything in the extreme. Minimum custody, and the camp. My chances for parole are greatly increased. So I dare not think maybe ...? Enough of this. With time off for 'good behavior,' I now have two years left to serve. That is at this point the basic reality. That, and – my God, I'm leaving this place!

The cell mates I am leaving. I will get them on paper before my mind, in defense, forces me to forget even their names.

Joe, decorated in the Second World War, fifteen years for smuggling birds from South America. *Birds?* About every month or so, some guards would come into the cell and take away all of Joe's newspapers and magazines. He hoarded them to the point where there was room for little else in the cell. Twice he dropped a match into the pile, let it get burning, then jumped up with a great shouting and commotion, and put the fire out, 'saving' us all from catastrophe. At night he would pace the cell in the nude. He was convinced that the CIA had put him in jail ...

Chuck, thirty-nine, professional burglar. The joker of the cell, always talking, laughing, doing his best to keep the place as cheerful as possible. A 'Cadillac driver' – one who constantly told tales of how well he had been doing until being busted. Five years for white slavery. Korean veteran. I always thought if Chuck could have had a son, he wouldn't have been a criminal. Maybe just because he was my father surrogate.

Art, twenty-nine, five feet seven inches, over two hundred pounds. In for theft of federal property – electronic equipment. He was building his own computer. Alcoholic, insecure. Lost himself in electronics and math, his professional fields. Accomplished electrical engineer, a job waiting for him when he gets out. Quite well read. Have never been able to understand him. He is most likely a genius.

Larry, thirty-four, Korean vet, ten years for possession and sale of marihuana, handsome, cool, self-assured. In on various 'business' propositions and goings-on within the prison. When he laughed – usually at one of Chuck's jokes – the bars, walls, guards, gun towers disappeared, and we all laughed together.

Jim. What a beautiful man! Twenty-five, labeled 'incorrigible,' escaped twice from other prisons, in for car theft. Tall, good-looking, healthy, spends a lot of time lifting weights and playing basketball. I've seen his counterparts in junior and senior high schools – the kid who it was easier to send out of class or expel from school than to deal with in a direct, intimate relationship. He's incorrigible all right – incorrigibly *alive.* At fourteen, his parents couldn't handle him so he existed on the streets. Just a few weeks ago his caseworker thought he'd counsel Jim. Jim asked him why, why was he interested in helping. 'Because it's my job,' said the caseworker. Jim walked out. He has accumulated, over the past year, the works of Proust, Mann, Hesse, Sartre, Camus, Gide, Faulkner, Genet – and read them all. I can't keep up with him in discussions of literature. What an amazing man! Is there no other place for him in this world, other than a prison?

Drake. Withdrawal personified. In his case to the point of extreme introversion, morbid self-concern. Incarcerated since the age of twelve, now thirty-two, in and out of boys homes, state and federal prisons, mental institutions, county jails. A lifetime in jail, doing nothing but smoking, eating, sleeping. Doesn't read. Freaks out every so often and goes to the hole for a few days; comes back to the cell more withdrawn than when he left. Seldom speaks. No desire to live. When he's released, he'll steal a car or forge a check, come back to jail after pleading guilty. An absolute nonentity. Or so it seems. Why?

Bob. This is his first offense – two years for impersonating an FBI agent. Twenty-four, from Alabama, on his own since he was thirteen or fourteen. Worked in carnivals for a while as 'the ugly man' – his face would cause a traffic jam. Extremely disoriented, afraid of other cons. Spent time in the hole for stealing paint thinner for glue-sniffing – he doesn't practice, but was, under threat, getting it for another con. His suicidal tendencies are obvious – I pulled him away from the edge of the tier one time shortly after he got assigned to the cell. During the night he'd scream. After several fights and arguments with guards, sent to the hole again. Now in the hospital isolation ward after attempting suicide by swallowing pieces of razor blade.

Why, why why? A friend of mine here, Moose, once told me that if he was *convinced*, if he really *believed*, was *sure* of the existence of God, he would kill himself. I think, how, having been here for what seems a very long time, in these surroundings, I am beginning to understand that, and why he said it.

Transferred to camp. Before leaving, saw Moose; checked out at laundry, commissary, library, records department. Waited in corridor for officer taking me to camp. Sitting with my bag and box of belongings – books, writing materials, sketches, cigarettes – every inmate coming through the hallway stared at me; some made comments. A person *leaving* is an occasion here, even for the others staying behind. I once watched a man dress out for the streets and I too had to stare with fascination. Going home! to the streets! But my time has not yet come – I am only halfway home.

At camp, going through procedures of assignment to job and dormitory, checking out clothing, etc., I felt detached, drunk, not with it. I was merely being moved, not moving. Here too there are stares – not from envy or fascination, but from curiosity; I am a new member of the group, I am being sized up in one glance. An officer takes me quickly around the farm in his truck; we get stuck in mud and snow. I walk back to alert another officer, who phones for a tow.

Walking alone, later, everything is quiet. It is snowing lightly. From an enclosed area filled with eleven hundred men to an open, fenceless hilltop, where somewhere around me there are three hundred others. Very quiet. Few men around. Will be more after work crews return to the dormitories. But now, about three thirty on a late winter afternoon, in the open air, with no gun towers or guards in sight, I am coming back to earth. I am beginning to move myself.

January 30, 1969
There are other draft resisters here. Seems odd, after being the only one in the penitentiary for seven months, to come here where there are nearly thirty of us. Three of us, Wills, Colwell, and myself, walked away from camp today, after supper. It was dark, and we were taking a chance on being caught, which could get us into trouble. Walked to the woods behind the dairy, and there we sat, saying nothing, holding onto the moment. The dark night was clear, stars flashing pins of light, wind walking through the empty branches. Colwell stared up at the stars ... Wills got up, went and encircled a tree trunk with his arms, stood there. I asked if everything was all right. 'Sure,' he said. 'I just wanted to hold something that's alive.'

My emotions are becoming erratic, extreme. Close to weeping many times, or laugh without reason. Either very up or very down. But I must hide it well. Wills asked me the other day how I managed to stay so calm.

At times I'm really concerned about my sanity. The last three or four weeks have been terrible: insomnia. I sleep – fitfully – about three hours each night. Daytime I try to snatch half an hour at lunch and again before dinner. But it's never sound, healthy sleep. I can't figure out what's causing the insomnia. I've had it before; never this bad or this long. I'm not paranoid – not in the sense that I'm afraid of anything happening to me which might be painful.

The routine might be causing it. Everything is always the same. Seldom am I successful in getting away, for something breaks my spell and brings me back to the dull order of things. Dullness is bearable; what is not is the meaninglessness of our existence, our forced activities. As much as I love the contemplative life, I could never be a monk, for their routine effaces the beauty of their life, for me ...

July 15, 1969
The parole board has 'met' and is now considering cases for possible release. Prior to his meeting with the representative of the board, a report on the man being considered is written and submitted by his caseworker. Nothing of value is entered into the report, really, since it is merely another one of those many bureaucratic formalities which dictate much of our lives. My job assignment here at camp has been as secretary to both the superintendent and the caseworker, so I've become quite familiar with administrative procedure. Most of the men eligible for parole do not meet personally with the board, which is composed of seven members, only one of whom appears at the institution six times a year. Those who do meet with the board member are given about five to ten minutes of his time. For the most part, then, the board's decision is arrived at through a perusal of those forms and annual reports submitted by the caseworker at the institution. The contents of these reports are the same from one man to the next, and procedures have become so standardized that very soon a man's freedom will depend on a decision by a computer.

My own report was submitted to the board in June. Within the next month or two I will know whether I've been paroled or whether I remain here for another year, possibly another two. The average time served by draft resisters has been eighteen months, so I'm fairly confident that I'll get paroled. If so, I will leave sometime between September and January. Nothing is sure, however; for some reason or other, maybe for no reason at all, I could be kept here until my maximum release date, March 23, 1971. In any case, I am under federal supervision until June 7, 1972. Four years of my life, for refusing to kill! ...

Having time. Bright, sunny days, warm and fragrant. Blackberries beginning to ripen on the vines that spread over the entire island. Hours move slowly, and even though I'm on a prison farm, I relish every moment. Each has its own beauty. I've been spending much of my time wandering over the island. Working for the two key men at the farm, I get away with things others might be punished for, such as being 'out of bounds.' The boundaries are so arbitrary that each prisoner's supervisor can set his own. Consequently, I've got a lot of 'freedom' to walk the fields, orchards, pastures, and woods, supposedly on some errand for one of my bosses.

This evening I walked to the field that had been partially cut earlier today, behind the hill west of the camp. The sun was near the horizon, so it was still warm and bright, but with that particular lightness which comes in late summer when harvest dust diffuses the sun's rays. The scene of cut grass overwhelmed me. Confident I was alone and unobserved, I stripped off my clothes and literally rolled in the hay ...

An example of how beautiful convicts can be: I went to the hospital today for dental work – cleaning and polishing. (No cavities in the past seventeen years!) One of the inmates did the work on my teeth. He's a man about thirty, perfect physical specimen, gentle face, and a very good technician. I mentioned to him that he had moved into my old bunk in the main cellblock, and asked about my cell mates. He told me about Drake.

Drake [see p. 447 above] is a fellow in his mid-thirties who's been in and out of various institutions – juvenile homes, prison farms, penitentiaries, foster homes – since he was twelve, when he ran away from an orphanage. He's a quietly tormented man, withdrawn, uncommunicative, subject to depressions that completely incapacitate him. He has been for the most part simply ignored. Not any more. My friend – for he is my friend simply because he's a good man – the dental technician, along with the others in the cell, have undertaken the task of bringing Drake back into the fellowship of men. In less than a year they have succeeded in doing what institutions and the 'authorities' have failed to do. They have helped Drake find his identity – or at least begin to build one – and have through their love and acceptance of him brought about major changes in what had been an empty shell of a personality.

How did they do it? They themselves don't know. In my friend's words: 'We talked to him a lot at first. He had to answer, so he started talking himself. Then we started talking *with* him. Then we listened to him. We did things with him. Played cards, Scrabble, taught him chess, practically dragged him to some English classes at night and helped him with that when we could. Chuck and he designed a house. Joe taught him how to play poker, and the guy's getting sharp. Johansen is teaching him Spanish. We've got the guy going and now we can't stop him. He's playing softball and giving speeches at Toastmasters Club.

When he's finished with a typing class he's going to file a writ to get himself out, or maybe at least a sentence reduction. The guy's a miracle.'

Miracle? No, just a sample of something that happens whenever someone finds there are a few people who honestly would like to be his friends. *Friend.* Where have they all gone, why have free people lost the meaning of friendship? Here was a man – Drake – who had nothing, absolutely nothing, and found there were persons who didn't care what he had – they cared about *who he was, and who he could become.* Not a name, or a title, or a personage, but a man. A man. One who could speak, and answer, and listen, and advise, and care, and love. A man, and a friend of men.

My friend the dental technician, and his friends, and their friends, and Drake. Here, within these walls, among the outcasts of society, dangerous men guarded by fences and towers and guns, among a mass of humanity where stabbings and beatings and unspeakable acts are perpetrated, here, in this cesspool of rejects festering in their wounds, real and imagined, here, *here! in prison,* love steals in unnoticed and makes princes of men.

September 10, 1969

Since June, when my case was reviewed for parole, I have been waiting for word from the board. Much of the time has been painful, a dull pain just out of reach of anything that might soothe it. ...

Today I received from the caseworker a slip of paper, with my name and number on it, and the words: *Parole Effective December 11, 1969.* It is impossible to say how I feel.

September 22, 1969

Have written letters to all those on my correspondence list, telling of my parole date. I now enter yet another period of *waiting,* but this will be the last.

An odd thing: I have felt vaguely guilty since getting a parole date. Guilty about those I leave behind in this prison. Do I have a right to be free while they remain behind bars? ...

Thanksgiving, 1969

I came to prison – the Federal Penitentiary on McNeil Island, in the State of Washington – late in the spring of 1968. For me there was no summer, no autumn, that year. Winter was nearly over before I was transferred to the Federal Prison camp on the island. Two miles apart they lie, the penitentiary and the prison camp; two worlds apart on an island of barely seven square miles. Of course there are differences, and naturally the physical differences are first to command one's attention. Inside, there are eleven hundred men living and working in a compound of less than ten acres. Here there are fewer than three hundred in jobs that spread them over the forty-four hundred acres of the island. So the first thing one notices, after being transferred here from inside, is the absence of other people. This comparative quiet struck me quite forcefully, coming after long months of bells and clanging steel and the voices of over a thousand men in constant babble from six in the morning until after midnight. The quiet, the absence of others, the totally different array of sights and smells, came upon me like a sudden dose of powerful medicine, and I was left for several days in a state of detached, floating, inner confusion. I simply did not know what to do with myself. So I walked. I started a habit that has carried me over these long months on this prison island, until I can see ahead the day when I shall be released, from this island and from myself.

The camp proper consists of the six-dormitory main building, which also includes the mess hall, kitchen, offices, clothing room, laundry and storage rooms. Thirty paces north (behind) the main building is the vocational training building, where no training is done; but groups that occasionally tour the facilities are told, 'This is our vocational training building,' and they naturally assume that it is used for its original purpose. It is used, rather, to house a small reading room, music room, hobby shop, meeting rooms, and gymnasium. These two buildings are, seven days a week, the hub of camp activity.

Recreational facilities are much the same as they are 'inside': tennis, handball, softball, gym activities, and horseshoe pits. Lately there is even a nine-hole golf course. (There has been an increase in recent years of income-tax offenders.) There is one luxury that is inestimable in its effect: the absence of fences and towers with guns.

On the hill a quarter mile west of the compound are the dairy barns, silos, maintenance shops, and barns. To the north are chicken coops, to the northwest a piggery. Surrounding the camp are several hundred acres of pasture, and to the southeast are forty acres of vegetable garden. In a valley between the camp proper and the dairy barns lies a small sawmill, the likes of which used to dot the Pacific Coast from San Francisco Bay to Queen Charlotte Sound, but which are now disappearing in this age of largeness.

The external, physical differences are basic and easy to define. More difficult to realize and understand are the subtle, internal differences.

One of these is the effect of the daily sight of someone leaving for the streets. During nearly a year inside, I saw one person leave to go home. Here it's a daily and very obvious occurrence, and anyone who has a long spell in front of him is naturally going to take notice, however much he might deny it, of these daily departures.

Another subtle influence is the seeming presence of freedom. No manned towers, no high fences, no bars, and one willingly accepts the charade of free activity. Until, as it does every two hours, the counting bell rings and one must remain frozen to his position or return to his dormitory to be counted. Still another is the depressive effect of the insistence on the part of staff members that inmates remember at all times that they are still wards of the government. This type of officer–inmate relationship gives rise to an anti-authoritarian prejudice that carries over to later activities of the freed convict, in addition to laying the seeds of dependency upon authority in weaker individuals. Prisons tend to further weakness and dependency by their emphasis on authority ...

Winter, 1970

I was released from prison on Thursday, December 11, 1969, after serving eighteen months and four days. It is a simple but numbing experience, being given your 'freedom.' At 9:30 a.m. I went to the dress-out room where I was issued civilian clothes, a coat, and a handbag for personal items. An hour later I boarded the boat for the twenty-minute ride to the mainland. It was a harsh, windy, cold day; the waters were choppy, the boat lurching and rocking. For the length of the trip I stared back at the prison, set on the edge of McNeil Island, as it grew smaller in my sight. In this way I had hoped to make its memory fade within until it would one day become a speck in my total life's experience ...

I live now in a room on Seattle's Capitol Hill. It is a small room, but the house is large, and there are others in it. I read much, and write, and listen to music, though my tastes in all three are not those of my generation. I have a calico cat named Maggie, and a white canary, Mozart. The three of us get along just fine.

Notes

Source: J.K. Osborne, *I Refuse* (Philadelphia: Westminster Press, 1971), 67–71, 73,74, 77–83, 86–8, 92, 93, 95–7, 99–102, 119, 120, 123, 124, 138–41, 146, 147, 160–6, 200–5, 207–9, 221, 226.

1 For another account by a CO of life around this time in the McNeil Island Federal Penitentiary, see Meldon Acheson in Murray Polner, ed., *When Can I Come Home? A Debate on Amnesty for Exiles, Antiwar Prisoners and Others* (Garden City, NY: Doubleday Anchor Books, 1972), 167–87. Sentenced to three years in jail, Acheson, an ex-Methodist Christian anarchist, was paroled after seventeen months. From the moment when, on a sunny day with a view of 'the Olympic Mountains in the distance' and with 'a smile on my face despite my inner fears,' he made the boat journey to the penitentiary, his impressions of 'McNeil' are fairly similar to Osborne's, though his style is usually more prosaic. When, aged 18, he had registered as a CO, 'prison frightened me,' he tells us, 'having been brainwashed in school as everyone is that prison is the worst of all possible experiences' (p. 164). Neither for Acheson nor for Osborne did McNeil bear out this ominous view. But of course it remains very much a personal matter.

Paul W. Keve, in his *The McNeil Century: The Life and Times of an Island Prison* (Chicago: Nelson-Hall, 1984), makes no mention of either the Second World War or the Vietnam War COs who were incarcerated in this penitentiary. For these two war periods, see 243, 246–53.

'JOHNSON'

Within a year of J.K. Osborne's release from the Federal Penitentiary on McNeil Island another 'refusenik' – we know him as 'Johnson' – had arrived there to serve a two-year sentence. He spent his time on the Island in an angry and rebellious mood very different from that of the gentle and soft-spoken Osborne. As one might expect, their views of the same institution and its inmates differ considerably.

Osborne had committed his impressions of prison to paper even before he got out, long before their memory faded 'within until it would one day become a speck in [his] total life's experience.' Johnson, by contrast, waited two decades until he was interviewed by a professor of English at the University of Washington in Seattle, who was preparing an oral history of conscientious objection during the Vietnam War. In that conflict the future Professor Tollefson had been a CO: 'one of the privileged few,' as he calls himself in the introduction to his book which first appeared in 1993, one out of the 'approximately 170,000 individuals ... receiving deferments from the draft as conscientious objectors.' Johnson, however, had been non-collaborative and the authorities did not like that. Thus his two-year sentence! 'I didn't want to conform to social institutions,' he told Tollefson. 'I wanted to purely be me, even at the risk of social ostracism or punishment.' Looking back on the threshold of middle age he remarks: 'In a way, I was a chump, a dummy, a patsy, a dupe to let myself get into a goddamned Federal penitentiary for moral and ethical beliefs.' But further reflection led him to assert: 'from my point of view, it was the only thing I could have done.'

As a student at Western Washington University in Bellingham, Johnson had adopted a hippy lifestyle, which shocked his conventional middle-class Catholic family in New Jersey. He began to read all the antiwar literature he could get hold of, including Gandhi, Martin Luther King, and Thomas Merton, and he 'started to attend demonstrations, listening to speeches and watching people burn draft cards.' 'I felt a kinship with them,' he says. Finally, after long hesitation he decided to become a CO himself if drafted, rejecting the idea of escaping across the near-by border into Canada.

Like so many of his generation he had become a drug user, and this led to his other clash with the law. 'In January of '70,' he relates, 'I got busted for having a fair amount of marijuana, so it was bust with intent to sell. That, plus waiting for the appeal of my draft case, meant I had really painted myself into a corner.' He received six months on the marijuana charge but the authorities kindly allowed him to graduate before he had to turn himself in. 'My mom came out for my graduation. That was the first contact we had had in years. Everyone else was talking about their jobs and graduate studies and traveling in Europe. "What are you going to do?" people asked me. "Well, I'm going to jail next Monday for six months, and after that I'm going to the Federal penitentiary for two years."'

Johnson's subsequent prison career is told briefly in the document that follows.

The 'forty solitary individuals' interviewed by Tollefson for his oral history include selective objectors and draft-file burners as well as religious and humanist pacifists of different shades of belief. (Johnson's pacifism seems rather hard to define but it was enough to see him through.) Some went to prison; others received CO status doing alternative civilian service or serving as non-combatants in the armed forces; still others fled to Canada to evade the draft. They were united by their 'principled opposition to war in Vietnam.' (Though 'many women opposed the war ... none faced military induction,' so that they appear in Tollefson's book only 'in the COs' stories.') The editor preserved anonymity throughout, sometimes though referring to an interviewee by a pseudonym like Johnson. In the stories of the interviewees who were jailed, it is clear that in almost all cases prison made a lasting impression. How indeed could it not?

[I]

I served part of the drug sentence and then got out on probation. Almost immediately, I heard that there were people on campus asking questions about me. I assumed they were FBI, because they looked straight, they were large, and they wore shiny black shoes. I was unofficially and illegally living on college property twenty miles out of town. A few people knew it, but no one would tell them.

At some point, the FBI thought they had notified me to turn myself in on the draft sentence. One day, when I went to see my probation officer, FBI agents jumped out from behind closed doors, handcuffed me, and took me into custody with a new federal charge of being a felony fugitive from justice. My bail was set at $100,000. They were convinced I had left the country or gone underground. My guess is that they also knew I had been involved with helping war resisters go to Canada.

I had hoped to have a few farewell parties, get high one last time, kiss all the girls goodbye, and then go off in a blaze of glory. Instead, I was locked down right back in the same Whatcom County jail where I had been for the marijuana bust.

After a few days there, I was moved to King County jail for two weeks, and then to Rocky Butte jail in Multnomah County in Oregon. Rocky Butte was a hellhole, built at the turn of the century and first condemned as unfit for human habitation in 1946. It was rotting old masonry and brick, with rusty iron bars. On my first night there, I saw one guy have his eye put out and another guy have his jaw broken. I saw a rat run over a guy in the bunk next to mine. In less than two months, I saw people stabbed, I got tear-gassed, and I had a shotgun stuck in my stomach by a guard as I was trying to get away from a riot.

I got clinically depressed. I slept fourteen to sixteen hours a day. When I was awake, I would read or hold a book over my face and try to make believe I wasn't in a giant tank with sixty other prisoners. I withdrew socially, didn't have much of an appetite, lost weight, and didn't exercise. Finally, just after Thanksgiving, 1970, I was transferred to McNeil Island Federal Penitentiary.

My first day at McNeil, I went through rituals to make me less of an individual and more of an animal. My clothes were taken away and I was given standard issue. My head was shaved, I got sprayed for body lice, and I had body-cavity searches. For me, the worst was getting sprayed with insecticide. It was like I was a cow, I was a piece of meat, I was just a slab going down the conveyor belt, getting poked, prodded, and sprayed.

I was scared shitless at McNeil. I didn't want to have anything to do with those bad-ass people. They were bank robbers, father stabbers, and mother rapers. Of course, that was my own misconception, because some of them were just like me, lightweight drug offenders and hippies at the wrong place at the wrong time. A couple of bank robbers had master's degrees in literature and were really great people, enlightened damned-near Buddhists. But I didn't know that then.

Until one evening, when a group of five guys approached my bunk.

One said, 'We know who you are and what you're here for. You may or may not know us and what we are here for. You are trying to do time the hard way. You might as well be in a single cell for as much contact as you've had in this tank of sixty people. You can make a pretty good time out of being here if you lighten up and trust people to communicate.'

'That makes sense, guys,' I said, 'but look around.' I pointed to one guy who was just totally gone, flat-out psychotic and withering away in his bunk. There was another guy with bandages on his wrists from his most recent suicide attempt and still another guy in the bunk below me who had been so depressed and so ill it seemed like he was willing himself to death in front of me. 'Maybe, guys, we'll see,' I said.

Then someone said, 'You probably like to get high, don't you?' At that point, all I imagined was people shooting up, which appalled me. I never liked needles, I never liked opiate addicts, and I was chagrined that here I was in a penitentiary and I could see people shooting up heroin everyday.

Surprisingly, he said, 'Two hundred of us are dropping acid tomorrow. Would you like to join us?'

Well, I did.

I had taken LSD over a hundred times, but that was probably the second or third strongest, highest microgrammage, purest LSD I've ever taken. It was god-awful, mind-melting strong. I went totally bananas. Almost immediately, I went to my bunk and started screaming. I had the good sense to put my face in my pillow so I wouldn't attract the guards. The most intense part of the trip was a vision of a biblical God with flowing beard and hair, who was holding a big book listing every interaction I had ever had in my life. As he flipped the pages, he frowned and muttered and made 'tsk-tsk' sounds. After he turned the last page, he pointed thumbs down. Suddenly an execution squad of prison guards appeared with shotguns, and I was blown away and killed.

God knows how many eons had passed when I felt I was looking out a window that looked like the window that I used to look out when I used to be in prison years and years and years before. I turned to the person in the bunk next to me and said, 'What year is this?'

He laughed and said, 'How long do you think it has been?'

I said. 'Twenty years.'

He said, 'It's been about seven hours. It's still the same day as when you first tripped.'

I looked around and realized then that I really was in prison. I really had made a set of choices to end up sentenced to two years in a federal penitentiary. That moment was a breakthrough, an acceptance. And at that point I decided to make friends.

I never took LSD again in prison. My God, it was way too intense. But about once a month, I'd get together with other guys out in the pasture to share one tiny, thin joint. We'd be high for a whole day because we made so much of it. As I got to know more people, I learned there could be camaraderie in prison. We could play Scrabble and exchange books. We even started a religious and social-awareness discussion group that met weekly with a Lutheran minister from Tacoma named Jeff Smith, who years later became the Frugal Gourmet on TV.

Still, going to prison meant my parents wanted nothing to do with me. My mother and sister were forbidden by my father to write to me or even acknowledge that I existed. My folks had incorporated my sister's boyfriend as my replacement in the family – as the idealized other son. He was even the same age as me. He had gotten engaged to my sister, then he enlisted and went to Nam. Just two weeks before he was supposed to come home, the same week I entered prison, he was killed in action.

[II]

In retrospect, prison was my rite of passage for manhood. True, it was a long adolescence, and true, it wasn't over until my middle twenties. But I made it. I made it.

Towards the end of my time in prison, I really started to push the limits. I was a short-timer getting cocky. I hadn't been beaten up. I hadn't gotten raped. I had survived. Prison was going to be something I would remember for the rest of my life.

Just before my release, I let my hair and my sideburns and my mustache grow out to the max. I didn't want to walk out of prison looking like I had just come out of military drill camp. The prison authorities had to keep telling me to keep my hair within acceptable parameters ...

The last place you muster out of prison is the storeroom, where they keep the civilian clothes of everyone who has come in, all cleaned and hung in racks. You get to pick out a snappy outfit – a suit and a pair of shoes. The majority of stuff was three-piece suits, none of it appropriate for how I wanted to dress. No bell-bottom jeans. No fringed leather vests. But at least I could pick out my own clothes, and they did not look like prison issue. I would walk out looking like I was becoming something other than a prisoner. In a small way, I began to regain my individuality. That was a great feeling.

On the day I left, my buddies threw a party for me in the back of the tank. We smoked three kinds of hash and two types of marijuana and drank two types of wine, literally having a get-down, fucked-up party. The last day in prison, you give away to your best friends any of your possessions – a favorite book, a pillow, a blanket. You have very few material possessions that are yours, so everything has great value, especially if it's one of a kind. People brought presents, like little pieces of jewelry they had made, a ring, or a necklace, and books to exchange. I had commissioned paintings from prisoners who were artists and hung them at the foot of my bunk. I gave away all of them except one, which I still have. It's a painting of the Tibetan word 'om.'

Our cell block was a three-mile drive away from the landing for the boat to the mainland. The driver of the van was outside waiting for me, beeping his horn. He couldn't believe that I wasn't there at the door, waiting to go. The guard had to come back and break up the party. 'I don't believe it, you stupid shit,' he said. 'You're going to miss the boat.' Then he said, 'I'll walk out of here as if I haven't seen what you're doing, and you'd better be on the van in two minutes or you'll spend a lot more time here.' I thought, 'God, let me out of here,' and I ran out in a cloud of smoke. I hopped on the van, and the driver and I laughed all the way to the boat.

The ride across the bay to the mainland was great. The skipper let me captain the boat, so I got to work the wheel and toot the horn and pull up to the dock for my very last time. It was wonderful, commanding an eighty-five-foot boat on my release.

My girlfriend's father, my future father-in-law, was waiting for me. He was active in the Lutheran Church and worked for the homeless a decade before it became a topical issue. He took me back to his family for my first dinner of freedom. He didn't know me well, but he respected what I stood for and he was proud of his daughter for loving me. I remember how good it felt to be accepted by him.

Society puts the squeeze on prisoners. We are at the bottom of the pile, suffering the most pressure. I came out of prison angry and raw ... But, thank God, I didn't come out hating. I didn't hate the guards. I didn't hate the prison administration. Some of them were rotten SOBs. But you can't hate people for their institutional roles. To hate is to trap yourself in a way that perpetuates and gives power and recognition to what you are hating. To not stay stuck in a stifling cycle of embitterment – that's the lesson I learned in prison. The challenge was: could I survive a truly alien environment, a different culture and a different set of societal rules that nothing in my prior background had prepared me for, and still land on my feet and keep running and survive? I could. I did ...

For a long while, I was sure I would never forget my prison number. But one day, a few years after my release, I realized I knew some of the digits, but not the exact pattern. I was amazed, because for so long, nothing could happen in my life unless I used that number.

But I haven't forgotten the feeling of being in prison. In my job today, I go in and out of jails a lot to do mental health evaluations. Every time I hear the sound of the large metal gates clang shut into the concrete walls behind me, I feel a deep reverberation inside myself and I want to yell, 'Let me the hell out of here!'

[III]

My father was a lieutenant during the Second World War. Three boats were torpedoed out from under him. Once, he was missing in action, washed up on an island, and rescued weeks later. He never talked much about it. During the Korean War, he was called up again. He was very patriotic.

My un-American ways really pissed him off. We finally had a horrible scene where he began to choke me in front of Mom. So I had to leave. I walked out of the house and didn't return for nearly six years.

When I was on trial, my folks wanted nothing to do with me. My father was mortified that we had the same name. My going to prison was so antithetical to his world view that the only way he could deal with it for a long time was to act as if I didn't exist.

As time passed in prison, I started corresponding with my parents, telling them about day-to-day life there, and injecting a bit of my radical social perspective. Eventually, my mom came to visit me at McNeil Island. I got to pilot the boat that brought her from the mainland to the prison. I deliberately put the boat sideways in some rolling chop, so both rails went under the water and people got sick. I got in trouble, but I sure had fun. And my mom liked the ride. She knew what I was doing.

Finally, my father came to visit me, too. By that point, he had digested my sister's fiancé's death in Vietnam and he realized that maybe there was some validity to the questions I had asked and the choices I had made. His visit was an acknowledgment that I was still a member of his family and I still had his name. He tried, very haltingly and with great difficulty, to communicate that to me.

The fact that my father came to prison, sat next to me, and acknowledged my existence was a kind of reconciliation, or at least an acceptance of why I did what I did. My father was still horrified by my actions, and he certainly wished I wasn't in jail, but at least he came to some awareness of my reasons for refusing to fight. And I could appreciate his point of view, that going to prison was the last thing I should have done. But from my point of view, it was the only thing I could have done.

Sometimes, today, I really get down on myself. Why the hell did I waste my time in prison twenty years ago? At the time, I thought I was doing something noble and good, but maybe I just threw away nearly two years of my life. But usually I get over that feeling and remember that there are many more people today willing to say 'Wait a minute' before the first bomb is dropped. So I see a glimmer of hope.

Yet I question myself. Since Vietnam, I haven't done a goddamned thing politically. I'm now a father of two, a tax-paying, all-American working stiff ... I worry that people may discount what I say because of the interwoven tapestry of being an outlaw, a hippie, and a drug taker. Drugs did influence my thinking and my perceptions. I make no bones about it. It bothers me that some people will discount what I say. Part of me would like to polish up my story and delete portions of it. But I believe I should put out the whole story – warts, blemishes, tarnishes, and idiosyncrasies. Unless I lay out everything sincerely and honestly, there is no real relationship, no real communication. I am who I am, with all my parts.

My wife says there is no greater act of faith in the future of humanity than getting married and having kids. I do have a strong sense of optimism. I think there are many branchings of alternative realities, perhaps one where there is no life because of thermonuclear war, another where feudal city-states are in a constant state of warfare. Maybe I've read too much science fiction, or perhaps I'm brain-dead from too many drugs. But I sure hope I'm on the pathway that ends in peace, where human beings become an enlightened, collaborative species moving out into the stars.

My children are amazed that bad people are arrested and punished by society. And they say, 'Dad, you don't seem like a bad guy, but you must have been bad if you were in jail.'

'I wasn't really a bad guy,' I tell them. 'But I wasn't the nicest of guys, either.'

Three years ago, when my son was four, as part of my job I had to go to the State hospital, which is just a mile or two away from the boat landing to McNeil Island Penitentiary. I took my son and pointed out the prison where Daddy had been in jail. He said, 'You were in that place? They locked you up?' I told him, 'Yes, that's where I was locked up.' At the time, he didn't say much more about it.

About a year later, he started making up songs. He sang me the first song he made up. It went:

I'm a jailbird.
I'm a jailbird.
They said I was bad.
I wasn't going to be glad.
They locked me away.
I'm a jailbird.

'This song is for you, Dad,' he said.

Source: James W. Tollefson, ed., *The Strength Not to Fight: Conscientious Objectors of the Vietnam War in Their Own Words* (Washington: Brassey's, 2000), 78–80, 176, 178–80, 231–3; see also 47–51, 73–7, 177.

DAVID MILLER

Going to Jail emerged from the collaboration of two men who had challenged the American military establishment and found themselves in prison as a result. Using their own carceral experience as a basis, the authors aimed primarily at providing a 'training manual,' as it were, for Selective Service violators, whose numbers were expected to increase as the Vietnam War dragged on.[1] While Howard Levy had disobeyed military orders not as a pacifist but as a medical ethicist, David Miller had in October 1965 publicly burned his draft card as a conscientious objector whose pacifism was rooted in the movement centring around Dorothy Day and the *Catholic Worker*.[2]

In addition to the topics included below (either under joint authorship or by one or other author), the manual includes a number of other themes like entering prison, food and clothing, correspondence and visiting, recreation and religion, education and medical care, punishment and parole, resistance, and race relations. Almost every page of the book reflects the authors' perceptive observation of prison life. Thus, although their ostensible purpose was a practical one, their finished product fulfils all the prerequisites of a memoir and may, I think, justifiably be regarded as such.

Preface

I am not the same man today that I was on June 2, 1967, when I began to serve time. Twenty-six months in prison change a man.

While serving as a physician in the U.S. Army, I was outspoken in my opposition to the war in Vietnam; I refused a direct order to train Special Forces (so-called) medics. I went to jail because to have obeyed that order would have compelled me to violate canons of medical ethics which were deeply significant to me. David Miller was imprisoned for twenty-two months because he burned his draft card in opposition to the draft and the war in Vietnam. These acts were of the kind which are intensely personal. We were moral witnesses, and our acts, though not entirely without political import, were firmly rooted in individualistic soil.

Prison either breaks or nurtures political prisoners, and while most have not been broken, a few have. ...

Our aim in writing this book was twofold. First, to provide a conceptual framework through which those who have never been in prison can comprehend and then challenge the prison system – a system totally lacking in socially redeeming qualities. Second, to proffer a sort of 'training manual' for prospective political prisoners. Literally millions of Americans, in particular young Americans, are in revolt against the government of the United States. Many of these men and women may unfortunately be going to jail. It seems worthwhile to let them know what to expect, as well as to suggest some guidelines which might allow them to continue their revolt while incarcerated.

This book is, therefore, analytical in tone, ... detached and dispassionate. David and I have indeed referred to our personal experiences, but only for illustrative purposes. We have alluded, occasionally angrily, to various prison administrators. It is not our intent to provide an image of these poorly misguided men as personifications of evil. They, like us, are trapped in an evil system. They have chosen to defend that system; we have elected to transform it.

We have chosen to examine the military and Federal prison systems because we can claim a certain degree of expertise concerning them. At some time or other during our prison careers we have been confined at the United States Disciplinary Barracks, Fort Leavenworth, Kansas; Allenwood Prison Farm Camp, Allenwood, Pennsylvania; and Lewisburg Federal Penitentiary and Farm Camp, Lewisburg, Pennsylvania ...

The Federal prison system is America's model, but that is not saying much. Those concerned with reforming state prisons – and they are pitifully few – often wish to see the Federal system adopted. Our experience has taught us that while this may result in a superficial improvement, it will not approach the ideal: a penal system which deters crime and rehabilitates criminals. Federal prisons do neither; furthermore, although acts of blatant physical brutality are infrequent in the Federal system, that system still cruelly dehumanizes its inmates. Moreover, we are not convinced that physical violence will not be resorted to if Federal authorities think it required to maintain good order and discipline. The Federal government can be ruthless and may well be expected to match the state prison system's brutality blow for blow. For the time being, psychological manipulation suffices, but that should be no cause for rejoicing. If behavioral techniques fail, the whip will be cracked ...

We hope that this book will do justice to the forgotten men behind concrete walls and steel bars. Justice is their due, but for most prisoners it remains a rare commodity indeed.

(Howard Levy)

Going to Jail is not an academic, well-researched exposé of prison life. It is a biased document of opinions, anecdotes, and conclusions drawn from two years' experience in the Federal and military prison systems with the idea of quickly putting these insights into the hands of people who might face a similar experience. We feel strongly about our observations, as the reader shall see ...

There is a distinction made in the following pages between political prisoners and nonpolitical prisoners. The only purpose of this distinction is to provide the reader with a clear idea of the primary focus of the analysis. When the term 'political prisoner' arises, it refers to the roughly three hundred war resisters in prison on any given day. They are the Selective-Service violators, the anti-war GIs, and the draft-file destroyers. Of course, the vast majority of inmates in American prisons are political prisoners in the wider sense of the word. Prisons reflect the class bias of the society which they serve, and the inmates are its victims: it is our continuing responsibility to point out the political nature of the courts and prisons.

Personally, I was not prepared in any real way to deal effectively with my term of imprisonment: there were reasons for this, one, certainly, having to do with my own psychology and experience. But there was more than that. I feel that I – and many other political activists – have been let down by political prisoners before us. As I recall, when speaking with friends and acquaintances who had recently served time, they either gave a superficial appraisal of prison life or they did not want to speak about it at all. I may not be entirely fair to everyone but I think that this was the general trend.

This trend is understandable but it must be overcome. The prison experience is an intensely humiliating experience; prison life is difficult to communicate to people who have not experienced 'total institution' life; one would like to forget about the whole thing; if one is pressured into talking about prison, the focus will most often be on the very bad or the very good; the life style of inmates does not emerge. But if an individual is to survive the prison experience – and perhaps even make some good use of the time served – he *must* gain an appreciation of the life style of prisoners. The daily routine, the mundane details, the minor concerns, the serious problems – these are the things that Howard and I have attempted to set forth in the following pages, if only briefly.

Most of the work for the book was done at the Lewisburg farm camp while Howard and I were there together: we collabaorated closely and thank the prison authorities for putting us together so that we could work to common purpose on something that neither of us probably would have set out upon alone.

(David Miller)

Contraband

I was no exception in the need for contraband to make life a little more pleasant. For the twelve months that a roommate of mine said that I had a cereal 'Jones' (a habit), I possessed a bowl and spoon that I had lifted from the dining hall; I kept them in my locker. At breakfast I would steal a few of the individual-portion boxes of cereal put out. Cheerios and Wheaties were my favorites, but if all they had were Rice Toasties, they had to do. I also stole sugar, which I placed in an empty cereal box. I did not learn the best techniques for 'swagging' these things until after some trial-and-error methods. One morning I came bopping out of the dining hall with half-a-dozen Cheerios under my arm – and ran smack into the farm administrator. Shamefaced, I had to return them to the cereal rack. After doing so, he walked into the dining hall and bragged to the hacks on duty, 'Ha, ha, I just caught Miller with an armload of cereal.' Later, under the careful tutelage of a friend with years of experience at Macy's and Bloomingdale's, I learned to wear a shirt or jacket loosely and tuck the merchandise inside, around my waist. My friend, Marty, commented that I came to the penitentiary as green as a new kid on the block and would leave nickel slick.

After the 8:30 p.m. count at the farm camp, the kitchen was opened to let in the dairy crew that had done the seven o'clock milking. A few others might get in if they, for some reason, had worked late. These inmates were given a bag that normally contained two pathetic sandwiches of a single slice each of something that passed for lunch meat, and a couple of stale cookies: but they were also allowed two large dippers of milk. Depending on the whim of the night hack and his assistants, other inmates could get on the milk line. For one six-month period, the night officer permitted anyone to get milk. So, along with the crowd, I filled a glass jar that I had rescued from the dump, went back upstairs to my room, and ate my cereal. Good things never seem to last very long in prison and the milk ration came to an end. Many hacks are moved around in their jobs every six months precisely in order not to become too familiar with the inmates they work with. When this particular night hack was moved, one inmate made up a card saying that we were sorry to see him go but good luck, etc. I was among those who signed the card. The new night hack was much tighter.

(David Miller)

Rats and Snitches

Every new prisoner must learn to appreciate three things concerning rats and snitches in prison. The first is how to recognize those inmates most likely to be snitches; the second is to realize that one is going to have to live in close personal contact with them; the third is to see how, and the extent to which, the administration uses them.

Don't take anyone in prison at face value. The most militant-looking and tough-rapping prisoner may be the biggest snitch. Although it is not always true, a lot of snitches have the best jobs in each institution: they are the closest to the seat of power and they have 'the ear of the king,' so to speak. A likely snitch can also be spotted by the amount of time he got for a particular crime, if the sentence is much less than it should normally be. For instance, a first bust for selling heroin nets you a 'pound' (five years). If a man comes in with two years for dope, one can guess that he ratted someone out in court. If a man comes in with two or three years for bank robbery or post-office robbery, and his partners got fifteen or twenty, it's a good bet that his testimony in court 'buried' them. In the end, however, one has to rely on a few inmates whose integrity one trusts to point out the snitches; one must also rely on his own experience.

Snitches are despised, but contrary to the movies, the majority of them are not bumped off once they become known; they remain very much alive and kicking. A good number of them may be moved from the penitentiary to the farm camp for safer keeping, but even inside the wall there are plenty of them. Though some are in serious danger of being hurt, most inmates are realistic enough not to want to try and beat a murder charge – even if they would like to kill someone who snitched on them. The result is that snitches go on living: you might end up sleeping right next to one, in which case, at least a few pleasantries have to be exchanged once in awhile, even though this may be repugnant. If you aren't ready to 'call him out,' then you have to live with him. It certainly isn't wise to hang out with a snitch but in the closeness of prison life one finds it necessary to accept the fact that they are almost ever present.

Any time that one inmate snitches on another, that fact is entered in the former's record: there is then a permanent notation of that inmate's cooperation with the authorities. The inmate who has once snitched will be used by prison officials as often as they need him; they know that he will snitch again if they hold something over his head – parole, good time, a new charge, or a few privileges. We recall that one well-known snitch at the farm camp was 'given' a passive homosexual: the latter was allowed to move into his room.

With the 'ground rules,' and depending on what they think they can get away with, prison officials will try to get any inmate to snitch. The sad fact is that there are plenty of inmates ready to cut your throat for the price of a few extra good days, or a telephone call – certainly for a parole. You had better believe that there are cutthroats in the penitentiary, made that way by a cutthroat society. The administration encourages them and uses them ruthlessly. They are not the primary enemy but be wary: not paranoid, but wary.

(David Miller)

Violence [The General Problem]

Violence in prison is a serious and constant threat that all prisoners must live with. There are two kinds of violence, that between inmate and inmate, and that between staff and inmate. We should preface this chapter by saying that both authors – as well as most other political prisoners – have done their entire bits without one physical fight. But although we may have avoided fighting, the fear and the ever present threat of violence was unavoidable. In some ways, the constant state of preparedness was harder on our minds and bodies than actual physical violence might have been.[3]

The amount of prison violence would be hard to guess: perhaps it is no greater than it is in any other situation – especially in our cities. There might be several murders and stabbings a year, along with several fights every few weeks. But the near misses, the verbal fights, the times that tremendous urges toward violence are suppressed by sheer will power – these would be impossible to tabulate. One of the most amazing things about prison is the seemingly successful suppression of enormous frustrations and destructive urges: it is a very unhealthy but very necessary suppression. No inmate can afford to go around fighting all the time if he wants to survive. He who does has the label 'no understanding' applied to him ...

Homosexuality

Different institutions pose different problems. An adult penitentiary (i.e., Lewisburg) differs from a youth institution (i.e., Petersburg or El Reno). In the adult penitentiary, the approaches are more sophisticated than at the youth institutions. The experienced adults have developed the combination technique more effectively, whereas at the youth institutions the hard sell prevails. However, there are advantages to this. If the newcomer acts quickly and decisively the danger is over sooner, because the young men at these institutions are less accomplished and less persistent than penitentiary prisoners.

The minimum-security farm camps pose the least threat of all. In the case of a young political prisoner, once he reaches the farm or prison camp where he will find other political prisoners of his own age, the danger is almost nonexistent. Only if a particular individual is extremely naive will any difficulty develop. This does not, of course, imply that the sexually torturing atmosphere behind the wall is not also operative at the farm camps: it most assuredly is. The danger is less but the sexual agony is the same on all levels of imprisonment.

In relating the whole question of prison homosexuality to political prisoners we would like to list and describe various factors that conspire to make many political prisoners potential targets for homosexual advances. We would then like to offer some advice on how to deal with them.

The first factor is that most political prisoners are young. Being young in prison is of itself tantamount to being sexually attractive. A concomitant of the attractiveness of youth is the aura of inexperience that is associated with youth. The inexperience of political prisoners with prison life seems more noticeable than is the inexperience of young prisoners convicted of other crimes. The latter are more likely to be wise in the ways of the street and are more likely to put up a defense of violent self-assertiveness. Political prisoners, in comparison, tend to be gentle, and do not project a super-masculine image of toughness. To be both young and gentle is to be in danger.[4]

A second factor is the candor that these prisoners tend to exhibit. Political prisoners are polite, intelligent, articulate, and usually pleased to explain their position and actions to anyone who will listen, or to anyone who questions them. Politics and religion are their business. These brought them to prison and because of that it is felt that an explanation is due. Bank-robbing needs no similar defense; it is self-explanatory. But in prison there is a danger in being too candid. New inmates are sized up by established prisoners very quickly. First impressions are lasting, and an initial blunder may be costly in terms of the problems it may engender, conceivably, for the duration of one's confinement. Being too open and talkative is usually considered a come-on by aggressive homosexuals.

A third factor is the independence generally exhibited by most political prisoners. The independence we speak of is a tendency, almost a practice, not to identify strongly or quickly with a particular clique. Hillbillies hang out with one another, narcotics pushers talk to each other about the business of selling dope, inmates who were involved in so-called organized crime associate with one another, block 'homies' (men from the same city or town), those from Washington or New York stick together, etc. The political prisoner, on the other hand, tends to be, though affable, more of a loner. But there is a danger in being a loner because a loner sticks out; in more practical terms, the loner finds it more difficult to protect himself.

A fourth factor specifically concerns the manner by which white political prisoners relate to the black-liberation struggle. White political prisoners tend to be sympathetic to that struggle and on occasion, a black aggressive homosexual can use the white political prisoner's sympathy as an inroad to a homosexual relationship. This is especially likely to occur when naïveté outstrips clear thinking. The point must be starkly presented: it is dangerous in the first stages of imprisonment for a young white prisoner to associate freely with black inmates. If a young white prisoner is seen fraternizing extensively with black inmates, and especially if he is seen talking with well-known black homosexuals, the majority of white inmates is preconditioned to believe the worst. As a matter of fact, some black inmates will themselves interpret what may essentially be an inexperienced liberal attitude as being an overture for protection. If one flaunts his pretentious liberal attitudes, and eats and talks with black inmates, he will only get himself in trouble; in fact, black inmates couldn't care less about eating with him. The response will most likely be the same as that received by one political prisoner in the penitentiary: he was approached by a brother who said, 'I hear you're a nigger lover, prove it.' This response is less of a reflection on the brother and more of a reflection on the inexperience and poor judgment of the white inmate.

The fifth factor is the inability or reluctance of many political prisoners to act decisively and forcefully in the face of homosexual advances. There may be many reasons for this outlook but it must be realized that to vacillate or to appear hesitant only serves as an invitation.

It is clear that a young prisoner cannot alter his age, but he *can* be more self-conscious about his person. For example, a young prisoner simply cannot afford to allow himself to project any characteristic that might be considered effeminate: this includes forms of posture, speech, and grooming. Experienced prisoners have an uncanny ability to size up new prisoners. Because of the perverted situation in which many inmates affect an exaggerated masculinity, effeminacy stands out immediately. The novice must realize that what is not noticed on the outside, such as long hair, may be seized upon as an indication of homosexuality in prison.

In the case of a passive homosexual who clearly flaunts effeminate characteristics, he is immediately spotted. If such an individual swishes into the county jail or the A&O [admission and orientation] section of the penitentiary, the chances are very high indeed that he will be approached and taken to bed by one, and often by more than one, inmate before his first night is over. Word of the 'new homo' spreads like wildfire and the effeminate passive homosexual has little chance against the odds he faces. It seems that resignation is the usual course taken by these individuals, with the hope that a better arrangement can be worked out later on.

The young prisoner, who in lieu of a shortage of passive homosexuals might face advances himself, is well advised to acquire a good degree of modesty about his body. He should dress and undress quickly, and not hang around the shower room, but shower with dispatch, preferably when the shower room is least crowded. If he does not mind his ass, somebody else will.

It sometimes happens in the penitentiary that political prisoners get themselves into a jam. By making any one of the mistakes touched upon, they find themselves in situations that they have to get out of fast. Such situations develop most frequently in the A&O section of the penitentiary and in the 'jungle' dormitories where some political prisoners spend a few weeks before going to the farm camp. At such times one of the most commonly employed means of extricating oneself from a possible jam is by checking into the segregation unit. This can be done in a number of ways: one can refuse to report to work, one can tell the lieutenant that he is being bothered and wants out, one can have a friend tell the lieutenant for him. *Under no circumstances* do we advise anyone to point out to prison officials those specific individuals who might be making threats, nor do we advise that anyone threaten an inmate with such a report. But if a situation seems to have gotten out of hand, and if the prisoner thinks that he can't handle it, then he should feel no shame and make no hesitation in checking into segregation. However, our hope is that future political prisoners will be wise enough *not* to get themselves into jams. Also, if the first time an advance is made, one acts as if he is ready to 'bust some motherfuckin' ass,' that is, in our opinion, better than having to check into segregation.

The candor that most political prisoners exhibit must be significantly curtailed. We do not suggest that one make a practice of insulting people, but we do say that one must be wary, uncommunicative, and sometimes rude with a majority of inmates. As the political inmate becomes jail-wise, he can alter this approach, but in the beginning it is necessary. It may seem strange at first but one must discipline oneself so as to ignore a large number of people with whom one is in close physical proximity. We mean that it is sometimes necessary to avert one's eyes from direct eye contact with other inmates, and avoid visual as well as verbal communication. *Friendly attitudes just will not do.*

Group solidarity must be substituted for independence. At almost every Federal institution, there are several political prisoners. The novice and the established political prisoner must seek one another out. They should dine together, spend leisure time together, and rap together. The established political prisoner must awaken the novice to the major aspects of life in the institution. Among other things, the novice must have pointed out, for his benefit, those inmates with whom it might be dangerous to associate. If there are no political prisoners around, the novice should find the next safest groups of inmates to associate with. These would be the white-collar criminals, potheads, acid heads, and select JW's [Jehovah's Witnesses]. However, trying to categorize 'safe' groups is risky. Decisions must be made individually, and with one's eyes open.

In avoiding possible homosexual advances, there are two groups of inmates one should take special pains to sidestep. They are the notorious aggressive homosexuals and the obvious passive homosexuals. We have tried to make it clear why one should avoid the former, but there are also good reasons to avoid the latter as well. Most political prisoners do not feel compelled to hate passive homosexuals. On the contrary, liberal, humanitarian, civil-libertarian views tend to make political prisoners sympathetic to their plight, and often lead to attempts to befriend them: this is risky on two counts. One might be accused of trying to mess with someone else's 'woman'; or, one may be placed in the same category by virtue of guilt by association. We were acquainted with one political prisoner who had his face slapped by an aggressive homosexual simply because he had quite innocently said 'hello' while passing the homosexual's 'woman' in the hallway. He was accused of having tried to get a 'piece of the action.'

Finally, there is an aspect of the homosexual scene called 'blocking.' Blocking means that a third party deliberately moves between a homosexual advancer and his object. This is done by rapping, eating, and taking recreation with the intended trick, while the advancer is trying to do the same in the hope of making a score. Blocking is a dangerous pastime, especially in the penitentiary. Someone blocking a potential score may find himself in a worse jam than the score is in. But the authors' experience has shown that a limited form of blocking is necessary if experienced political prisoners are to protect some of the more naive new ones. Even at the farm camps blocking may be required, especially if word gets around that a newly arrived young man had 'trouble' inside the penitentiary. When it may become necessary to do some blocking, it has to be done with caution and in a very cool manner: one must take pains to act as if he is not aware of what he is doing.

If the above cautions are heeded, it is hoped that homosexual advances can be avoided altogether; that is best, by far. But if such advances do occur, it is important to meet them forcefully and decisively. Curt, even hostile, remarks are in order. 'No, man. You must be crazy.' 'Get out of my face.' 'You can try whatever you want if you want your head busted.' If possible, one may be able to turn the situation around by making a joke; a joke helps the other guy save face. That is, it doesn't put him in the position, necessarily, of having to respond to a counter-threat or else back down. At the same time, a good joke gives the impression that one is not as naive as he looks and that he would fight if pressed. One might smile and say, 'Sure, man, you can have all the ass you want after I stick my dick in *your* cakes. Tit for tat, right?'

Our experience has shown us that verbal and physical force, in response to aggressive homosexual advances, has almost always ended successfully for the intended victim. The aggressor was not beaten; he was repulsed and went away. He may have said, 'This isn't the end. I'll get you later.' But if he and his friends were subsequently studiously avoided by the intended victim, the latter would usually be left alone after that. A grudge or bad feelings may have been held for a time, but in due time even they dissipate. One does not have to be a killer to ward off these advances. A show of force is usually sufficient. If extreme trouble occurs, we recommend that the individual defend himself physically, but we wish to emphasize that a physical defense is a last resort. Inmates should, whenever possible, avoid fighting with one another. Inmate fights mainly benefit the prison authorities, and weaken the likelihood that inmate solidarity against their common oppressor will develop.

This brings us to our final consideration, the role of the administration in prison homosexuality. The prison officials' role is crucial and determinant since it is they who possess the power.

Officially, consenting homosexual relations are forbidden by prison regulations. At the USDB [United States Disciplinary Barracks], even masturbation is forbidden. Needless to say, forced homosexual relations are also forbidden and may be punished by law. But the official position of the administration, and their protestations to the effect that they are combating the problem, do not correspond with their real practices and desires.

The more notorious passive homosexuals are usually quartered in a specific cell block, where supposedly they can be watched more closely. Periodically, consenting homosexuals may be busted if they are too indiscreet, or if a tightening of the strings is deemed necessary. They might lose some good time and perhaps, temporarily, some other privileges. In the case of homosexual rape, it is the practice of the prison administration to admit as little as possible. If they can, they will try to discredit the reputation of the *victim*. They may allege that he was always a passive homosexual and invited the attack. If the administrators cannot do that, they will do everything they can to see to it that 'rape' cases are never brought into Federal court, where the lights burn too brightly.

Often, the prison authorities will admit that homosexuality exists in prison but that it is hard to deal with and eradicate; they say that it is difficult to detect and hence, control. When asked specifically about the problems of young prisoners, they say that they have no idea who may or who may not have problems. We do not buy the administration line. Our experience has brought us to the conclusion that the administrators profit by the perverted and poisonous atmosphere which they themselves maintain. We further believe that they consciously use the exploitable homosexual atmosphere to further their own ends.

To begin with, the prison administration is thoroughly committed to punishment by sexual deprivation. It is the single most important component of our punitive and vindictive prison system. Secondly, the administration allows the homosexual vigilante aura to exist because it acts as a threat to inmates. Specifically, the jungle dormitories of every penitentiary are used by officials to threaten and intimidate prisoners with homosexual rape. When the prison officials place a young prisoner, political or not, in the jungle, they are saying in effect, 'Go ahead men, see what you can do with him.' It may not serve the administration's purpose to have a young prisoner actually assaulted but the *threat* of rape does serve its purpose. It induces all inmates, especially the younger, less apathetic ones, to cooperate, to get out of the jungle and stay out. The message is, 'Keep in line, boy, or lose your ass.' Finally, preoccupation with their sexual frustration acts to divert the prisoners from confronting the enemy – the prison administration. It also plays havoc with inmate solidarity, because some inmates are forced to prey upon other inmates. As a result, all inmates must be on guard against being taken advantage of.

One final fact that liberals, radicals, and revolutionaries must appreciate is that a simple exposé of the problem – including proof of homosexual rape attempts – is not enough. The administration is ruthless. In order to appease and mollify public opinion, it will punish unmercifully the alleged homosexual attackers who are themselves victims and who have been severely punished in the first place by the penal system. The exposé approach, in the absence of concomitant legal and political pressure, simply results in punishment for *all* the victims. The enemy – the prison Establishment – is left virtually unconfronted.

There is a position with which the authors are familiar and that should be raised in this chapter. It concerns those political activists who are homosexuals and who, finding themselves in prison, think they should take an open stand on the issue while there. These men say that fulfilling sexual desires greatly increases one's ability to deal with the dehumanizing life of prison; they say that an open stand on homosexuality is a better political position than hiding it.

However, homosexual activity in prison is contrary to regulations. If inmates are caught in such activity, or if they are ratted upon by other inmates, the 'culprits' can lose good time and a reasonable chance for parole. They can be put in segregation, conceivably for long periods of time, if they are constant offenders. Redress to the courts for these rights does not seem to help. ... It is clear, therefore, that even if an individual admits and defends his homosexuality among inmates and staff, actual participation must be pursued in secret – or one must be prepared for further punishment. A very important consideration that must be taken into account is that known homosexuals, i.e., those who have been caught, are not given the opportunity of residing at the farm camps: they are kept behind the walls of the penitentiary or the correctional institute. If inmates at a farm camp are caught in homosexual activity, they are busted back to the wall.

We have indicated that passive homosexuals are held in derision by the vast majority of inmates. As a rule, they find themselves the prey of tough, sexually deprived inmates. But we want to make clear that passive homosexuals do not necessarily face constant, unwanted, and adverse attention: some are constant prey but others are not. Two inmates come to mind: the first a slight, thin brother in his early thirties who bore exaggerated feminine affectations – he was a freewheeling 'home' who played the field. But it was clear from all accounts that this inmate called his own shots. He was a tough-minded but exuberant person with a strong personality. A comment by another inmate that stuck in our minds was, 'You better believe that ——— can take care of "herself."' About the second, we heard the following story. A big, muscular inmate approached him and intimidated him into performing homosexual relations. At a not much later date the offended individual went up to his attacker while the latter slept and with three razor blades between the fingers of a clenched fist ran them down the man's face. No one bothers that passive homosexual anymore. This may be just a 'prison story' but the spirit of it is true. Along with the description of the man we know, it brings home our point. It *is* possible for a passive homosexual in prison to avoid exploitation; but it is a hard row to hoe. Both of the men above can defend themselves, but they seem to be exceptions. Most of the homosexuals we know both in and out of prison are not determined enough to be able to 'control their own bodies' in a prison setting.

However, if homosexual militancy continues to grow, then the political activist, who may also be a militant homosexual, may be sufficiently prepared to deal openly with the issue of homosexuality if he finds himself in prison. Militant homosexuality, prepared verbally and physically to defend itself, is a good and important development. If it can be done successfully in prison, we think that it is better – psychologically *and* politically – for all concerned that homosexuality be placed out in the open and defended.

(The following addendum is by David Miller.)
When I came through Lewisburg the first time, I was in a low frame of mind. The walled penitentiary was imposing. In A&O I was apprehensive when night came. I heard inmates talking about 'taking people off,' and stayed awake in my bunk until 3:00 or 4:00 a.m. What actually happened that night was that eight or ten inmates took turns in bed with a tall, thin brother who had arrived that day. I don't know whether the brother encouraged them or was pressured into it; he possessed many of the 'feminine' affectations of speech and posture that make such an individual an immediate target of aggressive homosexuals. I was shipped out to Allenwood in a few days. There was not much danger of physical homosexual attack there and my fears receded quickly. It wasn't until seven months later, when I was transferred back to the penitentiary, that I ran into trouble. One might have expected that in seven months, even at Allenwood, I would have gained enough insight not to fall into any traps. Unfortunately, that was not so.

Back at the penitentiary I was quartered in a dreary basement dormitory called K-1. We had to look up to see the sidewalk outside. It wasn't quite a 'jungle' dormitory but it wasn't far from it. I was put to work in the kitchen, first in the dish room, then wiping tables and mopping. I had decided to work and to live in 'population' instead of refusing work and going into segregation, even though there were a dozen political prisoners already there. I knew I wouldn't be put in with them even if I refused work, and I wanted to avoid, if possible, a transfer out of the area, to Sandstone, Minnesota, for instance. I was in the population at Lewisburg for a month; trouble developed during that time because of my naïveté and also because I was a victim of circumstances. I made several mistakes and I had mistakes made for me.

I tended to stay alone a lot and didn't bother to seek out one or two 'rap partners' to hang around with. I was too friendly with black inmates, even though I didn't hang out with any in particular. (I got to know black inmates right away because I started playing both intramural and all-star basketball, and the vast majority of the basketball players were black.) Often I would get on the black line in the dining hall. I was also too friendly with the black passive homosexual working in the same section of the dining hall as I; and he was the most sought after passive homosexual in the joint. But the associations that were the source of the most trouble were with two young, white, Selective-Service violators. One was an introverted quiet guy from the D.C. area, at Lewisburg for a ninety-day psychiatric-observation period before going back to court for sentencing. The psychiatric-observation cases are kept behind the wall, and are usually quartered in one of the jungle dormitories; it was a bad place for this young man to be. The second Selective-Service violator was also from the D.C. area. He was in A&O and I saw him in the dining hall and at yard time. Both of these men were harassed, often by aggressive homosexuals, almost from the day they each came to the penitentiary. To associate with them conspired to make me into a target.

A brother who was moving in on the quiet guy (although I didn't know it at the time), approached me and asked me if I knew him. I said I did. He said that a lot of guys were talking about him and that it would be a good idea if I hung out with him more – as a kind of protection for him. I said that I would, not appreciating that it was part of a setup. A partner of this brother also approached me and said the same thing. He added that some guys had expressed interest in me, too, and did I know how to handle that. I said yes, *still* not appreciating what was going on, nor how to handle it. At another point the latter asked if I would meet him at the movies. I didn't; the movies are a notorious homosexual rendezvous.

I found myself, a day or two later, having a talk with these two brothers. Their game was as follows: I was putting them in a bad spot; they said that they were being pressured from some guys who wanted to take me off; but those guys would lay off if these two and I let it be known that we had an 'arrangement.' They put in a few scare stories about being ripped off, like how bad it was at Marion (the penitentiary). They made up an idiotic story about how some guys thought I was a snitch because I was sent back to the penitentiary and then, right after that, twelve political prisoners were sent back too. I told them that I wasn't interested in an arrangement. I started to tell them something about myself and to ask them about themselves but soon realized that it was ridiculous. I finally said there was no arrangement and that I would think of a way to avoid any rip off. They didn't think I could avoid it, and we parted on that 'cordial' note.

I didn't sleep well that night. I had gotten myself into a jam. I wasn't sure about fighting if it came to that; I still did not think in terms of violent self-defense. Anyway, it seemed that the odds were against me – the lies that these guys were spreading seemed to have taken hold. I decided to avoid the trouble by going to segregation, so in the morning I refused to go to work in the kitchen. Instead, I sat down in front of the gate at the control center that leads to the associate warden's offices, and sang a freedom song. (I didn't have to go through the sit-in thing to get locked up but I did it anyway.) In five minutes I was carried to the hole by several hacks. One called me a lot of names to try to get me to react so that the others would have an excuse to beat me. I didn't react and was sent up to the segregation unit on the third floor.

Meanwhile, the second young draft-resister had already gone to segregation and subsequently had been shipped out to Allenwood: he had been even more naive than I. Guys in A&O would offer him a full pack of cigarettes after he had tried to bum only one – and he would take the pack. One guy tried to force him to the floor in the john but he held his ground successfully, without hitting back, and the guy gave up. He told me at dinner that he was going to be moved that afternoon from A&O to E-1, a jungle dorm. I told him that that wasn't a bright prospect, and he said that somebody had to confront the situation. Fortunately, a friend of his told the lieutenant on duty that this young man was having trouble. After the 10:00 p.m. count, a hack went to E-1 and fetched him. After being in segregation for a day, he was sent to Allenwood.

The other Selective-Service violator did not fare as well. A week or so after I went to segregation I heard that the quiet guy had been forced into relations with a group of ten inmates, and was now in the hospital. I was saddened and angry. Evidently, he had not seen the situation building up as it had. He didn't take the necessary step of getting out of it by going to segregation; maybe he hadn't realized or had refused to admit to himself the seriousness of the situation. Later, when he went back to court for sentencing, this incident and the report of the psychiatrist saved him from a prison sentence: he was given probation. But it was a hard way to get out of prison.

I stayed in segregation for a month. Locked in a cell twenty-four hours a day except for a shower once a week and for visits from my wife, I read (a few books floated around the segregation unit) and sang country songs with a couple of guys in cells near mine. I intended to stay there for two months, then ask to be sent to the farm outside the wall or transferred to another joint. I knew they wouldn't send me back to Allenwood; certainly, it was highly unlikely. But before I requested anything, an associate warden called me to his office and said that he had gotten a call from a friend of mine on the outside asking if I had 'trouble' with other prisoners at Lewisburg. (I was annoyed because I didn't ask anyone to do that for me; the person did it on his own, probably after talking with my wife.) I didn't admit to anything in front of the associate warden [AW], but I did say that I was willing to work if I were sent to the farm camp, and that I preferred not to be put back in population. Which, translated, meant that I would sooner be transferred anywhere than live and work in the population at that time. The AW was not stupid and knew the reason I didn't want to return to population, even though I didn't admit it. He asked if I had heard about the young man who had been physically assaulted. I said yes. He said it was terrible and I agreed. Then he tried to get me to agree that the men who did it were 'animals.' Two days later, after more than a month in segregation, I was moved to the farm camp.

When I arrived, I immediately sought out Howard Levy and [another war resister] Donald Baty. I knew that they were there since I had met them when they came 'through the wall.' I caught up with them at suppertime. That evening I ran the whole thing down to them, and from then on hung out nearly exclusively with Howard and Don, except of course during working hours. I carved out my niche with the two white political prisoners at the camp, and avoided almost every other inmate or cut conversations short if begun. It was necessary for me to do this at that time, since I had to regain my standing. I was aware that some dudes were talking behind my back, but because I was uncommunicative and hung out only with Howard and Don, the talk faded. It took less than a month for this unfavorable attention to be neutralized. After that, I found my place, and I could be more relaxed and move more freely among the inmates. What Howard and Don offered was group status – which is more powerful than a lone man, no matter how much of a killer he may be. I gained that status in a short time. But I was aware that I had had to work for it and could not make any more mistakes.

Soon I had acquired all of the affectations and attitudes necessary. I knew how to be cool and curt, and how to side-step those inmates who were dangerous – especially inside the wall; I knew how to give and take and roll with the jokes about who was going to suck whose dick and who was going to put his foot up whose ass; I knew which inmates *not* to joke with. I went back inside the wall many times, mainly to play intramural and all-star basketball, but also for visits and to attend college-seminar classes. I didn't go back inside on a regular basis until several months after going to the farm camp, when the basketball season rolled around. I noticed some talk at first but it disappeared quickly because I 'carried' myself much differently than before. The combination of in-group status, carrying myself better, being a good dude and minding my business, and being a 'smoker' on the court proved to eliminate any further trouble.

It is clear that there are differing kinds of help and advice that certain political prisoners need. The two young men inside the wall at Lewisburg could have been given no advice other than to check into segregation and go to the farm camp: it would not have worked for one or two political prisoners inside the wall to hang around with these men to protect them from unwanted advances – that would have jeopardized everyone. The two inmates in question were too naive at the time to help themselves, and they couldn't adapt fast enough to be able to deal successfully with penitentiary life: they simply had to get out. Other political prisoners might be heading for trouble but a few words of advice and redirection on whom to associate with would usually be sufficient in order for them to side-step potential difficulties. This was the case with me after I learned what was up.

Later, the roles changed. I was a member of the in group, and another political prisoner and I took each new political prisoner that came to the camp under our wing. There was one young man who came out to the camp several weeks before I was released; he had had trouble in the wall, and it was well known. A brother at the camp, a very gregarious person, came up to me and suggested that I take this new guy under my wing, that he was really a good kid; I was doing it anyway. Whenever I heard that a new political prisoner had arrived inside the wall, I did my best to get inside and see him as soon as possible. For as long as we had to talk – whether in the yard or at lunch – I hipped him to the prison scene, including advice on homosexual advances. Most of them would say 'Yeah, yeah' – but I didn't think that it had sunk in. I found it difficult to communicate the necessary survival techniques to guys who had not been well prepared enough before coming to prison.

I knew that they would be hardened by the end of their bits, but I wanted to help them avoid a long, stormy road. A few times, however, I received word that so and so had checked into segregation and was shipped to Allenwood the next day. Certainly, the hipping and hardening process should start before prison.

Work

While in prison, I held five different jobs. At Allenwood I was on the general farm detail and also on a construction detail; at the penitentiary I worked in food service; at the farm camp outside the penitentiary I worked on the general farm crew as well as in the power plant. I never did any more than I had to, and always carried a book or periodical small enough to conceal so that I could take every opportunity to R&R (rest and read).

The job that I'll remember for a long time to come was at Lewisburg while on the farm crew. First, there was the cabbage patch: several of us spent weeks hoeing a couple of acres of cabbage that had gotten completely out of hand; later we harvested. We worked as slowly as possible, and sat down as soon as the detail officer drove away to check something else. Ray, an ex-marine and gifted gold-bricker, Jimmy King, a brother from Newark, Jerry, a frustrated soccer player from Baltimore, and I played football with cabbages, usually kicking field goals which Jerry won. But the worst of it was the potato patch.

There were sixteen acres of potatoes. When harvested and stored in the root cellar at the rear of the penitentiary, they would last the institution for three months. The potato digger turned the earth over and laid the potatoes on the ground. We had to pick them by hand with buckets, fill 100-pound bags, and transport them to the root cellar. The whole job could have been done in less than two weeks; we worked so hard at avoiding work that we managed to stretch the job over a two-month period. It was excruciating, and incredibly boring, but we were determined. We sat down whenever the hack was out of sight; we played games: throwing a bucket high in the air and trying to hit it with potatoes before it hit the ground; we threw potatoes at one another's feet, saying, 'Dance, motherfucker!' We were so slow that frost got two rows of potatoes before we got them into the cellar.

One advantage that I had on the farm crew was to tend the little vegetable garden next to our tool- and tractor-sheds. With seeds and plants provided by a hack, we had three dozen tomato plants, a dozen bell pepper plants, two dozen hot pepper plants, a few rows of cucumbers, and some watermelon and cantaloupe hills. I watered and hoed and protected against thieves as much as possible; and I saw to it that each man got his share of the produce.

My favorite pastime during working hours – when I could manage it – was fishing. If the hack was working with a couple of inmates on a tractor or if he left us alone for a while in the farm shop, I would walk down the road 100 yards to a creek that ran adjacent to the reservation the penitentiary was on. I had a few hooks and some line that an inmate on the grounds crew found alongside the creek, and I dug worms next to the creek. I caught rock bass, sunfish, and bullheads. They were pan-size, but it would have been too much of a hassle to clean them and cook them on a hot plate back at camp. (It was a different story in the winter with the pheasants.) In the spring, the carp come up the creek to spawn, and feed close to the shore line. I speared a six-pounder – with a silage fork. On a later try I threw the silage fork too far and it still lies on the bottom of the creek.

The last job I had in prison was at the power plant just outside the penitentiary wall. I requested a transfer out of the farm crew as soon as the weather turned cold since I saw that instead of letting us sit by the pot-bellied stove in the farm shop, as he should have done, the detail officer intended to get us out in the cold to cut brush. I didn't want any part of that and asked for an indoor job. For the last four months of my sentence, I cleaned the basement of the power plant. (I don't like the look of electric floor brushes anymore.) Again, I turned a two-week into a two-month job: it was truly 'make-work.'

(David Miller)

Short Time

There is a period of time toward the end of a term of imprisonment when an inmate is called a 'short-timer.' The term may be applied to anyone with less than ninety days to go, although sometimes a prisoner may not be greeted by his fellows with, 'Hello short-timer,' until he has less than sixty days to go. But without question, if one has less than thirty days left to serve, he will think of himself by no other name than 'short-timer.'

The period of short time has specific problems and anxieties peculiar to it, missing or less apparent at other times. On the one hand, short time is a relief: you know that you've got them beat. The time is over.

You've done the bit and you're ready to go home. Friends might say, 'Well, ya got it licked, kid. This is it.' Unfortunately, it is not *quite* it. There remain a month or two of imprisonment: time seems to stand still. It is quite common during these last days to develop exaggerated fears of being busted on some account, losing a lot of good time, and thereby prolonging one's imprisonment.

There also lurks in the back of the mind of a short-timer the nagging suspicion that maybe the authorities are never going to let him out! After being in prison for a few years or longer, the routine becomes so embedded as to make one think, 'Was it ever any different than this?' It's hard to imagine oneself anywhere else *except* in prison: it's a chilling feeling, we guarantee.[5]

During the last sixty days of an inmate's sentence, every institution has some sort of pre-release program. It usually consists of half-a-dozen hour-long meetings. At these meetings, films are shown on subjects like VD and safe driving habits. At one meeting, a parole officer is available to answer questions about parole supervision on the street. The pre-release program is a sham, and is hardly given passing notice by the staff that runs it. Sometimes the person in charge of a particular meeting simply fails to show up.

But if the prison administration does not give a damn about the inmates, the inmates themselves should, because readjustment to liberty after many months or years in prison is no joke. Whether it is conscious or not, short time causes serious anxieties about how one is going to make it again on the outside. The most common revolve around the pressures of earning a living and readjusting to a wife and children. If work and family life were anywhere near problematic before prison, they may be insurmountable after release. The alienation that prisoners feel is clear to many. Less clearly understood is the bitterness and alienation that occurs within an inmate's family during its struggle during the enforced separation. Both the inmate and his family feel this, and short time – provided wife and children are still waiting – heightens the anxieties for both.

Some men become so upset at the prospect of facing the streets again that they seem to deliberately get into trouble either immediately before release or shortly thereafter. Inmates like this strike us as the ostensible 'successes' of the penal system, as that system is constituted to function. Everyone in prison is humiliated and made into dependent beings. Those who finally become so demoralized as to be unable to deal with their freedom for more than a few months at a time (between bits) must make many prison administrators and employees feel complete satisfaction at the thought that their jobs are secure.

A personal account by one of the authors [David Miller] might illuminate the anxieties of short time:

A little over a month before I was released, my wife and our children came to visit me at Lewisburg as they had, two or three times a month, since I had been there. The three hours' visiting time per month was usually divided into three separate visits; with two children, aged three and one, an hour in a crowded room was all they could take anyway. (Visiting is difficult at best. Catherine said that coming to the penitentiary to visit often produced in her what she called 'Federal diarrhea.')

When she and our daughters arrived at 9:00 a.m. they were forced to wait until 10:30. For inmates at the farm camp, like me, the procedure runs: the officer on duty in the visiting room calls the farm camp and an officer there locates and transports the inmate to the back gate of the penitentiary. He then goes inside the penitentiary, gets an officer to take him to the visiting room, and is strip-searched before going into the visiting room. All this takes about fifteen minutes. There was no excuse for my not being called promptly; it was simply harassment. Such delays are not uncommon when inmates are out of favor with the hacks, or when visitors are those whom the hacks dislike. Catherine fell into the latter category and I into the former.[6]

The children became restless and so did Catherine as time passed and I didn't show. She went down the hall to the warden's office to ask for me. She was upset, but asked the warden in a civilized tone the reason for the delay. He replied that he didn't know where I was and ventured that perhaps I was hiding – that I might be playing games with them. It was a tactless, ridiculous statement and Catherine became very upset. She shouted, the children cried, and Catherine cursed the warden in front of visitors and hacks.

I got to the visiting room about that time and was subsequently able to calm the situation down. Catherine and the children and I visited for a time and then they left. I was called into the associate warden's office after the visit – as I knew I would be. I had assured Catherine (and it proved true) that they would not do anything to me since I had not done anything out of line. The associate warden advised me that Catherine was to be refused permission to visit in the future. He indicated that if she made an apology, in writing, to the warden the matter might be rethought: I was to inform her of this in a letter. I wrote that evening and told her several things: that I had not been punished, that she was not going to be allowed in without an apology, that I did not think she would or that she should apologize, that I was not worried about the visiting because I had only four or five weeks to go, and that I would worry more if she came up to the penitentiary and tried to get in than if we simply forgot about visiting for the remainder of the time. Since there was no way to communicate other than by mail, I had to be frank even though I knew the letter would be read by the associate warden.

The day after I mailed the letter was February 26. (I was scheduled to be released on March 27.) While at work at the power plant that afternoon, one of the officers came to me and said that I had to go back to the dorm and pack my things, that I was going home the next day. He had gotten a call from the farm dormitory officer who, in turn, had gotten a call from someone in the penitentiary.

I was surprised and pleased – to say the least! I went back to the dorm, started shaking people's hands, then packed the things I wanted to take home. Driven to the back gate of the penitentiary with my belongings, I proceeded to the R&D (Receiving & Discharge) section. The R&D officer expected me and told the inmate workers to rush me through 'dress out' because I was going home the next day. A few minutes later, in the middle of trying on a pair of pants, the R&D officer came and said that I need not rush after all: he just got a call that it was all a mistake. I was going home next month, not this one.

I went back to the farm dorm and told the story to my friends. They didn't believe it at first, but after a while they did; everyone thought that it was a pretty mean trick, and a reprisal for what Catherine had said the day before in the visiting room. Most of the inmates already knew of that incident through the fast-traveling prison 'wire.' I don't know whether it was reprisal or not: it's difficult in prison at times to distinguish between incompetence and baseness. But whichever it was, it did tend to make me a bit anxious during the last days. It was nothing too difficult to overcome, but the nagging suspicion that they might never let me out became a little more pronounced beause of the 'mistake.'[7]

Notes

Source: Howard Levy and David Miller, *Going to Jail: The Political Prisoner* (New York: Grove Press, [1970]), vii–xii, 32, 33, 117–19, 145–63, 214–16, 221–5.

1 Cf. the advice to conscientious draft-law violators on the best way to do 'good time,' given two years earlier by Arlo Tatum and Joseph S. Tuchinsky in their *Guide to the Draft* (Boston: Beacon Press, 1969), 264, 265; 'A few months or years in prison is not a fate worse than death, if only because it has a court-determined time limit ... A prison experience is always difficult but ... [even] in a totalitarian society, as each prison is, interesting and worthwhile things can be done.'

2 For an overview of Catholic pacifism in the United States during the 1960s and 1970s, see William A. Au, *The Cross, the Flag, and the Atom Bomb: American Catholics Debate War and Peace, 1960–1986* (Westport, CT, and London, UK: Greenwood Press, 1986), 105–62. A few days after Miller burned his draft card, a colleague from the Catholic Worker movement, along with several others, did the same thing. For this 'crime' Tom Cornell received a five-month sentence, which he served in Danbury Prison. (Cornell, 31 years old, had already been classified as a conscientious objector. Therefore, although he also now burned his classification certificate, because of his age he was no longer liable to call-up.) Murray Polner, in his *When Can I Come Home? A Debate on Amnesty for Exiles, Antiwar Prisoners and Others* (Garden City, NY: Doubleday Anchor Books, 1972), 188–201, has included a short account by Cornell of his time in jail. 'I did good time,' the latter writes, due primarily to the support of wife and 'faithful friends.' Nevertheless, he found that 'much of what happens in a prison is so trivial that it cannot bear translation' (190). Incessant boredom, a painful sense of isolation, and 'a Byzantine complex of arbitrary and useless regulations' created 'a sterile environment' (192) with 'the erosion of [the inmate's] identity' (193). His comments on such aspects of prison life as homosexuality and the illicit use of drugs, the barely suppressed violence, 'hacks,' and medical care are as negative as most of those recorded at greater length by Levy and Miller in their *Going to Jail*.

3 One of the psychiatrist Dr Willard Gaylin's 'gentle felons,' 'Matthew' Morris (C-42893), in jail for two years as a Vietnam War resister, told Gaylin: 'Two or three times I've had people walk over and hit me for no reason ... The only safe response is to ignore it, because in any kind of physical combat both parties are judged equally guilty and locked up. It's unimportant who started it. The last time this happened to me, a guy had been talking very noisily during a TV program and I didn't say anything. All I did was shift my chair a little so that I could see around his head. He leaned back and said something like mother-fucker and slugged me very hard, knocking my glasses off and cutting my lip. I must have been close to passing out. My head was buzzing and I grew faint, but I just sat there. I didn't say a word.

Everyone was talking, wondering if the guard saw it [which he evidently did not].' See Willard Gaylin, *In the Service of Their Country: War Resisters in Prison* (New York: Viking Press, 1970), 69, 70. A journalist, reared in a middle-class Quaker home and educated at Swarthmore College, Matthew refused to claim Quakerism as the basis of his conscientious objection to military service.' My views were a combination of ethical and moral, religious, social and philosophical ... I was not distinguishable in categories. They all coalesce in my personality, who I am.' Matthew, as Gaylin presented him, was sensitive and deeply emotional, articulate and intellectually alert. Though the psychiatrist had the impression he was 'close to a model prisoner,' yet obviously he had maintained his integrity and self-esteem vis-à-vis the prison administration. He resented the regimentation he encountered, especially during the time he spent in the penitentiary before becoming a clerk in the parole office: 'the standing up, always in line, standing up for the count – the patronizing.' There was always the feeling he was an inmate, 'and they can do practically anything to me.' 'I don't like being treated as if I were a "thing,"' he protested. In the penitentiary at least, the prevailing atmosphere was 'dehumanizing,' with the 'hacks' (prison officers) shouting: 'No talking in the halls! Button your shirt up! Get that haircut – I mean now!' Throughout his time in jail Matthew's relationship with the hacks, he told Gaylin, had been 'very perfunctory and matter-of-fact ... I've never said "yes, sir" since I've been here. It's a very conscious thing on my part.' See ibid., 41, 42, 60–2, 68, 69.

4 As Gaylin's 'gentle felon,' Matthew, soon discovered. Another CO he met in jail was beaten up by a gang of convicts and then raped. 'Most of those who approached me,' Matthew told Gaylin, 'were willing to take no for an answer.' Still, he continued to feel frightened. One 'big tough-looking guy' did persist: 'homosexual in jail but not on the outside,' he ended by advising Matthew: '"Don't just stand there,"' if someone makes homosexual overtures, '"break a chair over his head. That's the best way to stop it. Or else ... let it be known that you have some very large friends who will beat the shit out of him."' Matthew followed this advice and had no more trouble over this issue. 'Maybe I've just been lucky in avoiding that kind of thing,' he conceded. See Gaylin, *In the Service of Their Country*, 71, 72. Basing himself on his observation of conditions in Graterford Prison (Pennsylvania) during the 1980s, Victor Hassine (Inmate AM4737) stresses that young prisoners – 'innocent,' 'naive,' 'cute-looking' – are particularly exposed to gang-rape in institutions of this kind. He writes: 'Rape is no longer a random act of violence that occurs occasionally in prison: it is now a common event behind bars. Few inmates are free from the fear of rape.' He attributes

this deplorable situation to the mounting overcrowding of federal prisons and to the increase in America's jails from the 1970s on of violent young drug addicts with their gang warfare. Levy and Miller were writing at the outset of this new crisis in the American prison world. See Hassine's startling prison memoir, *Life without Parole*, 2nd ed. (Los Angeles: Roxbury Publishing Co., 1999), 133, 134.

5 The response to a similar situation of a twenty-year-old draft resister, who served two years in a minimum-security prison in Arizona around the same time as Levy and Miller were in jail, was as follows: 'There's only one thing that people occupy themselves with in prison, and that's getting out. That is the focus of everybody's minds, that's what people talk about ... I worked very hard in prison; it was set up for punitive labor. I was set digging ditches, building a road, ... and I even broke rocks. I pushed myself hard because I wanted to keep my mind off prison. You don't want to dwell on every little second ([which is] called "doing hard time"), because the time goes by slowly enough as it is.' From Sherry Gershon Gottlief, ed., *Hell No, We Won't Go: Resisting the Draft during the Vietnam War* (New York: Viking Penguin, 1991), 207, 208.

6 Due to the 'dislike' of a mailroom officer, of whom 'Matthew' Morris had complained to the warden of the jail, for tampering with a letter of his, his visiting experiences were even more unpleasant than were David Miller's. 'The mailroom officer spread the word around to the other [hacks] that I had ratted him out,' Matthew told Gaylin (*Service*, 70, 71). Though indeed 'a routine frisk' by a guard was normal on the conclusion of a visit, in Matthew's case he was 'taken into a room, where he was forced to strip, to have his mouth searched, to bend over so that his rectum could be probed.' This humiliating procedure continued for months and proved 'a constant source of anguish' to Matthew. It 'succeeded in destroying the anticipations and pleasures of each visit.' Gaylin branded this kind of retaliation on the part of the prison officers as 'malicious and psychologically very sophisticated.' No violence was employed: 'no beatings, no marks, no physical abuses' (ibid., 70). But the pain inflicted was equally great. Eventually Matthew told the guard that he had considered he had become the victim of 'a personal vendetta,' and the guard reported him to the warden for 'insolence.' This in fact brought only a reprimand, since it was 'the first time.' But, as Matthew explained to Gaylin, he really got off easily, for 'a report like that could bring a number of punishments. They could lock you in the hole. They could take away your good time. They could do any of a number of things.' And Matthew, the near-model prisoner, took care not to repeat his offence. See Gaylin, ibid., 75. Of course strip searches, including

probings of a prisoner's rectum, were nothing new in prison history. In his prison memoir, Albert Škarvan, a conscript doctor in the Austro-Hungarian army, has described the daily 'turning-over' of rank-and-file military prisoners as they came back from work outside the jail where he was incarcerated – as a privileged inmate – in mid-1895. 'The prisoners,' writes Škarvan, 'lined up for the search. Then they took off all their clothes and stood naked while the warder ... went through the clothing, fingered the prisoners' bodies, made them open their mouths for examination and peered into the recesses of their ears. Indeed they often examined parts of the body which modesty precludes me from mentioning. Every day I watched this nasty procedure.' *Life in an Austro-Hungarian Military Prison: The Slovak Tolstoyan Dr. Albert Škarvan's Story*, trans. from the Slovak and ed. Peter Brock (distributed by Syracuse University Press, Syracuse NY, 2002), 15, 16. This 'nasty procedure' was, we see, to be found almost unchanged three-quarters of a century later and on another continent.

7 Some COs responded less traumatically to American prison life than David Miller (or 'Matthew' Morris) did. In 1971, for example, William A. Eagles from North Carolina, while still a Baptist and a graduate student at his state university, refused induction into the army. Denied exemption by his local draft board ('which had never found anyone to be a conscientious objector'), he subsequently spent seventeen months in prison. Unlike some imprisoned American COs, he did not encounter any physical threats or abuse. His carceral experience was in fact comparatively uneventful, perhaps in part because of his serene temperament and lively sense of humor. At Reception, he recalls, 'I sat across a gray metal desk from an older guard who filled out forms. He asked what I was in for; I said I had refused induction. Looking up from his forms, he said, "You aren't one of those fanatics, are you?" I replied, "I guess I must be or I wouldn't be here." He smiled and said, "You'll be all right." And, I knew it was true.' Eventually Eagles became a lawyer and joined the Quaker Society of Friends. See Chuck Fager, ed., *Friends and the Vietnam War* (Wallingford, PA: Pendle Hill, 1998), 40–45.

Appendix

In October 1982 the twenty-six-year-old East Berliner Michael Frenzel received his call-up papers. The authorities knew already of his conscientious objection to military service. Trained as a chemical technician, Frenzel had been active in social work organized by the Evangelical Church in East Berlin, and he had received training from it that qualified him to become a 'social deacon' (*Sozialdiakon*), a counsellor among the city's disoriented youth. Frenzel was one of the minority of young people in his church who espoused pacifism; the church authorities now supported them in their stand, even while most church leaders did not share their views on war and peace. It was indeed to accommodate religious dissent of this kind that the communist government of the German Democratic Republic (DDR) had instituted a system of alternative, non-combatant army service.

Yet not all COs, when conscripted into the East German army, were ready to accept this way out and become 'construction soldiers,' for these construction units were closely integrated into the country's war-making machine. The JWs of course, were unwilling – and, as a result, found themselves in jail. Frenzel too became a 'total resister'; and his church stood by him in this, so that he was able to return to his social deaconry after serving his sentence of twenty months. He had had to complete the full term – in various jails – since the authorities rejected his lawyer's plea for a four months' remission. Seven years later communism collapsed.

My wife and I had already realized some time ago that I would not be able to do military service. My conscience and my responsibilities towards other people would make it impossible for me to participate in any 'organized training to kill.' In spite of this, however, we were more than a little apprehensive when, in October of the year in which I turned 26, a letter arrived calling me up for service in one of the construction units of the National People's Army.

Once again we reviewed all the arguments. Only to come to the same conclusion: 'total resistance' was the only way. Which meant that preparations had to be made ... My wife was going to be solely responsible for the daily life of our family, including a second child just a few weeks old. I needed to find a replacement on the job. I had to say goodbye to my friends and relatives, visits that would likely lead to long discussions about whether my decision made sense, and questions about what it meant to me to go to jail. I also had to talk to my lawyer and try and make arrangements concerning the trial and conditions of my detention. What else did we need to do? Whose help did we still need? The nights were short and we were busy all the time. Was everything taken care of? What if ... we wondered again and again.

There was no end to our questions ... and then the day of departure arrived – November 2, 1982. No words can describe how I felt or the myriad thoughts that crossed my mind. Tucking in my one-and-a-half-year-old son for his afternoon nap, I wondered whether he knew what was happening. What would he say when he got up? Would he understand why his father had suddenly disappeared? I said goodbye to my wife – for how long? The road to the local induction centre, 200 metres from my home, seemed endless.

'Good morning, I am ...' – 'No, I won't,' followed by long explanations. I don't know how many times I repeated them in the hours that followed. Always in the hope of being understood, yet knowing that the person across from me could not possibly understand me. He was after all wearing the uniform I would always refuse to put on. They remained friendly, however. 'Are you really sure of this? Have you thought it through? Won't you reconsider?' 'No, I have made my decision! I am unwilling to participate. I will not serve in any army that makes war possible, not now and not here in Central Europe. All words and actions aimed at confrontation, whether psychological, pedagogical, political or economic, are preparation for war. I am convinced that any compulsory service, whether military or alternative, is degrading. Coercion equals disempowerment, especially in combination with the requirement for unquestioning obedience.'

At the time there were posters everywhere declaring, 'My battleground for peace? My job!' I fully agreed with this. My being drafted, however, denied this truth. How could my work be considered important, if it could be suspended for two years? This reasoning was beyond me. I was, after all, a church youth counsellor engaged in helping people, young people, scarred by lack of love, social disadvantages, and human shortcomings, to put their life back together. These folks trusted me and had begun to feel the stirring of hope through our contact. Now our dialogue was going to be interrupted, and the hope destroyed. This could not possibly be in the interest of anyone! Abandoning people, breaking off relationships – how could that contribute to peace?

I tried to explain and kept bumping up against the laws, 'Do you know what to expect?' 'I do.' 'So you want to abandon your wife and children?' 'I don't want to! That is your decision.' Back and forth it went, without bringing understanding – neither side was able to comprehend the other. Every conversation led to the same impasse. However, I often had the impression that neither side wanted this.

What finally happened? I remember statements, signatures, more discussions, followed again and again by 'Please, wait outside.' A soldier guarding the door. Why a guard? Had I not come here of my own free will? Did he know why I was here? When I was leaving to be taken to prison while awaiting trial, the guard in front of the military courthouse stood up and saluted. I smiled at the irony of the situation. In the parking lot of the prison, it still was 'Please, follow me.' But inside, after many steel doors had closed behind me, the tone changed. 'Face the wall,' a policewoman yelled. When I didn't realize that she was addressing me, she screamed even louder and, so it seemed, more aggressively. With my hands against the wall, my legs spread wide, I was searched from head to toe. 'Name!' – 'Date of birth!' ... The orders were always shouted.

It had an impact, I was scared, although I didn't understand why. Later I realized that all this was a means to an end. There were more steel doors, bolts, officials, I was ordered to empty my pockets and the contents were confiscated. Then more statements and signatures ... Finally my first encounter with a cell, a kind of waiting room, except that I didn't know what I was waiting for. The room was windowless, its walls and ceiling covered in greenish oil paint, its only furnishings fluorescent tubes and two bolted-down benches. The room was already occupied. When those inside didn't get up when the door opened, the guard shouted at them. They looked unsure. Eventually they and I learned to get up automatically whenever the door opened. In the beginning, though, we had to think about it. The others were also total resisters, mostly Jehovah's Witnesses. Little did we know then that in the next year or two we would keep running into each other, share other cells like this one, become friends.

It was in this cell, however, that I became for the first time aware of the suspicion people feel in such a situation. Everyone was wary of everyone else. 'Who is he?' 'Can he be trusted?' This made it hard to relate. It was also impossible at that time to determine whether the suspicion was justified. Not until later, when I was sitting out my sentence [along with ordinary prisoners], did I come to see that denunciations in exchange for small favours were the norm. We watched each other like hawks, noticed the slightest abnormality, recorded any discrepancy – someone without shoelaces, another one with a tie. No one, however, was able to interpret the differences. I realized for the first time that another logic had to be at work.

After hours of waiting we were finally each given a basin with soap, a shaving brush, bedding, and our own cell. Forbidden to call them cells, however, we had to refer to them as 'custodial rooms.' We had been taken into custody, were being kept safe ... From whom? For what purpose?

Alone in my custodial room, I wondered what to do. What was expected of me? I didn't want to provoke anyone, I wanted to show my willingness to co-operate. But what to do when you don't know what is against the rules and what is allowed? I picked one of the beds, the other remained empty. Now I had time, lots of time. How much time, I didn't know. I had not yet discovered how long a day can be when there is nothing to do but sit down, walk around the room, think, brood ... After the hectic pace of the last few weeks, this total lack of activity was all the more trying. And then there was the anxiety every time I heard the two bolts and the lock being opened.

Within a week, however, habit had set in. I had identified a system. I was even getting used to the rough treatment. I had begun to recognize the officers and could vaguely visualized the entire building. I had been given a cellmate and we were getting along well, fortunately. It would have been terrible to live in such close proximity and not understand each other. Intimacy was forced upon us at all times in that tiny space. Even the toilet offered no privacy. We lived together 24 hours a day – certainly at home I didn't spend that much time with my own family.

I could never have imagined that a cell holding 24 inmates – which is where I ended up after sentencing – would be better than a small cell. The hardest thing there, too, was the lack of privacy. Every word was heard, every gesture noticed.

Even the letters I wrote or received were not private. Why did their content matter to the prison authorities? At first this censorship kept many a phrase from being written. I had to learn to adjust my writing to the eyes of both my family and the censors, and often I wondered whether I might not be able to influence my jailors just a little. The latter thought eventually made me love writing letters. It became my favourite pastime. And I had all the time in the world to ponder every word. Letters from outside were also held back. I learned, for instance, during one of those monthly one-hour visits I was allowed, that my wife had sent me a poem by the East German author Hanns Cibulka. When I asked my 'Educator,' the police officer assigned to me, about the reasons for not having received it, he answered, 'The letter was of no pedagogical value.' 'But it contained a poem by Cibulka. His book has just been published in the DDR.' 'I decide what is or what is not of pedagogical value.' I left it at that. Why point out that the book was available for borrowing in the prison library?

'I preferred my time as a convict to the time spent in detention awaiting trial,' said those who had ended up in jail. I had to remind myself of this, lying in bed upon arriving at my final destination. My private things had been taken away and added to my 'personal effects.' I was now wearing a worn and wrinkled faded brown-to-burgundy uniform. Two hours earlier my hair had 'succumbed,' while in the seven weeks before the trial, I had been able to escape this fate. Now a stranger stared back at me from the mirror. For nineteen months, I would have to start each morning looking at him.

... Would I be forever marked? Would I still be 'me' when I left here? Would I endure? Would the others endure? Every other inmate was probably pondering the same questions. I had yet to learn how hard it would be to live the sermon on the Mount on a daily basis in jail. Fortunately, the others were just as insecure. Conversations were short. 'How long have you been here?' 'How long did you get?' My sentence was the longest, except for one. He shot someone, he told me; nothing more. Strange that it was with him that I ended up chatting for an hour ...

'You were lucky,' the others said when I was assigned to the infirmary. I was relieved when I finally knew what I was going to be doing. I was also looking forward to doing something meaningful. Little did I know that I could be transferred any day.

It took six months before I was reassigned to the cement plant penal detachment – a thorough change and a completely new start. Fortunately, I had already met many of these people in the infirmary and treated them well. That paid off now. I didn't have to sleep on the top bunk of the triple bunks like the other newcomers; the air up there was thick enough to slice. But I was still a newcomer. 'Why are you here?' 'How much time have you already done?' A newcomer always created a welcome diversion. Of course, I was always asked why I chose prison. Then a dialogue ensued. Some agreed with me, others thought I was a nutcase.

'At least he knows why he's here!' That, however, was my only advantage over my fellow inmates. I was in jail of my own free will, so to speak, but this did not free me from doubt. Why was I putting myself through this? Was it going to make the world a better place? Who was helped by my decision? These questions tormented me. The situation often seemed hopeless. I was all alone: nothing could change that. Hiding was not possible. Only one thing helped and that was remembering that if I had not chosen prison, I would have been in the army. It was a choice between two evils. I could avoid only one of them. But the bad taste in my mouth remained. The questions and a profound sadness remained, too.

My days in prison started with [the shouted] 'Time to leave,' get off to work. In lines of three we marched to the gate. 'Halt.' We stopped automatically. My name and number were called. 'I am not a number,' I thought, mindlessly repeating its six digits while passing the prison guard, who by then was no longer paying attention to me, having already moved on to the next name, the next number.

The ride to the plant offered some relief from the monotony of prison. Trees, bushes, fields, people. The world was continuing without us. We saw women waiting at a bus stop. Excitement inside the bus. 'Quiet,' shouted the prison guard. He knew it was in vain, but he had to do his duty. The plant was ancient. Since there were still civilians working there, however, I assumed that it was no worse than other chemical plants.

Working while in jail may seem like punishment to many, but I saw it differently. The work helped me pass the time; there was even some variety. Almost no job was in itself degrading. Activities that violated the safety requirements could be refused. But people did them anyway – mostly of their own accord – because they were reckless, preferred to choose the easy way out or liked to show off. Or because there was a reward – a pail of black tea, for example. It is easy to cast judgment on this. But who could be said to be 'truly voluntarily' carting away great mountains of cement or knocking stones out of an oven that was still hot? Was not each one of us hoping for some recognition or praise, for a favour or even early release?

Returning from work, we were standing at the gate to be let in and locked up. Nothing happened. 'They must be having coffee!' someone shouted. 'Open up,' others yelled repeatedly. There was swearing. The atmosphere was tense. It did not really matter on which side of the gate we found ourselves, but it was the waiting that got at us. 'It's all prison time,' one man growled. Another one responded with 'It should be punishment, too.' Everyone laughed. The atmosphere was still tense, however, when we were finally locked up.

Visiting time. Another month gone, another hour with my wife or someone else I loved. Scent freedom! Sense life! And then back to the cell. Refuse to react to stupid questions, motivated by fear. 'What did you sneak in? Come on, let's see.' ... Pretend you don't hear. I crawl now into bed quickly, and pull the covers over my head ...

Coming home from the night shift dead tired late one evening, someone at the front of the line shouted 'Search!' Shit, everyone thought, when they entered the cell. Everything had been turned upside down, including the beds. 'I'm missing a letter,' someone said; someone else was looking for a photo. The swearing got louder. Not everything was found, not only forbidden goods were missing. It was not clear who had taken them. Someone could simply have taken advantage of the chaos. 'They didn't find my package of tea,' one of us said out loud, without thinking. The next day there was another search and the tea was gone. We never knew who was the informer. It was rare for informers to be unmasked. However, each one of us was convinced that special favours were not granted for free. Mistrust was the inevitable result.

In spite of the fact that I had been granted a special favour [by the prison authorities] – I was allowed to read professional literature in a separate room – my cell mates trusted me more than they did their other mates. Was that because of the nature of my offence, or because reading was not considered a special favour? Or was it because I had treated all my fellow inmates fairly?

Four months before the end of my sentence I was told that my lawyer had applied for early release. I was anxious to know the outcome. There could be no objections because of my behaviour in prison, but I was not going to count on it being granted. In the same month in which my application was denied, three total resisters willing to live in exile left the DDR for West Germany. This raised more questions without answers. Who could have provided answers, anyway?

And then came the day of my release. I was made to wait, forced once more to line up, be counted, ordered about. Once more it was being made clear to me that I would only be free when the prison gates had shut behind me. I was being released because I had finished my sentence, but what would come of it?

I still don't believe that the song of peace can be played on the instrument of violence. Peace can only grow from trust and a mature attitude. What has been the effect of my decison? The world has not changed. Many children still have to make do without their dad while he is in the army? But maybe my example will encourage some of them to follow along the same path. It was and still is the only right one, of that I am convinced.

Translated by Miriam Jarsky.

Source: Heinz Janning et al., *Kriegs-/Ersatzdienst-Verweigerung in Ost und West* (Essen: Klartext Verlag, 1990), 255–61.

Further Reading

Baker, George. *The Soul of a Skunk: The Autobiography of a Conscientious Objector.* London: Scholartis Press, 1930.

Barker, Rachel. *Conscience, Government and War: Conscientious Objection in Great Britain 1939–45.* London: Routledge and Kegan Paul, 1982.

Barnes, Harry Elmer. 'Conscientious Objectors as a Correctional Problem in the Second World War.' *The Prison World* 6, no. 4 (July–August 1944), 12, 27–31.

Baskir, Lawrence M., and William A. Strauss. *Chance and Circumstance; The Draft, the War, and the Vietnam Generation.* New York: Alfred A. Knopf, 1978.

Bennett, Scott H. '"Free American Political Prisoners": Pacifist Activism and Civil Liberties, 1945–1948.' *Journal of Peace Research* 40, no. 4 (July 2003), 413–33.

Benney, Mark. *Gaol Delivery.* London: Longman, Green and Co., 1948.

Boulton, David. *Objection Overruled.* London: MacGibbon and Kee, 1967.

Braithwaite, Constance. *Conscientious Objection to Various Compulsions under British Law.* York, UK: William Sessions Ltd, 1995.

Brock, Peter. 'Prison Samizdat of British Conscientious Objectors in the First World War.' *Journal of Prisoners on Prisons* 12 (2003), 8–21.

– *Varieties of Pacifism: A Survey from Antiquity to the Outset of the Twentieth Century.* Syracuse, NY: Syracuse University Press, 1998.

– ed. *Liberty and Conscience: A Documentary History of the Experiences of Conscientious Objectors in America through the Civil War.* New York: Oxford University Press, 2002.

– ed. *Pacifism since 1914: An Annotated Reading List.* Toronto: privately printed, 2000.

Brock, Peter, and Thomas P. Socknat, eds. *Challenge to Mars: Essays on Pacifism from 1918 to 1945.* Toronto: University of Toronto Press, 1999.

Brock, Peter, and Nigel Young. *Pacifism in the Twentieth Century.* Syracuse, NY: Syracuse University Press, 1999.

Brockway, Fenner. *Inside the Left: Thirty Years of Platform, Press, Prison and Parliament*. London: George Allen and Unwin, 1942.

– *Towards Tomorrow*. London: Hart-Davis, MacGibbon, 1977.

Cantine, Holley, and Dachine Rainer, eds. *Prison Etiquette: The Convict's Compendium of Useful Information*. Bearsville, NY: Retort Press, 1950.

Carter, Charles F. *Snail's Progress: The English Local Prison*. London: Penal Reform Committee of the Society of Friends, 1948.

Catchpool, T. Corder. *Letters of a Prisoner for Conscience Sake*. London: George Allen and Unwin, 1941.

– *On Two Fronts*. London: Headley Bros., 1918.

Chambers, John Whiteclay. *To Raise an Army: The Draft Comes to Modern America*. New York: Free Press, 1987.

The *Conscientious Objector* (1939–1946). 2 vols. Ed. Stephen Siteman. New York: Greenwood Reprint Corp., 1968.

Cooney, Robert, and Helen Michalowski, eds. *The Power of the People: Active Nonviolence in the United States*. Philadelphia: New Society Publishers, 1987.

Davis, Chandler. 'So You're Going to Prison! Some Tips from a Political Prisoner.' *The Nation*, 3 December 1960: 435–7.

Dellinger, David. *From Yale to Jail: The Life Story of a Moral Dissenter*. New York: Pantheon Books, 1993.

Duckers, James Scott. *'Handed Over': The Prison Experiences of Mr. J. Scott Duckers, Solicitor, of Chancery Lane, under the Military Service Act*. London: C.W. Daniels, [1917].

Early, Frances H. *A World without War: How U.S. Feminists and Pacifists Resisted World War I*. Syracuse, NY: Syracuse University Press, 1997.

Eichel, Julius. *The Judge Said '20 Years': The Story of a Conscientious Objector in World War I*. Yonkers, NY: AMP & R, 1981.

Elder, Alexander, ed. *Louis Taylor, 1917–2000: Friends Remember ... Memorial Meeting 3.10.2001*. New York: privately printed, n.d.

Elliff, Nathan T. 'The Prosecution of Conscientious Objectors under the Selective Service Act.' *Federal Bar Journal* 6, no. 1 (October 1944), 41–50.

The Flowery 1942–4: The Scrubs 'Conchie' Review. London: Central Board for Conscientious Objectors, 1945.

Flynn, George Q. *Conscription and Democracy: The Draft in France, Great Britain and the United States*. Westport, CT: Greenwood Press, 2002.

Gara, Larry, and Lenna Mae Gara, eds. *A Few Small Candles: War Resisters of World War II Tell Their Stories*. Kent, OH: Kent State University Press, 1999.

Gaucher, Robert. 'Inside Looking Out: Writers in Prison.' *Journal of Prisoners on Prisons* 10, no. 1/2 (1999), 14–31.

Gaylin, Willard. *In the Service of Their Country: War Resisters in Prison*. New York: Viking Press, 1970.

Gilbert, Martin, ed. *Plough My Own Furrow: The Story of Lord Allen of Hurt-wood as Told through His Writings and Correspondence*. London: Longmans, 1965.

Goodall, Felicity. *A Question of Conscience: Conscientious Objection in the Two World Wars*. Stroud, UK: Sutton Publishing, 1997.

Goossen, Rachel Waltner. *Women against the Good War: Conscientious Objection and Gender on the American Home Front, 1941–1947*. Chapel Hill: University of North Carolina Press, 1997.

Graham, John W. *Conscription and Conscience: A History, 1916–1919*. London: George Allen and Unwin, 1922.

Grant, David. *Out in the Cold: Pacifists and Conscientious Objectors in New Zealand during World War II*. Auckland: Reed Methuen, 1986.

Gray, Harold Studley. *Character 'Bad': The Story of a Conscientious Objector*. Ed. Kenneth Irving Brown. New York: Harper, 1934.

Harding, Christopher, et al. *Imprisonment in England and Wales: A Concise History*. London: Croom Helm, 1985.

Hayes, Denis. *Challenge of Conscience: The Story of the Conscientious Objectors of 1939–1949*. London: George Allen and Unwin, 1949.

Hobhouse, Stephen, and A. Fenner Brockway, eds. *English Prisons Today: Being the Report of the Prison System Enquiry Committee*. London: Longmans, Green and Co., 1922.

Horeman, Bart, and Marc Stolwijk. *Refusing to Bear Arms: A World Survey of Conscription and Conscientious Objection to Military Service*. London: War Resisters' International, 1998.

Kellam, John R. *An American Prisoner of Conscience in World War Two*. Ed. Caroline Besse Webster. Providence, RI: self-published, 2002.

Kennedy, Thomas C. *The Hound of Conscience: A History of the No-Conscription Fellowship, 1914–1919*. Fayetteville: University of Arkansas Press, 1981.

Kock, Uwe, and Stephan Eschler, eds. *Zähne hoch – Kopf zusammenbeissen: Dokumente zur Kriegsdienstverweigerung in der DDR 1962–1990*. Kückenshagen: Scheunen-Verlag, 1994.

Kohn, Stephen M. *Jailed for Peace: The History of American Draft Law Violators, 1658–1985*. Westport, CT: Greenwood Press, 1986.

Lynd, Staughton, and Alice Lynd, eds. *Nonviolence in America: A Documentary History*. Maryknoll, NY: Orbis Books, 1995.

Marwick, Arthur. *Clifford Allen: The Open Conspirator*. Edinburgh and London: Oliver and Boyd, 1964.

Meyer, Ernest L. *'Hey! Yellowbacks!' The War Diary of a Conscientious Objector*. New York: John Day Company, 1930.

Miller, Melissa, and Phil M. Shenk. *The Path of Most Resistance: Stories of Mennonite Objectors Who Did Not Cooperate with the Vietnam War Draft.* Scottdale, PA: Herald Press, 1982.

Moore, Howard W. *Plowing My Own Furrow.* New York: W.W. Norton, 1985.

Morris, Norval, and David J. Rothman, eds., *The Oxford History of the Prison: The Practice of Punishment in Western Society.* New York and Oxford: Oxford University Press, 1998.

Moskos, Charles C., and John Whiteclay Chambers II, eds. The New *Conscientious Objection: From Sacred to Secular Resistance.* New York: Oxford University Press, 1993.

O'Connor, P.S. 'The Awkward Ones: Dealing with Conscience, 1916–1918.' *New Zealand Journal of History* 8, no. 2 (October 1974), 118–36.

Pearce, Cyril. *Comrades in Conscience: The Story of an English Community's Opposition to the Great War.* London: Francis Boutle Publishers, 2001.

Peck, James. *We Who Would Not Kill.* New York: Lyle Stuart, 1958.

Peterson, H.C., and Gilbert C. Fite. *Opponents of War, 1917–1918.* Madison: University of Wisconsin Press, 1957.

Polner, Murray, ed. *When Can I Come Home? A Debate on Amnesty for Exiles, Antiwar Prisoners, and Others.* Garden City, NY: Doubleday Anchor Books, 1972.

Priestley, Philip, ed. *Jail Journeys: The English Prison Experience since 1918.* London and New York: Routledge, 1989.

Rae, John. *Conscience and Politics: The British Government and the Conscientious Objector to Military Service, 1916–1919.* London: Oxford University Press, 1970.

Reeves, George B. *Men against the State.* Washington and Chicago: Human Events, 1946.

Richards, Edward C.M. *They Refuse to Be Criminals: Parole and the Conscientious Objector.* West Chester, PA: privately printed, 1946.

Rittenhouse, Ruth Rue. 'The Role of Conscientious Objectors in American Prisons.' M.A. thesis, University of Illinois at Urbana, 1958.

Ross, Jeffrey Ian, and Stephen C. Richards, eds. *Convict Criminology.* Belmont, CA: Wadsworth/Thomson Learning, 2003.

Satterthwait, Charles S., et al. *Federal Convicts Numbers 1128 and 1129: College to Prison.* Philadelphia: privately printed, 1942.

Sayre, Robert L. 'Rhetorical Defenses: The Autobiographies of World War I Conscientious Objectors.' *a/b: Auto/Biography Studies* 7, no. 1 (Spring 1992), 62–81.

Schlissel, Lillian, ed. *Conscience in America: A Documentary History of Conscientious Objection in America, 1757–1967.* New York: E.P. Dutton, 1968.

Serge, Victor. *Men in Prison.* Trans. from the French by Richard Greeman. London: Writers and Readers Publishing Cooperative, 1977.

Sibley, Mulford Q., and Philip E. Jacob. *Conscription of Conscience: The American State and the Conscientious Objector, 1940–1947.* Ithaca, NY: Cornell University Press, 1952.

Sibley, Mulford Q., and Ada Wardlaw. *Conscientious Objectors in Prison, 1940–1945.* Philadelphia: Pacifist Research Bureau, 1945.

Socknat, Thomas P. *Witness against War: Pacifism in Canada, 1900–1945.* Toronto: University of Toronto Press, 1987.

Stockdale, William. *Jehovah's Witnesses in American Prisons.* Putnam, CT: Wilda Press, 1946.

– *The Prison Experiences of Jehovah's Witnesses and Conscientious Objectors Now Told for the First Time in* 'The Government Is the Criminal.' Putnam, CT: Wilda Press, 1947.

Thomas, Norman. *Is Conscience a Crime?* New York: Vanguard Press, 1927.

Tietz, J.B. 'Jehovah's Witnesses: Conscientious Objectors.' *Southern California Law Review* 28, no. 2 (February 1955), 123–37.

Tollefson, James W., ed. *The Strength Not to Fight: Conscientious Objectors of the Vietnam War in Their Own Words.* Washington: Brassey's, 2000.

Tracy, James. *Direct Action: Radical Pacifism from the Union Eight to the Chicago Seven.* Chicago: University of Chicago Press, 1996.

The Tribunal. Ed. John G. Slater. New York: Kraus Reprint Co., 1970.

Wachs, Theodore Rickard. 'Conscription, Conscientious Objection, and the Context of American Pacifism, 1940–1945.' PhD thesis, University of Illinois at Urbana, 1976.

Wherry, Neal M. *Conscientious Objection.* 2 vols. Washington: Selective Service System (Special Monograph no. 11), 1950.

Wittner, Lawrence S. *Rebels against War: The American Peace Movement, 1933–1983.* Philadelphia: Temple University Press, 1984.

www.ingramcontent.com/pod-product-compliance
Lightning Source LLC
Chambersburg PA
CBHW051549100726
47898CB00001B/28

9780802086617